UNDERSTANDING
ARGUMENTS

UNDERSTANDING ARGUMENTS

An Introduction to Informal Logic

EIGHTH EDITION

WALTER SINNOTT-ARMSTRONG

Dartmouth College

ROBERT J. FOGELIN

Dartmouth College

WADSWORTH
CENGAGE Learning™

Australia • Brazil • Japan • Korea • Mexico • Singapore • Spain • United Kingdom • United States

WADSWORTH
CENGAGE Learning™

**Understanding Arguments:
An Introduction to Informal Logic,
Eighth Edition
Walter Sinnott-Armstrong and
Robert J. Fogelin**

Publisher/Executive Editor: Clark Baxter

Senior Sponsoring Editor: Joann Kozyrev

Associate Media Editor: Diane Akerman

Assistant Editor: Nathan Gamache

Editorial Assistant: Michaela Henry

Marketing Manager: Mark Haynes

Marketing Coordinator: Josh Hendrick

Marketing Communications
  Manager: Kim Soltero

Project Manager, Editorial
  Production: Abigail Greshik

Creative Director: Rob Hugel

Art Director: Faith Brosnan

Print Buyer: Betsy Donaghey

Permissions Editors: Scott Bragg/
  Karyn L. Morrison

Production Service: Pre-PressPMG

Photo Researcher: John Hill

Copy Editor: Pre-PressPMG

Cover Designer: RHDG

Cover Image: Getty Images/Stella Salazar

Compositor: Pre-PressPMG

For product information and technology assistance,
contact us at **Cengage Learning
Academic Resource Center, 1-800-423-0563.**

For permission to use material from this text or
product, submit all requests online at
www.cengage.com/permissions.
Further permissions questions can be emailed to
permissionrequest@cengage.com.

Library of Congress Control Number: 2008939692

ISBN-13: 978-0-495-60395-5

ISBN-10: 0-495-60395-3

Wadsworth Cengage Learning
10 Davis Drive
Belmont, CA 94002-3098
USA

Cengage Learning products are represented in Canada by
Nelson Education, Ltd.
For your course and learning solutions, visit
academic.cengage.com.
Purchase any of our products at your local college store or
at our preferred online store **www.ichapters.com.**

Printed in Canada
1 2 3 4 5 6 7 8 12 11 10 09

To Eric, John, Lars, Miranda, and Nicholas
and the colleges of their choice

———————————■———————————

CONTENTS

CHAPTER 4
THE ART OF CLOSE ANALYSIS   77

CHAPTER 5
DEEP ANALYSIS   105

PART II HOW TO EVALUATE ARGUMENTS: DEDUCTIVE STANDARDS   139

CHAPTER 6
PROPOSITIONAL LOGIC   141

PART IV FALLACIES 315

CHAPTER 13
FALLACIES OF VAGUENESS 317

CHAPTER 14
FALLACIES OF AMBIGUITY 333

CHAPTER 15
FALLACIES OF RELEVANCE 353

CHAPTER 16
FALLACIES OF VACUITY 369

CHAPTER 17
REFUTATION 381

PREFACE

Traditionally, logic has been considered the most general science dealing with arguments. The task of logic is to discover the fundamental principles for distinguishing good arguments from bad ones.

For certain purposes, arguments are best studied as abstract patterns of reasoning. Logic can then focus on these general forms rather than on particular arguments, such as your attempt to prove to the bank that they, not you, made a mistake. The study of those general principles that make certain patterns of argument valid and other patterns of argument invalid is called *formal logic*. Two chapters of this work are dedicated to formal logic.

A different but complementary way of viewing an argument is to treat it as a particular use of language: Presenting arguments is one of the important things we do with words. This approach stresses that arguing is a linguistic activity. Instead of studying arguments as abstract patterns, it examines them as they occur in concrete settings. It raises questions of the following kind:

What is the place of argument within language as a whole?

What words or phrases are characteristic of arguments?

How do these words function?

What task or tasks are arguments supposed to perform?

When an approach to argument has this emphasis, the study is called *informal logic*. Though it contains a substantial treatment of formal logic, *Understanding Arguments*, as its subtitle indicates, is primarily a textbook in informal logic.

The eighth edition of *Understanding Arguments* differs from the seventh edition in a number of significant ways. The uses of arguments have been brought right up front for emphasis. The chapters have been split up and reorganized for clarity. Some of the more difficult and confusing topics have been dropped to simplify and streamline the text. This edition also contains new readings on scientific reasoning in Chapter 20 and on religious reasoning in Chapter 21. These new readings make the text more relevant to contemporary debates. Finally, this edition includes a large-scale updating of examples, exercises, and discussion questions throughout the text, including a liberal sprinkling of quotations from Jon Stewart and Stephen Colbert as well as Colin Powell's argument that Iraq was seeking weapons of mass destruction.

This new edition has been influenced by our teaching of this material with various colleagues, including visitors, at Dartmouth College. In this regard, we would like to thank three student assistants—Ben Rump, Jane Tucker, and especially David Lamb—in addition to the many others who helped us on previous editions. We are also indebted to the following reviewers: André Ariew, University of Missouri, Columbia; John Zillmer, Michigan State University; K. D. Borcoman, Coastline College; Barbara A. Brown, Community College of Allegheny County; Marina F. Bykova, North Carolina State University; Eric Parkinson, Syracuse University; and Alison Reiheld, Michigan State University. At Wadsworth and Cengage Learning, we received expert advice and assistance from Worth Hawes, former Acquisitions Editor for Wadsworth; Joann Kozyrev, Sponsoring Editor for Philosophy and Religion; Sarah Perkins, Assistant Editor; Deborah Bader, copy editor; and Abigail Greshik, Pre-PressPMG Project Manager. Finally, we owe a great debt to Bill Fontaine (librarian) as well as Sarah Kopper and Kier Olsen DeVries (research assistants). Without all of these people, this book would contain many more mistakes than it undoubtedly still does.

Walter Sinnott-Armstrong
Robert J. Fogelin

HOW TO ANALYZE
ARGUMENTS

Arguments are all around us. They bombard us constantly in advertisements; in courtrooms; in political, moral, and religious debates; in academic courses on mathematics, science, history, literature, and philosophy; and in our personal lives when we make decisions about our careers, finances, and families. These crucial aspects of our lives cannot be understood fully without understanding arguments. The goal of this book, then, is to help us understand arguments and, thereby, to understand our lives.

We will view arguments as tools. To understand a tool, we need to know the purposes for which it is used, the material out of which it is made, and the forms that it takes. For example, hammers are normally used to drive nails or to pound malleable substances. Hammers are usually made out of a metal head and a handle of wood, plastic, or metal. A typical hammer's handle is long and thin, and its head is perpendicular to its handle. Similarly, in order to understand arguments, we need to investigate their purposes, materials, and forms.

Chapter 1 discusses the main purposes or uses of arguments. The material from which arguments are made is language, so Chapters 2–3 explore language in general and then the language of argument in particular. Chapters 4–5 use the lessons learned by then to analyze concrete examples of arguments in detail. The following chapters turn to the forms of arguments, including deductive forms in Part II (Chapters 6–7) and inductive forms in Part III (Chapters 8–12). Each form of argument comes with its own standards of adequacy. Part IV (Chapters 13–17) will then consider the main ways in which arguments can go astray, including fallacies of clarity, relevance, and vacuity. Finally, Part V (Chapters 18–22) will explore examples of arguments in different fields—law, morality, religion, science, and philosophy—in order to see both how such arguments differ and how they share common features of arguments in general. By the end of this journey, we should understand arguments much better.

USES OF ARGUMENTS

What are arguments? In our view, arguments are tools, so the first step toward understanding arguments is to ask what they are used for—what people are trying to accomplish when they give arguments. This brief chapter will propose a definition of arguments and then explore two main purposes of arguments: justification and explanation. Both justifications and explanations try to provide reasons, but reasons of different kinds. Justifications are supposed to give reasons to believe their conclusions, whereas explanations are supposed to give reasons why their conclusions are true. Each of these purposes is more complicated and fascinating than is usually assumed.

WHAT ARGUMENTS ARE

The word *"argument"* may suggest quarrels or squabbles. That is what a child means when she reports that her parents are having an argument. Arguments of that sort often include abuse, name-calling, and yelling. That is not what this book is about. The goal here is not to teach you to yell louder, to be more abusive, or to beat your opponents into submission.

Our topic is the kind of argument defined by Monty Python in their justly famous "Argument Clinic." In this skit, a client enters a clinic and pays for an argument. In the first room, however, all he gets is abuse, which is not argument. When he finally finds the right room to get an argument, the person who is supposed to give him an argument simply denies whatever the client says, so the client complains that mere denial is different from argument, because "an argument is a connected series of statements to establish a definite proposition." This definition is almost correct. As we will see, the purpose of an argument need not always be to "establish" its conclusion, both because some conclusions were established in advance and because many reasons are inconclusive. Nonetheless, Monty Python's definition needs to be modified only a little in order to arrive at an adequate definition:

> An argument is a connected series of sentences, statements, or propositions (called "premises") that are intended to give reasons of some kind for a sentence, statement, or proposition (called the "conclusion").

This definition does not pretend to be precise, but it does tell us what arguments are made of (sentences, statements, or propositions) and what their purpose is (to give reasons).

Another virtue of this definition is that it is flexible enough to cover the wide variety of arguments that people actually give. Different arguments are intended to give reasons of very different sorts. These reasons might be justificatory reasons to believe or to disbelieve some claim. They might, instead, be explanatory reasons why something happened. They might even be practical reasons to do some act. Because reasons come in so many kinds, arguments are useful in a great variety of situations in daily life. Trying to determine why your computer crashed, why your friend acted the way she did, and whether it will rain tomorrow as well as trying to decide which political candidate to vote for, which play to use at a crucial point in a football game, where to go to college, and whether to support or oppose capital punishment—all involve weighing and evaluating reasons.

It is inaccurate, therefore, to think of arguments as serving only one single simple purpose. People often assume that you always use every argument to make other people believe what you believe and what they did not believe before hearing or reading the argument. Actually, however, some arguments are used for that purpose, but others are not. To fully understand arguments in all their glory, then, we need to distinguish different uses of argument. In particular, we will focus on two exemplary purposes: justification and explanation.

JUSTIFICATIONS

One of the most prominent uses of arguments is to justify a disputed claim. For example, if I claim that September 11, 2001, was a Tuesday, and you deny this or simply express some doubt, then we might look for a calendar. But suppose we don't have a calendar for 2001. Luckily, we do find a calendar for 2002. Now I can justify my claim to you by presenting this argument: The calendar shows that September 11 was on Wednesday in 2002; 2002 was not a leap year, since 2002 is not divisible by four; nonleap years have 365 days, which is 1 more day than 52 weeks; so September 11 must have been on Tuesday in 2001. You should now be convinced.

What have I done? My utterance of this argument has the *effect* of changing your mind by getting you to believe a conclusion that you did not believe before. Of course, I might also be able to change your mind by hypnotizing you. But normally I do not want to use hypnosis. I also do not want to change your mind by manufacturing a fake calendar for 2002 with the wrong dates. Such tricks would not satisfy my goals fully. This shows that changing your mind is not all that I am trying to accomplish. What else do I want? My additional aim is to show you that you *should* change your mind, and why. I want to give you a *good reason* to change your mind. I want my argument not only to make you believe my conclusion but also to make you *justified* in believing my conclusion.

The above example is typical of one kind of justification, but there are other patterns. Suppose that I share your doubts about which day of the week it was on September 11, 2001. Then I might use the same argument to justify my belief as well as yours. Indeed, you don't even need to be present. If I am all alone, and I just want to figure out which day of the week it was on September 11, 2001, then I might think in terms of this same argument. Here the goal is not to convince anybody else, but the argument is still used to find a good reason to believe the conclusion.

In cases like these, we can say that the argument is used for *impersonal normative justification.* The justification is normative because the goal is to find a reason that is a good reason. It is impersonal because what is sought is a reason that is or should be accepted as a good reason by everyone capable of grasping this argument, regardless of who they are. The purpose is to show that there *is* a reason to believe the conclusion, regardless of who *has* a reason to believe it. Other arguments, in contrast, are aimed at specific people, and the goal is to show that those particular people are committed to the conclusion or have a reason to believe the conclusion. Such individualized uses of arguments seek what can be called *personal justification.*

There should be nothing surprising about different people having different reasons. I might climb a mountain to appreciate the view at the top, whereas you climb it to get exercise, and your friend climbs it to be able to talk to you while you climb it. Different people can have different reasons for the same action. Similarly, different people can have different reasons to believe the same conclusion. Suppose that someone is murdered in the ballroom with a revolver. I might have good reason to believe that Miss Peacock did not commit the murder, because I saw her in the library at the time the murder was committed. You might not trust me when I tell you that I saw her, but you still might have good reason to believe that she is innocent, because you believe that Colonel Mustard did it alone. Even if I doubt that Colonel Mustard did it, we still each have our own reasons to agree that Miss Peacock is innocent.

When different people with different beliefs are involved, we need to ask who is supposed to accept the reason that is given in an argument. A speaker might give an argument to show a listener that the speaker has a reason to believe something, even though the speaker knows that the audience does not and need not accept that reason. Suppose that you are an atheist, but I am an evangelical Christian, and you ask me why I believe that Jesus rose from the dead. I might respond that the Bible says that Jesus rose from the dead, and what the Bible says must be true, so Jesus rose from the dead. This argument tells you what *my* reasons are for believing what I believe, even if *you* do not accept those reasons. My argument can be used to show you that I have reasons and what my reasons are, regardless of whether you believe that my reasons are good ones and also regardless of whether my reasons really are good ones.

The reverse can also happen. A speaker might give an argument to show a listener that the listener has a reason to believe something, even though the speaker does not accept that reason. Suppose that you often throw loud parties late into the night close to my bedroom. I want to convince you to stop or at least quiet down. Fortunately, you think that every citizen ought to obey the law. I disagree, for I am an anarchist bent on undermining all governments and laws. Still, I want to get a good night's sleep before the protest tomorrow, so I might argue that it is illegal to make that much noise so late, and you ought to obey the law, so you ought to stop throwing such loud parties. This argument can show you that *you* are committed to its conclusion, even if *I* believe that its premises are false.

Of course, whether I succeed in showing my audience that they have a reason to believe my conclusion depends on who my audience is. My argument won't work against loud neighbors who don't care about the law. Consequently, we need to know who the audience is and what they believe in order to be able to show them what reason they have to believe a conclusion.

In all of these cases, arguments are used to show that someone has a reason to believe the conclusion of the argument. That is why all of these uses can be seen as providing different kinds of justification. The differences become crucial when we try to evaluate such arguments. If my goal is to show you that you have a reason to believe something, then I can be criticized for using a premise that you reject. Your beliefs are no basis for criticism, however, if all I want is to show my own reasons for believing the conclusion. Thus, to evaluate an argument properly, we often need to determine not only whether the argument is being used to justify a belief but also which kind of justification is sought and who the audience is.

EXERCISE I

Write the best brief argument you can to justify each of the following claims to someone who does not believe them.

1. Nine is not a prime number.
2. Seven is a prime number.
3. A molecule of water has three atoms in it.
4. Water is not made up of carbon.
5. The U.S. president lives in Washington.
6. The Earth is not flat.
7. Humans have walked on the moon.
8. Most bicycles have two wheels.

When, if ever, is it legitimate to try to convince someone else to believe something on the basis of a premise that you yourself reject? Consider a variety of cases.

EXPLANATIONS

A different but equally important use of arguments is to provide explanations. Explanations answer questions about how or why something happened. We explain how a mongoose got out of his cage by pointing to a hole he dug under the fence. We explain why Smith was acquitted by saying that he got off on a technicality. The purpose of explanations is not to prove that something happened, but to make sense of things.

An example will bring out the difference between justification and explanation. One person claims that a school's flagpole is thirty-five feet tall, and someone else asks her to justify this claim. In response, she might produce a receipt from the Allegiance Flagpole Company acknowledging payment for a flagpole thirty-five feet in height. Alternatively, she may put a stick straight up into the ground, measure the stick's length and its shadow's length, then measure the length of the flagpole's shadow, and calculate the length of the flagpole. Neither of these justifications, however, will answer a different question: *Why* is the flagpole thirty-five feet tall? This new question could be answered in all sorts of ways, depending on context: The school could not afford a taller one. It struck the committee as about the right height for the location. That was the only size flagpole in stock. There is a state law limiting flagpoles to thirty-five feet. And so on. These answers help us understand why the flagpole is thirty-five feet tall. They explain its height.

Sometimes simply filling in the details of a story provides an explanation. For example, we can explain how a two-year-old girl foiled a bank robbery by saying that the robber tripped over her while fleeing from the bank. Here we have made sense out of an unusual event by putting it in the context of a plausible *narrative*. It is unusual for a two-year-old girl to foil a bank robbery, but there is nothing unusual about a person tripping over a child when running recklessly at full speed in a crowded area.

Although the narrative is probably the most common form of explanation in everyday life, we also often use arguments to give explanations. We can explain a certain event by deriving it from established principles and accepted facts. This argument then has the following form:

    (1) General principles or laws
    (2) A statement of initial conditions
∴ (3) A statement of the phenomenon to be explained

The symbol "∴" is pronounced "therefore" and indicates that the premises above the line are supposed to give a reason for the conclusion below the line. By "initial conditions" we mean those facts in the context that, together with appropriate general principles and laws, allow us to derive the result that the event to be explained occurs.

This sounds quite abstract, but an example should clarify the basic idea. Suppose we put an ice cube into a glass and then fill the glass with water to the brim. The ice will stick out above the surface of the water. What will happen when the ice cube melts? Will the water overflow? Will it remain at the same level? Will it go down? Here we are asking for a *prediction,* and it will, of course, make sense to ask a person to *justify* whatever prediction he or she makes. Stumped by this question, we let the ice cube melt to see what happens. We observe that the water level remains unchanged. After a few experiments, we convince ourselves that this result always occurs. We now have a new question: *Why* does this occur? Now we want an explanation of this phenomenon. The explanation turns upon the law of buoyancy, which says that an object in water is buoyed up by a force equal to the weight of the water it displaces. This law implies that, if we put an object in water, it will continue to sink until it displaces a volume of water whose weight is equal to its own weight (or else the object hits the bottom of the container). With this in mind, go back to the original problem. An ice cube is itself simply water in a solid state. Thus, when it melts, it will exactly fill in the volume of water it displaced, so the water level will remain unchanged.

We can now see how this explanation conforms to the argumentative pattern mentioned above:

(1) General principles or laws (Primarily the law of buoyancy)
(2) Initial conditions (An ice cube in a glass of water filled to the brim)
∴ (3) Phenomenon explained (The level of the water remaining unchanged after the ice cube melts)

This explanation is fairly good. People with only a slight understanding of science can follow it and see why the water level remains unchanged. We should also notice that it is not a *complete* explanation, because certain things are simply taken for granted—for example, that things do not change weight when they pass from a solid to a liquid state. To put the explanation into perfect argumentative form, this assumption and many others would have to be stated explicitly. This is never done in everyday life and is only rarely done in the most exact sciences.

Is this explanation any good? Explanations are satisfactory if they remove bewilderment or surprise by telling us *how* or *why* something happened in a way that is relevant to the concerns of a particular context. Our example does seem to accomplish that much. However, it might seem that even the best explanations are not very useful because they take so much for granted. In explaining why the water level remains the same when the ice cube melts, we cited the law of buoyancy. Now, why should that law be true? What explains *it*? To explain the law of buoyancy, we would have to derive it from other laws that are more general and, perhaps, more intelligible. In fact, this has been done. Archimedes simultaneously proved and explained the law of buoyancy by deriving it from the laws of the lever. How about the laws of the lever? Can they be proved and explained by deriving them from still higher and more comprehensive laws? Perhaps. Yet reasons give out, and sooner or later explanation (like justification) comes to an end. It is the task of science and all rational inquiry to move that boundary further and further back. But even when there is more to explain, that does not show that a partial explanation is totally useless. As we have seen, explanations can be useful even when they are incomplete, and even though they are not used to justify any disputed claim. Explanation is, thus, a separate use of arguments.

EXERCISE II

Houses in Indonesia sometimes have their electrical outlets in the middle of the wall rather than at floor level. Why? A beginning of an explanation is that flooding is a danger in the Netherlands. Citing this fact does not help much, however, unless one remembers that Indonesia was formerly a Dutch colony. We can understand why the Dutch might put their electrical outlets above floor level in the Netherlands. It is safer in a country where flooding is a danger. Is flooding, then, a similar danger in Indonesia? Apparently not; so why did the Dutch continue this practice in Indonesia? The answer is that colonial settlers tend to preserve their home customs, practices, and styles. The Dutch continued to build Dutch-style houses with the electrical outlets where (for them) they are normally placed—that is, in the middle of the wall rather than at floor level. Restate this explanation in the form of an argument (that is, specify its premises and conclusion).

EXERCISE III

Write a brief argument to explain each of the following. Indicate what facts and what general principles are employed in your explanations. (Do not forget those principles that may seem too obvious to mention.)

1. Why a lighter-than-air balloon rises.
2. Why there is an infield fly rule in baseball.
3. Why there is an international date line.
4. Why there are more psychoanalysts in New York City than in any other city or, for that matter, in most countries in the world.
5. Why average temperatures tend to be higher closer to the equator.
6. Why there are usually more college freshmen who plan to go to medical school than there are seniors who still plan to go to medical school.
7. Why almost no textbooks are more than eighteen inches high.
8. Why most cars have four tires (instead of more or fewer).
9. Why paintings by Van Gogh cost so much.
10. Why wages go up when unemployment goes down.

COMBINATIONS: AN EXAMPLE

Although justification and explanation are distinct uses of arguments, we often want to know both *what* happened and also *why* it happened. Then we need to combine justifications and explanations. We can see how this works by considering a fictional example.

Imagine that Madison was arrested for murdering her husband, Victor. Now she is on trial, and you are on the jury. Presumably, the police and the prosecuting attorneys would not have arrested and prosecuted her if they did not believe that Madison committed the murder, but are their beliefs justified? Should she be convicted and sent to prison? That's up to you and the other jurors to decide.

You do not want to convict her arbitrarily, of course, so you need arguments to justify you in believing that Madison is guilty. The goal of prosecuting attorneys is to provide such justification. Their means of reaching this goal is to present evidence and arguments during the trial. Although their ultimate conclusion is that you should find Madison guilty of murder, the prosecutors need to justify lots of little claims along the way.

It might seem too obvious to mention, but the prosecution first needs an argument to show that the victim died. After all, if nobody died, nobody was killed. This first argument can be pretty simple: This person was walking and talking before he was shot in the head; now his heart has stopped beating for a long time; so he must be dead. There can be complications, since some gunshot victims can be revived, but let's assume that an argument like this justifies the claim that the victim is dead.

We also want to know who the victim was. The body was identified by several of Victor's friends, we assume, so all the prosecution needs to argue is that identifications like this are usually correct, so it was Victor who died. This second argument also provides a justification, but it differs from the first argument in several ways. The first argument referred directly to the facts about Victor that show he died, whereas this second argument does not say which features of the victim show that it was Victor. Instead, this argument relies on trusting other people—Victor's friends—without knowing what it was about the victim's face that made them think it was Victor. Such appeals to authority will be discussed in more detail in Chapters 3 and 15.

The third issue is the cause of death. Here it is common to appeal to a medical authority. In our case, the coroner or medical examiner makes observations or runs scientific tests that provide premises for another argument that is supposed to justify the conclusion that Victor's death was caused by a bullet to the head. This argument is also an appeal to an authority, but here the authority is a scientific expert rather than a friend.

Yet another argument, possibly based on firing marks on the bullet, can then justify you in believing that the bullet came from a certain gun. More arguments, possibly based on eyewitnesses, then justify the claims that Madison was the person who fired that gun at Victor. And so on.

All of these arguments depend on background assumptions. When you see the marks on the bullet that killed Victor line up with the marks on another bullet that was fired from the alleged murder weapon, you assume that guns leave distinctive marks on bullets and that nobody switched the bullets. A good prosecutor will provide arguments for these assumptions, but nobody can prove everything. Arguments always start from assumptions. This problem will occupy us at several points later, including parts of Chapters 3 and 5. The point for now is just that the prosecution needs to produce several arguments of various kinds in order to justify the claim that Madison killed Victor.

It is also crucial that killing violates the law. If not, then Madison should not be found guilty for killing Victor. So, how can the prosecutor justify the assumption that such killing is illegal? Prosecutors usually just quote a statute or cite a common law principle and apply it to the case, but that argument assumes a lot of background information. In the case of a statute, there must be a duly elected legislature, it must have jurisdiction over the place and time where and when the killing occurred, it must follow required procedures, and the content of the law must be constitutionally permissible. Given such a context, if the legislature says that a certain kind of killing is illegal, then it is illegal. It is fascinating that merely announcing that something is illegal thereby makes it illegal. We will explore such performatives and speech acts in Chapter 2. For now we will simply assume that all of these arguments could be provided if needed.

Even so, Madison might have had some justification for killing Victor, such as self-defense. This justification for her act can be presented in an argument basically like this: I have a reason to protect my own life, and I need to kill Victor first in order to protect my own life, so I have a reason to kill Victor. This justification differs in several ways from the kind of justification that we have been discussing so far. For one thing, this argument provides a reason for a different person—a reason for Madison—whereas the preceding arguments provided a reason for you as a juror. This argument also provides a reason with a different kind of object, since it justifies an action (killing Victor) whereas the previous arguments justified a belief (the belief that Madison did kill Victor). It provides a practical reason instead of an intellectual reason. Despite these differences, however, if her attorneys want to show that Madison has this new kind of justification, they need to give an argument to show that she was justified in doing what she did.

Even if Madison had no justification, she still might have had an excuse. Whereas a justification is supposed to show that the act was the right thing to do, an excuse admits that the act was wrong but tries to show that the agent was not fully responsible for doing it. Madison might, for example, argue that she honestly believed that Victor was going to kill her if she did not kill him first. If she offers this only as an excuse, she can admit that her belief was mistaken, so she had no justification for killing Victor. Her claim is, instead, that she was not fully responsible for his death because she was only trying to defend herself.

Excuses like this are, in effect, explanations. By citing her mistake, Madison explains why she did what she did. If she had killed Victor because she hated him or because she wanted to take his money, then she would have no excuse. Her act is less blameworthy, however, if she was mistaken. Of course, you should be careful before you shoot someone, so Madison could still be guilty of carelessness or negligence. But that is not as bad as killing someone out of hatred or for money. Her mistake might even be reasonable. If Victor was aiming a gun at her, then, even if it turned out not to be loaded, any rational person in her position might have thought that Victor was on the attack. Such reasonable mistakes might reduce or even remove responsibility. Thus, by explaining her act as a mistake, Madison puts her act in a better light than it would appear without that explanation. In general, an excuse is just an explanation of an act that puts that act in a better light by reducing the agent's responsibility.

To offer an excuse, then, Madison's defense attorneys will need to give arguments whose purpose is not justification but explanation. This excuse will then determine what she is guilty of. Whether Madison is guilty of first-degree murder or some lesser charge, such as second-degree murder or manslaughter, or even no crime at all, depends on the explanation for her act of killing Victor.

Several of the earlier arguments also provided explanations. The medical examiner cited the head wound to explain why Victor stopped breathing. The victim's identity explained why his friends said he was Victor. The fact that the bullet came out of a particular gun explained why it had certain markings. The legislature's vote explained why the killing was illegal. And so on.

In this way, what appears appears at first to be a simple case actually depends on a complex chain of arguments that mixes justifications with explanations. All of these justifications and explanations can be understood by presenting them explicitly in the form of arguments.

One final point is crucial. Suppose that Madison has no justification or excuse for killing Victor. It is still not enough for the prosecutor to give any old argument that Madison killed Victor. The prosecution must prove guilt beyond a reasonable doubt. This burden of proof makes the strength of the argument crucial. You as a juror should not convict, even if you think Madison is guilty, unless the prosecution's argument meets this high standard. In this case, as in many others, it is not enough just to be able to identify the argument and to understand its purpose. You also need to determine how strong it is.

For such reasons, we all need to understand arguments and to be able to evaluate them. This need arises not only in law but also in life, such as when we decide which candidate to vote for, what course to take, whether to believe that your spouse is cheating on you, and so on. The goal of this book is to teach the skills needed for understanding and assessing arguments about important issues like these.

DISCUSSION QUESTIONS

The following arguments mix justification with explanation. For each part of the argument, determine whether it is a justification or an explanation. How does each sub-argument work? How strong is it? How would you respond if you disagreed? How would you defend that part against criticisms?

It will, of course, be difficult to answer these questions before studying the rest of this book. However, it is worthwhile to reflect on how much you already understand at the start. It is also useful to have some concrete examples to keep in mind as you study arguments in more depth.

1. Dinosaurs are fascinating, and we cannot help but wonder what killed these magnificent creatures. The following argument tries to show that they were killed when a giant meteor struck the earth, but first the authors need to argue against alternatives to this impact hypothesis.

AN EXTRATERRESTRIAL IMPACT
------------■------------

by Walter Alvarez and Frank Asaro
from *Scientific American* (October 1990), pp. 78–92

About 65 million years ago something killed half of all the life on the earth. This sensational crime wiped out the dinosaurs, until then undisputed masters of the animal kingdom, and left the humble mammals to inherit their estate. Human beings, descended from those survivors, cannot avoid asking who or what committed the mass murder and what permitted our distant ancestors to survive. . . .

Murder suspects typically must have means, motive and opportunity. An impact [of a giant meteor, probably in the Yucatan peninsula] certainly had the means to cause the Cretaceous extinction, and the evidence that an impact occurred at exactly the right time points to opportunity.

The impact hypothesis provides, if not motive, then at least a mechanism behind the crime. How do other suspects in the killing of dinosaurs fare?

Some have an air-tight alibi: they could not have killed all the different organisms that died at the KT boundary. The venerable notion that mammals ate the dinosaurs' eggs, for example, does not explain the simultaneous extinction of marine foraminifera and ammonites.

(continued)

Stefan Gartner of Texas A&M University once suggested that marine life was killed by a sudden huge flood of fresh water from the Arctic Ocean, which apparently was isolated from other oceans during the late Cretaceous and filled with fresh water. Yet this ingenious mechanism cannot account for the extinction of the dinosaurs or the loss of many species of land plants.

Other suspects might have had the ability to kill, but they have alibis based on timing. Some scientific detectives have tried to pin the blame for mass extinction on changes in climate or sea level, for example. Such changes, however, take much longer to occur than did the extinction; moreover, they do not seem to have coincided with the extinction, and they have occurred repeatedly throughout the earth's history without accompanying extinctions.

Others consider volcanism a prime suspect. The strongest evidence implicating volcanoes is the Deccan Traps, an enormous outpouring of basaltic lava in India that occurred approximately 65 million years ago. Recent paleomagnetic work by Vincent E. Courtillot and his colleagues in Paris confirms previous studies. They show that most of the Deccan Traps erupted during a single period of reversed geomagnetic polarity, with slight overlaps into the preceding and succeeding periods of normal polarity. The Paris team has found that the interval in question is probably 29R, during which the KT extinction occurred, although it might be the reversed-polarity interval immediately before or after 29R as well.

Because the outpouring of the Deccan Traps began in one normal interval and ended in the next, the eruptions that gave rise to them must have taken place over at least 0.5 Myr. Most workers interested in mass extinction therefore have not considered volcanism a serious suspect in a killing that evidently took place over 0.001 Myr or less. . . .

Moreover, basaltic spherules in the KT boundary argue against explosive volcanism in any case; spherules might be generated by quieter forms of volcanism, but then they could not be transported worldwide. The apparent global distribution of the iridium anomaly, shocked quartz and basaltic spherules is strong evidence exonerating volcanism and pointing to impact. Eruptions take place at the bottom of the atmosphere; they send material into the high stratosphere at best. Spherules and quartz grains, if they came from an eruption, would quickly be slowed by atmospheric drag and fall to the ground.

Nevertheless, the enormous eruptions that created the Deccan Traps did occur during a period spanning the KT extinction. Further, they represent the greatest outpouring of lava on land in the past quarter of a billion years (although greater volumes flow continually out of mid-ocean ridges). No investigator can afford to ignore that kind of coincidence.

It seems possible that impact triggered the Deccan Traps volcanism. A few minutes after a large body hit the earth the initial crater would be 40 kilometers deep, and the release of pressure might cause the hot rock of the underlying mantle to melt. Authorities on the origin of volcanic provinces, however, find it very difficult to explain in detail how an impact could trigger large-scale basaltic volcanism.

In the past few years the debate between supporters of each scenario has become polarized: impact proponents have tended to ignore the Deccan Traps as irrelevant, while volcano backers have tried to explain away evidence for impact by suggesting that it is also compatible with volcanism.

Our sense is that the argument is a Hegelian one, with an impact thesis and a volcanic antithesis in search of a synthesis whose outlines are as yet unclear. . . .

2. In his famous testimony to the United Nations Security Council on February 5, 2003, which was 42 days before U.S. troops entered Iraq, Secretary of Defense Colin Powell gave several arguments for his main conclusion that Saddam Hussein was at that time still trying to obtain fissile material for a nuclear weapons program.

. . . Let me turn now to nuclear weapons. We have no indication that Saddam Hussein has ever abandoned his nuclear weapons program. On the contrary, we have more than a decade of proof that he remains determined to acquire nuclear weapons.

To fully appreciate the challenge that we face today, remember that in 1991 the inspectors searched Iraq's primary nuclear weapons facilities for the first time, and they found nothing to conclude that Iraq had a nuclear weapons program. But, based on defector information, in May of 1991, Saddam Hussein's lie was exposed. In truth, Saddam Hussein had a massive clandestine nuclear weapons program that covered several different techniques to enrich uranium, including electromagnetic isotope separation, gas centrifuge and gas diffusion.

We estimate that this illicit program cost the Iraqis several billion dollars. Nonetheless, Iraq continued to tell the IAEA that it had no nuclear weapons program. If Saddam had not been stopped, Iraq could have produced a nuclear bomb by 1993, years earlier than most worst case assessments that had been made before the war.

In 1995, as a result of another defector, we find out that, after his invasion of Kuwait, Saddam Hussein had initiated a crash program to build a crude nuclear weapon, in violation of Iraq's UN obligations. Saddam Hussein already possesses two out of the three key components needed to build a nuclear bomb. He has a cadre of nuclear scientists with the expertise, and he has a bomb design.

Since 1998, his efforts to reconstitute his nuclear program have been focused on acquiring the third and last component: sufficient fissile material to produce a nuclear explosion. To make the fissile material, he needs to develop an ability to enrich uranium. Saddam Hussein is determined to get his hands on a nuclear bomb.

He is so determined that he has made repeated covert attempts to acquire high-specification aluminum tubes from 11 different countries, even after inspections resumed. These tubes are controlled by the Nuclear Suppliers Group precisely because they can be used as centrifuges for enriching uranium.

By now, just about everyone has heard of these tubes and we all know that there are differences of opinion. There is controversy about what these tubes are for. Most U.S. experts think they are intended to serve as rotors in centrifuges used to enrich uranium. Other experts, and the Iraqis themselves, argue that they are really to produce the rocket bodies for a conventional weapon, a multiple rocket launcher.

(continued)

Let me tell you what is not controversial about these tubes. First, all the experts who have analyzed the tubes in our possession agree that they can be adapted for centrifuge use.

Second, Iraq had no business buying them for any purpose. They are banned for Iraq.

I am no expert on centrifuge tubes, but this is an old army trooper. I can tell you a couple things.

First, it strikes me as quite odd that these tubes are manufactured to a tolerance that far exceeds U.S. requirements for comparable rockets. Maybe Iraqis just manufacture their conventional weapons to a higher standard than we do, but I don't think so.

Second, we actually have examined tubes from several different batches that were seized clandestinely before they reached Baghdad. What we notice in these different batches is a progression to higher and higher levels of specification, including in the latest batch an anodized coating on extremely smooth inner and outer surfaces.

Why would they continue refining the specifications? Why would they go to all that trouble for something that, if it was a rocket, would soon be blown into shrapnel when it went off?

The high-tolerance aluminum tubes are only part of the story. We also have intelligence from multiple sources that Iraq is attempting to acquire magnets and high-speed balancing machines. Both items can be used in a gas centrifuge program to enrich uranium.

In 1999 and 2000, Iraqi officials negotiated with firms in Romania, India, Russia and Slovenia for the purchase of a magnet production plant. Iraq wanted the plant to produce magnets weighing 20 to 30 grams. That's the same weight as the magnets used in Iraq's gas centrifuge program before the Gulf War.

This incident, linked with the tubes, is another indicator of Iraq's attempt to reconstitute its nuclear weapons program.

Intercepted communications from mid-2000 through last summer showed that Iraqi front companies sought to buy machines that can be used to balance gas centrifuge rotors. One of these companies also had been involved in a failed effort in 2001 to smuggle aluminum tubes into Iraq.

People will continue to debate this issue, but there is no doubt in my mind. These illicit procurement efforts show that Saddam Hussein is very much focused on putting in place the key missing piece from his nuclear weapons program, the ability to produce fissile material. . . .

THE WEB OF LANGUAGE

Arguments are made up of language, so we cannot understand arguments without first understanding language. This chapter will examine some of the basic features of language, stressing three main ideas. First, language is conventional. *Words acquire meaning within a rich system of linguistic conventions and rules. Second, the uses of language are* diverse. *We use language to communicate information, but we also use it to ask questions, issue orders, write poetry, keep score, formulate arguments, and perform an almost endless number of other tasks. Third, meaning is often conveyed* indirectly. *To understand the significance of many utterances, we must go beyond what is literally said to examine what is conversationally implied by saying it.*

LANGUAGE AND CONVENTION

The preceding chapter stressed that arguing is a *practical* activity. More specifically, it is a *linguistic* activity. Arguing is one of the many things that we can do with words. In fact, unlike things that we can accomplish both with words and without words (like making people happy, angry, and so forth), arguing is something we can *only* do with words or other meaningful symbols. That is why nonhuman animals never give arguments. To understand how arguments work, then, it is crucial to understand how language works.

Unfortunately, our understanding of human language is far from complete, and linguistics is a young science in which disagreement exists on many important issues. Still, certain facts about language are beyond dispute, and recognizing them will provide a background for understanding how arguments work.

As anyone who has bothered to think about it knows, language is conventional. There is no reason why we, as English speakers, use the word "dog" to refer to a dog rather than to a cat, a tree, or the number of planets in our solar system. It seems that any word might have been used to stand for anything. Beyond this, there seems to be no reason why we put words together the way we do. In English, we put adjectives before the nouns they modify. We thus speak of a "green salad." In French, adjectives usually follow the noun, and so, instead of saying "verte salade," the French say "salade verte." The conventions of our own language are so much with us that it strikes us as odd when we discover that other languages have different conventions. A French diplomat once praised his own language because, as he said, it followed the natural order of thought. This strikes English speakers as silly, but in seeing why it is silly, we see that the word order in our own language is conventional as well.

Although it is important to realize that language is conventional, it is also important not to misunderstand this fact. From the idea that language is conventional, it is easy to conclude that language is totally arbitrary. If language is totally arbitrary, then it might seem that it really does not matter which words we use or how we put them together. It takes only a little thought to see that this view, however daring it might seem, misrepresents the role of conventions in language. If we wish to communicate with others, we must follow the system of conventions that others use. Grapefruits are more like big lemons than like grapes, so you might want to call them "mega-lemons." Still, if you order a glass of mega-lemon juice in a restaurant, you will get stares and smirks but no grapefruit juice. The same point lies behind this famous passage in *Through the Looking Glass,* by Lewis Carroll:

> "There's glory for you!"
> "I don't know what you mean by 'glory'," Alice said.
> Humpty Dumpty smiled contemptuously.
> "Of course you don't—till I tell you. I meant 'there's a nice knock-down argument for you!'"
> "But 'glory' doesn't mean 'a nice knock-down argument'," Alice objected.
> "When I use a word," Humpty Dumpty said, in a rather scornful tone, "it means just what I choose it to mean—neither more nor less."
> "The question is," said Alice, "whether you can make words mean so many different things."

The point, of course, is that Humpty Dumpty cannot make a word mean whatever he wants it to mean, and he cannot communicate if he uses words in his own peculiar way without regard to what those words themselves mean. Communication can take place only within a shared system of conventions. Conventions do not destroy meaning by making it arbitrary; conventions bring meaning into existence.

A misunderstanding of the conventional nature of language can lead to pointless disputes. Sometimes, in the middle of a discussion, someone will declare that "the whole thing is just a matter of definition" or "what you say is true by your definition, false by mine." There are times when definitions are important and the truth of what is said turns on them, but usually this is not the case. Suppose someone has fallen off a cliff and is heading toward certain death on the rocks below. Of course, it is a matter of convention that we use the word "death" to describe the result of the sudden, sharp stop at the end of the fall. We might have used some other word—perhaps "birth"—instead. But it certainly will not help a person who is falling to his certain death to shout out, "By 'birth' I mean death." It will not help even if *everyone* agrees to use these words in this new way. If we all decided to adopt this new convention, we would then say, "He is falling from the cliff to his certain birth" instead of "He is falling from the cliff to his certain death." But speaking in this way will not change the facts. It will not save him from perishing. It will not make those who care for him feel better.

The upshot of this simple example is that the *truth* of what we say is rarely just a matter of definition. Whether what we have said is true or not will depend, for the most part, on how things stand in the world. Abraham Lincoln, during his days as a trial lawyer, is reported to have cross-examined a witness like this:

> "How many legs does a horse have?"
> "Four," said the witness.
> "Now, if we call a tail a leg, how many legs does a horse have?"
> "Five," answered the witness.
> "Nope," said Abe, "calling a tail a leg don't make it a leg."

In general, then, though the *meaning of* what we say is dependent on convention, the *truth* of what we say is not.

In the preceding sentence we used the qualifying phrase, "in general." To say that a claim holds *in general* indicates that there may be exceptions. This qualification is needed because sometimes the truth of what we say *is* simply a matter of definition. Take a simple example: The claim that a triangle has three sides is true by definition, because a triangle is defined as "a closed figure having three sides." Again, if someone says that sin is wrong, he or she has said something that is true by definition, for a sin is defined as, among other things, "something that is wrong." In unusual cases like these, things are true merely as a matter of convention. Still, in general, the truth of what we say is settled not by appealing to definitions but, instead, by looking at the facts. In this way, language is not arbitrary, even though it is conventional.

LINGUISTIC ACTS

In the previous section we saw that a language is a system of shared conventions that allows us to communicate with one another. If we examine language, we will see that it contains many different kinds of conventions. These conventions govern what we will call linguistic acts, speech acts, and conversational acts. We will discuss linguistic acts first.

We have seen that words have meanings conventionally attached to them. The word "dog" is used conventionally to talk about dogs. Given what our words mean, it would be incorrect to call dogs "airplanes." Proper names are also conventionally assigned, for Harry Jones could have been named Wilbur Jones. Still, given that his name is not Wilbur, it would be improper to call him Wilbur. Rules like these, which govern meaning and reference, can be called *semantic* rules.

Other conventions concern the ways words can be put together to form sentences. These are often called *syntactic* or *grammatical* rules. Using the three words "John," "hit," and "Harry," we can formulate sentences with very different meanings, such as "John hit Harry" and "Harry hit John." We recognize that these sentences have different meanings, because we understand the grammar of our language. This grammatical understanding also allows us to see that the sentence "Hit John Harry" has no determinate meaning, even though the individual words do. (Notice that "Hit John, Harry!" *does* mean something: It is a way of telling Harry to hit John.) Grammatical rules are important, for they play a part in giving a meaning to combinations of words, such as sentences.

Some of our grammatical rules play only a small role in this important task of giving meaning to combinations of words. It is bad grammar to say, "If I was you, I wouldn't do that," but it is still clear what information the person is trying to convey. What might be called stylistic rules of grammar are of relatively little importance for logic, but grammatical rules that affect the meaning or content of what is said are essential to logical analysis. Grammatical rules of this kind can determine whether we have said one thing rather than another, or perhaps failed to say anything at all and have merely spoken nonsense.

It is sometimes hard to tell what is nonsense. Consider "The horse raced past the barn fell." This sentence usually strikes people as nonsense when they hear it for the first time. To show them that it actually makes sense, all we need to do is insert two words: "The horse that was raced past the barn fell." Since English allows us to drop "that was," the original sentence means the same as the slightly expanded version. Sentences like these are called "garden path sentences," because the first few words "lead you down the garden path" by suggesting that some word plays a grammatical role that it really does not play. In this example, "The horse raced . . ." suggests at first that the main verb is "raced." That makes it hard to see that the main verb really is "fell."

Another famous example is "Buffalo buffalo buffalo." Again, this seems like nonsense at first, but then someone points out that "buffalo" can be a verb meaning "to confuse." The sentence "Buffalo buffalo buffalo" then means "North American bison confuse North American bison." Indeed, we can even make sense out of "Buffalo buffalo Buffalo buffalo buffalo buffalo Buffalo buffalo Buffalo buffalo buffalo." This means "North American bison from Buffalo, New York, that North American bison from Buffalo, New York, confuse also confuse North American bison from Buffalo, New York, that North American bison from Buffalo, New York, confuse."

Examples like these show that sentences can have linguistic meaning when they seem meaningless. To be meaningful, sentences need to follow both *semantic* conventions that govern meanings of individual words and also *syntactic* or *grammatical* conventions that lay down rules for combining words into meaningful wholes. When a sentence satisfies essential semantic and syntactic conventions, we will say that the person who uttered that sentence performed a *linguistic act:* The speaker said something meaningful in a language.[1] The ability to perform linguistic acts shows a command of a language. What the speaker says may be false, irrelevant, boring, and so on; but, if in saying it linguistic rules are not seriously violated, then that person can be credited with performing a linguistic act.

Later, in Chapters 13–14, we will look more closely at semantic and syntactic conventions, for they are common sources of fallacies and other confusions. In particular, we shall see how these conventions can generate fallacies of ambiguity and fallacies of vagueness. Before examining the defects of our language, however, we should first appreciate that language is a powerful and subtle tool that allows us to perform a wide variety of jobs important for living in the world.

EXERCISE I

Read each of the following sentences aloud. Did you perform a linguistic act? If so, explain what the sentence means and why it might not seem meaningful.

1. The old man the ship.
2. Colorless green ideas sleep furiously.
3. Time flies like an arrow. Fruit flies like bananas.
4. The cotton clothing is made of grows in Mississippi.
5. The square root of pine is tree.
6. The man who whistles tunes pianos.
7. To force heaven, Mars shall have a new angel. (from Monk)
8. "'Twas brillig, and the slithy toves did gyre and gimble in the wabe." (from Lewis Carroll)

And now some weird examples from Dan Wegner's Hidden Brain Damage Scale. If these make sense to you, it might be a sign of hidden brain damage. If they don't make sense, explain why:

9. People tell me one thing one day and out the other.
10. I feel as much like I did yesterday as I do today.
11. My throat is closer than it seems.
12. Likes and dislikes are among my favorites.
13. I've lost all sensation in my shirt.
14. There's only one thing for me.
15. I don't like any of my loved ones.

1. When an actor on a stage says lines such as "To be or not to be, that is the question," does the actor perform a linguistic act?
2. When someone hums (but does not sing) the "Star-Spangled Banner," does she perform a linguistic act? Why or why not?
3. Can a speaker mispronounce a word in a sentence without performing any linguistic act? Why or why not?

THE FAR SIDE® By GARY LARSON

Understanding only German, Fritz was unaware that the clouds were becoming threatening.

SPEECH ACTS

When we are asked about the function of language, it is natural to reply that we use language to communicate ideas. This is, however, only one of the purposes for which we use language. Other purposes become obvious as soon as we look at the ways in which our language actually works. Adding up a column of figures is a linguistic activity—though it is rarely looked at in this way—but it does not communicate any ideas to others. When I add the figures, I am not even communicating anything to myself: I am trying to figure something out. A look at our everyday conversations produces a host of other examples of language being used for different purposes. Grammarians, for example, have divided sentences into various moods, among which are:

Indicative: Barry Bonds hit a home run.

Imperative: Get in there and hit a home run, Barry!

Interrogative: Did Barry Bonds hit a home run?

Expressive: Hurray for Barry Bonds!

The first sentence states a fact. We can use it to communicate information about something that Barry Bonds did. If we use it in this way, then what we say will be either true or false. Notice that none of the other sentences can be called either true or false even though they are all meaningful.

PERFORMATIVES

The different types of sentences recognized by traditional grammarians indicate that we use language to do more than convey information. But this traditional classification of sentences gives only a small idea of the wide variety of things that we can accomplish using language. Sometimes, for example, in using language we actually *do* things in the sense of bringing something about. In one familiar setting, if one person says, "I do," and another person says, "I do," and finally a third person says, "I now pronounce you husband and wife," the relationship between the first two people changes in a fundamental way: They are thereby married. With luck, they begin a life of wedded bliss, but they also alter their legal relationship. For example, they may now file joint income tax returns and may not legally marry other people without first getting divorced.

In uttering sentences of this kind, the speaker thereby *does* something more than merely *stating* something. The philosopher J. L. Austin labeled such utterances *performatives* in order to contrast performing an action with simply describing something.[2] For example, if an umpire shouts, "You're out!" then the batter is out. The umpire is not merely describing the situation but *declaring* the batter out. By way of contrast, if someone in the stands shouts, "He's out!" the batter is not *thereby* out, although the person who shouts this may be encouraging the umpire to call the batter out or complaining because he didn't.

Performatives come in a wide variety of forms. They are often in the first person (like "I do"), but not always. "You're all invited to my house after the game" is in the second person, but uttering it performs the act of inviting. In some circumstances, one person can speak for another person, a group, or an institution. At political conventions, heads of delegations say things like this: "The delegates from Kentucky, the Bluegrass State and the home of the Kentucky Derby, cast their votes for the next President of the United States, Joe W. Blodgett." In saying this, the speaker performs the act of casting Kentucky's votes in favor of Blodgett. Even silence can amount to a performative act in special situations. When the chairperson of a meeting asks if there are any objections to a ruling and none is voiced, then the voters, through their silence, have accepted the ruling.

Because of this diversity of forms that performatives can take, it is not easy to formulate a definition that covers them all. To avoid this difficulty, we will not even try to define performatives here. Instead, we will concentrate on one particularly clear subclass of performatives, what J. L. Austin called *explicit performatives*. All explicit performatives are utterances in the first-person singular indicative noncontinuous[3] present. But not all utterances of that form are explicit performatives. There is one more requirement:

> An utterance of that form is an explicit performative if and only if it yields a true statement when plugged into the following pattern:
> In saying "I _____" in appropriate circumstances, I thereby _____.

For example, "I congratulate you" expresses an explicit performative, because, in saying "I congratulate you," I thereby congratulate you. Here a quoted expression occurs on the left side of the word "thereby" but not on the right side. This reflects the fact that the formula takes us from the words (which are quoted) to the world (the actual act that is performed). The *saying*, which is referred to on the left side of the pattern, amounts to the *doing* referred to on the right side of the word "thereby." We will call this the *thereby test* for explicit performatives. It provides a convenient way of identifying explicit performatives.

The thereby test includes an important qualification: *The context of the utterance must be appropriate.* You have not congratulated anyone if you say, "I congratulate you," when no one is around, unless you are congratulating yourself. Congratulations said by an actor in a play are not real congratulations, and so on. Later in this chapter, we will try to clarify what makes a context appropriate.

Assuming an appropriate context, all of the following sentences meet the thereby test:

I promise to meet you tomorrow.

I bid sixty-six dollars. (said at an auction)

I bid one club. (said in a bridge game)

I resign from this club.

I apologize for being late.

Notice that it doesn't make sense to *deny* any of these performatives. If someone says, "I bid sixty-six dollars," it is not appropriate for someone to reply "No, you don't" or "That's false." It could, however, be appropriate for someone to reply, "You can't bid sixty-six dollars, because the bidding is already up to seventy dollars." In this case, the person tried to make a bid, but failed to do so.

Several explicit performatives play important roles in constructing arguments. These include sentences of the following kind:

I *conclude* that this bill should be voted down.

I *base* my conclusion on the assumption that we do not want to hurt the poor.

I *stipulate* that anyone who earns less than $10,000 is poor.

I *assure* you that this bill will hurt the poor.

I *concede* that I am not absolutely certain.

I *admit* that there is much to be said on both sides of this issue.

I *give my support* to the alternative measure.

I *deny* that this alternative will hurt the economy.

I *grant* for the sake of argument that some poor people are lazy.

I *reply* that most poor people contribute to the economy.

I *reserve comment* on other issues raised by this bill.

We will call this kind of performative an *argumentative performative.* Studying such argumentative performatives can help us to understand what is going on in arguments (which is one main reason why we are studying performatives here).

In contrast to the above utterances, which pass the thereby test, none of the following utterances does:

I agree with you. (This describes one's thoughts or beliefs, so, unlike a performative, it can be false.)

I am sorry for being late. (This describes one's feelings and could be false.)

Yesterday I bid sixty dollars. (This is a statement about a past act and might be false.)

I'll meet you tomorrow. (This utterance may only be a prediction that can turn out to be false.)

Questions, imperatives, and exclamations are not explicit performatives, because they cannot sensibly be plugged into the thereby test at all. They do not have the right form, since they are not in the first-person singular indicative noncontinuous present.

EXERCISE II

Using the thereby test as described above, indicate which of the following sentences express explicit performatives (EP) and which do not express explicit performatives (N) in appropriate circumstances:

1. I pledge allegiance to the flag.
2. We pledge allegiance to the flag.
3. I pledged allegiance to the flag.
4. I always pledge allegiance at the start of a game.
5. You pledge allegiance to the flag.

(continued)

6. He pledges allegiance to the flag.

7. He doesn't pledge allegiance to the flag.

8. Pledge allegiance to the flag!

9. Why don't you pledge allegiance to the flag?

10. Pierre is the capital of South Dakota.

11. I state that Pierre is the capital of South Dakota.

12. I order you to leave.

13. Get out of here!

14. I didn't take it.

15. I swear that I didn't take it.

16. I won't talk to you.

17. I refuse to talk to you.

18. I'm out of gas.

19. I feel devastated.

20. Bummer!

21. I claim this land for England.

22. I bring you greetings from home.

KINDS OF SPEECH ACTS

Recognizing explicit performatives helps break the spell of the idea that language functions only to transmit information. It also introduces us to a kind of act distinct from linguistic acts. We will call them *speech acts*.[4] They include such acts as stating, promising, swearing, and refusing. A speech act is the conventional move that a remark makes in a language exchange. It is what is done *in* saying something.

It is difficult to give a precise definition of a speech act, but we can begin by contrasting speech acts with linguistic acts. A linguistic act, we said, is the act of saying something meaningful in a language. It is important to see that the same linguistic act can play different roles as it occurs in different contexts. This is shown by the following brief conversations.

A: Is there any pizza left?

B: Yes.

A: Do you promise to pay me back by Friday?

B: Yes.

A: Do you swear to tell the truth?

B: Yes.

A: Do you refuse to leave?

B: Yes.

Here the same linguistic act, uttering the word "yes," is used to do four different things: to state something, to make a promise, to take an oath, and to refuse to do something.

We can make this idea of a speech act clearer by using the notion of an explicit performative. Explicit performatives provide a systematic way of identifying different kinds of speech acts. The basic idea is that different speech acts are named by the different verbs that occur in explicit performatives. We can thus use the thereby test to search for different kinds of speech acts. For example:

If I say, "I promise," I thereby promise. So "I promise" is a performative, and *promising* is a kind of speech act.

If I say, "I resign," I thereby resign. So "I resign" is a performative, and *resigning* is a kind of speech act.

If I say, "I apologize," I thereby apologize. So "I apologize" is a performative, and *apologizing* is a kind of speech act.

If I say, "I question his honesty," I thereby question his honesty. So "I question his honesty" is a performative, and *questioning* is a kind of speech act.

If I say, "I conclude that she is guilty," I thereby conclude that she is guilty. So "I conclude that she is guilty" is a performative, and *concluding* is a kind of speech act.

The main verbs that appear in such explicit performatives can be called *performative verbs*. Performative verbs name kinds of speech acts.[5]

Still, the same speech act can also be performed without any performative verb. I can deny my opponent's claim by saying either "I deny that" or simply "No way!" Both utterances perform the speech act of denying, even though only the former is a performative. The latter is not a performative and does not contain any performative verb, but it still performs a speech act. Similarly, I can assure you by saying either "I assure you that I am right" or "There's no doubt about it." Both utterances perform the speech act of assuring, even though only the former is a performative.

Thus far, we have emphasized that we do a great deal more with language than make statements, assert facts, and describe things—that is, we do more with language than put forward claims that are either true or false. But we also use language to do these things, so stating, asserting, and describing are themselves kinds of speech acts. This can be shown by using the thereby test:

If I say, "I state that I am a U.S. citizen," I thereby state that I am a U.S. citizen.

If I say, "I assert that the defendant was in Detroit at the time of the crime," I thereby assert that the defendant was in Detroit at that time.

If I say, "I describe him as being dark haired and just over six feet tall," I thereby describe him as being dark haired and just over six feet tall.

We now have a more accurate conception of the way in which language functions than the common conception that the function of language is to convey ideas. Making claims that are either true or false is one important kind of speech act, but we perform a great many other kinds of speech acts that are also important.

EXERCISE III

Which of the following verbs names a speech act?

1. *capture* the suspect
2. *assert* that the suspect is guilty
3. *stare* accusingly at the suspect
4. *find* the defendant guilty
5. *take* the defendant away
6. *punish* the defendant
7. *revoke* the defendant's driver's license
8. *welcome* the prisoner to prison
9. *order* the prisoner to be silent
10. *lock* the cell door

EXERCISE IV

Using a dictionary, find ten verbs that can be used to construct explicit performatives that have not yet been mentioned in this chapter.

SPEECH ACT RULES

The distinctive feature of a performative utterance is that, in a sense we have tried to make clear, the saying constitutes a doing of something. In saying, "I pronounce you husband and wife," a minister is not simply describing a marriage ceremony, she is performing it. Here, however, an objection might arise. Suppose someone who is a supporter of family values goes about the streets pronouncing random couples husband and wife. Unless this person is a member of the clergy, a justice of the peace, a ship's captain, or the like, that person will have no right to make such pronouncements. Furthermore, even if this person is, say, a crazed member of the clergy, the pronouncement will still not come off—that is, the utterance will not succeed in making any-one husband and wife. The parties addressed have to say, "I do," they must have a proper license, and so on. This example shows that a speech act will *fail to come off* or will be *void* unless certain rules or conventions are satisfied. These rules or conventions that must be satisfied for a speech act to come off and not be void will be called *speech act rules*.

The main types of speech act rules can be discovered by considering the following questions:

1. *Must the speaker use any special words or formulas to perform the speech act?*

Sometimes a speech act will come off only if certain words or formulas are used. In baseball the umpire must say, "Strike two," or something very close to this, in order to call a second strike. In a pickup game it might be all right to say instead, "Hey, that's two bad ones on you, baby!" but that way of calling strikes is not permitted in serious play. Similarly, certain legal documents are not valid if they are not properly signed, endorsed, notarized, and so forth.

2. *Is any response or uptake by the audience needed in order to complete the speech act?*

Sometimes a speech act will come off only if there is an uptake by another person. A person can *offer* a bet by saying, "I bet you ten dollars that the Angels will win today," but this person will have *made* a bet only if the other person says, "Done" or "You're on," shakes hands, or in some other way accepts the bet. A marriage ceremony is completely void if one of the parties does not say, "I do," but instead says, "Well, maybe I should think about this for a while."

3. *Must the (a) speaker or (b) audience hold any special position or role in order for the speaker to perform the speech act?*

Sometimes a speech act will come off only if it is performed by someone with an official position. We have already seen that, for someone to make two people husband and wife by pronouncing them husband and wife, that person must hold a certain official position. Similarly, even if a body is plainly dead when it arrives at the hospital, a janitor cannot pronounce it dead on arrival. That is the job of a doctor or a coroner. In the same way, although a shortstop can perform the linguistic act of *shouting*, "You're out," a shortstop cannot perform the speech act of *calling* someone out. Only an umpire can do that. Moreover, even an umpire cannot call out the catcher or a spectator, so sometimes the audience of the speech also needs to have some special position.

4. *Are any other special circumstances required for the speech act?*

Most speech acts also involve assumptions or presuppositions that certain *facts* obtain. A father cannot bequeath an antique car to his son if he does not own such a car. You cannot resign from the American Civil Liberties Union or the Veterans of Foreign Wars if you are not a member. These special circumstances might sometimes include the audience's desires. In promising someone to do something, for example, we usually do so in the belief that the person *wants* us to do it. For example, I will promise to drive someone to the airport only if I believe that person wants to go the airport and would like me to drive her there. Sometimes, however, we do promise to do things a person does not want done. I can promise to throw someone out if he doesn't behave himself. Here, however, I am making a threat, not a promise. Different answers to this question, thus, reveal differences among speech acts.

5. *What feelings, desires, or beliefs is the speaker expected to have?*

If we apologize for something, we are expected to feel sorry for what we have done. If we congratulate someone, we are usually supposed to be pleased with that person's success. If we state something, we are expected to believe what we say. In all these cases—in apologizing, congratulating, and stating—if the speaker lacks the expected feelings, desires, or beliefs, the speaker still does succeed in performing the speech act, but that speaker and speech act are subject to criticism. In this respect, this rule differs from the preceding rules. Those preceding rules reflected conventions that must be satisfied for the speech act to come off (for it not to be void). In contrast, the person who says, "I apologize," has apologized even if he or she does not feel sorry. The speech act does come off and is not void, even though the apology can be criticized as insincere.

6. *What general purpose or purposes are served by this kind of speech act?*

This final question asks why a certain kind of speech act exists at all. Why, for example, is there the speech act of promising? That is a rather complicated question, but the primary reason for the institution of promising is that it helps people coordinate their activities. People who make promises place themselves under an obligation to do something. When promises are contractual, this obligation is a legal obligation. Promise making, then, increases the confidence we can have that someone will do what they said they will do, and, for legal promises at least, provides remedies when they do not. To cite another example of the purpose of a speech act, apologizing expresses regret for harming or insulting someone. One of its purposes is to normalize relations between the speaker and the person harmed or insulted.

Answering the six questions listed above for a particular kind of speech act is called giving a *speech act analysis*. For example, here is a brief speech act analysis of "to appoint," as in, "I appoint you to the judiciary committee":

1. Appointments are usually made by using the word "appoint," but other words can be used as well; for example, "name" and "designate" can also be used to do this job. You cannot, however, say, "I wish you were on the judiciary committee."

2. Sometimes further actions by others are necessary for an appointment to come off. Perhaps ratification is needed. Before ratification, the word "nominate" is often used. In such cases, only after the nomination is ratified has the appointment been made. Usually the appointment does not come off if the person declines the appointment.

3. Normally, someone who appoints a person to something must have the *power* to make such appointments. For example, Queen Elizabeth II does not have the power to appoint the commissioner of baseball.

4. This speech act presupposes a wide variety of facts, for example, that a position exists, that the person appointed to it is eligible for this appointment, and so on.

5. Appointments are often made with the belief that the person appointed will do a good job. This is not always the case, however, as appointments are made for all sorts of different reasons—rewarding an important supporter, for example.

6. An important purpose of an appointment is to explicitly designate someone to play a particular role. For example, it is often important to know who is in charge. It can also be important that the person who gains this role does so through regular, authorized procedures.

EXERCISE V

Give a speech act analysis of the ten verbs below by writing two or three sentences in response to each of the six questions above. Speech act analyses can go on much longer, but your goal here is just to bring out the most interesting features of the speech act named by each verb.

1. to bet
2. to promise
3. to congratulate
4. to state
5. to apologize

6. to deny
7. to vote
8. to give up (in a fight)
9. to thank
10. to invite

DISCUSSION QUESTIONS

1. Imagine that an actor on stage during a modern play screams, "Fire! No, I really mean it. " The audience realizes that he is just acting, so they laugh. Then the actor sees a real fire behind the stage out of view of the audience. The actor again screams, "Fire! No, I really mean it. *Fire!*" Which speech act, if any, does the actor perform in uttering these words the second time? Why? What does this show about speech acts?

2. *Do* the speech acts in which people get married presuppose that the people who are getting married are of different sexes? *Should* these speech acts presuppose this fact? Why or why not?

3. The importance of deciding what kind of speech act has been performed is illustrated by a classic case from the law of contracts, *Hawkins v. McGee.*[6] McGee performed an operation on Hawkins that proved unsuccessful, and Hawkins sued for damages. He did not sue on the basis of malpractice, however, but on the basis of breach of contract. His attorney argued that the doctor initiated a contractual relationship in that he tried to persuade Hawkins to have the operation by saying things such as "I will guarantee to make the hand a hundred percent perfect hand." He made statements of this kind a number of times, and Hawkins finally agreed to undergo the operation on the basis of these remarks. Hawkins's attorney maintained that these exchanges, which took place in the doctor's office on a number of occasions, constituted an offer of a contract that Hawkins explicitly accepted. The attorney for the surgeon replied that these words, even if uttered, would not constitute an offer of a contract, but merely

(continued)

expressed a *strong belief,* and that reasonable people should know that doctors cannot guarantee results.

It is important to remember that contracts do not have to be written and signed to be binding. A proper verbal offer and acceptance are usually sufficient to constitute a contract. The case, then, turned on two questions: (1) Did McGee utter the words attributed to him? In other words, did McGee perform the *linguistic act* attributed to him? The jury decided that he did. (2) The second, more interesting question was whether these words, when uttered in this particular context, amounted to an offer of a contract, as Hawkins's attorney maintained, or merely were an expression of strong belief, as McGee's attorney held. In other words, the fundamental question in this case was what kind of *speech act* McGee performed when trying to convince Hawkins to have the operation.

Explain how you would settle this case. (The court actually ruled in favor of Hawkins, but you are free to disagree.)

CONVERSATIONAL ACTS[7]

In examining linguistic acts (saying something meaningful in a language) and then speech acts (doing something in using words), we have largely ignored some central features of language: It is usually—though not always—a *social* activity that takes place among people. It is also normally a *practical* activity with certain goals. We use language in order to inform people of things, get them to do things, amuse them, calm them down, and so on. We can capture these social and practical aspects of language by introducing the notion of a *conversational exchange,* that is, a situation where various speakers use speech acts in order to bring about some effects in each other. We will call this act of using a speech act to cause a standard effect in another a *conversational act.*

Suppose, for example, Amy says to Bobbi, "Someone is following us." In this case, Amy has performed a linguistic act; that is, she has uttered a meaningful sentence in the English language. Amy has also performed a speech act—specifically, she has *stated* that they are being followed. The point of performing this speech act is to produce in Bobbi a particular belief—namely, that they are being followed. (Amy's utterance might also have other purposes, such as to alert Bobbi to some danger, but it accomplishes those other purposes by means of getting Bobbi to believe they are being followed.) If Amy is successful in this, then Amy has successfully performed the conversational act of producing this belief in Bobbi. Amy, of course, might fail in her attempt to do this. Amy's linguistic act could be successful and her speech act successful as well, yet, for whatever reason, Bobbi might not accept as true what Amy is telling her. Perhaps Bobbi thinks that Amy is paranoid or just trying to frighten her as some kind of joke. In that case, Amy failed to perform her intended conversational act, even though she did perform her intended linguistic and speech acts.

Here are some other examples of the difference between performing a speech act and performing a conversational act:

> We can *warn* people about something in order to *put them on guard* concerning it.
> Here warning is the speech act; putting them on guard is the intended conversational act.

> We can *urge* people to do things in order to *persuade* them to do these things.
> Here urging is the speech act; persuading is the intended conversational act.

> We can *assure* people concerning something in order to *instill confidence in them*.
> Here assuring is the speech act; instilling confidence is the intended conversational act.

> We can *apologize* to people in order to *make them feel better about us.*
> Here apologizing is the speech act; making them feel better about us is the intended conversational act.

In each of these cases, our speech act may not succeed in having its intended conversational effect. Our urging, warning, and assuring may, respectively, fail to persuade, put on guard, or instill confidence. Indeed, speech acts may bring about the opposite of what was intended. People who brag (a speech act) in order to impress others (the intended conversational act) often actually make others think less of them (the actual effect). In many ways like these, we can perform a speech act without performing the intended conversational act.

The relationship between conversational acts and speech acts is confusing, because both of them can be performed at once by the same utterance. Suppose Carl says, "You are invited to my party." By means of this single utterance, he performs a linguistic act of uttering this meaningful sentence, a speech act of inviting you, and perhaps also a conversational act of getting you to come to his party. Indeed, he would not be able to perform this conversational act without also performing such a speech act, assuming that you would not come to his party if you were not invited. He would also not be able to perform this speech act without performing this linguistic act or something like it, since he cannot invite you by means of an inarticulate grunt or by asking, "Are you invited to my party?"

As a result, we cannot sensibly ask whether Carl's utterance of "You are invited to my party" is a linguistic act, a speech act, or a conversational act. That single utterance performs all three acts at once. Nonetheless, we can distinguish those kinds of acts that Carl performs in terms of the verbs that describe the acts. Some verbs describe speech acts; other verbs describe conversational acts. We can tell which verbs describe which kinds of acts by asking whether the verb passes the thereby test (in which case the verb describes a speech act) or whether, instead, it describes a standard effect of the utterance (in which case the verb describes a conversational act).

Indicate whether the verbs in the following sentences name a speech act, a conversational act, or neither. Assume a standard context. Explain your answers.

1. She *thought* that he did it.
2. She *asserted* that he did it.
3. She *convinced* them that he did it.
4. She *condemned* him in front of everyone.
5. She *challenged* his integrity.
6. She *embarrassed* him in front of them.
7. He *denied* doing it.
8. They *believed* her.
9. They *encouraged* him to admit it.
10. She *told* him to get lost.
11. He *praised* her lavishly.
12. His praise *made* her happy.
13. He *threatened* to reveal her secret.
14. He *submitted* his resignation.
15. Her news *frightened* him half to death.
16. He *advised* her to go into another line of work.
17. She *blamed* him for her troubles.
18. His lecture *enlightened* her.
19. His jokes *amused* her.
20. His book *confused* her.

CONVERSATIONAL RULES

Just as there are rules that govern linguistic acts and other rules that govern speech acts, so too there are rules that govern conversational acts. This should not be surprising, because conversations can be complicated interpersonal activities in need of rules to make them effective in attaining their goals. These underlying rules are implicitly understood by users of the language, but the philosopher Paul Grice was the first person to examine them in careful detail.

We can start by examining standard or normal conversational exchanges where conversation is a cooperative venture—that is, where the people involved in the conversation have some common goal they are trying to achieve in talking with one another. (A prisoner being interrogated and a shop owner being robbed are *not* in such cooperative situations.) According to Grice, such exchanges are governed by what he calls the *Cooperative Principle*. This principle states that the parties involved should use language in a way that contributes toward achieving their common goal. It tells them to cooperate.[8]

This general principle gains more content when we consider other forms of cooperation. Carpenters who want to build a house need enough nails and wood, but not too much. They need the right kinds of nails and wood. They also need to put the nails and wood together in the relevant way—that is, according to their plans. And, of course, they also want to perform their tasks quickly and in the right order. Rational people who want to achieve common goals must follow similar general restrictions in other practical activities. Because cooperative conversations are one such practical activity, speakers who want to cooperate with one another must follow rules analogous to those for carpenters.

Grice spells out four such rules. The first he calls the rule of *Quantity*. It tells us to give the right amount of information. More specifically:

1. Make your contribution as informative as is required (for the current purposes of the exchange).

and possibly:

2. Do not make your contribution more informative than is required.

Here is an application of this rule: A person rushes up to you and asks, "Where is a fire extinguisher?" You know that there is a fire extinguisher five floors away in the basement, and you also know that there is a fire extinguisher just down the hall. Suppose you say that there is a fire extinguisher in the basement. Here you have said something true, but you have violated the first part of the rule of Quantity. You have failed to reveal an important piece of information that, under the rule of Quantity, you should have produced. A violation of the second version of the rule would look like this: As smoke billows down the hall, you say where a fire extinguisher is located on each floor, starting with the basement. Eventually you will get around to saying that there is a fire extinguisher just down the hall, but you bury the point in a mass of unnecessary information.

Grice's second rule is called the rule of *Quality*. In general: Try to make your contribution one that is true. More specifically:

1. Do not say what you believe to be false.
2. Do not say that for which you lack adequate evidence.

In a cooperative activity, you are not supposed to tell lies. Beyond this, you are expected not to talk off the top of your head either. When we make a statement, we can be challenged by someone asking, "Do you really believe that?" or "Why do you believe that?" That a person has the right to ask such questions shows that statement making is governed by the rule of Quality.

In a court of law, witnesses promise to tell the whole truth and nothing but the truth. The demand for *nothing but the truth* reflects the rule of Quality. The demand for *the whole truth* roughly reflects the rule of Quantity. Obviously, nobody really tells every truth he or she knows. Here the *whole* truth concerns all the known truths that are relevant in the context.

This brings us to our next rule, the rule of *Relevance*. Simply stated, the rule of Relevance says:

Be relevant!

Though easy to state, the rule is not easy to explain, because relevance itself is a difficult notion. It is, however, easy to illustrate. If someone asks me where he can find a doctor, I might reply that there is a hospital on the next block. Though not a direct answer to the question, it does not violate the rule of Relevance because it provides a piece of useful information. If, however, in response I tell the person that I like his haircut, then I have violated the rule of Relevance. Clear-cut violations of this principle often involve *changing the subject*.

Another rule concerns the manner of our conversation. We are expected to be clear in what we say. Under the general rule of *Manner* come various special rules:

1. Avoid obscurity of expression.

2. Avoid ambiguity.

3. Be brief.

4. Be orderly.

As an example of the fourth part of this rule, when describing a series of events, it is usually important to state them in the order in which they occurred. It would certainly be misleading to say that two people had a child and got married when, in fact, they had a child after they were married.

Many other rules govern our conversations. "Be polite!" is one of them. "Be charitable!" is another. That is, we should put the best interpretation on what others say, and our replies should reflect this. We should avoid quibbling and being picky. For the most part, however, we will not worry about these other rules.

EXERCISE VII

Indicate which, if any, of Grice's conversational rules are violated by the italicized sentence of each of the following conversations. Assume a standard context. More than one rule might be violated.

1. "What did you get on the last test?" "*A grade.*"

2. "Did you like her singing?" "*Her costume was beautiful.*"

3. "*The governor has the brains of a three-year-old.*"

4. "*The Lone Ranger rode into the sunset and jumped on his horse.*"

5. "*Without her help, we'd be up a creek without a paddle.*"

6. "Where is Palo Alto?" "*On the surface of the Earth.*"

7. "*It will rain tomorrow.*" "How do you know?" "I just guessed."

8. "*Does the dog need to go out for a W-A-L-K [spelled out]?*"

9. "Why did the chicken cross the road?" "*To get to the other side.*"

10. Psychiatrist: "You're crazy." Patient: "I want a second opinion." Psychiatrist: "Okay. *You're ugly,* too."

THE FAR SIDE® By GARY LARSON

When dumb animals attempt murder

CONVERSATIONAL IMPLICATION

In a normal setting where people are cooperating toward reaching a shared goal, they often conform quite closely to Grice's conversational rules. If, on the whole, people did not do this, we could not have the linguistic practices we do. If we thought, for example, that people very often lied (even about the most trivial matters), the business of exchanging information would be badly damaged.

Still, people do not always follow these conversational rules. They withhold information, they elaborate needlessly, they assert what they know to be false, they say the first thing that pops into their heads, they wander off the subject, and they talk vaguely and obscurely. When we observe actual conversations, it is sometimes hard to tell how any information gets communicated at all.

The explanation lies in the same conversational rules. Not only do we usually follow these conventions, we also (1) implicitly realize that we are following them, and (2) expect others to assume that we are following them. This mutual understanding of the commitments involved in a conversational act has the following important consequence: People are able to convey a great deal of information without actually saying it.

A simple example will illustrate this point. Again suppose that a person, with smoke billowing behind him, comes running up to you and asks,

"Where's a fire extinguisher?" You reply, "There's one in the lobby." Through a combination of conversational rules, notably relevance, quantity, and manner, this commits you to the claim that this is the closest, or at least the most accessible, fire extinguisher. Furthermore, the person you are speaking to assumes that you are committed to this. Of course, you have not actually *said* that it is the closest fire extinguisher; but you have, we might say, *implied* this. When we do not actually say something but imply it by virtue of a mutually understood conversational rule, the implication is called a *conversational implication*.

It is important to realize that conversational implication is a pervasive feature of human communication. It is not something we employ only occasionally for special effect. In fact, virtually every conversation relies on these implications, and most conversations would fall apart if people refused to go beyond literal meanings to take into account the implications of saying things. In the following conversation, B is literal-minded in just this way:

A: Do you know what time it is?

B: Not without looking at my watch.

B has answered A's question, but it is hard to imagine that A has received the information she was looking for. Presumably, she wanted to know what time it was, not merely whether B, at that very moment, knew the time. Finding B rather obtuse, A tries again:

A: Can you tell me what time it is?

B: Oh, yes, all I have to do is look at my watch.

Undaunted, A gives it another try:

A: Will you tell me what time it is?

B: I suppose I will as soon as you ask me.

Finally:

A: What time is it?

B: Two o'clock. Why didn't you ask me that in the first place?

Notice that in each of these exchanges B gives a direct and accurate answer to A's question; yet, in all but the last answer, B does not provide A with what A wants. Like a computer in a science-fiction movie, B is taking A's questions too literally. More precisely, B does nothing *more* than take A's remarks literally. In a conversational exchange, we expect others to take our remarks in the light of the obvious purpose we have in making them. We expect them to share our commonsense understanding of why people ask questions. At the very least, we expect people to respond to us in ways that are *relevant* to our purposes. Except at the end, B seems totally oblivious to the point of A's questions. That is what makes B unhelpful and annoying.

Though all the conversational rules we have examined can be the basis of conversational implication, the rule of Relevance is particularly powerful in this respect. Normal conversations are dense with conversational implications that depend on the rule of Relevance. Someone says, "Dinner's ready," and that is immediately taken to be a way of asking people to come to the table. Why? Because dinner's being ready is a transparent *reason* to come to the table to eat. This is an ordinary context that most people are familiar with. Change the context, however, and the conversational implications can be entirely different. Suppose the same words, "Dinner's ready," are uttered when guests have failed to arrive on time. In this context, the conversational implication, which will probably be reflected in an annoyed tone of voice, will be quite different.

To cite another example of context dependence, if someone says, "I broke a finger," people will naturally assume that it is the speaker's own finger that was broken. Why? Because when people break fingers, it is almost always their own fingers that they break. That is the standard context in which this remark is made. If, however, we shift the context, that conversational implication can be lost and another can take its place. Suppose the speaker is a mobster in an extortion racket, that is, someone who physically harms people who do not pay protection money. Among his fellow extortionists, the conversational implication of "I broke a finger" is likely to be that it was someone who refused to pay up who had his finger broken. (We can imagine the extortionist canceling this implication by saying, "No, no, it was *my* finger that got broken when I slugged the guy.")

EXERCISE VIII

Assuming a natural conversational setting, what might a person intend to conversationally imply by making the following remarks? Briefly explain why each of these conversational implications holds; that is, explain the relationship between what the speaker *literally* says and what the speaker intends to convey through conversational implication. Finally, for each example, find a context where the standard conversational implication would fail and another arise in its place.

1. It's getting a little chilly in here. (Said by a visitor in your home)
2. Do you mind if I borrow your pen? (Said to a friend while studying)
3. We are out of soda. (Said by a child to her parents)
4. I got here before he did. (Said in a ticket line)
5. Don't blame me if you get in trouble. (Said by someone who advised you not to do it)
6. Has this seat been taken? (Said in a theater before a show)
7. These sweet potatoes are very filling. (Said when the cook asks if you want more)
8. Don't ask me. (Said in response to a question)
9. Does your dog bite? (Said to a man standing next to a dog)
10. I will be out of town that day. (Said in response to a party invitation)

VIOLATING CONVERSATIONAL RULES

If we look at basic conversational rules, we notice that these rules sometimes clash, or at least push us in different directions. The rule of Quantity encourages us to give as much information as possible, but this is constrained by the rule of Quality, which restricts our claims to things we believe to be true and can back up with good reasons. The demands of the rule of Quantity can also conflict with the demand for brevity. In order to be brief, we must sometimes simplify and even falsify, and this can come into conflict with the rule of Quality, which demands that we say only what we believe to be true. Sometimes it is not important to get things exactly right; sometimes it is. An ongoing conversation can be a constant series of adjustments to this background system of rules.

Because conversational rules can come into conflict with one another, speakers can sometimes *seem* to be violating the Cooperative Principle by violating one of its maxims. This can happen when one conversational rule is overridden by another. Grasping the resolution of such a conflict can generate interesting conversational implications. This may sound complicated, but an example from Grice should make it clear. Suppose *A* tells *B*, "I'm planning to visit *C*; where does he live?" *B* replies, "Somewhere in the south of France." If *A* is interested in visiting *C*, then *B*'s reply really does not give her the information she needs and thus seems to violate the first part of the rule of Quantity. We can explain this departure on the assumption that *B* does not know *exactly* where *C* lives and would thus violate the rule of Quality if he said anything more specific. In this case, *B*'s reply conversationally implies that he does not know exactly where *C* lives.

In a more extreme case, a person may even *flout* one of these conventions, that is, may openly violate a conversational rule without, as in the previous example, there being any other conversational rule that overrides it. Here is an adaptation of one of Grice's examples and his explanation of it:

> *A* is writing a letter of recommendation about one of his students who is applying to law school, and the letter reads as follows: "Dear Sir: Mr. *X*'s command of English is excellent, and his attendance in class has been regular. Yours, etc." (Gloss: *A* cannot be opting out, since if he wished to be uncooperative, why write at all? He cannot be unable, through ignorance, to say more, since the person is his student; moreover, he knows that more information is wanted. He must, therefore, be wishing to impart information he is reluctant to write down. This supposition is only tenable on the assumption that he thinks that Mr. *X* is not a good student. This, then, is what he is implicating.)

This is a case of *damning with faint praise*. Faint praise can be damning because, under the first part of the rule of Quantity, it conversationally implies that no stronger praise is warranted.

We can intentionally violate the rule of Relevance by pointedly changing the subject. Here is variation on another one of Grice's examples:

> Standing outside a classroom, *A* says, "Professor *X* is a moron." There is a moment of shocked silence; then *B* says, "Nice day, isn't it?"

A would have to be fairly dim not to realize that Professor *X*, whom he has just called a moron, may be somewhere nearby. Why else would *B* reply in such an irrelevant manner? So in saying, "Nice day, isn't it?" *B* conversationally implies that Professor *X* is nearby.

Winston Churchill reportedly provided a famous example of intentionally violating the rule of Manner. When criticized for ending a sentence with a preposition, he is said to have replied, "That is the type of criticism up with which I will not put."

EXERCISE IX

These sentences appeared in Exercise VII. For each, explain what the speaker is conversationally implying and how that conversational implication is generated.

1. "What did you get on the last test?" "*A grade.*"
2. "Did you like her singing?" "*Her costume was beautiful.*"
3. "*The governor has the brains of a three-year-old.*"
4. "*Does the dog need to go out for a W-A-L-K* [spelled out]?"

EXERCISE X

For each of the following paired questions and answers, what do the answers conversationally imply in a normal context? Explain why these conversational implications hold. (Try to rely on the content of what is said, rather than on the tone of voice in which it is uttered. In particular, don't think of these remarks being uttered with heavy sarcasm.)

1. Are you going to vote for a Republican? I just might.
2. Are you going to vote for a Republican? You can bet on it.
3. Are you going to vote for a Republican? Not unless hell freezes over.
4. Are you going to vote for a Republican? Don't be silly.
5. Are you going to vote for a Republican? I am voting for an independent.
6. Are you going to vote for a Republican? There is no other choice.
7. Did you vote for a Republican? Maybe yes, maybe no.
8. Did you vote for a Republican? I voted for the winner.

RHETORICAL DEVICES

Many rhetorical devices work by flouting conversational rules in order to generate conversational implications. Consider exaggeration. When someone claims to be hungry enough to eat a horse, it does not dawn on us to treat this as a literal claim about how much she can eat. To do so would be to attribute to the speaker a blatant violation of Grice's first rule of Quality—namely, do not say what you believe to be false. Consequently, her audience will naturally interpret her remark figuratively, rather than literally. They will assume that she is exaggerating the amount she can eat in order to conversationally imply that she is very hungry. This rhetorical device is called *overstatement* or *hyperbole*. It is commonly employed, often in heavy-handed ways.

We sometimes use the opposite ploy and attempt to achieve rhetorical effect by *understating* things. We say that something is pretty good or not too bad when, as all can see, it is terrific. In these cases the speaker is violating something akin to the rule of Quantity. He is not saying just how good something really is. He expects his audience to recognize this and say (inwardly, at least) something like this: "Oh, it is much better than that." Understatement is often used as a way of fishing for compliments.

Sometimes, then, we do not intend to have others take our words at face value. Even beyond this, we sometimes expect our listeners to interpret us as claiming just the *opposite* of what we assert. This occurs, for example, with *irony* and *sarcasm*. Suppose at a crucial point in a game, the second baseman fires the ball ten feet over the first baseman's head, and someone shouts, "Great throw." Literally, it was not a great throw; it was the opposite of a great throw, and this is just what the person who says "Great throw" is indicating. How do the listeners know they are supposed to interpret it in this way? Sometimes this is indicated by tone of voice. A sarcastic tone of voice usually indicates that the person means the opposite of what he or she is saying. Even without the tone of sarcasm, the remark "Great throw" is not likely to be taken literally. The person who shouts this knows that it was not a great throw, as do the people who hear it. Rather than attributing an obviously false belief to the shouter, we assume that the person is blatantly violating the rule of Quality to draw our attention to just how bad the throw really was.

Metaphors and similes are perhaps the most common forms of figurative language. A *simile* is, roughly, an explicit figurative comparison. A word such as "like" or "as" makes the comparison explicit, and the comparison is figurative because it would be inappropriate if taken literally. To say that the home team fought like tigers does not mean that they clawed the opposing team and took large bites out of them. To call someone as dumb as a post is not to claim that they have no brain at all.

With a *metaphor,* we also compare certain items, but without words such as "like" or "as." Metaphorical comparisons are still figurative because the vocabulary, at a literal level, is not appropriate to the subject matter. George Washington was not literally the father of his country. Taken literally, it hardly makes sense to speak of someone fathering a country. But the metaphor is so natural (or so familiar) that it does not cross our minds to treat the remark literally, asking, perhaps, who the mother was.

Taken literally, metaphors are usually obviously false, and then they violate Grice's rule of Quality. Again, as with irony, when someone says something obviously false, we have to decide what to make of that person's utterance. Perhaps the person is very stupid or a very bad liar, but often neither suggestion is plausible. In such a situation, sometimes the best supposition is that the person is speaking metaphorically rather than literally.

Not all metaphors, however, are literally false. In John Donne's Meditation XVII, "No man is an island" is literally true. We treat this remark as a metaphor because, taken literally, it is so obviously and boringly true that we cannot imagine why anyone would want to say it. Taken literally, it would make no greater contribution to the conversation than any other irrelevant, obvious truth—for example, that no man is a socket wrench. Taken literally, this metaphor violates the rule of Relevance and, perhaps, the second part of the rule of Quantity. Taken figuratively, it is an apt, if somewhat overworked, way of indicating that no one is isolated and self-contained.

EXERCISE XI

Here are some more true metaphors. Explain what they mean and how they work.

1. "Blood is thicker than water."
2. "Cream rises to the top."
3. "People who live in glass houses should not throw stones."
4. Robert Frost's poem "The Road Not Taken" begins, "Two roads diverged in a yellow wood."
5. China's Chairman Mao Tse-tung is reported to have said, "A revolution is not the same as inviting people to dinner, or writing an essay, or painting a picture, or doing fancy needle-work."
6. Cuba's Fidel Castro is supposed to have said, "A revolution is not a bed of roses. A revolution is a struggle between the future and the past." (Is this different from item 5?)

EXERCISE XII

Identify each of the following sentences as irony, metaphor, or simile. For each sentence, write another expressing its literal meaning.

1. He missed the ball by a mile.
2. He acted like a bull in a china shop.
3. The exam blew me away.
4. He had to eat his words.
5. It was a real team effort. (Said by a coach after his team loses by forty points.)
6. They are throwing the baby out with the bathwater.
7. The concert was totally awesome.
8. A midair collision can ruin your whole day.
9. This is a case of the tail wagging the dog.
10. "Religion is the opiate of the masses." (Marx)

EXERCISE XIII

Metaphors do not appear only in statements. They also appear in imperatives. For example, "Don't rock the boat" can be employed literally in a context where someone is moving around in a canoe in a way that could tip it. It can also be used metaphorically to tell someone not to do something that will cause a fuss. For each of the following metaphors, find a context where the imperative can be used in its literal way and another context where it is used metaphorically.

1. Keep your eye on the ball.
2. Don't put all your eggs in one basket.
3. Look before you leap.
4. Make hay while the sun shines.
5. Don't count your chickens before they hatch.
6. Don't change horses in midstream.

EXERCISE XIV

Unpack the following political metaphors by giving their literal content.

1. We can't afford a president who needs on-the-job training.
2. It's time for people on the welfare wagon to get off and help pull.
3. If you can't stand the heat, get out of the kitchen.
4. We need to restore a level playing field.
5. The special interests have him in their pockets.
6. The bill was passed through typical horse trading.
7. He's a lame duck.

1. A classic example of rhetoric occurs in Marc Antony's funeral oration in William Shakespeare's play, *Julius Caesar* (act III, scene ii). Brutus and other conspirators had killed Julius Caesar. At Caesar's funeral, Brutus first argued that they needed to kill Caesar to prevent him from becoming too powerful and taking away the freedoms of Roman citizens. Brutus concludes, "As Caesar loved me, I weep for him; as he was fortunate, I rejoice in it; as he was valiant, I honor him. But as he was ambitious, I slew him." On the other side, Marc Antony sees Brutus as a traitor, but Brutus now has power, so Antony does not dare to call Brutus a traitor openly. The central part of Antony's speech is reprinted below. Indicate which lines are ironic, and comment on any other rhetorical devices in this speech. Why was it so effective (and famous) as a speech?

   Come I to speak in Caesar's funeral.

   He was my friend, faithful and just to me.

   But Brutus says he was ambitious,

   And Brutus is an honorable man.

   He hath brought many captives home to Rome,

   Whose ransoms did the general coffers fill.

   Did this in Caesar seem ambition?

   When that the poor have cried, Caesar hath wept—

   Ambition should be made of sterner stuff.

   Yet Brutus says he was ambitious,

   And Brutus is an honorable man.

   You all did see that on the Lupercal

   I thrice presented him a kingly crown,

   Which he did thrice refuse. Was this ambition?

   Yet Brutus says he was ambitious,

   And, sure, he is an honorable man.

   I speak not to disprove what Brutus spoke,

   But here I am to speak what I do know.

   You all did love him once, not without cause.

   What cause withholds you then to mourn for him?

2. At the start of the U.S. war with Iraq in 2003, some described Iraq as another Vietnam, while others described Saddam Hussein (Iraq's president) as another Hitler. Which metaphor was used by supporters of the war? Which was used by opponents? How can you tell? How do these metaphors work?

DECEPTION

In the preceding examples, a speaker openly violates a conversational rule. The listeners recognize that a rule is being intentionally broken, and the speaker knows that the listeners recognize the violation. At other times, however, speakers intentionally break conversational rules because they are trying to mislead their listeners. A speaker may violate the first part of Grice's rule of Quality by uttering something she knows to be false with the intention of producing a false belief in her listeners. That is called *lying*. Notice that lying depends on the general acceptance of the Cooperative Principle. Because audiences generally assume that speakers are telling the truth, speakers can sometimes get away with lying.

Flat-out lying is not the only way (and often not the most effective way) of intentionally misleading people. We can say something literally true that, at the same time, conversationally implies something false. This is sometimes called making a *false suggestion*. If a son tells his parents that he "has had some trouble with the car," that could be true but deeply misleading if, in fact, he had totaled it. It would be misleading because it would violate the rule of Quantity. In saying only that he has had some trouble with the car, he conversationally implies that nothing very serious happened. He conversationally implies this because, in this context, he is expected to come clean and reveal all that actually happened.

A more complex example of false suggestion arose in a lawsuit that reached the United States Supreme Court.

BRONSTON V. UNITED STATES

(409 U.S. 352, 1973)

MR. CHIEF JUSTICE BURGER delivered the opinion of the Court:

Petitioner's perjury conviction was founded on the answers given by him as a witness at that bankruptcy hearing, and in particular on the following colloquy with a lawyer for a creditor of Bronston Productions:

> **Q.** Do you have any bank accounts in Swiss banks, Mr. Bronston?
>
> **A.** No, sir.
>
> **Q.** Have you ever?
>
> **A.** The company had an account there for about six months, in Zurich.
>
> **Q.** Have you any nominees who have bank accounts in Swiss banks?
>
> **A.** No, sir.
>
> **Q.** Have you ever?
>
> **A.** No, sir.

It is undisputed that for a period of nearly five years, between October 1959 and June 1964, petitioner had a personal bank account at the International Credit Bank in Geneva, Switzerland, into which he made deposits and upon which he drew checks totalling more than $180,000. It is likewise undisputed that petitioner's answers were literally truthful. (i) Petitioner did not at the time of questioning have a Swiss bank account. (ii) Bronston

Productions, Inc., did have the account in Zurich described by petitioner. (iii) Neither at the time of questioning nor before did petitioner have nominees who had Swiss accounts. The government's prosecution for perjury went forward on the theory that in order to mislead his questioner, petitioner answered the second question with literal truthfulness but unresponsively addressed his answer to the company's assets and not to his own—thereby implying that he had no personal Swiss bank account at the relevant time.

It is hard to read the witness's response to the second question in any other way than as a deliberate attempt to mislead the Court, for his response plainly suggests that he did not have a personal account in a Swiss bank, when, in fact, he did. But the issue before the Court was not whether he intentionally misled the Court, but whether in doing so he committed perjury. The relevant statute reads as follows:

> Whoever, having taken an oath before a competent tribunal . . . that he will testify . . . truly, . . . willfully and contrary to such oath states or subscribes to any material matter which he does not believe to be true, is guilty of perjury.
>
> (18 U.S.C. 1621)

The lower courts ruled that Bronston violated this statute and, thus, committed perjury. The Supreme Court reversed this decision, in part for the following reasons:

> It should come as no surprise that a participant in a bankruptcy proceeding may have something to conceal and consciously tries to do so, or that a debtor may be embarrassed at his plight and yield information reluctantly. It is the responsibility of the lawyer to probe; testimonial interrogation, and cross-examination in particular, is a probing, prying, pressing form of inquiry. If a witness evades, it is the lawyer's responsibility to recognize the evasion and to bring the witness back to the mark, to flush out the whole truth with the tools of adversary examination.
>
> (409 U.S. 352 at 358–359 [1973])

In other words, in a courtroom, where the relationship is typically adversarial rather than cooperative, not all the standard conversational rules are in force or fully in force. In particular, it would be unrealistic to assume that the rule of Quantity will be consistently honored in a courtroom clash; therefore, it becomes the task of the cross-examiner to force the witness to produce all the relevant facts.

DISCUSSION QUESTIONS

Refer back to the dialogue quoted in *Bronston v. United States*. Because it is difficult to read the witness's second response as anything but a willful attempt to deceive, why should this case be treated differently from lying? Alternatively, why not even drop the demand that witnesses tell the truth and make it the responsibility of the lawyers to get at the truth itself (rather than just the whole truth) through "probing, prying, pressing" inquiry?

SUMMARY

In this chapter we have developed a rather complex picture of the way our language functions. In the process, we have distinguished three kinds or levels of acts that are performed when we employ language. We have also examined the rules associated with each kind or level of act. The following table summarizes this discussion:

THREE LEVELS OF LANGUAGE

Kinds of Acts	Governing Rules
A LINGUISTIC ACT is an act of saying something meaningful in a language. It is the basic act that is needed to make anything part of language.	Semantic rules (such as definitions) and syntactic rules (as in grammar).
A SPEECH ACT concerns the move a person makes *in* saying something. Different kinds of speech acts are indicated by the various verbs found in explicit performatives.	Speech act rules about special agents, formulas, circumstances, responses, and feelings appropriate to different kinds of speech acts, discovered by speech act analysis.
A CONVERSATIONAL ACT is a speaker's act of causing a standard kind of effect in the listener; it is what I do *by* saying something—for example, I persuade someone to do something.	Conversational rules (the Cooperative Principle; Quantity, Quality, Relevance, and Manner).

EXERCISE XV

1. It is late, and *A* is very hungry. *A* asks *B*, "When will dinner be ready?" Describe the linguistic act, the speech act, and some of the conversational acts this person may be performing in this context.

2. Someone is trying to solve the following puzzle: One of thirteen balls is heavier than the others, which are of equal weight. In no more than three weighings on a balance scale, determine which ball is the heavier one. The person is stumped, so someone says to her: "Begin by putting four balls in each pan of the scale." Describe the linguistic act, the speech act, and the conversational act of the person who makes this suggestion.

NOTES

[1] J. L. Austin used the phrase "locutionary act" to refer to a level of language closely related to what we refer to as a "linguistic act." See J. L. Austin, *How to Do Things with Words,* 2nd ed. (Cambridge, MA: Harvard University Press, 1975), 94–109.

[2] See, for example, J. L. Austin's *How to Do Things with Words.*

[3] An example of the continuous present is "I bet ten dollars every week in the lottery." Since this sentence is not used to make a bet, this sentence and others with the continuous present do not pass the thereby test or express explicit performatives.

[4] Austin calls speech acts "illocutionary acts." See *How to Do Things with Words*, 98–132.

[5] Although performative verbs name kinds of speech acts, not every kind of speech act has a corresponding performative verb. For example, insulting seems to be a kind of speech act, but "insult" is not a performative verb, because you cannot insult someone simply by saying, "I insult you." We might have had a convention that enabled us to insult people just by saying, "I insult you." In English, however, we do not.

[6] Supreme Court of New Hampshire, 1929, 84 N.H. 114, A. 641.

[7] This discussion of conversational rules and implications is based on Paul Grice's important essay, "Logic and Conversation," which appears as the second chapter of his *Studies in the Way of Words* (Cambridge, MA: Harvard University Press, 1989). To avoid British references that an American reader might find perplexing, we have sometimes altered Grice's wording.

[8] Grice states the Cooperative Principle in these words: "Make your conversational contribution such as is required, at the stage at which it occurs, by the accepted purpose or direction of the talk exchange in which you are engaged."

3

THE LANGUAGE OF ARGUMENT

Using the techniques developed in Chapter 2, this chapter will examine the use of language to formulate arguments and will provide methods to analyze genuine arguments in their richness and complexity. The first stage in analyzing an argument is the discovery of its basic structure. *To do this, we will examine the words, phrases, and special constructions that indicate the premises and conclusions of an argument. The second stage is to explore the* standards *that arguments are supposed to meet. Here we will focus on validity, truth, and soundness. The third stage is the study of techniques used to* protect *an argument. These include* guarding *premises so that they are less subject to criticism,* offering *assurances* concerning debatable claims, and *discounting possible criticisms in advance.*

ARGUMENT MARKERS

In Chapter 2, we saw that language is used for a great many different purposes. One important thing that we do with language is construct arguments. Arguments are constructed out of statements, but arguments are not just lists of statements. Here is a simple list of statements:

Socrates is a man.

All men are mortal.

Socrates is mortal.

This list is not an argument, because none of these statements is presented as a reason for any other statement. It is, however, simple to turn this list into an argument. All we have to do is to add the single word "therefore":

Socrates is a man.

All men are mortal.

Therefore, Socrates is mortal.

Now we have an argument. The word "therefore" converts these sentences into an argument by signaling that the statement following it is a *conclusion,* and the statement or statements that come before it are offered as *reasons* on behalf of this conclusion. The argument we have produced in this way is a good one, because the conclusion follows from the reasons stated on its behalf.

There are other ways of linking these sentences to form an argument. Here is one:

Since Socrates is a man,

and all men are mortal,

Socrates is mortal.

Notice that the word "since" works in roughly the opposite way that "therefore" does. The word "therefore" is a *conclusion marker*, because it indicates that the statement that follows it is a conclusion. In contrast, the word "since" is a *reason marker*, because it indicates that the following statement or statements are reasons. In our example, the conclusion comes at the end, but there is a variation on this. Sometimes the conclusion is given at the start:

Socrates is mortal, since all men are mortal and Socrates is a man.

"Since" flags reasons; the remaining connected statement is then taken to be the conclusion, whether it appears at the beginning or at the end of the sentence.

Many other terms are used to introduce an argumentative structure into language by marking either reasons or conclusions. Here is a partial list:

REASON MARKERS	CONCLUSION MARKERS
since	therefore
because	hence
for	thus
as	then

We shall call such terms "argument markers," because each presents one or more statements as part of an argument or backing for some other statement.

It is important to realize that these words are not always used as argument markers. The words "since" and "then" are often used as indicators of time, as in, "He's been an American citizen since 1973" and "He ate a hot dog, then a hamburger." The word "for" is often used as a preposition, as in "John works for IBM." Because some of these terms have a variety of meanings, it is not possible to identify argument markers in a mechanical way just by looking at words. It is necessary to examine the function of words in the context in which they occur. One test of whether a word is functioning as an argument marker in a particular sentence is whether you can substitute another argument marker without changing the meaning of the sentence. In the last example, it makes no sense to say, "John works since IBM."

Many *phrases* are also available to signal that an argument is being given. Here is just a small sample:

from which it follows that . . .

from which we may conclude that . . .

from which we see that . . .

which goes to show that . . .

which establishes that . . .

We can also indicate conclusions and reasons by using *argumentative perfor-matives,* which we examined briefly in Chapter 2. If someone says, "I conclude that . . . ," the words that follow are given the status of a conclusion. More pretentiously, if someone says, "Here I base my argument on the claim that . . . ," what comes next has the status of a reason.

Examination of actual arguments will show that we have a great many ways of introducing an argumentative structure into our language by using the two forms of argument markers: reason markers and conclusion markers. The first, and in many ways the most important, step in analyzing an argument is to identify the conclusion and the reasons given on its behalf. We do this by paying close attention to these argument markers.

IF . . . , THEN . . .

If-then sentences, which are also called *conditionals,* often occur in arguments, but they do not present arguments by themselves. To see this, consider the following conditional:

If the Dodgers improve their hitting, then they will win the
    Western Division.

The sentence between the "if" and the "then" is called the *antecedent* of the conditional. The sentence after the "then" is called its *consequent.* In uttering such a conditional, we are not asserting the truth of its antecedent, and we are not asserting the truth of its consequent either. Thus, the person who makes the above remark is not claiming that the Dodgers will win the Western Division. All she is saying is that *if* they improve their hitting, *then* they will win. Furthermore, she is not saying that they will improve their hitting. Because the speaker is not committing herself to either of these claims, she is not presenting an argument. This becomes clear when we contrast this conditional with a statement that does formulate an argument:

CONDITIONAL: *If* the Dodgers improve their hitting, *then* they will win the
    Western Division.

ARGUMENT: *Since* the Dodgers will improve their hitting, they will win the
    Western Division.

The sentence that follows the word "since" is asserted. That is why "since" is an argument marker, whereas the connective "if . . . then . . ." is not an argument marker.

Even though conditionals by themselves do not mark arguments, there is a close relationship between conditionals and arguments: Indicative conditionals provide *patterns* that can be converted into an argument whenever the antecedent is said to be true. (We also get an argument when the consequent is said to be false, but we will focus here on the simpler case of asserting the antecedent.) Thus, we often hear people argue in the following way:

> If inflation continues to grow, there will be an economic crisis. But inflation will certainly continue to grow, so an economic crisis is on the way.

The first sentence is an indicative conditional. It makes no claims one way or the other about whether inflation will grow or whether an economic crisis will occur. The next sentence asserts the antecedent of this conditional and then draws a conclusion signaled by the argument marker "so." We might say that when the antecedent of an indicative conditional is found to be true, the conditional can be *cashed in* for an argument.

Often the antecedent of a conditional is not asserted explicitly but is conversationally implied. When asked which player should be recruited for a team, the coach might just say, "If Deon is as good as our scouts say he is, then we ought to go for Deon." This conditional does not actually assert that Deon is as good as the scouts report. Nonetheless, it would be irrelevant and pointless for the coach to utter this conditional alone if he thought that the scouts were way off the mark. The coach might immediately add that he disagrees with the scouting reports. But unless the coach cancels the conversational implication in some way, it is natural to interpret him as giving an argument that we ought to pick Deon. In such circumstances, then, an indicative conditional can conversationally imply an argument, even though it does not state the argument explicitly.

This makes it easy to see why indicative conditionals are a useful feature of our language. By providing patterns for arguments, they prepare us to draw conclusions when the circumstances are right. Much of our knowledge of the world around us is contained in such conditionals. Here is an example: If your computer does not start, the plug might be loose. This is a useful piece of practical information, for when your computer does not start, you can immediately infer that the plug might be loose, so you know to check it out.

Other words function in similar ways. When your computer fails to start, a friend might say, "Either the plug is loose or you are in deep trouble." Now, if you also assert, "The plug is not loose," you can conclude that you are in deep trouble. "Either . . . or . . ." sentences thus provide patterns for arguments, just as conditionals do. However, neither if-then sentences nor either-or sentences by themselves explicitly assert enough to present a complete argument, so "if . . ., then . . ." and "either . . . or . . ." should not be labeled as argument markers.

EXERCISE I

Indicate which of the following italicized words or phrases is a reason marker, a conclusion marker, or neither.

1. He apologized, *so* you should forgive him.
2. He apologized. *Accordingly,* you should forgive him.
3. *Since* he apologized, you should forgive him.
4. *Provided that* he apologized, you should forgive him.
5. *In view of the fact that* he apologized, you should forgive him.
6. He apologized. *Ergo,* you should forgive him.
7. *Given that* he apologized, you should forgive him.
8. He apologized, and *because of that* you should forgive him.
9. *After* he apologizes, you should forgive him.
10. He apologized. *As a result,* you should forgive him.
11. *Seeing as* he apologized, you should forgive him.
12. He apologized. *For that reason alone,* you should forgive him.

EXERCISE II

Indicate whether each of the following sentences is an argument.

1. Charles went bald, and most men go bald.
2. Charles went bald because most men go bald.
3. My roommate likes to ski, so I do, too.
4. My roommate likes to ski, and so do I.
5. I have been busy since Tuesday.
6. I am busy, since my teacher assigned lots of homework.

ARGUMENTS IN STANDARD FORM

Because arguments come in all shapes and forms, it will help to have a standard way of presenting arguments. For centuries, logicians have used a format of the following kind:

(1) All men are mortal.
(2) Socrates is a man.
∴ (3) Socrates is mortal. (from 1–2)

The reasons (or premises) are listed and numbered. Then a line is drawn below the premises. Next, the conclusion is numbered and written below the line. The symbol "∴", which is read "therefore," is then added to the left of the conclusion in order to indicate the relation between the premises and the conclusion. Finally, the premises from which the conclusion is supposed to be derived are indicated in parentheses. Arguments presented in this way are said to be in *standard form*.

The notion of a standard form is useful because it helps us see that the same argument can be expressed in different ways. For example, the following three sentences formulate the argument that was given in standard form above.

Socrates is mortal, since all men are mortal, and Socrates is a man.

All men are mortal, so Socrates is mortal, because he is a man.

All men are mortal, and Socrates is a man, which goes to show that
Socrates is mortal.

More important, by putting arguments into standard form, we perform the most obvious, and in some ways most important, step in the analysis of an argument: the identification of its premises and conclusion.

EXERCISE III

Identify which of the following sentences expresses an argument. For each that does, (1) circle the argument marker (or markers), (2) indicate whether it is a reason marker or a conclusion marker, and (3) restate the argument in standard form.

1. Since Chicago is north of Boston, and Boston is north of Charleston, Chicago is north of Charleston.

2. Toward evening, clouds formed and the sky grew darker; then the storm broke.

3. Texas has a greater area than Topeka, and Topeka has a greater area than the Bronx Zoo, so Texas has a greater area than the Bronx Zoo.

4. Both houses of Congress may pass a bill, but the president may still veto it.

5. Other airlines will carry more passengers, because United Airlines is on strike.

6. Since Jesse James left town, taking his gang with him, things have been a lot quieter.

7. Things are a lot quieter, because Jesse James left town, taking his gang with him.

8. Witches float because witches are made of wood, and wood floats.

9. The hour is up, so you must hand in your exams.

10. Joe quit, because his boss was giving him so much grief.

SOME STANDARDS FOR EVALUATING ARGUMENTS

Not all arguments are good arguments; so, having identified an argument, the next task is to evaluate the argument. Evaluating arguments is a complex business. In fact, this entire book is aimed primarily at developing procedures for doing so. There are, however, certain basic terms used in evaluating arguments that should be introduced from the start. They are validity, truth, and soundness. Here they will be introduced informally. Later (in Chapters 6–7) they will be examined with more rigor.

VALIDITY

In some good arguments, the conclusion is said to follow from the premises. However, this commonsense notion of *following from* is hard to pin down precisely. The conclusion follows from the premises only when the content of the conclusion is related appropriately to the content of the premises, but which relations count as appropriate?

To avoid this difficult question, most logicians instead discuss whether an argument is *valid*. Calling something "valid" can mean a variety of things, but in this context validity is a technical notion. Here "valid" does not mean "good," and "invalid" does not mean "bad." This will be our definition of validity:

> An argument is *valid* if and only if it is not possible that all of its premises are true and its conclusion false.

Alternatively, one could say that its conclusion *must* be true if its premises are all true (or, again, that at least one of its premises *must* be false if its conclusion is false). The point is that a certain combination—true premises and a false conclusion—is ruled out as impossible.

The following argument passes this test for validity:

> (1) All senators are paid.
> (2) Sam is a senator.
> ∴(3) Sam is paid. (from 1–2)

Clearly, if the two premises are both true, there is no way for the conclusion to fail to be true. To see this, just try to tell a coherent story in which every single senator is paid and Sam is a senator, but Sam is not paid. You can't do it.

Contrast this example with a different argument:

> (1) All senators are paid.
> (2) Sam is paid.
> ∴(3) Sam is a senator. (from 1–2)

Here the premises and the conclusion are all in fact true, let's assume, but that is still not enough to make the argument valid, because validity concerns what is possible or impossible, not what happens to be true. This conclusion *could* be false even when the premises are true, for Sam *could* leave the Senate but still be paid for some other job, such as lobbyist. That possibility shows that this argument is invalid.

Another very common form of argument is called *modus ponens:*

> (1) If it is snowing, then the roads are slippery.
> (2) It is snowing.
> ∴(3) The roads are slippery. (from 1–2)

This argument is valid, because it is not possible for its premises to be true when its conclusion is false. We can show that by assuming that the conclusion is false and then reasoning backwards. Imagine that the roads are not slippery. Then there are two possibilities. Either it is snowing or it is not snowing. If it is not snowing, then the second premise is false. If it is snowing, then the first premise must be false, since we are supposing that it is snowing and that the roads are not slippery. Thus, at least one premise has to be false when the conclusion is false. Hence, this argument is valid.

This argument might seem similar to another:

> (1) If it is snowing, then the roads are slippery.
> (2) It is not snowing.
> ∴(3) The roads are not slippery. (from 1–2)

This argument is clearly invalid, because there are several ways for its premises to be true when its conclusion is false. It might have just stopped snowing or ice might make the roads slippery. Then the roads are slippery, so the conclusion is false, even if both premises are true.

Yet another form of argument is often called *process of elimination:*

> (1) Either Joe or Jack or Jim or Jerry committed the murder.
> (2) Joe didn't do it.
> (3) Jack didn't do it.
> (4) Jim didn't do it.
> ∴(5) Jerry committed the murder. (from 1–4)

The first premise asserts that at least one of these four suspects is guilty. That couldn't be true if all of the other premises were true and the conclusion were false, because that combination would exclude all four of these suspects. So this argument is valid.

Now compare this argument:

> (1) Either Joe or Jack or Jim or Jerry committed the murder.
> (2) Joe did it.
> ∴(3) Jerry did not commit the murder. (from 1–2)

To show that this argument is invalid, all we have to do is explain how the premises could be true and the conclusion false. Here's how: Joe and Jerry did it together. In that case, Jerry did it, so the conclusion is false; Joe also did it, so the second premise is true; and the first premise is true, because it says that at least one of these four suspects did it, and that is true when more than one of the suspects did it. That possibility of complicity, thus, makes this argument invalid.

We will explore many more forms of argument in Chapters 6–7. The goal for now is just to get a feel for how to determine validity. In all of these examples, an argument is said to be *valid* if and only if there is no possible situation in which its premises are true and its conclusion is false. You need to figure out whether there could be any situation like this in order to determine whether an argument is valid. If so, the argument is invalid. If not, it is valid.

This definition shows why validity is a valuable feature for an argument to possess: There can be no valid argument that leads one from true premises to a false conclusion. This should square with your commonsense ideas about reasoning. If you reason well, you should not be led from truth into error.

What are known as *deductive* arguments are put forward as meeting this standard of validity, so validity is one criterion for a good deductive argument. Other arguments—so-called *inductive* arguments—are not presented as meeting this standard. Roughly, an inductive argument is presented as providing strong support for its conclusion. The standards for evaluating inductive arguments will be examined in Chapter 8. For now we will concentrate on deductive arguments.

TRUTH

Although a deductive argument must be valid in order to be a good argument, validity is not enough. One reason is that an argument can be valid even when some (or all) of the statements it contains are false. For example:

(1) No fathers are female.
(2) Sam is a father.
∴ (3) Sam is not female. (from 1–2)

Suppose that Sam has no children or that Sam is female, so premise 2 is false. That would be a serious defect in this argument. Nonetheless, this argument satisfies our definition of validity: If the premises were true, then the conclusion could not be false. There is no way that Sam could be female if Sam is a father and no fathers are female. This example makes it obvious that validity is not the same as truth. It also makes it obvious that another requirement of a good argument is that *all of its premises must be true.*

SOUNDNESS

We thus make at least two demands of a deductive argument:

1. The argument must be valid.

2. The premises must be true.

When an argument meets both of these standards, it is said to be *sound*. If it fails to meet either one or the other, then it is *unsound*. Thus, an argument is unsound if it is invalid, and it is also unsound if at least one of its premises is false.

	ALL PREMISES TRUE	AT LEAST ONE FALSE PREMISE
Valid	Sound	Unsound
Invalid	Unsound	Unsound

Soundness has one great benefit: A sound argument must have a true conclusion. We know this because its premises are true and, since it is valid, it is not possible that its premises are true and its conclusion is false. This is why people who seek truth want sound arguments, not merely valid arguments.

A TRICKY CASE

Our definition of validity yields a surprising result. Consider the following argument:

> (1) Frogs are green.
> (2) Frogs are not green.
> ∴(3) I am president. (from 1–2)

It is obviously not possible for both premises to be true, so it is also not possible that both premises are true when the conclusion is false. Consequently, this argument fits our definition of validity. So does any other argument whose premises cannot be true. Such arguments cannot ever take us from truths to falsehoods, because they never start with truths.

This weird example illustrates some of the ways in which the technical notion of *validity* differs from the commonsense notion of *following from*. The content of its premises has no relation to the content of the conclusion. Frogs have nothing to do with who is president. Hence, the conclusion does not follow from the premises. But that does not prevent the argument from being valid.

This example also shows the importance of distinguishing validity from soundness. Any argument whose premises cannot all be true is *valid*, no matter how ridiculous its conclusion. However, an argument cannot be *sound* if its premises can't be true, and a valid argument that is unsound cannot show that its conclusion is true. Consequently, this strange case won't cause any trouble.

EXERCISE IV

Indicate whether each of the following arguments is valid and whether it is sound. Explain your answers where necessary.

1. Most professors agree that they are paid too little, so they are.
2. David Letterman is over four feet tall, so he is over two feet tall.
3. Lee can't run a company right, because he can't do anything right.
4. Barack Obama is smart and good-looking, so he is smart.
5. Barack Obama is either a Democrat or a Republican, so he is a Democrat.
6. Since Jimmy Carter was president, he must have won an election.
7. Since Gerald Ford was president, he must have won an election.
8. Pat is either a mother or a father. If Pat is a mother, then she is a parent. If Pat is a father, he is a parent. So, either way, Pat is a parent. (Assume that this conclusion is true.)
9. People who live in the Carolinas live in either North Carolina or South Carolina. Hillary Clinton does not live in North Carolina or South Carolina. Hence, she does not live in the Carolinas.
10. If all of Illinois were in Canada, then Chicago would be in Canada. But Chicago is not in Canada. Therefore, not all of Illinois is in Canada.
11. If George lives in Crawford, then George lives in Texas. If George lives in Texas, then George lives in the United States. Hence, if George lives in Crawford, he lives in the United States.
12. There can't be a largest six-digit number, because six-digit numbers are numbers, and there is no largest number.

EXERCISE V

Assume that the following sentences are either true (T) or false (F) as indicated.

All my children are teenagers. (T)

All teenagers are students. (T)

All teenagers are my children. (F)

All my children are students. (T)

Using these assigned values, label each of the following arguments as (a) either valid or invalid, and (b) either sound or unsound.

1. All my children are teenagers.
   All teenagers are students.
   _____
   ∴ All my children are students.

2. All my children are students.
   All teenagers are students.
   _____
   ∴ All my children are teenagers.

(continued)

3. All teenagers are my children.
   All my children are students.

∴ All teenagers are students.

4. All teenagers are students.
   All my children are students.

∴ All my children are students.

EXERCISE VI

Indicate whether each of the following sentences is true. For those that are true, explain why they are true. For those that are false, show why they are false by giving a counterexample.

F 1. Every argument with a false conclusion is invalid.

F 2. Every argument with a false premise is invalid.

F 3. Every argument with a false premise and a false conclusion is invalid.

F 4. Every argument with a false premise and a true conclusion is invalid.

T 5. Every argument with true premises and a false conclusion is invalid.

F 6. Every argument with a true conclusion is sound.

T 7. Every argument with a false conclusion is unsound.

DISCUSSION QUESTION

Compare these arguments:

(1) Al Gore was president.   (1*) George W. Bush was president.

∴(2) Frogs are frogs.   ∴(2*) Frogs are frogs.

Are these arguments valid? Why or why not? Are they sound? Why or why not? Is anything wrong with the argument on the right side? If so, what?

A PROBLEM AND SOME SOLUTIONS

Although soundness guarantees a true conclusion, we usually expect even more from an argument than soundness. In the first place, an argument can be sound but trivially uninteresting:

(1) Nigeria is in Africa.

∴(2) Nigeria is in Africa. (from 1)

Here the premise is true. The argument is also valid, because the premise cannot be true without the conclusion (which repeats it) being true as well. Yet the argument is completely worthless as a proof that Nigeria is in Africa. The reason is that this argument is *circular*. We will examine circular arguments in detail in Chapter 16, but it should already be clear why such arguments are useless. If *A* is trying to justify something to *B* that *B* has doubts about, then citing the very matter in question will not do any good. Explanations of a phenomenon that cite that very phenomenon itself also fail to increase our understanding. In general, for *A* to argue successfully, *A* must marshal facts that *B* accepts and then show that they justify or explain the conclusion. In circular arguments, the worries about the conclusion immediately turn into worries about the premise as well.

Now, however, *A* seems to run into a problem. *A* cannot cite a proposition as a reason for *itself,* for that would be circular reasoning. If, however, *A* cites some *other* propositions as premises leading to the conclusion, then the question naturally arises why these premises should be accepted. Does *A* not have to present arguments for them as well? Yet if *A* does that, then *A* will introduce further premises that are also in need of proof, and so on indefinitely. It now looks as if every argument, to be successful, will have to be infinitely long.

This potential regress causes deep problems in theoretical philosophy. In everyday life, however, we try to avoid these problems by relying on shared beliefs—beliefs that will not be challenged. Beyond this, we expect people to believe us when we cite information that only we possess. But there are limits to this expectation, for we all know that people sometimes believe things that are false and sometimes lie about what they know to be true. This presents a practical problem: How can we present our reasons in a way that does not produce just another demand for an argument—a demand for more reasons? Here we use three main strategies:

1. *Assuring*: Indicating that there are backup reasons even though we are not giving them fully right now.
2. *Guarding*: Weakening our claims so that they are less subject to attack.
3. *Discounting*: Anticipating criticisms and dismissing them.

In these three ways we build a defensive perimeter around our premises. Each of these defenses is useful, but each can also be abused.

ASSURING

When will we want to give assurances about some statement we have made? If we state something that we know everyone believes, assurances are not necessary. For that matter, if everyone believes something, we may not even state it at all; we let others fill in this step in the argument. We offer assurances when we think that someone might doubt or challenge what we say.

There are many ways to give assurances. Sometimes we cite authorities:

Doctors agree . . .

Recent studies have shown . . .

An unimpeachable source close to the White House says . . .

It has been established that . . .

Here we indicate that authorities have these reasons without specifying what their reasons are. We merely indicate that good reasons exist, even if we ourselves cannot—or choose not to—spell them out. When the authority cited can be trusted, this is often sufficient, but authorities often can and should be questioned. This topic will be discussed more fully in Chapter 15.

Another way to give assurances is to comment on the strength of our own belief:

I'm certain that . . .

I'm sure that . . .

I can assure you that . . .

I'm not kidding. . . .

Over the years, I have become more and more convinced that . . .

Again, when we use these expressions, we do not explicitly present reasons, but we conversationally imply that there are reasons that back our assertions.

A third kind of assurance abuses the audience:

Everyone with any sense agrees that . . .

Of course, no one will deny that . . .

It is just common sense that . . .

There is no question that . . .

Nobody but a fool would deny that . . .

These assurances not only do not give any reason; they also suggest that there is something wrong with you if you ask for a reason. We call this the *trick of abusive assurances*.

Just as we can give assurances that something is true, we can also give assurances that something is false. For example,

It is no longer held that . . .

It is wholly implausible to suppose that . . .

No intelligent person seriously maintains that . . .

You would have to be pretty dumb to think that . . .

The last three examples clearly involve abusive assurances.

Although many assurances are legitimate, we as critics should always view assurances with some suspicion. People tend to give assurances only when they have good reasons to do so. Yet assuring remarks often mark the weakest parts of the argument, not the strongest. If someone says "I hardly need argue that . . . ," it is often useful to ask why she has gone to the trouble of saying this. When we distrust an argument—as we sometimes do—this is precisely the place to look for weakness. If assurances are used, they are used for some reason. Sometimes the reason is a good one. Sometimes, however, it is a bad one. In honest argumentation, assurances save time and simplify discussion. In a dishonest argument, they are used to paper over cracks.

GUARDING

Guarding represents a different strategy for protecting premises from attack. We reduce our claim to something less strong. Thus, instead of saying "all," we say "many." Instead of saying something straight out, we use a qualifying phrase, such as "it is likely that . . ." or "it is very possible that. . . ." Law school professors like the phrase "it is arguable that. . . ." This is wonderfully noncommittal, for it does not indicate how strong the argument is, yet it does get the statement into the discussion.

Broadly speaking, there are three main ways of guarding what we say:

1. Weakening the *extent* of what has been said: retreating from "all" to "most" to "a few" to "some," and so on.

2. Introducing *probability* phrases such as "It is virtually certain that . . . ," "It is likely that . . . ," "It might happen that . . . ," and so on.

3. Reducing our *level of commitment:* moving from "I know that . . ." to "I believe that . . ." to "I suspect that . . . ," and so on.

Such terms guard premises when they are used in place of stronger alternatives. "Madison probably quit the volleyball team" is weaker than "She definitely quit" but stronger than "She could have quit." Thus, if the context makes one expect a strong claim, such as "I know she quit," then it is guarding to say, "She probably quit." In contrast, if the context is one of speculating about who might have quit the team, then it is not guarding to say, "She probably quit." That is a relatively strong claim when others are just guessing. Thus, you need to pay careful attention to the context in order to determine whether a term has the function of guarding. When a term is used for guarding, you should be able to specify a stronger claim that the guarding term replaces and why that stronger term would be expected in the context.

Guarding terms and phrases are often legitimate and useful. If you want to argue that a friend needs fire insurance for her house, you do not need to claim that her house *will* burn down. All you need to claim is that there is a significant *chance* that her house will burn down. Your argument is better if you start with this weaker premise, because it is easier to defend and it is enough to support your conclusion.

If we weaken a claim sufficiently, we can make it completely immune to criticism. What can be said against a remark of the following kind: "There is some small chance that perhaps a few politicians are honest on at least some occasions"? You would have to have a *very* low opinion of politicians to deny this statement. On the other hand, if we weaken a premise too much, we pay a price. The premise no longer gives strong support to the conclusion.

The goal in using guarding terms is to find a middle way: We should weaken our premises sufficiently to avoid criticism, but not weaken them so much that they no longer provide strong enough evidence for the conclusion. Balancing these factors is one of the most important strategies in making and criticizing arguments.

Just as it was useful to zero in on assuring terms, so it is also useful to keep track of guarding terms. One reason is that, like assuring terms, guarding terms are easily corrupted. A common trick is to use guarding terms to *insinuate* things that cannot be stated explicitly in a conversation. Consider the effect of the following remark: "Perhaps the secretary of state has not been candid with the Congress." This does not actually say that the secretary of state has been less than candid with the Congress, but, by the rule of Relevance, clearly suggests it. Furthermore, it suggests it in a way that is hard to combat.

A more subtle device for corrupting guarding terms is to introduce a statement in a guarded form and then go on to speak as if it were not guarded at all.

> Perhaps the secretary of state has not been candid with the Congress. Of course, he has a right to his own views, but this is a democracy where officials are accountable to Congress. It is time for him to level with us.

The force of the guarding term "perhaps" that begins this passage disappears at the end, where it is taken for granted that the secretary of state has not been candid. This can be called *the trick of the disappearing guard.*

What is commonly called *hedging* is a sly device that operates in the opposite direction from our last example. With hedging, one shifts ground from a strong commitment to something weaker. Things, as they say, get "watered down" or "taken back." Strong statements made at one stage of an argument are later weakened without any acknowledgment that the position has thereby been changed in a significant way. A promise to *pass* a piece of legislation is later whittled down to a promise to *bring it to a vote.*

DISCOUNTING

The general pattern of discounting is to cite a possible criticism in order to reject it or counter it. Notice how different the following statements sound:

> The ring is beautiful, but expensive.

> The ring is expensive, but beautiful.

Both statements assert the same facts—that the ring is beautiful and that the ring is expensive. Both statements also suggest that there is some opposition between these facts. Yet these statements operate in different ways. We might use the first as a reason for *not* buying the ring; we can use the second as a reason *for* buying it. The first sentence acknowledges that the ring is beautiful, but overrides this by pointing out that it is expensive. In reverse fashion, the second statement acknowledges that the ring is expensive, but overrides this by pointing out that it is beautiful. Such assertions of the form "*A* but *B*" thus have four components:

1. The assertion of *A*
2. The assertion of *B*
3. The suggestion of some opposition between *A* and *B*
4. The indication that the truth of *B* is more important than the truth of *A*

The word "but" thus discounts the statement that comes before it in favor of the statement that follows it.

"Although" is also a discounting connective, but it operates in reverse fashion from the word "but." We can see this, using the same example:

Although the ring is beautiful, it is expensive.

Although the ring is expensive, it is beautiful.

Here the statement following the word "although" is discounted in favor of the connected statement.

A partial list of terms that typically function as discounting connectives includes the following conjunctions:

although	even if	but	nevertheless
though	while	however	nonetheless
even though	whereas	yet	still

These terms are not always used to discount. The word "still," for example, is used for discounting in (a) "He is sick; still, he is happy" but not in (b) "He is still happy" (or "Sit still"). We can tell whether a term is being used for discounting by asking whether the sentence makes sense when we substitute another discounting term: It makes sense to say, "He is sick, but he is happy." It makes no sense to say, "He is but happy." It is also illuminating to try to specify the objection that is being discounted. If you cannot say which objection is discounted, then the term is probably not being used for discounting.

The clearest cases of discounting occur when we are dealing with facts that point in different directions. We discount the facts that go against the position we wish to take. But discounting is often more subtle than this. We sometimes use discounting to block certain conversational implications of what we have said. This comes out in examples of the following kind:

Jones is an aggressive player, but he is not dirty.

The situation is difficult, but not hopeless.

The Republicans have the upper hand in Congress, but only for the
  time being.

A truce has been declared, but who knows for how long?

Take the first example. There is no opposition between Jones being aggressive and his not being dirty. Both would be reasons to pick Jones for our team. However, the assertion that Jones is aggressive might *suggest* that he is dirty. The "but" clause discounts this suggestion without, of course, denying that Jones is aggressive.

The nuances of discounting terms can be subtle, and a correct analysis is not always easy. All the same, the role of discounting terms is often important. It can be effective in an argument to beat your opponents to the punch by anticipating and discounting criticisms before your opponents can raise them. The proper use of discounting can also help you avoid side issues and tangents.

Still, discounting terms, like the other argumentative terms we have examined, can be abused. People often spend time discounting *weak* objections to their views in order to avoid other objections that they know are harder to counter. Another common trick is to discount objections no one would raise. This is called *attacking straw men*. Consider the following remark: "A new building would be great, but it won't be free." This does not actually say that the speaker's opponents think we can build a new building for free, but it does conversationally imply that they think this, because otherwise it would be irrelevant to discount that objection. The speaker is thus trying to make the opponents look bad by putting words in their mouths that they would never say themselves. To counter tricks like this, we need to ask whether a discounted criticism is one that really would be raised, and whether there are stronger criticisms that should be raised.

EXERCISE VII

For each of the numbered words or expressions in the following sentences, indicate whether it is an argument marker, an assuring term, a guarding term, a discounting term, or none of these. For each argument marker, specify what the conclusion and the reasons are, and for each discounting term, specify what criticism is being discounted and what the response to this criticism is.

1. *Although* [1] no mechanism has been discovered, *most* [2] *researchers in the field agree* [3] that smoking *greatly increases the chances* [4] of heart disease.
2. *Since* [5] *historically* [6] public debt leads to inflation, *I maintain* [7] that, *despite* [8] recent trends, inflation will return.
3. *Take it from me* [9], there hasn't been a decent center fielder *since* [10] Joe DiMaggio.
4. *Whatever anyone tells you* [11], there is *little* [12] to the rumor that Queen Elizabeth II will step down *for* [13] her son, Prince Charles.

5. The early deaths of Janis Joplin and Jimi Hendrix *show* [14] that drugs are *really* [15] dangerous.

6. I *think* [16] he is out back somewhere.

7. I *think* [17], *therefore* [18] I am.

8. I *concede* [19] that the evidence is *hopelessly* [20] weak, *but* [21] I still think he is guilty.

9. I *deny* [22] that I had *anything* [23] to do with it.

10. The wind has shifted to the northeast, *which means* [24] that snow is *likely* [25].

EXERCISE VIII

1. Construct three new and interesting examples of statements containing assuring terms.

2. Do the same for guarding terms.

3. Do the same for discounting terms, and indicate which statement is being discounted in favor of the other.

4. Do the same for argument markers, and indicate what is presented as a reason for what.

EVALUATIVE LANGUAGE

Arguments are often filled with evaluation. The clearest cases of evaluative language occur when we say that something is *good* or *bad,* that some course of action is *right* or *wrong,* or that something *should* or *should not* (or *ought to* or *ought not to*) be done. The meaning of such evaluative terms is very controversial, but we can begin to understand evaluative language by asking which acts—linguistic, speech, and conversational—it is used to perform.

Evaluative terms often come into play when one is faced with a choice or decision. If you are deciding which shirt to buy, and a friend tells you, "That one's nice," your friend would normally be taken to be prescribing that you buy it. A passenger who says, "That's the wrong turn," is telling the driver not to turn that way. In such contexts, evaluative statements are action guiding—that is, they are used to direct someone to do or refrain from doing some action. Evaluative terms do not, however, have such direct prescriptive force when applied to things in remote times or places. Saying that it was wrong for James Earl Ray to assassinate Martin Luther King does not tell Ray not to do anything, for it is idle to address imperatives to people in the past. Someone who says that it would be wrong for the president to pursue a particular policy is not telling the president not to pursue it, unless she happens to be speaking or writing to the president. Nevertheless, even in cases where evaluations lack direct prescriptive force, they sometimes have prescriptive force indirectly. Calling Ray's past action bad or wrong might, through analogy, be a way of telling someone not to do future acts like it. Evaluative language is, in these ways, used to perform speech acts of *prescribing action*.

Evaluative language is also often used for other speech acts. When a fan says, "That band is great," this usually expresses admiration for their music and a desire to hear more. After a meal, someone who announces, "That was horrible," is often expressing aversion or even disgust at the food. To say, "That's too bad," is often to express disappointment or sadness. In these ways, evaluative language is used to perform speech acts of *expressing emotion*.

These speech acts do not, however, exhaust the meaning of evaluative language. For one thing, evaluative language is typically also used to bring about certain effects. When a mother tells her son that that he ought to keep his promises, she not only prescribes that her son not lie; she also standardly intends to have an effect on his behavior—she tries to get him to keep his promises. And when war protesters express their disapproval by calling a war immoral, they are normally trying to get anyone listening to feel the same way about the war. Thus, evaluative language is used to perform conversational acts of *changing people's behavior and feelings*.

There is still more to the meaning of evaluative language. Our lives consist of a constant stream of choices of varying kinds and of various levels of importance. Because we often have to make these choices or decisions under time pressure, it is not possible to make all of them on a case-by-case basis. It is for this reason, among others, that we come to rely on *standards* in making evaluations. In most cases, we call something "good" or "right" because we believe that it meets or satisfies relevant standards, and we call something "bad" or "wrong" because we believe that it violates some relevant standard. This is, roughly, the content of the *linguistic* act of uttering evaluative language.

On this account, calling something good or bad by itself can be fairly empty of content. Such remarks gain content—sometimes a very rich content—by virtue of the particular standards they invoke. This explains why the word "good" can be applied to so many different kinds of things. When we say that Hondas are good cars, we are probably applying standards that involve reliability, efficiency, comfort, and so on. We call someone a good firefighter because we think the person is skilled at the tasks of a firefighter, is motivated to do those tasks, works well with other firefighters, and so on. Our standards for calling someone an ethically good person concern honesty, generosity, fairness, and so on. The standards we have for calling something a good car, a good firefighter, and an (ethically) good person have little in common. Even so, the word "good" functions in the same way in all three cases: It invokes the standards that are relevant in a given context and indicates that something adequately satisfies these standards.

Because evaluative statements invoke standards, they stand in contrast to utterances that *merely* express personal feelings. If I say that I like a particular singer, then I am expressing a personal taste. Unless I were being accused of lying or self-deception, it would be very odd for someone to reply, "No, you don't like that singer." On the other hand, if I call someone a good singer (or the best singer in years), then I am going beyond expressing my personal tastes. I am saying something that others may accept or reject. Of course, the standards for judging singers may be imprecise, and they may shift from culture to culture. Still, to call someone a good singer is to evaluate that person as a singer, which goes beyond merely expressing feelings, because it invokes standards and indicates that the person in question meets them.

The words "good" and "bad" are general evaluative terms. Other evaluative terms are more restrictive in their range of application. The word "delicious" is usually used for evaluating the taste of foods; it means "good-tasting." A *sin* is a kind of wrong action, but, more specifically, it is an action that is wrong according to religious standards. A *bargain* has a good price. An *illegal* action is one that is legally wrong. Our language contains a great many specific terms of evaluation like these. Here are a few more examples:

beautiful	dangerous	wasteful	sneaky	cute
murder	prudent	nosy	sloppy	smart

Each of these words expresses either a positive or a negative evaluation of a quite specific kind.

Positive and negative evaluations can be subtle. Consider a word like "clever." It presents a positive evaluation in terms of quick mental ability. In contrast, "cunning" often presents a negative evaluation of someone for misusing mental abilities. It thus makes a difference which one of these words we choose. It also makes a difference where we apply them. When something is supposed to be profound and serious, it is insulting to call it merely clever. Prayers, for example, should not be clever.

Sometimes seemingly innocuous words can shift evaluative force. The word "too" is the perfect example of this. This word introduces a negative evaluation, sometimes turning a positive quality into a negative one. Compare the following sentences:

John is smart.	John is too smart.
John is honest.	John is too honest.
John is ambitious.	John is too ambitious.
John is nice.	John is too nice.
John is friendly.	John is too friendly.

The word "too" indicates an excess, and thereby contains a criticism. If you look at the items in the second column, you will see that the criticism is sometimes rather brutal—for example, calling someone "too friendly."

The difference between an evaluative term and a descriptive term is not always obvious. To see this, consider the terms "homicide" and "murder." The words are closely related but do not mean the same thing. "Homicide" is a descriptive term meaning "the killing of a human being." "Murder" is an evaluative term meaning, in part at least, "the *wrongful* killing of a human being." It takes more to show that something is a murder than it does to show that something is a homicide.

Just as it is easy to miss evaluative terms because we fail to recognize the evaluative component built into their meanings, it is also possible to interpret neutral words as evaluative because of positive or negative associations that the words might evoke. The word "nuclear," for example, has bad connotations for some people because of its association with bombs and wars, but the word itself is purely descriptive. To call people nuclear scientists is not to say that they are bad in any way. The test for an evaluative term is this: Does the word mean that something is good or bad (right or wrong) in a particular way?

Farcus

by David Waisglass
Gordon Coulthart

**"Let's hope corporate communications
can put a positive spin on this."**

SPIN DOCTORING

Evaluation need not be problematic, but it is often hidden and abused, most notoriously in *spin doctoring*. The expression "spin doctor" seems to combine two metaphors. The first concerns putting the right spin on things—that is, presenting things in ways that make them look good or bad, depending on how one wants them to be perceived. The second concerns doctoring things up to accomplish this. Spin doctoring often involves trying to find the right way of labeling something.

A classic example comes from Shakespeare's play, *Julius Caesar* (act III, scene i). After Brutus and others killed Caesar, Brutus announced, "So are we Caesar's friends that have abridged his time of fearing death." By redescribing his act in terms of a minor benefit to Caesar, Brutus tries to make people see his treacherous act of killing his friend as a generous act of doing his friend a favor!

Spin doctoring is still rampant in politics today. Referring to the Iraq war, those who favored it spoke of the "liberation" of Iraq, whereas those who opposed it called it an "invasion" or an "occupation." Each label involves evaluation, so the disagreement over what to call it was really about how to evaluate it. This verbal dispute is not purely verbal, because the label can affect attitudes and behaviors by associating the Iraq war with good military actions (liberations) or bad military actions (invasions and occupations).

Often spin doctoring involves attributing questionable views or attitudes to opponents. Supporters of President Bush sometimes refer to his detractors as "the blame-America-first crowd" and describe their policies for getting out of Iraq as "cut and run." These negative labels are applied even to policies, such as partial staged redeployment, that are far from cowardly in the way suggested by "cut and run." Similarly, in 2006, conservative commentator David Brooks described opposition to Joe Lieberman's campaign as a "liberal inquisition." Stephen Colbert lampooned this label in a segment of "The Word" where he joked that, if incumbents like Lieberman continued to be attacked so harshly, then they would actually be forced to defend their records. Colbert concluded, "There is only one word for that—inquisition." But the sidebar read "democracy." Sometimes parody is the most effective response to spin doctoring.

Of course, liberal democrats are often just as guilty of spin doctoring. When discussing a measure that would repeal a large number of environmental regulations, President Clinton sarcastically referred to it as the "Polluter's Bill of Rights"—not exactly a generous way of describing a bill based on the belief that environmental regulations had gone too far. And, to quote Stephen Colbert again, "Affirmative action is a prime example of the Leftist campaign to make ideas seem less dangerous than they are, through the strategic use of positive words. Think about it. How can something be bad if it is 'affirmative'? and how can we ignore it if is it 'action'?" [from *I Am America (and So Can You!)*, New York: Grand Central Publishing, 2007, p. 174].

Spin doctoring like this makes it harder to discuss the real benefits and costs of such laws and policies, because nobody wants to argue against liberation or affirmation or in favor of invasion, inquisition, or pollution. The task of critical analysis is to see through such slogans to the important issues that lie behind them, so that we can intelligently address the real values at stake.

EXERCISE IX

Indicate whether the following italicized terms are positively evaluative (E+), negatively evaluative (E–), or simply descriptive (D). Remember, the evaluations need not be moral evaluations.

1. Janet is an *excellent* golfer.
2. The group was playing very *loudly*.
3. The group was playing *too* loudly.
4. William was *rude* to his parents.
5. William *shouted* at his parents.
6. They mistakenly turned *right* at the intersection.
7. *Fascists* ruled Italy for almost twenty years.
8. That's a *no-no*.
9. *Bummer.*
10. Debbie *lied*.
11. Debbie *said something false*.
12. Joe *copped out*.
13. Jake is a *bully*.
14. Mary Lou was a *gold medalist*.
15. She is *sick*.
16. He suffers from a hormonal *imbalance*.

EXERCISE X

For each of the following sentences, construct two others—one that reverses the evaluative force, and one that is as neutral as possible. The symbol "0" stands for neutral, "+" for positive evaluative force, and "–" for negative evaluative force. Try to make as little change as possible in the descriptive content of the sentence.

Example:　　　– Professor Conrad is rude.

+ Professor Conrad is uncompromisingly honest in his criticisms.

0 Professor Conrad often upsets people with his criticisms.

1. – Larry is a lazy lout.
2. + Brenda is brave.
3. – Sally is a snob.
4. + Bartlett is a blast.
5. – George is a goody-goody.
6. – Walter is a weenie.
7. + Carol is caring.
8. – Bill is bossy.
9. – Oprah is opinionated.
10. – This is a Mickey Mouse exercise.

EXERCISE XI

Be a spin doctor yourself by writing upbeat, good-sounding titles or descriptions for the following proposals. Remember that, as a professional spin doctor, you should be able to make things you personally hate sound good.

1. Imposing a $1,000 fee on graduating seniors
2. Requiring all students to participate in a twenty-one-meal-per-week food plan

3. Abolishing coed dormitories

4. Abolishing fraternities

5. Requiring women students to return to their dormitories by midnight (such rules were once quite common)

6. Abolishing failing grades

7. Restoring failing grades

8. Requiring four years of physical education

9. Abolishing intercollegiate football

10. Introducing a core curriculum in Western civilization

11. Abolishing such a curriculum

12. Abolishing faculty tenure

DISCUSSION QUESTIONS

1. What precisely does "That's too bad" mean?
2. In the Democratic presidential candidate debate on September 26, 2007, Representative Dennis Kucinich was asked the following question by MSNBC correspondent Tim Russert. Was Kucinich's answer spin doctoring? Was it legitimate or illegitimate? Why?

RUSSERT: . . . Congressman Kucinich, when you were mayor of Cleveland, you let Cleveland go into bankruptcy, the first time that happened since the Depression. The voters of Cleveland rewarded you by throwing you out of office and electing a Republican mayor of Cleveland. How can you claim that you have the ability to manage the United States of America, when you let Cleveland go bankrupt?

REP. KUCINICH: You know, Tim, that was NBC's story. Now I want the people to know what the real story was. I took a stand on behalf of the people of Cleveland to save a municipal electric system. The banks and the utilities in Cleveland, the private utilities, were trying to force me to sell that system. And so on December 15th, 1978, I told the head of the biggest bank, when he told me I had to sell the system in order to get the city's credit renewed, that I wasn't going to do it. . . . I put my job on the line. How many people would be willing to put their job on the line in the face of pressure from banks and utilities? As this story gets told, people will want me to be their next president because they'll see in me not only the ability to take a stand, but the ability to live with integrity.

4

THE ART OF CLOSE ANALYSIS

This chapter will largely be dedicated to a single purpose: the close and careful analysis of a speech drawn from the Congressional Record, *using argumentative devices introduced in Chapter 3. The point of this chapter is to show in detail how these methods of analysis can be applied to an actual argument of some richness and complexity.*

AN EXTENDED EXAMPLE

It is now time to apply all of our previously discussed notions to a genuine argument. Our example will be a debate that occurred in the House of Representatives on the question of whether there should be an increase in the allowance given to members of the House for clerical help—the so-called clerk hire allowance. The argument against the increase presented by Representative Kyl (Republican, Iowa) will be examined in detail. We will put it under an analytic microscope.

The choice of this example may seem odd, for the question of clerk hire allowance is not one of the burning issues of our time. This, in fact, is one reason for choosing it. It will be useful to begin with an example about which feelings do not run high to learn the habit of objective analysis. Later on we shall examine arguments about which almost everyone has strong feelings and try to maintain an objective standpoint even there.

The example is good for two other reasons: 1. It contains most of the argumentative devices we have listed, and 2. relatively speaking, it is quite a strong argument. This last remark may seem ironic after we seemingly tear the argument to shreds. However, in comparison to other arguments we shall examine, it stands up well.

We begin by reading through a section of the *Congressional Record* (vol. 107, part 3, March 15, 1961, pp. 4059–60) without comment:

CLERK HIRE ALLOWANCE, HOUSE OF REPRESENTATIVES

Mr. FRIEDEL. Mr. Speaker, by direction of the Committee on House Administration, I call up the resolution (H. Res. 219) to increase the basic clerk hire allowance of each Member of the House, and for other purposes, and ask for its immediate consideration.

The Clerk read the resolution as follows:

Resolved, That effective April 1, 1961, there shall be paid out of the contingent fund of the House, until otherwise provided by law, such sums as may be necessary to increase the basic clerk hire allowance of each Member and the Resident Commissioner from Puerto Rico by an additional $3,000 per annum, and each such Member and Resident Commissioner shall be entitled to one clerk in addition to those to which he is otherwise entitled by law.

Mr. FRIEDEL. Mr. Speaker, this resolution allows an additional $3,000 per annum for clerk hire and an additional clerk for each Member of the House and the Resident Commissioner from Puerto Rico. Our subcommittee heard the testimony, and we were convinced of the need for this provision to be made. A few Members are paying out of their own pockets for additional clerk hire. This $3,000 is the minimum amount we felt was necessary to help Members pay the expenses of running their offices. Of course, we know that the mail is not as heavy in some of the districts as it is in others, and, of course, if the Member does not use the money, it remains in the contingent fund.

Mr. KYL. Mr. Speaker, will the gentleman yield?

Mr. FRIEDEL. I yield to the gentleman from Iowa [Mr. Kyl] for a statement.

Mr. KYL. Mr. Speaker, I oppose this measure. I oppose it first because it is expensive. I further oppose it because it is untimely.

I do not intend to belabor this first contention. We have been presented a budget of about $82 billion. We have had recommended to us a whole series of additional programs or extensions of programs for priming the pump, for depressed areas, for the needy, for the unemployed, for river pollution projects, and recreation projects, aid to education, and many more. All are listed as "must" activities. These extensions are not within the budget. Furthermore, if business conditions are as deplorable as the newspapers indicate, the Government's income will not be as high as anticipated. It is not enough to say we are spending so much now, a little more will not hurt. What we spend, we will either have to recover in taxes, or add to the staggering national debt.

The amount of increase does not appear large. I trust, however, there is no one among us who would suggest that the addition of a clerk would not entail allowances for another desk, another typewriter, more materials, and it is not beyond the realm of possibility that the next step would then be a request for additional office space, and ultimately new buildings. Some will say, "All the Members will not use their maximum, so the cost will not be great." And this is true. If the exceptions are sufficient in number to constitute a valid argument, then there is no broad general need for this measure. Furthermore, some Members will use these additional funds to raise salaries. Competition will force all salaries upward in all offices and then on committee staffs, and so on. We may even find ourselves in a position of paying more money for fewer clerks and in a tighter bind on per person workload.

This measure proposes to increase the allowance from $17,500 base clerical allowance to $20,500 base salary allowance. No member of this House can tell us what this means in gross salary. That computation is almost impossible. Such a completely absurd system has developed through the years on salary computations for clerical hire that we have under discussion a mathematical monstrosity. We are usually told that the gross allowed is approximately $35,000. This is inaccurate. In one office the total might be less than $35,000 and in another, in complete compliance with the law and without any conscious padding, the amount may be in excess of $42,000. This is possible because of a weird set of formulae which determines that three clerks at $5,000 cost less than five clerks at $3,000. Five times three might total the same as three times five everywhere else in the world—but not in figuring clerk hire in the House.

This is an application of an absurdity. It is a violation of bookkeeping principles, accounting principles, business principles and a violation of common sense. Listen to the formula:

First, 20 percent increase of first $1,200; 10 percent additional from $1,200 to $4,600; 5 percent further additional from $4,600 to $7,000.

Second, after applying the increases provided in paragraph 1, add an additional 14 percent or a flat $250, whichever is the greater, but this increase must not exceed 25 percent.

Third, after applying the increases provided in both paragraphs 1 and 2, add an additional increase of 10 percent in lieu of overtime.

Fourth, after applying the increases provided in paragraphs 1, 2, and 3, add an additional increase of $330.

Fifth, after applying the increases provided in paragraphs 1, 2, 3, and 4, add an additional increase of 5 percent.

Sixth, after applying the increases provided in paragraphs 1, 2, 3, 4, and 5, add an additional increase of 10 percent but not more than $800 nor less than $300 a year.

Seventh, after applying the increases provided in paragraphs, 1, 2, 3, 4, 5, and 6, add an additional increase of 7½ percent.

Eighth, after applying the increases provided in paragraphs, 1, 2, 3, 4, 5, 6, and 7, add an additional increase of 10 percent.

Ninth, after applying the increases provided in paragraphs 1, 2, 3, 4, 5, 6, 7, and 8, add an additional increase of 7½ percent.

The Disbursing Office has a set of tables to figure House salaries for office staffs and for about 900 other employees. It contains 45 sheets with 40 entries per sheet. In the Senate, at least, they have simplified the process some by figuring their base in multiples of 60, thus eliminating 11 categories. Committee staffers, incidentally, have an $8,880 base in comparison to the House $7,000 base limitation.

Now, Mr. Speaker, I have planned to introduce an amendment or a substitute which would grant additional clerk hire where there is a demonstrable need based on heavier than average population or "election at large" and possible other factors. But after becoming involved in this mathematical maze, I realize the folly of proceeding one step until we have corrected this situation. We can offer all kinds of excuses for avoiding a solution. We cannot offer reasonable arguments that it should not be done or that it cannot be done.

Someone has suggested that the Members of this great body prefer to keep the present program because someone back in the home district might object to the gross figures. I know this is not so. When a Representative is busy on minimum wage, or aid to education, or civil rights, such matters of housekeeping seem too picayune to merit attention. The Member simply checks the table and hires what he can hire under the provisions and then forgets the whole business. But I know the Members also want the people back home to realize that what we do here is open and frank and accurate, and that we set an example in businesslike procedures. The more we can demonstrate responsibility the greater will be the faith in Congress.

May I summarize. It is obvious that some Members need more clerical help because of large population and large land area. I have been working for some time with the best help we can get, on a measure which would take these items into consideration. Those Members who are really in need of assistance should realize that this temporary, hastily conceived proposition we debate today will probably obviate their getting a satisfactory total solution.

First, we should await redistricting of the Nation.

Second, we should consider appropriate allowance for oversize districts considering both population and total geographic area.

Finally, I hope we can develop a sound and sensible formula for computing salaries of office clerks and other statutory employees in the same category.

————————————■————————————

Before going any further, it will be useful to record your general reactions to this speech. Perhaps you think that on the whole Kyl gives a well-reasoned argument on behalf of his position. Alternatively, you might think that he is making a big fuss over nothing, trying to confuse people with numbers, and just generally being obnoxious. When you are finished examining this argument in detail, you can look back and ask yourself why you formed this original impression and how, if at all, you have changed your mind.

The first step in the close analysis of an argument is to go through the text, labeling the various argumentative devices we have examined. Here some abbreviations will be useful:

argument marker	M
assuring term	A
guarding term	G
discounting term	D
argumentative performative	AP
evaluative term	E (+ *or* –)
rhetorical device	R

The last label is a catchall for the various rhetorical devices discussed in Chapter 1, such as overstatement, understatement, irony or sarcasm, metaphor, simile, rhetorical questions, and so on.

If you want to make your analysis extra close, it is illuminating to specify which rhetorical device is deployed whenever you mark something with "R."

It is also useful to specify whether each argument marker marks a reason or a conclusion (and what the argument is), which stronger term is replaced by each guarding term marked "G," and which objection is discounted whenever you mark a discounting term with "D."

This simple process of labeling brings out features of an argument that could pass by unnoticed. It also directs us to ask sharp critical questions. To see this, we can look at each part of the argument in detail.

> M   Mr. KYL. Mr. Speaker, (I oppose) this measure. I (oppose) it   AP
>   first (because) it is expensive. I further (oppose) it (because) it is   AP
>   untimely.   M

This is a model of clarity. By the use of a performative utterance in the opening sentence, Kyl makes it clear that he opposes the measure. Then by twice using the argument marker "because," he gives his two main reasons for opposing it: It is expensive and it is untimely. We must now see if he makes good on each of these claims.

The next paragraph begins the argument for the claim that the measure is expensive:

> (I do not intend to belabor this first contention.) We have been   A
> presented a budget of about $82 billion. We have had recom-
> mended to us a whole series of additional programs or ex-
> tensions of programs for priming the pump, for depressed
> areas, for the needy, for the unemployed, for river pollution
> projects, and recreation projects, aid to education, and many
> more. All are listed as ⊘must⊘ activities. These extensions are   R
> not within the budget. (Furthermore), if business conditions   M
> are as deplorable as the newspapers indicate, the Govern-
> ment's income will not be as high as anticipated. (It is not   D
> enough to say) we are spending so much now, a little more
> will not hurt. What we spend, we will either have to recover
> in taxes, or add to the staggering national debt.

a. "I do not intend to belabor this first contention." This is an example of *assuring*. The conversational implication is that the point is so obvious that little has to be said in its support. Yet there is something strange going on here. Having said that he will *not* belabor the claim that the bill is expensive, Kyl actually goes on to say quite a bit on the subject. It is a good idea to look closely when someone says that he or she is not going to do something, for often just the opposite is happening. For example, saying "I am not suggesting that Smith is dishonest" is one way of suggesting that Smith *is* dishonest. If no such suggestion is being made, why raise the issue at all?

b. Kyl now proceeds in a rather flat way, stating that the proposed budget comes to $82 billion and that it contains many new programs and extensions of former programs. Because these are matters of public record and nobody is likely to deny them, there is no need for guarding or assuring. Kyl also claims, without qualification, that these extensions are not within the budget. This recital of facts does, however, carry an important conversational implication: Since the budget is already out of balance, any further extensions should be viewed with suspicion.

c. Putting the word "must" in quotation marks, or saying it in a sarcastic tone of voice, is a common device for denying something. The plain suggestion is that some of these measures are *not* must activities at all. Kyl here suggests that some of the items already in the budget are not necessary. He does this, of course, without defending this suggestion.

d. "Furthermore, if business conditions are as deplorable as the newspapers indicate, the Government's income will not be as high as anticipated." The word "furthermore" suggests that an argument is about to come. However, the following sentence as a whole is an *indicative conditional* (with the word "then" dropped out). As such, the sentence does not produce an argument, but instead provides only a pattern for an argument.

To get an argument from this pattern, one would have to assert the antecedent of the conditional. The argument would then come to this:

> (1) If business conditions are as deplorable as the newspapers indicate, then the Government's income will not be as high as anticipated.
> (2) Business conditions are as deplorable as the newspapers indicate.
> ∴ (3) The Government's income will not be as high as anticipated.

The first premise seems perfectly reasonable, so, if Kyl could establish the second premise, then he would have moved the argument along in an important way. Yet he never explicitly states that business conditions are so deplorable. All he says is that "the newspapers *indicate*" this. Moreover, this appeal to authority (see Chapter 15) does not mention any specific newspaper, so he does not endorse any specific authority. Still, Kyl never questions what the newspapers claim, and it would be misleading to bring up these newspaper reports without questioning them if he thought they were way off the mark. So Kyl does seem to have in mind something like the argument (1)–(3).

e. "It is not enough to say we are spending so much now, a little more will not hurt." The opening phrase is, of course, used to deny what follows it. Kyl is plainly rejecting the argument that, since we are spending so much now, a little more will not hurt. Yet his argument has a peculiar twist, for who would come right out and make such an argument? If you stop to think for a minute, it should be clear that nobody would want to put it that way. An opponent, for example, would use quite different phrasing. He might say something like this: "Considering the large benefits that will flow from this measure, it is more than worth the small costs." What Kyl has done is attribute a bad argument to his opponents and then reject it in an indignant tone. This is a common device, and when it is used, it is often useful to ask whether anyone would actually argue or speak in the way suggested. When the answer to this question is no, as it often is, we have what was called "the trick of discounting straw men" in Chapter 3 (see also Chapter 17). In such cases, it is useful to ask what the speaker's opponent would have said instead. This leads to a further question: Has the arguer even addressed himself to the *real* arguments of his opponents?

So far, Kyl has not addressed himself to the first main point of his argument: that the measure is *expensive*. This is not a criticism, because he is really making the preliminary point that the matter of expense is significant. Here he has stated some incontestable facts—for example, that the budget is already out of balance. Beyond this he has indicated, with varying degrees of strength, that the financial situation is grave. It is against this background that the detailed argument concerning the cost of the measure is actually presented in the next paragraph.

> The amount of increase does not appear large. I trust, however, there is no one among us who would suggest that the addition of a clerk would not entail allowances for another desk, another typewriter, more materials, and it is not beyond the realm of possibility that the next step would then be a request for additional office space, and ultimately new buildings. Some will say, "All the Members will not use their maximum, so the cost will not be great." And this is true. If the exceptions are sufficient in number to constitute a valid argument, then there is no broad general need for this measure. Furthermore, some Members will use these additional funds to raise salaries. Competition will force all salaries upward in all offices and then on committee staffs, and so on. We may even find ourselves in a position of paying more money for fewer clerks and in a tighter bind on per person workload.

D *A* *G* *D* *M* *G* *G*

a. "The amount of increase does not appear large." Words like "appear" and "seem" are sometimes used for guarding, but we must be careful not to apply labels in an unthinking way. The above sentence is the beginning of a discounting argument. As soon as you hear this sentence, you can feel that a word like "but" or "however" is about to appear. Sure enough, it does.

b. "I trust, however, there is no one among us who would suggest that the addition of a clerk would not entail allowances for another desk, another typewriter, more materials. . . ." This is the beginning of Kyl's argument that is intended to rebut the argument that the increase in expenses will not be large. Appearances to the contrary, he is saying, the increase *will* be large. He then ticks off some additional expenses that are entailed by hiring new clerks. Notice that the whole sentence is covered by the assuring phrase

"I trust . . . there is no one among us who would suggest. . . ." This implies that anyone who would make such a suggestion is merely stupid. But the trouble with Kyl's argument so far is this: He has pointed out genuine additional expenses, but they are not, after all, very large. It is important for him to get some genuinely large sums of money into his argument. This is the point of his next remark.

c. ". . . and it is not beyond the realm of possibility that the next step would then be a request for additional office space, and ultimately new buildings." Here, at last, we have some genuinely large sums of money in the picture, but the difficulty is that the entire claim is totally guarded by the phrase "it is not beyond the realm of possibility." There are very few things that *are* beyond the realm of possibility. Kyl's problem, then, is this: There are certain additional expenses that he can point to without qualification, but these tend to be small. On the other hand, when he points out genuinely large expenses, he can only do so in a guarded way. So we are still waiting for a proof that the expense will be large. (Parenthetically, it should be pointed out that Kyl's prediction of new buildings actually came true.)

d. "Some will say, 'All the Members will not use their maximum, so the cost will not be great.' And this is true. If the exceptions are sufficient in number to constitute a valid argument, then there is no broad general need for this measure." This looks like a "trick" argument, and for this reason alone it demands close attention. The phrase "some will say" is a standard way of beginning a discounting argument. This *is*, in fact, a discounting argument, but its form is rather subtle. Kyl cites what some will say, and then he adds, somewhat surprisingly: "And this is true." To understand what is going on here, we must have a good feel for conversational implication. Kyl imagines someone reasoning in the following way:

> All the Members will not use their maximum.
> So, the cost will not be great.
> Therefore, we should adopt the measure.

Given the same starting point, Kyl tries to derive just the *opposite* conclusion along the following lines:

> All the Members will not use their maximum.
> If the exceptions are not sufficient, then the cost will be too great.
> But if the exceptions are sufficient, there is no broad general need for this measure.
> Therefore, whether it is expensive or not, we should reject this measure.

In order to get clear about this argument, we can put it into schematic form:

Kyl's argument:

If (1) the measure is expensive, then *reject* it.

If (2) the measure is inexpensive, then, because that shows there is no general need, *reject* it.

The opposite argument:

If (1) the measure is inexpensive, then *accept* it.

If (2) the measure is expensive, then, because that demonstrates a general need, *accept* it.

When the arguments are spread out in this fashion, it should be clear that they have equal strength. Both are no good. The question that must be settled is this: Does a genuine need exist that can be met in an economically sound manner? If there is no need for the measure, then it should be rejected, however inexpensive. Again, if there is a need, then some expense is worth paying. The real problem is to balance need against expense and then decide on this basis whether the measure as a whole is worth adopting.

Kyl's argument is a sophistry, because it has no tendency to answer the real question at hand. A *sophistry* is a clever but fallacious argument intended to establish a point through trickery. Incidentally, it is one of the marks of a sophistical argument that, though it may baffle, it almost never convinces. We think that few readers will have found this argument persuasive even if they cannot say exactly what is wrong with it. The appearance of a sophistical argument (or even a complex and tangled argument) is a sign that the argument is weak. Remember, when a case is strong, people usually argue in a straightforward way.

e. "Furthermore, some Members will use these additional funds to raise salaries. Competition will force all salaries upward in all offices and then on committee staffs, and so on." The word "furthermore" signals that further reasons are forthcoming. Here Kyl returns to the argument that the measure is more expensive than it might appear at first sight. Although Kyl's first sentence is guarded by the term "some," he quickly drops his guard and speaks in an unqualified way about *all* salaries in *all* offices. Yet the critic is bound to ask whether Kyl has any right to make these projections. Beyond this, Kyl here projects a *parade of horrors.* (See Chapter 13.) He pictures this measure leading by gradual steps to quite disastrous consequences. Here the little phrase "and so on" carries a great burden in the argument. Once more, we must simply ask ourselves whether these projections seem reasonable.

f. "We may even find ourselves in a position of paying more money for fewer clerks and in a tighter bind on per person workload." Once more, the use of a strong guarding expression takes back most of the force of the argument. Notice that if Kyl could have said straight out that the measure *will* put us in a position of paying more money for fewer clerks and in a tighter bind on per-person workload, that would have counted as a very strong objection. You can hardly do better in criticizing a position than showing that it will have just the opposite result from what is intended. In fact, however, Kyl has not established this; he has only said that this is something that we "may even find."

Before we turn to the second half of Kyl's argument, which we shall see in a moment is much stronger, we should point out that our analysis has not been entirely fair. Speaking before the House of Representatives, Kyl is in an *adversarial* situation. He is not trying to prove things for all time; rather, he is responding to a position held by others. Part of what he is doing is *raising objections,* and a sensitive evaluation of the argument demands a detailed understanding of the nuances of the debate. But even granting this, it should be remembered that objections themselves must be made for good reasons. The problem so far in Kyl's argument is that the major reasons behind his objections have constantly been guarded in a very strong way.

Turning now to the second part of Kyl's argument—that the measure is untimely—we see that he moves along in a clear and direct way with little guarding.

> This measure proposes to increase the allowance from $17,500 base clerical allowance to $20,500 base salary allowance. No member of this House can tell us what this means in gross salary. That computation is almost impossi- **G**
> ble. Such a completely absurd system has developed **E—**
> through the years on salary computations for clerical hire that we have under discussion a mathematical monstrosity. **E—**
> We are usually told that the gross allowed is approximately $35,000. This is inaccurate. In one office the total might be less than $35,000 and in another, in complete compliance with the law and without any conscious padding, the amount may be in excess of $42,000. This is possible because of a weird set of formulae which determines that three **E—**
> clerks at $5,000 cost less than five clerks at $3,000. Five times **R**
> three might total the same as three times five everywhere else in the world—but not in figuring clerk hire in the House.
> This is an application of an absurdity. It is a violation of **E—**
> bookkeeping principles, accounting principles, business prin- ciples and a violation of common sense. Listen to the formula. **E—**

The main point of the argument is clear enough: Kyl is saying that the present system of clerk salary allowance is utterly confusing, and this matter should be straightened out before *any* other measures in this area are adopted. There is a great deal of negative evaluation in this passage. Notice the words and phrases that Kyl uses:

a completely absurd system

weird set of formulae

violation of common sense

mathematical monstrosity

an absurdity

There is also a dash of irony in the remark that five times three might total the same as three times five everywhere else in the world, but not in figuring clerk hire in the House. Remember, there is nothing wrong with using negative evaluative and expressive terms if they are deserved. Looking at the nine-step formula in Kyl's speech, you can decide for yourself whether he is on strong grounds in using this negative language.

> Now, Mr. Speaker, I have planned to introduce an amendment or a substitute which would grant additional clerk hire where there is a demonstrable need based on heavier than average population or "election at large" and possible other factors.

a. This passage discounts any suggestion that Kyl is unaware that a genuine problem does exist in some districts. It also indicates that he is willing to do something about it.

b. The phrase "and possible other factors" is not very important, but it seems to be included to anticipate other reasons for clerk hire that should at least be considered.

> D — (But) after becoming involved in this (mathematical maze) I — E—
> A — (realize) the (folly) of proceeding one step until we have corrected this situation. — E—

a. Here Kyl clearly states his reason for saying that the measure is untimely. Notice that the reason offered has been well documented and is not hedged in by qualifications.

b. The phrases "mathematical maze" and "folly" are again negatively evaluative.

> We can offer all kinds of (excuses) for avoiding a solution. — E—
> (We cannot offer reasonable arguments that) it should not be — A
> done or that it cannot be done.

Notice that the first sentence ridicules the opponents' arguments by calling them *excuses*, a term with negative connotations. The second sentence gives assurances that such a solution can be found.

> Someone has suggested that the Members of this great body prefer to keep the present program because someone back in the home district might object to the gross figures. (I know) — A
> this is not so. When a Representative is busy on minimum wage, or aid to education, or civil rights, such matters of housekeeping seem too picayune to merit attention. The Member simply checks the table and hires what he can hire under the provisions and then forgets the whole business.

D (But) (I know) the Members also want the people back home A

to realize that what we do here is (open and frank and accu- E+

rate,) and that we set an example in businesslike procedures.

The more we can demonstrate responsibility the greater will

be the faith in Congress.

    a. Once more the seas of rhetoric run high. Someone (though not Kyl himself) has suggested that the members of the House wish to conceal information. He disavows the very thought that he would make such a suggestion by the sentence "I know this is not so." All the same, he has gotten this suggestion into the argument.

    b. Kyl then suggests another reason why the members of the House will not be concerned with this measure: It is "too picayune." The last two sentences rebut the suggestion that it is too small to merit close attention. Even on small matters, the more the House is "open and frank and accurate," the more it will "set an example in businesslike procedures" and thus "demonstrate responsibility" that will increase "the faith in Congress." This is actually an important part of Kyl's argument, for presumably his main problem is to get the other members of the House to take the matter seriously.

    May I summarize. (It is obvious that) some Members need A

M more clerical help (because) of large population and large

land area. (I have been working for some time with the best A

help we can get,) on a measure which would take these items

into consideration. Those Members who are really in need of

A assistance should (realize) that this (temporary, hastily con- E–

ceived) proposition we debate today will (probably) obviate G

their getting a satisfactory total solution.

    a. This is a concise summary. Kyl once more assures the House that he is aware that a genuine problem exists. He also indicates that he is working on it.

    b. The phrase "temporary, hastily conceived proposition we debate today" refers back to his arguments concerning untimeliness.

    c. The claim that "it will probably obviate their getting a satisfactory total solution" refers back to the economic argument. Notice, however, that, as before, the economic claim is guarded by the word "probably."

E+ First, we (should) await redistricting of the Nation.

E+ Second, we (should) consider appropriate allowance for

oversize districts considering both population and total

geographic area.

    Finally, I hope we can develop a (sound and sensible) for- E+

mula for computing salaries of office clerks and other statu-

tory employees in the same category.

This is straightforward except that a new factor is introduced: We should await redistricting of the nation. This was not mentioned earlier in the argument, and so seems a bit out of place in a summary. Perhaps the point is so obvious that it did not need any argument to support it. On the other hand, it is often useful to keep track of things that are smuggled into the argument at the very end. If redistricting was about to occur in the *near* future, this would give a strong reason for delaying action on the measure. Because the point is potentially so strong, we might wonder why Kyl has made so little of it. Here, perhaps, we are getting too subtle.

Now that we have looked at Representative Kyl's argument in close detail, we can step back and notice some important features of the argument as a whole. In particular, it is usually illuminating to notice an argument's *purpose, audience*, and *standpoint*.

First, Kyl's overall *purpose* is clear. As his opening sentence indicates, he is presenting an argument intended to justify his opposition to an increase in the clerk hire allowance. Virtually everything he says is directed toward this single goal. In other cases, arguers pursue multiple goals, and sorting things out can be a complex matter. Sometimes it is hard to tell what an argument is even intended to establish. This is usually a sign that the person presenting the argument is confused or, perhaps, trying to confuse his audience.

Second, Kyl's argument is addressed to a specific *audience*. He is not speaking to an enemy of the United States who would love to see our government waste its money. Nor is he speaking to clerks or to those U.S. citizens who might be hired as clerks if the clerk hire allowance were raised. He is presenting his argument to other representatives in Congress. He is trying to show this group that they and he have reasons to oppose this increase in the clerk hire allowance. His task, then, is to present reasons that *they* accept—or should accept—for rejecting an increase in the clerk hire allowance.

Third, Kyl not only addresses his argument to a particular audience, he also adopts a particular *standpoint* to it. Good arguments are usually presented not only *to* specific audiences but also *from* particular standpoints. Kyl's standpoint is clear and powerful. He puts himself across as a tough-minded, thoroughly honest person who is willing to stand up against majority opinion. This, in fact, may be an accurate representation of his character, but by adopting this standpoint he gains an important argumentative advantage: He suggests that those who disagree with him are a bit soft-minded, not altogether candid, and, anyway, mere tools of the Democratic majority that runs the Congress. By adopting this stance, Kyl casts his opponents in a light that is hardly flattering.

By specifying the purpose, audience, and standpoint of an argument, we get a clearer sense of what the argument needs to accomplish in order to succeed in its goals. By looking closely at special words in the argument, as well as at what is conversationally implied, we get a better idea of how the argument is supposed to achieve its goals. All of this together helps us understand the argument. It will sometimes remain unclear how well the argument succeeds. It will always require care and skill to apply these methods. Still, the more you practice, the more you will be able to understand arguments.

EXERCISE I

Read the following passage. Then, for each of the numbered expressions, either answer the corresponding question or label the main argumentative move, if any, using these abbreviations:

M = argument marker
A = assuring term
G = guarding term
D = discounting term
E– = negative evaluative term
E+ = positive evaluative term
R = rhetorical device
N = none of the above

This letter to the editor appeared in *The Dartmouth* on September 23, 1992, although references to the author's college have been removed. The author was president of the student assembly and a member of a single-sex fraternity at the time.

GREEKS SHOULD BE CO-ED
■
by Andrew Beebe

For some time now, people have been asking the question "Why should the Greek [fraternity and sorority] system go co-ed?" To them, *I pose an answer* [1] in a question, *"Why not?"* [2]

Learning in college extends beyond the classrooms, onto the athletic fields, into the art studios, and into our social environs. [3] *In fact* [4], *some* [5] say that *most* [6] of what we learn at college comes from interaction with people and ideas during time spent outside of the lecture halls. The concept of segregating students in their social and residential environments by gender directly contradicts the *ideals* [7] of a college experience. This is *exactly* [8] what the fraternity and sorority system does.

With all the *benefits* [9] of a small, closely-bonded group, the potential for strong social education would seem *obvious* [10]. *But* [11] is it *fair* [12] for us to remove the other half of our community from that education? [13] In many colleges, this voluntary segregation exists in fraternities and sororities.

From the planning of a party or involvement in student activities to the sharing of living and recreational space, the fraternity and sorority system is a social environment *ripe* [14] with *educational potential* [15]. The idea that women and men would receive as complete an experience from these environments while *virtually* [16] separated is *implausible* [17].

But [18] *what do women and men learn from one another that they don't already know?* [19] Problems in gender relations between all ages *prove* [20] that our society is *plagued by gender-based prejudice* [21]. *Since* [22] *prejudice is the ignorance of one group by another* [23], it will best be addressed by education. The question *then* [24] becomes: Which way is best to educate one another?

Sexism, homophobia, date rape, eating disorders, and other social *problems* [25] are *often* [26] connected to gender-relation issues. As campus experience *shows* [27], we have a long way to go in combating these problems. Defenders of fraternities and sororities *may* [28] argue that they do not, solely by nature of being single sex, promote sexism or other prejudices. *But* [29], if we can recognize that these problems exist in our society, it is not important to find the blame, *but* [30] rather to offer a solution. It is *clear* [31] that separating people by gender is not the *right* [32] way to promote *better* [33] understanding between the sexes. To the contrary, bringing different people together is the only way prejudice, *no matter what the cause (or result) may be* [34], can be overcome.

Acknowledging that breaking down walls of separation *may* [35] help foster better understanding, it is important to look at what *might* [36] change for the worse. There would be *some* [37] *obvious* [38] logistical changes in rush, pledging, relationships with national organization, and house leadership. *But* [39] where are the real consequences? [40] Men *could* [41] still cultivate strong bonds with other men. Women *could* [42] still bond with other women. The difference is that there would be a *well-defined* [43] environment where men and women *could* [44] create strong, lasting bonds and friendships between one another.

There are many more *benefits* [45] to a co-ed system than there are *sacrifices* [46]. Men and women could share the responsibilities of running what is now a *predominantly* [47] male-controlled social structure. First-year men and women could interact with older students in a social environment beyond the classroom or the dining halls. People in a co-ed system could find a strong support group that extends beyond their own sex. With these *advantages* [48] and more, it is *clear* [49] that the all-co-ed system offers everything found in a single-sex organization and more. *Although* [50] there are *some* [51] minor sacrifices to be made, they are insignificant in comparison to the *gain* [52] for all.

College is the last place we want to isolate ourselves. The entire idea of the "holistic education" is *based on* [53] expanding our knowledge, not separating ourselves from one another. Our fraternity and sorority system includes *many* [54] different types of students. *So* [55] why should some houses refuse women simply *because* [56] they are women? Why do some houses refuse men solely *because* [57] they are men? The only solution is desegregation of the fraternity and sorority system. *After all* [58], when it comes to challenging one another to learn, *what are we afraid of?* [59]

(continued)

QUESTIONS:

[1]: Is this sentence an explicit performative?

[2]: Explain the difference between asking "Why?" and asking "Why not?" in this context.

[3]: Why does the author begin with this point?

[4]–[12]: Write labels.

[13]: What is the expected answer to this rhetorical question?

[14]: What kind of rhetorical device is this? What is its point?

[15]–[18]: Write labels.

[19]: Who is supposed to be asking this question?

[20]–[22]: Write labels.

[23]: What is the point of this definition?

[24]–[33]: Write labels.

[34]: Why does this author add this dependent clause?

[35]–[39]: Write labels.

[40]: What does this question imply in this context?

[41]–[58]: Write labels.

[59]: What is the expected answer to this rhetorical question?

EXERCISE II

Read the following passage from *The Washington Post* (November 25, 1997), page A19. Then, for each of the numbered expressions, label the main argumentative move, if any, using the same abbreviations as in Exercise I:

A PIECE OF "GOD'S HANDIWORK"

■

by Robert Redford

Just over a year ago, President Clinton created the Grand Staircase-Escalante National Monument *to* [1] *protect* [2] once and for all *some* [3] of Utah's extraordinary red rock canyon country. *In response to* [4] plans of the Dutch company Andalex to mine coal on the Kaiparowits Plateau, President Clinton used his authority under the Antiquities Act to establish the new monument, setting aside for protection what he described as "some of the most remarkable land in the world." *I couldn't agree more.* [5] For over two decades, many have fought *battle after battle* [6] to keep mining conglomerates from *despoiling* [7] the unique *treasures* [8] of this stunning red rock canyon country. *Now* [9], we thought at least some of it was safe.

Not so. *Shocking* [10] as it sounds, Clinton's Bureau of Land Management (BLM) has approved oil drilling within the monument. BLM has given Conoco Inc., a subsidiary of the corporate giant DuPont, permission to drill for oil and gas in the *heart* [11] of the new monument. You *may* [12] wonder, as I do, *how can this happen?* [13] Wasn't the whole purpose of creating the monument to preserve its colorful cliffs, sweeping arches and other extraordinary *resources* [14] from large-scale mineral development? Didn't the president say he was *saving* [15] these lands from mining companies for our children and grandchildren?

The BLM says *its hands are tied.* [16] Why? *Because* [17] these lands were set aside subject to "valid existing rights," and Conoco has a lease that gives it the right to drill. *Sure* [18] Conoco has a lease—more than one, *in fact* [19]—*but* [20] those leases were originally issued without sufficient environmental study or public input. *As a result* [21], none of them conveyed a valid right to drill. *What's more* [22], in deciding to issue a permit to drill now, the BLM did not conduct a full analysis of the environmental impacts of drilling in these incomparable lands, *but instead* [23] determined there would be no significant environmental harm on the basis of an abbreviated review that didn't even look at drilling on the other federal leases.

Sounds like [24] Washington *double-speak* [25] to me. I've spent considerable time on these extraordinary lands for years, and I *know* [26] that an oil rig in their midst would have a major impact. *What's more* [27], Conoco wants to drill a well to find oil. *Inevitably* [28], more rigs, more roads, new pipelines, *toxic* [29] wastes and bright lights would follow to get the oil out. The BLM couldn't see this, *but* [30] the U.S. Fish and Wildlife Service and the Environmental Protection Agency did. Both of those agencies *recognized* [31] the *devastating* [32] effects extensive oil drilling would have on this area and urged the BLM to refuse to allow it, *in order to* [33] protect the monument.

Maybe [34] the *problem* [35] comes from giving management responsibility for this monument to the BLM. This is the BLM's first national monument; *almost* [36] all the others are managed by the National Park Service. The Park Service's mission is to *protect the resources* [37] under its care while the bureau has always sought to accommodate economic uses of those under its. *Even so* [38], the BLM *seemed* [39] to be getting off to a *good* [40] start by enlisting *broad* [41] public involvement in developing a management plan for the area. *Yet* [42] the agency's decision to allow oil drilling in the monument completely *undercuts* [43] this process just as it is beginning.

What we're talking about is, in the words of President Clinton, a small piece of "God's handiwork." *Almost* [44] 4 1/2 million acres of irreplaceable red rock wilderness remain outside the monument. Let us at least protect what is within it. The many *roadless* [45] areas within the monument *should* [46] remain so—protected as wilderness. The monument's designation means little *if* [47] a pattern of exploitation is allowed to continue.

Environmentalists—including the Southern Utah Wilderness Alliance, the Natural Resources Defense Council, and the Wilderness Society—appealed BLM's decision to the Interior Department's Board of Land Appeals. This appeal, *however* [48], was rejected earlier this month. This is a *terrible mistake* [49]. We shouldn't be drilling in our national monuments. Period. As President Clinton said when dedicating the new monument, "Sometimes progress is measured in mastering frontiers, but *sometimes* [50] we must measure progress in protecting frontiers for our children and children to come."

Allowing drilling to go forward in the Grand Staircase-Escalante Monument would permanently stain what might otherwise have been a defining legacy of the Clinton presidency.

Read the following advertisement from *Equal Exchange* (Copyright © 1997, 1998, 1999). For each of the numbered expressions, label the main argumentative move, if any, using the same abbreviations as in Exercise I. Then state what you take to be the central conclusions and premises. What criticisms, if any, do you have of this argument?

It *may* [1] be a little early in the morning to bring this up, *but* [2] *if* [3] you buy coffee from *large corporations* [4], you are inadvertently maintaining the system which keeps small farmers *poor* [5] *while* [6] *lining the pockets* [7] of rich corporations. *By* [8] choosing Equal Exchange coffee, you *can* [9] help to make a change. We believe in trading directly with small farming cooperatives at mutually agreed-upon prices with a fixed minimum rate. *Then* [10], *should* [11] the coffee market decline, the farmers are still guaranteed a *fair* [12] price. *So* [13] have a cup of Equal Exchange Coffee and make a small farmer *happy* [14]. *Of course* [15], your decision to buy Equal Exchange need not be completely altruistic. *For* [16] we take as much pride in refining the taste of our *gourmet* [17] coffees *as* [18] we do in *helping* [19] the farmers who produce them. *For* [20] more information about Equal Exchange or to order our line of gourmet, organic, and shade-grown coffee directly, call 1 800 406 8289.

"Excuse me waiter, there's the blood and misery of a thousand small farmers in my coffee."

From *Equal Exchange*. Advertisement. Copyright 1997, 1998, 1999.

EXERCISE IV

This advertisement appeared in various national magazines in 2008. Circle and label each of its key argumentative terms. State its central premises and conclusion, and then put them into standard form. Is the result a good argument? Why or why not?

Provide a close analysis of the following passages by circling and labeling each of the key argumentative terms. Then state what you take to be the central conclusions and premises. What criticisms, if any, do you have of each argument?

PASSAGE 1

The following encomium was written by an art critic for the *New York Times,* in which this review appeared (June 6, 1992, pp. 1, 31). If you are not familiar with Eakins's work, looking at some reproductions might help you appreciate this argument. You might also look up the rest of the essay, as only a small part is reproduced here.

IS EAKINS OUR GREATEST PAINTER?

by John Russell

There never was a painter like Thomas Eakins, who was born in 1844, died in 1916, and is the subject of a great exhibition that has just opened in the Philadelphia Museum of Art. It is not simply that in his hands painting became an exact science, so that if he paints two men rowing on a river, we can tell the month, day, and the hour that they passed under a certain bridge. We admire Eakins for that, but we prize him above all for the new dimension of moral awareness that he brought to American painting.

The question that he asks is not "What do we look like?" It is "What have we done to one another?" And it is because he gives that question so full and so convincing an answer that we ask ourselves whether Thomas Eakins was not the greatest American painter who ever lived. Even if the question strikes us as meaningless, we find it difficult after an exhibition such as this to think of a convincing rival. . . .

PASSAGE 2

The following passage is an excerpt from an essay that appeared in the *Boston Review* (vol. 7, no. 5 [October 1982], pp. 13–19), which is funded by the National Endowment for the Humanities, a government agency that supports scholarship and the arts. Its author was professor of drama at Stanford University.

BEYOND THE WASTELAND: WHAT AMERICAN TV CAN LEARN FROM THE BBC

by Martin Esslin

What are the advantages and disadvantages of a public TV service as compared to a completely commercial system? One of the dangers inherent in a public service system is paternalism: Some authority decides what the viewers should see and hear simply on the basis of what it arbitrarily feels would be good for them. Yet in countries where a highly developed public system exists alongside a commercial one, that danger is minimized because of the market pressure on the commercial system to give its audience what it wants. Indeed, in a dual system the danger is often that the public service may be tempted to ignore its stated purpose to serve the public interest and instead pander to mass preferences because of a sense of competition with the commercial networks.

Another problem that plagues public TV service is that it may run short of money, which in turn can increase its dependence on the government. The extent of government dependence is intimately connected to how the public broadcasting service is financed. In West Germany and Italy, for example, the public broadcasting service takes advertising, but it is usually confined to a clearly delimited area of the network's programming. In Britain the BBC . . . relies entirely on its annual license fee, which guarantees it a steady income and allows long-term planning. In periods of severe inflation, the license-fee system leaves the BBC in a dangerous position vis-a-vis the government, and the network's income may decline in real terms. In countries where the public broadcasting service is financed by an annual allocation in the national budget, long-term planning becomes more difficult and the dependence on the government is far greater. Nevertheless, public TV services financed on that pattern, such as the ABC in Australia and the CBC in Canada, provide programs of high quality that are genuine alternatives to the fare on the numerous popular and prosperous commercial networks. In Canada, this includes programs from the three commercial American networks.

One of the most important positive features of services under public control is their ability to provide planned, high-quality viewing alternatives. The BBC, for example, has two television channels, BBC 1 and BBC 2. The program planning on these two networks is closely coordinated so that highly popular material on one channel is regularly paired with more specialized or demanding fare on the other. And though the percentage of the audience that tunes in to the challenging programming may be small, the scale of magnitude operative in the mass media is such that even a small percentage of the viewing audience represents a very large number of people indeed. A popular dramatic series on BBC 1, for instance, may reach an audience of 20 percent of the adult population of Britain—about ten million people. A play by Shakespeare on BBC 2 that may attract an audience of only 5 percent nonetheless reaches about two-and-a-half million people—a substantial audience for a work of art. It would take a theater with a seating capacity of 1,000 about seven years, or 2,500 performances, to reach an equivalent number of people! Nor should it be overlooked that this audience will include people whose influence may be greater in the long run than that of the ten million who watched the entertainment program. In this system, no segment of the viewing public is forced to compromise with any other. In our example, not only did BBC 1 provide a popular entertainment program as an alternative to the Shakespeare, but, in addition, the commercial network offered still another popular program. By careful—perhaps paternalistic—planning the general audience satisfaction was substantially increased.

(continued)

One of the difficulties of the American situation is that the size of the United States favors decentralization and the fragmentation of initiatives for the more ambitious programming of the public service network. A revitalized PBS would need a strong central governing body that could allocate to local producing stations the substantial sums of money they require for ambitious projects—projects that could compete with the best offerings of the rich commercial competitors.

Using existing satellite technology, such a truly national network of public service television could be made available to the entire country. If a public service television organization was able to provide simultaneous, alternative programming along the lines of BBC 1 and BBC 2, the cultural role of television in the United States could be radically improved, and the most powerful communication medium in history could realize its positive potential to inform, educate, and provide exposure to diverse cultural ideas.

PASSAGE 3

This article was published in the *New York Times* (January 15, 2004, p. A33).

LIFE (AND DEATH) ON MARS

■

by Paul Davies

Sydney, Australia—President Bush's announcement yesterday that the United States will soon be pointing its rockets toward Mars will doubtless be greeted with delight by space scientists. . . . And yet the scientific community's enthusiasm will surely be tempered by skepticism. Scientists, it's worth remembering, rejoiced when President George H. W. Bush unveiled a Mars project in 1989. The same scientists then despaired when the plan quickly evaporated amid spiraling projected costs and shifting priorities. . . .

Why is going to Mars so expensive? Mainly it's the distance from Earth. At its closest point in orbit, Mars lies 35 million miles away from us, necessitating a journey of many months, whereas reaching the Moon requires just a few days' flight. On top of this, Mars has a surface gravity that, though only 38 percent of Earth's, is much greater than the Moon's. It takes a lot of fuel to blast off Mars and get back home. If the propellant has to be transported there from Earth, costs of a launching soar. . . .

There is, however, an obvious way to slash the costs and bring Mars within reach of early manned exploration. The answer lies with a one-way mission.

Most people react with instinctive horror at the suggestion. I recall my own sense of discomfort when I met an aging American scientist who claimed to have trained for a one-way mission to the Moon in the pre-Apollo days. And in the case of the barren Moon, that reaction is largely justified. There is little on the Moon to sustain human life. Mars, however, is a different story. Because of the planet's relatively benign environment, it is theoretically able to support a permanent human presence. If provided with the right equipment, astronauts would have a chance of living there for years. A one-way trip to Mars need not mean a quick demise.

Every two years the orbit of Mars creates a window of opportunity to send fresh supplies at a reasonable cost. An initial colony of four astronauts, equipped with a small nuclear reactor and a couple of rover vehicles, could make their own oxygen, grow some food and even initiate building projects using local raw materials. Supplemented by food shipments, medical supplies and replacement gadgets from home, the colony could be sustained indefinitely. To be sure, the living conditions would be uncomfortable, but the colonists would have the opportunity to do ground-breaking scientific work and blaze a trail that would ensure them a permanent place in the annals of discovery.

Obviously this strategy carries significant risks in addition to those faced by a conventional Mars mission. Major equipment failure could leave the colony without enough power, oxygen or food. An accident might kill or disable an astronaut who provided some vital expertise. A supply drop might fail, condemning the colonists to starve in a very public way. Even if nothing went wrong, the astronauts' lives would certainly be shortened by the harsh conditions. . . .

Would it be right to ask people to accept such conditions for the sake of science, or even humanity? The answer has to be yes. We already expect certain people to take significant risks on our behalf, such as special forces operatives or test pilots. Some people gleefully dice with death in the name of sport or adventure. Dangerous occupations that reduce life expectancy through exposure to hazardous conditions or substances are commonplace. . . .

Who would put their hand up for a one-way ticket to Mars? I work among people who study astrobiology and planetary science, and there is no lack of eager young scientists who would sign up right now, given half a chance. But it would make more sense to pick mature, older scientists with reduced life expectancy. Other considerations, like weight, emotional stability and scientific credentials, would of course have to be factored in.

The early outpost wouldn't be left to wither and die. Rather, it would form the basis for a much more ambitious colonization program. Over the years new equipment and additional astronauts would be sent to join the original crew. In time, the colony would grow to the point of being self-sustaining.

When this stage was reached, humanity would have a precious insurance policy against catastrophe at home. During the next millennium there is a significant chance that civilization on Earth will be destroyed by an asteroid, a killer plague or a global war. A Martian colony could keep the flame of civilization and culture alive until Earth could be reverse-colonized from Mars.

Would NASA entertain a one-way policy for human Mars exploration? Probably not. But other, more adventurous space agencies in Europe or Asia might. The next giant leap for mankind won't come without risk.

PASSAGE 4

The following letter to the editor was written by Charlie Buttrey, a lawyer, and published in the White River Junction, Vermont, *Valley News* on Wednesday, August 29, 2001.

(continued)

THREE FALLACIES ABOUT GUN RIGHTS

by Charlie Buttrey

In the never-ending debate on these pages over gun ownership, those who favor expansive gun rights appear to have adopted one (or more) of three lines of argument:

The Constitution protects the individual right to gun ownership.

The crime rate in Great Britain (where gun ownership is strictly controlled) is "skyrocketing."

In colonial days, the vast majority of people owned guns.

Each premise, however, is erroneous.

In our constitutional system, the ultimate arbiter of what the Constitution says is the Supreme Court. One may not agree with its rulings (for example, many people do not approve of its ruling extending First Amendment protections to flag burning or Fourth Amendment protections to the decision to terminate a pregnancy), but, under our system of government, once the Supreme Court has ruled a certain way, that ruling stands as the law of the land. On the issue of whether the Second Amendment encompasses an individual's right to possess firearms, the Supreme Court has spoken. And the answer is that it does not. Like it or not, that is the law of the land. It is true that the state constitutions in both Vermont and New Hampshire provide for the protection of individual gun ownership. In neither instance, however, is such a right absolute. For example, the New Hampshire Supreme Court has ruled that a law prohibiting felons from possessing firearms is not unconstitutional. Similarly, a Vermont law prohibiting people from carrying loaded firearms in their vehicles was held to be permissible.

The notion that Great Britain's crime rate is skyrocketing is belied by the facts. British government statistics reveal a steady increase in most crime categories between 1980 and 1995 and a gradual leveling off in the last five years. Of course, gun-related crimes are minuscule when compared with those in the United States. Guns are used in robberies in Great Britain less than 5 percent of the time. And from 1980 to 1999, annual gun-related homicides in Britain ranged from a low of 7 to a high of 42. In comparison, according to U.S. Bureau of Justice statistics, an average of 10,000 gun-related homicides occurred each year in this country during the same period.

Finally, the suggestion that our colonial forebears were almost universally armed has been thoroughly repudiated. In his recent book, *Arming America*, Emory University historian Michael Bellesiles reveals that the average colonial citizen had virtually no access to or training in the use of firearms, and that the few guns that did exist were kept under strict control. The fewer than 10 percent of Americans who did possess guns in the years prior to the Civil War were generally neglectful of the weapons and those guns were expensive, clumsy, unreliable, and hard to maintain.

There may be sound policy grounds that can be advanced in favor of relatively unrestricted gun ownership. Those arguments should be made, however, from a perspective of historical truth and legal accuracy.

PASSAGE 5

The following extract comes from *Compulsory Mis-Education and the Community of Scholars* (New York: Vintage Books, 1966). Copyright © 1962, 1964 by Paul Goodman. Used by permission of Random House, Inc.

A PROPOSAL TO ABOLISH GRADING

■

by Paul Goodman

Let half a dozen of the prestigious universities—Chicago, Stanford, the Ivy League—abolish grading, and use testing only and entirely for pedagogic purposes as teachers see fit.

Anyone who knows the frantic temper of the present schools will understand the transvaluation of values that would be effected by this modest innovation. For most of the students, the competitive grade has come to be the essence. The naïve teacher points to the beauty of the subject and the ingenuity of the research; the shrewd student asks if he is responsible for that on the final exam.

Let me at once dispose of an objection whose unanimity is quite fascinating. I think that the great majority of professors agree that grading hinders teaching and creates a bad spirit, going as far as cheating and plagiarizing. I have before me the collection of essays, *Examining in Harvard College,* and this is the consensus. It is uniformly asserted, however, that the grading is inevitable; for how else will the graduate schools, the foundations, the corporations *know* whom to accept, reward, hire? How will the talent scouts know whom to tap? By testing the applicants, of course, according to the specific task-requirements of the inducting institution, just as applicants for the Civil Service or for licenses in medicine, law, and architecture are tested. Why should Harvard professors do the testing *for* corporations and graduate schools? . . .

There are several good reasons for testing, and kinds of test. But if the aim is to discover weakness, what is the point of down-grading and punishing, and thereby inviting the student to conceal his weakness, by faking and bulling, if not cheating? The natural conclusion of [education] is the insight itself, not a grade for having had it. For the important purpose of placement, if one can establish in the student the belief that one is testing *not* to grade and making invidious comparisons but for his own advantage, the student should normally seek his own level, where he is challenged and yet capable, rather than trying to get by. If the student dares to accept himself as he is, a teacher's grade is a crude instrument compared with a student's self-awareness. But it is rare in our universities that students are encouraged to notice objectively their vast confusion. Unlike Socrates, our teachers rely on power-drives rather than shame and ingenuous idealism.

Many students are lazy, so teachers try to goad or threaten them by grading. In the long run this must do more harm than good. Laziness is a character-defense. It may be a way of avoiding learning, in order to protect the conceit that one is already perfect. . . . It may be a way of avoiding just the risk of

(continued)

failing and being down-graded. Sometimes it is a way of politely saying, "I won't." But since it is the authoritarian grown-up demands that have created such attitudes in the first place, why repeat the trauma? There comes a time when we must treat people as adults, laziness and all. It is one thing courageously to fire a do-nothing out of your class; it is quite another thing to evaluate him with a lordly F.

Most important of all, it is often obvious that balking in doing the work, especially among bright young people who get to great universities, means exactly what it says: The work does not suit me, not this subject, or not at this time, or not in this school, or not in school altogether. The student might not be bookish; he might be school-tired; perhaps his development ought now to take another direction. Yet, unfortunately, if such a student is intelligent and is not sure of himself, he *can* be bullied into passing, and this obscures everything. My hunch is that I am describing a common situation. What a grim waste of young life and teacherly effort! Such a student will retain nothing of what he has "passed" in. Sometimes he must get mononucleosis to tell his story and be believed.

And, ironically, the converse is also probably commonly true. A student flunks and is mechanically weeded out, who is really ready and eager to learn in a scholastic setting, but he has not quite caught on. A good teacher can recognize the situation, but the computer wreaks its will.

PASSAGE 6

The following op-ed appeared in *The Dartmouth* on April 30, 2007. The author was a college student at the time.

MAKE IT 18
■

by Ben Selznick

Did you get wasted this weekend? Are you under the age of 21? Don't fret, my underage friends, you are not alone. Across America, hundreds of thousands of underage men and women enjoyed booze this weekend—illegally. In response to a recent news article in *The Dartmouth* ("Ex-Middlebury president: lower drinking age to 18," April 25), I would like to agree with the former president of Middlebury College that states should try once again lowering the drinking age to 18.

We must first get our facts straight. The drinking age is not set by the federal government; it is set by the states. Currently, each state has its law set at 21. However, this figure neither necessarily reflects research and careful consideration nor appeals to constituents. Instead, it reflects the fact that drinking age became tied to highway funds somewhere along the way. Because of this, were a state to lower their drinking age, they would also have to significantly raise taxes to offset the lost highway funds from the government. This hand-tying is asinine. If the drinking age is a state decision, it should be made by states independently of funds for highways. Before any progress can be made, lawmakers must sever this illogical connection.

Were drinking age to become a true state consideration, states could engage in open debate about the issue. Several arguments could then be made in favor of lowering the age to 18.

First: A fair portion of drinkers between the ages of 18 and 21 are at colleges where alcohol can be easily obtained. Just think about this weekend and all the people without wristbands—because they forgot their IDs at home I'm sure—who were able to obtain alcohol. This easy availability leads to a very danger-ous game of cat and mouse between colleges and their students. In this game, colleges know full well that underage drinking exists. Students know that they are drinking underage and therefore illegally. And yet, the game continues with colleges trying to make sure that no alcohol-related tragedies occur. This game isn't the fault of colleges, nor is it the fault of students. Instead, it is the fault of our law, which classifies part of this college-age set as "underage" and the rest as "of age." When it comes to colleges, our law simply doesn't reflect reality. It must therefore be changed.

Second: At present, keeping the drinking age at 21 prevents America from having an open and honest conception of alcohol the way, say, continental Europe does. In France, where the drinking age is 16, alcohol is understood as a complement to a meal as well as an intoxicant. Though people certainly drink to get drunk, the concept of binge drinking beer through a funnel is seen as a bar-baric abuse of alcohol. More importantly, France's policy reflects the understand-ing that people are going to drink alcohol whether the activity is legal or not. America stubbornly refuses to accept this fact. Perhaps it is our long history of teetotalers, prohibition and general dislike of alcohol by various groups. What-ever our past, our present situation is one where binge drinking is the norm and alcohol education to college students reeks of being too little too late.

Third: The main concern against lowering the drinking age comes from Mothers Against Drunk Driving. MADD has statistics to back up their claim that a lower drinking age yields more drunk driving accidents. But if the drinking age were lowered and then supplemented with honest, not pander-ing, alcohol education programs in schools, perhaps over time our approach towards alcohol as a culture would change.

America has the highest drinking age of any country on Earth. Although in-tended to protect us, in the end this high barrier leads to unsafe abuse of alco-hol nationwide. States must engage in true conversation with their constituents and consider arguments from frustrated college administrators as well as MADD.

In the end, a state may conclude that 21 is a good age. But they may also conclude that lowering the drinking age is a practical solution to a pressing problem. After all, by changing the definition of "underage drinking," we could alleviate its negative effects.

EXERCISE VI

Practice close analysis some more by doing close analyses of:

1. one of the passages in the Discussion Questions at the end of Chapter 1,
2. one of the articles in Part V of this book,
3. an editorial or advertisement from your local paper,
4. something that you read for another course,
5. a lecture by your professor in another course (or this course!), or
6. a paper by you or by a friend in another course.

EXERCISE VII

Describe the purpose of, intended audience for, and standpoint in each of the arguments in Exercises I-VI.

DISCUSSION QUESTIONS

1. If, as some social critics have maintained, the pervasive nature of television has created generation upon generation of intellectually passive automatons, why study close analysis?
2. Television commercials are often arguments in miniature. Recount several recent television commercials and identify the argumentative devices at work.

5

DEEP ANALYSIS

Arguments in everyday life rarely occur in isolation. They usually come in the middle of much verbiage that is not essential to the argument itself. Everyday arguments are also rarely complete. Essential premises are often omitted. Many such omissions are tolerable because we are able to convey a great deal of information indirectly by conversational implication. Nevertheless, to give a critical evaluation of an argument, it is necessary to isolate the argument from extraneous surroundings, to make explicit unstated parts of the argument, and to arrange them in a systematic order. This puts us in a better position to decide on the soundness or unsoundness of the argument in question. This chapter will develop methods for reconstructing arguments so that they may be understood and evaluated in a fair and systematic fashion. These methods will then be illustrated by applying them to a disagreement that depends on fundamental principles.

GETTING DOWN TO BASICS

To understand an argument, it is useful to put it into standard form. As we saw in Chapter 3, this is done simply by writing down the numbered premises, drawing a line, adding "∴" followed by the conclusion, and indicating which premises are supposed to be reasons for the conclusion. That is all we write down in standard form, but there is often a lot more in the passage that includes the argument. It is not uncommon for the stated argument to stretch over several pages, whereas the basic argument has only a few premises and a single conclusion.

One reason for this is that people often go off on *tangents*. They start to argue for one claim, but that reminds them of something else, so they talk about that for a while; then they finally return to their original topic. One example occurred during the Republican presidential candidates' debate on October 9, 2007, when Governor Mitt Romney said,

> . . . We're also going to have to get serious about treating Ahmadinejad [the President of Iran] like the rogue and buffoon that he is. And it was outrageous for the United Nations to invite him to come to this country. It was outrageous for Columbia to invite him to speak at their university. This is a person who denied the Holocaust, a person who has spoken about genocide, is seeking the

means to carry it out. And it is unacceptable to this country to allow that individual to have control of launching a nuclear weapon. And so we will take the action necessary to keep that from happening . . .

Romney's criticisms of the United Nations and Columbia are not really part of his argument, because they do not support his conclusion that the United States needs to keep nuclear weapons out of the hands of Ahmadinejad.

Such tangents can be completely irrelevant or unnecessary, and they often make it hard to follow the argument. Some people even go off on tangents on purpose to confuse their opponents and hide gaping holes in their arguments. The irrelevant diversion is sometimes called a *red herring* (after a man who, when pursued by hounds, threw them off his scent by dragging a red herring across his trail). More generally, this maneuver might be called the *trick of excess verbiage*. It violates the conversational rules of Quantity, Relevance, or Manner, which were discussed in Chapter 2.

To focus on the argument itself, we need to look carefully at each particular sentence to determine whether it affects the validity or strength of the argument or the truth of its premises. If we decide that a sentence is not necessary for the argument, then we should not add it when we list the premises and conclusion in standard form. Of course, we have to be careful not to omit anything that would improve the argument, but we also do not want to include too much, because irrelevant material simply makes it more difficult to analyze and evaluate the argument.

Another source of extra material is repetition. Consider Senator John Edwards's response to a question about the Defense of Marriage Act in the Democratic presidential candidates' debate on January 22, 2004:

> These are issues that should be left [to the states]. Massachusetts, for example, has just made a decision—the Supreme Court at least has made a decision—that embraces the notion of gay marriage. I think these are decisions the states should have the power to make. And the Defense of Marriage Act, as I understand it—you're right, I wasn't there when it was passed—but as I understand it, would have taken away that power. And I think that's wrong—that power should not be taken away from the states. . . .

Now compare:

> These are issues that should be left to the states.
>
> These are decisions that states should have the power to make.
>
> That power should not be taken away from the states.

All three of these sentences say pretty much the same thing, so we do not need them all.

Why do people repeat themselves like this? Sometimes they just forget that they already made the point before, but often repetition accomplishes a goal. Good speakers regularly repeat their main points to remind their audience of what was said earlier. Repetition is subtler when it is used to explain something. A point can often be clarified by restating it in a new way. Repetition can also function as a kind of assurance, as an expression of confidence, or as an indication of how important a point is. Some writers seem to think that if they say something often enough, people will come to believe it. Whether or not this trick works, if two sentences say equivalent things, there is no need to list both sentences when the argument is put into standard form. Listing the same premise twice will not make the argument any better from a logical point of view.

Sometimes *guarding* terms can also be dropped. If I say, "I think Miranda is at home, so we can probably meet her there," this argument might be represented in standard form thus:

(1) I think Miranda is at home.

∴ (2) We can probably meet her there. (from 1)

This is misleading. My *thoughts* are not what make us able to meet Miranda at home. My thoughts do not even increase the probability that she is at home or that we can meet her there. It is the *fact* that Miranda is at home that provides a reason for the conclusion. Thus, it is clearer to drop the guarding phrase ("I think") when putting the argument into standard form. But you have to be careful, for not all guarding phrases can be dropped. When I say "We can *probably* meet her there," I might not want to say simply, "We *can* meet her there." After all, even if she is there now, we might not be able to get there before she leaves. Then to drop "probably" from my conclusion would distort what I meant to say and would make my argument more questionable, so you should not drop that guarding term if you want to understand my argument charitably and accurately.

Here's another example: If a friend says that you ought to buckle your seat belt because you could have an accident, it would distort her argument to drop the guarding term ("could"), because she is not claiming that you definitely will have an accident, or even that you probably will have one. The *chance* of an accident is significant enough to show that you ought to buckle your seat belt, so this guarding term should be kept when the argument is put into standard form.

It is also possible to drop *assuring* terms in some cases. Suppose someone says, "You obviously cannot play golf in Alaska in January, so there's no point in bringing your clubs." There is no need to keep the assuring term ("obviously") in the premise. It might even be misleading, because the issue is whether the premise is true, not whether it is obvious. The argument cannot be refuted by showing that, even though you in fact cannot play golf in Alaska in January, this is not obvious, since there might be indoor golf courses. In contrast, assuring terms *cannot* be dropped in some other cases. For example, if someone argues, "We know that poverty causes crime, because many studies have shown that it does," then the assuring terms ("We know that . . ." and "studies have shown that . . .") cannot be dropped without turning the argument into an empty shell: "Poverty causes crime, because it does." The point of this argument is to cite the sources of our knowledge ("studies") and to show that we have knowledge instead of just a hunch. That point is lost if we drop the assuring terms.

Unfortunately, there is no mechanical method for determining when guarding or assuring terms and phrases can be dropped, or whether certain sentences are unnecessary tangents or repetition. We simply have to look closely at what is being said and think hard about what is needed to support the conclusion. It takes great skill, care, and insight to pare an argument down to its essential core without omitting anything that would make it better. And that is the goal: If you want to understand someone's argument, you should try to make that argument as good as it can be. You should interpret it charitably. Distorting and oversimplifying other people's arguments might be fun at times and can win points in debates, but it cannot help us understand or learn from other people's arguments.

EXERCISE I

Put the following arguments into standard form and omit anything that does not affect the validity of the argument or the truth of its premises.

1. Philadelphia is rich in history, but it is not now the capital of the United States, so the United States Congress must meet somewhere else.

2. Not everybody whom you invited is going to come to your party. Some of them won't come. So this room should be big enough.

3. I know that my wife is at home, since I just called her there and spoke to her. We talked about our dinner plans.

4. I'm not sure, but Joseph is probably Jewish. Hence, he is a rabbi if he is a member of the clergy.

5. Some students could not concentrate on the lecture, because they did not eat lunch before class, although I did.

6. The most surprising news of all is that Johnson dropped out of the race because he thought his opponent was better qualified than he was for the office.

7. The Democrat is likely to win, since experts agree that more women support him.

8. It seems to me that married people are happier, so marriage must be a good thing, or at least I think so.

DISCUSSION QUESTION

In the quotation above, is it fair to drop "I think" from the start of Edwards's sentences "I think these are decisions the states should have the power to make" and "I think that's wrong—that power should not be taken away from the states"? Why or why not? Is this phrase "I think" used for guarding or assuring or some other purpose in this context? Explain why Edwards adds these words.

CLARIFYING CRUCIAL TERMS

After the essential premises and conclusion are isolated, we often need to clarify these claims before we can begin our logical analysis. The goal here is not perfect clarity, for there probably is no such thing. It is, however, often necessary to eliminate ambiguity and reduce vagueness before we can give an argument a fair assessment. In particular, it is usually helpful to specify the referents of pronouns, because such references can depend on a context that is changed when the argument is put into standard form. "You are wrong" or "That's wrong" can be perfectly clear when said in response to a particular claim, but they lose their clarity when they are moved into the conclusion of an argument in standard form. We also often need to specify whether a claim is about all, most, many, or just some of its subject matter. When people say, "Blues music is sad," do they mean all, most, some, or typical blues music?

Another common problem arises when someone argues like this:

You should just say "No" to drugs, because drugs are dangerous.

What counts as a drug? What about penicillin or aspirin? The speaker might seem to mean "drugs like cocaine," but "like" them in which respects? Maybe what is meant is "addictive drugs," but what about alcohol and nicotine (which are often addictive)? You might think that the speaker means "dangerous drugs," but then the premise becomes empty: "Dangerous drugs are dangerous." Or maybe the idea is "illegal drugs," but that seems to assume that the law is correct about what is dangerous. In any case, we cannot begin to evaluate this argument if we do not know the extent of what it claims.

Of course, we should not try to clarify every term in the argument. Even if this were possible, it would make the argument extremely long and boring. Instead, our goal is to clarify anything that seems likely to produce confusion later if it is not cleared up now. As our analysis continues, we can always return and clarify more if the need arises, but it is better to get the most obvious problems out of the way at the start.

Some problems, however, just won't go away. Don't get frustrated if you cannot figure out how to clarify a crucial term in someone else's argument. The fault might lie with the person who gave the argument. Often an argument leaves a crucial term vague or ambiguous, because serious defects in the argument would become apparent if its terms were made more precise. We will discuss such tricks in detail in Chapters 13–14. For now, we just need to try our best to understand and clarify the essential terms in the argument.

DISSECTING THE ARGUMENT

A single sentence often includes several clauses that make separate claims. When this happens, it is usually useful to dissect the sentence into its smallest parts, so that we can investigate each part separately. Because simpler steps are easier to follow than complex ones, we can understand the argument better when it is broken down. Dissection makes us more likely to notice any flaws in the argument. It also enables us to pinpoint exactly where the argument fails, if it does.

The process of dissecting an argument is a skill that can be learned only by practice. Let's start with a simple example:

> Joe won his bet, because all he had to do was eat five pounds of oysters, and he ate nine dozen oysters, which weigh more than five pounds.

The simplest unpacking of this argument yields the following restatement in standard form:

> (1) All Joe had to do was eat five pounds of oysters, and he ate nine dozen oysters, which weigh more than five pounds.
> ∴(2) Joe won his bet. (from 1)

If we think about the premise of this argument, we see that it actually contains three claims. The argument will be clearer if we separate these claims into independent premises and add a few words for the sake of clarity. The following, then, is a better representation of this argument:

> (1) All Joe had to do (to win his bet) was eat five pounds of oysters.
> (2) Joe ate nine dozen oysters.
> (3) Nine dozen oysters weigh more than five pounds.
> ∴(4) Joe won his bet. (from 1–3)

With the premise split up in this way, it becomes obvious that there are three separate ways in which the argument could fail. One possibility is that the first premise is false because Joe had to do more than just eat five pounds of oysters to win his bet: Maybe what he bet was that he could eat five pounds in five minutes. Another possibility is that the second premise is false because Joe did not really eat nine dozen oysters: Maybe he really ate one dozen oysters cut into nine dozen pieces. A final way in which the argument could fail is if the third premise is false because nine dozen oysters do not weigh more than five pounds: Maybe the oysters that Joe ate were very small, or maybe nine dozen oysters weigh more than five pounds only when they are still in their shells, but Joe did not eat the shells. In any case, breaking down complex premises into simpler ones makes it easier to see exactly where the argument goes wrong, if it does. Consequently, we can be more confident that an argument does not go wrong if we do not see any problem in it even after we have broken it down completely.

Although it is a good idea to break down the premises of an argument when this is possible, we have to be careful not to do this in a way that changes the logical structure of the argument. Suppose someone argues like this:

> Socialism is doomed to failure because it does not provide the incentives that are needed for a prosperous economy.

The simplest representation of this argument yields the following standard form:

> (1) Socialism does not provide the incentives that are needed for a prosperous economy.
> ∴ (2) Socialism is doomed to failure. (from 1)

It is tempting to break up the first premise into two parts:

> (1) Socialism does not provide incentives.
> (2) Incentives are needed for a prosperous economy.
> ∴ (3) Socialism is doomed to failure. (from 1–2)

In this form, the argument is open to a fatal objection: Socialism *does* provide *some* incentives. Workers often get public recognition and special privileges when they produce a great deal in socialist economies. But this does not refute the original argument. The point of the original argument was not that socialism does not provide any incentives at all, but only that socialism does not provide enough incentives or the right kind of incentives to create a prosperous economy. This point is lost if we break up the premise in the way suggested. A better attempt is this:

> (1) Socialism does not provide adequate incentives.
> (2) Adequate incentives are needed for a prosperous economy.
> ∴ (3) Socialism is doomed to failure. (from 1–2)

The problem now is to specify when incentives are *adequate*. What kinds of incentives are needed? How much of these incentives? The answer seems to be "enough for a prosperous economy." But then premise 2 reduces to "Enough incentives for a prosperous economy are needed for a prosperous economy." This is too empty to be useful. Thus, we are led back to something like the original premise:

> (1) Socialism does not provide enough incentives for a prosperous economy.
> ∴ (2) Socialism is doomed to failure. (from 1)

In this case, we cannot break the premise into parts without distorting the point.

ARRANGING SUBARGUMENTS

When the premises of an argument are dissected, it often becomes clear that some of these premises are intended as reasons for others. The premises then form a chain of simpler arguments that culminate in the ultimate conclusion, but only after some intermediate steps. Consider this argument:

> There's no way I can finish my paper before the 9 o'clock show, since I have to do the reading first, so I won't even start writing until at least 9 o'clock.

It might seem tempting to put this argument into standard form as:

(1) I have to do the reading first.
(2) I won't even start writing until at least 9 o'clock.
∴(3) I can't finish my paper before the 9 o'clock show. (from 1–2)

This reformulation does include all three parts of the original argument, but it fails to indicate the correct role for each part. The two argument markers in the original argument indicate that there are really *two* conclusions. The word "since" indicates that what precedes it is a conclusion, and the word "so" indicates that what follows it is also a conclusion. We cannot represent this as a single argument in standard form, because each argument in standard form can have only one conclusion. Thus, the original sentence must have included two arguments. The relationship between these arguments should be clear: The conclusion of the first argument functions as a premise or reason in the second argument. To represent this, we let the two arguments form a chain. This is the first argument:

(1) I have to do the reading first.
∴(2) I won't even start writing until at least 9 o'clock. (from 1)

This is the second argument:

(2) I won't even start writing until at least 9 o'clock.
∴(3) I can't finish my paper before the 9 o'clock show. (from 2)

If we want to, we can then write these two arguments in a chain like this:

(1) I have to do the reading first.
∴(2) I won't even start writing until at least 9 o'clock. (from 1)
∴(3) I can't finish my paper before the 9 o'clock show. (from 2)

This chain of reasoning can also be diagrammed like this:

(1)

(2)

(3)

The arrows indicate which claims are supposed to provide reasons for which other claims.

Although it is often illuminating to break an argument into stages and arrange them in a single series, this can be misleading if done incorrectly. For example, the first sentences of Kyl's speech cited in Chapter 4 read as follows:

Mr. Speaker, I oppose this measure. I oppose it first because it is expensive. I further oppose it because it is untimely.

If we try to force this into a simple chain, we might get this:

(1) <u>This measure is expensive.</u>

∴(2) <u>This measure is untimely.</u> (from 1)

∴(3) I oppose this measure. (from 2)

This reconstruction suggests that the measure's being expensive is what makes it untimely. That might be true (say, during a temporary budget crisis), but it is not what Kyl actually says. Instead, Kyl is giving two separate reasons for the same conclusion. First,

(1) <u>This measure is expensive.</u>

∴(2) I oppose this measure. (from 1)

Second,

(1*) <u>This measure is untimely.</u>

∴(2) I oppose this measure. (from 1*)

The structure of this argument can now be diagrammed as a branching tree:

(1)　　(1*)

(2)

The two arrows indicate that there are two separate reasons for the conclusion. We have to be careful not to confuse branching arguments like this with chains of arguments that do not branch.

We also need to distinguish this branching structure from cases where several premises work together to support a single conclusion. Consider this:

My keys must be either at home or at the office. They can't be at the office, because I looked for them there. So they must be at home.

With some clarifications, we can put this argument in standard form:

(1) My keys are either at my home or at my office.
(2) <u>My keys are not at my office.</u>

∴(3) My keys are at my home. (from 1–2)

Although this argument has two premises, it does not give two separate reasons for its conclusion. Neither premise by itself, without the other, is enough to give us any reason to believe the conclusion: "My keys are either at my home or at my office" alone is not enough to support "My keys are at my home," and "My keys are not at my office" alone is also not enough to support "My keys are at my home." The premises work only when they work together. Thus, it would be misleading to diagram this argument in the same way as Kyl's argument.

Instead, we need to indicate that the premises work together. Here's a simple way:

(1) + (2)

(3)

The symbol "+" with a single arrow indicates that the two premises together provide a single reason for the conclusion. The line under the premises that are joined together makes it clear that those are the premises that lead to the conclusion at the end of the arrow. If three or more premises provided a single reason, then we could simply add to the list—(1) + (2) + (3), and so on—then draw a line under the premises to show which ones work together.

The argument that we are diagramming included one part that we have not incorporated yet:

They can't be at the office, because I looked for them there.

The standard form is this:

(2*) I looked for my keys at my office.

∴ (2) My keys can't be at my office. (from 2*)

By itself, this argument has this diagram:

(2*)

(2)

Since the conclusion of this background argument is a premise in the other part of the argument, we can put the diagrams together like this:

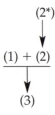

(2*)

(1) + (2)

(3)

The fact that the arrow goes from (2*) to (2) but not to (1) indicates that this background argument supports premise (2), but not the other premise. In cases like this, you need to be careful where you draw your arrows.

Argument structures can get very complex, but we can diagram most arguments by connecting the simple forms that we illustrated. Begin by identifying the premises and conclusions. Give each different claim a different number. When two premises work together to support a single conclusion, put a "+" between the premises and a line under them connected to a single arrow that points to the conclusion. When two or more premises (or sets of premises) provide separate reasons for a conclusion, draw separate arrows from each reason to the conclusion. When a conclusion of one argument is a premise in another, put it in the middle of a chain. The whole diagram together will then show how the parts of the argument fit together.

EXERCISE II

Put the following arguments into standard form. Break up the premises and form chains of arguments wherever this can be done without distorting the argument. Then diagram the argument.

1. I know that Pat can't be a father, because she is not a male. So she can't be a grandfather either.

2. Either Jack is a fool or Mary is a crook, because she ended up with all of his money.

3. Our team can't win this Saturday, both because they are not going to play, and because they are no good, so they wouldn't win even if they did play.

4. Mercury is known to be the only metal that is liquid at room temperature, so a pound of mercury would be liquid in this room, which is at room temperature, and it would also conduct electricity, since all metals do. Therefore, some liquids do conduct electricity.

5. Since he won the lottery, he's rich and lucky, so he'll probably do well in the stock market, too, unless his luck runs out.

6. Joe is not a freshman, since he lives in a fraternity, and freshmen are not allowed to live in fraternities. He also can't be a senior, since he has not declared a major, and every senior has declared a major. And he can't be a junior, because I never met him before today, and I would have met him before now if he were a junior. So Joe must be a sophomore.

7. Since many newly emerging nations do not have the capital resources necessary for sustained growth, they will continue to need help from industrial nations to avoid mass starvation.

EXERCISE III

In "A Piece of 'God's Handiwork'" (Exercise II in Chapter 4), Robert Redford argues that the Bureau of Land Management (BLM) should not allow Conoco to drill for oil in Utah's Grand Staircase-Escalante National Monument. The following passage is a crucial part where Redford answers an objection. Arrange its subarguments in standard form so as to reveal the structure of his argument. Then diagram the overall argument.

> The BLM says its hands are tied. Why? Because these lands were set aside subject to "valid existing rights," and Conoco has a lease that gives it the right to drill. Sure Conoco has a lease—more than one, in fact—but those leases were originally
>
> *(continued)*

issued without sufficient environmental study or public input. As a result, none of them conveyed a valid right to drill. What's more, in deciding to issue a permit to drill now, the BLM did not conduct a full analysis of the environmental impacts of drilling in these incomparable lands, but instead determined there would be no significant environmental harm on the basis of an abbreviated review that didn't even look at drilling on the other federal leases. Sounds like Washington double-speak to me.

EXERCISE IV

During the Republican candidates' debate on October 9, 2007, Chris Matthews asked Senator John McCain, ". . . Do you believe that Congress has to authorize a strategic attack, not an attack on—during hot pursuit, but a strategic attack on weaponry in Iran—do you need congressional approval as commander and chief?" Read McCain's response, then arrange its subarguments in standard form so as to reveal the structure of his argument. Then diagram the overall argument.

> McCain: We're dealing, of course, with hypotheticals. If the situation is that it requires immediate action to ensure the security of the United States of America, that's what you take your oath to do, when you're inaugurated as president of the United States. If it's a long series of build-ups, where the threat becomes greater and greater, of course you want to go to Congress; of course you want to get approval, if this is an imminent threat to the security of the United States of America. So it obviously depends on the scenario. But I would, at minimum, consult with the leaders of Congress because there may come a time when you need the approval of Congress. And I believe that this is a possibility that is, maybe, closer to reality than we are discussing tonight.

SUPPRESSED PREMISES

Arguments in everyday life are rarely completely explicit. They usually depend on unstated assumptions that are understood by those involved in the conversation. Thus, if we are told that Chester Arthur was a president of the United States, we have a right to conclude a great many things about him—for example, that at the time he was president, he was a live human being. Appeals to facts of this kind lie behind the following argument:

> Benjamin Franklin could not have been our second president, because he died before the second election was held.

This argument obviously turns on a question of fact: Did Franklin die before the second presidential election was held? (He did.) The argument would not be sound if this explicit premise were not true. But the argument also depends on a more general principle that ties the premise and conclusion together:

> The dead cannot be president.

This new premise is needed to make the argument valid in the technical sense.

This new premise is also needed to explain *why* the premise supports the conclusion. You could have made the original argument valid simply by adding this:

> If Franklin died before the second election was held, then he could not have been our second president.

Indeed, you can always make an argument valid simply by adding a conditional whose antecedent is the premises and whose consequent is the conclusion. However, this trick is often not illuminating; it does not reveal how the argument works. In our example, there is nothing special about Franklin, so it is misleading to add a conditional that mentions Franklin in particular. In contrast, when we add the general principle, "The dead cannot be president," this new premise not only makes the argument valid but also helps us understand how the conclusion is supposed to follow from the premise.

Traditionally, logicians have called premises that are not stated but are needed (to make the argument valid and explain how it works) *suppressed premises*. An argument depending on suppressed premises is called an *enthymeme* and is said to be *enthymematic*. If we look at arguments that occur in daily life, we discover that they are, almost without exception, enthymematic. Therefore, to trace the pathway between premises and conclusion, it is usually necessary to fill in these suppressed premises that serve as links between the stated premises and the conclusion.

CONTINGENT FACTS

Suppressed premises come in several varieties. They often concern facts or conventions that might have been otherwise—that are contingent rather than necessary. Our example assumed that the dead are not eligible for the presidency, but we can imagine a society in which the deceased are elected to public office as an honor (something like posthumous induction into the Baseball Hall of Fame). Our national government is not like that, however, and this is something that most Americans know. This makes it odd to come right out and say that the deceased cannot hold public office. In most settings, this would involve a violation of the conversational rule of Quantity, because it says more than needs to be said.

Even though it would be odd to state it, this fact plays a central role in the argument. To assert the conclusion without believing the suppressed premise would involve a violation of the conversational rule of Quality, because the speaker would not have adequate reasons for the conclusion. Furthermore, if this suppressed premise were not believed to be true, then to give the explicit premise as a reason for the conclusion would violate the conversational rule of Relevance (just as it would be irrelevant to point out that Babe Ruth is dead when someone asks whether he is in the Baseball Hall of Fame). For these reasons, anyone who gives the original argument conversationally implies a commitment to the suppressed premise.

Suppressed premises are not always so obvious. A somewhat more complicated example is this:

> Arnold Schwarzenegger cannot become president of the United States, because he was born in Austria.

Why should being from Austria disqualify someone from being president? It seems odd that the Founding Fathers should have something against that particular part of the world. The answer is that the argument depends on a more general suppressed premise:

> Only a natural-born United States citizen may become president of the United States.

It is this provision of the United States Constitution that lies at the heart of the argument. Knowing this provision is, of course, a more specialized piece of knowledge than knowing that you have to be alive to be president. For this reason, more people will see the force of the first argument (about Franklin) than the second (about Schwarzenegger). The second argument assumes an audience with more specialized knowledge.

The argument still has to draw a connection between being born in Austria and being a natural-born United States citizen. So it turns out that the argument has three stages:

> (1) Schwarzenegger was born in Austria.
> (2) Austria has never been part of the United States.
> ∴(3) Schwarzenegger was born outside of the United States. (from 1–2)
> (4) Anyone who was born outside of the United States is not a natural-born United States citizen.
> ∴(5) Schwarzenegger is not a natural-born United States citizen. (from 3–4)
> (6) Only a natural-born United States citizen may become president of the United States.
> ∴(7) Schwarzenegger cannot become president of the United States. (from 5–6)

With the addition of suppressed premises (2), (4), and (6), the argument is technically valid, for, if (1)–(2) are true, (3) must be true; if (3)–(4) are true, (5) must also be true; and if (5)–(6) are true, then (7) must be true.

The argument is still not sound, however, because some of the suppressed premises that were added are not true. In particular, there is an exception to the suppressed premise about who is a natural-born United States citizen. This exception is well known to United States citizens who live overseas.

People who were born in Austria are United States citizens if their parents were United States citizens. They also seem to count as natural-born citizens, since they are not naturalized. This is not completely settled, but it does not matter here, as Arnold Schwarzenegger's parents were not United States citizens when he was born. Thus, the second stage of the above argument can be reformulated as follows:

(3)   Schwarzenegger was born outside of the United States.

(4*) Schwarzenegger's parents were not United States citizens when he was born.

(4**) Anyone who was born outside of the United States and whose parents were not United States citizens at the time is not a natural-born United States citizen.

∴(5)   Schwarzenegger is not a natural-born United States citizen. (from 3, 4*, and 4**)

This much of the argument is now sound.

An argument with a single premise has grown to include three stages with at least four suppressed premises. Some of the added premises are obvious, but others are less well known, so we cannot assume that the person who gave the original argument had the more complete argument in mind. Many people would be convinced by the original argument even without all these added complexities. Nonetheless, the many suppressed premises are necessary to make the argument sound. Seeing this brings out the assumptions that must be true for the conclusion to follow from the premises. This process of making everything explicit enables us to assess these background assumptions directly.

EXERCISE V

There is one obscure exception to the premise that only a natural-born citizen may become president of the United States. The Constitution does allow a person who is not a natural-born citizen to become president if he or she was "a citizen of the United States at the time of the adoption of this Constitution." This exception is said to have been added to allow Alexander Hamilton to run for president, but it obviously does not apply to Schwarzenegger or to anyone else alive today. Nonetheless, this exception keeps the argument from being sound in its present form. Reformulate the final stage of the argument to make it sound.

LINGUISTIC PRINCIPLES

Often an argument is valid, but it is still not clear *why* it is valid. It is not clear *how* the conclusion follows from the premises. Arguments are like pathways between premises and conclusions, and some of these pathways are more complicated than others. Yet even the simplest arguments reveal hidden complexities when examined closely. For example, there is no question that the following argument is valid:

(1) Harriet is in New York with her son.

∴(2) Harriet's son is in New York.

It is not possible for the premise to be true and the conclusion false. If asked why this conclusion follows from the premise, it would be natural to reply that:

You cannot be someplace with somebody unless that person is there, too.

This is not something we usually spell out, but it is the principle that takes us from the premise to the conclusion.

One thing to notice about this principle is that it is quite general—that is, it does not depend on any special features of the people or places involved. It is also true that if Benjamin is in St. Louis with his daughter, then Benjamin's daughter is in St. Louis. Although the references have changed, the general pattern that lies behind this inference will seem obvious to anyone who understands the words used to formulate it. For this reason, principles of this kind are basically *linguistic* in character.

If we look at arguments as they occur in everyday life, we will discover that almost all of them turn on unstated linguistic principles. To cite just one more example: Alice is taller than her husband, so there is at least one woman who is taller than at least one man. This inference relies on the principles that husbands are men and wives are women. We do not usually state these linguistic principles, for to do so will often violate the rule of Quantity. (Try to imagine a context in which you would come right out and say, "Husbands, you know, are men." Unless you were speaking to someone just learning the language, this would be a peculiar remark.) Nonetheless, even if it would usually be peculiar to come right out and state such linguistic principles, our arguments still typically presuppose them. This observation reveals yet another way in which our daily use of language moves within a rich, though largely unnoticed, framework of linguistic rules, as we emphasized in Chapter 2.

EVALUATIVE SUPPRESSED PREMISES

We have examined two kinds of suppressed premises, factual and linguistic. Many arguments also contain unstated evaluative premises. As we saw in Chapter 3, evaluation comes in many kinds. The following argument involves moral evaluation:

It is immoral to buy pornography, because pornography leads to violence toward women.

This argument clearly relies on the moral principle that it is immoral to buy anything that leads to violence toward women. A different example contains religious premises:

You shouldn't take the name of the Lord in vain, for this shows disrespect.

The suppressed premise here is that you should not do anything that shows disrespect (to the Lord). One more example is about economics:

> It is unwise to invest all of your money in one stock, since this increases the risk that you will lose everything.

The suppressed premise here is that it is unwise to increase the risk that you will lose everything. More examples could be given, but the point should be clear. Most arguments depend on unstated assumptions, and many of these assumptions are evaluative in one way or another.

USES AND ABUSES OF SUPPRESSED PREMISES

Talk about *suppressed* premises may bring to mind suppressing a rebellion or an ugly thought, and using *hidden* premises may sound somewhat sneaky. However, the way we are using them, these expressions do not carry such negative connotations. A suppressed or hidden premise is simply an *unstated* premise. It is often legitimate to leave premises unstated. It is legitimate if (1) those who are given the argument can easily supply these unstated premises for themselves, and (2) the unstated premises are not themselves controversial. If done properly, the suppression of premises can add greatly to the efficiency of language. Indeed, without the judicious suppression of obvious premises, many arguments would become too cumbersome to be effective.

On the other hand, suppressed premises can also be used improperly. People sometimes suppress questionable assumptions so that their opponents will not notice where an argument goes astray. For example, when election debates turn to the topic of crime, we often hear arguments like this:

> My opponent is opposed to the death penalty, so he must be soft on crime.

The response sometimes sounds like this:

> Since my opponent continues to support the death penalty, he must not have read the most recent studies, which show that the death penalty does not deter crime.

The first argument assumes that anyone who is opposed to the death penalty is soft on crime, and the second argument assumes that anyone who read the studies in question would be convinced by them and would turn against the death penalty. Both of these assumptions are questionable, and the questions they raise are central to the debate. If we want to understand these issues and address them directly, we have to bring out these suppressed premises openly.

The following arguments depend for their validity on suppressed premises of various kinds. For each of them, list enough suppressed premises to make the argument valid and also to show why it is valid. This might require several suppressed premises of various kinds.

> **EXAMPLE:** Carol has no sisters, because all her siblings are brothers.
>
> **SUPPRESSED PREMISES:** A sister would be a sibling.
>
> A brother is not a sister.

1. Britney Spears is under age thirty-five. Therefore, she cannot run for president of the United States.
2. Nixon couldn't have been president in 1950 because he was still in the Senate.
3. 81 is not a prime number, because 81 is divisible by 3.
4. There's no patient named Rupert here; we have only female patients.
5. Columbus did not discover the New World because the Vikings explored Newfoundland centuries earlier.
6. There must not be any survivors, since they would have been found by now.
7. Lincoln could not have met Washington, because Washington was dead before Lincoln was born.
8. Philadelphia cannot play Los Angeles in the World Series, since they are both in the National League.
9. Mildred must be over forty-three, since she has a daughter who is thirty-six years old.
10. He cannot be a grandfather because he never had children.
11. That's not modern poetry; you can understand it.
12. Harold can't play in the Super Bowl, because he broke his leg.
13. Shaquille must be a basketball player, since he is so tall.
14. Dan is either stupid or very cunning, so he must be stupid.
15. Susan refuses to work on Sundays, which shows that she is lazy and inflexible.
16. Jim told me that Mary is a professor, so she can't be a student, since professors must already have degrees.
17. This burglar alarm won't work unless we are lucky or the burglar uses the front door, so we can't count on it.
18. His natural talents were not enough; he still lost the match because he had not practiced sufficiently.

THE METHOD OF RECONSTRUCTION

We can summarize the discussion so far by listing the steps to be taken in reconstructing an argument. The first two steps were discussed in Chapters 4 and 3, respectively.

1. Do a *close analysis* of the passage containing the argument.
2. List all explicit premises and the conclusion in *standard form*.
3. *Clarify* the premises and the conclusion where necessary.
4. *Break up* the premises and the conclusion into smaller parts where this is possible.
5. *Arrange* the parts of the argument into a chain or tree of subarguments where this is possible.
6. Assess each argument and subargument for *validity*.[1]
7. If any argument or subargument is not valid, or if it is not clear why it is valid, add *suppressed premises* that will show how to get from the premises to the conclusion.
8. Assess the *truth* of the premises.

Remember that the goal of reconstruction is not just technical validity but is, instead, to understand why and how the conclusion is supposed to follow from the premises.

After reconstructing the argument, it is often helpful to add some indication of its structure. This can be done by numbering the premises and then, after each conclusion, listing the premises from which that conclusion follows. (We did this in our examples.) The argument's structure can also be shown by a diagram like those discussed above. Either way, we need to make it clear exactly how the separate parts of the argument are supposed to fit together.

This method is not intended to be mechanical. Each step requires care and intelligence. As a result, a given argument can be reconstructed in various ways with varying degrees of illumination and insight. The goal of this method is to reveal as much of the structure of an argument as possible and to learn from it as much as you can. Different reconstructions approach this goal more or less closely.

The whole process is more complex than our discussion thus far has suggested. This is especially clear in the last three steps of reconstruction, which must be carried out simultaneously. In deciding whether an argument is acceptable, we try to find a set of true suppressed premises that, if added to the stated premises, yields a sound argument for the conclusion. Two problems typically arise when we make this effort:

1. We find a set of premises strong enough to support the conclusion, but at least one of these premises is false.
2. We modify the premises to avoid falsehood, but the conclusion no longer follows from them.

The reconstruction of an argument typically involves shifting back and forth between the demand for a valid argument and the demand for true premises. Eventually, either we show the argument to be sound or we abandon the effort. In the latter case, we conclude that the argument in question has no sound reconstruction. It is still possible that *we* were at fault in not finding a reconstruction that showed the argument to be sound. Perhaps we did not show enough ingenuity in searching for a suppressed premise that would do the trick. There is, in fact, no purely formal or mechanical way of dealing with this problem. A person presenting an argument may reasonably leave out steps, provided that they can easily be filled in by those to whom the argument is addressed. So, in analyzing an argument, we should be charitable, but our charity has limits. After a reasonable search for those suppressed premises that would show the argument to be sound, we should not blame ourselves if we fail to find them. Rather, the blame shifts to the person who formulated the argument for not doing so clearly.

EXERCISE VII

Reconstruct and diagram the main arguments in:

1. The passages in the Discussion Questions at the end of Chapter 1.
2. The passages in Exercises I and V in Chapter 4.
3. An editorial from your local paper.
4. Your last term paper or a friend's last term paper.
5. Part of one of the readings in Part V.

EXERCISE VIII

Not all arguments are serious or good. The following silly argument comes from a famous scene in *Monty Python and the Holy Grail*. Reconstruct the argument that is supposed to show that the woman is a witch.

CROWD: We have found a witch. May we burn her? . . .

WOMAN: I'm not a witch! I'm not a witch! . . .

LEADER: What makes you think she is a witch?

MAN #1: She turned me into a newt!

LEADER: A newt?

MAN #1: I got better.

CROWD: Burn her anyway!

LEADER: Quiet! Quiet! There are ways of telling whether she is a witch.

CROWD: Are there? What are they? Tell us. Do they hurt?

LEADER: Tell me, what do you do with witches?

CROWD: Burn them!

LEADER: And what do you burn apart from witches?

MAN #2: More witches!

MAN #3: Wood.

LEADER: So, why do witches burn?

MAN #1: 'Cause they're made of wood.

LEADER: Good! . . . So, how do we tell whether she is made of wood?

CROWD: Build a bridge out of her.

LEADER: Ah, but can you not also make bridges out of stone?

CROWD: Oh yeah.

LEADER: Does wood sink in water?

CROWD: No, it floats. Throw her into the pond!

LEADER: What also floats in water?

CROWD: Bread. Apples. Very small rocks. Cider! Great gravy. Cherries. Mud. Churches. Lead.

ARTHUR: A duck!

LEADER: Exactly. So, logically, —

MAN #3: If she weighs the same as a duck, she's made of wood.

LEADER: And therefore?

CROWD: A witch! . . . A duck. A duck. Here's a duck!

LEADER: We shall use my largest scales.

CROWD: Burn the witch! (Woman is placed on scales opposite a duck.)

LEADER: Remove the supports. (Woman balances duck.)

CROWD: A witch!

WOMAN: It's a fair cop.

DIGGING DEEPER

After we have reconstructed an argument as well as we can, doubts still might arise about its premises. If we agree with its premises, others might deny them or ask why they are true. If we disagree with its premises, we might be able to understand the source of our disagreement better if we determine why those premises are believed by other people—including the person who gave the argument. Either way, it is useful to try to construct supporting arguments for the premises that may be questioned. These supporting arguments are not parts of the explicit argument or even of its reconstruction, but are arguments further back in a chain of arguments.

When we look for further arguments to support the premises in an argument, we might then wonder whether the premises of each new argument can be accepted without supporting arguments as well. We seem faced with the unpleasant task of producing endless chains of argument. (A similar problem was mentioned in Chapter 3.) When pressed in this way to give reasons for our reasons, and reasons for our reasons for our reasons, we eventually come upon *fundamental principles*—principles for which we cannot give any more basic argument. These fundamental principles can concern morality, religion, politics, or our general views concerning the nature of the world. We often argue within a framework of such principles without actually stating them, because we assume (sometimes incorrectly) that others accept them as well. When someone argues that environmental destruction should be stopped because it will lead to the annihilation of the human race, he or she will not feel called on to say explicitly, "And the annihilation of the human race would be a very bad thing." That, after all, is something that most people take for granted.

Though fundamental principles are often obvious and generally accepted, at times it is not clear which principles are being assumed and just how acceptable they really are. Then we need to make our assumptions explicit and look for deeper arguments, continuing the process as far as we can. There is a limit to how far we can go, but the deeper we go, the better we will understand both our own views and the views of our opponents.

EXERCISE IX

The following arguments depend on suppressed premises for their validity. (a) State what these underlying premises might be. In some cases, there might be more than one. (b) Indicate whether these premises are fundamental principles in the sense just described. (c) For each premise that is not fundamental, give a supporting argument that is as plausible as you can make it. Remember, you do not have to accept an argument to detect its underlying principles and to understand the kind of argument that could be used to support it.

EXAMPLE: General Snork has no right to rule, because he came to power by a military coup.

SUPPRESSED PREMISE: Someone who came to power by a military coup has no right to rule.

SUPPORTING ARGUMENT: Someone has a right to rule only if he or she has been elected by the people.

Someone who comes to power by a military coup has not been elected by the people.

∴ Someone who came to power by a military coup has no right to rule.

(Further support for the first premise might be provided by some general theory of democracy, such as that all rights to use power come from the people, and the only legitimate way for the people to delegate these rights is in elections.)

1. You shouldn't call Kirk guilty, because he has not even been tried yet.

2. Cows cannot live in a desert, because they eat grass.

3. The liquid in this glass must not be water, since the sugar I put in it isn't dissolving.

4. People can vote and be drafted at age eighteen, so they should also be allowed to drink at eighteen.

5. We have no right to attack Muslim dictatorships if we support Christian dictatorships. So we should not attack Muslim dictatorships.

6. That chair won't hold you, since it almost broke a few minutes ago when your little sister sat in it.

7. Bringing down our deficits should be a high priority, because inflation will return if high deficits continue.

8. The thought of eating ostrich meat will seem strange to most people, so your ostrich farm is bound to go broke.

9. Getting good grades must be hard, since, if it were easy, more people would get good grades.

10. Morris does not deserve his wealth, for he merely inherited it.

11. Frank should not be punished, because it is wrong to punish someone just to make an example of him.

12. There can't be UFOs (unidentified flying objects), because there is no life on other planets.

13. The sky is red tonight, so it isn't going to rain tomorrow.

14. Parents take care of their children when they are young, so their children should take care of them when they get old.

DISCUSSION QUESTION

How can you tell when you have reached a fundamental principle? Must every argument start with some basic claim for which no further argument can be given or for which you can give no argument? Why or why not?

AN EXAMPLE OF DEEP ANALYSIS: CAPITAL PUNISHMENT

We can illustrate these methods of deep analysis by examining the difficult question of the constitutionality of capital punishment. It has been argued that the Supreme Court should declare the death penalty unconstitutional because it is a cruel and unusual punishment. The explicitly stated argument has the following basic form:

(1) The death penalty is a cruel and unusual punishment.

∴(2) The death penalty should be declared unconstitutional. (from 1)

The argument plainly depends on two suppressed premises:

SP1: The Constitution prohibits cruel and unusual punishments.

SP2: Anything that the Constitution prohibits should be declared unconstitutional.

So the argument, more fully spelled out, looks like this:

(1) The death penalty is a cruel and unusual punishment.
(2) SP: The Constitution prohibits cruel and unusual punishments.
∴(3) The Constitution prohibits the death penalty. (from 1–2)
(4) SP: Anything that the Constitution prohibits should be declared unconstitutional.
∴(5) The death penalty should be declared unconstitutional. (from 3–4)

This reconstruction seems to be a fair representation of the intent of the original argument.

We can now turn to an assessment of this argument. First, the argument is valid: Given the premises, the conclusion does follow. All that remains is to determine the truth of the premises one by one.

Premise 4 seems uncontroversial. Indeed, it might sound like a truism to say that anything that violates a constitutional provision should be declared unconstitutional. But in fact, this notion was once controversial, for nothing in the Constitution explicitly gives the courts the right to declare acts of legislators unconstitutional and hence void. The courts have acquired and consolidated this right in the years since 1789, and it is still sometimes challenged by those who think that it gives the courts too much power. But even if the judiciary's power to declare laws unconstitutional is not itself a constitutionally stated power, it is so much an accepted part of our system that no one would challenge it in a courtroom proceeding today.

The second premise is clearly true, for the Constitution does, in fact, prohibit cruel and unusual punishments. Its Eighth Amendment reads, "Excessive bail shall not be required, nor excessive fines imposed, nor cruel and unusual punishments inflicted." It is not clear, however, just what this prohibition amounts to. In particular, does the punishment have to be *both* cruel *and* unusual to be prohibited, or is it prohibited whenever it is *either* cruel *or* unusual? This would make a big difference if cruel punishments were usual, or if some unusual punishments were not cruel. For the moment, let us interpret the language as meaning "both cruel and unusual."

The first premise—"The death penalty is a cruel and unusual punishment"—obviously forms the heart of the argument. What we would expect, then, is a good supporting argument to be put forward on its behalf. The following argument by Supreme Court Justice Potter Stewart (in *Furman v. Georgia*, 408 U.S. 239 at 309–310 [1972]) was intended to support this claim in particular cases in which the death penalty was imposed for rape and murder:

> In the first place, it is clear that these sentences are "cruel" in the sense that they excessively go beyond, not in degree but in kind, the punishments that the state legislatures have determined to be necessary. . . . In the second place, it is equally clear that these sentences are "unusual" in the sense that the penalty of death is infrequently imposed for murder, and that its imposition for rape is extraordinarily rare. But I do not rest my conclusion upon these two propositions alone. These death sentences are cruel and unusual in the same way that being struck

by lightning is cruel and unusual. For, of all the people convicted of rapes and murders in 1967 and 1968, many just as reprehensible as these, the petitioners are among a capriciously selected random handful upon whom the sentence of death has in fact been imposed. My concurring brothers [the Justices who agree with Stewart] have demonstrated that, if any basis can be discerned for the selection of these few to be sentenced to die, it is the constitutionally impermissible basis of race.

The first sentence argues that the death penalty is *cruel*. The basic idea is that punishments are cruel if they inflict harms that are much worse than what is necessary for any legitimate and worthwhile purpose. Stewart then seems to accept the state legislatures' view that the death penalty does go far beyond what is necessary. This makes it cruel.

Now let us concentrate on the part of this argument intended to show that the death penalty is an *unusual* punishment. Of course, in civilized nations, the death penalty is reserved for a small range of crimes, but this is hardly the point at issue. The point of the argument is that the death penalty is unusual even for those crimes that are punishable by death, including first-degree murder. Moreover, Stewart claims that, among those convicted of crimes punishable by death, who actually receives a death sentence is determined either capriciously or on the basis of race. The point seems to be that whether a person who is convicted of a capital crime will be given the death penalty depends on the kind of legal aid he or she receives, the prosecutor's willingness to offer a plea bargain, the judge's personality, the beliefs and attitudes of the jury, and many other considerations. At many points in the process, choices that affect the outcome could be based on mere whim or caprice, or even on the race of the defendant or the victim. Why are these factors mentioned? Because, as Stewart says, it is unconstitutional for sentencing to be based on caprice or race.

We can then restate this supporting argument more carefully:

(1) Very few criminals who were found guilty of crimes that are punishable by death are actually sentenced to death.
(2) Among those found guilty of crimes punishable by death, who is sentenced to death depends on caprice or race.
(3) It is unconstitutional for sentencing to depend on caprice or race.
(4) A punishment is unusual if it is imposed infrequently and on an unconstitutional basis.

∴ (5) The death penalty is an unusual punishment. (from 1–4)

This conclusion is part of the first premise in our original argument. Now we can spread the entire argument out before us:

(1) An act is cruel if it inflicts harms that are much worse than what is necessary for any legitimate and worthwhile purpose.
(2) The death penalty inflicts harms that are much worse than what is necessary for any legitimate and worthwhile purpose.

∴ (3) The death penalty is cruel. (from 1–2)

(4) Very few criminals who were found guilty of crimes that are punishable by death are sentenced to death.

(5) Among those found guilty of crimes punishable by death, who is sentenced to death depends on caprice or race.

(6) It is unconstitutional for sentencing to depend on caprice or race.

(7) A punishment is unusual if it is imposed infrequently and on an unconstitutional basis.

∴(8) The death penalty is an unusual punishment. (from 4–7)

∴(9) The death penalty is both cruel and unusual. (from 3 and 8)

(10) The Constitution prohibits cruel and unusual punishments.

∴(11) The Constitution prohibits the death penalty. (from 9–10)

(12) Anything that the Constitution prohibits should be declared unconstitutional.

∴(13) The death penalty should be declared unconstitutional. (from 11–12)

These propositions provide at least the skeleton of an argument with some force. The conclusion does seem to follow from the premises, and the premises themselves seem plausible. We have produced a charitable reconstruction of the argument.

We can now see how an opponent might respond to it. One particularly probing objection goes like this:

> It is sadly true that caprice and race sometimes determine who, among those found guilty of crimes punishable by death, is given the death sentence. However, this fact reflects badly not on the law but on its administration. If judges and juries met their obligations, these factors would not affect who receives the death penalty, and this punishment would no longer be unusual in any relevant sense. What is needed, then, is judicial reform and not the removal of the death penalty on constitutional grounds.

This response is probing because it insists on a distinction between a law itself and the effects of its application—or, more pointedly, its misapplication. Because this distinction was not drawn in the argument above, it is not clear which premise is denied in this response. Probably the best interpretation is that this response denies premise 7, because it is not the death penalty itself that is unusual in the relevant sense when the conditions in premise 7 are met. Instead, it is the present administration of the death penalty that is problematic.

To meet this objection, the original argument could be strengthened in the following way:

> A law should not be judged in isolation from the likely effects of implementing it. Because of the very nature of our system of criminal justice, for the foreseeable future, the death penalty will almost certainly continue to be applied in a capricious and racially discriminatory manner, and who receives it will be determined partly by factors that the Constitution forbids as a basis for sentencing. The death penalty will therefore remain an unusual punishment, so it should be declared unconstitutional.

This argument suggests ways to avoid the above objection by strengthening premises 5–7 of the above argument. The new versions of these premises can be spelled out in the following way:

(5*) It is very likely in the foreseeable future that, among those found guilty of crimes punishable by death, who is given the death sentence will continue to depend on either caprice or race.

(6) It is unconstitutional for sentencing to depend on caprice or race.

(7*) A punishment is unusual if it is very likely in the foreseeable future that it will continue to be imposed infrequently and on an unconstitutional basis.

∴(8) The death penalty is an unusual punishment. (from 5*–7*)

Of course, an opponent can still respond that these premises are false if he or she can show that there is some way to avoid the problems that are raised by premise (5*). This will not be easy to show, however, if the argument is right about "the very nature of our system of criminal justice."

Another kind of question is raised by premise (7*). Should a law be declared unconstitutional whenever there is a good chance that it will be abused in ways that infringe on constitutional rights? Many laws have this potential—for example, all laws involving police power. This is why certain police powers have been limited by court rulings. Strict rules governing interrogations and wiretaps are two results. But only an extremist would suggest that we should abolish all police powers because of the inevitable risk of unconstitutional abuse. Accordingly, those who argue in favor of the death penalty might try to show that the problems in the application of the death penalty are not sufficiently important to be constitutionally intolerable.

The supporter of the death penalty also might take a very different tack:

Those who argue against the constitutionality of the death penalty on the grounds that it is a cruel and unusual punishment use the expression "cruel and unusual" in a way wholly different from that intended by the framers of the Eighth Amendment. By "cruel" they had in mind punishments that involved torture. By "unusual" they meant bizarre or ghoulish punishments of the kind that often were part of public spectacles in barbaric times. Modern methods of execution are neither cruel nor unusual in the constitutionally relevant senses of these words. Therefore, laws demanding the death penalty cannot be declared unconstitutional on the grounds that they either directly or indirectly involve a punishment that is cruel and unusual.

The core of this counterargument can be expressed as follows:

(1) In appeals to the Constitution, its words should be taken as they were originally intended.

(2) Modern methods of carrying out a death penalty are neither "cruel" nor "unusual" if these words are interpreted as they were originally intended.

∴(3) The death penalty should not be declared unconstitutional on the ground that it violates the prohibition against cruel and unusual punishments. (from 1–2)

The second premise of this argument states a matter of historical fact that might not be altogether easy to verify. Chances are, however, that it comes close to the truth, because the Constitution refers to the death penalty without criticism, and the death penalty was rarely questioned at the time. Given this, the opponent of the death penalty must either attack the first premise or find some other grounds for holding that the death penalty should be declared unconstitutional.

The first premise might seem like a truism, for how can a document guide conduct if anyone can reinterpret its words regardless of what was intended? Isn't the literal meaning of the document simply what was meant at the time, with everything else being interpretation? Of course, there are times when it is not easy to discover what its meaning was. (In the present case, for example, it is not clear whether the Eighth Amendment prohibits punishments that are either cruel or unusual or only those that are both cruel and unusual.) It seems unlikely, however, that those who drafted the Eighth Amendment used either the word "cruel" or the word "unusual" in the ways in which they are employed in the argument against the death penalty.

Does this last concession end the debate in favor of those who reject the anti–capital punishment argument that we have been examining? The argument certainly seems to be weakened, but there are those who would take a bold course by simply denying the first premise of the argument used to refute them. They would deny, that is, that we are bound to read the Constitution in the way intended by its framers. An argument in favor of this position might look something like this:

> The great bulk of the Constitution was written in an age almost wholly different from our own. To cite just two examples: Women were denied fundamental rights of full citizenship, and slavery was a constitutionally accepted feature of national life. The Constitution has remained a live and relevant document just because it has undergone constant reinterpretation. So, even if it is true that the expression "cruel and unusual" meant something quite special to those who framed the Eighth Amendment, plainly a humane desire to make punishment more civilized lay behind it. The present reading of this amendment is in the spirit of its original intention and simply makes it applicable to our own times.

The argument has now moved to an entirely new level, one concerning whether the Constitution should be read strictly in accord with the original intentions of those who wrote it or more freely to accommodate modern realities.

We shall not pursue the discussion further into these complex areas. Instead, we should consider how we were led into them. Recall that our original argument did not concern the general question of whether capital punishment is morally right or wrong. The argument turned on a much more specific point: Does the death penalty violate the prohibition against cruel and unusual punishments in the Eighth Amendment to the

Constitution? The argument with which we began seemed to be a straightforward proof that it does. Yet as we explored principles that lay in back of this deceptively simple argument, the issue became broader and more complex. We finally reached a point at which the force of the original argument was seen to depend on what we consider the proper way to interpret the Constitution—strictly or more freely. If we now go on to ask which method of interpretation is best, we will have to look at the role of the courts and, more generally, the purpose of government. Eventually we will come to fundamental principles for which we can give no further argument.

In examining the question of the constitutionality of capital punishment, we have had to compress a complicated discussion into a few pages. We have only begun to show how the issues involved in this complex debate can be sorted out and then addressed intelligently. There is, however, no guarantee that these procedures, however far they are carried out, will eventually settle this or any other fundamental dispute. It is entirely possible that the parties to a dispute may reach a point where they encounter a fundamental or rock-bottom disagreement that they cannot resolve. They simply disagree and cannot conceive of any deeper principles that could resolve their disagreement. But even if this happens, they will at least understand the source of their disagreement. They will not be arguing at cross-purposes, as so often happens in the discussion of important issues. Finally, even if they continue to disagree, they may come to appreciate that others may view things quite differently from the way they do. This may in turn help them deal with their basic disagreements in an intelligent, humane, and civilized way.

EXERCISE X

What is the best argument that Justice Stewart could give in support of the premise that the death penalty "excessively go[es] beyond" what is necessary for any legitimate and worthwhile purpose? Is this argument adequate to justify this premise? (For one such argument, see Justice Brennan's opinion in *Furman v. Georgia*.)

EXERCISE XI

How could one best argue in support of premise (5*), that it is very likely in the foreseeable future that, among those found guilty of crimes punishable by death, who is given the death sentence will continue to depend on either caprice or race? How could defenders of the death penalty try to refute this argument?

Formulate the best argument you can in support of the premise that, in appeals to the Constitution, its words should be taken as they were originally intended. Is this argument adequate to justify this premise? Why or why not?

The final argument in our examination of whether or not the death penalty violates the Constitution attempts to show that the Constitution must be read in a free or liberal way that makes it relevant to present society. Filling in suppressed premises where necessary, restate this argument as a sequence of explicit steps. After you have given the argument the strongest restatement you can, evaluate it for soundness.

To solve a mystery, you need to determine which facts are crucial and then argue from those facts to a solution. Solve the following mysteries and reconstruct your own argument for your solution. These stories come from *Five-Minute Whodunits*, by Stan Smith (New York: Sterling, 1997). The first passage introduces our hero:

Even those acquainted with Thomas P. Stanwick are often struck by his appearance. A lean and lanky young man, he stands six feet two inches tall. His long, thin face is complemented by a full head of brown hair and a droopy mustache. Though not husky in build, he is surprisingly strong and enjoys ruggedly good health. His origins and early life are obscure. He is undeniably well educated, however, for he graduated with high honors from Dartmouth College as a philosophy major. . . .

MYSTERY 1: A MERE MATTER OF DEDUCTION
———————————■———————————

Thomas P. Stanwick, the amateur logician, removed a pile of papers from the extra chair and sat down. His friend Inspector Matthew Walker had just returned to his office from the interrogation room, and Stanwick thought he looked unusually weary.

"I'm glad you dropped by, Tom," said Walker. "We have a difficult case on hand. Several thousand dollars' worth of jewelry was stolen from Hoffman's Jewel Palace yesterday morning. From some clues at the scene and a few handy tips, we have it narrowed down to three suspects: Addington, Burke, and Chatham. We know that at least one of them was involved, and possibly more than one."

"Burke has been suspected in several other cases, hasn't he?" asked Stanwick as he filled his pipe.

"Yes, he has," Walker replied, "but we haven't been able to nail him yet. The other two are small potatoes, so what we really want to know is whether Burke was involved in this one."

"What have you learned about the three of them?"

"Not too much. Addington and Burke were definitely here in the city yesterday. Chatham may not have been. Addington never works alone, and carries a snub-nosed revolver. Chatham always uses an accomplice, and he was seen lurking in the area last week. He also refuses to work with Addington, who he says once set him up."

"Quite a ragamuffin crew!" Stanwick laughed. "Based on what you've said, it's not too hard to deduce whether Burke was involved."

Was Burke involved or not?

MYSTERY 2: MURDER IN A LONDON FLAT

Lord Calinore was gunned down in his London flat by a robber, who then ransacked the flat. The case was placed in the capable hands of Inspector Gilbert Bodwin of Scotland Yard. Bodwin's investigation revealed that one man had planned the crime, another had carried it out, and a third had acted as lookout.

Bodwin discussed the case at length one evening over dinner at his club with an old friend, Thomas P. Stanwick, the amateur logician, visiting from America.

"It's quite a case," Stanwick remarked. "Have you any suspects?"

Bodwin sliced his roast beef with relish. "Yes, indeed. Four. We have conclusive evidence that three of those four were responsible for the crime."

"Really! That's remarkable progress. What about the fourth?"

"He had no prior knowledge of the crime and is completely innocent. The problem is that we're not sure which of the four are the planner, the gunman, the lookout, and the innocent bystander."

"I see." Stanwick took more Yorkshire pudding. "What do you know about them at this point?"

"Well, the names of the four are Merrick, Cross, Llewellyn, and Halifax. Halifax and Cross play golf together every Saturday. They're an odd pair! Halifax can't drive, and Cross has been out of Dartmoor Prison for only a year."

"What was he in for?"

"Forgery. We know that Merrick and Halifax kept the flat under surveillance for several days just before the day the crime was committed, the 17th. Llewellyn and Merrick, with their wives, had dinner together on the Strand on the 12th."

"An interesting compilation," said Stanwick, "but hardly conclusive. Is that all of it?"

(continued)

"Not quite. We know that the gunman spent the week before the crime in Edinburgh, and that the innocent bystander was acquainted with the planner and the gunman, but not with the lookout."

"That is very helpful," said Stanwick with a smile. He raised his wine glass. "Bodwin, old fellow, your case is complete."

Who are the planner, the gunman, and the lookout?

MYSTERY 3: A THEFT AT THE ART MUSEUM

The theft of several valuable paintings from the Royston Art Museum created a sensation throughout New England. Two days after Stanwick's return from a visit to Scotland, he was visited by Inspector Matt Walker, who was in charge of the case. As Stanwick poured tea, Walker quickly brought his friend up to date on the case.

"We've identified the gang of five thieves who must have done this job," Walker reported. "Archie McOrr, who never finished high school, is married to another one of the five, Charlayne Trumbull. The other three are Beverly Cuttle, Ed Browning, and Douglas Stephens."

"I thought you told me earlier that only four people were involved in the robbery," said Stanwick.

"That's right. One stayed in the car as the driver, another waited outside and acted as lookout, and two others entered the museum and carried out the actual theft. One of the five gang members was not involved in this particular job at all."

"And the question, I hope," said Stanwick with a smile, "is who played what part, if any, in the theft."

"Exactly." Walker flipped open his notebook. "Though I'm glad to say that our investigation is already bearing some fruit. For example, we have good reason to believe that the lookout has a Ph.D. in art history, and that the driver was first arrested less than two years ago."

"A remarkable combination," Stanwick chuckled.

"Yes, indeed. We know that Douglas was on the scene during the robbery. One of the actual thieves (who entered the museum) is the sister of Ed Browning. The other thief is either Archie or his wife."

"What else do you have on Douglas?" asked Stanwick.

"Not much. Although he's never learned to drive, he used to be a security guard at the Metropolitan Museum of Art in New York."

"Interesting. Please go on."

"The rest is mainly odds and ends." Walker thumbed through a few more pages of notes. "Charlayne, an only child, is very talented on the saxophone. Beverly and Ed both have criminal records stretching back a decade or more. We've also learned that the driver has a brother who is not a member of the gang."

"Most interesting indeed," remarked Stanwick. He handed Walker a mug of tea and sat down with his own. "Your investigation has made excellent progress. So much, in fact, that you already have enough to tell who the thieves, the lookout, and the driver are."

Who are they?

MYSTERY 4: TRIVIA AND SIGNIFICA

———————————■———————————

"For April, this is starting out to be a pretty quiet month," remarked Inspector Walker as he rummaged in his desk drawer for a cigar.

Thomas P. Stanwick, the amateur logician, finished lighting his pipe and leaned back in his chair, stretching his long legs forward.

"That is indeed unusual," he said. "Spring usually makes some young fancies turn to crime. The change is welcome."

"Not that we police have nothing to do." Walker lit his cigar. "A couple of the youth gangs, the Hawks and the Owls, have been screeching at each other lately. In fact, we heard a rumor that they were planning to fight each other this Wednesday or Thursday, and we're scrambling around trying to find out whether it's true."

"The Hawks all go to Royston North High, don't they?" asked Stanwick.

"That's right. The Owls are the street-smart dropouts who hang out at Joe's Lunch Cafe on Lindhurst. You know that only those who eat at Joe's collect green matchbooks?"

Stanwick blinked and smiled. "I beg your pardon?"

"That's right." Walker picked up a few papers from his desk. "That's the sort of trivia I'm being fed in my reports. Not only that, but everyone at Royston North High wears monogrammed jackets. What else have I got here? Only kids who hang out on Laraby Street fight on weekdays. Laraby is three blocks from Lindhurst. The Hawks go out for pizza three times a week."

"Keep going," chuckled Stanwick. "It's wonderful."

"A hog for useless facts, eh? No one who eats at Joe's wears a monogrammed jacket. The Owls elect a new leader every six months, the Hawks every year. Elections! Furthermore, everyone who hangs out on Laraby Street collects green matchbooks. Finally, the older (but not wiser) Owls buy beer at Johnny's Package Store."

Stanwick laughed heartily. "Lewis Carroll," he said, "the author of *Symbolic Logic* and the 'Alice in Wonderland' books, taught logic at Oxford, and he used to construct soriteses, or polysyllogisms [that is, chains of categorical syllogisms], out of material like that. In fact, his were longer and much wilder and more intricate, but of course they were fiction.

"As it is, the information you've cited should ease your worries. Those gangs won't get together to fight until at least Saturday."

How does he know?

NOTE

[1] We assess inductive arguments for *strength* instead of validity, but here we focus on deductive arguments. Inductive arguments will be examined in Part III, Chapters 8–12.

How to Evaluate Arguments: Deductive Standards

After isolating, laying out, and filling in an argument, the next step is to determine whether that uncovered argument is any good. This assessment, like other evaluations, requires standards. There are two main standards for evaluating arguments: the deductive standard of validity and the inductive standard of strength. Part II (which includes Chapters 6 and 7) will investigate the deductive standard of validity. Part III (which includes Chapters 8–12) will then explore the inductive standard of strength.

We already saw in Chapter 3 that an argument is valid in our technical sense if and only if it is not possible that its premises are true and its conclusion false. That standard sounds simple, but it is not so easy to say how to determine whether this combination of truth values is or is not possible in a particular case. Sometimes the validity of an argument can be seen simply by looking at the premises and conclusion viewed as whole propositions. That is the approach of propositional (or sentential) logic, which is the topic of Chapter 6. Another possibility is that the validity of an argument can be seen only by looking inside premises and conclusions to their parts, including their subjects and predicates. That is the approach of categorical (or syllogistic) logic, which is the topic of Chapter 7.

These relatively simple examples of formal logic do not, of course, exhaust the possibilities. There are many more kinds of formal logic. Many arguments remain valid, even though their validity is not captured by either propositional or categorical logic. That creates problems that we will face throughout Chapters 6 and 7. Still, by exploring some simple ways in which arguments can be valid by virtue of their form alone, we can gain greater insight into the nature of validity and, thereby, into the standards for assessing arguments.

6

Propositional Logic

This chapter begins our investigation of evaluating arguments by means of formal deductive logic. The first part of the chapter will show how the crucial standard of validity, which was introduced in Chapter 3, can be developed rigorously in one area—what is called propositional logic. This branch of logic deals with connectives such as "and" and "or," which allow us to build up compound propositions from simpler ones. Throughout most of the chapter, the focus will be theoretical rather than immediately practical. It is intended to provide insight into the concept of validity by examining it in an ideal setting. The chapter will close with a discussion of the relationship between the ideal language of symbolic logic and the language we ordinarily speak.

THE FORMAL ANALYSIS OF ARGUMENTS

When we carry out an informal analysis of an argument, we pay close attention to the key words used to present the argument and then ask ourselves whether these key terms have been used properly. So far, we have no exact techniques for answering the question of whether a word is used correctly. We rely, instead, on linguistic instincts that, on the whole, are fairly good.

In a great many cases, people can tell whether an argument marker, such as "therefore," is used correctly in indicating that one claim follows from another. However, if we go on to ask the average intelligent person *why* one claim follows from the other, he or she will probably have little to say except, perhaps, that it is just obvious. In short, it is often easy to see *that* one claim follows from another, but to explain *why* can be difficult. The purpose of this chapter is to provide such an explanation for some arguments.

This quality of "following from" is elusive, but it is related to the technical notion of validity, which was introduced in Chapter 3. The focus of our attention will be largely on the *concept* of validity. We are not, for the time being at least, interested in whether this or that argument is valid; we want to understand validity itself. To this end, the arguments we will examine are so simple that you will not be able to imagine anyone not understanding them at a glance. Who needs logic to deal with arguments of this kind? There is, however, good reason for dealing with simple—trivially simple—arguments at the start. The analytic approach to a complex issue is first to break it down into subissues, repeating the process until we reach problems simple enough to be solved. After these simpler problems are solved, we can reverse the process and construct solutions to larger and more complex problems. When done correctly, the *result* of such an analytic process may seem dull and obvious—and it often is. The *discovery* of such a process, in contrast, often demands the insight of genius.

The methods of analysis to be discussed here are *formal* in a specific way. In Chapter 3, we gave the following argument as an example of a valid argument: "All Senators are paid, and Sam is a Senator, so Sam is paid." The point could have been made just as well with many similar examples: (a) "All Senators are paid, and Sally is a Senator, so Sally is paid." (b) "All plumbers are paid, and Sally is a plumber, so Sally is paid." (c) "All plumbers are dirty, and Sally is a plumber, so Sally is dirty." These arguments are all valid (though not all are sound). Thus, we can change the person we are talking about, the group that we say the person is in, and the property that we ascribe to the person and to the group, all without affecting the validity of the argument at all. That flexibility shows that the validity of this argument does not depend on the particular content of its premises and conclusion. Instead, the validity of this argument results solely from its form. Formal validity of this kind is what formal logics try to capture.

BASIC PROPOSITIONAL CONNECTIVES

CONJUNCTION

The first system of formal logic that we will examine concerns propositional (or sentential) connectives. *Propositional connectives* are terms that allow us to build new propositions from old ones, usually combining two or more propositions into a single proposition. For example, given the propositions "John is tall" and "Harry is short," we can use the term "and" to *conjoin* them, forming a single compound proposition: "John is tall and Harry is short."

Let us look carefully at the simple word "and" and ask how it functions. "And" is a curious word, for it does not seem to stand for anything, at least in the way in which a proper name ("Churchill") and a common noun ("dog") seem to stand for things. Instead of asking what this word stands for, we can ask a different question: What *truth conditions* govern this connective? That is, under what conditions are propositions containing this connective true? To answer this question, we imagine every possible way in which the component propositions can be true or false. Then, for each combination, we decide what truth value to assign to the entire proposition. This may sound complicated, but an example will make it clear:

John is tall.	Harry is short.	John is tall and Harry is short.
T	T	T
T	F	F
F	T	F
F	F	F

Here the first two columns cover every possibility for the component propositions to be either true or false. The third column states the truth value of the whole proposition for each combination. Clearly, the conjunction of two propositions is true if both of the component propositions are true; otherwise, it is false.

Our reflections have not depended on the particular propositions in our example. We could have been talking about dinosaurs instead of people, and we still would have come to the conclusion that the conjunction of two propositions is true if both propositions are true, but false otherwise. This neglect of the particular content of propositions is what makes our account *formal*.

To reflect the generality of our concerns, we can drop the reference to particular sentences altogether and use variables instead. Just as the lowercase letters "x," "y," and "z" can be replaced by any numbers in mathematics, so we can use the lowercase letters "p," "q," "r," "s," and so on as variables that can be replaced by any propositions in logic. We will also use the symbol "&" (called an *ampersand*) for "and."

Consider the expression "p & q." Is it true or false? There is obviously no answer to this question. This is not because we do not know what "p" and "q" stand for, for in fact "p" and "q" do not stand for any proposition at all. Just as "$x + y$" is not any particular number in mathematics, so "p & q" is not a proposition. Instead, "p & q" is a pattern for a whole series of propositions. To reflect this, we will say that "p & q" is a *propositional form*. It is a pattern, or form, for a whole series of propositions, including "John is tall and Harry is short" as well as many other propositions.

To specify precisely which propositions have the form "p & q," we need a little technical terminology. The central idea is that we can pass from a proposition to a propositional form by replacing propositions with propositional variables.

Proposition	*Propositional Form*
John is tall and Harry is short.	p & q

When we proceed in the opposite direction by uniformly substituting propositions for propositional variables, we get what we will call a *substitution instance* of that propositional form.

Propositional Form	*Substitution Instance*
p & q	Roses are red and violets are blue.

Thus, "John is tall and Harry is short" and "Roses are red and violets are blue" are both substitution instances of the propositional form "*p* & *q*."

To get clear about these ideas, it is important to notice that "*p*" is also a propositional form, with *every* proposition, including "Roses are red and violets are blue," among its substitution instances. There is no rule against substituting compound propositions for propositional variables. Perhaps a bit more surprisingly, our definitions allow "Roses are red and roses are red" to be a substitution instance of "*p* & *q*." This example makes sense if you compare it to variables in mathematics. Using only positive integers, how many solutions are there to the equation "*x* + *y* = 4"? There are three: 3 + 1, 1 + 3, and 2 + 2. The fact that "2 + 2" is a solution to "*x* + *y* = 4" shows that "2" can be substituted for both "*x*" and "*y*" in the same solution. That's just like allowing "Roses are red" to be substituted for both "*p*" and "*q*," so that "Roses are red and roses are red" is a substitution instance of "*p* & *q*" in propositional logic.

In general, then, we get a substitution instance of a propositional form by uniformly replacing the same variable with the same proposition throughout, but different variables do not have to be replaced with different propositions. The rule is this:

> Different variables may be replaced with the same proposition, but different propositions may not be replaced with the same variable.

According to this rule:

> "Roses are red and violets are blue" is a substitution instance of "*p* & *q*."
>
> "Roses are red and violets are blue" is also a substitution instance of "*p*."
>
> "Roses are red and roses are red" is a substitution instance of "*p* & *q*."
>
> "Roses are red and roses are red" is a substitution instance of "*p* & *p*."
>
> "Roses are red and violets are blue" is *not* a substitution instance of "*p* & *p*."
>
> "Roses are red" is *not* a substitution instance of "*p* & *p*."

We are now in a position to give a perfectly general definition of conjunction with the following truth table, using propositional variables where previously we used specific propositions.

p	*q*	*p* & *q*
T	T	T
T	F	F
F	T	F
F	F	F

There is no limit to the number of propositions we can conjoin to form a new proposition. "Roses are red and violets are blue; sugar is sweet and so are you" is a substitution instance of "*p* & *q* & *r* & *s*." We can also use parentheses to group propositions. This last example could be treated as a substitution instance of "$(p \ \& \ q) \ \& \ (r \ \& \ s)$"—that is, as a conjunction of two conjunctions. Later we will see that, just as in mathematics, parentheses can make an important difference to the meaning of a total proposition.

One cautionary note: The word "and" is not always used to connect two distinct sentences. Sometimes a sentence has to be rewritten for us to see that it is equivalent to a sentence of this form. For example,

Serena and Venus are tennis players.

is simply a short way of saying

Serena is a tennis player, and Venus is a tennis player.

At other times, the word "and" is *not* used to produce a conjunction of propositions. For example,

Serena and Venus are playing each other.

does *not* mean that

Serena is playing each other, and Venus is playing each other.

That does not even make sense, so the original sentence cannot express a conjunction of two propositions. Instead, it expresses a single proposition about two people taken as a group. Consequently, it should not be symbolized as "$p \ \& \ q$." Often, unfortunately, it is unclear whether a sentence expresses a conjunction of propositions or a single proposition about a group. The sentence

Serena and Venus are playing tennis.

could be taken either way. Maybe Serena and Venus are playing each other. If that is what it means, then the sentence expresses a single proposition about a group, so it should not be symbolized as "$p \ \& \ q$." But maybe Serena is playing one match, while Venus is playing another. If that would make it true, then the sentence expresses a conjunction of propositions, so it may be symbolized as "$p \ \& \ q$."

When a sentence containing the word "and" expresses the conjunction of two propositions, we will say that it expresses a *propositional conjunction*. When a sentence containing "and" does not express the conjunction of two propositions, we will say that it expresses a *nonpropositional conjunction*. In this chapter we are concerned only with sentences that express propositional conjunctions. A sentence should be translated into the symbolic form "$p \ \& \ q$" only if it expresses a propositional conjunction. There is no mechanical procedure that can be followed to determine whether a certain sentence expresses a conjunction of two propositions. You must think carefully about what the sentence means and about the context in which that sentence is used. This takes practice.

EXERCISE I

The proposition "The night is young, and you're so beautiful" is a substitution instance of which of the following propositional forms?

1. p 5. $p \& q \& r$
2. q 6. $p \& p$
3. $p \& q$ 7. p or q
4. $p \& r$

EXERCISE II

Which of the following propositions is a substitution instance of "$p \& q \& q$"?

1. The night is young, and you're so beautiful, and my flight leaves in thirty minutes.
2. The night is young, and you're so beautiful, and my flight leaves in thirty minutes, and my flight leaves in thirty minutes.
3. You're so beautiful, and you're so beautiful, and you're so beautiful.

EXERCISE III

For each of the following propositions, give three different propositional forms of which that proposition is a substitution instance.

1. The night is young, and you're so beautiful, and my flight leaves in thirty minutes.
2. The night is young, and you're so beautiful, and you're so beautiful.

EXERCISE IV

Indicate whether each of the following sentences expresses a propositional conjunction or a nonpropositional conjunction—that is, whether or not it expresses a conjunction of two propositions. If the sentence could be either, then specify a context in which it would naturally be used to express a propositional conjunction and a different context in which it would naturally be used to express a nonpropositional conjunction.

1. A Catholic priest married John and Mary.
2. Fred had pie and ice cream for dessert.
3. The winning presidential candidate rarely loses both New York and California.

> 4. Susan got married and had a child.
>
> 5. Jane speaks both French and English.
>
> 6. Someone who speaks both French and English is bilingual.
>
> 7. Ken and Naomi are two of my best friends.
>
> 8. Miranda and Nick cooked dinner.
>
> 9. I doubt that John is poor and happy.

Now we can look at an argument involving conjunction. Here is one that is ridiculously simple:

Harry is short and John is tall.
∴ Harry is short.

This argument is obviously valid. But why is it valid? Why does the conclusion follow from the premise? The answer in this case seems obvious, but we will spell it out in detail as a guide for more difficult cases. Suppose we replace these particular propositions with propositional forms, using a different variable for each distinct proposition throughout the argument. This yields what we will call an *argument form*. For example:

$$p \,\&\, q$$
$$\therefore p$$

This is a pattern for endlessly many arguments, each of which is called a substitution instance of this argument form. Every argument that has this general form will also be valid. It really does not matter which propositions we put into this schema; the resulting argument will be valid—so long as we are careful to substitute the same proposition for the same variable throughout.

Let's pursue this matter further. If an argument has true premises and a false conclusion, then we know at once that it is invalid. But in saying that an argument is *valid*, we are not only saying that it does not have true premises and a false conclusion; we are also saying that the argument *cannot* have a false conclusion when the premises are true. Sometimes this is true because the argument has a structure or form that rules out the very possibility of true premises and a false conclusion. We can appeal to the notion of an argument form to make sense of this idea. A somewhat more complicated truth table will make this clear:

		PREMISE	CONCLUSION
p	q	$p \,\&\, q$	p
T	T	T	T
T	F	F	T
F	T	F	F
F	F	F	F

The first two columns give all the combinations for the truth values of the propositions that we might substitute for "*p*" and "*q*." The third column gives the truth value of the premise for each of these combinations. (This column is the same as the definition for "&" given above.) Finally, the fourth column gives the truth value for the conclusion for each combination. (Here, of course, this merely involves repeating the first column. Later on, things will become more complicated and interesting.) If we look at this truth table, we see that no matter how we make substitutions for the variables, we never have a case in which the premise is true and the conclusion is false. In the first line, the premise is true and the conclusion is also true. In the remaining three lines, the premise is not true, so the possibility of the premise being true and the conclusion false does not arise.

Here it is important to remember that a valid argument can have false premises, for one proposition can follow from another proposition that is false. Of course, an argument that is sound cannot have a false premise, because a sound argument is defined as a valid argument with true premises. But our subject here is validity, not soundness.

Let's summarize this discussion. In the case we have examined, validity depends on the form of an argument and not on its particular content. A first principle, then, is this:

An *argument* is valid if it is an instance of a valid argument form.

Hence, the argument "Harry is short and John is tall; therefore, Harry is short" is valid because it is an instance of the valid argument form "*p* & *q*; ∴ *p*."

Next we must ask what makes an argument form valid. The answer to this is given in this principle:

An argument *form* is valid if and only if it has no substitution instances in which the premises are true and the conclusion is false.

We have just seen that the argument form "*p* & *q*; ∴ *p*" passes this test. The truth table analysis showed that. Incidentally, we can use the same truth table to show that the following argument is valid:

John is tall.	p
Harry is short.	q
∴ John is tall and Harry is short.	∴ p & q

The argument on the left is a substitution instance of the argument form on the right. A glance at the truth table will show that there can be no cases for which all the premises could be true and the conclusion false. This pretty well covers the logical properties of conjunction.

Notice that we have not said that *every* argument that is valid is so in virtue of its form. There may be arguments in which the conclusion follows from the premises but we cannot show how the argument's validity is a matter of logical form. There are, in fact, some obviously valid arguments that have yet to be shown to be valid in terms of their form. Explaining validity by means of logical form has long been an ideal of logical theory, but there are arguments—many of them quite common—where this ideal has yet to be adequately fulfilled. Many arguments in mathematics fall into this category. At present, however, we will only consider arguments in which the strategy we used for analyzing conjunction continues to work.

EXERCISE V

Are the following arguments valid by virtue of their propositional form? Why or why not?

1. Donald owns a tower in New York and a palace in Atlantic City. Therefore, Donald owns a palace in Atlantic City.
2. Tom owns a house. Therefore, Tom owns a house and a piece of land.
3. Ilsa is tall. Therefore, Ilsa is tall, and Ilsa is tall.
4. Bernie has a son and a daughter. Bernie has a father and a mother. Therefore, Bernie has a son and a mother.
5. Mary got married and had a child. Therefore, Mary had a child and got married.
6. Bess and Katie tied for MVP. Therefore, Bess tied for MVP.

EXERCISE VI

For each of the following claims, determine whether it is true or false. Defend your answers.

1. An argument that is a substitution instance of a valid argument form is always valid.
2. An argument that is a substitution instance of an invalid argument form is always invalid.
3. An invalid argument is always a substitution instance of an invalid argument form.

DISCUSSION QUESTION

Is a valid argument always a substitution instance of a valid argument form? Why or why not?

DISJUNCTION

Just as we can form a conjunction of two propositions by using the connective "and," we can form a *disjunction* of two propositions by using the connective "or," as in the following compound sentence:

John will win or Harry will win.

Again, it is easy to see that the truth of this whole compound proposition depends on the truth of the component propositions. If they are both false, then the compound proposition is false. If just one of them is true, then the compound proposition is true. But suppose they are both true. What shall we say then?

Sometimes when we say "either-or," we seem to rule out the possibility of both. When a waiter approaches your table and tells you, "Tonight's dinner will be chicken or steak," this suggests that you cannot have both. In other cases, however, it does not seem that the possibility of both is ruled out—for example, when we say to someone, "If you want to see tall mountains, go to California or Colorado."

One way to deal with this problem is to say that the English word "or" has two meanings: one *exclusive*, which rules out both, and one *inclusive*, which does not rule out both. Another solution is to claim that the English word "or" always has the inclusive sense, but utterances with "or" sometimes conversationally imply the exclusion of both because of special features of certain contexts. It is, for example, our familiarity with common restaurant practices that leads us to infer that we cannot have both when the waiter says, "Tonight's dinner will be chicken or steak." If we may have both, then the waiter's utterance would not be as informative as is required for the purpose of revealing our options, so it would violate Grice's conversational rule of Quantity (as discussed in Chapter 2). That explains why the waiter's utterance seems to exclude both.

Because such explanations are plausible, and because it is simpler as well as traditional to develop propositional logic with the inclusive sense of "or," we will adopt that inclusive sense. Where necessary, we will define the exclusive sense using the inclusive sense as a starting point. Logicians symbolize disjunctions using the connective "∨" (called a *wedge*). The truth table for this connective has the following form:

p	q	$p \vee q$
T	T	T
T	F	T
F	T	T
F	F	F

We will look at some arguments involving this connective in a moment.

NEGATION

With conjunction and disjunction, we begin with two propositions and construct a new proposition from them. There is another way in which we can construct a new proposition from just one proposition—by *negating* it.

Given the proposition "John is clever," we can get a new proposition, "John is not clever," simply by inserting the word "not" in the correct place in the sentence.

What, exactly, does the word "not" mean? This can be a difficult question to answer. Does it mean "nothing" or, maybe, "nothingness"? Although some respectable philosophers have sometimes spoken in this way, it is important to see that the word "not" does not stand for anything at all. It has an altogether different function in the language. To see this, think about how conjunction and disjunction work. Given two propositions, the word "and" allows us to construct another proposition that is true only when both original propositions are true, and false otherwise. With disjunction, given two propositions, the word "or" allows us to construct another proposition that is false only when both of the original propositions are false, and true otherwise. (Our truth table definitions reflect these facts.) Using these definitions as models, how should we define negation? A parallel answer is that the negation of a proposition is true just in the cases in which the original proposition is false, and it is false just in the cases in which original proposition is true. Using the symbol "~" (called a *tilde*) to stand for negation, this gives us the following truth table definition:

p	$\sim p$
T	F
F	T

Negation might seem as simple as can be, but people quite often get confused by negations. If Diana says, "I could not breathe for a whole minute," she might mean that there was a minute when something made her unable to breathe (maybe she was choking) or she might mean that she was able to hold her breath for a whole minute (say, to win a bet). If "A" symbolizes "Diana could breathe sometime during this minute," then "$\sim A$" symbolizes the former claim (that Diana was unable to breathe for this minute). Consequently, the latter claim (that Diana could hold her breath for this minute) should not also be symbolized by "$\sim A$." Indeed, this interpretation of the original sentence is not a negation, even though the original sentence did include the word "not." Moreover, some sentences are negations even though they do not include the word "not." For example, "Nobody owns Mars" is the negation of "Somebody owns Mars." If the latter is symbolized as "A," the former can be symbolized as "$\sim A$," even though the former does not include the word "not."

The complexities of negation can be illustrated by noticing that the simple sentence "Everyone loves running" can include negation at four distinct places: "Not everyone loves running," "Everyone does not love running," "Everyone loves not running," and the colloquial "Everyone loves running— not!" Some of these sentences can be symbolized in propositional logic as negations of "Everyone loves running," but others cannot.

To determine whether a sentence can be symbolized as a negation in propositional logic, it is often useful to reformulate the sentence so that it starts with "It is not the case that . . . ." For example, "I did none of the homework" would be reformulated as "It is not the case that I did any of the homework." If the resulting sentence means the same as the original (as it does in this example), then the original sentence can be symbolized as a propositional negation. In contrast, "I promise not to leave you" means something very different from "It is not the case that I promise to leave you," so "I promise not to leave you" should not be symbolized as a propositional negation.

Unfortunately, this test will not always work. There is no complete mechanical procedure for determining whether an English sentence can be symbolized as a negation. All you can do is think carefully about the sentence's meaning and context. The best way to get good at this is to practice.

EXERCISE VII

Explain the differences in meaning among "Not everyone loves running," "Everyone does not love running," "Everyone loves not running," and "Everyone loves running—not!" For each, is it a negation of "Everyone loves running"? Why or why not?

EXERCISE VIII

Negative terms or prefixes can often be interpreted in more than one way. Explain two ways to interpret each of the following sentences. Describe a context in which it would be natural to interpret it in each way.

1. You may not go to the meeting.
2. I cannot recommend him too highly.
3. He never thought he'd go to the Himalayas.
4. Have you not done all of your homework?
5. All of his friends are not students.
6. I will not go to some football games next season.
7. No smoking section available.
8. The lock on his locker was unlockable.

EXERCISE IX

Put each of the following sentences in symbolic form. Be sure to specify exactly which sentence is represented by each capital letter, and pay special attention to the placement of the negation. If the sentence could be interpreted in more than one way, symbolize each interpretation and describe a context in which it would be natural to interpret it in each way.

1. It won't rain tomorrow.
2. It might not rain tomorrow.
3. There is no chance that it will rain tomorrow.
4. I believe that it won't rain tomorrow.
5. Joe is not too smart or else he's very clever.
6. Kristin is not smart or rich.
7. Sometimes you feel like a nut; sometimes you don't. (from an advertisement for Mounds and Almond Joy candies, which are made by the same company and are exactly alike except that only one of them has a nut)

PROCESS OF ELIMINATION

Using only negation and disjunction, we can analyze the form of one common pattern of reasoning, which is called *process of elimination* or, more technically, *disjunctive syllogism*. As an example, consider this argument:

> Her phone line is busy, so she must either be talking on the phone or using her modem. She is not using her modem, since I just tried to e-mail her and she did not respond. So she must be talking on the phone.

After trimming off assurances and subarguments that support the premises, the core of this argument can be put in standard form:

  (1) She is either using her modem or talking on the phone.
  (2) She is not using her modem.
  ∴(3) She is talking on the phone. (from 1–2)

This core argument is then an instance of this argument form:

  1. $p \vee q$
   $\sim p$
  ∴ q

It does not matter if we change the order of the disjuncts so that the first premise is "She must be either talking on the phone or using her modem." Then the argument takes this form:

  2. $p \vee q$
   $\sim q$
  ∴ p

Both of these argument forms are valid, so the core of the original argument is also valid.

Explain why argument forms 1–2 are valid. Use common language that would be understandable to someone who has not read this chapter.

Process of elimination is sometimes confused with a similar but crucially different pattern of reasoning, which can be called *affirming a disjunct*. This pattern includes both of these forms:

3. $p \vee q$
   p _____
   $\therefore ~q$

4. $p \vee q$
   q _____
   $\therefore ~p$

These forms of argument are invalid. This can be shown by the following single instance:

> She is either using her modem or talking on the phone.
> She is using her modem.
> $\therefore$ She is not talking on the phone.

This argument might seem valid if one assumes that she cannot talk on the phone while using her modem. The premises, however, do not specify that she has only one phone line. If she talks on one phone line while using her modem on a different phone line, then the premises are true and the conclusion is false. Because this is possible, the argument is invalid, and so is its form, 3. Moreover, this argument would remain invalid if the disjuncts were listed in a different order, so that the argument took the form of 4. Thus, affirming a disjunct is a fallacy.

Give other instances of argument forms 3–4 that are not valid. Explain why these instances are invalid and why they show that the general argument form is invalid.

HOW TRUTH-FUNCTIONAL CONNECTIVES WORK

We have now defined conjunction, disjunction, and negation. That, all by it-self, is sufficient to complete the branch of modern logic called propositional logic. The definitions themselves may seem peculiar. They do not look like the definitions we find in a dictionary. But the form of these definitions is important, for it tells us something interesting about the character of such words as "and," "or," and "not." Two things are worth noting: (1) These expressions are used to construct a new proposition from old ones; (2) the newly constructed proposition is always a *truth function* of the original propositions—that is, the truth value of the new proposition is always determined by the truth value of the original propositions. For this reason, these connectives are called *truth-functional connectives*. (Of course, with negation, we start with a *single* proposition, so there are not really two things to connect.) For example, suppose that "*A*" and "*B*" are two true propositions and "*G*" and "*H*" are two false propositions. We can then determine the truth values of more complex propositions built from them using conjunction, disjunction, and negation. Sometimes the correct assignment is obvious at a glance:

A & *B*	True
A & *G*	False
~*A*	False
~*G*	True
A ∨ *H*	True
G ∨ *H*	False
~*A* & *G*	False

As noted earlier, parentheses can be used to distinguish groupings. Sometimes the placement of parentheses can make an important difference, as in the following two expressions:

~*A* & *G*

~(*A* & *G*)

Notice that in one expression the negation symbol applies only to the proposition "*A*," whereas in the other expression it applies to the entire proposition "*A* & *G*." Thus, the first expression above is false, and the second expression is true. Only the second expression can be translated as "Not both *A* and *G*." Both of these expressions are different from "~*A* & ~*G*," which means "Neither *A* nor *G*."

As expressions become more complex, we reach a point where it is no longer obvious how the truth values of the component propositions determine the truth value of the entire proposition. Here a regular procedure is helpful. The easiest method is to fill in the truth values of the basic propositions and then, step-by-step, make assignments progressively wider, going from the inside out. For example:

~((*A* ∨ *G*) & ~(~*H* & *B*))

~((*T* ∨ *F*) & ~(~*F* & *T*))

~((*T* ∨ *F*) & ~(*T* & *T*))

~(*T* & ~(*T*))

~(*T* & *F*)

~(*F*)

T

With a little practice, you can master this technique in dealing with other very complex examples.

> ### EXERCISE XII
>
> Given that "A," "B," and "C" are true propositions and "X," "Y," and "Z" are false propositions, determine the truth values of the following compound propositions:
>
> 1. ~X ∨ Y
> 2. ~(X ∨ Y)
> 3. ~(Z ∨ Z)
> 4. ~(Z ∨ ~Z)
> 5. ~ ~(A ∨ B)
> 6. (A ∨ Z) & B
> 7. (A ∨ X) & (B ∨ Z)
> 8. (A & Z) ∨ (B & Z)
>
> 9. ~(A ∨ (Z ∨ X))
> 10. ~(A ∨ ~(Z ∨ X))
> 11. ~A ∨ ~(Z ∨ X)
> 12. ~Z ∨ (Z & A)
> 13. ~(Z ∨ (Z & A))
> 14. ~((Z ∨ Z) & A)
> 15. A ∨ ((~B & C) ∨ ~(~B ∨ ~(Z ∨ B)))
> 16. A & ((~B & C) ∨ ~(~B ∨ ~(Z ∨ B)))

TESTING FOR VALIDITY

What is the point of all this? In everyday life, we rarely run into an expression as complicated as the one in our example at the end of the previous section. Our purpose here is to sharpen our sensitivity to how truth-functional connectives work and then to express our insights in clear ways. This is important because the validity of many arguments depends on the logical features of these truth-functional connectives. We can now turn directly to this subject.

Earlier we saw that every argument with the form "p & q; ∴ p" will be valid. This is obvious in itself, but we saw that this claim could be justified by an appeal to truth tables. A truth table analysis shows us that an argument with this form can never have an instance in which the premise is true and the conclusion is false. We can now apply this same technique to arguments that are more complex. In the beginning, we will examine arguments that are still easy to follow without the use of technical help. In the end, we will consider some arguments that most people cannot follow without guidance.

Consider the following argument:

Valerie is either a doctor or a lawyer.
Valerie is neither a doctor nor a stockbroker.

∴ Valerie is a lawyer.

We can use the following abbreviations:

D = Valerie is a doctor.
L = Valerie is a lawyer.
S = Valerie is a stockbroker.

Using these abbreviations, the argument and its counterpart argument form look like this:

$$D \lor L \qquad\qquad p \lor q$$
$$\underline{\sim(D \lor S)} \qquad\qquad \underline{\sim(p \lor r)}$$
$$\therefore L \qquad\qquad\qquad \therefore q$$

The expression on the right gives the argument form of the argument presented on the left. To test the argument for validity, we ask whether the argument form is valid. The procedure is cumbersome, but perfectly mechanical:

p	q	r	PREMISE $(p \lor q)$	$(p \lor r)$	PREMISE $\sim(p \lor r)$	CONCLUSION q	
T	T	T	T	T	F	T	
T	T	F	T	T	F	T	
T	F	T	T	T	F	F	
T	F	F	T	T	F	F	
F	T	T	T	T	F	T	
F	T	F	T	F	T	T	OK
F	F	T	F	T	F	F	
F	F	F	F	F	T	F	

Notice that there is only one combination of truth values for which both premises are true, and in that case the conclusion is true as well. So the original argument is valid because it is an instance of a valid argument form—that is, an argument form with no substitution instances for which true premises are combined with a false conclusion.

This last truth table may need some explaining. First, why do we get eight rows in this truth table where before we got only four? The answer to this is that we need to test the argument form for *every possible combination of truth values* for the component propositions. With two variables, there are four possible combinations: (TT), (TF), (FT), and (FF). With three variables, there are eight possible combinations: (TTT), (TTF), (TFT), (TFF), (FTT), (FTF), (FFT), and (FFF). The general rule is this: If an argument form has n variables, the truth table used in its analysis must have 2^n rows. For four variables there will be sixteen rows; for five variables, thirty-two rows; for six variables, sixty-four rows; and so on. You can be sure that you capture all possible combinations of truth values by using the following pattern in constructing the columns of your truth table under each individual variable:

First column	Second column	Third column . . .
First half Ts,	First quarter Ts,	First eighth Ts,
second half Fs.	second quarter Fs,	second eighth Fs,
	and so on.	and so on.

A glance at the earlier examples in this chapter will show that we have been using this pattern, and it is the standard way of listing the possibilities.

Of course, as soon as an argument becomes at all complex, these truth tables become very large indeed. But there is no need to worry about this, because we will not consider arguments with many variables. Those who do so turn to a computer for help.

The style of the truth table above is also significant. The premises are plainly labeled, and so is the conclusion. A line is drawn under every row in which the premises are all true. (In this case, there is only one such row— row 6.) If the conclusion on this line is also true, it is marked "OK." If every line in which the premises are all true is OK, then the argument form is valid. Marking all this may seem rather childish, but it is worth doing. First, it helps guard against mistakes. More importantly, it draws one's attention to the purpose of the procedure being used. Cranking out truth tables without understanding what they are about—or even why they might be helpful—does not enlighten the mind or elevate the spirit.

For the sake of contrast, we can next consider an invalid argument:

> (1) Valerie is either a doctor or a lawyer.
> (2) Valerie is not both a lawyer and a stockbroker.
> ∴(3) Therefore, Valerie is a doctor.

Using the same abbreviations as earlier, this becomes:

$$D \lor L \qquad p \lor q$$
$$\underline{\sim(L \& S)} \qquad \underline{\sim(q \& r)}$$
$$\therefore D \qquad\quad \therefore p$$

The truth table for this argument form looks like this:

p	q	r	PREMISE $(p \lor q)$	$(q \& r)$	PREMISE $\sim(q \& r)$	CONCLUSION p	
T	T	T	T	T	F	T	
T	T	F	T	F	T	T	OK
T	F	T	T	F	T	T	OK
T	F	F	T	F	T	T	OK
F	T	T	T	T	F	F	
F	T	F	T	F	T	F	Invalid
F	F	T	F	F	T	F	
F	F	F	F	F	T	F	

This time, we find four rows in which all the premises are true. In three cases the conclusion is true as well, but in one of these cases (row 6), the conclusion is false. This line is marked "Invalid." Notice that every line in which all of the premises are true is marked either as "OK" or as "Invalid." If even one row is marked "Invalid," then the argument form as a whole is invalid. The argument form under consideration is thus invalid, because it is possible for it to have a substitution instance in which all the premises are true and the conclusion is false.

The labeling not only shows *that* the argument form is invalid, it also shows *why* it is invalid. Each line that is marked "Invalid" shows a combination of truth values that makes the premises true and the conclusion false. Row 6 presents the combination in which Valerie is not a doctor, is a lawyer, and is not a stockbroker. With these assignments, it will be true that she is either a doctor or a lawyer (premise 1), and also true that she is not both a lawyer and a stockbroker (premise 2), yet false that she is a doctor (the conclusion). It is this possibility that shows why the argument form is not valid.

In sum, we can test a propositional argument form for validity by following these simple steps:

1. Provide a column for each premise and the conclusion.
2. Fill in truth values in each column.
3. Underline each row where all of the premises are true.
4. Mark each row "OK" if the conclusion is true on that row.
5. Mark each row "Invalid" if the conclusion is false on that row.
6. If any row is marked "Invalid," the argument form is invalid.
7. If no row is marked "Invalid," the argument form is valid.

EXERCISE XIII

Using the truth table technique outlined above, show that argument forms 1–2 in the above section on process of elimination are valid and that argument forms 3–4 in the same section are invalid.

EXERCISE XIV

Using the truth table technique outlined above, explain why the "Tricky Case" that was mentioned in Chapter 2 is valid.

EXERCISE XV

Using the truth table technique outlined above, test the following argument forms for validity:

1. $\sim p \vee q$
   $\underline{p\hphantom{aaaaaaaa}}$
   $\therefore \sim q$

2. $\underline{\sim (p \vee q)\hphantom{aa}}$
   $\therefore \sim q$

3. $\sim (p \vee q)$
   $\underline{p\hphantom{aaaaaaaa}}$
   $\therefore q$

4. $\sim (p \vee q)$
   $\underline{p\hphantom{aaaaaaaa}}$
   $\therefore r$

(continued)

5. ~ (p & q)

$$q$$

∴ ~ p

6. ~ (p & q)

$$~q$$

∴ p

7. (p & q) ∨ (p & r)

∴ p & (q ∨ r)

8. (p ∨ q) & (p ∨ r)

∴ p & (q ∨ r)

9. p & q

∴ (p ∨ r) & (q ∨ r)

10. p ∨ q

∴ (p & r) ∨ (q & r)

SOME FURTHER CONNECTIVES

We have developed the logic of propositions using only three basic notions corresponding (perhaps roughly) to the English words "and," "or," and "not."
Now let us go back to the question of the two possible senses of the word "or":
one exclusive and the other inclusive. Sometimes "or" seems to rule out the
possibility that both alternatives are true; at other times "or" seems to allow this
possibility. This is the difference between exclusive and inclusive disjunction.

Suppose we use the symbol "$\underline{\vee}$" to stand for exclusive disjunction. This is
the same as the symbol for inclusive disjunction except that it is underlined.
(After this discussion, we will not use it again.) We could then give two truth
table definitions, one for each of these symbols:

		INCLUSIVE	EXCLUSIVE
p	q	$p \vee q$	$p \underline{\vee} q$
T	T	T	F
T	F	T	T
F	T	T	T
F	F	F	F

We could also define this new connective in the following way:

$$(p \underline{\vee} q) = \text{(by definition)} ((p \vee q) \& \sim(p \& q))$$

It is not hard to see that the expression on the right side of this definition
captures the force of exclusive disjunction. Because we can always define
exclusive disjunction when we want it, there is no need to introduce it into
our system of basic notions.

EXERCISE XVI

Construct a truth table analysis of the expression on the right side of the preceding definition, and compare it with the truth table definition of exclusive
disjunction.

Use truth tables to test the following argument forms for validity:

1. p _____   4. $\sim(p \mathbin{\&} q)$ _____

∴ $p \veebar q$ ∴ $p \veebar q$

2. $p \veebar q$ 5. $p \veebar q$ _____

p _____   ∴ $p \vee q$

∴ $\sim q$ 6. $p \vee q$ _____

3. $p \mathbin{\&} q$ _____   ∴ $p \veebar q$

∴ $\sim(p \veebar q)$

Actually, in analyzing arguments we have been defining new logical connectives without thinking about it much. For example, "not both p and q" was symbolized as "$\sim(p \mathbin{\&} q)$." "Neither p nor q" was symbolized as "$\sim(p \vee q)$." Let us look more closely at the example "$\sim(p \vee q)$." Perhaps we should have symbolized it as "$\sim p \mathbin{\&} \sim q$." In fact, we could have used this symbolization, because the two expressions amount to the same thing. Again, this may be obvious, but we can prove it by using a truth table in yet another way. Compare the truth table analysis of these two expressions:

p	q	$\sim p$	$\sim q$	$\sim p \mathbin{\&} \sim q$	$(p \vee q)$	$\sim(p \vee q)$
T	T	F	F	F	T	F
T	F	F	T	F	T	F
F	T	T	F	F	T	F
F	F	T	T	T	F	T

Under "$\sim p \mathbin{\&} \sim q$" we find the column (FFFT), and we find the same sequence under "$\sim(p \vee q)$." This shows that, for every possible substitution we make, these two expressions will yield propositions with the same truth value. We will say that these propositional forms are *truth-functionally equivalent*. The above table also shows that the expressions "$\sim q$" and "$\sim p \mathbin{\&} \sim q$" are *not* truth-functionally equivalent, because the columns underneath these two expressions differ in the second row, so some substitutions into these expressions will not yield propositions with the same truth value.

Given the notion of truth-functional equivalence, the problem of more than one translation can often be solved. If two translations of a sentence are truth-functionally equivalent, then it does not matter which one we use in testing for validity. Of course, some translations will seem more natural than others. For example, "$p \vee q$" is truth-functionally equivalent to

$\sim((\sim p \mathbin{\&} \sim p) \mathbin{\&} (\sim q \vee \sim q))$

Despite this equivalence, the first form of expression is obviously more natural than the second when translating sentences, such as "It is either cloudy or sunny."

EXERCISE XVIII

Use truth tables to test which of the following propositional forms are truth-functionally equivalent to each other:

1. $\sim(p \lor q)$
2. $\sim(\sim p \lor \sim q)$
3. $\sim p \& \sim q$
4. $p \& q$

EXERCISE XIX

Use truth tables to determine whether the expressions in each of the following pairs are truth-functionally equivalent:

1. "p" and "$p \& p$"
2. "p" and "$p \lor p$"
3. "$p \lor \sim p$" and "$\sim(p \& \sim p)$"
4. "p" and "$p \& (q \lor \sim q)$"
5. "p" and "$p \& (q \& \sim q)$"
6. "p" and "$p \lor (q \& \sim q)$"
7. "$p \& (q \lor r)$" and "$p \lor (q \& r)$"
8. "$p \& (q \& r)$" and "$(p \& q) \& r$"

9. "$\sim(p \lor q)$" and "$\sim p \lor q$"
10. "$\sim(p \lor q)$" and "$\sim p \& \sim q$"
11. "$\sim\sim(p \lor q)$" and "$\sim\sim p \& \sim\sim q$"
12. "$\sim(p \& q)$" and "$\sim p \lor q$"
13. "$\sim\sim(p \& q)$" and "$\sim\sim p \lor \sim\sim q$"
14. "$\sim\sim p \lor \sim\sim q$" and "$\sim(\sim p \& \sim q)$"
15. "$\sim\sim p \& \sim\sim q$" and "$\sim(\sim p \lor \sim q)$"
16. "$p \& \sim\sim q$" and "$\sim\sim p \& q$"

CONDITIONALS

So far in this chapter we have seen that by using conjunction, disjunction, and negation, it is possible to construct compound propositions out of simple propositions. A distinctive feature of compound propositions constructed in these three ways is that the truth of the compound proposition is always a function of the truth of its component propositions. Thus, these three notions allow us to construct truth-functionally compound propositions. Some arguments depend for their validity simply on these truth-functional connectives. When this is so, it is possible to test for validity in a purely mechanical way. This can be done through the use of truth tables. Thus, in this area at least, we are able to give a clear account of validity and to specify exact procedures for testing for validity.

This truth-functional approach might seem problematic in another area: *conditionals*. We will argue that an important group of conditionals can be handled in much the same way as negation, conjunction, and disjunction. We separate conditionals from the other connectives only because a truth-functional treatment of conditionals is more controversial and faces problems that are instructive.

Conditionals have the form "If _____, then _____." What goes in the first blank of this pattern is called the *antecedent* of the conditional; what goes in the second blank is called its *consequent*. Sometimes conditionals appear in the indicative mood:

If it rains, then the crop will be saved.

Sometimes they occur in the subjunctive mood:

If it had rained, then the crop would have been saved.

There are also conditional imperatives:

If a fire breaks out, then call the fire department first!

And there are conditional promises:

If you get into trouble, then I promise to help you.

Indeed, conditionals get a great deal of use in our language, often in arguments. It is important, therefore, to understand them.

Unfortunately, there is no general agreement among experts concerning the correct way to analyze conditionals. We will simplify matters and avoid some of these controversies by considering only indicative conditionals. We will not examine conditional imperatives, conditional promises, or subjunctive conditionals. Furthermore, at the start, we will examine only what we will call *propositional conditionals*. We get a propositional conditional by substituting indicative sentences that express propositions—something either true or false—into the schema "If _____, then _____." Or, to use technical language already introduced, a propositional conditional is a substitution instance of "If p, then q" in which "p" and "q" are propositional variables. Of the four conditional sentences listed above, only the first is clearly a propositional conditional.

Even if we restrict our attention to propositional conditionals, this will not avoid all controversy. Several competing theories claim to provide the correct analysis of propositional conditionals, and no consensus has been reached concerning which is right. It may seem surprising that theorists disagree about such a simple and fundamental notion as the if-then construction, but they do. In what follows, we will first describe the most standard treatment of propositional conditionals, and then consider alternatives to it.

TRUTH TABLES FOR CONDITIONALS

For conjunction, disjunction, and negation, the truth table method provides an approach that is at once plausible and effective. A propositional conditional is also compounded from two simpler propositions, and this suggests that we might be able to offer a truth table definition for these conditionals as well. What should the truth table look like? When we try to answer this question, we get stuck almost at once, for it is unclear how we should fill in the table in three out of four cases.

p	q	If p, then q
T	T	?
T	F	F
F	T	?
F	F	?

It seems obvious that a conditional cannot be true if the antecedent is true and the consequent is false. We record this by putting "F" in the second row. But suppose "p" and "q" are replaced by two arbitrary true propositions— say, "Two plus two equals four" and "Chile is in South America." Consider what we shall say about the conditional:

If two plus two equals four, then Chile is in South America.

This is a *very* strange statement, because the arithmetical remark in the antecedent does not seem to have anything to do with the geographical remark in the consequent. So this conditional is odd—indeed, extremely odd—but is it true or false? At this point, a reasonable response is bafflement.

Consider the following argument, which is intended to solve all these problems by providing reasons for assigning truth values in each row of the truth table. First, it seems obvious that, if "If p, then q" is true, then it is not the case that both "p" is true and "q" is false. That in turn means that "$\sim(p \ \& \ \sim q)$" must be true. The following, then, seems to be a valid argument form:

If p, then q.
∴ $\sim(p \ \& \ \sim q)$

Second, we can also reason in the opposite direction. Suppose we know that "$\sim(p \ \& \ \sim q)$" is true. For this to be true, "$p \ \& \ \sim q$" must be false. We know this from the truth table definition of negation. Next let us suppose that "p" is true. Then "$\sim q$" must be false. We know this from the truth table definition of conjunction. Finally, if "$\sim q$" is false, then "q" itself must be true. This line of reasoning is supposed to show that the following argument form is valid:

$\sim(p \ \& \ \sim q)$
∴ If p, then q.

The first step in the argument was intended to show that we can validly derive "$\sim(p \ \& \ \sim q)$" from "If p, then q." The second step was intended to show that the derivation can be run in the other direction as well. But if each of these expressions is derivable from the other, this suggests that they are equivalent. We use this background argument as a justification for the following definition:

If p, then q = (by definition) not both p and not q.

We can put this into symbolic notation using "⊃" (called a *horseshoe*) to symbolize the conditional connective:

$p \supset q$ = (by definition) $\sim(p \ \& \ \sim q)$

Given this definition, we can now construct the truth table for propositional conditionals. It is simply the truth table for "$\sim(p \ \& \sim q)$":

p	q	$\sim(p \ \& \sim q)$	$p \supset q$	$\sim p \lor q$
T	T	T	T	T
T	F	F	F	F
F	T	T	T	T
F	F	T	T	T

Notice that "$\sim(p \ \& \sim q)$" is also truth-functionally equivalent to the expression "$\sim p \lor q$." We have cited it here because "$\sim p \lor q$" has traditionally been used to define "$p \supset q$." For reasons that are now obscure, when a conditional is defined in this truth-functional way, it is called a *material conditional*.

Let's suppose, for the moment, that the notion of a material conditional corresponds exactly to our idea of a propositional conditional. What would follow from this? The answer is that we could treat conditionals in the same way in which we have treated conjunction, disjunction, and negation. A propositional conditional would be just one more kind of truth-functionally compound proposition capable of definition by truth tables. Furthermore, the validity of arguments that depend on this notion (together with conjunction, disjunction, and negation) could be settled by appeal to truth table techniques. Let us pause for a moment to examine this.

One of the most common patterns of reasoning is called *modus ponens*. It looks like this:

If p, then q.	$p \supset q$
p	p
$\therefore q$	$\therefore q$

The truth table definition of a material conditional shows at once that this pattern of argument is valid:

Premise		Premise	Conclusion	
p	q	$p \supset q$	q	
T	T	T	T	OK
T	F	F	F	
F	T	T	T	
F	F	T	F	

EXERCISE XX

The argument form called *modus tollens* looks like this:

$$p \supset q$$
$$\sim q$$
$$\therefore \sim p$$

Use truth tables to show that this argument form is valid.

Farcus

by David Waisglass
Gordon Coulthart

WAISGLASS/COULTHART   © 1997 Farcus Cartoons

Reprinted by permission of LaughingStock Licensing Inc.

**"So, I say if it's not worth doing well,
it's not worth doing at all."**

These same techniques allow us to show that one of the traditional fallacies is, indeed, a fallacy. It is called the fallacy of *denying the antecedent,* and it has this form:

$p \supset q$

$\sim p$

$\therefore \sim q$

The truth table showing the invalidity of this argument form looks like this:

		PREMISE	PREMISE	CONCLUSION	
p	q	$p \supset q$	$\sim p$	$\sim q$	
T	T	T	F	F	
T	F	F	F	T	
F	T	T	T	F	Invalid
F	F	T	T	T	OK

EXERCISE XXI

A second standard fallacy is called *affirming the consequent.* It looks like this:

$p \supset q$

q

$\therefore p$

Use truth tables to show that this argument form is invalid.

In his radio address to the nation on April 17, 1982, President Ronald Reagan argued that the United States should not accept a treaty with the Soviet Union that would mutually freeze nuclear weapons at current levels, because he believed that the United States had fallen behind. Here is a central part of his argument:

> It would be wonderful if we could restore the balance of power with the Soviet Union without increasing our military power. And, ideally, it would be a long step towards assuring peace if we could have significant and verifiable reductions of arms on both sides. But let's not fool ourselves. The Soviet Union will not come to any conference table bearing gifts. Soviet negotiators will not make unilateral concessions. To achieve parity, we must make it plain that we have the will to achieve parity by our own effort.

Put Reagan's central argument into standard form. Then symbolize it and its form. Does his argument commit any fallacy? If so, identify it.

The relations among these last four argument forms can be seen in this diagram:

	Antecedent	Consequent
Affirming	Affirming the Antecedent = *Modus Ponens* (valid)	Affirming the Consequent (invalid)
Denying	Denying the Antecedent (invalid)	Denying the Consequent = *Modus Tollens* (valid)

Another argument form that has been historically significant is called a *hypothetical syllogism:*

$$p \supset q$$
$$q \supset r$$
$$\therefore p \supset r$$

Because we are dealing with an argument form containing three variables, we must perform the boring task of constructing a truth table with eight rows:

p	q	r	PREMISE $p \supset q$	PREMISE $q \supset r$	CONCLUSION $p \supset r$	
T	T	T	T	T	T	OK
T	T	F	T	F	F	
T	F	T	F	T	T	
T	F	F	F	T	F	
F	T	T	T	T	T	OK
F	T	F	T	F	T	
F	F	T	T	T	T	OK
F	F	F	T	T	T	OK

This is fit work for a computer, not for a human being, but it is important to see that it actually works.

Why is it important to see that these techniques work? Most people, after all, could see that hypothetical syllogisms are valid without going through all of this tedious business. We seem only to be piling boredom on top of triviality. This protest deserves an answer. Suppose we ask someone *why* he or she thinks that the conclusion follows from the premises in a hypothetical syllogism. The person might answer that anyone can see that—which, by the way, is false. Beyond this, he or she might say that it all depends on the meanings of the words or that it is all a matter of definition. But if we go on to ask, "which words?" and "what definitions?" then most people will fall silent. We have discovered that the validity of some arguments depends on the meanings of such words as "and," "or," "not," and "if-then." We have then gone on to give explicit definitions of these terms—definitions, by the way, that help us see how these terms function in an argument. Finally, by getting all these *simple* things right, we have produced what is called a *decision procedure* for determining the validity of every argument depending only on conjunctions, disjunctions, negations, and propositional conditionals. Our truth table techniques give us a mechanical procedure for settling questions of validity in this area. In fact, truth table techniques have practical applications, for example, in computer programming. But the important point here is that, through an understanding of how these techniques work, we can gain a deeper insight into the notion of validity.

EXERCISE XXIII

Two more classic, common, and useful argument forms combine conditionals with disjunction. Using truth tables, test them for validity.

Constructive Dilemma	*Destructive Dilemma*
$p \vee q$	$\sim p \vee \sim q$
$p \supset r$	$r \supset p$
$q \supset r$	$r \supset q$
$\therefore r$	$\therefore \sim r$

EXERCISE XXIV

Using the truth table techniques employed above, test the following argument forms for validity. (For your own entertainment, guess whether the argument form is valid or invalid before working it out.)

1. $p \supset q$

$\therefore q \supset p$

2. $p \supset q$

$\therefore \sim q \supset \sim p$

3. $\sim q \supset \sim p$

$\therefore p \supset q$

4. $p \supset q$

$q \supset r$

$\therefore p \supset (q \ \& \ r)$

5. $p \supset q$
   $q \supset r$
   $\sim r$
   _____
   $\therefore \sim p$

6. $p \supset q$
   $q \supset r$
   _____
   $\therefore \sim r \supset \sim p$

7. $p \vee q$
   $p \supset q$
   $q \supset r$
   _____
   $\therefore r$

8. $p \supset (q \vee r)$
   $\sim q$
   $\sim r$
   _____
   $\therefore \sim p$

9. $(p \vee q) \supset r$
   _____
   $\therefore p \supset r$

10. $(p \& q) \supset r$
    _____
    $\therefore p \supset r$

11. $p \supset (q \supset r)$
    _____
    $\therefore (p \& q) \supset r$

12. $(p \& q) \supset r$
    _____
    $\therefore p \supset (q \supset r)$

13. $p \supset (q \supset r)$
    q
    $\sim r$ *valid*
    _____
    $\therefore \sim p$

14. $p \supset (q \supset r)$ *invalid*
    $p \supset q$
    _____
    $\therefore r$

15. $(p \vee q) \& (p \vee r)$ *invalid*
    $\sim r$
    _____
    $\therefore \sim q$

16. $(p \supset q) \& (p \supset \sim r)$
    $q \& r$
    _____
    $\therefore \sim p$

17. $(p \vee q) \supset p$ *invalid*
    _____
    $\therefore \sim q$

18. $(p \vee q) \supset (p \& q)$ *valid*
    _____
    $\therefore (p \supset q) \& (q \supset p)$

19. $(p \& q) \supset (p \vee q)$
    _____
    $\therefore (p \supset q) \vee (q \supset p)$

20. r *valid*
    _____
    $\therefore (p \supset q) \vee (q \supset p)$

(handwritten truth-value tables in margin)

14. | p | q | r |
    | F | T | F |
    | F | F | F |

15. | p | q | r |
    | T | T | F |

17. | p | q |
    | T | T |

LOGICAL LANGUAGE AND EVERYDAY LANGUAGE

Early in this chapter we started out by talking about such common words as "and" and "or," and then we slipped over to talking about *conjunction* and *disjunction*. The transition was a bit sneaky, but intentional. To understand what is going on here, we can ask how closely these logical notions we have defined match their everyday counterparts. We will start with conjunction, and then come back to the more difficult question of conditionals.

At first sight, the match between conjunction as we have defined it and the everyday use of the word "and" may seem fairly bad. To begin with, in everyday discourse, we do not go about conjoining random bits of information. We do not say, for example, "Two plus two equals four and Chile is in South America." We already know why we do not say such things, for unless the context is quite extraordinary, this is bound to violate the conversational rule of Relevance. But if we are interested in validity, the rule of Relevance—like all other conversational (or pragmatic) rules—is simply beside the point. When dealing with validity, we are interested in only one question: If the premises of an argument are true, must the conclusion be true as well? Conversational rules, as we saw in Chapter 2, do not affect truth.

The truth-functional notion of conjunction is also insensitive to another important feature of our everyday discourse: By reducing all conjunctions to their bare truth-functional content, the truth-functional notion often misses the argumentative point of a conjunction. As we saw in Chapter 3, each of the following remarks has a different force in the context of an argument:

The ring is beautiful, but expensive.

The ring is expensive, but beautiful.

These two remarks point in opposite directions in the context of an actual argument, but from a purely truth-functional point of view, we treat them as equivalent. We translate the first sentence as "$B \& E$" and the second as "$E \& B$." Their truth-functional equivalence is too obvious to need proof. Similar oddities arise for all discounting terms, such as "although," "whereas," and "however."

It might seem that if formal analysis cannot distinguish an "and" from a "but," then it can hardly be of any use at all. This is not true. A formal analysis of an argument will tell us just one thing: whether the argument is valid or not. If we expect the analysis to tell us more than this, we will be sorely disappointed. It is important to remember two things: (1) We expect deductive arguments to be valid, and (2) usually we expect much more than this from an argument. To elaborate on the second point, we usually expect an argument to be sound as well as valid; we expect the premises to be true. Beyond this, we expect the argument to be informative, intelligible, convincing, and so forth. Validity, then, is an important aspect of an argument, and formal analysis helps us evaluate it. But validity is not the only aspect of an argument that concerns us. In many contexts, it is not even our chief concern.

We can now look at our analysis of conditionals, for here we find some striking differences between the logician's analysis and everyday use. The following argument forms are both valid:

1. p _____
   $\therefore q \supset p$

2. $\sim p$ _____
   $\therefore p \supset q$

EXERCISE XXV

Check the validity of the argument forms above using truth tables.

Though valid, both argument forms seem odd—so odd that they have actually been called *paradoxical*. The first argument form seems to say this: If a proposition is true, then it is *implied by* any proposition whatsoever. Here is an example of an argument that satisfies this argument form and is therefore valid:

Lincoln was president.

∴ If the moon is made of cheese, Lincoln was president.

This is a peculiar argument to call valid. First, we want to know what the moon has to do with Lincoln's having been president. Beyond this, how can his having been president depend on a blatant falsehood? We can give these questions even more force by noticing that even the following argument is valid:

Lincoln was president.

∴ If Lincoln was not president, then Lincoln was president.

Both arguments are instances of the valid argument form "p; ∴ $q \supset p$."

The other argument form is also paradoxical. It seems to say that a false proposition implies any proposition whatsoever. The following is an instance of this argument form:

Columbus was not president.

∴ If Columbus was president, then the moon is made of cheese.

Here it is hard to see what the falsehood that Columbus was president has to do with the composition of the moon.

At this point, nonphilosophers become impatient, whereas philosophers become worried. We started out with principles that seemed to be both obvious and simple. Now, quite suddenly, we are being overwhelmed with a whole series of peculiar results. What in the world has happened, and what should be done about it? Philosophers remain divided in the answers they give to these questions. The responses fall into two main categories: (1) Simply give up the idea that conditionals can be defined by truth-functional techniques and search for a different and better analysis of conditionals that avoids the difficulties involved in truth-functional analysis; or (2) take the difficult line and argue that there is nothing wrong with calling the aforementioned argument forms valid.

The first approach is highly technical and cannot be pursued in detail in this book, but the general idea is this: Instead of identifying "If p, then q" with "Not both p and not q," identify it with "Not *possibly* both p and not q." This provides a stronger notion of a conditional and avoids some—though not all—of the problems concerning conditionals. This theory is given a systematic development by offering a logical analysis of the notion of possibility. This branch of logic is called *modal* logic, and it has shown remarkable development in recent decades.

The second line has been taken by Paul Grice, whose theories played a prominent part in Chapter 2. He acknowledges—as anyone must—that the two argument forms above are decidedly odd. He denies, however, that this oddness has anything to do with *validity*. Validity concerns one thing and one thing only: a relationship between premises and conclusion. An argument is valid if the premises cannot be true without the conclusion being true as well. The above arguments are valid by this definition of "validity."

Of course, arguments can be defective in all sorts of other ways. Look at the first argument form: (1) p; $\therefore$ $q \supset p$. Because "q" can be replaced by any proposition (true or false), the rule of Relevance will often be violated. It is worth pointing out violations of the rule of Relevance, but, according to Grice, this issue has nothing to do with validity. Beyond this, arguments having this form can also involve violations of the rule of Quantity. A conditional will be true whenever the consequent is true. Given this, it does not matter to the truth of the whole conditional whether the antecedent is true or false. Yet it can be misleading to use a conditional on the basis of this logical feature. For example, it would be misleading for a museum guard to say, "If you give me five dollars, then I will let you into the exhibition," when, in fact, he will admit you in any case. For Grice, this is misleading because it violates the rule of Quantity. Yet strictly speaking, it is not false. Strictly speaking, it is true.

The Grice line is attractive because, among other things, it allows us to accept the truth-functional account of conditionals, with all its simplicity. Yet sometimes it is difficult to swallow. Consider the following remark:

If God exists, then there is evil in the world.

If Grice's analysis is correct, even the most pious person will have to admit that this conditional is true provided only that he or she is willing to admit that there is evil in the world. Yet this conditional plainly suggests that there is some connection between God's existence and the evil in the world—presumably, that is the point of connecting them in a conditional. The pious will wish to deny this suggestion. All the same, this connection is something that is conversationally implied, not asserted. So, once more, this conditional could be misleading—and therefore is in need of criticism and correction—but it is still, strictly speaking, true.

Philosophers and logicians have had various responses to Grice's position. No consensus has emerged on this issue. The authors of this book find it adequate, at least in most normal cases, and therefore have adopted it. This has two advantages: (1) The appeal to conversational rules fits in well with our previous discussions, and (2) it provides a way of keeping the logic simple and within the range of a beginning student. Other philosophers and logicians continue to work toward a definition superior to the truth table definition for indicative conditionals.

OTHER CONDITIONALS IN ORDINARY LANGUAGE

So far we have considered only one form in which propositional conditionals appear in everyday language: the conditional "If p, then q." But propositional conditionals come in a variety of forms, and some of them demand careful treatment.

We can first consider the contrast between constructions using "if" and those using "only if":

1. I'll clean the barn if Hazel will help me.
2. I'll clean the barn only if Hazel will help me.

Adopting the following abbreviations:

B = I'll clean the barn

H = Hazel will help me

the first sentence is symbolized as follows:

$H \supset B$

Notice that in the prose version of item 1, the antecedent and consequent appear in reverse order; "q if p" means the same thing as "If p, then q."

How shall we translate the second sentence? Here we should move slowly and first notice what seems incontestable: If Hazel does not help me, then I will not clean the barn. This is translated in the following way:

$\sim H \supset \sim B$

And that is equivalent to:

$B \supset H$

If this equivalence is not obvious, it can quickly be established using a truth table.

A more difficult question arises when we ask whether an implication runs the other way. When I say that I will clean the barn only if Hazel will help me, am I committing myself to cleaning the barn if she does help me? There is a strong temptation to answer the question "yes" and then give a fuller translation of item 2 in the following way:

$(B \supset H) \, \& \, (H \supset B)$

Logicians call such two-way implications *biconditionals,* and we will discuss them in a moment. But adding this second conjunct is almost surely a mistake, for we can think of parallel cases where we would not be tempted to include it. A government regulation might read as follows:

A student may receive a New York State Scholarship only if the student attends a New York State school.

From this it does not follow that anyone who attends a New York State school may receive a New York State Scholarship. There may be other requirements as well—for example, being a New York State resident.

Why were we tempted to use a biconditional in translating sentences containing the connective "only if"? Why, that is, are we tempted to think that the statement "I'll clean the barn only if Hazel will help me" implies "If Hazel helps me, then I will clean the barn"? The answer turns on the notion of conversational implication first discussed in Chapter 2. If I am *not* going to clean the barn whether Hazel helps me or not, then it will be misleading—a violation of the rule of Quantity—to say that I will clean the barn only if Hazel helps me. For this reason, in many contexts, the *use* of a sentence of the form "p only if q" will conversationally imply a commitment to "p if and only if q."

To appreciate the complexities of the little word "only," it is useful to notice that it fits at every point in the sentence "I hit him in the eye":

Only I hit him in the eye.

I only hit him in the eye.

I hit only him in the eye.

I hit him only in the eye.

I hit him in only the eye.

I hit him in the only eye.

I hit him in the eye only.

Explain what each of these sentences means.

We can next look at sentences of the form "*p* if and only if *q*"—so-called biconditionals. If I say that I will clean the barn if and only if Hazel will help me, then I am saying that I will clean it if she helps and I will not clean it if she does not. Translated, this becomes:

$(H \supset B) \& (\sim H \supset \sim B)$

This is equivalent to:

$(H \supset B) \& (B \supset H)$

We thus have an implication going both ways—the characteristic form of a biconditional. In fact, constructions containing the expression "if and only if" do not often appear in everyday speech. They appear almost exclusively in technical or legal writing. In ordinary conversation, we capture the force of a biconditional by saying something like this:

I will clean the barn, but only if Hazel helps me.

The decision whether to translate a remark of everyday conversation into a conditional or a biconditional is often subtle and difficult. We have already noticed that the use of sentences of the form "*p* only if *q*" will often conversationally imply a commitment to the biconditional "*p* if and only if *q*." In the same way, the *use* of the conditional "*p* if *q*" will often carry this same implication. If I plan to clean the barn whether Hazel helps me or not, it will certainly be misleading—again, a violation of the rule of Quantity—to say that I will clean the barn *if* Hazel helps me.

We can close this discussion by considering one further, rather difficult case. What is the force of saying "*p* unless *q*"? Is this a biconditional, or just a conditional? If it is just a conditional, which way does the implication go? There is a strong temptation to treat this as a biconditional, but the following example shows this to be wrong:

McCain will lose the election unless he carries the South.

This sentence clearly indicates that McCain will lose the election if he does not carry the South. Using abbreviations, we get the following:

N = McCain will carry the South.

L = McCain will lose the election.

$\sim N \supset L$

The original statement does not imply—even conversationally—that McCain will win the election if he does carry the South. Thus,

p unless $q = \sim q \supset p$

In short, "unless" means "if not." We can also note that "$\sim p$ unless q" means the same thing as "p only if q," and they both are translated thus:

$p \supset q$

Our results can be diagrammed as follows:

	Translates As	Often Conversationally Implies
p if q	$q \supset p$	$(p \supset q)$ & $(q \supset p)$
p only if q	$p \supset q$	$(p \supset q)$ & $(q \supset p)$
p unless q	$\sim q \supset p$	$(p \supset \sim q)$ & $(\sim q \supset p)$

EXERCISE XXVII

Translate each of the following sentences into symbolic notation, using the suggested symbols as abbreviations.

1. The Reds will win only if the Dodgers collapse. (R, D)
2. The Steelers will win if their defense holds up. (S, D)
3. If it rains or snows, the game will be called off. (R, S, O) $(R \lor S) \supset O$
4. If she came home with a trophy and a prize, she must have won the tournament. (T, P, W) $(T \& P) \supset W$
5. If you order the dinner special, you get dessert and coffee. (S, D, C) $S \supset (D \& C)$
6. If you order the dinner special, you get dessert; but you can have coffee whether or not you order the dinner special. (S, D, C)
7. If the house comes up for sale, and if I have the money in hand, I will bid on it. (S, M, B) $(S \& M) \supset B$ $S \supset (M \supset B)$
8. If you come to dinner, I will cook you a lobster, if you want me to. (D, L, W) $D \supset (W \supset L)$
9. You can be a success if only you try. (S, T) $T \supset S$
10. You can be a success only if you try. (S, T) $S \supset T$
11. Only if you try can you be a success. (S, T) $S \supset T$
12. You can be a success if you are the only one who tries. (S, O) $O \supset S$

(continued)

13. Unless there is a panic, stock prices will continue to rise. (P, R) $\sim P \supset R$
14. I won't scratch your back unless you scratch mine. (I, Y)
15. You will get a good bargain provided you get there early. (B, E)
16. You cannot lead a happy life without friends. (Let H = You can lead a happy life, and let F = You have friends.) $\sim F \supset \sim H$ $H \supset F$
17. The only way that horse will win the race is if every other horse drops dead. (Let W = That horse will win the race, and let D = Every other horse drops dead.)
18. You should take prescription drugs if, but only if, they are prescribed for you. (T, P) $(T \supset P) \cdot (P \supset T)$
19. The grass will die without rain. (D, R = It rains.) $\sim R \supset D$
20. Given rain, the grass won't die. (R, D = The grass will die.) $R \supset \sim D$
21. Unless it doesn't rain, the grass won't die. (R, D = The grass will die.)
    $\sim \sim R \supset \sim D$
    $R \supset \sim D$

EXERCISE XXVIII

(a) Translate each of the following arguments into symbolic notation. Then (b) test each argument for truth-functional validity using truth table techniques, and (c) comment on any violations of conversational rules.

Example: Harold is clever; so, if Harold isn't clever, then Anna isn't clever either. (H, A)

(a) H _____   _____

∴ ~H ⊃ ~A   ∴ ~p ⊃ ~q

(b) PREMISE   CONCLUSION

p	q	~p	~q	~p ⊃ ~q	
T	T	F	F	T	OK
T	F	F	T	T	OK
F	T	T	F	F	
F	F	T	T	T	

(c) The argument violates the rule of Relevance, because Anna's cleverness is irrelevant to Harold's cleverness.

1. Jones is brave, so Jones is brave or Jones is brave. (J)

2. The Republicans will carry either New Mexico or Arizona; but, since they will carry Arizona, they will not carry New Mexico. (A, N)

3. The Democrats will win the election whether they win Idaho or not. Therefore, they will win the election. (D, I)

4. The Democrats will win the election. Therefore, they will win the election whether they win Idaho or not. (D, I)

5. The Democrats will win the election. Therefore, they will win the election whether they win a majority or not. (D, M)

$M \supset L$ valid

$\sim L$

$\therefore \sim M$

6. If Bobby moves his queen there, he will lose her. Bobby will not lose his queen. Therefore, Bobby will not move his queen there. (*M, L*)

7. John will play only if the situation is hopeless. But the situation is hopeless. So John will play. (*P, H*)

8. Although Brown will pitch, the Rams will lose. If the Rams lose, their manager will get fired. So their manager will get fired. (*B, L, F*)

9. America will win the Olympics unless China does. China will win the Olympics unless Germany does. So America will win the Olympics unless Germany does. (*A, R, E*)

$\sim R \supset A$
$\sim E \supset R$
$\therefore \sim E \supset A$
valid
$A R E$
$F T F$

10. If you dial 0, you will get the operator. So, if you dial 0 and do not get the operator, then there is something wrong with the telephone. (*D, O, W*)

11. The Democrats will run either Jones or Borg. If Borg runs, they will lose the South. If Jones runs, they will lose the North. So the Democrats will lose either the North or the South. (*J, B, S, N*)

12. I am going to order either the fish special or the meat special. Either way, I will get soup. So I'll get soup. (*F, M, S*)

$J \vee B$
$B \supset S$
$J \supset N$
$N \vee S$
valid

13. The grass will die if it rains too much or it does not rain enough. If it does not rain enough, it won't rain too much. If it rains too much, then it won't not rain enough. So the grass will die. (*D* = The grass will die, *M* = It rains too much, *E* = It rains enough.)

14. If you flip the switch, then the light will go on. But if the light goes on, then the generator is working. So if you flip the switch, then the generator is working. (*F, L, G*) (This example comes from Charles L. Stevenson.)

$\supset (M \vee \sim E) \supset D$
$\sim E \supset \sim M$
$M \supset \sim \sim E$
$\therefore D$
invalid
$D \ M \ E$
$F \ F \ T$

DISCUSSION QUESTIONS

1. If "~*p* unless *q*" is translated as "*p* ⊃ *q*," then "*p* unless *q*" can be translated as "*p* ∨ *q*." Why?

2. Symbolize the following argument and give its form. Does this example show that *modus ponens* is not always valid? Why or why not?

   Opinion polls taken just before the 1980 election showed the Republican Ronald Reagan decisively ahead of the Democrat Jimmy Carter, with the other Republican in the race, John Anderson, a distant third. Those apprised of the poll results believed, with good reason:

   1. If a Republican wins the election, then if it's not Reagan who wins it will be Anderson.
   2. A Republican will win the election.

   Yet they did not have reason to believe:

   3. If it's not Reagan who wins, it will be Anderson.[1]

   (continued)

3. Symbolize the following argument and give its form. Does this example show that *modus tollens* is not always valid? Why or why not?

> (1) If it rained, it didn't rain hard.
> (2) It rained hard.
> ∴ (3) It didn't rain.[2]

4. In order to avoid logical mistakes, it is useful to study our own psychological tendencies. One experiment asked subjects whether the following arguments are valid:

> If the card has an "A" on the left, then it has a "3" on the right. The card has an "A" on the left. Therefore, the card has a "3" on the right. (95–100 percent)

> If the card has an "A" on the left, it has a "3" on the right. The card does not have a "3" on the right. Therefore, it does not have an "A" on the left. (70–75 percent)

> If the card does not have an "A" on the left, then it has a "3" on the right. The card does not have a "3" on the right. Therefore, it has an "A" on the left. (40–50 percent)

The figures in parentheses give the percentage of people who correctly identified that argument as valid. In another experiment, the indicated percentage of subjects gave the correct answer to these questions:

> If she meets her friend, she will go to a play. She meets her friend. What follows? (96 percent)

> If she meets her friend, she will go to a play. If she has enough money, she will go to a play. She meets her friend. What follows? (38 percent)

Again, subjects often deny the validity of arguments with implausible conclusions, like this:

> If her pet is a fish, then it is a phylone. If her pet is a phylone, then it is a whale. So, if her pet is a fish, then it is a whale.

Finally, the Wason Selection Task uses cards with a capital letter on one side and a single-figure number on the other side. Four such cards are placed on a table with, say, "B," "L," "2," and "9" on the top side in this order, then subjects are asked:

> Which cards need to be turned over to check whether the following rule is true or false?
> (1) If a card has a "B" on one side, it has a "2" on other side. (10 percent)
> (2) If a card has a "B" on one side, it does *not* have a "2" on other side. (100 percent)

The figure in parentheses indicates how many subjects on average give the correct answer for each of the rules. What are the correct answers?

How can you explain why so many people make these mistakes? How can you avoid making these mistakes yourself?

NOTES

[1] Vann McGee, "A Counterexample to *Modus Ponens*," *Journal of Philosophy 82*, no. 9 (September 1985): 462. See also Walter Sinnott-Armstrong, James Moor, and Robert Fogelin, "A Defense of *Modus Ponens*," *Journal of Philosophy 83*, no. 5 (May 1986): 296–300.

[2] Ernest Adams, "*Modus Tollens* Revisited," *Analysis 48*, no. 3 (1988): 122–28. See also Walter Sinnott-Armstrong, James Moor, and Robert Fogelin, "A Defense of *Modus Tollens*," *Analysis 50*, no. 1 (1990): 9–16.

CATEGORICAL LOGIC

In Chapter 6, we saw how validity can depend on the external connections among propositions. This chapter will demonstrate how validity can depend on the internal structure of propositions. In particular, we will examine two types of categorical arguments—immediate inferences and syllogisms—whose validity or invalidity depends on relations among the subject and predicate terms in their premises and conclusions. Our interest in these kinds of arguments is mostly theoretical. Understanding the theory of the syllogism deepens our understanding of validity, even if this theory is, in some cases, difficult to apply directly to complex arguments in daily life.

BEYOND PROPOSITIONAL LOGIC

Armed with the techniques developed in Chapter 6, let's look at the following argument:

> All squares are rectangles.
> All rectangles have parallel sides.
> ∴ All squares have parallel sides.

It is obvious at a glance that the conclusion follows from the premises, so this argument is valid. Furthermore, it seems to be valid in virtue of its form. But it is not yet clear what the form of this argument is. To show the form of this argument, we might try something of the following kind:

> $p \supset q$
> $q \supset r$
> ∴ $p \supset r$

But this is a mistake—and a bad mistake. We have been using the letters "*p*," "*q*," and "*r*" as *propositional variables*—they stand for arbitrary propositions. But the proposition "All squares are rectangles" is not itself composed of two propositions. Nor does it contain "if," "then" or any other propositional connective. In fact, if we properly translate the above argument into the language of propositional logic, we get the following result:

> p
> q
> ∴ r

This, of course, is *not* a valid argument form. But if we look back at the original argument, we see that it is obviously valid. This shows that propositional logic—however adequate it is in its own area—is not capable of explaining the validity of all valid arguments. There is more to logic than propositional logic.

CATEGORICAL PROPOSITIONS

To broaden our understanding of the notion of validity, we will examine a modern version of a branch of logic first developed in ancient times—categorical logic. Categorical logic concerns immediate inferences and syllogisms that are composed of categorical propositions, so we need to begin by explaining what a categorical proposition is.

In the argument above, the first premise asserts some kind of relationship between squares and rectangles; the second premise asserts some kind of relationship between rectangles and things with parallel sides; finally, in virtue of these asserted relationships, the conclusion asserts a relationship between squares and things having parallel sides. Our task is to understand these relationships as clearly as possible so that we can discover the *basis* for the validity of this argument. Again, we shall adopt the strategy of starting from simple cases and then use the insights gained there for dealing with more complicated cases.

A natural way to represent the relationships expressed by the propositions in an argument is through diagrams. Suppose we draw one circle standing for all things that are squares and another circle standing for all things that are rectangles. The claim that all squares are rectangles may be represented by placing the circle representing squares completely inside the circle representing rectangles.

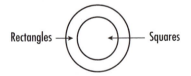

Another way of representing this relationship is to begin with overlapping circles.

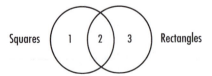

We then shade out the portions of the circles in which nothing exists, according to the proposition we are diagramming. If all squares are rectangles, there is nothing that is a square that is not a rectangle—that is, there is nothing in region 1. So our diagram looks like this:

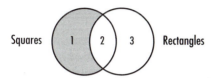

Either method of representation seems plausible. Perhaps the first seems more natural. We shall, however, use the system of overlapping circles, because they will work better when we get to more complex arguments. They are called *Venn diagrams*, after their inventor, John Venn, a nineteenth-century English logician.

Having examined one relationship that can exist between two classes, it is natural to wonder what other relationships might exist. Going to the opposite extreme from our first example, two classes may have *nothing* in common. This relationship could be expressed by saying, "All triangles are not squares," but it is more common and natural to say, "No triangles are squares." We diagram this claim by indicating that there is nothing in the overlapping region of things that are both triangles and squares:

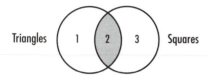

This is one of the relationships that could not be diagrammed by putting one circle inside another. (Just try it!)

In these first two extreme cases, we have indicated that one class is either completely included in another ("All squares are rectangles") or completely excluded from another ("No triangles are squares"). Sometimes, however, we claim only that two classes have at least *some* things in common. We might say, for example, "Some aliens are spies." How shall we indicate this relationship in the following diagram?

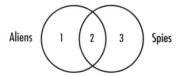

In this case, we do not want to cross out any whole region. We do not want to cross out region 1 because we are not saying that *all* aliens are spies. Plainly, we do not want to cross out region 2, for we are actually saying that some persons *are* both aliens and spies. Finally, we do not want to cross out region 3, for we are not saying that all spies are aliens. Saying that some aliens are spies does not rule out the possibility that some spies are homegrown. So we need some new device to represent claims that two classes have at least *some* members in common. We shall do this in the following way:

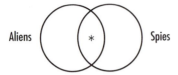

Here the asterisk indicates that there is at least one person who is both an alien and a spy. Notice, by the way, that we are departing a bit from an everyday way of speaking. "Some" is usually taken to mean "more than one"; here we let it mean "at least one." This makes things simpler and will cause no trouble, so long as we remember that this is what we are using "some" to mean.

Given this new method of diagramming class relationships, we can immediately think of other possibilities. The following diagram indicates that there is someone who is an alien but not a spy. In more natural language, it represents the claim that *some aliens are not spies.*

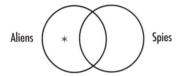

Next we can indicate that there is someone who is a spy but not an alien. More simply, the claim is that *some spies are not aliens,* and it is represented like this:

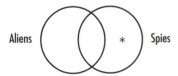

These last three claims are, of course, compatible, because there might be some aliens who are spies, some aliens who are not spies, and some spies who are not aliens.

THE FOUR BASIC CATEGORICAL FORMS

Although two classes can be related in a great many different ways, it is possible to examine many of these relationships in terms of four basic propositional forms:

A: All *S* is *P*.   E: No *S* is *P*.

I: Some *S* is *P*.   O: Some *S* is not *P*.

These forms are called *categorical forms*, and propositions with these forms are called *categorical propositions*.

As with the propositional forms discussed in the previous chapter, the A, E, I, and O forms for categorical propositions are not themselves propositions, so they are neither true nor false. Instead, they are patterns for whole groups of propositions. We get propositions from these forms by uniformly replacing the variables S and P with terms that refer to classes of things. For example, "Some spies are not aliens" is a substitution instance of the O propositional form. Nonetheless, we will refer to propositions with the A, E, I, or O form simply as A, E, I, or O propositions, except where this might cause confusion.

A and E propositions are said to be *universal* propositions (because they are about *all S*), and I and O propositions are called *particular* propositions (because they are about *some S*). A and I propositions are described as *affirmative* propositions (because they say what *is P*), and E and O propositions are referred to as *negative* propositions (because they say what is *not P*). Thus, these four basic propositional forms can be described this way:

A = Universal Affirmative E = Universal Negative

I = Particular Affirmative O = Particular Negative

These four forms fit into the following table:

	Affirmative	Negative
Universal	A: All S is P.	E: No S is P.
Particular	I: Some S is P.	O: Some S is not P.

Here are the Venn diagrams for the four basic categorical forms:

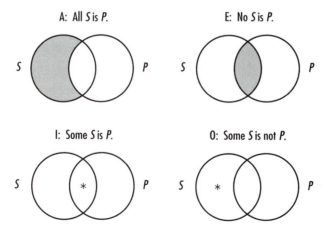

These basic categorical forms, together with their labels, classifications, and diagrams, should be memorized, because they will be referred to often in the rest of this chapter.

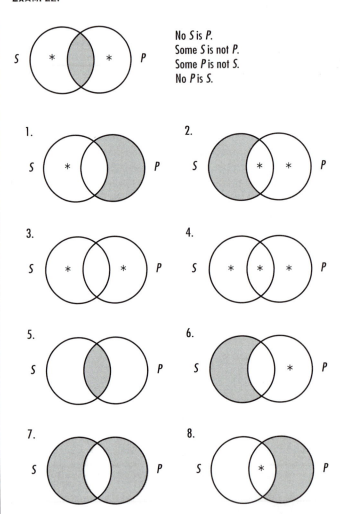

EXERCISE I

Using just the four basic categorical forms, indicate what information is given in each of the following diagrams:

EXAMPLE:

No S is P.
Some S is not P.
Some P is not S.
No P is S.

1.

2.

3.

4.

5.

6.

7.

8.

TRANSLATION INTO THE BASIC CATEGORICAL FORMS

Propositions with the specific A, E, I, and O forms do not appear often in everyday conversations. Normal people rarely say things like "All whales are mammals. All mammals breathe air. Therefore, all whales breathe air." Most people talk more like this: "Whales breathe air, since they're mammals." Thus, if our logical apparatus could be applied only to propositions with the explicit forms of A, E, I, and O, then it would apply to few arguments in everyday life.

Fortunately, however, many common statements that are not explicitly in a categorical form can be translated into a categorical form. For example, when someone says, "Whales are mammals," the speaker presumably means to refer to *all* whales, so this statement can be translated into "All whales are mammals," which is an A proposition. We need to be careful, however. If someone says, "Whales are found in the North Atlantic," the speaker probably does *not* mean to refer to *all* whales, because there are many whales in the Pacific as well. Similarly, if someone says, "A whale is a mammal," this can usually be translated as "All whales are mammals," which is an A proposition, but this translation would be inappropriate for "A whale is stranded on the beach," which seems to mean "One whale is stranded on the beach." Thus, we can be misled badly if we look only at the surface structure of what people say. We also need to pay attention to the context when we translate everyday talk into the basic categorical forms.

Despite these complications, it is possible to give some rough-and-ready guides to help in translating many common forms of expression into propositions with the A, E, I, and O forms. Let's begin with one problem that arises for all these categorical forms: They all require a class of things as a predicate. Thus, "All whales are big" and "No whales live on land" should strictly be reformulated as "All whales are big things" and "No whales are things that live on land" or "No whales are land dwellers." This much is easy.

Things get more complicated when we look at the word "all" in A propositions. We have already seen that the word "all" is sometimes dropped in everyday conversation, as in "Whales are mammals." The word "all" can also be moved away from the start of a sentence. "Democrats are all liberal" usually means "All Democrats are liberal," which is an A proposition. Moreover, other words can be used in place of "all." Each of the following claims can, in standard contexts, be translated into an A proposition with the form "All *S* is *P*":

Every Republican is conservative.

Any investment is risky.

Anyone who is human is mortal.

Each ant is precious to its mother.

To translate such claims, we sometimes need to construct noun phrases out of adjectives and verbs. These transformations are often straightforward, but sometimes they require ingenuity, and even then they can seem somewhat contorted. For example, both "Only a fool would bungee jump" and "Nobody but a fool would bungee jump" can usually be translated into "All people who bungee jump are fools." This translation might not seem as natural as the originals, but, since the translation has the A form, it explicitly shows that this claim has the logical properties shared by other A propositions.

With some stretching, it is also possible to translate statements about individuals into categorical form. The standard method is to translate "Socrates is a man" as the A proposition "All things that are Socrates are men." Similarly,

"The cannon is about to go off" in a typical context must not be translated as the I proposition "Some cannon is about to go off," because the original statement is about a particular cannon. Instead, the original statement should be translated as the A proposition "All things that are that cannon are about to go off." These translations might seem stilted, but they are necessary in order to apply syllogistic logic to everyday forms of expression.

Similar difficulties arise with the other basic propositional forms. If a woman says, "I am looking for a man who is not attached," and a friend responds, "All of the men in my church are not attached," then this response should probably be translated as "No men in my church are attached," which is an E proposition. In contrast, "All ocean dwellers are not fish" should usually be translated not as the E proposition "No ocean dwellers are fish" but rather as "Not all ocean dwellers are fish." This means "Some ocean dwellers are not fish," which is an O proposition. Thus, some statements with the form "All S are not P" should be translated as E propositions, but others should be translated as O propositions. (This ambiguity in the form "All S are not P" explains why it is standard to give E propositions in the less ambiguous form "No S is P.") Other sentences should also be translated as E propositions even though they do not explicitly contain the word "no." "Underground cables are not easy to repair" and "If a cable is underground, it is not easy to repair" and "There aren't any underground cables that are easy to repair" can all be translated as the E proposition "No underground cables are easy to repair."

Similar complications also arise for I and O propositions. We already saw that "Whales are found in the North Atlantic" should be translated as the I proposition "*Some* whales are found in the North Atlantic." In addition, some common forms of expression can be translated as O propositions even though they do not contain either the word "not" or the word "some." For example, "There are desserts without chocolate" can be translated as "Some desserts are not chocolate," which is an O proposition.

Because of such complications, there is no mechanical procedure for translating common English sentences into A, E, I, and O propositions. To find the correct translation, you need to think carefully about the sentence and its context.

EXERCISE II

Translate each of the following sentences into an A, E, I, or O proposition. Be sure that the subjects and predicates in your translations use nouns that refer to classes of things (rather than adjectives or verbs). If the sentence can be translated into different forms in different contexts, give each translation and specify a context in which it seems natural.

1. Real men eat ants.

2. Bats are not birds.

3. The hippo is charging.

4. The hippo is a noble beast.

5. Not all crabs live in water.

6. All crabs do not live in water.

7. Movie stars are all rich.

8. If anybody hits me, I will hate them.

9. If anything is broken, it does not work.

10. Somebody loves you.

11. Somebody does not love you.

12. Nobody loves me but my mother.

13. Anybody who is Mormon believes in God.

14. My friends are the only ones who care.

15. Only seniors may take this course.

16. Our pit bull is a good pet.

17. Everything that is cheap is no good.

18. Some things that are expensive are no good.

19. Some things that are cheap are good.

20. Some things that are not cheap are good.

21. Some things that are cheap are not good.

22. Some things that are not cheap are not good.

23. Not all cars have four wheels.

24. There are couples without children.

25. There are no people who hate chocolate.

26. There are people who hate chocolate.

27. Nothing that is purple is an apple.

28. Nothing that is not white is snow.

29. There aren't any runners who are slow.

30. Flamingos aren't friendly.

CONTRADICTORIES

Once we understand A, E, I, and O propositions by themselves, the next step is to ask how they are related to each other. From their diagrams, some relationships are immediately evident. Consider the Venn diagrams for the E and I propositional forms:

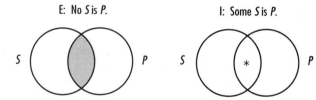

The first diagram has shading in the very same region that contains an asterisk in the second diagram. This makes it obvious that an E proposition and the corresponding I proposition (that is, the I proposition that has the same subject and predicate terms as the E proposition) cannot both be true. For an E proposition to be true, there must be *nothing* in the central region.

But for the corresponding I proposition to be true, there must be *something* in the central region. Thus, they cannot both be true. They also cannot both be false. The only way for an E proposition to be false is for there to be something in the central region, but then the corresponding I proposition is not false but true. The only way for the I proposition to be false is if there is nothing in the central region, and then the E proposition is not false but true. Thus, they cannot both be true, and they cannot both be false. In other words, they always have opposite truth values. This relation is described by saying that these propositions are *contradictories.*

More generally, we can produce a diagram for the denial of a proposition by a simple procedure. The only information given in a Venn diagram is represented either by shading out some region, thereby indicating that nothing exists in it, or by putting an asterisk in a region, thereby indicating that something does exist in it. We are given no information about regions that are unmarked. To represent the denial of a proposition, we simply reverse the information in the diagram. That is, where there is an asterisk, we put in shading; where there is shading, we put in an asterisk. Everything else is left unchanged. Thus, we can see at once that corresponding E and I propositions are denials of one another, so they must always have opposite truth values. This makes them contradictories.

The same relation exists between an A proposition and its corresponding O proposition. Consider their forms:

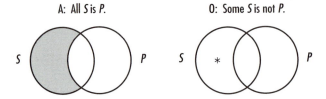

A: All *S* is *P.*   O: Some *S* is not *P.*

The diagram for an A proposition has shading exactly where the corresponding O proposition has an asterisk, and they contain no other information. Consequently, corresponding A and O propositions cannot both be false and cannot both be true, so they are contradictories.

EXERCISE III

1. Is an A proposition a contradictory of its corresponding E proposition? Why or why not?

2. Is an I proposition a contradictory of its corresponding O proposition? Why or why not?

3. If one proposition is the contradictory of another, is the latter always the contradictory of the former? Why or why not?

EXISTENTIAL COMMITMENT

It might also seem that an A proposition (with the form "All *S* is *P*") implies the corresponding I proposition (with the form "Some *S* is *P*"). This, however, raises a difficult problem that logicians have not fully settled. Usually when we make a statement, we are talking about certain specific things. If someone claims that all whales are mammals, that person is talking about whales and mammals and stating a relationship between them. In making this statement, the person seems to be taking the *existence* of whales and mammals for granted. The remark seems to involve what logicians call *existential commitment* to the things referred to in the subject and predicate terms. In the same way, stating an E proposition often seems to commit the speaker to the existence of things in the subject and predicate classes and, thus, to imply an O proposition. For example, someone who says, "No whales are fish" seems committed to "Some whales are not fish."

In other contexts, however, we seem to use universal (A and E) propositions without committing ourselves to the existence of the things referred to in the subject and predicate terms. For example, if we say, "All trespassers will be fined," we are not committing ourselves to the existence of any trespassers or to any actual fines for trespassing; we are only saying, "*If* there are trespassers, then they will be fined." Similarly, if we tell a sleepy child, "No ghosts are under your bed," we are not committing ourselves to the existence of ghosts or anything under the bed. Finally, when Newton said, "All bodies that are acted on by no forces are at rest," he did not commit himself to the existence of bodies that are acted on by no forces. Given these examples of A and E propositions that carry no commitment to the things referred to, it is easy to think of many others.

The question then arises whether we should include existential commitment in our treatment of universal propositions or not. Once more, we must make a decision. (Remember that we had to make decisions concerning the truth-table definitions of both disjunction and conditionals in Chapter 6.) *Classical* logic was developed on the assumption that universal (A and E) propositions carry existential commitment. *Modern* logic makes the opposite decision, treating the claim "All men are mortal" as equivalent to "If someone is a man, then that person is mortal," and the claim "No men are islands" as equivalent to "If someone is a man, then that person is not an island." This way of speaking carries no commitment to the existence of any men.

Which approach should we adopt? The modern approach is simpler and has proved more powerful in the long run. For these reasons, we will adopt the modern approach and *not* assign existential commitment to universal (A and E) propositions, so these propositions do not imply particular (I and O) propositions. All the same, there is something beautiful about the classical approach, and it does seem appropriate in some contexts to some people, so it is worth exploring in its own right. The Appendix to this chapter will show how to develop the classical theory by adding existential commitment to the modern theory.

EXERCISE IV

Give two new examples of contexts in which:

1. Stating an A proposition does not seem to commit the speaker to the existence of the things to which the subject term refers.

2. Stating an A proposition does not seem to commit the speaker to the existence of the things to which the predicate term refers.

3. Stating an E proposition does not seem to commit the speaker to the existence of the things to which the subject term refers.

4. Stating an E proposition does not seem to commit the speaker to the existence of the things to which the predicate term refers.

VALIDITY FOR CATEGORICAL ARGUMENTS

We have introduced Venn diagrams because they provide an efficient and illuminating way to test the validity of arguments made up of categorical (A, E, I, and O) propositions. The basic idea is simple: An argument made up of categorical propositions is valid if all the information contained in the Venn diagram for the conclusion is already contained in the Venn diagram for the premises. There are only two ways to put information into a Venn diagram: We can either shade out an area or put an asterisk in an area. Hence, to test the validity of an argument made up of categorical propositions, we need only examine the diagram of the conclusion for its information (its shading or asterisks) and then check to see if the diagram for the premises contains this information (the same shading or asterisks).

The following simple example will give a general idea of how this works:

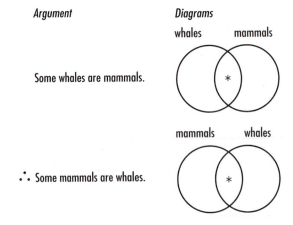

Argument

Some whales are mammals.

∴ Some mammals are whales.

Diagrams

whales   mammals

mammals   whales

Notice that the only information contained in the diagram for the conclusion is the asterisk in the overlap between the two circles, and that information is already included in the diagram for the premise. Thus, the argument is valid.

The same method can be used to test argument *forms* for validity. The form of the previous argument and the corresponding diagrams look like this:

Argument Form   *Diagrams*

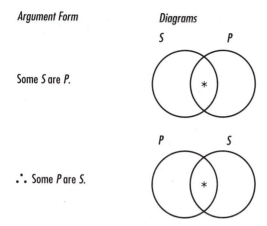

Some *S* are *P.*

∴ Some *P* are *S.*

This argument form is valid, because all the information contained in the Venn diagram for the conclusion is contained in the Venn diagram for the premise. And any argument that is a substitution instance of a valid argument form is valid.

Notice that we did not say that an argument is *invalid* if it fails these tests—that is, if some of the information in the Venn diagram for the conclusion (or its form) is not contained in the Venn diagram for the premises (or their forms). As with truth tables in propositional logic (see Chapter 6), Venn diagrams test whether arguments are valid by virtue of a certain form, but some arguments will be valid on a different basis, even though they are not valid by virtue of their categorical form. Here is one example:

Argument   *Diagrams*

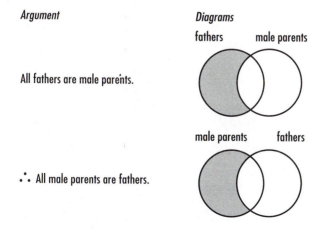

All fathers are male parents.

∴ All male parents are fathers.

The Venn diagram for the conclusion includes shading in the circle for male parents, whereas the Venn diagram for the premise includes shading in the circle for fathers, so the premise does not contain the information for the conclusion. Thus, this *form* of argument is *not* valid, and some arguments of this form are not valid. Nonetheless, this particular argument *is* clearly valid, since it is not possible for the premise to be true when the conclusion is false, for the simple reason that the conclusion cannot be false. Because of such cases, Venn diagrams can show us that an argument is valid, but they cannot prove that an argument is invalid.

Despite this limitation, the method of Venn diagrams can be used to test many different kinds of arguments and argument forms for validity. We will show how this method works for two main kinds of argument: immediate inferences and syllogisms.

CATEGORICAL IMMEDIATE INFERENCES

A categorical *immediate inference* is an argument with the following features:

1. It has a single premise. (That is why the inference is called *immediate.*)
2. It is constructed from A, E, I, and O propositions. (That is why the inference is called *categorical.*)

These arguments deserve attention because they occur quite often in everyday reasoning.

We will focus on the simplest kind of immediate inference, which is *conversion.* We *convert* a proposition (and produce its *converse*) simply by reversing the subject term and the predicate term. By the *subject term,* we mean the term that occurs as the grammatical subject; by the *predicate term,* we mean the term that occurs as the grammatical predicate. In the A proposition "All spies are aliens," "spies" is the subject term and "aliens" is the predicate term; the converse is "All aliens are spies."

In this case, identifying the predicate term is straightforward because the grammatical predicate is a noun—a predicate nominative. Often, however, we have to change the grammatical predicate from an adjective to a noun phrase in order to get a noun that refers to a class of things. "All spies are dangerous" becomes "All spies are dangerous things." Here "spies" is the subject term and "dangerous things" is the predicate term. Although this change is a bit artificial, it is necessary because, when we convert a proposition (that is, reverse its subject and predicate terms), we need a noun phrase to take the place of the grammatical subject. In English we cannot say, "All dangerous are spies," but we can say, "All dangerous things are spies."

Having explained what conversion is, we now want to know when this operation yields a *valid* immediate inference. To answer this question, we use Venn diagrams to examine the relationship between each of the four basic categorical propositional forms and its converse. The immediate inference is valid if the information contained in the conclusion is also contained in the premise—that is, if any region that is shaded in the conclusion is shaded in the premise, and if any region that contains an asterisk in the conclusion contains an asterisk in the premise.

Two cases are obvious: Both I and E propositions validly convert. From an I proposition with the form "Some S is P," we may validly infer its converse, which has the form "Some P is S."

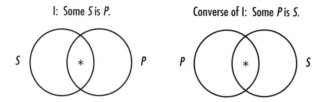

From an E proposition with the form "No S is P," we may validly infer its converse, which has the form "No P is S."

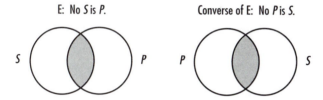

Notice that in both these cases, the information (the asterisk or shading) is in the center of the original diagram, and the diagram for the converse flips the original diagram. Thus, the two diagrams contain the same information, since the diagram for the converse has exactly the same markings in the same areas as does the diagram for the original propositional form. This shows that E and I propositions not only logically *imply* their converses but are also logically *implied by* them. Because the implication runs both ways, these propositions are said to be *logically equivalent* to their converses, and they always have the same truth values as their converses.

The use of a Venn diagram also shows that an O proposition cannot always be converted validly. From a proposition with the form "Some S is not P," we may not always infer its converse, which has the form "Some P is not S."

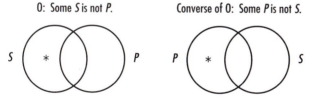

Notice that in this case the information is not in the center but is instead off to one side. As a result, the information changes when the diagram is flipped. The asterisk is in a different circle—it is in the circle for S in the diagram for an O proposition, but it is in the circle for P in the diagram for the converse of the O proposition. That shows that an argument from an O proposition to its converse is not always valid.[1]

Finally, we can see that A propositions also do not always validly convert. From a proposition with the form "All *S* is *P*," we may not always infer its converse, which has the form "All *P* is *S*."

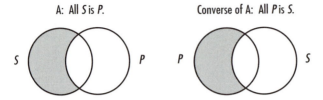

A: All *S* is *P*.   Converse of A: All *P* is *S*.

Since the diagram is not symmetrical, the information changes when the diagram is flipped; the shading ends up in a different circle. That shows why this form of argument is not always valid.

Traditionally, other immediate inferences have also been studied, but we will not run through them all here. The single example of conversion is enough to illustrate how Venn diagrams can be used to test some arguments for validity.

EXERCISE V

Use Venn diagrams to determine whether the following immediate inferences are valid:

1. All dinosaurs are animals. Therefore, all animals are dinosaurs.
2. Some pterodactyls can fly. Therefore, some flying things are pterodactyls.
3. Some eryopses are not meat eaters. Therefore, some things that eat meat are not eryopses.
4. No tyrannosaurus is a king. Therefore, no king is a tyrannosaurus.
5. Some dinosaurs are reptiles. Therefore, all dinosaurs are reptiles.
6. Some dinosaurs are not alive today. Therefore, no dinosaurs are alive today.
7. All dimetrodons eat meat. Therefore, some dimetrodons eat meat.
8. No dinosaurs are warm-blooded. Therefore, some dinosaurs are not warm-blooded.

THE THEORY OF THE SYLLOGISM

In an immediate inference, we draw a conclusion directly from a single A, E, I, or O proposition. Moreover, when two categorical propositions are contradictories, the falsity of one can be validly inferred from the truth of the other, and the truth of one can be validly inferred from the falsity of the other. All these forms of argument contain only one premise. The next step in understanding categorical propositions is to consider arguments with two premises.

An important group of such arguments is called *categorical syllogisms*. The basic idea behind these arguments is commonsensical. Suppose you wish to prove that all squares have four sides. A proof should present some *link* or *connection* between squares and four-sided figures. This link can be provided by some intermediate class, such as rectangles. You can then argue that, because the set of squares is a subset of the set of rectangles and rectangles are a subset of four-sided figures, squares must also be a subset of four-sided figures.

Of course, there are many other ways to link two terms by means of a third term. All such arguments with categorical propositions are called categorical syllogisms. More precisely, a categorical syllogism is any argument such that:

1. The argument has exactly two premises and one conclusion;
2. The argument contains only basic A, E, I, and O propositions;
3. Exactly one premise contains the predicate term;
4. Exactly one premise contains the subject term; and
5. Each premise contains the middle term.

The *predicate term* is simply the term in the predicate of the conclusion. It is also called the *major term,* and the premise that contains the predicate term is called the *major premise.* The *subject term* is the term in the subject of the conclusion. It is called the *minor term,* and the premise that contains the subject term is called the *minor premise.* It is traditional to state the major premise first, the minor premise second.

Our first example of a categorical syllogism then looks like this:

All rectangles are things with four sides.	(Major premise)
All squares are rectangles.	(Minor premise)
∴ All squares are things with four sides.	(Conclusion)

Subject term = "Squares"

Predicate term = "Things with four sides"

Middle term = "Rectangles"

To get the form of this syllogism, we replace the terms with variables:

All *M* is *P.*
All S is M.
∴ All S is *P.*

Of course, many other arguments fit the definition of a categorical syllogism. Here is one with a negative premise:

No ellipses are things with sides.
All circles are ellipses.
∴ No circles are things with sides.

The next categorical syllogism has a particular premise:

All squares are things with equal sides.
Some squares are rectangles.
∴ Some rectangles are things with equal sides.

VENN DIAGRAMS FOR SYLLOGISMS. In a previous section, we used Venn diagrams to test the validity of immediate inferences. Immediate inferences contain only two terms or classes, so the corresponding Venn diagrams need only two overlapping circles. Categorical syllogisms contain three terms or classes. To reflect this, we will use diagrams with three overlapping circles. If we use a bar over a letter to indicate that things in the area are not in the class (so that $\bar{S}$ indicates what is not in *S*), then our diagram looks like this:

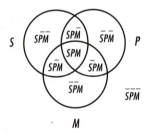

This diagram has eight different areas, which can be listed in an order that resembles a truth table:

S	P	M
S	P	M
S	P	$\bar{M}$
S	$\bar{P}$	M
S	$\bar{P}$	$\bar{M}$
$\bar{S}$	P	M
$\bar{S}$	P	$\bar{M}$
$\bar{S}$	$\bar{P}$	M
$\bar{S}$	$\bar{P}$	$\bar{M}$

Notice that, if something is neither an *S* nor a *P* nor an *M*, then it falls completely outside the system of overlapping circles. In every other case, a thing is assigned to one of the seven compartments within the system of overlapping circles.

TESTING SYLLOGISMS FOR VALIDITY. To test the validity of a syllogism using a Venn diagram, we first fill in the diagram to indicate the information
contained in the premises. Remember that the only information contained
in a Venn diagram is indicated either by shading out an area or by putting
an asterisk in it. The argument is valid if the information expressed by the
conclusion is already contained in the diagram for the premises.[2] To see
this, consider the diagrams for examples that we have already given:

> All rectangles have four sides.
> All squares are rectangles.
> ∴ All squares have four sides.

Here's the diagram for the premises:

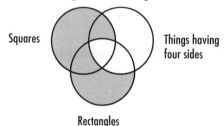

Here's the diagram for the conclusion:

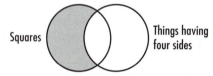

This diagram for the conclusion contains only the information that nothing is
in the circle for squares that is not also in the circle for things having four
sides. In the diagram for the premises, all the things that are squares are cor-
ralled into the region of things that have four sides. Thus, the diagram for the
premises contains all of the information in the diagram for the conclusion.
That shows that this syllogism is valid.

Next, let's try a syllogism with a negative premise:

> No ellipses have sides.
> All circles are ellipses.
> ∴ No circles have sides.

Here's the diagram for the premises:

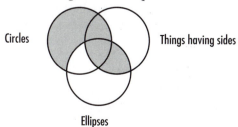

We diagram the conclusion "No circles have sides" as follows:

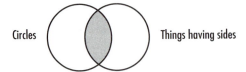

That information is clearly already contained in the Venn diagram for the premises, so this syllogism is also valid.

Let's try a syllogism with a particular premise:

> All squares have equal sides.
> Some squares are rectangles.
> ∴ Some rectangles have equal sides.

It is a good strategy to diagram a universal premise *before* diagramming a particular premise. The diagram for the above argument then looks like this:

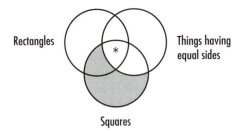

Here's the diagram for the conclusion—that there is something that is a rectangle that has equal sides:

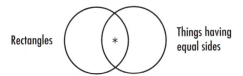

The asterisk in the middle area of this diagram says that something is in both circles, and that information already appears in the diagram for the premises, so this argument is valid.

So far we have looked only at valid syllogisms. Let's see how this method applies to invalid syllogisms. Here is one:

> All pediatricians are doctors.
> All pediatricians like children.
> ∴ All doctors like children.

We can diagram the premises at the left and the conclusion at the right:

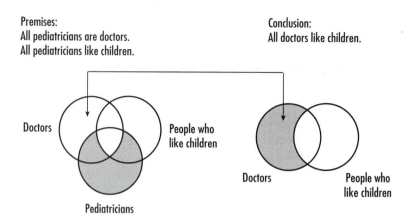

Premises:
All pediatricians are doctors.
All pediatricians like children.

Conclusion:
All doctors like children.

It is evident that the information in the diagram for the conclusion is *not* already contained in the diagram for the premises. The arrow shows differences in informational content. Thus, this form of syllogism is not valid.

Notice that the difference between these diagrams not only tells us *that* this form of syllogism is invalid; it also tells us *why* it is invalid. In the diagram for the premises, there is no shading in the upper left area, which includes people who are doctors but are not pediatricians and do not like children. This shows that the premises do not rule out the possibility that some people are doctors without being pediatricians or liking children. But if anyone is a doctor and not a person who likes children, then it is not true that all doctors like children. Because this is the conclusion of the syllogism, the premises do not rule out all of the ways in which the conclusion might be false. As a result, this conclusion does not follow by virtue of categorical form.[3]

Here is an example of an invalid syllogism with particular premises:

> Some doctors are golfers.
> Some fathers are doctors.
> ∴ Some fathers are golfers.

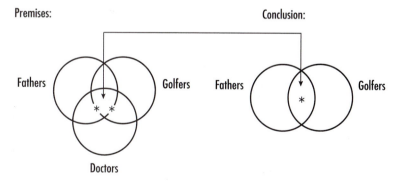

Premises:

Conclusion:

Examine this diagram closely. Notice that in diagramming "Some doctors are golfers," we had to put an asterisk *on the boundary* of the circle for fathers, because we were not given information saying whether anything falls into the category of fathers or not. For the same reason, we had to put an asterisk on the boundary of the circle for golfers when diagramming "Some fathers are doctors." The upshot was that we did not indicate that anything exists in the region of overlap between fathers and golfers. But this is what the conclusion demands, so the form of this syllogism is not valid.

Here is an invalid syllogism with negative premises:

> No babies are golfers.
> No fathers are babies.
> ∴ No fathers are golfers.

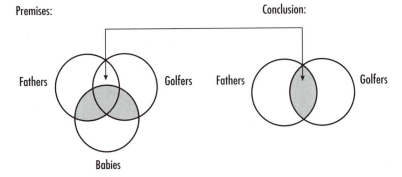

Again, we see that the form of this syllogism is not valid, because the entire area of overlap between the circles is shaded in the diagram for the conclusion, but part of that area is not shaded in the diagram for the premises.

The method of Venn diagrams is adequate for deciding the validity or invalidity of all possible forms of categorical syllogism. To master this method, all you need is a little practice.

EXERCISE VII

Using Venn diagrams, test the following syllogistic forms for validity:

1. All *M* is *P*.
   All *M* is *S*.
   ∴ All *S* is *P*.

2. All *P* is *M*.
   All *M* is *S*.
   ∴ All *S* is *P*.

3. All *M* is *P*.
   Some *M* is *S*.
   ∴ Some *S* is *P*.

4. All *P* is *M*.
   Some *M* is *S*.
   ∴ Some *S* is *P*.

5. All *P* is *M*.
   Some *S* is *M*.
   ∴ Some *S* is *P*.

6. All *P* is *M*.
   Some *S* is not *M*.
   ∴ Some *S* is not *P*.

7. All *M* is *P.*
 Some *S* is not *M.*

∴ Some *S* is not *P.*

8. All *M* is *P.*
 Some *M* is not *S.*

∴ Some *S* is not *P.*

9. No *M* is *P.*
 Some *S* is *M.*

∴ Some *S* is not *P.*

10. No *P* is *M.*
 Some *S* is *M.*

∴ Some *S* is not *P.*

11. No *P* is *M.*
 Some *S* is not *M.*

∴ Some *S* is not *P.*

12. No *M* is *P.*
 Some *S* is not *M.*

∴ Some *S* is not *P*

13. No *P* is *M.*
 Some *M* is not *S.*

∴ Some *S* is not *P.*

14. No *P* is *M.*
 No *M* is *S.*

∴ No *S* is *P.*

15. No *P* is *M.*
 All *M* is *S.*

∴ No *S* is *P.*

16. No *P* is *M.*
 All *S* is *M.*

∴ No *S* is *P.*

17. All *P* is *M.*
 No *S* is *M.*

∴ No *S* is *P.*

18. All *M* is *P.*
 No *S* is *M.*

∴ No *S* is *P.*

19. Some *M* is *P.*
 Some *M* is not *S.*

∴ Some *S* is not *P.*

20. Some *P* is *M.*
 Some *S* is not *M.*

∴ Some *S* is *P.*

EXERCISE VIII

Explain why it is a good strategy to diagram a universal premise before diagramming a particular premise in a syllogism with both.

PROBLEMS IN APPLYING THE THEORY OF THE SYLLOGISM. After mastering the techniques for evaluating syllogisms, students naturally turn to arguments that arise in daily life and attempt to use these newly acquired skills. They are often disappointed with the results. The formal theory of the syllogism seems to bear little relationship to everyday arguments, and there does not seem to be any easy way to bridge the gap.

This gap between formal theory and its application occurs for a number of reasons. First, as we saw in Chapters 2 and 5, our everyday discourse leaves much unstated. Many things are conversationally implied rather than explicitly asserted. We do not feel called on to say many things that are matters of common agreement. Before we can apply the theory of the syllogism to everyday arguments, these things that are simply understood must be made explicit. This is often illuminating, and sometimes boring, but it usually involves a great deal of work. Second, the theory of the syllogism applies to statements only in a highly stylized form. Before we apply the theory of the syllogism to an argument, we must cast its premises and conclusion into the basic A, E, I, and O forms. As we saw earlier in this chapter, the needed translation is not always simple or obvious. It may not always be possible. For these and related reasons, modern logicians have largely abandoned the project of reducing all reasoning to syllogisms.

Why study the theory of the syllogism at all, if it is hard to apply in some circumstances and perhaps impossible to apply in others? The answer to this question was given at the beginning of Chapter 6. The study of formal logic is important because it deepens our insight into a central notion of logic: *validity*. Furthermore, the argument forms we have studied do underlie much of our everyday reasoning, but so much else is going on in a normal conversational setting that this dimension is often hidden. By examining arguments in idealized forms, we can study their validity in isolation from all the other factors at work in a rich conversational setting.

There is a difference, then, between the techniques developed in Chapters 1–5 and the techniques developed in Chapters 6–7. The first five chapters presented methods of informal analysis that may be applied directly to the rich and complex arguments that arise in everyday life. These methods of analysis are not wholly rigorous, but they do provide practical guides for the analysis and evaluation of actual arguments. The chapters concerning formal logic have the opposite tendency. In comparison with the first five chapters, the level of rigor is very high, but the range of application is correspondingly smaller. In general, the more rigor and precision you insist on, the less you can talk about.

DISCUSSION QUESTIONS

1. What are the chief differences between the logical procedures developed in this chapter and those developed in the chapter on propositional logic?

2. If we evaluate arguments as they occur in everyday life by using the exact standards developed in Chapters 6 and 7, we discover that our everyday arguments rarely satisfy these standards, at least explicitly. Does this show that most of our ordinary arguments are illogical? What else might it show?

APPENDIX: THE CLASSICAL THEORY

The difference between classical and modern logic is simply that the classical approach adds one more assumption—namely, that every categorical
proposition is about something. More technically, the assumption is that A,
E, I, and O propositions all carry commitment to the existence of something
in the subject class and something in the predicate class. To draw Venn diagrams for categorical propositions on the classical interpretation, then, all
we need to do is add existential commitment to the diagrams for their modern interpretations, which were discussed above.

But how should we add existential commitment to Venn diagrams? The
answer might seem easy: Just put an asterisk wherever there is existential
commitment. The story cannot be quite so simple, however, for the following reason. The Venn diagram for the E propositional form on the modern
interpretation is this:

Modern E: No *S* is *P*.

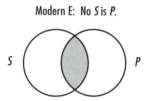

The classical interpretation adds existential commitment in both the subject
and the predicate, so if we represent existential commitment with an asterisk,
we get this diagram:

Classical E: No *S* is *P*. (???)

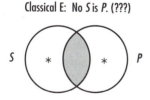

Although this diagram might seem to work, it breaks down when we perform
operations on it. We are supposed to be able to diagram the contradictory of a
proposition simply by substituting shading for asterisks and asterisks for shading. If we perform this operation on the previous diagram, we get this:

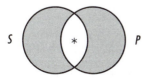

This diagram is very different from the Venn diagram for the I propositional form, which is the same on both classial and modern interpretations:

I: Some S is P.

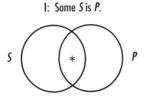

An I proposition, however, is supposed to be the contradictory of the corresponding E proposition even on the classical interpretation. So something has
gone wrong. This problem shows that existential commitment cannot be
treated exactly like explicit existential assertion, as in I and O propositions. As
a result, we cannot use the same asterisk to represent existential commitment
in Venn diagrams. Instead, we will use a plus sign: "+." With this new symbol, we can diagram the E propositional form on the classical interpretation
this way:

Classical E: No S is P.

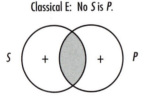

The plus sign indicates that an E proposition carries commitment to the existence of something in each class, even though it does not explicitly assert
that something exists in either class.

From this new diagram, we can get the contradictory of a proposition by
substituting shading for asterisks and asterisks for shading, as long as we
also add plus signs to ensure that no class is empty, and drop plus signs that
are no longer needed to indicate this existential commitment. When this procedure is applied to the previous diagram, the shading becomes an asterisk
in the central area, and we can then drop the plus signs in the side areas because the central asterisk already assures us that something exists in both
circles. Thus, we get the (modern and classical) diagram for the I propositional form. Moreover, when this procedure is applied to the diagram for the
I propositional form, it yields the above diagram for the E propositional
form on the classical interpretation.

It might not be so clear, however, that E and I propositions are contradictories on their classical interpretations; let us see why this is so. Two

propositions are contradictories if and only if they cannot both be true and also cannot both be false. The diagram for an E proposition has shading in the same area in which the diagram for its corresponding I proposition has an asterisk, so they cannot both be true. It is harder to see why these propositions cannot both be false on the classical interpretation, but this can be shown by the following argument. Suppose that an I proposition is false. Then there is nothing in the central area, so that area should be shaded. The classical interpretation insists that the subject and predicate classes are not empty, so if there is nothing in the central area, there must be something in each side area, which is indicated by a plus sign in each side area. That gives us the diagram for the corresponding E proposition, so that proposition is true. Thus, if an I proposition is false, its corresponding E proposition is true. That means that they cannot both be false. We already saw that they cannot both be true. So they are contradictories.

The same procedure yields a classical O proposition when it is applied to a classical A proposition, and a classical A proposition when it is applied to a classical O proposition:

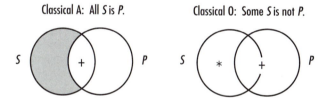

Classical A: All S is P.   Classical O: Some S is not P.

(The plus sign on the line indicates that the commitment is to something in the right-hand circle, but not to anything in either specific part of that circle.) Propositions of these forms on their classical interpretations cannot both be true and cannot both be false, so they are contradictories. Thus, this method of diagramming seems to capture the classical interpretation of the basic propositions.

EXERCISE IX

Explain why an A proposition and its corresponding O proposition are contradictories on their classical interpretations, using the diagrams above.

THE CLASSICAL SQUARE OF OPPOSITION

In addition to the contradictories, there is a more extensive and elegant set of logical relationships among categorical propositions on the classical interpretation. This system of relationships produces what has been called the *square of opposition.*

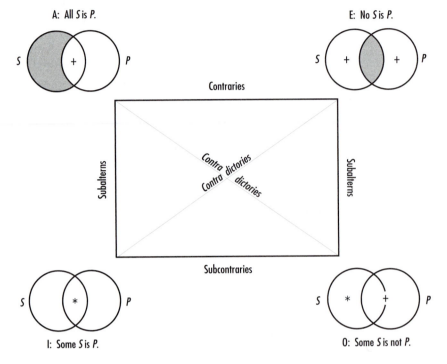

The lines in this diagram show the logical relationships that each proposition has to the other three. These relationships are explained below. Throughout the discussion, it is important to remember that all of the basic propositions are interpreted as carrying existential commitment in both their subjects and their predicates.

CONTRADICTORIES.   Two propositions are *contradictories* of each other (and they contradict each other) when they are related in the following way:

1. They cannot both be true, and
2. They cannot both be false.

More simply, contradictory pairs of propositions always have opposite truth values. We have already seen that the E and I propositions are contradictories of one another, as are the A and O propositions. This relationship holds on both the modern interpretation and the classical interpretation.

CONTRARIES.   Two propositions are said to be *contraries* of one another if they are related in this way:

1. They cannot both be true, but
2. They can both be false.

On the classical interpretation (but not the modern interpretation), A and E propositions with the same subject and predicate are contraries of one another.

In common life, the relationship between such corresponding A and E propositions is captured by the notion that one claim is the *complete opposite* of another. The complete opposite of "Everyone is here" is "No one is here." Clearly, such complete opposites cannot both be true at once. We see this readily if we look at the diagrams for A and E propositions on the classical interpretation. The middle region of the diagram for an A proposition shows the existence of something that is both S and P, whereas the middle region of the diagram for the corresponding E proposition is shaded, showing that nothing is both S and P. It should also be clear that these A and E propositions can both be false. Suppose that there is some S that is P and also some S that is not P:

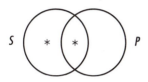

Going from left to right, the first asterisk shows that the A proposition of the form "All S is P" is false; the second asterisk shows that the corresponding E proposition of the form "No S is P" is also false. Thus, these propositions can both be false, but they cannot both be true. This makes them contraries.

SUBCONTRARIES.   Propositions are *subcontraries* of one another when

1. They can both be true, and
2. They cannot both be false.

On the classical approach (but not the modern approach), corresponding I and O propositions are subcontraries. To see how this works, compare the diagrams for I and O propositions:

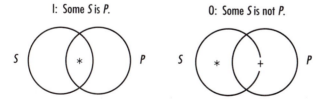

It should be clear that corresponding propositions with these forms can both be true, since there can be some S that is P and another S that is not P. But why can't they both be false? Consider the left side of the following diagram:

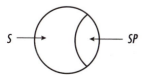

We know that, on the classical approach, there must be something in this circle somewhere. If there is something in the overlapping region *SP*, then the I proposition is true. If there is something in the nonoverlapping region of *S*, then there must be something else in the circle for *P*, because *P* cannot be empty on the classical approach; therefore, the O proposition is true. Thus, either the I proposition or the corresponding O proposition must be true, so they cannot both be false. We already saw that they can both be true. Consequently, corresponding I and O propositions are subcontraries.

SUBALTERNS.   *Subalternation* is the relationship that holds down the sides of the classical square of opposition. Quite simply, an A proposition implies the corresponding I proposition, and an E proposition implies the corresponding O proposition. This relationship depends on the existential commitment found on the classical approach and does not hold on the modern approach.

The validity of subalternation is illustrated by the following diagrams:

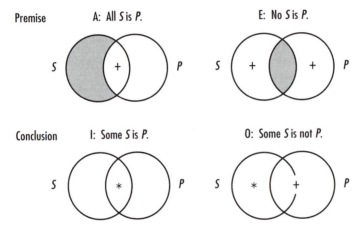

An A proposition includes a plus sign where the corresponding I proposition includes an asterisk, but both symbols indicate that something lies in the middle area. Thus, the information for the I proposition is already included in the diagram for the A proposition, which means that the A proposition implies the I proposition.

The same point applies to the implication on the right-hand side, because the diagram for an E proposition includes a plus sign in the same area as the asterisk in the diagram for the corresponding O proposition. The diagram for the E proposition also has a plus sign in the rightmost area. If something exists in that area, then something exists in either that area or the middle area, which is what is meant by the plus sign on the line in the diagram for the O proposition. Thus, an E proposition implies its corresponding O proposition.

The information given by the classical square of opposition can now be summarized in two charts. We shall ask two questions. First, for each propositional form, if we assume that a proposition with that form is *true*, what consequences follow for the truth or falsity of a corresponding proposition with a different form?

		A	E	I	O
	A	T	F	T	F
Assumed true	E	F	T	F	T
	I	?	F	T	?
	O	F	?	?	T

"T" indicates that the corresponding proposition in that column is true, "F" indicates that it is false, and "?" indicates that it might have either truth value, because neither consequence follows.

Second, for each propositional form, if we assume that a proposition with that form is *false*, what consequences follow for the truth or falsity of a corresponding proposition with a different form?

		A	E	I	O
	A	F	?	?	T
Assumed false	E	?	F	T	?
	I	F	T	F	T
	O	T	F	T	F

THE CLASSICAL THEORY OF IMMEDIATE INFERENCE

The difference between the modern and classical approaches is simply that the classical approach assigns more information—specifically, existential commitment—to the basic propositions than the modern interpretation does. Because of this additional information, certain immediate inferences hold on the classical approach that do not hold on the modern approach. In particular, though conversion of an A proposition fails on both approaches, what is known as *conversion by limitation* holds on the classical approach but not on the modern approach. That is, from a proposition with the form "All S is P," we may not validly infer the proposition with the form "All P is S," but on the classical approach, we may validly infer "*Some P is S.*" The reason is simple: From a proposition with the form "All S is P" on the classical interpretation, we may infer a proposition with the form "*Some S is P,*" and then we may convert this to get a proposition with the form "*Some P is S.*"

EXERCISE X

Using the Venn diagrams for the classical interpretation of the A propositional form given above, show that conversion by limitation is classically valid for an A proposition.

THE CLASSICAL THEORY OF SYLLOGISMS

As in the case of immediate inferences, the premises of syllogisms will contain more information—specifically, existential commitment—on the classical interpretation than they do on the modern interpretation. This will make some syllogisms valid on the classical approach that were not valid on the modern approach.

We begin our study of this matter with an example that has had a curious history:

> All rectangles are four-sided.
> All squares are rectangles.
> ∴ *Some* squares are four-sided.

The argument is peculiar because its conclusion is weaker than it needs to be. We could, after all, conclude that *all* squares are four-sided. The argument thus violates the conversational rule of Quantity. Perhaps for this reason, this syllogism was often not included in traditional lists of valid syllogisms. Yet the argument is valid on the classical interpretation of existential commitment, and our diagram should show this.

Step I: Diagram the first premise

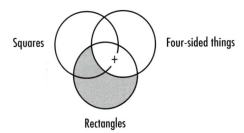

Squares   Four-sided things

Rectangles

Notice that the plus sign is placed on the outer edge of the circle for squares, because we are not in a position to put it either inside or outside that circle. We now add the information for the second premise:

Step II: Add the second premise

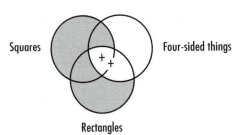

Squares   Four-sided things

Rectangles

As expected, the conclusion that some squares are four-sided is already dia-grammed, so the argument is valid—provided that we take A propositions to have existential commitment.

Because classical logicians tended to ignore the previous argument, their writings did not bring out the importance of existential commitment in eval-uating it. There is, however, an argument that did appear on the classical lists that makes clear the demand for existential commitment. These are syl-logisms with the following form:

> All *M* is *P*.
> All *M* is *S*.
> ∴ Some *S* is *P*.

This form of syllogism is diagrammed as follows:

Step I: Diagram the first premise

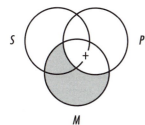

Step II: Add the second premise

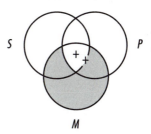

Again, we see that the conclusion follows, but only if we diagram A propo-sitions to indicate existential commitment. This, then, is an argument that was declared valid on the classical approach, but invalid on the modern approach.

EXERCISE XI

Use Venn diagrams to test the following syllogism forms for validity on the classical approach:

1. All *M* is *P*.
   No *M* is *S*.
   ∴ Some *S* is not *P*.

2. No *M* is *P*.
   All *M* is *S*.
   ∴ Some *S* is not *P*.

3. No *M* is *P*.
   All *S* is *M*.
   ∴ Some *S* is not *P*.

4. No *M* is *P*.
   No *M* is *S*.
   ∴ Some *S* is not *P*.

EXERCISE XII

Are the following claims true or false? Explain your answers.

1. Every syllogism that is valid on the modern approach is also valid on the classical approach.

2. Every syllogism that is valid on the classical approach but not on the modern approach has a particular conclusion that starts with "Some."

NOTES

[1] We say "not always" rather than simply "not," because there are some strange cases—logicians call them "degenerate cases"—for which inferences of this pattern are valid. For example, from "Some men are not men," we may validly infer "Some men are not men." Here, by making the subject term and the predicate term the same, we trivialize conversion. Keeping cases of this kind in mind, we must say that the inference from an O proposition to its converse is usually, but not always, invalid. In contrast, the set of valid arguments holds in all cases, including degenerate cases.

[2] We cannot say "only if" here because of degenerate cases of categorical syllogisms that are valid, but not by virtue of their syllogistic form. Here is one example: "All numbers divisible by two are even. No prime number other than two is divisible by two. Therefore, no prime number other than two is even." This syllogism is valid because it is not possible that its premises are true and its conclusion is false, but other syllogisms with this same form are not valid.

[3] We need to add *by virtue of its categorical form*, because, as we saw above, it still might be valid on some other basis. In this particular example, however, nothing else makes this argument valid.

How to Evaluate Arguments: Inductive Standards

Previous chapters have been concerned primarily with deductive arguments that aim at validity. Many arguments encountered in daily life, however, are not intended to meet this standard of validity. They are only supposed to provide reasons (perhaps very strong reasons) for their conclusions. Such arguments are called inductive and will be the focus of Part III. This part begins with a discussion of the nature of inductive standards and arguments followed by a survey of five forms of inductive argument: statistical generalizations, statistical applications, causal reasoning, inference to the best explanation, and arguments from analogy. The next topic is probability, because, as we will see, the inductive standard of strength can be understood in terms of probability. Part III will close by discussing how probabilities get deployed in decision making.

ARGUMENTS TO AND FROM GENERALIZATIONS

This chapter begins our investigation of inductive arguments by distinguishing the inductive standard of strength from the deductive standard of validity. Inductive arguments are defined as arguments that are intended to be strong rather than valid. Two common examples of inductive arguments are discussed next. In statistical generalizations, *a claim is made about a population on the basis of features of a sample of that population. In* statistical applications, *a claim is made about members of a population on the basis of features of the population. Statistical generalizations take us up from samples to general claims, and statistical applications then take us back down to individual cases.*

INDUCTION *VERSUS* DEDUCTION

The distinction between deductive arguments and inductive arguments can be drawn in a variety of ways, but the fundamental difference concerns the relationship that is claimed to hold between the premises and the conclusion for each type of argument. An argument is *deductive* insofar as it is intended or claimed to be *valid*. As we know from Chapter 3, an argument is valid if and only if it is impossible for the conclusion to be false when its premises are true. The following is a valid deductive argument:

All ravens are black.
∴ If there is a raven on top of Pikes Peak, then it is black.

Because the premise lays down a universal principle governing all ravens, if it's true, then it *must* be true of all ravens (if any) on top of Pikes Peak. This same relationship does not hold for invalid arguments. Nonetheless, arguments that are not valid can still be deductive if they are intended or claimed to be valid.

In contrast, inductive arguments are not intended to be valid, so they should not be criticized for being invalid. The following is an example of an inductive argument:

All ravens that we have observed so far are black.
∴ All ravens are black.

Here we have drawn an inductive inference from the characteristics of *observed* ravens to the characteristics of *all* ravens, most of which we have not observed. Of course, the premise of this argument *could be* true, yet the conclusion turn out to be false. A raven that has not yet been observed might be albino. The obviousness of this possibility suggests that someone who gives this argument does not put it forth as valid, so it is not a deductive argument. Instead, the premise is put forth as a *reason* or *support* for the conclusion. When an argument is not claimed to be valid but is intended only to provide a reason for the conclusion, the argument is *inductive.*

Because inductive arguments are supposed to provide reasons, and reasons vary in strength, inductive arguments can be evaluated as *strong* or *weak,* depending on the strength of the reasons that they provide for their conclusions. If we have seen only ten ravens, and all of them were in our backyard, then the above argument gives at most a very weak reason to believe that all ravens are black. But, if we have traveled around the world and seen over half the ravens that exist, then the above argument gives a strong reason to believe that all ravens are black. Inductive arguments are usually intended to provide strong support for their conclusions, in which case they can be criticized if the support they provide is not strong enough for the purposes at hand.

The most basic distinction, then, is not between two kinds of argument but is instead between two standards for evaluating arguments. The deductive standard is validity. The inductive standard is strength. Arguments themselves are classified as either deductive or inductive in accordance with the standard that they are intended or claimed to meet.

There are several important differences between deductive and inductive standards. One fundamental feature of the deductive standard of validity is that adding premises to a valid argument cannot make it invalid. The definition of validity guarantees this: In a valid argument, it is not possible for the premises to be true without the conclusion being true as well. If any further premises could change this, then it would be possible for this relationship not to hold, so the argument would not be valid after all. Additional information might, of course, lead us to question the truth of one of the premises, but that is another matter.

The situation is strikingly different when we deal with inductive arguments. To cite a famous example, before the time of Captain Cook's voyage to Australia, Europeans had observed a great many swans, and every one of them was white. Thus, up to that time Europeans had very strong inductive evidence to support the claim that all swans are white. Then Captain Cook discovered black swans in Australia. What happens if we add this new piece of information to the premises of the original inductive argument? Provided that we accept Cook's report, we now produce a sound *deductive* argument in behalf of the opposite claim that *not* all swans are white; for, if some swans are black, then not all of them are white. This, then, is a feature of the inductive standard of strength: No matter how strong an inductive argument is, the possibility remains open that further information can undercut, perhaps completely, the strength of the argument and the support that the premises give to the conclusion. Because inductive strength and inductive arguments can always be defeated in this way, they are described as *defeasible*. Valid deductive arguments do not face a similar peril, so they are called *indefeasible*.

A second important difference between inductive and deductive standards is that inductive strength comes in degrees, but deductive validity does not. An argument is either valid or invalid. There is no question of how much validity an argument has. In contrast, inductive arguments can be more or less strong. The more varied ravens or swans we observe, the stronger the inductive arguments above. Some inductive arguments are extremely strong and put their conclusions beyond any reasonable doubt. Other inductive arguments are much weaker, even though they still have some force.

Because of the necessary relationship between the premises and the conclusion of a valid deductive argument, it is often said that the premises of valid deductive arguments (if true) provide *conclusive* support for their conclusions, whereas true premises of strong inductive arguments provide only *partial* support for their conclusions. There is something to this. Because the premises of a valid deductive argument necessitate the truth of the conclusion, if those premises are definitely known to be true, then they do supply conclusive reasons for the conclusion. The same cannot be said for inductive arguments.

It would be altogether misleading, however, to conclude from this that inductive arguments are inherently inferior to deductive arguments in supplying a justification or ground for a conclusion. In the first place, inductive arguments often place matters beyond any reasonable doubt. It is possible that the next pot of water will not boil at any temperature, however high, but this is not something we worry about. We do not take precautions against it, and we shouldn't.

More important, deductive arguments normally enjoy no advantages over their inductive counterparts. We can see this by comparing the two following arguments:

DEDUCTIVE	INDUCTIVE
All ravens are black.	All observed ravens are black.
∴ If there is a raven on top of Pikes Peak, it is black.	∴ If there is a raven on top of Pikes Peak, it is black.

Of course, it is true for the deductive argument (and not true for the inductive argument) that if the premise is true, then the conclusion must be true. This may seem to give an advantage to the deductive argument over the inductive argument. But before we can decide how much support a deductive argument gives its conclusion, we must ask if its premises are, after all, true. That is not something we can just take for granted. If we examine the premises of these two arguments, we see that it is easier to establish the truth of the premise of the inductive argument than it is to establish the truth of the premise of the deductive argument. If we have observed carefully and kept good records, then we might be fully confident that all *observed* ravens have been black. On the other hand, how can we show that *all* ravens (observed and unobserved—past, present, and future) are black? The most obvious way (though there may be other ways) would be to observe ravens to see if they are black or not. This, of course, involves producing an inductive argument (called a statistical generalization) for the premise of the deductive argument. Here our confidence in the truth of the premise of the deductive argument should be no greater than our confidence in the strength of the inference in the statistical generalization. In this case—and it is not unusual—the deductive argument provides no stronger grounds in support of its conclusion than does its inductive counterpart, because any reservations we might have about the *strength* of the inductive inference will be paralleled by doubts concerning the *truth* of the premise of the deductive argument.

We will also avoid the common mistake of saying that deductive arguments always move from the general to the particular, whereas inductive arguments always move from the particular to the general. In fact, both sorts of arguments can move in either direction. There are inductive arguments intended to establish particular matters of fact, and there are deductive arguments that involve generalizations from particulars. For example, when scientists assemble empirical evidence to determine whether the extinction of the dinosaurs was caused by the impact of a meteor, their discussions are models of inductive reasoning. Yet they are not trying to establish a generalization or a scientific law. Instead, they are trying to determine whether a particular event occurred some 65 million years ago. Inductive reasoning concerning particular matters of fact occurs constantly in everyday life as well, for example, when we check to see whether our television reception is being messed up by someone using a hair dryer. Deductive arguments from the particular to the general also exist, though they tend to be trivial, and hence boring. Here's one:

> Benjamin Franklin was the first postmaster general; therefore, anyone who is identical with Benjamin Franklin was the first postmaster general.

Of course, many deductive arguments do move from the general to the particular, and many inductive arguments do move from particular premises to a general conclusion. It is important to remember, however, that this is not the *definitive* difference between these two kinds of arguments. What makes deductive arguments deductive is precisely that they are intended to meet the deductive standard of validity, and what makes inductive arguments inductive is just that they are not intended to be deductively valid but are, instead, intended to be inductively strong.

EXERCISE I

Assuming a standard context, label each of the following arguments as deductive or inductive. Explain what it is about the words or form of argument that indicates whether or not each argument is intended or claimed to be valid. If it is not clear whether the argument is inductive or deductive, say why.

1. The sun is coming out, so the rain will probably stop soon.
2. It's going to rain tomorrow, so it will either rain or be clear tomorrow.
3. No woman has ever been elected president. Therefore, no woman will ever be elected president.
4. Diet cola never keeps me awake at night. I know because I drank it just last night without any problems.
5. The house is a mess, so Jeff must be home from college.
6. If Harold were innocent, he would not go into hiding. Since he is hiding, he must not be innocent.
7. Nobody in Paris seems to understand me, so either my French is rotten or Parisians are unfriendly.
8. Because both of our yards are near rivers in Tennessee, and my yard has lots of mosquitoes, there must also be lots of mosquitoes in your yard.
9. Most likely, her new husband speaks English with an accent, because he comes from Germany, and most Germans speak English with an accent.
10. There is no even number smaller than 2, so 1 is not an even number.

DISCUSSION QUESTIONS

1. The following arguments are not clearly inductive and also not clearly deductive. Explain why.
   a. All humans are mortal, and Socrates is a human, so Socrates is likely to be mortal also.
   b. We checked every continent there is, and every raven in every continent was observed to be black, so every raven is black.
   c. If there's radon in your basement, this monitor will go off. The monitor is going off, so there must be radon in your basement. (Said by an engineer while running the monitor in your basement.)
2. In mathematics, proofs are sometimes employed using the method of *mathematical induction.* If you are familiar with this procedure, determine whether these proofs are deductive or inductive in character. Explain why.

STATISTICAL GENERALIZATIONS

One classic example of an inductive argument is an opinion poll. Suppose a candidate wants to know how popular she is with voters. Because it would be practically impossible to survey all voters, she takes a sample of voting opinion and then infers that the opinions of those sampled indicate the overall opinion of voters. Thus, if 60 percent of the voters sampled say that they will vote for her, she concludes that she will get around 60 percent of the vote in the actual election. As we shall see later, inferences of this kind often go wrong, even when made by experts, but the general pattern of this reasoning is quite clear: Statistical features of a sample are used to make statistical claims about the population as a whole.

Basically the same form of reasoning can be used to reach a universal conclusion. An example is the inductive inference discussed at the start of this chapter: All observed ravens are black, so all ravens are black. Again, we sample part of a population to draw a conclusion about the whole. Arguments of this form, whether the conclusion is universal or partial (as when it cites a particular percentage), are called *statistical generalizations*.

How do we assess such inferences? To begin to answer this question, we can consider a simple example of a statistical generalization. On various occasions, Harold has tried to use Canadian quarters in American payphones and found that they have not worked. From this he draws the conclusion that Canadian quarters do not work in American payphones. Harold's inductive reasoning looks like this:

> In the past, when I tried to use Canadian quarters in American payphones, they did not work.
> _____
> ∴ Canadian quarters do not work in American payphones.

The force of the conclusion is that Canadian quarters *never* work in American payphones.

In evaluating this argument, what questions should we ask? We can start with a question that we should ask of any argument.

SHOULD WE ACCEPT THE PREMISES?

Perhaps Harold has a bad memory, has kept bad records, or is a poor observer. For some obscure reason, he may even be lying. It is important to ask this question explicitly, because fairly often the premises, when challenged, will not stand up to scrutiny.

If we decide that the premises are acceptable (that is, true and justified), then we can shift our attention to the relationship between the premises and the conclusion and ask how much support the premises give to the conclusion. One commonsense question is this: "How many times has Harold tried to use Canadian quarters in American payphones?" If the answer is "Once," then our confidence in his argument should drop to almost nothing. So, for statistical generalizations, it is always appropriate to ask about the size of the sample.

IS THE SAMPLE LARGE ENOUGH?

One reason we should be suspicious of small samples is that they can be affected by runs of luck. Suppose Harold flips a Canadian quarter four times and it comes up heads each time. From this, he can hardly conclude that Canadian quarters always come up heads when flipped. He could not even reasonably conclude that *this* Canadian quarter would always come up heads when flipped. The reason for this is obvious enough: If you spend a lot of time flipping coins, runs of four heads in a row are not all that unlikely (the probability is actually one in sixteen), and therefore samples of this size can easily be distorted by chance. On the other hand, if Harold flipped the coin twenty times and it continued to come up heads, he would have strong grounds for saying that this coin, at least, will always come up heads. In fact, he would have strong grounds for thinking that he has a two-headed coin. Because an overly small sample can lead to erroneous conclusions, we need to make sure that our sample includes enough trials.

How many is enough? On the assumption, for the moment, that our sampling has been fair in all other respects, how many samples do we need to provide the basis for a strong inductive argument? This is not always an easy question to answer, and sometimes answering it demands subtle mathematical techniques. Suppose your company is selling 10 million computer chips to the Department of Defense, and you have guaranteed that no more than 0.2 percent of them will be defective. It would be prohibitively expensive to test all the chips, and testing only a dozen would hardly be enough to reasonably guarantee that the total shipment of chips meets the required specifications. Because testing chips is expensive, you want to test as few as possible; but because meeting the specifications is crucial, you want to test enough to guarantee that you have done so. Answering questions of this kind demands sophisticated statistical techniques beyond the scope of this text.

Sometimes, then, it is difficult to decide how many instances are needed to give reasonable support to inductive generalizations; yet many times it is obvious, without going into technical details, that the sample is too small. Drawing an inductive conclusion from a sample that is too small can lead to the fallacy of *hasty generalization.* It is surprising how common this fallacy is. We see a person two or three times and find him cheerful, and we immediately leap to the conclusion that he is a cheerful person. That is, from a few instances of cheerful behavior, we draw a general conclusion about his personality. When we meet him later and find him sad, morose, or grouchy, we then conclude that he has changed—thus swapping one hasty generalization for another.

This tendency toward hasty generalization was discussed over 200 years ago by the philosopher David Hume, who saw that we have a strong tendency to "follow general rules which we rashly form to ourselves, and which are the source of what we properly call prejudice."[1] More recently, this tendency toward hasty generalization has been the subject of extensive psychological investigation. The cognitive psychologists Amos Tversky and Daniel Kahneman put the matter this way:

> We submit that people view a sample randomly drawn from a population as highly representative, that is, similar to the population in all essential characteristics. Consequently, they expect any two samples drawn from a particular population to be more similar to one another and to the population than sampling theory predicts, at least for small samples.[2]

To return to a previous example, we make our judgments of someone's personality on the basis of a very small sample of his or her behavior and expect this person to behave in similar ways in the future when we encounter further samples of behavior. We are surprised, and sometimes indignant, when the future behavior does not match our expectations.

By making our samples sufficiently large, we can guard against distortions due to "runs of luck," but even very large samples can give us a poor basis for a statistical generalization. Suppose that Harold has tried hundreds of times to use a Canadian quarter in an American payphone, and it has never worked. This will increase our confidence in his generalization, but size of sample alone is not a sufficient ground for a strong inductive argument. Suppose that Harold has tried the same coin in hundreds of different payphones, or tried a hundred different Canadian coins in the same payphone. In the first case, there might be something wrong with this particular coin; in the second case, there might be something wrong with this particular payphone. In neither case would he have good grounds for making the general claim that *no* Canadian quarters work in *any* American payphones. This leads us to the third question we should ask of any statistical generalization.

IS THE SAMPLE BIASED?

When the sample, however large, is not representative of the population, then it is said to be unfair or biased. Here we can speak of the fallacy of *biased sampling.*

One of the most famous errors of biased sampling was committed by a magazine named the *Literary Digest.* Before the presidential election of 1936, this magazine sent out 10 million questionnaires asking which candidate the recipient would vote for: Franklin Roosevelt or Alf Landon. It received 2.5 million returns, and on the basis of the results, confidently predicted that Landon would win by a landslide: 56 percent for Landon to only 44 percent for Roosevelt. When the election results came in, Roosevelt had won by an even larger landslide in the opposite direction: 62 percent for Roosevelt to a mere 38 percent for Landon.

What went wrong? The sample was certainly large enough; in fact, by contemporary standards it was much larger than needed. It was the way the sample was selected, not its size, that caused the problem: The sample was randomly drawn from names in telephone books and from club membership lists. In 1936 there were only 11 million payphones in the United States, and many of the poor—especially the rural poor—did not have payphones. During the Great Depression there were more than 9 million unemployed in America; they were almost all poor and thus underrepresented on club membership lists. Finally, a large percentage of these underrepresented groups voted for Roosevelt, the Democratic candidate. As a result of these biases in its sampling, along with some others, the *Literary Digest* underestimated Roosevelt's percentage of the vote by a whopping 18 percent.

Looking back, it may be hard to believe that intelligent observers could have done such a ridiculously bad job of sampling opinion, but the story repeats itself, though rarely on the grand scale of the *Literary Digest* fiasco. In 1948, for example, the Gallup poll, which had correctly predicted Roosevelt's victory in 1936, predicted, as did other major polls, a clear victory for Thomas Dewey over Harry Truman. Confidence was so high in this prediction that the *Chicago Tribune* published a banner headline declaring that Dewey had won the election before the votes were actually counted.

What went wrong this time? The answer here is more subtle. The Gallup pollsters (and others) went to great pains to make sure that their sample was representative of the voting population. The interviewers were told to poll a certain number of people from particular social groups—rural poor, suburban middle class, urban middle class, ethnic minorities, and so on—so that the proportions of those interviewed matched, as closely as possible, the proportions of those likely to vote. (The *Literary Digest* went bankrupt after its incorrect prediction, so the pollsters were taking no chances.) Yet somehow bias crept into the sampling; the question was, "How?" One speculation was that a large percentage of those sampled did not tell the truth when they were interviewed; another was that a large number of people changed their minds at the last minute. So perhaps the data collected were not reliable. The explanation generally accepted was more subtle. Although Gallup's workers were told to interview specific numbers of people from particular classes (so many from the suburbs, for example), they were not instructed to choose people randomly from within each group. Without seriously thinking about it, they tended to go to "nicer" neighborhoods and interview "nicer" people. Because of this, they biased the sample in the direction of their own (largely) middle-class preferences and, as a result, under-represented constituencies that would give Truman his unexpected victory.

IS THE RESULT BIASED IN SOME OTHER WAY?

Because professionals using modern techniques can make bad statistical generalizations through biased sampling, it is not surprising that our everyday, informal inductive generalizations are often inaccurate. Sometimes we go astray because of small samples and biased samples. This happens, for example, when we form opinions about what people think or what people are like by asking only our friends. But bias can affect our reasoning in other ways as well.

One of the main sources of bias in everyday life is *prejudice*. Even if we sample a wide enough range of cases, we often reinterpret what we hear or see in light of some preconception. People who are prejudiced will find very little good and a great deal bad in those they despise, no matter how these people actually behave. In fact, most people are a mixture of good and bad qualities. By ignoring the former and dwelling on the latter, it is easy enough for a prejudiced person to confirm negative opinions. Similarly, stereotypes, which can be either positive or negative, often persist in the face of overwhelming counterevidence. Criticizing the beliefs common in Britain in his own day, David Hume remarked:

> An Irishman cannot have wit, and a Frenchman cannot have solidity; for which reason, though the conversation of the former in any instance be very agreeable, and of the latter very judicious, we have entertained such a prejudice against them, that they must be dunces and fops in spite of sense and reason.[3]

Although common stereotypes have changed somewhat since Hume's day, prejudice continues to distort the beliefs of many people in our own time.

Another common source of bias in sampling arises from phrasing questions in ways that encourage certain answers while discouraging others. Even if a fair sample is asked a question, it is well known that the way a question is phrased can exert a significant influence on how people will answer it. Questions like the following are not intended to elicit information, but instead to push people's answers in one direction rather than another.

> Which do you favor: (a) preserving a citizen's constitutional right to bear arms or (b) leaving honest citizens defenseless against armed criminals?

> Which do you favor: (a) restricting the sale of assault weapons or (b) knuckling under to the demands of the well-financed gun lobby?

In both cases, one alternative is made to sound attractive, the other unattractive. When questions of this sort are used, it is not surprising that different pollsters can come up with wildly different results.

Now we can summarize and restate our questions. Confronted with inductive generalizations, there are four questions that we should routinely ask:

1. Are the premises acceptable?
2. Is the sample too small?
3. Is the sample biased?
4. Are the results affected by other sources of bias?

EXERCISE II

By asking the preceding questions, specify what, if anything, is wrong with the following statistical generalizations:

1. This philosophy class is about logic, so most philosophy classes are probably about logic.
2. Most college students like to ski, because I asked a lot of students at several colleges in the Rocky Mountains, and most of them like to ski.
3. K-Mart asked all of their customers throughout the country whether they prefer K-Mart to Walmart, and 90 percent said they did, so 90 percent of all shoppers in the country prefer K-Mart.
4. A Swede stole my bicycle, so most Swedes are thieves.

5. I've never tried it before, but I just put a kiwi fruit in a tub of water. It floated. So most kiwi fruits float in water.

6. I have lots of friends. Most of them think that I would make a great president. So most Americans would probably agree.

7. In exit polls after people had just voted, most people told our candidate that they voted for her, so probably most people did vote for her.

8. Mary told me that all of her older children are geniuses, so her baby will probably be a genius, too.

9. When asked whether they would prefer a tax break or a bloated budget, almost everyone said that they wanted a tax break. So a tax break is overwhelmingly popular with the people.

10. When hundreds of convicted murderers in states without the death penalty were asked whether they would have committed the murder if the state had a death penalty, most of them said that they would not have done it. So most murders can be deterred by the death penalty.

DISCUSSION QUESTION

It is often easy to see that a sample is biased, but how can you tell that a sample is not biased? How can you determine whether a sample is big enough?

STATISTICAL APPLICATIONS

In a statistical generalization, we draw inferences concerning a population from information concerning a sample of that population. If 60 percent of the population sampled said that they would vote for candidate X, we might draw the conclusion that roughly 60 percent of the population will vote for candidate X. With a *statistical application* (sometimes called a *statistical syllogism*), we reason in the reverse direction: From information concerning a population, we draw a conclusion concerning a member or subset of that population. Here is an example:

> Ninety-seven percent of the Republicans in California voted for McCain.
> Marvin is a Republican from California.
>
> ∴ Marvin voted for McCain.

Such arguments have the following general form:

> X percent of Fs have the feature G.
> a is an F.
>
> ∴ a has the feature G.[4]

Obviously, when we evaluate the strength of a statistical application, the percentage of *F*s that have the feature *G* will be important. As the figure approaches 100 percent, the argument gains strength. Thus, our original argument concerning Marvin is quite strong. We can also get strong statistical applications when the figure approaches 0 percent. The following is a strong inductive argument:

> Three percent of the socialists from California voted for McCain.
> Maureen is a socialist from California.
>
> ∴ Maureen did *not* vote for McCain.

Statistical applications of the kind considered here are strong only if the figures are close to 100 percent or 0 percent. When the percentages are in the middle of this range, such statistical applications are weak.

A more interesting problem in evaluating the strength of a statistical application concerns the *relevance* of the premises to the conclusion. In the above schematic representation, *F* stands for what is called the *reference class.* In our first example, being a Republican from California is the reference class; in our second example, being a socialist from California is the reference class. A striking feature of statistical applications is that using different reference classes can yield incompatible results. To see this, consider the following example:

> Three percent of Obama's relatives voted for McCain.
> Marvin is a relative of Obama.
>
> ∴ Marvin did not vote for McCain.

We now have a statistical application that gives us strong support for the claim that Marvin did not vote for McCain. This is incompatible with our first statistical application, which gave strong support to the claim that he did. To overlook this conflict between arguments based on different reference classes would be a kind of fallacy. Which statistical application, if either, should we trust? This will depend on which of the reference classes we take to be more relevant. Which counts more, political affiliation or family ties? That might be hard to say.

One way of dealing with competing statistical applications is to combine the reference classes. We could ask, for example, what percentage of Republicans from California who are relatives of Obama voted for McCain? The result might come out this way:

> Forty-two percent of Republicans from California who were relatives of Obama voted for McCain.
> Marvin is a Republican from California who is a relative of Obama.
>
> ∴ Marvin voted for McCain.

This statistical application provides very weak support for its conclusion. Indeed, it supplies some weak support for the denial of its conclusion—that is, for the claim that Marvin did *not* vote for McCain.

This situation can be diagrammed with ellipses of varying sizes to represent the percentages of Californians and relatives of Obama who do or do not vote for McCain. First, we draw an ellipse to represent Republicans from California and place a vertical line so that it cuts off roughly (very roughly!) 97 percent of the area of that ellipse to represent the premise that 97 percent of the Republicans from California voted for McCain:

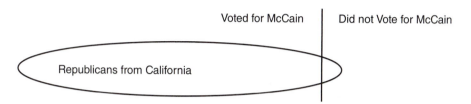

Next, we add a second ellipse to represent Obama's relatives:

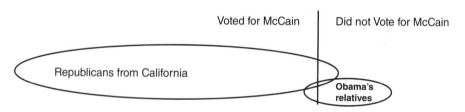

Only about 3 percent of the small ellipse is left of the line to represent the premise that 3 percent of Obama's relatives voted for McCain. The area that lies within both ellipses represents the people who are both Republicans from California and also relatives of Obama. About 42 percent of that area is left of the line to represent the premise that 42 percent of Republicans from California who were relatives of Obama voted for McCain. The whole diagram now shows how all of these premises can be true, even though they lead to conflicting conclusions.

This series of arguments illustrates in a clear way what we earlier called the defeasibility of inductive inferences: A strong inductive argument can be made weak by adding further information to the premises. Given that Marvin is a Republican from California, we seemed to have good reason to think that he voted for McCain. But when we added to this the additional piece of information that he was a relative of Obama, the original argument lost most of its force. And new information could produce another reversal. Suppose we discover that Marvin, though a relative of Obama, actively campaigned for McCain. Just about everyone who actively campaigns for a candidate votes for that candidate, so it seems that we again have good reason for thinking that Marvin voted for McCain.

It is clear, then, that the way we select our reference classes will affect the strength of a statistical application. The general idea is that we should define our reference classes in a way that brings all relevant evidence to bear on the subject. But this raises difficulties. It is not always obvious which factors are relevant and which are not. In our example, party affiliation is relevant to how people voted in the 2008 election; shoe size presumably is not. Whether gender is significant, and, if so, how significant, is a matter for further statistical research.

These difficulties concerning the proper way to fix reference classes reflect a feature of all inductive reasoning: To be successful, such reasoning must take place within a broader framework that helps determine which features are significant and which features are not. Without this framework, there would be no reason not to consider shoe size when trying to decide how someone will vote. This shows how statistical applications, like all of the other inductive arguments that we will study, cannot work properly without appropriate background assumptions.

EXERCISE III

Carry the story of Marvin two steps further, producing two more reversals in the strength of the statistical application with the conclusion that Marvin voted for McCain.

EXERCISE IV

For each of the following statistical applications, identify the reference class, and then evaluate the strength of the argument in terms of the percentages or proportions cited and the relevance of the reference class.

1. Less than 1 percent of the people in the world voted for McCain.
   Michelle is a person in the world.
   ∴ Michelle did not vote for McCain.

2. Very few teams repeat as Super Bowl champions.
   New England was the last Super Bowl champion.
   ∴ New England will not repeat as Super Bowl champion.

3. A very high percentage of people in the Senate are men.
   Hillary Clinton is in the Senate.
   ∴ Hillary Clinton is a man.

4. Three percent of socialists with blue eyes voted for McCain.
   Maureen is a socialist with blue eyes.
   ∴ Maureen did not vote for McCain.

5. Ninety-eight percent of what John says is true.
John said that his father is also named John.

∴ John's father is named John.

6. Ninety-eight percent of what John says is true.
John said that the Giants are going to win.

∴ The Giants are going to win.

7. Half the time he doesn't know what he is doing.
He is eating lunch.

∴ He does not know that he is eating lunch.

8. Most people do not understand quantum mechanics.
My physics professor is a person.

∴ My physics professor probably does not understand quantum mechanics.

9. Almost all birds can fly.
This penguin is a bird.

∴ This penguin can fly.

10. Most people who claim to be psychic are frauds.
Mary claims to be psychic.

∴ Mary is a fraud.

DISCUSSION QUESTION

Although both in science and in daily life, we rely heavily on the methods of inductive reasoning, this kind of reasoning raises a number of perplexing problems. The most famous problem concerning the legitimacy of induction was formulated by the eighteenth-century philosopher David Hume, first in his *Treatise of Human Nature* and then later in his *Enquiry Concerning Human Understanding*. A simplified version of Hume's skeptical argument goes as follows: Our inductive generalizations seem to rest on the assumption that *unobserved* cases will follow the patterns that we discovered in *observed* cases. That is, our inductive generalizations seem to presuppose that nature operates uniformly: The way things are observed to behave here and now are accurate indicators of how things behave anywhere and at any time. But by what right can we assume that nature is uniform? Because this claim itself asserts a contingent matter of fact, it could only be established by inductive reasoning. But because all inductive reasoning presupposes the principle that nature is uniform, any inductive justification of this principle would seem to be circular. It seems, then, that we have no ultimate justification for our inductive reasoning at all. Is this a good argument or a bad one? Why?

NOTES

[1] David Hume, *A Treatise of Human Nature*, 2nd ed. (1739; Oxford: Oxford University Press, 1978), 146.

[2] Amos Tversky and Daniel Kahneman, "Belief in the Law of Small Numbers," *Psychological Bulletin* 76, no. 2 (1971), 105.

[3] Hume, *A Treatise of Human Nature*, 146–47.

[4] We can also have a *probabilistic* version of the statistical syllogism:

> Ninety-seven percent of the Republicans from California voted for McCain.
> Marvin is a Republican from California.
> ∴ There is a 97 percent chance that Marvin voted for McCain.

We will discuss arguments concerning probability in Chapter 11.

9

CAUSAL REASONING

Statistical generalization can tell us that all ravens are black and that most Texans will vote for McCain, but these generalizations alone cannot tell us what makes ravens black or what makes most Texans vote for McCain. To determine what causes such phenomena, we need to engage in a new kind of inductive reasoning—causal reasoning—which is the topic of this chapter. We will show how causal reasoning is often based on negative and positive tests for necessary conditions and for sufficient conditions. After developing these tests and applying them to a concrete example, we will discuss concomitant variation as a method of drawing causal conclusions from imperfect correlations. Our goal throughout this chapter is to improve our ability to identify causes so that we can better understand why certain effects happened and also make better predictions about whether similar events will happen in the future.

REASONING ABOUT CAUSES

If our car goes dead in the middle of rush-hour traffic just after its 20,000-mile checkup, we assume that there must be some reason why this happened. Cars just don't stop for no reason at all. So we ask, "What caused our car to stop?" The answer might be that it ran out of gas. If we find, in fact, that it did run out of gas, then that will usually be the end of the matter. We will think that we have discovered why this particular car stopped running. This reasoning is about a particular car on a particular occasion, but it rests on certain *generalizations:* We are confident that our *car* stopped running when it ran out of gas, because we believe that all cars stop running when they run out of gas. We probably did not think about this, but our causal reasoning in this particular case appealed to a commonly accepted causal generalization: Lack of fuel causes cars to stop running. Many explanations depend on *causal generalizations.*

Causal generalizations are also used to *predict* the consequences of particular actions or events. A race car driver might wonder, for example, what would happen if he added just a bit of nitroglycerin to his fuel mixture. Would it give him better acceleration, blow him up, do very little, or what?

In fact, the driver may not be in a position to answer this question straight off, but his thinking will be guided by the causal generalization that igniting nitroglycerin can cause a dangerous explosion.

So a similar pattern arises for both causal explanation and causal prediction. These inferences contain two essential elements:

1. The facts in the particular case. (For example, the car stopped and the gas gauge reads empty; or I just put a pint of nitroglycerin in the gas tank of my Maserati, and I am about to turn the ignition key.)
2. Certain causal generalizations. (For example, cars do not run without gas, or nitroglycerin explodes when ignited.)

The basic idea is that causal inferences bring particular facts under causal generalizations.

This shows why causal generalizations are important, but what exactly are they? Although this issue remains controversial, here we will treat them as a kind of *general conditional*. A general conditional has the following form:

For all x, if x has the feature F, then x has the feature G.

We will say that, according to this conditional, x's having the feature F is a *sufficient condition* for its having the feature G; and x's having the feature G is a *necessary condition* for its having the feature F.

Some general conditionals are not *causal*. Neither of these two general conditionals expresses a causal relationship:

If something is a square, then it is a rectangle.

If you are eighteen years old, then you are eligible to vote.

The first conditional tells us that being a square is sufficient for being a rectangle, but this is a mathematical (or *a priori*) relationship, not a causal one. The second conditional tells us that being eighteen years old is a sufficient condition for being eligible to vote. The relationship here is legal, not causal.

Although many general conditionals are not causal, all causal conditionals are general, in our view. Consequently, if we are able to show that a causal conditional is false just by virtue of its being a general conditional, we will have refuted it. This will serve our purposes well, for in what follows we will be largely concerned with finding reasons for *rejecting* causal generalizations.

It is important to weed out false causal generalizations, because they can create lots of trouble. Doctors used to think that bloodletting would cure disease. They killed many people in the process of trying to heal them. Thus, although we need causal generalizations for getting along in the world, we also need to get them right. We will be more likely to succeed if we have proper principles for testing and applying such generalizations.

In the past, very elaborate procedures have been developed for this purpose. The most famous set of such procedures was developed by John Stuart Mill and has come to be known as Mill's methods.[1] Though inspired by Mill's methods, the procedures introduced here involve some fundamental simplifications; whereas Mill introduced five methods, we will introduce only three primary rules.

The first two rules are the sufficient condition test (SCT) and the necessary condition test (NCT). We will introduce these tests first at an abstract level. One advantage of formulating these tests abstractly is so that they can be applied to other kinds of sufficient and necessary conditions, for example, those that arise in legal and moral reasoning, the topics of Chapters 18 and 19. Once it is clear how these tests work in general, we will apply them specifically to causal reasoning.

SUFFICIENT CONDITIONS AND NECESSARY CONDITIONS

To keep our discussion as general as possible, we will adopt the following definitions of sufficient conditions and necessary conditions:

> Feature F is a *sufficient* condition for feature G if and only if anything that *has* feature F also *has* feature G.

> Feature F is a *necessary* condition for feature G if and only if anything that *lacks* feature F also *lacks* feature G.

These definitions are equivalent to those in the previous section, because, if anything that *lacks* feature F also *lacks* feature G, then anything that *has* feature G must also *have* feature F; and if anything that *has* feature G must also *have* feature F, then anything that *lacks* feature F also *lacks* feature G. It follows that feature F is a sufficient condition for feature G if and only if feature G is a necessary condition for feature F.

When F is sufficient for G, the relation between these features can be diagrammed like this:

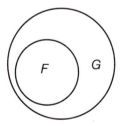

The inside circle represents the sufficient condition, because anything inside that inside circle must also be inside the outside circle. The outside circle represents the necessary condition, for anything outside the outside circle must also be outside the inside circle.

These diagrams, along with the preceding definitions, should make it clear that something can be a sufficient condition for a feature without being a necessary condition for that feature, and vice versa. For example, being the element mercury is a *sufficient* condition for being a metal, but it is not a *necessary* condition for being a metal, since there are other metals. Similarly, being a metal is a *necessary* condition for being mercury, but it is not a *sufficient* condition for being mercury. Of course, some necessary conditions are also sufficient conditions. Being mercury is both necessary and sufficient for being a metallic element that is liquid at twenty degrees Centigrade. Nonetheless, many necessary conditions are not sufficient conditions, and vice versa, so we need to be careful not to confuse the two kinds of conditions.

This distinction becomes complicated when conditions get complex. Our definitions and tests hold for all features, whether positive or negative (such as not having hair) and whether simple or conjunctive (such as having both a beard and a mustache) or disjunctive (such as having either a beard or a mustache). Thus, not having any hair (anywhere) on your head is a sufficient condition of not having a beard, so not having a beard is a necessary condition of not having any hair on your head. But not having any hair on your head is not necessary for not having a beard, because you can have some hair on the top of your head without having a beard. Negation can create confusion, so we need to think carefully about what is being claimed to be necessary or sufficient for what.

Even in simple cases without negation, conjunction, or disjunction, there is a widespread tendency to confuse necessary conditions with sufficient conditions. It is important to keep these concepts straight, for, as we will see, the tests concerning them are fundamentally different.

EXERCISE I

Which of the following claims are true? Which are false?

1. Being a car is a sufficient condition for being a vehicle.
2. Being a car is a necessary condition for being a vehicle.
3. Being a vehicle is a sufficient condition for being a car.
4. Being a vehicle is a necessary condition for being a car.
5. Being an integer is a sufficient condition for being an even number.
6. Being an integer is a necessary condition for being an even number.
7. Being an integer is a sufficient condition for being either an even number or an odd number.
8. Being an integer is a necessary condition for being either an even number or an odd number.
9. Not being an integer is a sufficient condition for not being an odd number.
10. Not being an integer is a sufficient condition for not being an even number.
11. Being both an integer and divisible by 2 without remainder is a sufficient condition for being an even number.

12. Being both an integer and divisible by 2 without remainder is a necessary condition for being an even number.

13. Being an integer divisible by 2 without remainder is a necessary condition for being an even number.

14. Driving seventy-five miles per hour (for fun) is a sufficient condition for violating a legal speed limit of sixty-five miles per hour.

15. Driving seventy-five miles per hour (for fun) is a necessary condition for violating a legal speed limit of sixty-five miles per hour.

16. Cutting off Joe's head is a sufficient condition for killing him.

17. Cutting off Joe's head is a necessary condition for killing him.

18. Cutting off Joe's head and then holding his head under water for ten minutes is a sufficient condition for killing him.

EXERCISE II

Indicate whether the following principles are true or false and why.

1. If having feature F is a *sufficient* condition for having feature G, then having feature G is a *necessary* condition for having feature F.

2. If having feature F is a *sufficient* condition for having feature G, then lacking feature F is a *necessary* condition for lacking feature G.

3. If lacking feature F is a *sufficient* condition for having feature G, then having feature F is a *necessary* condition for lacking feature G.

4. If lacking feature F is a *sufficient* condition for having feature G, then lacking feature F is a *necessary* condition for having feature G.

5. If having either feature F or feature G is a *sufficient* condition for having feature H, then having feature F is a *sufficient* condition for having feature H.

6. If having either feature F or feature G is a *sufficient* condition for having feature H, then having feature G is a *sufficient* condition for having feature H.

7. If having either feature F or feature G is a *sufficient* condition for having feature H, then not having feature F is a *necessary* condition for not having feature H.

8. If having both feature F and feature G is a *necessary* condition for having feature H, then lacking feature F is a *sufficient* condition for lacking feature H.

9. If not having both feature F and feature G is a *sufficient* condition for having feature H, then lacking feature F is a *sufficient* condition for having feature H.

10. If having either feature F or feature G is a *sufficient* condition for having feature H, then having both feature F and feature G is a *sufficient* condition for having feature H.

THE SUFFICIENT CONDITION TEST

We can now formulate tests to determine when something meets our definitions of sufficient conditions and necessary conditions. It will simplify matters if we first state these tests formally using letters. We will also begin with a simple case where we consider only four *candidates*—A, B, C, and D—for sufficient conditions for a *target* feature, G. A will indicate that the feature is present; ~A will indicate that this feature is absent. Using these conventions, suppose that we are trying to decide whether any of the four features—A, B, C, or D—could be a sufficient condition for G. To this end, we collect data of the following kind:

TABLE 1

Case 1:	A	B	C	D	G
Case 2:	~A	B	C	~D	~G
Case 3:	A	~B	~C	~D	~G

We know by definition that, for something to be a sufficient condition of something else, when the former is present, the latter must be present as well. Thus, to test whether a candidate really is a sufficient condition of G, we only have to examine cases in which the target feature, G, is absent, and then check to see whether any of the candidate features are present. The sufficient condition test (SCT) can be stated as follows:

SCT: Any candidate that is present when G is absent is eliminated as a possible sufficient condition of G.

The test applies to Table 1 as follows: Case 1 need not be examined because G is present, so there can be no violation of SCT in Case 1. Case 2 eliminates two of the candidates, B and C, for both are present in a situation in which G is absent. Finally, Case 3 eliminates A for the same reason. We are thus left with D as our only remaining candidate for a sufficient condition for G.

Now let's consider feature D. Having survived the application of the SCT, does it follow that D is a sufficient condition for G? No! On the basis of what we have been told so far, it remains entirely possible that the discovery of a further case will reveal an instance where D is present and G absent, thus showing that D is also not a sufficient condition for G.

Case 4:	~A	B	C	D	~G

In this way, it is always possible for new cases to refute any inference from a limited group of cases to the conclusion that a certain candidate is a sufficient condition. In contrast, no further case can change the fact that A, B, and C are not sufficient conditions, because they fail the SCT.

This observation shows that, when we apply the SCT to rule out a candidate as a sufficient condition, our argument is *deductive*. We simply find a counterexample to the universal claim that a certain feature is sufficient. (See Chapter 17 on counterexamples.) However, when a candidate is not ruled out and we draw the positive conclusion that that candidate *is* a sufficient condition, then our argument is *inductive.* Inductive inferences, however well confirmed, are always defeasible. (Recall Captain Cook's discovery of black swans at the start of Chapter 8.) That is why our inductive inference to the conclusion that *D* is a sufficient condition could be refuted by the new data in Case 4.

THE NECESSARY CONDITION TEST

The necessary condition test (NCT) is like the SCT, but it works in the reverse fashion. With SCT we eliminated a candidate *F* from being the sufficient condition for *G*, if *F* was ever present when *G* was absent. With the necessary condition test, we eliminate a candidate *F* from being a necessary condition for *G* if we can find a case where *G* is present, but *F* is not. This makes sense, because if *G* can be present when *F* is not, then *F* cannot be necessary for the occurrence of *G*. Thus, in applying the necessary condition test, we only have to examine cases in which the target feature, *G*, is present, and then check to see whether any of the candidate features are absent.

> **NCT:** Any candidate that is absent when *G* is present is eliminated as a possible necessary condition of *G*.

The following table gives an example of an application of this test:

TABLE 2

Case 1:	*A*	*B*	*C*	*D*	~*G*
Case 2:	~*A*	*B*	*C*	*D*	*G*
Case 3:	*A*	~*B*	*C*	~*D*	*G*

Because Case 1 does not provide an instance where *G* is present, it cannot eliminate any candidate as a necessary condition of *G*. Case 2 eliminates *A* as a necessary condition of *G*, since it shows that *G* can be present without *A* being present. Case 3 then eliminates both *B* and *D*, leaving *C* as the only possible candidate for being a necessary condition for *G*.

From this, of course, it does not follow that *C is* a necessary condition for *G*, for, as always, new cases might eliminate it as well. The situation is the same as with the SCT. An argument for a negative conclusion that a candidate is not a necessary condition, because that candidate fails the NCT, is a deductive argument that cannot be overturned by any further cases. In contrast, an argument for a positive conclusion that a candidate is a necessary condition, because that candidate passes the NCT, is an inductive argument that can be overturned by a further case where this candidate fails the NCT. For example, suppose we find:

Case 4:	~*A*	~*B*	~*C*	~*D*	*G*

The information in this new Case 4 is enough to show that *C* cannot be a necessary condition of the target feature *G*, regardless of what we found in Cases 1–3.

In applying both the SCT and the NCT, it is crucial to specify the target feature. Case 4 shows that candidate *C* is not a necessary condition for target feature *G*. Nonetheless, candidate *C* still might be necessary for the opposite target feature, ~G. It also might be necessary for features A, B, and D. Nothing in Cases 1–4 rules out these possibilities. Thus, even after Case 4, we cannot say simply that C is not a necessary condition. Case 4 shows that candidate feature C is not a necessary conditions for target feature G, but C still might be necessary for something else. The same point applies to sufficient conditions as well. In Table 1, Case 2 ruled out the possibility that candidate feature B is sufficient for target feature G, but none of the cases in Table 1 show that B is not sufficient for target feature C. To avoid confusion, then, it is always important to specify the target feature when talking about what is or is not a necessary or sufficient condition.

THE JOINT TEST

It is also possible to apply these rules simultaneously in the search for possible conditions that are both sufficient and necessary. Any candidate cannot be both sufficient and necessary if it fails either the SCT or the NCT. In Table 2, C is the only possible necessary condition for G, and it is not also a possible sufficient condition for G, since C fails the SCT in Case 1, where C is present and G is absent. In Table 1, however, D is a possible sufficient condition of G, because D is never present when G is absent; and D might also be a necessary condition for G, since G is never present when D is absent. Thus, none of Cases 1–3 in Table 1 eliminates D as a candidate for a condition that is both sufficient and necessary for G. As before, this possibility still might be refuted by Case 4, so any inference to a positive conclusion that some candidate is a necessary and sufficient condition must be defeasible and, hence, inductive.

EXERCISE III

For each of the following tables determine

a. Which, if any, of the candidates—A, B, C, or D—is not eliminated by the *sufficient* condition test as a sufficient condition for target feature G?

b. Which, if any, of the candidates—A, B, C, or D—is not eliminated by the *necessary* condition test as a necessary condition for target feature G?

c. Which, if any, of the candidates—A, B, C, or D—is not eliminated by *either* test?

EXAMPLE:					
Case 1:	A	B	~C	D	~G
Case 2:	~A	B	C	D	G
Case 3:	A	~B	C	D	G

a. Only C passes the SCT.

b. Only C and D pass the NCT.

c. Only C passes both tests.

1. Case 1:	*A*	*B*	*C*	*D*	*G*
Case 2:	~*A*	*B*	~*C*	*D*	~*G*
Case 3:	*A*	~*B*	*C*	~*D*	*G*
2. Case 1:	*A*	*B*	*C*	~*D*	*G*
Case 2:	~*A*	*B*	*C*	*D*	*G*
Case 3:	*A*	~*B*	*C*	~*D*	*G*
3. Case 1:	*A*	*B*	*C*	*D*	~*G*
Case 2:	~*A*	*B*	*C*	*D*	*G*
Case 3:	*A*	~*B*	*C*	~*D*	*G*
4. Case 1:	*A*	*B*	~*C*	*D*	*G*
Case 2:	~*A*	~*B*	*C*	*D*	*G*
Case 3:	*A*	*B*	~*C*	~*D*	~*G*
5. Case 1:	*A*	~*B*	*C*	*D*	~*G*
Case 2:	~*A*	*B*	*C*	~*D*	~*G*
Case 3:	*A*	~*B*	~*C*	*D*	*G*
6. Case 1:	*A*	*B*	~*C*	*D*	*G*
Case 2:	~*A*	~*B*	*C*	*D*	~*G*
Case 3:	*A*	~*B*	*C*	~*D*	~*G*
7. Case 1:	*A*	*B*	~*C*	*D*	~*G*
Case 2:	~*A*	*B*	~*C*	*D*	~*G*
Case 3:	*A*	*B*	~*C*	~*D*	~*G*
8. Case 1:	*A*	*B*	*C*	*D*	~*G*
Case 2:	~*A*	~*B*	*C*	*D*	*G*
Case 3:	*A*	~*B*	~*C*	~*D*	~*G*

EXERCISE IV

Imagine that your desktop computer system won't work, and you want to find out why. After checking to make sure that it is plugged in, you experiment with a new central processing unit (CPU), a new monitor (MON), and new system software (SSW) in the combinations on the table below. The candidates for necessary conditions and sufficient conditions of failure are the plug position (in or out), the CPU (old or new), the monitor (old or new), and the software (old or new). For each candidate, say (1) which cases, if any, eliminate it as a sufficient condition of your computer's failure and (2) which cases, if any, eliminate it as a necessary condition of your computer's failure. Which candidates, if any, are not eliminated as a sufficient condition of failure? As a necessary condition of failure? Does it follow that these candidates are necessary conditions or sufficient conditions of failure? Why or why not?

(continued)

	Plug	CPU	Monitor	Software	Result
Case 1	In	Old CPU	Old MO	Old SW	~~Works~~ *Fails*
Case 2	In	Old CPU	Old MO	New SW	Works
Case 3	In	Old CPU	New MO	Old SW	Fails
Case 4	In	Old CPU	New MO	New SW	Works
Case 5	In	Old CPU	Old MO	Old SW	Works
Case 6	In	Old CPU	Old MO	New SW	Works
Case 7	In	Old CPU	New MO	Old SW	Fails
Case 8	In	Old CPU	New MO	New SW	Works
Case 9	In	New CPU	Old MO	Old SW	Fails
Case 10	In	New CPU	Old MO	New SW	Works
Case 11	In	New CPU	New MO	Old SW	Fails
Case 12	In	New CPU	New MO	New SW	Works

EXERCISE V

After a banquet, several diners get sick and die. You suspect that something they ate or drank caused their deaths. The following table records their meals and fates. The target feature is death. The candidates for necessary conditions and sufficient conditions of death are the soup, entrée, wine, and dessert. For each candidate, say (1) which cases, if any, eliminate it as a sufficient condition of death and (2) which cases, if any, eliminate it as a necessary condition of death. Which candidates, if any, are not eliminated as a sufficient condition of death? Which candidates, if any, are not eliminated as a necessary condition of death? Does it follow that these candidates are necessary conditions or sufficient conditions of death? Why or why not?

Diners	Soup	Entrée	Wine	Dessert	Result
Ann	Tomato	Chicken	White	Pie	Alive
Barney	Tomato	Fish	Red	Cake	Dead
Cathy	Tomato	Beef	Red	Ice Cream	Alive
Doug	Tomato	Beef	Red	Cake	Alive
Emily	Tomato	Fish	Red	Pie	Dead
Fred	Tomato	Fish	Red	Cake	Dead
Gertrude	Leek	Fish	White	Pie	Alive
Harold	Tomato	Beef	White	Cake	Alive
Irma	Leek	Fish	Red	Pie	Dead
Jack	Leek	Beef	Red	Ice Cream	Alive
Ken	Leek	Chicken	Red	Ice Cream	Alive
Leslie	Tomato	Chicken	White	Cake	Alive

RIGOROUS TESTING

Going back to Table 1, it is easy to see that candidates A, B, C, and D are not eliminated by the NCT as necessary conditions of target G, as G is present in only one case (Case 1) and A, B, C, and D are present there as well. So far, so good. But if we wanted to test these features more rigorously, it would be important to find more cases in which target G was present and see whether these candidates are also present and thus continue to survive the NCT.

The following table gives a more extreme example of nonrigorous testing:

TABLE 3

Case 1:	A	~B	C	D	G
Case 2:	A	~B	~C	~D	~G
Case 3:	A	~B	C	~D	~G
Case 4:	A	~B	~C	D	G

Here candidate feature A is eliminated by SCT (in Cases 2 and 3) but is not eliminated by NCT, so it is a possible necessary condition but not a possible sufficient condition for target feature G. B is not eliminated by SCT but is eliminated by NCT (in Cases 1 and 4), so it is a possible sufficient condition but not a possible necessary condition for target feature G. C is eliminated by both rules (in Cases 3 and 4). Only D is not eliminated by either test, so it is the only candidate for being both a necessary and a sufficient condition for G.

The peculiarity of this example is that candidate A is always present whether target G is present or not, and candidate B is always absent whether target G is absent or not. Now if something is always present, as A is, then it cannot possibly fail the NCT; for there cannot be a case where the target is present and the candidate is absent if the candidate is *always* present. If we want to test candidate A rigorously under the NCT, then we should try to find cases in which A is absent and then check to see whether G is absent as well.

In reverse fashion, but for similar reasons, if we want to test candidate B rigorously under the SCT, then we should try to find cases in which B is present and then check to see if G is present as well. If we restrict our attention to cases where B is always absent, as in Table 3, then B cannot possibly fail the SCT, but passing that test will be trivial for B and so will not even begin to show that B is a sufficient condition for G.

Now consider two more sets of data just like Table 2, except with regard to the target feature, G:

TABLE 4

Case 1:	A	B	C	D	G
Case 2:	~A	B	C	D	G
Case 3:	A	~B	C	~D	G

TABLE 5

Case 1:	A	B	C	D	~G
Case 2:	~A	B	C	D	~G
Case 3:	A	~B	C	~D	~G

Because G is present in all of the cases in Table 4, no candidate can be eliminated by the SCT as a sufficient condition for target feature G. This result is trivial, however. Table 4 does not provide rigorous testing for a sufficient condition of G, because our attention is restricted to a range of cases that is too narrow. Nothing could possibly be eliminated as a sufficient condition of G as long as G is always present.

Similarly, G is absent in all of the cases in Table 5, so no candidate can be eliminated by the NCT as a necessary condition of target feature G. Still, because this data is so limited, its failure to eliminate candidates does not even begin to show that anything is a necessary condition of G.

For both rules, then, rigorous testing involves seeking out cases in which failing the test is a live possibility. For the SCT, this requires looking both at cases in which the candidates are present and also at cases in which the target is absent. For the NCT, rigorous testing requires looking both at cases in which the candidates are absent and also at cases in which the target is present. Without cases like these, passing the tests is rather like a person bragging that he has never struck out when, in fact, he has never come up to bat.

REACHING POSITIVE CONCLUSIONS

Suppose that we performed rigorous testing on candidate C, and it passed the SCT with flying colors. Can we now draw the positive conclusion that C is a sufficient condition for the target G? That depends on which kinds of candidates and cases have been considered. Since rigorous testing was passed, these three conditions are met:

1. We have tested some cases in which the candidate, C, is present.
2. We have tested some cases in which the target, G, is absent.
3. We have not found any case in which the candidate, C, is present and the target, G, is absent.

For it to be reasonable to reach a positive conclusion that C is sufficient for G, this further condition must also be met:

4. We have tested enough cases of the various kinds that are likely to include a case in which C is present and G is absent if there is any such case.

This new condition cannot be applied in the mechanical way that conditions 1–3 could be applied. To determine whether condition 4 is met, we need to rely on *background information* about how many cases are "enough" and about which kinds of cases "are likely to include a case in which C is present and G is absent, if there is any such case." For example, if we are trying to figure out whether our new software is causing our computer to crash, we do not need to try the same kind of computer in different colors. What we need to try are different kinds of CPUs, monitors, software, and so on, because we know that these are the kinds of factors that can affect performance. Background information like this is what tells us when we have tested enough cases of the right kinds.

Of course, our background assumptions might turn out to be wrong. Even if we have tested many variations of every feature that we think might be relevant, we still might be surprised and find a further case in which C and $\sim G$ are present. All that shows, however, is that our inference is defeasible, like all inductive arguments. Despite the possibility that future discoveries might undermine it, our inductive inference can still be strong if our background beliefs are justified and if we have looked long and hard without finding any case in which C is present and G is absent.

Similar rules apply in reverse to positive conclusions about necessary conditions. We have good reason to suppose that candidate C is a necessary condition for target G, if the following conditions are met:

1. We have tested some cases in which the candidate, C, is absent.
2. We have tested some cases in which the target, G, is present.
3. We have not found any case in which the candidate, C, is absent and the target, G, is present.
4. We have tested enough cases of the various kinds that are likely to include a case in which C is absent and G is present, if there is any such case.

This argument again depends on background assumptions in determining whether condition 4 is met. This argument is also defeasible, as before. Nonetheless, if our background assumptions are justified, the fact that conditions 1–4 are all met can still provide a strong reason for the positive conclusion that candidate C is a necessary condition for target G.

The SCT and NCT themselves are still negative and deductive; but that does not make them better than the positive tests encapsulated in conditions 1–4. The negative SCT and NCT are of no use when we need to argue that some condition *is* sufficient or *is* necessary. Such positive conclusions can be reached only by applying something like condition 4, which will require background information. These inductive arguments might not be as clear-cut or secure as the negative ones, but they can still be inductively strong under the right circumstances. That is all they claim to be.

APPLYING THESE METHODS TO FIND CAUSES

In stating the SCT and NCT and applying these tests to abstract patterns of conditions to eliminate candidates, our procedure was fairly mechanical. We cannot be so mechanical when we try to reach positive conclusions that certain conditions are necessary, sufficient, or both. Applying these rules to actual concrete situations introduces a number of further complications, especially when using our tests to determine causes.

NORMALITY

First, it is important to keep in mind that, in our ordinary understanding of causal conditions, we usually take it for granted that the setting is normal. It is part of common knowledge that if you strike a match, then it will light.

Thus, we consider striking a match sufficient to make it light. But if someone has filled the room with carbon dioxide, then the match will not light, no matter how it is struck. Here one may be inclined to say that, after all, striking a match is not sufficient to light it. We might try to be more careful and say that if a match is struck *and* the room is not filled with carbon dioxide, then it will light. But this new conditional overlooks other possibilities—for example, that the room has been filled with nitrogen, that the match has been fireproofed, that the wrong end of the match was struck, that the match has already been lit, and so forth. It now seems that the antecedent of our conditional will have to be endlessly long in order to specify a true or genuine sufficient condition. In fact, however, we usually feel quite happy with saying that if you strike a match, then it will light. We simply do not worry about the possibility that the room has been filled with carbon dioxide, the match has been fireproofed, and so on. Normally we think that things are normal, and give up this assumption only when some good reason appears for doing so.

These reflections suggest the following *contextualized* restatement of our original definitions of sufficient conditions and necessary conditions:

F is a sufficient condition for G if and only if, whenever F is present in a normal context, G is present there as well.

F is a necessary condition for G if and only if, whenever F is absent from a normal context, G is absent from it as well.

What will count as a normal context will vary with the type and the aim of an investigation, but all investigations into causally sufficient conditions and causally necessary conditions take place against the background of many factors that are taken as fixed.

BACKGROUND ASSUMPTIONS

If we are going to subject a causal hypothesis to rigorous testing with the SCT and the NCT, we have to seek out a wide range of cases that might refute that hypothesis. In general, the wider the range of possible refuters the better. Still, some limit must be put on this activity or else testing will get hopelessly bogged down. If we are testing a drug to see whether it will cure a disease, we should try it on a variety of people of various ages, medical histories, body types, and so on, but we will not check to see whether it works on people named Edmund or check to see whether it works on people who drive Volvos. Such factors, we want to say, are plainly irrelevant. But what makes them irrelevant? How do we distinguish relevant from irrelevant considerations?

The answer to this question is that our reasoning about causes occurs within a framework of beliefs that we take to be established as true. This framework contains a great deal of what is called *common knowledge*—knowledge we expect almost every sane adult to possess. We all know, for example, that human beings cannot breathe underwater, cannot walk through walls, cannot be in two places at once, and so on. The stock of these commonplace beliefs is almost endless. Because they are commonplace beliefs, they tend not to be mentioned; yet they play an important role in distinguishing relevant factors from irrelevant ones.

Specialized knowledge also contains its own principles that are largely taken for granted by experts. Doctors, for example, know a great deal about the detailed structure of the human body, and this background knowledge constantly guides their thought in dealing with specific illnesses. Even if someone claimed to discover that blood does not circulate, no doctor would take the time to refute that claim.

It might seem close-minded to refuse to consider a possibility that someone else suggests. However, giving up our basic beliefs can be very costly. A doctor who took seriously the suggestion that blood does not circulate, for example, would have to abandon our whole way of viewing humans and other animals, along with the rest of biology and science. It is not clear how this doctor could go on practicing medicine. Moreover, there is usually no practical alternative in real life. When faced with time pressure and limited information, we have no way to judge new ideas without taking some background assumptions for granted.

A DETAILED EXAMPLE

To get a clearer idea of the complex interplay between our tests and the reliance on background information, it will be helpful to look in some detail at actual applications of these tests. For this purpose, we will examine an attempt to find the cause of a particular phenomenon, an outbreak of what came to be known as Legionnaires' disease. The example not only shows how causal reasoning relies on background assumptions, it has another interesting feature as well: In the process of discovering the cause of Legionnaires' disease, the investigators were forced to *abandon* what was previously taken to be a well-established causal generalization. In fact, until it was discarded, this false background principle gave them no end of trouble.

The story began at an otherwise boring convention:

> The 58th convention of the American Legion's Pennsylvania Department was held at the Bellevue-Stratford Hotel in Philadelphia from July 21 through 24, 1976. . . . Between July 22 and August 3, 149 of the conventioneers developed what appeared to be the same puzzling illness, characterized by fever, coughing and pneumonia. This, however, was an unusual, explosive outbreak of pneumonia with no apparent cause. . . . Legionnaires' disease, as the illness was quickly named by the press, was to prove a formidable challenge to epidemiologists and laboratory investigators alike.[2]

Notice that at this stage the researchers begin with the assumption that they are dealing with a single illness and not a collection of similar but different illnesses. That assumption could turn out to be wrong; but, if the symptoms of the various patients are sufficiently similar, this is a natural starting assumption. Another reasonable starting assumption is that this illness had a single causative agent. This assumption, too, could turn out to be false, though it did not. The assumption that they were dealing with a single disease with a single cause was at least a good simplifying assumption, one to be held onto until there was good reason to give it up. In any case, we now have a clear specification of our target feature, *G:* the occurrence of a carefully described illness that came to be known as Legionnaires' disease. The situation concerning it was puzzling because people had contracted a disease with symptoms much like those of pneumonia, yet they had not tested positive for any of the known agents that cause such diseases.

The narrative continues as follows:

> The initial step in the investigation of any epidemic is to determine the character of the illness, who has become ill and just where and when. The next step is to find out what was unique about the people who became ill: where they were and what they did that was different from other people who stayed well. Knowing such things may indicate how the disease agent was spread and thereby suggest the identity of the agent and where it came from.

Part of this procedure involves a straightforward application of the NCT: Was there any interesting feature that was always present in the history of people who came down with the illness? Progress was made almost at once on this front:

> We quickly learned that the illness was not confined to Legionnaires. An additional 72 cases were discovered among people who had not been directly associated with the convention. They had one thing in common with the sick conventioneers: for one reason or another they had been in or near the Bellevue-Stratford Hotel.

Strictly speaking, of course, all these people who had contracted the disease had more than one thing in common. They were, for example, all alive at the time they were in Philadelphia, and being alive is, in fact, a necessary condition for getting Legionnaires' disease. But the researchers were not interested in this necessary condition because it is a normal background condition for the contraction of any disease. Furthermore, it did not provide a condition that distinguished those who contracted the disease from those who did not. The overwhelming majority of people who were alive at the time did not contract Legionnaires' disease. Thus, the researchers were not interested in this necessary condition because it would fail so badly when tested by the SCT as a sufficient condition. On the basis of common knowledge and specialized medical knowledge, a great many other conditions were also kept off the candidate list.

One prime candidate on the list was presence at the Bellevue-Stratford Hotel. The application of the NCT to this candidate was straightforward. Everyone who had contracted the disease had spent time in or near that hotel. Thus, presence at the Bellevue-Stratford could not be eliminated as a necessary condition of Legionnaires' disease.

The application of the SCT was more complicated, because not everyone who stayed at the Bellevue-Stratford contracted the disease. Other factors made a difference: "Older conventioneers had been affected at a higher rate than younger ones, men at three times the rate for women." Since some young women (among others) who were present at the Bellevue-Stratford did not get Legionnaires' disease, presence at that hotel could be eliminated as a sufficient condition of Legionnaires' disease. Nonetheless, it is part of medical background knowledge that susceptibility to disease often varies with age and gender. Given these differences, some people who spent time at the Bellevue-Stratford were at higher risk for contracting the disease than others. The investigation so far suggested that, for some people, being at the Bellevue-Stratford was connected with a sufficient condition for contracting Legionnaires' disease. Indeed, the conjunction of spending time at the Bellevue-Stratford and being susceptible to the disease could not be ruled out by the SCT as a sufficient condition of getting the disease.

As soon as spending time at the Bellevue-Stratford became the focus of attention, other hypotheses naturally suggested themselves. Food poisoning was a reasonable suggestion, since it is part of medical knowledge that diseases are sometimes spread by food. It was put on the list of possible candidates, but failed. Investigators checked each local restaurant and each function where food and drink were served. Some of the people who ate in each place did not get Legionnaires' disease, so the food at these locations was eliminated by the SCT as a sufficient condition of Legionnaires' disease. These candidates were also eliminated by the NCT as necessary conditions because some people who did get Legionnaires' disease did not eat at each of these restaurants and functions. Thus, the food and drink could not be the cause.

Further investigation turned up another important clue to the cause of the illness.

> Certain observations suggested that the disease might have been spread through the air. Legionnaires who became ill had spent on the average about 60 percent more time in the lobby of the Bellevue-Stratford than those who remained well; the sick Legionnaires had also spent more time on the sidewalk in front of the hotel than their unaffected fellow conventioneers. . . . It appeared, therefore, that the most likely mode of transmission was airborne.

Merely breathing air in the lobby of the Bellevue-Stratford Hotel still could not be a necessary or sufficient condition, but the investigators reasoned that something in the lobby air probably caused Legionnaires' disease, since the rate of the disease varied up or down in proportion to the time spent in the lobby (or near it on the sidewalk in front). This is an application of the method of concomitant variation, which will be discussed soon.

Now that the focus was on the lobby air, the next step was to pinpoint a specific cause in that air. Again appealing to background medical knowledge, there seemed to be three main candidates for the airborne agents that could have caused the illness: "heavy metals, toxic organic substances, and infectious organisms." Examination of tissues taken from patients who had died from the disease revealed "no unusual levels of metallic or toxic organic substances that might be related to the epidemic," so this left an infectious organism as the remaining candidate. Once more we have an application of NCT. If the disease had been caused by heavy metals or toxic organic substances, then there would have been unusually high levels of these substances in the tissues of those who had contracted the disease. Because this was not always so, these candidates were eliminated as necessary conditions of the disease.

Appealing to background knowledge once more, it seemed that a bacterium would be the most likely source of an airborne disease with the symptoms of Legionnaires' disease. But researchers had already made a routine check for bacteria that cause pneumonia-like diseases, and they had found none. For this reason, attention was directed to the possibility that some previously unknown organism had been responsible but had somehow escaped detection.

It turned out that an undetected and previously unknown bacterium *had* caused the illness, but it took more than four months to find this out. The difficulties encountered in this effort show another important fact about the reliance on a background assumption: Sometimes it turns out to be false. To simplify, the standard way to test for the presence of bacteria is to try to grow them in culture dishes—flat dishes containing nutrients that bacteria can live on. If, after a reasonable number of tries, a colony of a particular kind of bacterium does not appear, then it is concluded that the bacterium is not present. As it turned out, the bacterium that caused Legionnaires' disease would not grow in the cultures commonly used to detect the presence of bacteria. Thus, an important background assumption turned out to be false.

After a great deal of work, a suspicious bacterium was detected using a live-tissue culture rather than the standard synthetic culture. The task, then, was to show that this particular bacterium in fact caused the disease. Again to simplify, when people are infected by a particular organism, they often develop antibodies that are specifically aimed at this organism. In the case of Legionnaires' disease, these antibodies were easier to detect than the bacterium itself. They also remained in the patients' bodies after the infection had run its course. We thus have another chance to apply the NCT: If Legionnaires' disease was caused by this particular bacterium, then whenever the disease was present, this antibody should be present as well. The suspicious bacterium passed this test with flying colors and was named, appropriately enough, *Legionella pneumophila*. Because the investigators had worked so hard to test such a wide variety of candidates, they assumed that the disease must have some cause among the candidates that they checked. So, since only one candidate remained, they felt justified in reaching a positive conclusion that the bacterium was a necessary condition of Legionnaires' disease.

The story of the search for the cause of Legionnaires' disease brings out two important features of the use of inductive methods in the sciences. First, it involves a complicated interplay between what is already established and what is being tested. Confronted with a new problem, established principles can be used to suggest theoretically significant hypotheses to be tested. The tests then eliminate some hypotheses and leave others. If, at the end of the

investigation, a survivor remains that fits in well with our previously established principles, then the stock of established principles is increased. The
second thing that this example shows is that the inductive method is fallible.
Without the background of established principles, the application of inductive principles like the NCT and the SCT would be undirected; yet sometimes
these established principles let us down, for they can turn out to be false. The
discovery of the false background principle that hindered the search for
the cause of Legionnaires' disease led to important revisions in laboratory
techniques. The discovery that certain fundamental background principles
are false can lead to revolutionary changes in science. (See Chapter 20.)

CALLING THINGS CAUSES

After their research was finally completed, with the bacterium identified,
described, and named, it was then said that *Legionella pneumophila* was the
cause of Legionnaires' disease. What was meant by this? To simplify a bit,
suppose *L. pneumophila* (as it is abbreviated) entered the bodies of *all* those
who contracted the disease: Whenever the disease was present, *L. pneumophila*
was present. Thus, *L. pneumophila* passes the NCT for the disease. We will
further suppose, as is common in bacterial infections, that some people's
immune systems were successful in combating *L. pneumophila,* and they
never actually developed the disease. Thus, the presence of *L. pneumophila*
would not pass the SCT for the disease. This suggests that we sometimes call
something a cause of an effect if it passes the NCT for that effect, even if it
does not pass the SCT for that effect.

But even if we sometimes consider necessary conditions to be causes, we
certainly do not consider *all* necessary conditions to be causes. We have already
noted that to get Legionnaires' disease, one has to be alive, yet no one thinks
that being alive is the cause of Legionnaires' disease. To cite another example,
this time one that is not silly, it might be that another necessary condition for developing Legionnaires' disease is that the person be in a run-down condition—
healthy people might always be able to resist *L. pneumophila.* Do we then want
to say that being in a run-down condition is the cause of Legionnaires' disease?
As we have described the situation, almost certainly not, but we might want to
say that it is an important *causal factor* or *causally relevant factor.*

Although the matter is far from clear, what we call *the* cause rather than simply *a* causal factor or causally relevant factor seems to depend on a number of
considerations. We tend to reserve the expression "the cause" for *changes* that
occur prior to the effect, and describe *permanent* or *standing* features of the context as "causal factors" instead. That is how we speak about Legionnaires' disease. Being exposed to *L. pneumophila,* which was a specific event that occurred
before the onset of the disease, *caused it.* Being in a run-down condition, which
was a feature that patients possessed for some time before they contracted the
disease, was not called the cause, but instead called a causal factor.

It is not clear, however, that we always draw the distinction between
what we call the cause and what we call a causal factor based on whether

something is a prior event or a standing condition. For example, if we are trying to explain why certain people who came in contact with *L. pneumophila* contracted the disease whereas others did not, then we might say that the former group contracted the disease because they were in a run-down condition. Thus, by limiting our investigation only to those who came in contact with *L. pneumophila,* our perspective has changed. We want to know why some within that group contracted the disease and others did not. Citing the run-down condition of those who contracted the disease as the cause now seems entirely natural. These examples suggest that we call something *the* cause when it plays a particularly important role relative to the purposes of our investigation. Usually this will be an event or change taking place against the background of fixed necessary conditions; sometimes it will not.

Sometimes we call *sufficient* conditions causes. We say that short circuits cause fires because in many normal contexts, a short circuit is sufficient to cause a fire. Of course, short circuits are not necessary to cause a fire, because, in the same normal contexts, fires can be caused by a great many other things. With sufficient conditions, as with necessary conditions, we often draw a distinction between what we call the cause as opposed to what we call a causal factor, and we seem to draw it along similar lines. Speaking loosely, we might say that we sometimes call the *key* components of sufficient conditions *causes.* Then, holding background conditions fixed, we can use the SCT to evaluate such causal claims.

In sum, we can use the NCT to eliminate proposed necessary causal conditions. We can use the SCT to eliminate proposed sufficient causal conditions. Those candidates that survive these tests may be called causal conditions or causal factors if they fit in well with our system of other causal generalizations. Finally, some of these causal conditions or causal factors will be called causes if they play a key role in our causal investigations. Typically, though not always, we call something the cause of an event if it is a prior event or change that stands out against the background of fixed conditions.

▸ DISCUSSION QUESTION ◂

Reread the passage on what killed the dinosaurs in the Discussion Question at the end of Chapter 1. Where do the authors use the NCT? Where do they use the SCT? Where do they rely on background assumptions?

CONCOMITANT VARIATION

The use of the sufficient condition test and the necessary condition test depends on certain features of the world being sometimes present and sometimes absent. Some features of the world, however, are always present to

some degree. Because they are always present, the NCT will never eliminate them as possible necessary conditions of any event, and the SCT will
never eliminate anything as a sufficient condition for them. Yet the *extent*
or *degree* to which a feature exists in the world is often a significant phenomenon that demands causal explanation.

An example should make this clear. In recent decades, a controversy has
raged over the impact of acid rain on the environment of the northeastern
United States and Canada. Part of the controversy involves the proper interpretation of the data that have been collected. The controversy has arisen for
the following reason: The atmosphere always contains a certain amount of
acid, much of it from natural sources. It is also known that an excess of acid in
the environment can have severe effects on both plants and animals. Lakes are
particularly vulnerable to the effects of acid rain. Finally, it is also acknowledged that industries, mostly in the Midwest, discharge large quantities of
sulfur dioxide (SO_2) into the air, and this increases the acidity of water in the
atmosphere. The question—and here the controversy begins—is whether the
contribution of acid from these industries is the cause of the environmental
damage downwind of them.

How can we settle such a dispute? The two rules we have introduced provide no immediate help, for, as we have seen, they provide a rigorous test of a
causal hypothesis only when we can find contrasting cases with the presence
or the absence of a given feature. The NCT provides a rigorous test for a necessary condition only if we can find cases in which the feature does not occur
and then check to make sure that the target feature does not occur either. The
SCT provides a rigorous test for a sufficient condition only when we can find
cases in which the target phenomenon is absent and then check whether the
candidate sufficient condition is absent as well. In this case, however, neither
check applies, for there is always a certain amount of acid in the atmosphere,
so it is not possible to check what happens when atmospheric acid is completely absent. Similarly, environmental damage, which is the target phenomenon under investigation, is so widespread in our modern industrial society
that it is also hard to find a case in which it is completely absent.

So, if there is always acid in the atmosphere, and environmental damage
always exists at least to some extent, how can we determine whether the SO_2
released into the atmosphere is *significantly* responsible for the environmental
damage in the affected areas? Here we use what John Stuart Mill called the
Method of Concomitant Variation. We ask whether the amount of environmental
damage varies directly in proportion to the amount of SO_2 released into the
environment. If environmental damage increases with the amount of SO_2
released into the environment and drops when the amount of SO_2 is lowered,
this means that the level of SO_2 in the atmosphere is *positively correlated* with
environmental damage. We would then have good reason to believe that lowering SO_2 emissions would lower the level of environmental damage, at least
to some extent.

Arguments relying on the method of concomitant variation are difficult
to evaluate, especially when there is no generally accepted background

theory that makes sense of the concomitant variation. Some such variations are well understood. For example, most people know that the faster you drive, the more gasoline you consume. (Gasoline consumption varies *directly* with speed.) Why? There is a good theory here: It takes more energy to drive at a high speed than at a low speed, and this energy is derived from the gasoline consumed in the car's engine. Other correlations are less well understood. There seems to be a correlation between how much a woman smokes during pregnancy and how happy her children are when they reach age thirty. The correlation here is not nearly as good as the correlation between gasoline consumption and speed, for many people are very happy at age thirty even though their mothers smoked a lot during pregnancy, and many others are very unhappy at age thirty even though their mothers never smoked. Furthermore, no generally accepted background theory has been found to explain the correlation that does exist.

This reference to background theory is important, because two sets of phenomena can be correlated to a very high degree, even with no direct causal relationship between them. A favorite example that appears in many statistics texts is the discovered positive correlation in boys between foot size and quality of handwriting. It is hard to imagine a causal relation holding in either direction. Having big feet should not make you write better and, just as obviously, writing well should not give you big feet. The correct explanation is that both foot size and handwriting ability are positively correlated with age. Here a noncausal correlation between two phenomena (foot size and handwriting ability) is explained by a third common correlation (maturation) that *is* causal.

At times, it is possible to get causal correlations *backward.* For example, a few years ago, sports statisticians discovered a negative correlation between forward passes thrown and winning in football. That is, the more forward passes a team threw, the less chance it had of winning. This suggested that passing is not a good strategy, since the more you do it, the more likely you are to lose. Closer examination showed, however, that the causal relationship, in fact, went in the other direction. Toward the end of a game, losing teams tend to throw a great many passes in an effort to catch up. In other words, teams throw a lot of passes because they are losing, rather than the other way around.

Finally, some correlations seem inexplicable. For example, a strong positive correlation reportedly holds between the birth rate in Holland and the number of storks nesting in chimneys. There is, of course, a background theory that would explain this—storks bring babies—but that theory is not favored by modern science. For the lack of any better background theory, the phenomenon just seems weird.

So, given a strong correlation between phenomena of types *A* and *B*, four possibilities exist:

1. *A* is the cause of *B*.
2. *B* is the cause of *A*.

3. Some third thing is the cause of both.

4. The correlation is simply accidental.

Before we accept any one of these possibilities, we must have good reasons for preferring it over the other three.

One way to produce such a reason is to manipulate *A* or *B*. If we vary factor *A* up and down, but *B* does not change at all, this finding provides some reason against possibility 1, since *B* would normally change along with *A* if *A* did cause *B*. Similarly, if we manipulate *B* up and down, but *A* does not vary at all, this result provides some reason against alternative 2 and for the hypothesis that that *B* does not cause *A*. Together these manipulations can reduce the live options to items 3 and 4.

Many scientific experiments work this way. When scientists first discovered the correlation between smoking and lung cancer, some cigarette manufacturers responded that lung cancer might cause the desire to smoke or there might be a third cause of both smoking and lung cancer that explains the correlation. Possibly, it was suggested, smoking relieves discomfort due to early lung cancer or due to a third factor that itself causes lung cancer. To test these hypotheses, scientists manipulated the amount of smoking by lab animals. When all other factors were held as constant as possible, but smoking was increased, lung cancer increased; and when smoking went down, lung cancer went down. These results would not have occurred if some third factor had caused both smoking and lung cancer but remained stable as smoking was manipulated. The findings would also have been different if incipient lung cancer caused smoking, but had remained constant as scientists manipulated smoking levels. Such experiments can, thus, help us rule out at least some of the options 1–4.

Direct manipulation like this is not always possible or ethically permissible. The data would probably be more reliable if the test subjects were human beings rather than lab animals, but that is not an ethical option. Perhaps more complicated statistical methods could produce more reliable results, but they often require large amounts and special kinds of data. Such data is, unfortunately, often unavailable.

EXERCISE VI

In each of the following examples a strong correlation, either negative or positive, holds between two sets of phenomena, *A* and *B*. Try to decide whether *A* is the cause of *B*, *B* is the cause of *A*, both are caused by some third factor, *C*, or the correlation is simply accidental. Explain your choice.

1. For a particular United States president, there is a negative correlation between the number of hairs on his head (*A*) and the population of China (*B*).

(continued)

2. My son's height (A) increases along with the height of the tree outside my front door (B).

3. It has been claimed that there is a strong positive correlation between those students who take sex education courses (A) and those who contract venereal disease (B).

4. At one time there was a strong negative correlation between the number of mules in a state (A) and the salaries paid to professors at the state university (B). In other words, the more mules, the lower professional salaries.[3]

5. There is a high positive correlation between the number of fire engines in a particular borough in New York City (A) and the number of fires that occur there (B).[4]

6. "Washington (UPI)—Rural Americans with locked doors, watchdogs or guns may face as much risk of burglary as neighbors who leave doors unlocked, a federally financed study says. The study, financed in part by a three-year $170,000 grant from the Law Enforcement Assistance Administration, was based on a survey of nearly 900 families in rural Ohio. Sixty percent of the rural residents surveyed regularly locked doors [A], but were burglarized more often than residents who left doors unlocked [B]."[5]

7. The speed of a car (A) is exactly the same as the speed of its shadow (B).

8. The length of a runner's ring finger minus the length of the runner's index finger (A) is correlated with the runner's speed in the one-hundred-yard dash. (B)

DISCUSSION QUESTIONS

1. After it became beyond doubt that smoking is dangerous to people's health, a new debate arose concerning the possible health hazards of secondhand smoke on nonsmokers. Collect statements pro and con on this issue and evaluate the strength of the inductive arguments on each side.

2. The high positive correlation between CO_2 concentrations in the atmosphere and the Earth's mean surface temperatures is often cited as evidence that increases in atmospheric CO_2 cause global warming. This argument is illustrated by the famous "hockey stick" diagram in Al Gore's *An Inconvenient Truth*. Is this argument persuasive? How could skeptics about global warming respond?

3. In *Twilight of the Idols*, Nietzsche claims that the following examples illustrate "the error of mistaking cause for consequence." Do you agree? Why or why not?

Everyone knows the book of the celebrated Cornaro in which he recommends his meager diet as a recipe for a long and happy life—a virtuous one, too. . . . I do not doubt that hardly any book (the Bible rightly excepted) has done so much harm, has shortened so many lives, as this curiosity, which was so well meant.

The reason: mistaking the consequence for the cause. The worthy Italian saw in his diet the *cause* of his long life; while the prerequisite of long life, an extraordinarily slow metabolism, a small consumption, was the cause of his meager diet. He was not free to eat much *or* little as he chose, his frugality was *not* an act of "free will": he became ill when he ate more. But if one is not a bony fellow of this sort one does not merely do well, one positively needs to eat *properly*. A scholar of *our day*, with his rapid consumption of nervous energy, would kill himself with Cornaro's regimen. . . .

Long life, a plentiful posterity is *not* the reward of virtue, virtue itself is rather just that slowing down of the metabolism which also has, among other things, a long life, a plentiful posterity, in short *Cornarism*, as its outcome.—The Church and morality say: "A race, a people perishes through vice and luxury." My *restored* reason says: when a people is perishing, degenerating physiologically, vice and luxury (that is to say the necessity for stronger and stronger and more and more frequent stimulants, such as every exhausted nature is acquainted with) *follow* therefrom. A young man grows prematurely pale and faded. His friends say: this and that illness is to blame. I say: *that* he became ill, *that* he failed to resist the illness, was already the consequence of an impoverished life, an hereditary exhaustion. The newspaper reader says: this party will ruin itself if it makes errors like this. My *higher* politics says: a party which makes errors like this is already finished—it is no longer secure in its instincts. Every error, of whatever kind, is a consequence of degeneration of instinct, degeneration of will: one has thereby virtually defined the *bad*. Everything *good* is instinct—and consequently easy, necessary, free. Effort is an objection, the *god* is typically distinguished from the hero (in my language: *light* feet are the first attribute of divinity).[6]

NOTES

[1] Mill's "methods of experimental inquiry" are found in book 3, chap. 8 of his *A System of Logic* (London: John W. Parker, 1843). Mill's method of difference, method of agreement, and joint method parallel our SCT, NCT, and Joint Test, respectively. Our simplification of Mill's methods derives from Brian Skyrms, *Choice and Chance*, 3rd ed. (Belmont, CA: Wadsworth, 1986), chap. 4.

[2] These excerpts are drawn from David W. Fraser and Joseph E. McDade, "Legionellosis," *Scientific American*, October 1979, 82–99.

[3] From Gregory A. Kimble, *How to Use (and Misuse) Statistics* (Englewood Cliffs, NJ: Prentice-Hall, 1978), 182.

[4] From Kimble, *How to Use (and Misuse) Statistics*, 182.

[5] "Locked Doors No Bar to Crime, Study Says," *Santa Barbara* [California] *Newspress*, Wednesday, February 16, 1977. This title suggests that locking your doors will not increase safety. Is that a reasonable lesson to draw from this study?

[6] Friedrich Nietzsche, *Twilight of the Idols* and *The Anti-Christ*, trans. R. J. Hollingdale (1889; Harmondsworth: Penguin, 1968), 47–48.

10

INFERENCE TO THE BEST
EXPLANATION AND FROM ANALOGY

Once we know the cause of a phenomenon, we can cite this cause in a premise of an argument whose purpose is to explain the phenomenon (as we saw in Chapter 1). Explanation and causation are also related in a different way, for explanations can be used to pick out the cause from among various conditions correlated with the phenomenon (a problem faced at the end of Chapter 9). The general strategy is then to cite the explanatory value of a causal hypothesis as evidence for that hypothesis. This form of argument, which is described as an inference to the best explanation, *is the first topic in this chapter. It requires us to determine which explanation is best, so we will investigate common standards for assessing explanations, including falsifiability, conservativeness, modesty, simplicity, power, and depth. After explaining these standards, this chapter will turn to a related form of argument called an* argument from analogy, *in which the fact that two things have certain features in common is taken as evidence that they have further features in common. The chapter ends by suggesting that many, or maybe even all, arguments from analogy are ultimately based on implicit inferences to the best explanation.*

INFERENCES TO THE BEST EXPLANATION

One of the most common forms of inductive argument is *inference to the best explanation.*[1] The general idea behind such inferences is that a hypothesis gains inductive support if, when added to our stock of previously accepted beliefs, it enables us to explain something that we observe or believe, and no competing explanation works nearly as well.

To see how inferences to the best explanation work, suppose you return to your home and discover that the lock on your front door is broken and some valuables are missing. In all likelihood, you will immediately conclude that you have been burglarized. Of course, other things *could* have produced the mess. Perhaps the police mistakenly busted into your house looking for drugs and took your valuables as evidence. Perhaps your friends are playing a strange joke on you. Perhaps a meteorite struck the door and then vaporized your valuables. In fact, all of these things *could* have happened (even the last), and further investigation could show that one of them did. Why, then, do we so quickly accept the burglary hypothesis without even considering these competing possibilities? The reason is that the hypothesis that your home was robbed is not highly improbable; and this hypothesis, together with other things we believe, provides the best—the strongest and the most natural— explanation of the phenomenon. The possibility that a meteorite struck your door is so wildly remote that it is not worth taking seriously. The possibility that your house was raided by mistake or that your friends are playing a strange practical joke on you is not wildly remote, but neither fits the overall facts very well. If it was a police raid, then you would expect to find a police officer there or at least a note. If it is a joke, then it is hard to see the point of it. By contrast, burglaries are not very unusual, and that hypothesis fits the facts extremely well. Logically, the situation looks like this:

(1) OBSERVATION: Your lock is broken, and your valuables are missing.
(2) EXPLANATION: The hypothesis that your house has been burglarized, combined with previously accepted facts and principles, provides a suitably strong explanation of observation 1.
(3) COMPARISON: No other hypothesis provides an explanation nearly as good as that in 2.

(4) CONCLUSION: Your house was burglarized.

The explanatory power of the conclusion gives us reason to believe it because doing so increases our ability to understand our observations and to make reliable predictions. Explanation is important because it makes sense out of things—makes them more intelligible—and we want to understand the world around us. Prediction is important because it tests our theories with new data and sometimes allows us to anticipate or even control future events. Inference to the best explanation enables us to achieve such goals.

Here it might help to compare inferences to the best explanation with other forms of argument. Prior to any belief about burglars, you were already *justified* in believing *that* your lock was broken and your valuables were missing. You could see that much. What you could not see was *why* your lock was broken. That question is what the explanation answers. Explanations help us understand why things happen, when we are already justified in believing those things did happen. (Recall Chapter 1.)

Explanations often take the form of arguments. In our example, we could argue:

(1) Your house was burglarized.
(2) When houses are burglarized, valuables are missing.
∴(3) Your valuables are missing.

This explanatory argument starts with the hypothesis that was the conclusion of the inference to the best explanation, and it ends with the observation that was the first premise in that inference to the best explanation. The difference is that this new argument *explains* why its conclusion is true—why the valuables are missing—whereas the inference to the best explanation *justified* belief in its conclusion that your house was burglarized.

More generally, in an explanatory use of argument, we try to make sense of something by deriving it (sometimes deductively) from premises that are themselves well established. With an inference to the best explanation, we reason in the opposite direction: Instead of deriving an observation from its explanation, we derive the explanation from the observation. That a hypothesis provides the best explanation of something whose truth is already known provides evidence for the truth of that hypothesis.

Once we grasp the notion of an inference to the best explanation, we can see this pattern of reasoning everywhere. If you see your friend kick the wall, you infer that he must be angry, because there is no other explanation of why he would kick the wall. Then if he turns away when you say, "Hello," you might think that he is angry *at you,* if you cannot imagine any other reason why he would not respond. Similarly, when your car goes dead right after a checkup (as at the start of Chapter 9), you may conclude that it is out of fuel, if that is the best explanation of why your car stopped. Psychologists infer that people care what others think about them, even when they deny it, because that explains why people behave differently in front of others than when they are alone. Linguists argue that the original Indo-European language arose millennia ago in an area that was not next to the sea but did have lakes and rivers, because that is the best explanation of why Indo-European languages have no common word for seas but do share a common root "nav-" that connotes boats or ships. Astronomers believe that our Universe began with a Big Bang, because that hypothesis best explains the background microwave radiation and spreading of galaxies. All of these arguments and many more are basically inferences to the best explanation.

Solutions to murder mysteries almost always have the form of an inference to the best explanation. The facts of the case are laid out and then the clever detective argues that, given these facts, only one person could possibly have committed the crime. In the story "Silver Blaze," Sherlock Holmes concludes that the trainer must have been the dastardly fellow who stole Silver Blaze, the horse favored to win the Wessex Cup, which was to be run the following day. Holmes's reasoning, as usual, was very complex, but the key part of his argument was that the dog kept in the stable did not bark loudly when someone came and took away the horse.

> I had grasped the significance of the silence of the dog, for one true inference invariably suggests others. [I knew that] a dog was kept in the stables, and yet, though someone had been in and fetched out a horse, he had not barked enough to arouse the two lads in the loft. Obviously the midnight visitor was someone whom the dog knew well.[2]

Together with other facts, this was enough to identify the trainer, Straker, as the person who stole Silver Blaze. In this case, it is the fact that something *didn't* occur that provides the basis for an inference to the best explanation.

Of course, Holmes's inference is not absolutely airtight. It is possible that Straker is innocent and Martians with hypnotic powers over dogs committed the crime. But that only goes to show that this inference is neither valid nor deductive in our sense. It does not show anything wrong with Holmes's inference. Since his inference is inductive, it is enough for it to be strong.

Inferences to the best explanation are also defeasible. No matter how strong such an inference might be, it can always be overturned by future experience. Holmes might later find traces of a sedative in the dog's blood or someone else might confess or provide Straker with an alibi. Alternatively, Holmes (or you) might think up some better explanation. Still, unless and until such new evidence or hypothesis comes along, we have adequate reason to believe that Straker stole the horse, because that hypothesis provides the best available explanation of the information that we have now. The fact that future evidence or hypotheses always might defeat inferences to the best explanation does not show that such inferences are all bad. If it did show this, then science and everyday life would be in trouble, because so much of science and our commonsense view of the world depends on inferences to the best explanation.

To assess such inferences, we still need some standards for determining which explanation is the *best*. There is, unfortunately, no simple rule for deciding this, but we can list some factors that go into the evaluation of an explanation.[3]

First, the hypothesis should really *explain the observations*. A good explanation makes sense out of that which it is intended to explain. In our original example, the broken lock can be explained by a burglary but not by the hypothesis that a friend came to see you (unless you have strange friends). Moreover, the hypothesis needs to explain *all* of the relevant observations. The hypothesis of a mistaken police raid might explain the broken lock but not the missing valuables or the lack of any note or police officers when you return home.

The explanation should also be *deep*. An explanation is not deep but shallow when the explanation itself needs to be explained. It does not help to explain something that is obscure by citing something just as obscure. Why did the police raid your house? Because they suspected you. That explanation is shallow if it immediately leads to another question: Why did they suspect you? Because they had the wrong address. If they did not have the wrong address, then we would wonder why they suspected you. Without an explanation of their suspicions, the police raid hypothesis could not adequately explain even the broken lock.

Third, the explanation should be *powerful*. It is a mark of excellence in an explanation that the same kind of explanation can be used successfully over a wide range of cases. Many broken locks can be explained by burglaries. Explanatory range is especially important in science. One of the main reasons why Einstein's theory of relativity replaced Newtonian physics is that Einstein could explain a wider range of phenomena, including very small particles at very high speeds.

Explanations go too far, however, when they could explain any possible event. Consider the hypothesis that each particle of matter has its own individual spirit that makes it do exactly what it does. This hypothesis might seem to explain some phenomena that even Einstein's theory cannot explain. But the spirit hypothesis really explains nothing, because it does not explain why any particle behaves one way as opposed to another. Either behavior is compatible with the hypothesis, so neither is explained. To succeed, therefore, explanations need to be incompatible with some possible outcome. In short, they need to be *falsifiable*. (See Chapter 16 on self-sealers.)

Moreover, explanations should be *modest* in the sense that they should not claim too much—indeed, any more than is needed to explain the observations. When you find your lock broken and valuables gone, you should not jump to the conclusion that there is a conspiracy against you or that gangs have taken over your neighborhood. Without further information, there is no need to specify that there was more than one burglar in order to explain what you see. There is also no need to hypothesize that there was only one burglar. For this reason, the most modest explanation would not specify any number of burglars, so no inference to the best explanation could justify any claim about the number of burglars, at least until more evidence comes along.

Modesty is related to *simplicity*. One kind of simplicity is captured by the celebrated principle known as Occam's razor, which tells us not to multiply entities beyond necessity. Physicists, for example, should not postulate new kinds of subatomic particles or forces unless there is no other way to explain their experimental results. Similar standards apply in everyday life. We should not believe in ghosts unless they really are necessary to explain the noises in our attic or some other phenomenon. Simplicity is not always a matter of new kinds of entities. In comparison with earlier views, the theory that gases are composed of particles too small to see was simpler insofar as the particle theory allowed gas laws to be explained by the standard physical principles governing the motions of larger particles without having to add any new laws. Simplicity is a mark of excellence in an explanation partly because simple explanations are easier to understand and apply, but considerations of plausibility and aesthetics are also at work in judgments of which explanation is simplest.

The tests of modesty and simplicity might seem to be in tension with the test of power. This tension can be resolved only by finding the right balance. The best explanation will not claim any more than is necessary (so it will be modest), but it will claim enough to cover a wide range of phenomena (so it will be powerful). This is tricky, but the best explanations succeed in reconciling and incorporating these conflicting virtues as much as possible.

Finally, an explanation should be *conservative*. Explanations are better when they force us to give up fewer well-established beliefs. We have strong reasons to believe that cats cannot break metal locks. This rules out the hypothesis that your neighbor's cat broke your front-door lock. Explanations should also not contain claims that are themselves too unlikely to be true. A meteorite would be strong enough to break your lock, but it is very unlikely that a meteorite struck your lock. That makes the burglary hypothesis better, at least until we find other evidence (such as meteorite fragments) that cannot be explained except by a meteorite.

In sum, a hypothesis provides the best explanation when it is more explanatory, powerful, falsifiable, modest, simple, and conservative than any competing hypothesis. Each of these standards can be met to varying degrees, and they can conflict. As we saw, the desire for simplicity might have to be sacrificed to gain a more powerful explanation. Conservatism also might have to give way to explain some unexpected observations, and so on. These standards are not always easy to apply, but they can often be used to determine whether a particular explanation is better than its competitors.

Once we determine that one explanation is the best, we still cannot yet infer that it is true. It might turn out that the best explanation out of a group of weak explanations isn't good enough. For centuries people were baffled by the floods that occurred in the Nile River each spring. The Nile, as far as anyone knew, flowed from an endless desert. Where, then, did the flood waters come from? Various wild explanations were suggested—mostly about deities of one kind or another—but none was any good. Looking for the best explanation among these weak explanations would be a waste of time. It was only after it was discovered that central Africa contains a high mountain range covered with snow in the winter that a reasonable explanation became possible. That, in fact, settled the matter. So it must be understood that the best explanation must also be a *good enough* explanation.

Even when an explanation is both good and best, what it explains might be illusory. Many people believe that shark cartilage prevents cancer, because the best explanation of why sharks do not get cancer lies in their cartilage. One serious problem for this inference is that sharks *do* get cancer. They even get cancer in their cartilage. So this inference to the best explanation fails.

When a particular explanation is both good and much better than any competitor, and when the explained observation is accurate, then an inference to the best explanation will provide *strong* inductive support. At other times, no clear winner or even reasonable contender emerges. In such cases, an inference to the best explanation will be correspondingly *weak*.

Whether an inference to the best explanation is strong *enough* depends on the context. As contexts shift, standards of rigor can change. Evidence that is strong enough to justify my belief that my spouse took our car might not be strong enough to convict our neighbor of stealing our car. Good judgment is often required to determine whether a certain degree of strength is adequate for the purposes at hand.

Context can also affect the rankings of various factors. Many explanations, for example, depend on universal premises. In such cases, compatibility with observation is usually the primary test. The universal principle should not be refuted by counterexamples (see Chapter 17). But sometimes explanatory power will take precedence: If a principle has strong explanatory power, we may accept it even in the face of clear disconfirming evidence. We do not give up good explanations lightly—nor should we. To understand why, recall (from Chapter 9) that we do not test single propositions in isolation from other propositions in our system of beliefs. When faced with counterevidence to our beliefs, we often have a choice between what to give up and what to continue to hold on to. A simple example will illustrate this. Suppose that we believe the following things:

(1) Either John or Joan committed the crime.
(2) Whoever committed the crime must have had a motive for doing so.
(3) Joan had no motive to commit the crime.

From these three premises we can validly infer that John committed the crime. Suppose, however, that we discover that John could not have committed the crime. (Three bishops and two judges swear that John was somewhere else at the time.) Now, from the fact that John did not commit the crime, we could not immediately conclude that Joan committed it, for that would lead to an inconsistency. If she committed the crime, then, according to premise 3, she would have committed a motiveless crime, but that conflicts with premise 2, which says that motiveless crimes do not occur. So the discovery that John did not commit the crime entails that at least one of the premises in the argument must be abandoned, but it does not tell us which one or which ones.

This same phenomenon occurs when we are dealing with counterevidence to a complex system of beliefs. Counterevidence shows that there must be something wrong somewhere in the system, but it does not show exactly where the problem lies. One possibility is that the *supposed* counterevidence is itself in error. Imagine that a student carries out an experiment and gets the result that one of the fundamental laws of physics is false. This will not shake the scientific community even a little, for the best explanation of the student's result is that she messed things up. Given well-established principles, she could not have gotten the result she did if she had run the experiment correctly. Of course, if a great many reputable scientists find difficulties with a supposed law, then the situation is different. The hypothesis that all of these scientists, like the student, simply messed up is itself highly unlikely. But it is surprising how much contrary evidence will be tolerated when dealing with a strong explanatory theory. Scientists often continue to employ a theory in the face of counterevidence. Sometimes this perpetuates errors. For years, instruments reported that the levels of ozone above Antarctica were lower than before, but scientists attributed these measurements to bad equipment, until finally they announced an ozone hole there. Still, there is often good reason to hold on to a useful theory despite counterevidence, as long as its defects do not make serious trouble—that is, give bad results in areas that count. Good judgment is required to determine when it is finally time to shift to a different explanation.

Imagine that you offer an explanation, and a critic responds in the following way. Which virtue (explanatoriness, depth, power, falsifiability, modesty, simplicity, or conservativeness) is your critic claiming that your explanation lacks?

1. But that won't explain anything other than this particular case.
2. But that conflicts with everything we know about biology.
3. But you don't have to claim all of that in order to explain what we see.
4. But that just raises new questions that you need to answer.
5. But that explains only a small part of the story.
6. But that would apply whatever happened.

For each of the following explanations, specify which standard of a good explanation, if any, it violates. The standards require that a good explanation be explanatory, deep, powerful, falsifiable, modest, simple, and conservative. A single explanation might violate more than one standard.

1. Although we usually have class at this time in this room, I don't see anybody in the classroom, because a wicked witch made them all invisible.
2. Although we usually have class at this time in this room, I don't see anybody in the classroom, because they all decided to skip class today.
3. Although we usually have class at this time in this room, I don't see anybody in the classroom, because it's Columbus Day.
4. My house fell down, because it was painted red.
5. My house fell down, because of a powerful earthquake centered on my property that did not affect anything or anybody else.
6. My house fell down, because its boards were struck by a new kind of sub-atomic particle.
7. Although I fished here all day, I didn't catch any fish, because there are no fish in this whole river.
8. Although I fished here all day, I didn't catch any fish, because the river gods don't like me.
9. Although I fished here all day, I didn't catch any fish, because I was unlucky today.
10. That light far up in the night sky is moving quickly, because it is the daily United Airlines flight from Boston to Los Angeles.
11. That light far up in the night sky is moving quickly, because it is an alien space ship.
12. That light far up in the night sky looks like it is moving quickly, because there's something wrong with my eyes right now.

EXERCISE III

Give two competing hypotheses that might be offered to explain each of the following phenomena. Which of these hypotheses is better? Why?

1. You follow a recipe carefully, but the bread never rises.
2. Your house begins to shake so violently that pictures fall off your walls.
3. Your key will not open the door of your house.
4. People start putting television cameras on your lawn, and a man with a big smile comes walking up your driveway.
5. Virtually all of the food in markets has suddenly sold out.
6. You put on a shirt and notice that there is no pocket on the front like there used to be.
7. A cave is found containing the bones of both prehistoric humans and now-extinct predators.
8. A cave is found containing the bones of both prehistoric humans and now-extinct herbivores.
9. After being visited by lobbyists for cigarette producers, your senator votes in favor of tobacco price supports, although he opposed them before.
10. Large, mysterious patterns of flattened wheat appear in the fields of Britain. (Some people attribute these patterns to visitors from another planet.)
11. A palm reader foretells that something wonderful will happen to you soon, and it does.
12. A neighbor sprinkles purple powder on his lawn to keep away tigers, and, sure enough, no tigers show up on his lawn.

DISCUSSION QUESTIONS

1. Put the following inference to the best explanation in standard form, and then evaluate it as carefully as you can, using the tests discussed above.

[During the Archean Era, which extended from about 3.8 to 2.5 million years before the present,] the sun's luminosity was perhaps 25% less than that of today. . . . This faint young sun has led to a paradox. There is no evidence from the scant rock record of the Archean that the planetary surface was frozen. However, if Earth had no atmosphere or an atmosphere of composition like that of today, the amount of radiant energy received by Earth from the sun would not be enough to keep it from freezing. The way out of this dilemma is to have an atmosphere present during the early Archean that was different in composition that that of today. . . . For a variety of reasons, it has been concluded, although still debated, that the most likely gases present in greater abundance in the Archean atmosphere were carbon dioxide, water vapor (the most important greenhouse gas) and perhaps methane. The presence of these greenhouse gases warmed the atmosphere and planetary surface and prevented the early Archean Earth from being frozen.[4]

(continued)

2. Reread the passage on what killed the dinosaurs in the Discussion Questions at the end of Chapter 1. Reconstruct the argument as an inference to the best explanation. How well does that argument meet the standards for assessing explanations?

3. Also in the Discussion Questions at the end of Chapter 1, Colin Powell gives several arguments that in 2003 Saddam Hussein was still trying to obtain fissile material for a nuclear weapons program. Which of his arguments is an inference to the best explanation? How well do these arguments meet the standards for this form of argument?

4. Find three inferences to the best explanation in the readings on scientific reasoning in Chapter 20. This should be easy because scientists use this form of argument often. Put those inferences in standard form, and then evaluate them using the tests discussed above.

5. Sherlock Holmes was lauded for his ability to infer a great deal of information about strangers from simple observations of their clothing and behavior. He displays this ability in the following exchange with his brother, Mycroft, in front of his friend Dr. Watson, who is the first-person narrator. Reconstruct and evaluate the inferences to the best explanation by Holmes and Mycroft in the closing four paragraphs.

"THE GREEK INTERPRETER"

■

from *The Memoirs of Sherlock Holmes*
by Sir Arthur Conan Doyle

. . . The two sat down together in the bow-window of the club. "To anyone who wishes to study mankind this is the spot," said Mycroft. "Look at the magnificent types! Look at these two men who are coming towards us for example."

"The billiard-marker and the other?"

"Precisely. What do you make of the other?"

The two men had stopped opposite the window. Some chalk marks over the waistcoat pocket were the only signs of billiards which I could see in one of them. The other was a very small, dark fellow, with his hat pushed back and several packages under his arm.

"An old soldier, I perceive," said Sherlock.

"And very recently discharged," remarked the brother.

"Served in India, I see."

"And a non-commissioned officer."

"Royal Artillery, I fancy" said Sherlock.

"And a widower."

"But with a child."

"Children, my dear boy, children."

"Come," said I, laughing, "this is a little too much."

"Surely," answered Holmes, "it is not hard to say that a man with that bearing, expression of authority, and sun-baked skin, is a soldier, is more than a private, and is not long from India."

"That he has not left the service long is shown by his still wearing his ammunition boots, as they are called," observed Mycroft.

"He had not the cavalry stride, yet he wore his hat on one side, as is shown by the lighter skin on that side of his brow. His weight is against his being a sapper [a soldier who builds and repairs fortifications]. He is in the artillery."

"Then, of course, his complete mourning shows that he has lost someone very dear. The fact that he is doing his own shopping looks as though it were his wife. He has been buying things for children, you perceive. There is a rattle, which shows that one of them is very young. The wife probably died in childbed. The fact that he has a picture-book under his arm shows that there is another child to be thought of."

ARGUMENTS FROM ANALOGY

Another very common kind of inductive argument moves from a premise that two things are similar in some respects to a conclusion that they must also be analogous in a further respect. Such arguments from analogy can be found in many areas of everyday life. When we buy a new car, how can we tell whether it is going to be reliable? *Consumer Reports* might help if it is an old model; but if it is a brand-new model with no track record, then all we can go on is its similarities to earlier models. Our reasoning then seems to be that the new model is like the old model in various ways, and the old model was reliable, so the new model is probably reliable, too.

The same form of argument is used in science. Here's an example from geology:

> Meteorites composed predominantly of iron provide evidence that parts of other bodies in the solar system, presumably similar in origin to Earth, were composed of metallic iron. The evidence from meteorite compositions and origins lends support to the conclusion that Earth's core is metallic iron.[5]

The argument here is that Earth is analogous to certain meteors in their origins, and those meteors have a large percentage of iron, so the Earth as a whole probably contains about the same percentage of iron. Because a smaller amount of iron is present in the Earth's crust, the rest must lie in the Earth's core.

Similarly, archaeologists might argue that a certain knife was used in ritual sacrifices because it resembles other sacrificial knives in its size, shape, materials, carvings, and so on. The analogy in this case is between the newly discovered knife and the other knives. This analogy is supposed to support a conclusion about the function of the newly discovered knife.

Although such arguments from analogy have diverse contents, they share a common form that can be represented like this:

(1) Object *A* has properties *P, Q, R,* and so on.
(2) Objects *B, C, D,* and so on also have properties *P, Q, R,* and so on.

(3) Objects *B, C, D*, and so on have property *X*.

∴(4) Object *A* probably also has property *X*.

In the archaeological example, object *A* is the newly discovered knife, and objects *B, C, D*, and so on are previously discovered knives that are known to have been used in sacrifices. Properties *P, Q, R*, and so on are the size, shape, materials, and carvings that make *A* analogous to *B, C, D*, and so on. *X* is the property of being used as a sacrificial knife. Premise 3 says that the previously discovered artifacts have this property. The conclusion, on line 4, says that the newly discovered artifact probably also has this property.

Since arguments from analogy are inductive, they normally aren't valid. It is possible that, even though this knife is analogous to other sacrificial knives, this knife was used to shave the king or just to cut bread. These arguments are also defeasible. The argument about knives obviously loses all of its strength if we find "Made in China" printed on the newly discovered knife. Still, none of this shows that arguments from analogy are no good. Despite being invalid and defeasible, some arguments from analogy can still provide reasons—even strong reasons—for their conclusions.

How can we tell whether an argument from analogy is strong or weak? One obvious requirement is that the premises must be *true*. If the previously discovered knives were not really used in sacrifices, or if they do not really have the same carvings on their handles as the newly discovered knife, then this argument from analogy does not provide much, if any, support for its conclusion.

In addition, the cited similarities must be *relevant*. Suppose someone argues that his old car was red with a black interior and had four doors and a sunroof, and his new car also has these properties, so his new car is probably going to be as reliable as his old car. This argument is very weak because the cited similarities are obviously irrelevant to reliability. Such assessments of relevance depend on background beliefs, such as that reliability depends on the drive train and the engine rather than on the color or the sunroof.

The similarities must also be *important*. Similarities are usually more important the more specific they are. Lots of cars with four tires and a motor are reliable, but this is not enough to infer that, because this particular car also has four tires and a motor, it will be reliable, too. The reason is obvious: There are also lots of unreliable cars with four tires and a motor. In general, if many objects have properties *P, Q*, and *R*, and many of those lack property *X*, then arguments from these analogies will be weak. In contrast, if a smaller percentage of objects that have properties *P, Q*, and *R* lack property *X*, then the argument from these analogies will be strong.

If we are not sure which respects *are* important, we still might have some idea of which respects *might* be important. Then we can try to cite objects that are analogous in as many as possible of those respects. By increasing the number of potentially relevant respects for which the analogy holds, we can increase the likelihood that the important respects will be on our list. That shows why arguments from analogy are usually stronger when they cite *more and closer analogies* between the objects.

Another factor that affects the strength of an argument from analogy is the presence of *relevant disanalogies.* Because arguments from analogy are defeasible, as we saw, a strong argument from analogy can become weak if we add a premise that states an important disanalogy. Suppose my new car is like my old cars in many ways, but there is one difference: The new car has an electric motor, whereas the old cars were powered by gasoline. This one difference is enough to weaken any argument to the conclusion that the new car will be reliable. Of course, other disanalogies, such as a different color, won't matter to reliability; and it will often require background knowledge to determine how important a disanalogy is.

We need to be careful here. Some disanalogies that are relevant do not undermine an argument from analogy. If a new engine design was introduced by top engineers to increase reliability, then this disanalogy might not undermine the argument from analogy. Differences that point to more reliability rather than less might even make the argument from analogy stronger.

Other disanalogies can increase the strength of an argument from analogy in a different way. If the same markings are found on very different kinds of sacrificial knives, then the presence of those markings on the newly discovered knife is even stronger evidence that this knife was also used in sacrifices. Differences among the cases cited only in the premises as analogies (that is, B, C, D, and so on) can strengthen an argument from analogy.

Finally, the strength of an argument from analogy depends on its conclusion. Analogies to other kinds of cars provide stronger evidence for a weak conclusion (such as that the new model will probably be pretty reliable) and weaker evidence for a strong conclusion (such as that the new model will definitely be just as reliable as the old model). As with other forms of argument, an argument from analogy becomes stronger as its conclusion becomes weaker and vice versa.

These standards can be summarized by saying that an argument from analogy is stronger when:

1. It cites more and closer analogies that are more important.
2. There are fewer or less important disanalogies between the object in the conclusion and the other objects.
3. The objects cited only in the premises are more diverse.
4. The conclusion is weaker.

After learning about arguments from analogy, it is natural to wonder how they are related to inferences to the best explanation. Although this is sometimes disputed, it seems to us that arguments from analogy are often—if not always—implicit and incomplete inferences to the best explanation. As we pointed out, analogies don't support any conclusion unless they are relevant, and whether they are relevant depends on how they fit into explanations. The color of a car is irrelevant to its reliability, because color plays no role in explaining its reliability. What explains its reliability is its drive train design, materials, care in manufacturing, and so on. That is why analogies in those respects can support a conclusion about reliability. Similarly, the markings on an artifact are relevant to whether it is a sacrificial knife *if* the best explanation of why it has those markings is that it was used in sacrifices. What makes that explanation best is that it also explains similar markings on other sacrificial knives. Thus, such arguments from analogy can be seen as involving an inference to the best explanation of why objects *B, C, D,* and so on have property *X* followed by an application of that explanation to the newly discovered object *A.*

Sometimes the explanation runs in the other direction. Whereas the conclusion about the knife's use (*X*) is supposed to explain its shared markings (*P, Q, R*), sometimes it is the shared features (*P, Q, R*) that are supposed to explain the feature claimed in the conclusion (*X*). Here is a classic example:

> We may observe a very great [similarity] between this earth which we inhabit, and the other planets, Saturn, Jupiter, Mars, Venus, and Mercury. They all revolve around the sun, as the earth does, although at different distances and in different periods. They borrow all their light from the sun, as the earth does. Several of them are known to revolve around their axis like the earth, and, by that means, must have a like succession of day and night. Some of them have moons that serve to give them light in the absence of the sun, as our moon does to us. They are all, in their motions, subject to the same law of gravitation, as the earth is. From all this similarity it is not unreasonable to think that those planets may, like our earth, be the habitation of various orders of living creatures. There is some probability in this conclusion from analogy.[6]

The argument here seems to be that some other planet probably supports life, because Earth does and other planets are similar to Earth in revolving around the sun and around an axis, getting light from the sun, and so on. What makes certain analogies relevant is not, of course, that the motion of Earth is explained by the presence of life here. Rather, certain features of Earth explain why Earth is habitable. The argument suggests that the best explanation of why there is life on our planet is that certain conditions make life possible. That generalization can then be used to support the conclusion that other planets with the same conditions probably support life as well.

In one way or another, many (or maybe even all) arguments from analogy can be seen as inferences to the best explanation. But they are usually incomplete explanations. The argument for life on other planets did not have to commit itself to any particular theory about the origin of life or about which conditions are needed to support life. Nor did the car argument specify exactly what makes cars reliable. Such arguments from analogy merely list a number of similarities so that the list will be likely to include whatever factors are needed for life or for reliability. In this way, arguments from analogy can avoid depending on any complete theory about what is and what is not relevant.

This incompleteness makes arguments from analogy useful in situations where we do not yet know enough to formulate detailed theories or even to complete an inference to the best explanation. Yet the incompleteness of arguments from analogy also makes them more vulnerable to refutation, since the analogies that they list might fail to include a crucial respect. This does not mean that arguments from analogy are never any good. They can be strong. However, it does suggest that their strength will increase as they approach or approximate more complete inferences to the best explanation.

EXERCISE IV

For each of the following arguments, state whether the indicated changes would make the argument weaker or stronger, and explain why. The strength of the argument might not be affected at all. If so, say why it is not affected.

1. My friend and I have seen many movies together, and we have always agreed on whether they are good or bad. My friend liked the movie trilogy *The Lord of the Rings*. So I probably will like it as well.

Would this argument be weaker or stronger if:

   a. The only movies that my friend and I have watched together are comedies, and *The Lord of the Rings* is not a comedy.
   b. My friend and I have seen very many, very different movies together.
   c. My friend and I always watched movies together on Wednesdays, but my friend watched *The Lord of the Rings* on a weekend.
   d. The conclusion claims that I definitely will like *The Lord of the Rings* a lot.
   e. The conclusion claims that I probably won't totally dislike *The Lord of the Rings*.

2. All the students from Joe's high school with high grades and high board scores did well in college. Joe also had high grades and board scores. So he will probably do well in college.

Would this argument be weaker or stronger if:

   a. The other students worked hard, but Joe's good grades came easily to him, so he never learned to work hard.
   b. Joe is going to a different college than the students with whom he is being compared.
   c. Joe plans to major in some easy subject, but the other students were pre-med.
   d. Joe recently started taking drugs on a regular basis.
   e. Joe needs to work full-time to pay his college expenses, but the others had their expenses paid by their parents.

3. A new drug cures a serious disease in rats. Rats are similar to humans in many respects. Therefore, the drug will probably cure the same disease in humans.

Would this argument be weaker or stronger if:

   a. The disease affects the liver, and rat livers are very similar to human livers.

(continued)

b. The drug does not cure this disease in cats.

c.. The drug has to be injected into the rat's tail to be effective (that is, it does not work if it is injected anywhere else in the rat).

d. No drug of this general type has been used on humans before.

e. The effects of the drug are enhanced by eating cooked foods.

EXERCISE V

Using the criteria mentioned above, evaluate each of the following arguments as strong or weak. Explain your answers. Be sure to specify the properties on which the analogy is based, as well as any background beliefs on which your evaluation depends.

1. This landscape by Cézanne is beautiful. He did another painting of a similar scene around the same time. So it is probably beautiful, too.

2. My aunt had a Siamese cat that bit me, so this Siamese cat will probably bite me, too.

3. The students I know who took this course last year got grades of A. I am a lot like them, since I am also smart and hardworking; and the course this year covers very similar material. So I will probably get an A.

4. This politician was caught cheating in his marriage, and he will have to face similarly strong temptations in his public duties, so he will probably cheat in political life as well.

5. A very high minimum wage led to increased unemployment in one country. That country's economy is similar to the economy in a different country. So a very high minimum wage will probably lead to increased unemployment in the other country as well.

6. I feel pain when someone hits me hard on the head with a baseball bat. Your body is a lot like mine. So you would probably feel pain if I hit you hard on the head with a baseball bat. (This is related to the so-called "Problem of Other Minds.")

7. It is immoral for a doctor to lie to a patient about a test result, even if the doctor thinks that lying is in the patient's best interest. We know this because even doctors would agree that it would be morally wrong for a financial adviser to lie to them about a potential investment, even if the financial advisor thinks that this lie is in the doctor's best interests.

8. Chrysler was held legally liable for damages due to defects in the suspension of its Corvair. The defects in the Pinto gas tank caused injuries that were just as serious. Thus, Ford should also be held legally liable for damages due to those defects.

1. As we will see in Chapter 18 of Part V, legal reasoning often uses analogies to legal precedents. In the case of *Plessy v. Ferguson* (1896), Plessy cites similarities to a laundry ordinance in *Yick Wo v. Hopkins* to argue against segregation in public transportation. Later, in *Grutter and Gratz* (excerpted below), critics argue that affirmative action is unconstitutional because of analogies to other forms of racial discrimination that were found unconstitutional in precedents. Reconstruct these arguments from analogy and then evaluate them by applying the criteria discussed above.

2. As we will see in Chapter 19, moral reasoning also often depends on arguments from analogies. One famous example occurs when Judith Jarvis Thomson defends the morality of abortion by means of an analogy to a kidnapped violinist (in the excerpt below). Reconstruct Thomson's argument from analogy and then evaluate it by applying the criteria discussed above.

3. The following excerpt presents evidence that Neanderthals were cannibals. Put the central argument from analogy, which is italicized here, into standard form. Then reconstruct the argument as an inference to the best explanation. Which representation best captures the force of the argument, or are they equally good?

"A GNAWING QUESTION IS ANSWERED"

——■——

from *The Toronto Star*, October 10, 1999
by Michael Downey

Tim White is worried that he may have helped to pin a bad rap on the Neanderthals, the prehistoric Europeans who died out 25,000 years ago. "There is a danger that everyone will think that all Neanderthals were cannibals and that's not necessarily true," he says. White was part of a French-American team of paleoanthropologists who recently found conclusive evidence that at least some Neanderthals ate others about 100,000 years ago. But that doesn't mean they were cannibalistic by nature, he stresses. Most people don't realize that cannibalism is widespread throughout nature, says White, a professor at the University of California at Berkeley and the author of a book on prehistoric cannibalism.

The question of whether the Neanderthals were cannibals had long been a hotly debated topic among anthropologists. No proof had ever been found. That debate ended, however, with the recent analysis by the team of stone tools and bones found in a cave at Moula-Guercy in southern France. The cave is about the size of a living room, perched about 80 metres above the Rhone River. "This one site has all of the evidence right together," says White. "It's as if somebody put a yellow tape around the cave for 100,000 years and kept the scene intact." The bones of deer and other fauna show the clear markings of the nearby stone tools, indicating the deer had been expertly butchered; they were skinned, their body parts cut off and the meat and tendons sliced from the bone. Long bones were bashed open "to get at the fatty marrow inside," says White.

(continued)

So what does all this have to do with cannibalism? *The bones of the six (so far) humans in the same locations have precisely the same markings made by the same tools. That means these fairly modern humans were skinned and eaten in the same manner as the deer.*

And if you are thinking they were eaten after they just happened to die, they do represent all age groups. Two were children about 6 years old, two were teenagers and two were adults.

But maybe they were eaten at a time when food was unusually scarce, right? Not so. There is a large number of animal bones at the same dig, indicating that there were options to eating other Neanderthals.

Human bones with similar cut marks have been found throughout Europe, from Spain to Croatia, providing tantalizing hints of Neanderthal cannibalism activity over tens of thousands of years. But finding such clear evidence of the same preparation techniques being used on deer in the same cave site in France, will "necessitate reassessment of earlier finds," always attributed to ritual burial practices or some other explanation, says White.

It was not clear whether the Neanderthals ate human flesh of their own tribe or exclusively from an enemy tribe, White stresses. Nor was there any indication the purpose of the cannibalism involved nourishment. Eating human flesh could have had another purpose altogether, he says. Surprising to some, cannibalism has been found in 75 mammal species and in 15 primate groups. White says it has often been practiced for reasons not associated with normal hunger. White quotes an archeological maxim: "Actions fossilize, intentions don't." In other words, the reason for the cannibalism remains unknown. He notes that the flesh of other humans has sometimes been eaten to stave off starvation, to show contempt for an enemy or as part of a ritual of affection for the deceased. "Were the victims already dead or killed to be eaten?" he asks, "Were they enemies of the tribe or family members?" Learning these details is the "important and extremely difficult part."

This excavation represents a breakthrough in archeological practice. In a series of papers, White has long advocated the importance of treating a dig site like a crime scene, leaving every piece of evidence in place. In many earlier digs, animal bones were frequently pulled out and thrown away as being irrelevant and human bones were often coated with shellac. The human bones were all tossed into the same bag with no regard to their juxtaposition to each other or precise location. This is one of the first times that modern forensic techniques have been utilized in an archeological excavation, White says, and conclusions drawn have been much more precise than in previous digs that used cruder methods. The project team, which is headed by Alban Defleur of the Universite du Mediterrane at Marseilles, has been digging in the cave since 1991.

4. In the following passage, William Paley argues for the existence of God on the basis of an analogy to a watch. Reconstruct this argument from analogy and then evaluate it by applying the criteria discussed above. Could Paley's argument also be reconstructed as an inference to the best explanation? If so, would that reconstruction better capture the force of the argument?

"THE WATCH AND THE WATCHMAKER"
■

from *Natural Theology* (New York: Hopkins, 1836)
by William Paley

. . . In crossing a heath, suppose I pitched my foot against a stone and were asked how the stone came to be there, I might possibly answer that for anything I knew to the contrary it had lain there forever; nor would it, perhaps, be very easy to show the absurdity of this answer. But suppose I had found a watch upon the ground, and it should be inquired how the watch happened to be in that place, I should hardly think of the answer which I had before given, that for anything I knew the watch might have always been there. Yet why should not this answer serve for the watch as well as for the stone? Why is it not as admissible in the second case as in the first? For this reason, and for no other, namely, that when we come to inspect the watch, we perceive—what we could not discover in the stone—that its several parts are framed and put together for a purpose, e.g., that they are so formed and adjusted as to produce motion, and that motion so regulated as to point out the hour of the day; that if the different parts had been differently shaped from what they are, of a different size from what they are, or placed after any other manner or in any other order than that in which they are placed, either no motion at all would have been carried on in the machine, or none which would have answered the use that is now served by it. . . . This mechanism being observed—it requires indeed an examination of the instrument, and perhaps some previous knowledge of the subject, to perceive and understand it; but being once, as we have said, observed and understood—the inference we think is inevitable, that the watch must have had a maker—that there must have existed, at some time and at some place or other, an artificer or artificers who formed it for the purpose which we find it actually to answer, who comprehended its construction and designed its use. . . .

[E]very indication of contrivance, every manifestation of design, which existed in the watch, exists in the works of nature; with the difference, on the side of nature, of being greater and more, and that in a degree which exceeds all computation. I mean that the contrivances of nature surpass the contrivances of art, in the complexity, subtlety, and curiosity of the mechanism; and still more, if possible, do they go beyond them in number and variety; yet in a multitude of cases, are not less evidently mechanical, not less evidently contrivances, not less evidently accommodated to their end, or suited to their office, than are the most perfect productions of human ingenuity.

I know no better method of introducing so large a subject, than that of comparing a single thing with a single thing: an eye, for example, with a telescope. As far as the examination of the instrument goes, there is precisely the same proof that the eye was made for vision, as there is that the telescope was made for assisting it. They are made upon the same principles; both being adjusted to the laws by which the transmission and refraction of rays of light are regulated. I speak not of the origin of the laws themselves; but such laws being fixed, the construction in both cases is adapted to them. . . .

(continued)

To some it may appear a difference sufficient to destroy all similitude between the eye and the telescope, that the one is a perceiving organ, the other an unperceiving instrument. The fact is that they are both instruments. And as to the mechanism, at least as to mechanism being employed, and even as to the kind of it, this circumstance varies not the analogy at all. . . . The end is the same; the means are the same. The purpose in both is alike; the contrivance for accomplishing that purpose is in both alike. The lenses of the telescopes, and the humors of the eye, bear a complete resemblance to one another, in their figure, their position, and in their power over the rays of light, viz. in bringing each pencil to a point at the right distance from the lens; namely, in the eye, at the exact place where the membrane is spread to receive it. How is it possible, under circumstances of such close affinity, and under the operation of equal evidence, to exclude contrivance from the one; yet to acknowledge the proof of contrivance having been employed, as the plainest and clearest of all propositions, in the other? . . .

Were there no example in the world of contrivance except that of the *eye*, it would be alone sufficient to support the conclusion, which we draw from it, as to the necessity of an intelligent Creator. . . . The proof is not a conclusion that lies at the end of a chain of reasoning, of which chain each instance of contrivance is only a link, and of which, if one link fail, the whole fails; but it is an argument separately supplied by every separate example. An error in stating an example affects only that example. The argument is cumulative in the fullest sense of that term. The eye proves it without the ear; the ear without the eye. The proof in each example is complete; for when the design of the part and the conduciveness of its structure to that design is shown, the mind may set itself at rest; no further consideration can detract anything from the force of the example.

NOTES

[1] Gilbert Harman deserves much credit for calling attention to the importance of inferences to the best explanation; see, for example, his *Thought* (Princeton, NJ: Princeton University Press, 1973). A similar form of argument called abduction was analyzed long ago by Charles Sanders Peirce; see, for example, his *Collected Papers of Charles Sanders Peirce* (Cambridge, MA: Harvard University Press, 1931), 5: 189. A wonderful recent discussion is Peter Lipton, *Inference to the Best Explanation* (London: Routledge, 1991).

[2] Sir Arthur Conan Doyle, "Silver Blaze," *The Complete Sherlock Holmes* (Garden City, NY: Doubleday, 1930), 1: 349. The stories describe Holmes as a master of deduction, but his arguments are inductive as we define the terms.

[3] This discussion in many ways parallels and is indebted to the fifth chapter of W. V. Quine and J. S. Ullian, *The Web of Belief*, 2nd ed. (New York: Random House, 1978).

[4] From Fred T. Mackenzie, *Our Changing Planet* (Upper Saddle River, NJ: Prentice-Hall, 1998), 192.

[5] Mackenzie, *Our Changing Planet*, 42.

[6] Thomas Reid, *Essays on the Intellectual Powers of Man* (Cambridge, MA: MIT Press, 1969), essay I, section 4, 48.

11

Chances

The kinds of arguments discussed in the preceding three chapters are all inductive, so they need not meet the deductive standard of validity. They are, instead, intended to meet the inductive standard of strength. Whereas deductive validity hinges on what is possible, inductive strength hinges on what is probable. Roughly, an argument is inductively strong to the extent that its premises make its conclusion more likely or probable. Hence, just as we can get a better theoretical understanding of deductive validity by studying formal logic, as we did in Chapters 6–7, so we can get a better theoretical understanding of inductive strength by studying probability, as we will do in this chapter. To complete our survey of inductive arguments, this chapter offers an elementary discussion of probability. It begins by illustrating several common mistakes about probability. To help avoid these fallacies, we need to approach probability more carefully, so formal laws of probability are presented along with Bayes's theorem.

SOME FALLACIES OF PROBABILITY

Probability is pervasive. We all assume or make probability judgments throughout our lives. We do so whenever we form a belief about which we are not certain, as in all of the kinds of inductive arguments studied in Chapters 8–10. Such arguments do not pretend to reach their conclusions with certainty, even if their premises are true. They merely try to show that a conclusion is likely or probable. Judgments about probability are, thus, assumed in assessing such arguments and beliefs. Probability also plays a crucial role in our most important decisions. Mistakes about probability can then lead to disasters. Doctors lose patients' lives, stockbrokers lose clients' money, and coaches lose games because they overestimate or underestimate probabilities. Such mistakes are common and fall into several regular patterns. It is useful to understand these fallacies, so that we can learn to avoid them.

THE GAMBLER'S FALLACY

Casinos thrive partly because so many gamblers misunderstand probability. One mistake is so common that it has been dubbed *the gambler's fallacy*. When people have a run of bad luck, they often increase their bets because they assume that they are due for a run of good luck to even things out. Gambling systems are sometimes based on this fallacious idea. People keep track of the numbers that come up on a roulette wheel, trying to discover a number that has not come up for a long time. They then pile their money on that number on the assumption that it is due. They usually end up losing a bundle.

These gamblers seem to assume, "In the long run, things will even out (or average out)." Interpreted one way, this amounts to what mathematicians call *the law of large numbers*, and it is perfectly correct. When flipping a coin, we expect it to come up heads half the time, so it should come up heads five times in ten flips. If we actually check this out, however, we discover that the number of times it comes up heads in ten flips varies significantly from this predicted value—sometimes coming up heads more than five times, sometimes coming up fewer. What the law of large numbers tells us is that the actual percentage of heads will tend to come closer to the theoretically predicted percentage of heads the more trials we make. If you flipped a coin a million times, it would be very surprising if the percentage of heads were more than 1 percent away from the predicted 50 percent.

This law of large numbers is often misunderstood in a way that leads to the gambler's fallacy. Some people assume that each possible outcome will occur the average number of times in each series of trials. To see that this is a fallacy, we can go back to flipping coins. Toss a coin until it comes up heads three times in a row. (This will take less time than you might imagine.) What is the probability that it will come up heads a fourth time? Put crudely, some people think that the probability of it coming up heads again must be very small, because it is unlikely that a fair coin will come up heads four times in a row, so a tails is needed to even things out. That is wrong. The chances of getting heads on any given toss is the same, regardless of what happened on previous tosses. Previous results cannot affect the probabilities on this new toss.

STRANGE THINGS HAPPEN

Another common mistake is to ignore improbable events. It is very unlikely that a fair coin will come up heads nineteen times in a row, so you might think it could never happen. You would be wrong. Of course, if you sat flipping a single coin, you might spend a very long time before you hit a sequence of nineteen consecutive heads, but there is a way of getting this result (with a little help from your friends) in a single afternoon. You start out with $6,000 worth of pennies and put them in a large truck. (Actually, the truck need not be very large.) Dump the coins out and then pick up all the coins that come up heads. Put them back in the truck and repeat the procedure nineteen times, always returning only those coins that come up heads to the truck. With tolerably good luck, on the nineteenth dump of the coins, you will get at least one coin that comes up heads again. Any such coin will have come up heads nineteen times in a row.

What is the point of this silly exercise? It is intended to show that we often attribute abilities or the lack of abilities to people when, in fact, their performances may be statistically insignificant. When people invest with stockbrokers, they tend to shift to a new broker when they lose money. When they hit on a broker who earns them money, they stay and praise this broker's abilities. In fact, some financial advisers seem to be better than others—they have a long history of sound financial advice—but the financial community is, in many ways, like the truckload of pennies we have just examined. There are many brokers giving all sorts of different advice and, by chance alone, some of them are bound to give good advice. Furthermore, some of them are bound to have runs of success, just as some of the pennies dumped from the truck will have long strings of coming up heads. Thus, in some cases, what appears to be brilliance in predicting stock prices may be nothing more than a run of statistically expected good luck.

The gambling casinos of the world are like the truck full of pennies as well. With roulette wheels spinning in a great many places over a great deal of time, startlingly long runs are bound to occur. For example, in 1918, black came up twenty-six consecutive times on a roulette wheel in Monte Carlo. The odds against this are staggering. But before we can decide what to make of this event, we would have to judge it in the context of the vast number of times that the game of roulette has been played.

HONORS EXERCISE

Students familiar with computer programming should not find it difficult to write a program that will simulate a Monte Carlo roulette wheel and keep track long runs of black and long runs of red. On a Monte Carlo wheel, the odds coming up black are 18/37. The same odds hold for coming up red. Write a program; run it for a day; then report the longest runs.

HEURISTICS

In daily life, we often have to make decisions quickly without full information. To deal with this overload of decisions, we commonly employ what cognitive psychologists call *heuristics*. Technically, a heuristic is a general strategy for solving a problem or coming to a decision. For example, a good heuristic for solving geometry problems is to start with the conclusion you are trying to reach and then work backward.

Recent research in cognitive psychology has shown, first, that human beings rely very heavily on heuristics and, second, that we often have too much confidence in them. The result is that our probability judgments often go very wrong, and sometimes our thinking gets utterly mixed up. In this regard, two heuristics are particularly instructive: the representativeness heuristic and the availability heuristic.

THE REPRESENTATIVENESS HEURISTIC. A simple example illustrates how errors can arise from the representativeness heuristic. Imagine that you are randomly dealt five-card hands from a standard deck. Which of the following two hands is more likely to come up?

HAND #1	HAND #2
Three of clubs	Ace of spades
Seven of diamonds	Ace of hearts
Nine of diamonds	Ace of clubs
Queen of hearts	Ace of diamonds
King of spades	King of spades

A surprisingly large number of people will automatically say that the second hand is much less likely than the first. Actually, if you think about it for a bit, it should be obvious that any two specific hands have exactly the same likelihood of being dealt in a fair game. Here people get confused because the first hand is unimpressive; and, because unimpressive hands come up all the time, it strikes us as a representative hand. In many card games, however, the second hand is very impressive—something worth talking about—and thus looks unrepresentative. Our reliance on representativeness blinds us to a simple and obvious point about probabilities: Any specific hand is as likely to occur as any other.

DISCUSSION QUESTION

Linda is thirty-one years old, single, outspoken, and very bright. As a student, she majored in philosophy, was deeply concerned with issues of discrimination and social justice, and also participated in antinuclear demonstrations. Rank the following statements with respect to the probability that they are also true of Linda, then explain your rankings:

Linda is a teacher in elementary school.
Linda works in a bookstore and takes yoga classes.
Linda is active in the feminist movement.
Linda is a psychiatric social worker.
Linda is a bank teller.
Linda is an insurance salesperson.
Linda is a bank teller and is active in the feminist movement.[1]

THE AVAILABILITY HEURISTIC. Because sampling and taking surveys is costly, we often do it imaginatively, that is, in our heads. If you ask a baseball fan which team has the better batting average, Detroit or San Diego, that person might just remember, might go look it up, or might think about each team and try to decide which has the most good batters. The latter approach, needless to say, would be a risky business, but many baseball fans have remarkable knowledge of the batting averages of top hitters. Even with this knowledge, however, it is easy to go wrong. The players that naturally come to mind are the stars on each team. They are more available to our memory, and we are likely to make our judgment on the basis of them alone. Yet such a sample can easily be biased because all the batters contribute to the team average, not just the stars. The fact that the weak batters on one team are much better than the weak batters on the other can swing the balance.

DISCUSSION QUESTION

In four pages of a novel (about 2,000 words), how many words would you expect to find that have the form _ _ _ _ _n_ (seven-letter words with "n" in the sixth place)? Write down your answer. Now, how many words would you expect to find that have the form _ _ _ _ing (seven-letter words that end with "ing")? Explain your answers.[2]

The point of examining these heuristics and noting the errors that they produce is not to suggest that we should cease relying on them. First, there is a good chance that this would be psychologically impossible, because the use of such heuristics seems to be built into our psychological makeup. Second, over a wide range of standard cases, these heuristics give quick and largely accurate estimates. Difficulties typically arise in using these heuristics when the situation is nonstandard—that is, when the situation is complex or out of the ordinary.

To avoid such mistakes when making important judgments about probabilities, we need to ask, "Is the situation sufficiently standard to allow the use of heuristics?" Because this is a mouthful, we might simply ask, "Is this the sort of thing that people can figure out in their heads?" When the answer to that question is "No," as it often is, then we need to turn to more formal procedures for determining probabilities.

DISCUSSION QUESTION

In a remarkable study,[3] Thomas Gilovich, Robert Vallone, and Amos Tversky found a striking instance of people's tendency to treat things as statistically significant when they are not. In professional basketball, certain players have the reputation of being streak shooters. Streak shooters seem to score points in batches, then go cold and are not able to buy a basket. Stated more precisely, in streak shooting, "the performance of a player during a particular period is significantly better than expected on the basis of the player's overall record." To test whether streak shooting really exists, the authors made detailed study of a year's shooting record for the players on the Philadelphia 76ers. This team

(continued)

included Andrew Toney, noted around the league as being streak shooter. The authors found no evidence for streak shooting, not even for Andrew Toney. How would you go about deciding whether streak shooting exists or not? If, as Gilovich, Vallone, and Tversky have argued, belief phenomenon is a "cognitive illusion," why do so many people, including most professional athletes, believe that it does exist?

THE LANGUAGE OF PROBABILITY

The first step in figuring out probabilities is to adopt a more precise way of talking. Our common language includes various ways of expressing probabilities. Some of the guarding terms discussed in Chapter 3 provide examples of informal ways of expressing probability commitments. Thus, someone might say that it is unlikely that the New England Patriots will win the Super Bowl this year without saying how unlikely it is. We can also specify various degrees of probability. Looking out the window, we might say that there is a fifty-fifty chance of rain. More vividly, someone might have remarked that Ralph Nader does not have a snowball's chance in hell of ever winning a presidential election. In each case, the speaker is indicating the relative strength of the evidence for the occurrence or nonoccurrence of some event. To say that there is a fifty-fifty chance that it will rain indicates that we hold that the evidence is equally strong that it will rain rather than not rain. The metaphor in the third statement indicates that the person who uttered it believed that the probability of Nader winning a presidential election is essentially nonexistent.

We can make our probability claims more precise by using numbers. Sometimes we use percentages. For example, the weather bureau might say that there is a 75 percent chance of snow tomorrow. This can naturally be changed to a fraction: The probability is 3/4 that it will snow tomorrow. Finally, this fraction can be changed to a decimal expression: There is a 0.75 probability that it will snow tomorrow.

The probability scale has two end points: the absolute certainty that the event will occur and the absolute certainty that it will not occur. Because you cannot do better than absolute certainty, a probability can neither rise above 100 percent nor drop below 0 percent (neither above 1, nor below 0). (This should sound fairly obvious, but it is possible to become confused when combining percentages and fractions, as when Yogi Berra was supposed to have said that success is one-third talent and 75 percent hard work.) Of course, what we normally call probability claims usually fall between these two endpoints. For this reason, it sounds somewhat peculiar to say that there is a 100 percent chance of rain and just plain weird to say the chance of rain is 1 out of 1. Even so, these peculiar ways of speaking cause no procedural difficulties and rarely come up in practice.

A *PRIORI* **PROBABILITY**

When people make probability claims, we have a right to ask why they assign the probability they do. In Chapter 8, we saw how statistical procedures can be used for establishing probability claims. Here we will examine the so-called *a priori* approach to probabilities. A simple example will bring out the differences between these two approaches. We might wonder what the probability is of drawing an ace from a standard deck of fifty-two cards. Using the procedure discussed in Chapter 8, we could make a great many random draws from the deck (replacing the card each time) and then form a statistical generalization concerning the results. We would discover that an ace tends to come up roughly one-thirteenth of the time. From this we could draw the conclusion that the chance of drawing an ace is one in thirteen.

But we do not have to go to all this trouble. We can assume that each of the fifty-two cards has an equal chance of being selected. Given this assumption, an obvious line of reasoning runs as follows: There are four aces in a standard fifty-two-card deck, so the probability of selecting one randomly is four in fifty-two. That reduces to one chance in thirteen. Here the set of favorable outcomes is a subset of the total number of equally likely outcomes, and to compute the probability that the favorable outcome will occur, we merely divide the number of favorable outcomes by the total number of possible outcomes. This fraction gives us the probability that the event will occur on a random draw. Since all outcomes here are equally likely,

$$\text{Probability of drawing an ace} = \frac{\text{number of aces}}{\text{total number of cards}} = \frac{4}{52} = \frac{1}{13}$$

Notice that in coming to our conclusion that there is one chance in thirteen of randomly drawing an ace from a fifty-two-card deck, we used only mathematical reasoning. This illustrates the *a priori* approach to probabilities. It is called the *a priori* approach because we arrive at the result simply by reasoning about the circumstances.

In calculating the probability of drawing an ace from a fifty-two-card deck, we took the ratio of favorable equally likely outcomes to total equally likely outcomes. Generally, then, the probability of a hypothesis h, symbolized "$Pr(h)$," when all outcomes are equally likely, is expressed as follows:

$$Pr(h) = \frac{\text{favorable outcomes}}{\text{total outcomes}}$$

We can illustrate this principle with a slightly more complicated example. What is the probability of throwing an eight on the cast of two dice? The following table lists all of the equally likely ways in which two dice can turn up on a single cast. Notice that five of the thirty-six possible outcomes produce an eight. Hence, the probability of throwing an eight is 5/36.

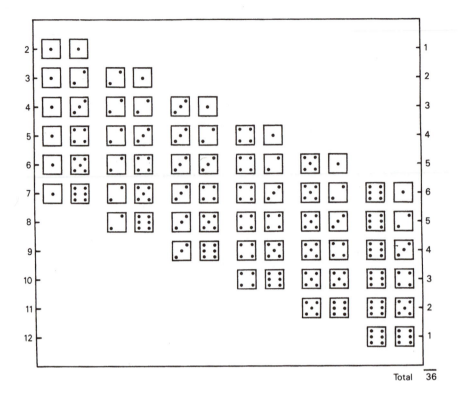

Total   36

Using the above chart, answer the following questions about the total on throw of two dice:

1. What is the probability of throwing a five?
2. Which number has the highest probability of being thrown? What is its probability?
3. What is the probability of throwing an eleven?
4. What is the probability of throwing either a seven or an eleven?
5. Which is more likely: throwing either a five or an eight?
6. Which is more likely: throwing a five or an eight, or throwing a two or a seven?
7. What is the probability of throwing a ten or above?
8. What is the probability of throwing an even number?
9. What is the probability of throwing an odd number?
10. What is the probability of throwing a value from four to six?
11. What is the probability of throwing either a two or a twelve?
12. What is the probability of throwing a value from two to twelve?

SOME RULES OF PROBABILITY

Suppose you have determined the probability that certain simple events will occur; how do you go about applying this information to combinations of events? This is a complex question and one that can be touched on only lightly in this text. There are, however, some simple rules of probability that are worth knowing because they can guide us in making choices when outcomes are uncertain.

By convention, events are assigned probabilities between 0 and 1 (inclusive). An event is going to either occur or not occur; that, at least, is certain (that is, it has a probability of 1). From this it is easy to see how to calculate the probability that the event will *not* occur given the probability that it will occur: We simply subtract the probability that it will occur from 1. This is our first rule:

RULE 1: NEGATION. The probability that an event will *not* occur is 1 minus the probability that it will occur. Symbolically:

$$\Pr(\text{not } h) = 1 - \Pr(h)$$

For example, the probability of drawing an ace from a standard deck is one in thirteen, so the probability of *not* drawing an ace is twelve in thirteen. This makes sense because there are forty-eight out of fifty-two ways of not drawing an ace, and this reduces to twelve chances in thirteen.

RULE 2: CONJUNCTION WITH INDEPENDENCE. Given two independent events, the probability of their *both* occurring is the product of their individual probabilities. Symbolically (where h_1 and h_2 are independent):

$$\Pr(h_1 \ \& \ h_2) = \Pr(h_1) \times \Pr(h_2)$$

Here the word "independent" needs explanation. Suppose you randomly draw a card from the deck, then put it back, shuffle, and draw again. In this case, the outcome of the first draw provides no information about the outcome of the second draw, so it is *independent* of it. What is the probability of drawing two aces in a row using this system? Using Rule 2, we see that the answer is $1/13 \times 1/13$, or 1 chance in 169.

The situation is different if we do *not* replace the card after the first draw. Rule 2 does not apply to this case because the two events are no longer independent. The chances of getting an ace on the first draw are still one in thirteen, but if an ace is drawn and not returned to the pack, then there is one less ace in the deck, so the chances of drawing an ace on the next draw are reduced to three in fifty-one. Thus, the probability of drawing two consecutive aces without returning the first draw to the deck is $4/52 \times 3/51$, or 1 in 221, which is considerably lower than 1 in 169.

If we want to extend Rule 2 to cover cases in which the events are *not* independent, then we will have to speak of the probability of one event occurring given that another has occurred. The probability that h_2 will occur given that h_1 has occurred is called the *conditional* probability of h_2 on h_1 and is usually symbolized thus: $\Pr(h_2 \mid h_1)$. This probability is calculated by considering only those cases where h_1 is true and then dividing the number of cases within that group where h_2 is also true by the total number of cases in that group. Symbolically:

$$Pr(h_2 \mid h_1) = \frac{\text{favorable outcomes where } h_1}{\text{total outcomes where } h_1} = \frac{\text{outcomes where } h_1 \text{ and } h_2}{\text{total outcomes where } h_1}$$

Using this notion of conditional probability, Rule 2 can be modified as follows to deal with cases in which events need not be independent:

RULE 2G: CONJUNCTION IN GENERAL. Given two events, the probability of their both occurring is the probability of the first occurring times the probability of the second occurring, given that the first has occurred. Symbolically:

$$Pr(h_1 \& h_2) = Pr(h_1) \times Pr(h_2 \mid h_1)$$

Notice that, in the event that h_1 and h_2 are independent, the probability of h_2 is not related to the occurrence of h_1, so the probability of h_2 on h_1 is simply the probability of h_2. Thus, Rule 2 is simply a special case of the more general Rule 2G.

We can extend these rules to cover more than two events. For example, with Rule 2, however many events we might consider, provided that they are independent of each other, the probability of all of them occurring is the product of each one of them occurring. For example, the chances of flipping a coin and having it come up heads is one chance in two. What are the chances of flipping a coin eight times and having it come up heads every time? The answer is:

$$1/2 \times 1/2 \times 1/2 \times 1/2 \times 1/2 \times 1/2 \times 1/2 \times 1/2$$

which equals 1 chance in 256.

Our next rule allows us to answer questions of the following kind: What are the chances of *either* an eight *or* a two coming up on a single throw of the dice? Going back to the chart, we saw that we could answer this question by counting the number of ways in which a two can come up (which is one) and adding this to the number of ways in which an eight can come up (which is five). We could then conclude that the chances of one or the other of them coming up is six chances in thirty-six, or $1/6$. The principle involved in this calculation can be stated as follows:

RULE 3: DISJUNCTION WITH EXCLUSIVITY. The probability that at least one of two mutually exclusive events will occur is the sum of the probabilities that each of them will occur. Symbolically (where h_1 and h_2 are mutually exclusive):

$$Pr(h_1 \text{ or } h_2) = Pr(h_1) + Pr(h_2)$$

To say that events are *mutually exclusive* means that they cannot both occur. You cannot, for example, get both a ten and an eight on the same cast of two dice. You might, however, throw neither one of them.

When events are not mutually exclusive, the rule for calculating disjunctive probabilities becomes more complicated. Suppose, for example, that exactly half the class is female and exactly half the class is over nineteen and the age distribution is the same for females and males. What is the probability that a randomly selected student will be either a female or over nineteen? If we simply add the probabilities ($1/2 + 1/2 = 1$), we would get the result that we are certain to pick someone who is either female or over nineteen. But that answer is wrong, because a quarter of the class is male and not over nineteen, and one of them might have been randomly selected. The correct answer is that the chances are $3/4$ of randomly selecting someone who is either female or over nineteen.

We can see that this is the correct answer by examining the following table:

	Over Nineteen	Not over Nineteen
Female	25%	25%
Male	25%	25%

It is easy to see that in 75 percent of the cases, a randomly selected student will be either female or over nineteen. The table also shows what went wrong with our initial calculation. The top row shows that 50 percent of the students are female. The left column shows that 50 percent of the students are over nineteen. But we cannot simply add these figures to get the probability of a randomly selected student being either female or over nineteen. Why not? Because that would double-count the females over nineteen. We would count them once in the top row and then again in the left column. To compensate for such double-counting, we need to subtract the students who are both female and over nineteen. The upper left figure shows that this is 25%. So the correct way to calculate the answer is $50\% + 50\% - 25\% = 75\%$.

This pattern is reflected in the general rule governing the calculation of disjunctive probabilities:

RULE 3G: DISJUNCTION IN GENERAL. The probability that at least one of two events will occur is the sum of the probabilities that each of them will occur, minus the probability that they will both occur. Symbolically:

$$Pr(h_1 \text{ or } h_2) = Pr(h_1) + Pr(h_2) - Pr(h_1 \& h_2)$$

If h_1 and h_2 are mutually exclusive, then $Pr(h_1 \& h_2) = 0$, and Rule 3G reduces to Rule 3. Thus, as with Rules 2 and 2G, Rule 3 is simply a special case of the more general Rule 3G.

Before stating Rule 4, we can think about a particular example. What is the probability of tossing heads at least once in eight tosses of a coin? Here it is tempting to reason in the following way: There is a 50 percent chance of getting heads on the first toss and a 50 percent chance of getting heads on the second toss, so after two tosses it is already certain that we will toss heads at least once, and thus after eight tosses there should be a 400 percent chance.

In other words, you cannot miss. There are two good reasons for thinking that this argument is fishy. First, probability can never exceed 100 percent. Second, there must be some chance, however small, that we could toss a coin eight times and not have it come up heads.

The best way to look at this question is to restate it so that the first two rules can be used. Instead of asking what the probability is that heads will come up at least once, we can ask what the probability is that heads will *not* come up at least once. To say that heads will not come up even once is equivalent to saying that tails will come up eight times in a row. By Rule 2 we know how to compute that probability: It is 1/2 multiplied by itself eight times, and that, as we saw, is 1/256. Finally, by Rule 1 we know that the probability that this will not happen (that heads will come up at least once) is 1 – (1/256). In other words, the probability of tossing heads at least once in eight tosses is 255/256. That comes close to a certainty, but it is not quite a certainty.

We can generalize these results as follows:

RULE 4: SERIES WITH INDEPENDENCE. The probability that an event will occur at least once in a series of independent trials is 1 minus the probability that it will not occur in that number of trials. Symbolically (where n is the number of independent trials):

$$\Pr(h \text{ at least once in } n \text{ trials}) = 1 - \Pr(\text{not } h)^n$$

Strictly speaking, Rule 4 is unnecessary, since it can be derived from Rules 1 and 2, but it is important to know because it blocks a common misunderstanding about probabilities: People often think that something is a sure thing when it is not.

Another common confusion is between permutations and combinations. A *permutation* is a set of items whose order is specified. A *combination* is a set of items whose order is not specified. Imagine, for example, that three cards—the jack, queen, and king of spades—are facedown in front of you. If you pick two of these cards in turn, there are three possible combinations: jack and queen, jack and king, and queen and king. In contrast, there are six possible permutations: jack then queen, queen then jack, jack then king, king then jack, queen then king, and king then queen.

Rule 2 is used to calculate probabilities of permutations—of conjunctions of events in a particular order. For example, if you flip a fair coin twice, what is the probability of its coming up heads and tails in that order (that is, heads on the first flip and tails on the second flip)? Since the flips are independent, Rule 2 tells us that the answer is $1/2 \times 1/2 = 1/4$. This answer is easily confirmed by counting the possible permutations (heads then heads, heads then tails, tails then heads, tails then tails). Only one of these four permutations (heads then tails) is a favorable outcome.

We need to calculate probabilities of combinations in a different way. For example, if you flip a fair coin twice, what is the probability of its landing heads and tails in *any* order? There are two ways for this to happen. The coin could come up either heads then tails or tails then heads. These alternatives are mutually exclusive, so the probability of this disjunction by Rule 3 is $1/4 + 1/4 = 1/2$. This is confirmed by counting two possibilities (heads then tails, tails then heads) out of four (heads then heads, heads then tails, tails then heads, tails then tails). Another way to calculate this probability is to realize that the first flip doesn't matter. Whatever you get on the first flip (heads or tails), you need the opposite on the second flip. You are certain to get either heads or tails on the first flip, so this probability is 1. Then, regardless of what happens on the first flip, the probability of getting the opposite on the second flip is $1/2$. These results are independent, so the probability of their conjunction by Rule 2 is the product $1 \times 1/2 = 1/2$.

We can also use our rules to calculate probabilities of combinations without independence. Rule 2G tells us that the probability of drawing an ace, not putting this card back in the deck, and then drawing a king is $4/52 \times 4/51 = 16/2{,}652$. But what is the probability of drawing an ace and a king in any order? It is the probability of drawing either an ace or a king and then drawing the other one given that you drew the first one. That probability by Rule 2G is $8/52 \times 4/51 = 32/2{,}652$. The difference between this result and the previous one, where the order was specified, shows why we need to determine whether we are dealing with permutations or combinations.

EXERCISE II

Use the rules of probability to calculate these probabilities:

1. What is the probability of rolling a five on one throw of a fair six-sided die?
2. What is the probability of *not* rolling a five on one throw of a fair six-sided die?
3. If you roll a five on your first throw of a fair six-sided die, what is probability of rolling *another* five on a second throw of that die?
4. If you roll two fair six-sided dice one time, what are the chances that *both* of the dice will come up a five?
5. If you roll two fair six-sided dice one time, what are the chances that *one or the other* (or both) of the dice will come up a five?
6. If you roll two fair six-sided dice one time, what are the chances that *one and only one* of the dice will come up a five?
7. If you roll two fair six-sided dice one time, what are the chances that *at least one* of the dice will come up a five?
8. If you roll two fair six-sided dice one time, what are the chances that *at least one* of the dice will *not* come up a five?
9. If you roll six fair six-sided dice one time, what are the chances that *at least one* of the dice will come up a five?
10. If you roll six fair six-sided dice one time, what are the chances that *at least one* of the dice will *not* come up a five?

Compute the probability of making the following draws from a standard fifty-two-card deck:

1. Drawing either a seven or a five on a single draw.

2. Drawing neither a seven nor a five on a single draw.

3. Drawing a seven and then, without returning the first card to the deck, drawing a five on the next draw.

4. Same as 3, but the first card is returned to the deck and the deck is shuffled after the first draw.

5. Drawing at least one spade in a series of three consecutive draws, when the card drawn is not returned to the deck.

6. Drawing at least one spade in a series of four consecutive draws, when the card drawn is not returned to the deck.

7. Same as 6, but the card is returned to the deck after each draw and the deck is reshuffled.

8. Drawing a heart and a diamond in that order in two consecutive draws, when the first card is returned to the deck and the deck is reshuffled the first draw.

9. Drawing a heart and a diamond in any order in two consecutive draws, when the first card is returned to the deck and the deck is reshuffled the first draw.

10. Drawing a heart and a diamond in any order in two consecutive draws, when the first card is not returned to the deck after the first draw.

Suppose there are two little lotteries in town, each of which sells exactly 100 tickets.

1. If each lottery has only one winning ticket, and you buy two tickets to the *same* lottery, what is the probability that you will have a winning ticket?

2. If each lottery has only one winning ticket, and you buy one ticket to *each* of the two lotteries, what is the probability that you will have at least one winning ticket?

3. If each lottery has only one winning ticket, and you buy one ticket to each of the two lotteries, what is the probability that you will have *two* winning tickets?

4. If each lottery has two winning tickets, and you buy one ticket to each of the two lotteries, what is the probability that you will have at least one winning ticket?

5. If each lottery has two winning tickets, and you buy two tickets to the same lottery, what is the probability that you will have two winning tickets?

6. If each lottery has two winning tickets, and you buy two tickets to the same lottery, what is the probability that you will have at least one winning ticket?

1. You are presented with two bags, one containing two ham sandwiches and the other containing a ham sandwich and a cheese sandwich. You reach in one bag and draw out a ham sandwich. What is the probability that the other sandwich in the bag is also a ham sandwich?

2. You are presented with three bags: two contain a chicken-fat sandwich and one contains a cheese sandwich. You are asked to guess which bag contains the cheese sandwich. You do so, and the bag you selected is set aside. (You obviously have one chance in three of guessing correctly.) From the two remaining bags, one containing a chicken-fat sandwich is then removed. You are now given the opportunity to switch your selection to the remaining bag. Will such a switch increase, decrease, or leave unaffected your chances of correctly ending up with the bag with the cheese sandwich in it?

In a fair lottery with a million tickets, the probability that ticket #1 will lose is 0.999999, the probability that ticket #2 will lose is also 0.999999, and so on for each ticket. On this basis, you might seem justified in believing each premise in the following argument:

> Ticket #1 will lose.
> Ticket #2 will lose.
> Ticket #3 will lose.
> [and so on, until:]
> Ticket #1,000,000 will lose.
> There are only 1,000,000 tickets.
> _____
> ∴ Every ticket will lose.

This conclusion must be false, since the lottery is fair. However, the conclusion follows from the premises, and each of the premises seems justified. Does this argument justify us in believing its conclusion? Why or why not?

BAYES'S THEOREM

Although dice and cards provide nice, simple models for learning how to calculate probabilities, real life is usually more complicated. One particularly interesting and important form of problem arises often in medicine. Suppose that Wendy tests positive for colon cancer. The treatment for colon cancer is painful and dangerous, so, before subjecting Wendy to that treatment, her doctor wants to determine how likely it is that Wendy really has colon cancer. After all, no test is perfect. Regarding the test that was used on Wendy, previous studies have revealed the following probabilities:

The probability that a person in the general population has colon cancer is 0.3 percent (or 0.003).

If a person has colon cancer, then the probability that the test is positive is 90 percent (or 0.9).

If a person does not have colon cancer, then the probability that the test is positive is 3 percent (or 0.03).

On these assumptions, what is the probability that Wendy actually has colon cancer, given that she tested positive? Most people guess that this probability is fairly high. Even most trained physicians would say that Wendy probably has colon cancer.[4]

What is the correct answer? To calculate the probability that a person who tests positive actually has colon cancer, we need to divide the number of favorable outcomes by the number of total outcomes. The favorable outcomes include everyone who tests positive and really has colon cancer. This outcome is not "favorable" to Wendy, so we will describe this group as *true positives*. The total outcomes include everyone who tests positive. This includes the true positives plus the *false positives*, which are those who test positive but do not have colon cancer. Given the stipulated probabilities, in a normal population of 100,000 people, there will be 270 true positives ($100,000 \times 0.003 \times 0.9$) and 2,991 false positives [$(100,000 - 300) \times 0.03$]. Thus, the probability that Wendy has colon cancer is about $270/(270 + 2,991)$. That is only about 8.3 percent, when most people estimate above 50 percent!

Why do people, including doctors, overestimate these probabilities so badly? Part of the answer seems to be that they focus on the rate of true positives (90 percent) and forget that, because there are so many people without colon cancer (99.7 percent of the total population), even a small rate of false positives (3 percent) will yield a large number of false positives (2,991) that swamps the much smaller number of true positives (270). (When the question about probability was reformulated in terms of the number of people in each group, most doctors come up with the correct answer.) For whatever reason, people have a strong tendency to make mistakes in cases like these, so we need to be careful, especially when so much is at stake.

One way to calculate probabilities like these uses a famous theorem that was first presented by an English clergyman named Thomas Bayes (1702–1761). A simple proof of this theorem applies the laws of probability from the preceding section. We want to figure out $\Pr(h \,|\, e)$, that is, the probability of the hypothesis h (e.g., Wendy has colon cancer), given the evidence e (e.g., Wendy tested positive for colon cancer). To get there, we start from Rule 2G:

1. $\Pr(e \ \& \ h) = \Pr(e) \times \Pr(h|e)$

Dividing both sides by Pr(e) gives us:

2. $\Pr(h|e) = \dfrac{\Pr(e \ \& \ h)}{\Pr(e)}$

If two formulas are logically equivalent, they must have the same probability. We can establish by truth tables (as in Chapter 6) that "e" is logically equivalent to "(e&h) ∨ (e&~h)." Consequently, we may replace "e" in the denominator of item 2 with "(e&h) ∨ (e&~h)" to get:

3. $\Pr(h|e) = \dfrac{\Pr(e \ \& \ h)}{\Pr[(e \ \& \ h) \lor (e \ \& \ \sim h)]}$

Since "e&h" and "e&~h" are mutually exclusive, we can apply Rule 3 to the denominator of item 3 to get:

4. $\Pr(h|e) = \dfrac{\Pr(e \ \& \ h)}{\Pr(e \ \& \ h) + \Pr(e \ \& \ \sim h)}$

Finally, we apply Rule 2G to item 4 and get:

BT: $\Pr(h \,|\, e) = \dfrac{\Pr(h) \times \Pr(e \,|\, h)}{[\Pr(h) \times \Pr(e \,|\, h)] + [\Pr(\sim h) \times \Pr(e \,|\, \sim h)]}$

This is a simplified version of Bayes's theorem.

This theorem enables us to calculate the desired probability in our original example:

h = the patient has colon cancer

e = the patient tests positive for colon cancer

$\Pr(h) = 0.003$

$\Pr(\sim h) = 1 - \Pr(h) = 0.997$

$\Pr(e|h) = 0.9$

$\Pr(e|\sim h) = 0.03$

If we substitute these values into Bayes's theorem, we get:

$\Pr(h \,|\, e) = \dfrac{0.003 \times 0.9}{[0.003 \times 0.9] + [0.997 \times 0.03]} = \text{about } 0.083$

In this way, we can calculate the conditional probability of the hypothesis given the evidence from its reverse, that is, from the conditional probability of the evidence given the hypothesis. That is what makes Bayes's theorem so useful.

Many people find a different method more intuitive. The first step is to set up a table. The two factors to be related are (1) whether the patient has colon cancer and (2) whether the patient tests positive for colon cancer.

To chart all possible combinations of these two factors, we need a table like this:

	Colon Cancer	Not Colon Cancer	Total
Test Positive			
Do Not Test Positive			
Total			

Next we need to enter a population size in the lower right box. The probabilities will not be affected by the population size, but it is cleaner to pick a population that is large enough to get whole numbers when the population is multiplied by the given probabilities. To determine the right size population, add the number of places to the right of the decimal point in the two most specific probabilities, then pick a population of 10 to the power of that sum. In our example, the most specific probabilities are 0.003 and 0.03, and $3 + 2 = 5$, so we can enter 10^5:

	Colon Cancer	Not Colon Cancer	Total
Test Positive			
Do Not Test Positive			
Total			100,000

This population size represents the total number of people who are tested. We have no information about the ones who are not tested, so they cannot figure into our calculations.

The bottom row can now be filled in by dividing the total population into those who have colon cancer and those who do not have colon cancer. Just multiply the population size by the probability of colon cancer in the general population [$\Pr(h)$] to get a number for the second box on the bottom row. This figure represents the total number of people with colon cancer in this population. Then subtract that product from the population size and put the remainder in the remaining box. This represents the total number of people without colon cancer in this population. Since these two groups exhaust the population, they must add up to the total population size. In our case, we were given that the probability that a person in the general population has colon cancer is 0.003. On this basis, we can fill in the bottom row of the table:

	Colon Cancer	Not Colon Cancer	Total
Test Positive			
Do Not Test Positive			
Total	300	99,700	100,000

Next, fill out the second column by dividing the total number of people with colon cancer into those who test positive and those who do not test positive. These numbers can be calculated with the given conditional probability of testing positive, given colon cancer [$Pr(e \mid h)$]. In our example, if a person has colon cancer, the probability that the test is positive is 0.9. Thus, 270 (=0.9 × 300) of the people in the colon cancer column will test positive and the rest (300 – 270 = 30) will not, so we get these figures:

	Colon Cancer	Not Colon Cancer	Total
Test Positive	270		
Do Not Test Positive	30		
Total	300	99,700	100,000

Similarly, we can fill out the third column by dividing the total number of people without colon cancer into those who test positive and those who do not test positive. Here we use the conditional probability of a positive test, given that a person does not have colon cancer [$Pr(e \mid {\sim}h)$]. This probability was given as 0.03, and 0.03 × 99,700 = 2,991. This number means that, out of a normal population of 99,700 without colon cancer, 2,991 will test positive. Since the figures in this column must add up to a total of 99,700, the remaining figure is 99,700 – 2,991 = 96,709:

	Colon Cancer	Not Colon Cancer	Total
Test Positive	270	2,991	
Do Not Test Positive	30	96,709	
Total	300	99,700	100,000

Finally, we can fill out the fourth column by calculating total numbers of people who test positive or do not test positive. Simply add across the rows:

	Colon Cancer	Not Colon Cancer	Total
Test Positive	270	2,991	3,261
Do Not Test Positive	30	96,709	96,739
Total	300	99,700	100,000

Check your calculations by adding the right column: 3,261 + 96,739 = 100,000.

Now that our population is divided up, the solution is staring you in the face. This table shows us that, in a normal population of 100,000 tested people distributed according to the given probabilities, a total of 3,261 will test positive. Out of those, 270 will have colon cancer. Thus, the probability that the patient has colon cancer, given that this patient tested positive, is 270/3,261, which is about 0.083 or 8.3 percent, just as before.

You can also read off other conditional probabilities. If you want to know the conditional probability of *not* having colon cancer, given that your test did *not* come out positive, then you need to look at the row for those who do *not* test positive. The figure at the right of this row tells you that a total of 96,739 out of the total population do not test positive. The column under "Not Colon Cancer" then tells you that 96,709 of these do not have colon cancer. Thus, the conditional probability of not having colon cancer given your test did not come out positive is 96,709/96,739 or about 0.9997. That means that, if you test negative, the odds are extremely high that you do not have colon cancer.

Tables like these work by dividing the population into groups. We already learned some names for these groups:

	Hypothesis (*h*)	Not Hypothesis (*~h*)	
Evidence (*e*)	True Positives	False positives	
Not Evidence (*~e*)	False Negatives	True Negatives	
			Population

False positives are sometimes also called *false alarms,* and false negatives are sometimes called *misses.* A little more terminology is also common:

$\Pr(h)$ = base rate or prevalence or prior probability

$\Pr(h \mid e)$ = solution or posterior probability

$\Pr(e \mid h)$ = sensitivity of the test

$\Pr(\sim e \mid \sim h)$ = specificity of the test

$1 - \Pr(e \mid h) = 1 -$ sensitivity = false negative rate

$1 - \Pr(\sim e \mid \sim h) = 1 -$ specificity = false positive rate

You don't need to use these terms in order to calculate the probabilities, but it is useful to learn them so that you will be able to understand people who discuss these issues.

One of the most important lessons of Bayes's theorem is that the base rate has big effects. To see how much it matters, let's recalculate the solution [$\Pr(h \mid e)$] in our colon cancer example for different values of the base rate [$\Pr(h)$] using the same test with the same sensitivity ($\Pr(e \mid h) = 0.9$) and specificity [$\Pr(\sim e \mid \sim h) = 0.97$]:

If $\Pr(h) = 0.003$, then $\Pr(h \mid e) = 0.083$

If $\Pr(h) = 0.03$, then $\Pr(h \mid e) = 0.48$

If $\Pr(h) = 0.3$, then $\Pr(h \mid e) = 0.93$

EXERCISE VI

Construct tables to confirm these calculations of $\Pr(h\,|\,e)$ for base rates of 0.03 and 0.3.

These calculations show that a positive test result for a given test means a lot more when the base rate is high than when it is low. Thus, if doctors use the specified test as a *screening test* in the general population, and if the rate of colon cancer in that general population is only 0.003, then a positive test result by itself does not show that the patient has cancer. In contrast, if doctors instead use the specified test as a *diagnostic test* only for people with certain symptoms, and if the rate of colon cancer among people with those symptoms is 0.3, then a positive test result does show that the patient probably has cancer, though the test still might be mistaken. Bayes's theorem, thus, reveals the right ways and the wrong ways to use and interpret such tests.

Notice also what happens to the probabilities when additional tests are performed. In our original example, one positive test result raises the probability of cancer from the base rate of 0.003 to our solution of 0.083. Now suppose that the doctor orders an additional independent test, and the result is again positive. To apply Bayes's theorem at this point, we can take the probability after the original positive test result (0.083) as the prior probability or base rate in calculating the probability after the second positive test result. This method makes sense because we are now interested not in the general population but only in the subpopulation that already tested positive on the first test. The solution after two tests [$\Pr(h\,|\,e)$], where "*e*" is now two independent positive test results in a row, is 0.731. Next, if the doctor orders a third independent test, and if the result is positive yet again, then $\Pr(h\,|\,e)$ increases to 0.988. Bayes's theorem, thus, reveals the technical rationale behind the commonsense practice of ordering additional tests. Problems arise only when doctors put too much faith in a single positive test result without doing any additional tests.

EXERCISE VII

Construct tables to confirm the above calculations of probabilities after a second and third positive test result.

EXERCISE VIII

1. What would Wendy's chances of having colon cancer be if the other probabilities remained the same as in the original example, except that the probability that a person in the general population has colon cancer only 0.1 percent (or 0.001)?

(continued)

2. What would Wendy's chances of having colon cancer be if the other probabilities remained the same as in the original example, except that the probability that a person in the general population has colon cancer 1 percent (0.01)?

3. What would Wendy's chances of having colon cancer be if the other probabilities remained the same as in the original example, except that the conditional probability that the test is positive, given that the patient has colon cancer, is only 50 percent (or 0.5)?

4. What would Wendy's chances of having colon cancer be if the other probabilities remained the same as in the original example, except that the conditional probability that the test is positive, given that the patient has colon cancer, is 99 percent (or 0.99)?

5. What would Wendy's chances of having colon cancer be if the other probabilities remained the same as in the original example, except that the conditional probability that the test is positive, given that the patient does not have colon cancer, is 1 percent (or 0.01)?

6. What would Wendy's chances of having colon cancer be if the other probabilities remained the same as in the original example, except that the conditional probability that the test is positive, given that the patient does not have colon cancer, is 10 percent (0.1)?

7. Chris tested positive for cocaine once in a random screening test. This test has a sensitivity and specificity of 95 percent, and 20 percent of the students in Chris's school use cocaine. What is the probability that Chris really did use cocaine?

8. As in problem 7, 20 percent of the students in Chris's school use cocaine, but this time Chris tests positive for cocaine on two independent tests, both of which have a sensitivity and specificity of 95 percent. Now what is the probability that Chris really did use cocaine?

9. In your neighborhood, 20 percent of the houses have high levels of radon gas in their basements, so you ask an expert to test your basement. An inexpensive test comes out positive in 80 percent of the basements that actually have high levels of radon, but it also comes out positive in 10 percent of the basements that do not have high levels of radon. If this inexpensive test comes out positive in your basement, what is the probability that there is a high level of radon gas in your basement?

10. A more expensive test for radon is also more accurate. It comes out positive in 99 percent of the basements that actually have high levels of radon. It also tests positive in 2 percent of the basements that do not high levels of radon. As in problem 7, 20 percent of the houses in your neighborhood have radon in their basement. If the expensive test comes out positive in your basement, what is the probability that there is a high level of radon gas in your basement?

11. Late last night a car ran into your neighbor and drove away. In your town, there are 500 cars, and 2 percent of them are Porsches. The only eyewitness to the hit-and-run says the car that hit your neighbor was a Porsche. Tested

under similar conditions, the eyewitness mistakenly classifies cars of other makes as Porsches 10 percent of the time, and correctly classifies Porsches as such 80 percent of the time. What are the chances that the car that hit your neighbor really was a Porsche?

12. Late last night a dog bit your neighbor. In your town, there are 400 dogs, 95 percent of them are black Labrador retrievers, and the rest are pit bulls. The only eyewitness to the event, a veteran dog breeder, says that the dog who bit your neighbor was a pit bull. Tested under similar low-light conditions, the eyewitness mistakenly classifies black Labs as pit bulls only 2 percent of the time, and correctly classifies pit bulls as pit bulls 90 percent of the time. What are the chances that dog who bit your neighbor really was a pit bull?

13. In a certain school, the probability that a student reads the assigned pages before a lecture is 80 percent (or 0.8). If a student does the assigned reading in advance, then the probability that the student will understand the lecture is 90 percent (or 0.9). If a student does not do the assigned reading in advance, then the probability that the student will understand the lecture is 10 percent (or 0.1). What is the probability that a student did the reading in advance, given that she did understand the lecture? What is the probability that a student did *not* do the reading in advance, given that she did *not* understand the lecture?

14. In a different school, the probability that a student reads the assigned pages before a lecture is 60 percent (or 0.6). If a student does the assigned reading in advance, then the probability that, when asked, the student will tell the professor that he did the reading is 100 percent (or 1.0). If a student does not do the assigned reading in advance, then the probability that, when asked, the student will tell the professor that he did the reading is 70 percent (or 0.7). What is the probability that a student did the reading in advance, given that, when asked, he told the professor that he did the reading? What is the probability that a student did not do the reading in advance, given that, when asked, he told the professor that he did not do the reading?

DISCUSSION QUESTION

Should Sally Clark be found guilty of murder? Why or why not? The following account of her case was extracted from http://pass.maths.org.uk/issue21/features/clark (10/22/04):

Five years ago, a young couple from Cheshire suffered one of the most devastating losses imaginable—their baby Christopher died in his sleep, aged 11 weeks. Doctors, neighbours, all were sympathetic, and the death was certified as natural causes—there was evidence of a respiratory infection, and no sign of any failure of care.

(continued)

But just a year later, in what must have felt like a horribly familiar nightmare, the Clarks' second child Harry died, aged 8 weeks. This time, there was no sympathy from the professionals. Four weeks after Harry's death the couple were arrested, and eventually Sally Clark was charged with murdering both children. She was tried and convicted in 1999 and is now almost three years into a life sentence.

The forensic evidence was slim to nonexistent—certainly neither case would have stood up alone. . . . So how come Sally Clark is serving life in prison? Simply put, because [of] a seemingly authoritative statement by pediatrician Sir Roy Meadow . . . that the chance of two children in the same (affluent nonsmoking) family both dying a cot death was 1 in 73 million. . . .

INDEPENDENCE

This statistic of 1 in 73 million came from the Confidential Enquiry for Stillbirths and Deaths in Infancy (CESDI), an authoritative and detailed study of deaths of babies in five regions of England between 1993 and 1996. There it is estimated that the chances of a randomly chosen baby dying a cot death are 1 in 1,303. If the child is from an affluent, nonsmoking family, with the mother over 26, the odds fall to around 1 in 8,500. The authors go on to say that *if* there is no link between cot deaths of siblings (because we have eliminated the biggest known and possibly shared factors influencing cot death rates) then we would be able to estimate the chances of two children from such a family both suffering a cot death by squaring 1/8,500—giving 1 chance in 73 million.

So far so good. But are cot deaths in the same family really independent? The website for the Foundation for the Study of Infant Death (FSID) says baldly that "second cot deaths in the same family are very rare." This is no help, because so are first-sibling cot deaths—what we need to know is, how comparatively rare? Does having one child die a cot death increase the chances that you will have another do so?

Ray Hill . . . estimates that siblings of children who die of cot death are between 10 and 22 times more likely than average to die the same way. Using the figure of 1 in 1,303 for the chance of a first cot death, we see that the chances of a second cot death in the same family are somewhere between 1 in 60 and 1 in 130. There isn't enough data to be more precise, or to take familial factors into account, but it seems reasonable to use a ballpark figure of 1 in 100. Multiplying 1/1,303 by 1/100 gives an estimate for the incidence of double cot death of around 1 in 130,000. . . .

BAYES'S THEOREM

. . . Very possibly, as you're reading this, you are . . . thinking "okay, so the odds aren't as extreme as 1 in 73 million, but they're still astronomically high. There's not that much difference between odds of 1 in 73 million and 1 in 100,000, so Sally Clark must still be guilty." If so, you're committing the "Prosecutor's Fallacy."

Simply put, this is the incorrect belief that the chance of a rare event happening is the same as the chance that the defendant is innocent. Even with the more accurate figure of 1 in 100,000 for the chance that a *randomly chosen* pair of siblings will both die of cot death, this is not the chance that Sally Clark is innocent. It is the chance that an *arbitrary* family will lose two children in cot deaths. . . .

In mathematical language, we need to find the *conditional probabilities* of the various possible causes of death, *given* the fact that the children died. If H is some hypothesis (for example, that both of Sally Clark's children died of natural causes) and D is some data (that both children are dead), we want to find the probability of the hypothesis given the data, which is written $P(H|D)$. Let's write A for the alternate hypothesis—that Sally Clark murdered both her children. We will discount all other possibilities, for example that someone else murdered both children, or that Sally Clark murdered only one of them.

$$P(H|D) = \frac{P(D|H)P(H)}{P(D|H)P(H) + P(D|A)P(A)}$$

This is not as complicated as it looks. We already have an estimate for $P(H)$ of $1/100,000$. . . . Trivially, both $P(D|H)$ and $P(D|A)$ are equal to 1. These numbers are the probabilities that two of the children are dead, given that that two of the children have died of natural causes, or been murdered, respectively.

A completely accurate version of Bayes's Theorem would take into account all sorts of factors—for example, the fact that social services had not been involved with the Clark family, their income level, and so on—but there isn't a sufficient amount of data available to do this. However, if we are only looking to analyse the case against Sally Clark, it is sufficient . . . to make reasonable estimates and show that these lead to reasonable doubt.

$P(A)$ is the most difficult figure to estimate. It is the probability that a randomly chosen pair of siblings will both be murdered. Statistics on such double murders are pretty much nonexistent, because child murders are so rare (far, far more rare than cot deaths) and because in most cases, someone known to have murdered once is not free to murder again. So we fall back on the Home Office statistic that fewer than 30 children are known to be murdered by their mother each year in England and Wales. Since 650,000 are born each year, and murders of pairs of siblings are clearly rarer than single murders, we should use a figure much smaller than $30/650,000 = 0.000046$. We will put a number ten times as small here— 0.0000046—which is almost certainly overestimating the incidence rate of double murder.

Now we get a rough and ready estimate of Sally Clark's innocence:

$$P(H|D) = \frac{P(H)}{P(H) + P(A)} = \frac{0.00001}{0.00001 + 0.0000046} > \frac{2}{3}$$

I must warn the reader that this figure isn't intended to be in any way an accurate estimate of the likelihood that Sally Clark is innocent. It is only meant to show that, with some reasonable estimates of the likelihoods of relevant events, the scales come down on the side of her innocence rather than her guilt. The only way to disagree with this analysis is to assume that literally hundreds, or thousands, of mothers murder their children undetected every year. The Campaign to Free Sally Clark say that nearly fifty families have contacted them to say that they have suffered double cot deaths. Are we to believe that the majority of these couples are murderers, confident or mad enough to draw attention to themselves in this way? . . .

Plus readers may be interested to know that Sally Clark's case has been referred to the Appeal Court for a second time. Evidence, not made available to her original defence team, has recently come to light that at the time of Harry's death, he was suffering from a bacterial blood infection known to cause sudden infant death.

NOTES

[1] Amos Tversky and Daniel Kahneman, "Extensional Versus Intuitive Reasoning: The Conjunction Fallacy in Probability Judgment." *Psychological Review* 90 (1983): 297.

[2] Ibid.

[3] Thomas Gilovich, Robert Vallone, and Amos Tversky, "The Hot Hand in Basketball: The Misperception of Random Sequences," *Cognitive Psychology* 17 (1985): 295–314. The quotation is from pages 295–6.

[4] See Gerd Gigerenzer, *Calculated Risk: How to Know When Numbers Deceive You* (New York: Simon & Schuster, 2003).

12

CHOICES

Probabilities are used not only when we determine what to believe but also when we choose what to do. Although we sometimes assume that we know how our actions will turn out, we often have to make decisions in the face of risk, when we do not know what the outcomes of our options will be, but we do know the probabilities of those outcomes. To help us assess reasoning about choices involving risk, this chapter will explain the notions of expected monetary value and expected overall value. Our most difficult choices arise, however, when we do not know even the probabilities of various outcomes. Such decisions under ignorance or uncertainty pose special problems, for which a number of rules have been proposed. Although these rules are useful in many situations, their limitations will also be noted.

EXPECTED MONETARY VALUE

It is obvious that having some sense of probable outcomes is important for running our lives. If we hear that there is a 95 percent chance of rain, this usually provides a good enough reason to call off a picnic. But the exact relationship between probabilities and decisions is complex and often misunderstood.

The best way to illustrate these misunderstandings is to look at lotteries in which the numbers are fixed and clear. A $1 bet in a lottery might make you as much as $10 million. That sounds good. Why not take a shot at $10 million for only a dollar? Of course, there is not much chance of winning the lottery—say, only 1 chance in 20 million—and that sounds bad. Why throw $1 away on nothing? So we are pulled in two directions. What we want to know is just how good the bet is. Is it, for example, better or worse than a wager in some other lottery? To answer questions of this kind, we need to introduce the notion of expected monetary value.

The idea of expected monetary value takes into account three features that determine whether a bet is financially good or bad: the probability of winning, the net amount you gain if you win, and the net amount you lose if you lose. Suppose that on a $1 ticket there is 1 chance in 20 million of winning the New York State Lottery, and you will get $10 million from the state if you do. First, it is worth noticing that, if the state pays you

$10 million, your net gain on your $1 ticket is only $9,999,999. The state, after all, still has your original $1. So the net gain equals the payoff minus the cost of betting. This is not something that those who win huge lotteries worry about, but taking into account the cost of betting becomes important when this cost becomes high relative to the size of the payoff. There is nothing complicated about the net amount that you lose when you lose on a $1 ticket: It is $1.[1]

We can now compute the expected monetary value or financial worth of a bet in the following way:

Expected monetary value =

(the probability of winning times the net gain in money of winning) minus

(the probability of losing times the net loss in money of losing)

In our example, a person who buys a $1 ticket in the lottery has 1 chance in 20 million of a net gain of $9,999,999 and 19,999,999 chances in 20 million of a net loss of a dollar. So the expected monetary value of this wager equals:

$$(1/20,000,000 \times \$9,999,999) - (19,999,999/20,000,000 \times \$1)$$

That comes out to −$0.50.

What does this mean? One way of looking at it is as follows: If you could somehow buy up all the lottery tickets and thus ensure that you would win, your $20 million investment would net you $10 million, or $0.50 on the dollar—certainly a bad investment. Another way of looking at the situation is as follows: If you invested a great deal of money in the lottery over many millions of years, you could expect to win eventually, but, in the long run, you would be losing fifty cents on every ticket you bought. One last way of looking at the situation is this: You go down to your local drugstore and buy a blank lottery ticket for $0.50. Since it is blank, you have no chance of winning, with the result that you lose $0.50 every time you bet. Although almost no one looks at the matter in this way, this is, in effect, what you are doing over the long run when you buy lottery tickets.

We are now in a position to distinguish favorable and unfavorable expected monetary values. The expected monetary value is favorable when it is greater than zero. Changing our example, suppose the chances of hitting a $20 million payoff on a $1 bet are 1 in 10 million. In this case, the state still has the $1 you paid for the ticket, so your gain is actually $19,999,999. The expected monetary value is calculated as follows:

$$(1/10,000,000 \times \$19,999,999) - (9,999,999/10,000,000 \times \$1)$$

That comes to $1. Financially, this is a good bet; for in the long run you will gain $1 for every $1 you bet in such a lottery.

The rule, then, has three parts: (1) If the expected monetary value of the bet is more than zero, then the expected monetary value is favorable. (2) If the expected monetary value of the bet is less than zero, then the expected monetary value is unfavorable. (3) If the expected monetary value of the bet is zero, then the bet is neutral—a waste of time as far as money is concerned.

Compute the probability and the expected monetary value for the following bets. Each time, you lay down $1 to bet that a certain kind of card will appear from a standard fifty-two-card deck. If you win, you collect the amount indicated, so your net gain is $1 less. If you lose, of course, you lose your $1.

Example: Draw a seven of spades. Win: $26.

Probability of winning = $1/52$

Expected value: $[1/52 \times \$(26–1)] – (51/52 \times \$1) = –\$0.50$

1. Draw a seven of spades or a seven of clubs. Win: $26.
2. Draw a seven of any suit. Win: $26.
3. Draw a face card (jack, queen, or king). Win: $4.
4. Do *not* draw a face card (jack, queen, or king). Win: $2.
5. On two consecutive draws without returning the first card to the deck, draw a seven of spades and then a seven of clubs. Win: $1,989.
6. Same as in problem 3, but this time the card is returned to the deck and the deck is shuffled before the second draw. Win: $1,989.
7. On two consecutive draws without returning the first card to the deck, do not draw a club. Win: $1.78.
8. Same as in problem 7, but this time the card is returned to the deck and the deck is shuffled before the second draw. Win: $1.78.
9. On four consecutive draws without returning any cards to the deck, a seven of spades, then a seven of clubs, then a seven of hearts, and then seven of diamonds. Win: $1,000,001.
10. On four consecutive draws without returning any cards to the deck, draw four sevens in any order. Win: $1,000,001.

Fogelin's Palace in Border, Nevada, offers the following unusual bet. If you win, you make a 50 percent profit on your bet; if you lose, you take a 40 percent loss. That is, if you bet $1 and win, then you get back $1.50; if you bet $1 and lose, you get back $0.60. The chances of winning are fifty-fifty. This sounds like a marvelous opportunity, but there is one hitch: To play, you must let your bet ride with its winnings, or losses, for four plays. For example, with $100, a four-bet sequence might look like this:

	Win	Win	Lose	Win
Total	$150	$225	$135	$202.50

At the end of this sequence, you can pick up $202.50, and thus make a $102.50 profit. It seems that Fogelin's Palace is a good place to gamble, but consider

(continued)

the following argument on the other side. Because the chances of winning are fifty-fifty, you will, on the average, win half the time. But notice what happens in such a case:

	Win	Lose	Lose	Win
Total	$150	$90	$54	$81

So, even though you have won half the time, you have come out $19 behind.

Surprisingly, it does not matter what order the wins and losses come in; if two are wins and two are losses, you come out behind. (You can check this.) So, because you are only going to win roughly half the time, and when you win half the time you actually lose money, it now seems to be a bad idea to gamble at Fogelin's Palace.

What should you do: gamble at Fogelin's Palace or not? Why?

EXPECTED OVERALL VALUE

Given that lotteries usually have an extremely unfavorable expected monetary value, why do millions of people invest billions of dollars in them each year? Part of the answer is that some people are stupid, superstitious, or both. People will sometimes reason, "Somebody has to win; why not me?" They can also convince themselves that their lucky day has come. But that is not the whole story, for most people who put down money on lottery tickets realize that the bet is a bad bet, but think that it is worth doing anyway. People fantasize about what they will do with the money if they win, and fantasies are fun. Furthermore, if the bet is only $1, and the person making the bet is not desperately poor, losing is not going to hurt much. Even if the expected monetary value on the lottery ticket is the loss of fifty cents, this might strike someone as a reasonable price for the fun of thinking about winning. (After all, you accept a sure loss of $8 every time you pay $8 to see a movie.) So a bet that is bad from a purely monetary point of view might be acceptable when other factors are considered.

The reverse situation can also arise: A bet may be unreasonable, even though it has a positive expected monetary value. Suppose, for example, that you are allowed to participate in a lottery in which a $1 ticket gives you 1 chance in 10 million of getting a payoff of $20 million. Here, as noted above, the expected monetary value of a $1 bet is a profit of $1, so from the point of view of expected monetary value, it is a good bet. This makes it sound reasonable to bet in this lottery, and a small bet probably is reasonable. But under these circumstances, would it be reasonable for you to sell everything you owned to buy lottery tickets? The answer to this is almost certainly no, for, even though the expected monetary value is positive, the odds of winning are still low, and the loss of your total resources would be personally catastrophic.

When we examine the effects that success or failure will have on a particular person relative to his or her own needs, resources, preferences, and so on, we are then examining what we shall call the *expected overall value* or *expected utility* of a choice. Considerations of this kind often force us to make adjustments in weighing the significance of costs and payoffs. In the examples we just examined, the immediate catastrophic consequences of a loss outweigh the long-term gains one can expect from participating in the lottery.

Another factor that typically affects the expected overall value of a bet is the phenomenon known as the *diminishing marginal value* or *diminishing marginal utility* of a payoff as it gets larger. Suppose someone offers to pay a debt by buying you a hamburger. Provided that the debt matches the cost of a hamburger and you feel like having one, you might go along with this. But suppose this person offers to pay off a debt ten times larger by buying you ten hamburgers? The chances are that you will reject the offer, for even though ten hamburgers cost ten times as much as one hamburger, they are not worth ten times as much to you. At some point you will get stuffed and not want any more. After one or two hamburgers, the marginal value of one more hamburger becomes pretty low. The notion of marginal value applies to money as well. If you are starving, $10 will mean a lot to you. You might be willing to work hard to get it. If you are wealthy, $10 more or less makes little difference; losing $10 might only be an annoyance.

Because of this phenomenon of diminishing marginal value, betting on lotteries is an even worse bet than most people suppose. A lottery with a payoff of $20 million sounds attractive, but it does not seem to be twenty times more attractive than a payoff of $1 million. So even if the expected monetary value of your $1 bet in a lottery is the loss of $0.50, the actual value to you is really something less than this, and so the bet is even worse than it seemed at first.

In general, then, when payoffs are large, the expected overall value of the payoff to someone is reduced because of the effects of diminishing marginal value. But not always. It is possible to think of exotic cases in which expected overall value increases with the size of the payoff. Suppose a witch told you that she would turn you into a toad if you did not give her $10 million by tomorrow. You believe her, because you know for a fact that she has turned others into toads when they did not pay up. You have only $1 to your name, but you are given the opportunity to participate in the first lottery described above, where a $1 ticket gives you 1 chance in 20 million of hitting a $10 million payoff. We saw that the expected monetary value of that wager was an unfavorable negative $0.50. But now consider the overall value of $1 to you if you are turned into a toad. Toads have no use for money, so to you, as a toad, the value of the dollar would drop to nothing. Thus, unless some other, more attractive alternatives are available, it would be reasonable to buy a lottery ticket, despite the unfavorable expected monetary value of the wager.

1. Though the situation is somewhat far-fetched, suppose you are going to the drugstore to buy medicine for a friend who will die without it. You have only $10—exactly what the medicine costs. Outside the drugstore a young man is playing three-card monte, a simple game in which the dealer shows you three cards, turns them over, shifts them briefly from hand to hand, and then lays them out, face down, on the top of a box. You are supposed to identify a particular card (usually the ace of spades); and, if you do, you are paid even money. You yourself are a magician and know the sleight-of-hand trick that fools most people, and you are sure that you can guess the card correctly nine times out of ten. First, what is the expected monetary value of a bet of $10? In this context, would it be reasonable to make this bet? Why or why not?

2. Provide an example of your own where a bet can be reasonable even though the expected monetary value is unfavorable. Then provide another example where the bet is unreasonable even though the expected monetary value is favorable. Explain what makes these bets reasonable or unreasonable.

Consider the following game: You flip a coin continuously until you get tails once. If you get no heads (tails on the first flip), then you are paid nothing. If you get one heads (tails on the second flip), then you are paid $2. If you get two heads (tails on the third flip), then you are paid $4. If you get three heads, then you are paid $8. And so on. The general rule is that for any number n, if you get n heads, then you are paid $\$2^n$. What is the expected monetary value of this game? What would you pay to play this game? Why that amount rather than more or less?

DECISIONS UNDER IGNORANCE

So far we have discussed choices where the outcomes of the various options are not certain, but we know their probabilities. Decisions of this kind are called *decisions under risk*. In other cases, however, we do not know the probabilities of various outcomes. Decisions of this kind are called *decisions under ignorance* (or, sometimes, *decisions under uncertainty*). If we do not have any idea where the probabilities of various outcomes lie, the ignorance is complete. If we know that these probabilities lie within some general range, the ignorance is partial.

As an example of partial ignorance, suppose that, just after graduating from college, you are offered three jobs. First, the Exe Company offers you a salary of $20,000. Exe is well-established and secure. The next offer comes from the Wye Company. Here the salary is $30,000, but Wye is a new company, so it is less secure. You think that this new company will probably do well, but you don't know how likely it is to last or for how long. Wye might go bankrupt, and then you will be left without a job. The final offer comes from the Zee Company, which is as stable as Exe and offers you a salary of $40,000 per year. These offers are summarized in the following table:

	Wye does not go bankrupt	Wye goes bankrupt
Take job at Exe	$20,000	$20,000
Take job at Wye	$30,000	$0
Take job at Zee	$40,000	$40,000

Let's assume that other factors (such as benefits, vacations, location, interest, working conditions, bonuses, raises, and promotions) are all equally desirable in the three jobs. Which job should you take?

The answer is clear: Take the job from the Zee Company. This decision is easy because you end up better off regardless of whether or not Wye goes bankrupt, so it doesn't matter how likely Wye's bankruptcy is. Everyone agrees that you should choose any option that is best whatever happens. This is called the *rule of dominance*.

The problem with the rule of dominance is that it can't help you make choices when no option is better regardless of what happens. Suppose you discover that the letter from the Zee Company is a forgery—part of a cruel joke by your roommate. Now your only options are Exe and Wye. The job with Wye will be better if Wye does not go bankrupt, but the job with Exe will be better if Wye does go bankrupt. Neither job is better no matter what happens, so the rule of dominance no longer applies.

To help you choose between Exe and Wye, you might look for a rational way to assign probabilities despite your ignorance of which assignments are correct. One approach of this kind uses the *rule of insufficient reason:* When you have no reason to think that any outcome is more likely than any other, assume that the outcomes are equally probable. This assumption enables us to calculate expected monetary value or utility, as in the preceding sections, and then we can choose the option with the highest expected utility. In our example, this rule of insufficient reason favors the job at Exe, because your expected income in that job is $20,000, whereas your expected income in the job at Wye is only $15,000 (= 0.5 × $30,000), assuming that the Wye company has as much chance of going bankrupt as of staying in business.

The problem with the rule of insufficient reason is that it may seem arbitrary to assume that unknown probabilities are equal. Often we suspect that the probabilities of various outcomes are not equal, even while we do not know what the probabilities are. Moreover, the rule of insufficient reason yields different results when the options are described differently. We can distinguish four possibilities: Wye goes bankrupt, Wye stays the same size, Wye increases in size, and Wye decreases in size but stays in business. If we do not have any reason to see any of these outcomes as more likely than any other, then the rule of insufficient reason tells us to assign them equal probabilities. On that assumption, and if you will keep your job as long as Wye stays in business, then you have only one chance in four of losing your job; so your expected income in the job at Wye is now $22,500 (= ¾ × $30,000). Thus, if we stick with the rule of insufficient reason, the expected value of the job at Wye and whether you should take that job seem to depend on how the options are divided. That seems crazy in this case.

Another approach tries to work without any assumptions about probability in cases of ignorance. Within this approach, several rules might be adopted. One possibility is the *maximax rule*, which tells you to choose the option whose best outcome is better than the best outcome of any other option. If you follow the maximax rule, then you will accept the job with the Wye Company, because the best outcome of that job is a salary of $30,000 when this new company does not go bankrupt, and this is better than any outcome with the Exe Company. Optimists and risk takers will favor this rule.

Other people are more pessimistic and tend to avoid risks. They will favor a rule more like the *maximin rule*, which says to choose the option whose worst outcome is better than the worst outcome of any other option. If you follow the maximin rule, you will accept the job with the Exe Company, because the worst outcome in that job is a steady salary of $20,000, whereas the worst outcome is unemployment if you accept the job with the Wye Company.

Each of these rules works by focusing exclusively on part of your information and disregarding other things that you know. The maximax rule considers only the best outcomes for each option—the best-case scenario. The maximin rule pays attention to only the worst outcome for each option—the worst-case scenario. Because they ignore other outcomes, the maximax rule strikes many people as too risky (since it does not consider how much you could lose by taking a chance), and the maximin rule strikes many people as too conservative (since it does not consider how much you could have gained if you had taken a small risk).

Another problem is that the maximax and maximin rules do not take probabilities into account at all. This makes sense when you know nothing about the probabilities. But when some (even if limited) information about probabilities is available, then it seems better to use as much information as you have. Suppose, for example, that each of two options might lead to disaster, and you do not know how likely a disaster is after either option, but you do know that one option is more likely to lead to disaster than another. In such situations, some decision theorists argue that you should choose the option that minimizes the chance that any disaster will occur. This is called the *disaster avoidance rule*.

To illustrate this rule, consider a different kind of case:

> A forty-year-old man is diagnosed as having a rare disease and consults the world's leading expert on the disease. He is informed that the disease is almost certainly not fatal but often causes serious paralysis that leaves its victims

bedridden for life. (In other cases it has no lasting effects.) The disease is so rare that the expert can offer only a vague estimate of the probability of paralysis: 20 to 60 percent. There is an experimental drug that, if administered now, would almost certainly cure the disease. However, it kills a significant but not accurately known percentage of those who take it. The expert guesses that the probability of the drug being fatal is less than 20 percent, and the patient thus assumes that he is definitely less likely to die if he takes the drug than he is to be paralyzed if he lets the disease run its course. The patient would regard bedridden life as preferable to death, but he considers both outcomes as totally disastrous compared to continuing his life in good health. Should he take the drug?[2]

Since the worst outcome is death, and this outcome will not occur unless he takes the drug, the maximin rule would tell him not to take the drug. In contrast, the disaster avoidance rule would tell him to take the drug, because both death and paralysis are disasters and taking the drug minimizes his chances that any disaster will occur. Thus, although the disaster avoidance rule opposes risk taking, it does so in a different way than the maximin rule.

We are left, then, with a plethora of rules: dominance, insufficient reason, maximax, maximin, and disaster avoidance. Other rules have been proposed as well. With all of these rules in the offing, it is natural to ask which is correct. Unfortunately, there is no consensus on this issue. Each rule applies and seems plausible in some cases but not in others. Many people conclude that each rule is appropriate to different kinds of situations. It is still not clear, however, which rule should govern decisions in which circumstances. The important problem of decision under ignorance remains unsolved.

DISCUSSION QUESTIONS

1. In the game of ignorance, you draw one card from a deck, but you do not know how many cards or which kinds of cards are in the deck. It might be a normal deck or it might contain only diamonds or only aces of spades or any other combination of cards. It costs nothing to play. If you bet that the card you draw will be a spade, and it is a spade, then you win $100. If you bet that the card you draw will not be a spade, and it is not a spade, then you win $90. You may make only one bet. Which bet would you make if you followed the maximax rule? The maximin rule? The disaster avoidance rule? The rule of insufficient reason? Which rule seems most plausible this case? Which bet should you make? Why?

2. In which circumstances do you think it is appropriate to use the dominance rule? The rule of insufficient reason? The maximax rule? The maximin rule? The disaster avoidance rule? Why?

3. Suppose that you may choose either of two envelopes. You know that one envelope contains twice as much money as the other, but you do not know the amount of money in either envelope. You choose an envelope, open it, and see that it contains $100. Now you know that the other envelope must

(continued)

contain either $50 or $200. At this point, you are given a choice: You may exchange your envelope for the other envelope. Should you switch envelopes, according to the rule of insufficient reason? Is this result plausible? Why or why not?

4. The following article raises a problem in dealing with infinity. How would you answer it?

PLAYING GAMES WITH ETERNITY: THE DEVIL'S OFFER[3]

by Edward J. Gracely

Suppose Ms C dies and goes to hell, or to a place that seems like hell. The devil approaches and offers to play a game of chance. If she wins, she can go to heaven. If she loses, she will stay in hell forever; there is no second chance to play the game. If Ms C plays today, she has a 1/2 chance of winning. Tomorrow the probability will be 2/3. Then 3/4, 4/5, 5/6, etc., with no end to the series. Thus, every passing day increases her chances of winning. At what point should she play the game?

The answer is not obvious: after any given number of days spent waiting, it will still be possible to improve her chances by waiting yet another day. And any increase in the probability of winning a game with infinite stakes has an infinite utility. For example, if she waits a year, her probability of winning the game would be approximately 0.997268; if she waits one more day, the probability would increase to 0.997275, a difference of only 0.000007. Yet even 0.000007 multiplied by infinity is infinite.

On the other hand, it seems reasonable to suppose the cost of delaying for a day to be finite—a day's more suffering in hell. So the infinite expected benefit from a delay will always exceed the cost.

This logic might suggest that Ms C should wait forever, but clearly such a strategy would be self-defeating: why should she stay forever in a place in order to increase her chances of leaving it? So the question remains: what should Ms C do?

5. Pascal is famous for invoking infinite utilities to argue for belief in God. Explain and evaluate his argument in the following passage.

THE WAGER[4]

by Blaise Pascal

... Let us weigh the gain and the loss in wagering that God is. Let us estimate these two chances. If you gain, you gain all; if you lose, you lose nothing.

Wager, then, without hesitation that He is.—"That is very fine. Yes, I must wager; but I may perhaps wager too much."—Let us see. Since there is an equal risk of gain and of loss, if you had only to gain two lives, instead of one, you might still wager. But if there were three lives to gain, you would have to play (since you are under the necessity of playing), and you would be imprudent, when you are forced to play, not to chance your life to gain three at a game where there is an equal risk of loss and gain. But there is an eternity of life and happiness. And this being so, if there were an infinity of chances, of which one only would be for you, you would still be right in wagering one to win two, and you would act stupidly, being obliged to play, by refusing to stake one life against three at a game in which out of an infinity of chances there is one for you, if there were an infinity of an infinitely happy life to gain. But there is here an infinity of an infinitely happy life to gain, a chance of gain against a finite number of chances of loss, and what you stake is finite. It is all divided; wherever the infinite is and there is not an infinity of chances of loss against that of gain, there is no time to hesitate, you must give all. And thus, when one is forced to play, he must renounce reason to preserve his life, rather than risk it for infinite gain, as likely to happen as the loss of nothingness. . . .

The end of this discourse.—Now, what harm will befall you in taking this side? You will be faithful, honest, humble, grateful, generous, a sincere friend, truthful. Certainly you will not have those poisonous pleasures, glory and luxury; but will you not have others? I will tell you that you will thereby gain in this life, and that, at each step you take on this road, you will see so great certainty of gain, so much nothingness in what you risk, that you will at last recognize that you have wagered for something certain and infinite, for which you have given nothing.

6. In the following passage, James Cargile responds to Pascal's argument. Explain Cargile's point. How could Pascal best respond? Is this response adequate? Why or why not?

Either (a) there is a god who will send only religious people to heaven or (b) there is not. To be religious is to wager for (a). To fail to be religious is to wager for (b). We can't settle the question whether (a) or (b) is the case, at least not at present. But (a) is clearly vastly better than (b). With (a), infinite bliss is *guaranteed,* while with (b) we are still in the miserable human condition of facing death with no assurance as to what lies beyond. So (a) is clearly the best wager. . . .

This argument just presented is formally similar to the following: Either (a) there is a god who will send you to heaven only if you commit a painful ritual suicide within an hour of first reading this, or (b) there is not. We cannot settle the question whether (a) or (b) is the case or it is at least not settled yet. But (a) is vastly preferable to (b), since in situation (a) infinite bliss is *guaranteed,* while in (b) we are left in the miserable human condition. So we should wager for (a) by performing ritual suicide.

It might be objected that we can be sure that there is not a god who will send us to heaven only if we commit suicide, but we can't be sure that there is not a god who will send us to heaven only if we are religious. However, a sceptic would demand proof of this. . . .[5]

NOTES

[1] If the lottery gave a consolation prize of a shiny new quarter to all losers, their net loss would be only seventy-five cents. Since most lotteries do not give consolation prizes, the net loss equals the cost of playing such lotteries.

[2] Gregory Kavka, "Deterrence, Utility, and Rational Choice," reprinted in *Moral Paradoxes of Nuclear Deterrence* (New York: Cambridge University Press, 1987), 65–66. Kavka uses this medical example to argue for his disaster avoidance rule and, by analogy, to defend the rationality of nuclear deterrence.

[3] From *Analysis* 48 (1988): 113.

[4] From *Pensées and the Provincial Letters,* trans. W. F. Trotter (New York: Modern Library, 1941).

[5] From "Pascal's Wager," *Philosophy* 41 (1966): 254.

FALLACIES

When inferences are defective, they are called fallacious. When defective styles of reasoning are repeated over and over, because people often get fooled by them, then we have an argumentative fallacy that is worth flagging with a name. The number and variety of argumentative fallacies are limited only by the imagination. Consequently, there is little point in trying to construct a complete list of fallacies. What is crucial is to get a feel for the most common and most seductive kinds of fallacy. Once this is done, we should be able to recognize many other kinds as well. The goal of Part IV is to develop that skill.

13

FALLACIES OF VAGUENESS

This chapter examines one of the main ways in which arguments can be defective or fallacious because language is not used clearly enough for the context. This kind of unclarity is vagueness. Vagueness occurs when, in a given context, a term is used in a way that allows too many cases in which it is unclear whether or not the term applies. Vagueness underlies several common fallacies, including three kinds of slippery-slope arguments.

USES OF UNCLARITY

In a good argument, a person states a conclusion clearly and then, with equal clarity, gives reasons for this conclusion. The arguments of everyday life often fall short of this standard. Usually, unclear language is a sign of unclear thought. There are times, however, when people are intentionally unclear. They might use unclarity for poetic effect or to leave details to be decided later. But often their goal is to confuse others. This is called *obfuscation*.

Before we look at the various ways in which language can be unclear, a word of caution is needed: There is no such thing as absolute clarity. Whether something is clear or not depends on the context in which it occurs. A botanist does not use common vocabulary in describing and classifying plants. At the same time, it would usually be foolish for a person to use botanical terms in describing the appearance of her backyard. Aristotle said that it is the mark of an educated person not to expect more rigor than the subject matter will allow. Because clarity and rigor depend on context, it takes judgment and good sense to pitch an argument at the right level.

Non Sequitur　　　　　　　　　　　　　　　　　　　**by Wiley**

VAGUENESS

Perhaps the most common form of unclarity is *vagueness*. It arises when a concept applies along a continuum or a series of very small changes. The standard example is baldness. A person with a full head of hair is not bald. A person without a hair on his head is bald. In between, however, is a range of cases in which we cannot say definitely whether the person is bald or not. These are called *borderline cases*. Here we say something less definite, such as that this person is "going bald."

Our inability to apply the concept of baldness in a borderline case is not due to ignorance of the number of hairs on the person's head. It will not help to count the number of hairs there. Even if we knew the exact number, we would still not be able to say whether the person was bald or not. The same is true of most adjectives that concern properties admitting of degrees—for example, "rich," "healthy," "tall," "wise," and "ruthless."

For the most part, imprecision—the lack of sharply defined limits— causes little difficulty. In fact, this is a useful feature of our language, for suppose we *did* have to count the number of grains of salt between our fingers to determine whether or not we hold a *pinch* of salt. It would take a long time to follow a simple recipe that calls for a pinch of salt.

Yet difficulties can arise when borderline cases themselves are at issue. Suppose that a state passes a law forbidding all actions that offend a large number of people. There will be many cases that clearly fall under this law and many cases that clearly do not fall under it. There will also be many cases in which it will not be clear whether or not they fall under this law. Laws are sometimes declared unconstitutional for this very reason. Here we shall say that the law is vague. In calling the law vague, we are criticizing it. We are not simply noticing the existence of borderline cases, for there will usually be borderline cases no matter how careful we are. Instead, we are saying that there are *too many* borderline cases for this context. More precisely, we shall say that an expression in a given context is *used vaguely* if it leaves open too wide a range of borderline cases for the successful and legitimate use of that expression in that context.

Vagueness thus depends on context. To further illustrate this context dependence, consider the expression "light football player." There are, of course, borderline cases between those football players who are light and those who are not light. But on these grounds alone, we would not say that the expression is vague. It is usually a perfectly serviceable expression, and we can indicate borderline cases by saying such things as "Jones is a bit light for a football player." Suppose, however, that Ohio State and Cal Tech wish to have a game between their light football players. It is obvious that the previous understanding of what counts as being light is too vague for this new context. At Ohio State, anyone under 210 pounds is considered light. At Cal Tech, anyone over 150 pounds is considered heavy. What is needed, then, is a ruling, such as that anyone under 175 pounds will be considered a lightweight. This example illustrates a common problem and its solution. A term that works perfectly well in one area becomes vague when applied in some other (usually more specialized) area. This vagueness can then be removed by adopting more precise rules in the problematic area. Vagueness is resolved by definition.

EXERCISE I

For each of the following terms, give one case to which the term clearly applies, one case to which the term clearly does not apply, and one borderline case. Then try to explain why the borderline case is a borderline case.

> Example: In the northern hemisphere, "summer month" clearly applies to July; clearly does not apply to January; and June is a borderline case, because the summer solstice is June 21, and schools usually continue into June, but June, July, and August are, nonetheless, often described as the summer months.

1. large animal
2. populous state
3. long book
4. old professor
5. popular singer
6. powerful person
7. difficult subject
8. late meeting
9. arriving late to a meeting

EXERCISE II

Each of the following sentences contains words or expressions that are potentially vague. Describe a context in which this vagueness might make a difference, and explain what difference it makes. Then reduce this vagueness by replacing the italicized expression with one that is more precise.

> Example: Harold has a *bad* reputation.
> Context: If Harold applies for a job as a bank security guard, then some but not all kinds of bad reputation are relevant. A reputation for doing bad construction work is irrelevant, but a reputation for dishonesty is relevant.
> Replacement: Harold is a known thief.

1. Ross has a *large* income.
2. Cocaine is a *dangerous* drug.
3. Ruth is a *clever* woman.
4. Andre is a *terrific* tennis player.
5. Mark is not doing *too well* (after his operation).

(continued)

6. Shaq's a *big* fellow.
7. Dan's grades are *low*.
8. Walter can't see *well*.
9. The earthquake was a *disaster*.
10. The news was *wonderful*.

HEAPS

The existence of borderline cases is essential to various styles of reasoning that have been identified and used since ancient times. One such argument was called the *argument from the heap* or the *sorites argument* (from the Greek word "soros," which means "heap"). The classic example was intended to show that it is impossible to produce a heap of sand by adding one grain at a time. As a variation on this, we will show that no one can become rich. The argument can be formulated as a long series like this:

(1) Someone with only one cent is not rich.
(2) If someone with only one cent is not rich, then someone with only two cents is not rich.
∴ (3) Someone with only two cents is not rich.

(4) If someone with only two cents is not rich, then someone with only three cents is not rich.
∴ (5) Someone with only three cents is not rich.

(6) If someone with only three cents is not rich, then someone with only four cents is not rich.
∴ (7) Someone with only four cents is not rich.

[and so on, until:]

∴ (199,999,999,999) Someone with only 100,000,000,000 cents is not rich.

The problem, of course, is that someone with 100,000,000,000 cents *is* rich. If someone denies this, we can keep on going. Or we can just sum up the whole argument like this:

(1*) Someone with only one cent is not rich.
(2*) For any number, n, if someone with only n cents is not rich, then someone with $n + 1$ cents is not rich.
∴ (3*) Someone with any number of cents is not rich.

Premise (2*) is, of course, just a generalization of premises (2), (4), (6), and so on.

Despite its plausibility, everyone should agree that there is something wrong with these arguments. If we hand over enough pennies to Peter, previously poor Peter will become the richest person in the world. Another sign of a problem is that a parallel argument runs in the other direction: Someone with 100 billion cents is rich. For any number, n, if someone with n cents is rich, then someone with $n - 1$ cents is also rich. Therefore, someone with no cents at all is rich. This is absurd (since we are not talking about how rich one's life can be as long as one has friends).

We can see that these arguments turn on borderline cases in the following way: The argument would fail if we removed borderline cases by laying down a ruling (maybe for tax purposes) that anyone with a million dollars or more is rich and anyone with less than this is not rich. A person with $999,999.99 would then pass from not being rich to being rich when given a single penny, so premise (2*) would be false at that point under this ruling. Of course, we do not usually use the word "rich" with this much precision. We see some people as clearly rich and others as clearly not rich, but in between there is a fuzzy area where we are not prepared to say that people either are or are not rich. In this fuzzy area, as well as in the clear areas, a penny one way or the other will make no difference.

That is how the argument works, but exactly where does it go wrong? This question is not easy to answer and remains a subject of vigorous debate. Here is one way to view the problem: Consider a person who is 80 pounds overweight, where we would all agree that that person would pass from being fat to not being fat by losing over 100 pounds. If he or she lost an ounce a day for five years, this would be *equivalent* to losing just over 114 pounds. An argument from the heap denies that this person would ever cease to be fat. (So what is the point of dieting?) Anyone who accepted that conclusion, or (3*), would seem to claim that a series of insignificant changes *cannot* be equivalent to a significant change. Surely, this is wrong. Here we might be met with the reply that every change must occur at some particular time (and place), but there would be no particular day on which this person would pass from being fat to not being fat. The problem with this reply is that, with concepts like this, changes seem to occur gradually over long stretches of time without occurring at any single moment. Anyway, however or whenever it occurs, the change does occur. Some people do cease to be fat if they lose enough weight.

This tells us that conclusions of arguments from the heap, such as (3*), are false, so these arguments cannot be sound. Almost everyone agrees to that much. Moreover, if an appropriate starting point is chosen, then premises like (1) and (1*) will also be accepted as true by almost everyone. So the main debate focuses on premise (2*) and on whether the argument is valid. Some philosophers reject premise (2*) and claim that there is a precise point at which a person becomes rich, even though we don't know where that point is. Others try to avoid any sharp cutoff point by developing some kind of alternative logic. Still others just admit that the premises seem true, and the argument seems valid, but the conclusion seems false, so the argument creates a paradox to which they have no solution. These views become complicated and technical, so we will not discuss them here. Suffice it to say that almost everyone agrees that conclusions like (3*) and (199,999,999,999) are false, so arguments from the heap are unsound for one reason or another. That is why such arguments are labeled *fallacies*.

DISCUSSION QUESTION

Where exactly do *you* think arguments from the heap go astray?

SLIPPERY SLOPES

Near cousins to arguments from the heap are *slippery-slope arguments*, but they reach different conclusions. Whereas heap arguments conclude that nothing has a certain property, such as baldness, a slippery-slope argument could be trotted out to try to show that there is no *real* or *defensible* or *significant* or *important* difference between being bald and not being bald. The claim is not that no change occurs because the person who loses all his hair is still not bald, as in an argument from the heap. Instead, the slippery-slope argument claims that we should not classify people as either bald or not bald, because there is no significant difference between these classifications.

Whether a difference is significant depends on a variety of factors. In particular, what is significant for one purpose might not be significant for other purposes. Different concerns then yield different kinds of slippery-slope arguments. We will discuss three kinds, beginning with conceptual slippery-slope arguments.

CONCEPTUAL SLIPPERY-SLOPE ARGUMENTS

Conceptual slippery-slope arguments try to show that things at opposite ends of a continuum do not differ in any way that would be important enough to justify drawing a distinction in one's concepts or theories. As an example, consider the difference between living and nonliving things.

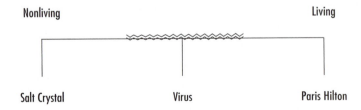

We all agree that a salt crystal is *not* alive. Yet a salt crystal is very similar to other more complex crystals, and these crystals are similar to certain viruses.

Still, a virus is on the borderline between living and nonliving things. A virus does not take nourishment and does not reproduce itself. Instead, a virus invades the reproductive mechanisms of cells, and these cells then produce the virus. As viruses become more complex, the differences between them and "higher" life forms become less obvious. Through a series of such small transitions, we finally reach a creature who is obviously alive: Paris Hilton. So far, we have merely described a series of gradual transitions along a *continuum*. We get a conceptual slippery-slope argument when we draw the following conclusion from these facts: There is no significant difference between living things and nonliving things.

To avoid this conclusion, we need to figure out where the argument goes wrong. Such arguments often seem to depend on the following principles:

1. We should not draw a distinction between things that are not significantly different.

2. If *A* is not significantly different from *B*, and *B* is not significantly different from *C*, then *A* is not significantly different from *C*.

This first principle is interesting, complicated, and at least *generally* true. We shall examine it more closely in a moment. The second principle is obviously false. As already noted, a series of insignificant differences can add up to a significant difference. Senator Everett Dirksen put the point well when he said, "A billion dollars here and a billion dollars there can add up to some real money." To the extent that conceptual slippery-slope arguments depend on this questionable assumption, they provide no more support for their conclusions than do arguments from the heap.

Unlike arguments from the heap, however, conceptual slippery-slope arguments do often lead people to accept their conclusions. Slippery-slope arguments have been used to deny the difference between sanity and insanity (some people are just a little weirder than others) and between amateur and professional athletics (some athletes just get paid a little more or more directly than other athletes). When many small differences make a big difference, such conceptual slippery-slope arguments are fallacious.

This fallacy is seductive, because it is often hard to tell when many small differences *do* make a big difference. Here is a recent controversial example: Some humans have very dark skin. Others have very pale skin. As members of these different groups marry, their children's skin can have any intermediate shade of color. This smooth spectrum leads some people to deny that any differences among races will be important to developed theories in biology. Their argument seems to be that the wealth of intermediate cases will make it difficult or impossible to formulate precise and exceptionless laws that apply to one racial group but not to others, so differences among races will play no important role in sciences that seek such laws. Critics respond that some scientific laws about races still might hold without exception even if skin color and other features do vary in tiny increments.

Whichever side one takes, this controversy shows that, even if there is a smooth spectrum between endpoints, this continuity is not enough *by itself* to show that there are no scientifically significant differences among races. That conclusion would need to be supported by more than just a conceptual slippery-slope argument. To show that certain concepts are useless for the purposes of a certain theory, one would need to add more information, particularly about the purposes of that theory and its laws. That is what determines which differences are important in that particular area. Conceptual slippery-slope arguments might work in conjunction with such additional premises, but they cannot work alone.

EXERCISE III

Whenever we find one thing passing over into its opposite through a gradual series of borderline cases, we can construct (a) an argument from the heap and (b) a conceptual slippery-slope argument by using the following method: Find some increase that will not be large enough to carry us outside the borderline area. Then use the patterns of argument given above. Applying this method, formulate arguments for the following claims. Then explain what is wrong with these arguments.

1. a. There are no heaps.
   b. There is no difference between a heap and a single grain of sand.
2. a. Nobody is tall.
   b. There is no difference between being tall and being short.
3. a. Books do not exist.
   b. There is no difference between a book and a pamphlet.
4. a. Heat is not real.
   b. There is no difference between being hot and being cold.
5. a. Taxes are never high.
   b. There is no difference between high taxes and low taxes.
6. a. Science is an illusion.
   b. There is no difference between science and faith.

DISCUSSION QUESTIONS

1. Do you think that differences among races have any role in developed theories in biology or sociology or any other science? Why or why not?
2. If animals evolve gradually from one species to another, does that show that there is no significant difference in biology between any species (say, horses and dogs)? Why or why not? Does it show that there is no important difference in moral theory between the rights of humans and the rights of animals in other species? Why or why not?

FAIRNESS SLIPPERY-SLOPE ARGUMENTS

When borderline cases form a continuum, if someone classifies a case at one end of the continuum, an opponent often challenges this classification by asking, "Where do you draw the line?" Sometimes this challenge is out of place. If I claim that Babe Ruth was a superstar, I will not be refuted if I cannot draw a sharp dividing line between athletes who are superstars and those who are not. There are some difficult borderline cases, but Babe Ruth is not one of them. Nor will we be impressed if someone tells us that the difference between Babe Ruth and the thousands of players who never made it to the major leagues is "*just* a matter of degree." What is usually wrong with this phrase is the emphasis on the word "just," which suggests that differences of degree do not count. Of course, it is a matter of degree, but the difference in degree is so great that it should be marked by a special word.

There are other occasions when a challenge to drawing a line is appropriate. For example, most schools and universities have grading systems that draw a fundamental distinction between passing grades and failing grades. Of course, a person who barely passes a course does not perform very differently from one who barely fails a course, yet they are treated very differently. Students who barely pass a course get credit for it; those who barely fail it do not. This, in turn, can lead to serious consequences in an academic career and even beyond. It is entirely reasonable to ask for a justification of a procedure that treats cases that are so similar in such strikingly different ways. We are not being tender-hearted; we are raising an issue of *fairness* or *justice*. It seems unfair to treat very similar cases in strikingly different ways.

The point is not that there is no difference between passing and failing. That is why this argument is not a conceptual slippery-slope argument. The claim, instead, is that the differences that do exist (as little as one point out of a hundred on a test) do not make it fair to treat people so differently (credit *versus* no credit for the course). This unfairness does not follow merely from the scores forming a continuum, but the continuum does put pressure on us to show why small differences in scores do justify big differences in treatment.

Questions about the fairness of drawing a line often arise in the law. For example, given reasonable cause, the police generally do not have to obtain a warrant to search a motor vehicle, for the obvious reason that the vehicle might be driven away while the police go to a judge to obtain a warrant. On the other hand, with few exceptions, the police may not search a person's home without a search warrant. In the case of *California v. Carney*,[1] the U.S. Supreme Court had to rule on whether the police needed a warrant to search for marijuana in an "oversized van, fully mobile," parked in a downtown parking lot in San Diego. Because the van was a fully mobile vehicle, it seemed to fall under the first principle; but because it also served as its owner's home, it seemed to fall under the second. The difficulty, as the Court saw, was that there is a gray area between those things that clearly are motor vehicles and not homes (for example, motorcycles) and those things that clearly are homes and not motor vehicles (for example, apartments). Chief Justice

Warren Burger wondered about a mobile home in a trailer park hooked up to utility lines with its wheels removed. Justice Sandra Day O'Connor asked whether a tent, because it is highly mobile, could also be searched without a warrant. As the discussion continued, houseboats (with or without motors or oars), covered wagons, and finally a house being moved from one place to another on a trailer truck came under examination. In the end, our highest court decided that the van in question was a vehicle and could be searched without first obtaining a warrant to do so. The court did not fully explain why it is fair to allow warrantless searches—and to send people to jail as a result—in cases of vans used as homes but not in other very similar cases.

Questions about where to draw a line often have even more important implications than in the case just examined. Consider the death penalty. Most societies have reserved the death penalty for those crimes they consider the most serious. But where should we draw the line between crimes punishable by death and crimes not punishable by death? Should the death penalty be given to murderers of prison guards? To rapists? To drug dealers? To drunk drivers who cause death? Wherever we draw the line, it seems to be an unavoidable consequence of the death penalty that similar cases will be treated in radically different ways. A defender of the death penalty can argue that it is not unfair to draw a line because, once the line is drawn, the public will have fair warning about which crimes are subject to the death penalty and which are not. It will then be up to each person to decide whether to risk his or her life by crossing this line. It remains a matter of debate, however, whether the law can be administered in a predictable way that makes this argument plausible.

The finality of death raises a profoundly difficult problem in another area, too: the legalization of abortion. There are some people who think abortion is never justified and ought to be declared totally illegal. There are others who think abortion does not need any justification at all and should be completely legalized. Between these extremes, there are many people who believe abortion is justified in certain circumstances but not in others (such as when abortion is the only way to save the life of the mother but not when it prevents only lesser harms to the mother). There are also those who think abortion should be allowed for a certain number of months of pregnancy, but not thereafter. People holding these middle positions face the problem of deciding where to draw a line, and this makes them subject to criticisms from holders of either extreme position.

This problem admits of no easy solution. Because every line we draw will seem arbitrary to some extent, a person who holds a middle position needs to argue that it is better to draw *some* line—even a somewhat arbitrary one—than to draw no line at all. The recognition that some line is needed, and why, can often help us locate the real issues. This is the first step toward a reasonable position.

Of course, this still does not tell us *where* to draw the line. A separate argument is needed to show that the line should be drawn at one point, or in one area, rather than another. In the law, such arguments often appeal to value judgments about the effects of drawing the line at one place rather than another.

For example, it is more efficient to draw a line where it is easy to detect, and drawing the line at one place will provide greater protection for some values or some people than will drawing it at another place. Different values often favor drawing different lines, and sometimes such arguments are not available at all. Thus, in the end, it will be difficult to solve many of these profound and important problems.

DISCUSSION QUESTION

Is it unfair for teachers to fail students who get one point out of a hundred less than others students who pass? Why or why not? Would an alternative grading system be fairer?

Farcus

by David Waisglass
Gordon Coulthart

© 1992 Farcus Cartoons

WAISGLASS/COULTHART

Reprinted by permission of LaughingStock Licensing Inc.

**What began with a few pencils
and paper clips ...**

CAUSAL SLIPPERY-SLOPE ARGUMENTS

Another common kind of argument is also often described as a slippery-slope argument. In these arguments, the claim is made that, once a certain kind of event occurs, other similar events will also occur, and this will lead eventually to disaster. The most famous (or infamous) argument of this kind was used by the U.S. government to justify its intervention in Vietnam in the 1960s. It was claimed that, if the communists took over Vietnam, they would then take over Cambodia, the rest of Asia, and other continents, until they ruled the whole world. This was called the domino theory, since the fall of one country would make neighboring countries fall as well. Arguments of this kind are sometimes called *domino arguments*. Such arguments claim that one event, which might not seem bad by itself, would lead to other, more horrible events, so such arguments can also be called *parades of horrors*.

Causal slippery slopes can also slide into good results. After all, someone who wants communists to take over the world might use the above domino argument to show why the United States should *not* intervene in Vietnam. Such optimistic slippery-slope arguments are, however, much less common than parades of horrors, so we will limit our discussion to the pessimistic versions.

These arguments resemble other slippery-slope arguments in that they depend on a series of small changes. The domino argument does not, however, claim that there is no difference between the first step and later steps—between Vietnam going communist and the rest of Asia going communist. Nor is there supposed to be anything unfair about letting Vietnam go communist without letting other countries also go communist. The point of a parade of horrors is that certain events will *cause* horrible effects because of their similarity or proximity to other events. Since the crucial claim is about causes and effects, these arguments will be called *causal slippery-slope arguments*.

We saw another example in Chapter 4. While arguing against an increase in the clerk hire allowance, Kyl says,

> The amount of increase does not appear large. I trust, however, there is no one among us who would suggest that the addition of a clerk would not entail allowances for another desk, another typewriter, more materials, and it is not beyond the realm of possibility that the next step would then be a request for additional office space, and ultimately new buildings.

Although this argument is heavily guarded, the basic claim is that increasing the clerk hire allowance is likely to lead to much larger expenditures that will break the budget. The argument can be represented more formally this way:

(1) If the clerk hire allowance is increased, other expenditures will also probably be increased.
(2) These other increases would be horrible.
∴(3) The clerk hire allowance should not be increased.

Opponents can respond in several ways. One response is to deny that the supposedly horrible effects really are so horrible. One might argue, for example, that additional office space and new buildings would be useful. This response is often foreclosed by describing the effects in especially horrible terms.

A second possible response would be to deny that increasing the clerk hire allowance really would have the horrible effects that are claimed in the first premise. One might argue, for example, that the old offices already have adequate room for additional clerks.

Often the best response is a combination of these. One can admit that certain claimed effects would be horrible, but deny that these horrible effects really are likely. Then one can acknowledge that some more minor problems will ensue, but argue that these costs are outweighed by the benefits of the program.

To determine which, if any, of these responses is adequate, one must look closely at each particular argument and ask the following questions:

Are any of the claimed effects really very bad?

Are any of these effects really very likely?

Do these dangers outweigh all the benefits of what is being criticized?

If the answers to all these questions are "Yes," then the causal slippery-slope argument is strong. But if any of these questions receives a negative answer, then the causal slippery-slope argument is questionable on that basis.

EXERCISE IV

Classify each of the following arguments as either (H) an argument from the heap, (C) a conceptual slippery-slope argument, (F) a fairness slippery-slope argument, or (S) a causal slippery-slope argument. Explain why you classify each example as you do.

1. We have to take a stand against sex education in junior high schools. If we allow sex education in the eighth grade, then the seventh graders will want it, and then the sixth graders, and pretty soon we will be teaching sex education to our little kindergartners.

2. People are found not guilty by reason of insanity when they cannot avoid breaking the law. But people who are brought up in certain deprived social circumstances are not much more able than the insane to avoid breaking the law. So it would be unjust to find them guilty.

3. People are called mentally ill when they do very strange things, but many so-called eccentrics do things that are just as strange. So there is no real difference between insanity and eccentricity.

4. If you try to smoke one cigarette a day, you will end up smoking two and then three and four and five, and so on, until you smoke two packs every day. So don't try even one.

5. A human egg one minute after fertilization is not very different from what it is one minute later, or one minute after that, and so on. Thus, there is really no difference between just-fertilized eggs and adult humans.

6. Since no moment in the continuum of development between an egg and a baby is especially significant, it is not fair to grant a right to life to a baby unless one grants the same right to every fertilized egg.

7. If we let doctors kill dying patients who are in great pain, then they will kill other patients who are in less pain and patients who are only slightly disabled. Eventually, they will kill anyone who is not wanted by society.

Explain the reasons, if any, for drawing a definite line in each of the following cases. Then further explain how this line can be drawn, if at all, in a reasonable way.

1. Minimum (or maximum?) age to drive a car
2. Minimum age to vote
3. Minimum age to enter (or be drafted into) the military
4. Minimum age to drink alcoholic beverages
5. Minimum age for election to the U.S. presidency
6. Maximum age before retirement becomes mandatory

Determine whether each of the following arguments provides adequate support, or any support, for its conclusion. Explain why.

1. I shouldn't get a speeding ticket for going fifty-six miles per hour, because my driving did not all of a sudden get more dangerous when I passed the speed limit of fifty-five.
2. No student should ever be allowed to ask a question during a lecture, because once one student asks a question, then another one wants to ask a question, and pretty soon the teacher doesn't have any time left to lecture.
3. Pornography shouldn't be illegal, because you can't draw a line between pornography and erotic art.
4. Marijuana should be legal, because it is no more dangerous than alcohol or nicotine.
5. Marijuana should be illegal, because people who try marijuana are likely to go on to try hashish, and then snorting cocaine, and then freebasing cocaine or shooting heroin.
6. The government should not put any new restrictions on free trade, because once they place some restrictions, they will place more and more until foreign trade is so limited that our own economy will suffer.
7. Governments should never bargain with any terrorist. Once they do, they will have to bargain with every other terrorist who comes along.
8. If assault weapons are banned, Congress will ban handguns next, and then rifles. Eventually, hunters will not be able to hunt, and law-abiding citizens will have no way to defend themselves against criminals.

DISCUSSION QUESTIONS

1. Explain and evaluate the following argument against restrictions on hate speech:

   To attempt to craft free speech exceptions only for racist speech would create a significant risk of a slide down the proverbial "slippery slope." . . . Censorial consequences could result from many proposed or adopted university policies, including the Stanford code, which sanctions speech intended to "insult or stigmatize" on the basis of race or other prohibited grounds. For example, certain feminists suggest that all heterosexual sex is rape because heterosexual men are aggressors who operate in a cultural climate of pervasive sexism and violence against women. Aren't these feminists insulting or stigmatizing heterosexual men on the basis of their sex and sexual orientation? And how about a Holocaust survivor who blames all ("Aryan") Germans for their collaboration during World War II? Doesn't this insinuation insult and stigmatize on the basis of national and ethnic origin? And surely we can think of numerous other examples that would have to give us pause.[2]

2. Explain and evaluate the following response to critics of college restrictions on hate speech:

   [Defenders of such restrictions] will ask whether an educational institution does not have the power . . . to enact reasonable regulations aimed at assuring equal personhood on campus. If one characterizes the issue this way, . . . a different set of slopes will look slippery. If we do not intervene to protect equality here, what will the next outrage be?[3]

3. When John Stewart interviewed William Bennett (former Secretary of Education under President Ronald Reagan) about gay marriage, both of them used slippery slopes and responded to each other's slippery slopes in the following exchange. What kinds of slippery slopes did they use? Was either argument better than the other? Was either response better than the other? Why or why not?

   BENNETT: The question is: How do you define marriage? Where do you draw the line? What do you say to the polygamist?

   STEWART: You don't say anything to the polygamist. That is a choice, to get three or four wives. That is not a biological condition that "I gots to get laid by different women that I am married to." That's a choice. Being gay is part of the human condition. There's a huge difference.

   BENNETT: Well, some people regard their human condition as having three women. Look, the polygamists are all over this.

   STEWART: Then let's go slippery slope the other way. If government says I can define marriage as between a man and a woman, what says they can't define it between people of different income levels, or they can decide whether or not you are a suitable husband for a particular woman?

   BENNETT: Because gender *matters* in marriage, it has mattered to every human society, it matters in every religion . . .

   STEWART: Race matters in every society as well. Isn't progress understanding?

4. What, if anything, is shown when slippery-slope arguments can be used on both sides of an issue?

NOTES

[1] 1471 U.S. 386 (1984). This case was reported by Linda Greenhouse, "Of Tents with Wheels and Houses with Oars," *New York Times*, May 15, 1985.

[2] Nadine Strossen, "Regulating Racist Speech on Campus: A Modest Proposal?" *Duke Law Journal* (1990): 537–38. When she wrote this, Strossen was on the National Board of Directors of the American Civil Liberties Union.

[3] Richard Delgado, "Campus Antiracism Rules: Constitutional Narratives in Collision," *Northwestern University Law Review* 85 (1991): 346.

FALLACIES OF AMBIGUITY

14

This chapter examines fallacies that arise from a second kind of unclarity: ambiguity. Ambiguity occurs when it is unclear which meaning of a term is intended in a given context. Ambiguity leads to the fallacy of equivocation, which will be defined and illustrated. The chapter closes with a discussion of different kinds of definitions that can be useful in avoiding or responding to fallacies of clarity.

AMBIGUITY

The idea of vagueness is based on a common feature of words in our language: Many of them leave open a range of borderline cases. The notion of *ambiguity* is also based on a common feature of our language: Words often have a number of different meanings. For example, the *New Merriam-Webster Pocket Dictionary* has the following entry under the word "cardinal":

> **cardinal** adj. 1: of basic importance; chief, main, primary,
> 2: of cardinal red color.
>
> n. 1: an ecclesiastical official of the Roman Catholic Church ranking next below the pope,
> 2: a bright red,
> 3: any of several American finches of which the male is bright red.

In the plural, "the Cardinals" is the name of an athletic team that inhabits St. Louis; "cardinal" also describes the numbers used in simple counting.

It is not likely that people would get confused about these very different meanings of the word "cardinal," but we might imagine a priest, a bird-watcher, and a baseball fan all hearing the remark "The cardinals are in town." The priest would prepare for a solemn occasion, the bird-watcher would get out binoculars, and the baseball fan would head for the stadium. In this context, the remark might be criticized as *ambiguous*. More precisely, we shall say that an expression in a given context is *used ambiguously* if and only if it is misleading or potentially misleading because it is hard to tell which of a number of possible meanings is intended in that context.

Using this definition, the word "bank" is *not* used ambiguously in the following sentence:

Joan deposited $500 in the bank and got a receipt.

Some writers, however, call an expression ambiguous simply if it admits of more than one interpretation, without adding that it is not possible to tell which meaning is intended. With this definition, the above sentence is ambiguous because it could mean that Joan placed $500 in a riverbank, and someone, for whatever reason, gave her a receipt for doing so. On this second definition of ambiguity, virtually every expression is ambiguous, because virtually every expression admits of more than one interpretation. On our first definition, only uses of expressions that are misleading or potentially misleading will be called ambiguous. In what follows, we will use the word "ambiguous" in accordance with the first definition. Ambiguity then depends on the context, because whether something is misleading also depends on context.

In everyday life, context usually settles which of a variety of meanings is appropriate. Yet sometimes genuine misunderstandings do arise. An American and a European discussing "football" may have different games in mind. The European is talking about what Americans call "soccer"; the American is talking about what Europeans call "American football." It is characteristic of the ambiguous use of a term that when it comes to light, we are likely to say something like, "Oh, you mean *that* kind of cardinal!" or "Oh, you were talking about *American* football!" This kind of misunderstanding can cause trouble. When it does, if we want to criticize the expression that creates the problem, we call it ambiguous.

Thus, "ambiguous" is both dependent on context and a term of criticism in much the same ways as "vague." But these kinds of unclarity differ in other ways. In a context where the use of a word is ambiguous, it is not clear which of two meanings to attach to a word. In a context where the use of a word is vague, we cannot attach *any* precise meaning to the use of a word.

Frank and Ernest

© 2000 Thaves. Reprinted with permission. Newspaper dist. by NEA, Inc.

So far we have talked about the ambiguity of individual terms or words. This is called *semantic ambiguity*. But sometimes we do not know which interpretation to give to a phrase or a sentence because its grammar or syntax admits of more than one interpretation. This is called *syntactic ambiguity* or *amphiboly*. Thus, if we talk about *the conquest of the Persians,* we might be referring either to the Persians' conquering someone or to someone's conquering the Persians. Sometimes the grammar of a sentence leaves open a great many possible interpretations. For example, consider the following sentence (from Paul Benacerraf):

Only sons marry only daughters.

One thing this might mean is that a person who is a male only child will marry a person who is a female only child. Again, it might mean that sons are the only persons who marry daughters and do not marry anyone else. Other interpretations are possible as well.

The process of rewriting a sentence so that one of its possible meanings becomes clear is called *disambiguating* the sentence. One way of disambiguating a sentence is to rewrite it as a whole, spelling things out in detail. That is how we disambiguated the sentence "Only sons marry only daughters." Another procedure is to continue the sentence in a way that supplies a context that forces one interpretation over others. Consider the sentence "Mary had a little lamb." Notice how the meaning changes completely under the following continuations:

1. Mary had a little lamb; it followed her to school.
2. Mary had a little lamb and then some broccoli.

Just in passing, it is not altogether obvious how we should describe the ambiguity in the sentence "Mary had a little lamb." The most obvious suggestion is that the word "had" is ambiguous, meaning "owned" on the first reading and "ate" on the second reading. Notice, however, that this also forces alternative readings for the expression "a little lamb." Presumably, it was a small, whole, live lamb that followed Mary to school, whereas it would have been a small amount of cooked lamb that she ate. So if we try to locate the ambiguity in particular words, we must say that not only the word "had" but also the word "lamb" are being used ambiguously. This is a reasonable approach, but another is available. In everyday speech, we often leave things out. Thus, instead of saying "Mary had a little *portion of meat derived from a* lamb *to eat*," we simply say "Mary had a little lamb," dropping out the italicized words on the assumption that they will be understood. In most contexts, such deletions cause no misunderstanding. But sometimes deletions are misunderstood, and this can produce ambiguity.

EXERCISE I

Show that each of the following sentences admits of at least two interpretations by (1) rewriting the sentence as a whole in two different ways and (2) expanding the sentence in two different ways to clarify the context:

Example:	Kenneth let us down.
Rewriting:	Kenneth lowered us.
	Kenneth disappointed us.
Expanding:	Kenneth let us down with a rope.
	Kenneth let us down just when we needed him.

(continued)

1. Barry Bonds (the baseball player) was safe at home.
2. I don't know what state Meredith is in.
3. Where did you get bitten?
4. The president sent her congratulations.
5. Visiting professors can be boring.
6. Wendy ran a marathon.
7. The meaning of the term "altering" is changing.
8. I don't want to get too close to him.
9. I often have my friends for dinner.
10. Slow Children Playing. (on a street sign.)
11. Save Soap and Waste Paper. (on a sign during World War II.)
12. In his will, he left $1,000 to his two sons, Jim and John.
13. There is some explanation for everything.
14. She is an Asian historian.
15. Nobody may be in the lounge this evening.
16. Nobody came to the concert at 8 PM.

EXERCISE II

Follow the same instructions for the following actual newspaper headlines, many of which come from Columbia Journalism Review, editors, *Squad Helps Dog Bite Victim and Other Flubs from the Nation's Press* (Garden City, NY: Doubleday, 1980).

1. Milk Drinkers Turn to Powder
2. Anti-busing Rider Killed by Senate
3. Mrs. Gandhi Stoned in Rally in India
4. College Graduates Blind Senior Citizen
5. Jumping Bean Prices Affect the Poor
6. Tuna Biting off Washington Coast
7. Time for Football and Meatball Stew
8. Police Kill Man with Ax
9. Squad Helps Dog Bite Victim
10. Child Teaching Expert to Speak
11. Prostitutes Appeal to Pope
12. Legalized Outhouses Aired by Legislature
13. Police Can't Stop Gambling
14. Judge Permits Club to Continue Sex Bar
15. Greeks Fine Hookers
16. Survivor of Siamese Twins Joins Parents

17. Caribbean Islands Drift to the Left

18. Teenage Prostitution Problem Is Mounting

19. Miners Refuse to Work After Death

20. Police Begin Campaign to Run Down Jaywalkers

21. Red Tape Holds Up New Bridges

22. Juvenile Court to Try Shooting Defendant

23. Kids Make Nutritious Snacks

24. Study of Obesity Looks for Larger Test Group

25. Hospitals Sued by Seven Foot Doctors

26. Local High School Dropouts Cut in Half

27. Iraqi Head Seeks Arms

28. Drunk Gets Nine Months in Violin Case

29. Teacher Strikes Idle Kids

30. British Left Waffles on Falkland Islands

31. Stolen Painting Found by Tree

32. New Vaccine May Contain Rabies

EXERCISE III

Poetry, songs, and jokes often intentionally exploit multiple meanings for effect. Find examples in poems, songs, and jokes that you like. Are these examples of ambiguity on the above definition? Why or why not?

EQUIVOCATION

Ambiguity can cause a variety of problems for arguments. Often it produces hilarious or embarrassing side effects, and it is hard to get your arguments taken seriously if your listeners are giggling over an unintended double entendre in which one of the double meanings has risqué connotations.

Ambiguity can also generate bad arguments that involve the *fallacy of equivocation*. An argument is said to commit this fallacy when it uses the same expression in different senses in different parts of the argument, and this ruins the argument. Here is a silly example (from Carl Wolf):

Six is an odd number of legs for a horse.
Odd numbers cannot be divided by two.

∴ Six cannot be divided by two.

Clearly, "odd" means "unusual" in the first premise, but it means "not even" in the second premise. Consequently, both premises are true, even though the conclusion is false, so the argument is not valid.

Let's consider another, more serious, example. In *Utilitarianism* (1861), John Stuart Mill claims to "prove" that "happiness is a good" with the following argument:

> The only proof capable of being given that an object is visible is that people actually see it. The only proof that a sound is audible is that people hear it. In like manner the sole evidence it is possible to produce that anything is desirable is that people actually desire it. . . . [E]ach person, so far as he believes it to be attainable, desires his own happiness. This, however, being a fact, we have not only all the proof which the case admits of, but all which it is possible to require, that happiness is a good.

Mill has sometimes been charged with committing a transparent fallacy in this passage. Specifically, the following argument is attributed to him:

(1) If something is desired, then it is desirable.
(2) If it is desirable, then it is good.
∴(3) If something is desired, then it is good.

Mill never presents his argument in this form, and it may be uncharitable to attribute it to him. Still, whether it is Mill's way of arguing or not, it provides a good specimen of a fallacy of equivocation.

The objection to this argument is that the word "desirable" is used in different senses in the two premises. Specifically, in the first premise, it is used to mean "capable of being desired," whereas in the second premise, it is used to mean "worthy of being desired." If so, the argument really amounts to this:

(1*) If something is desired, then it is capable of being desired.
(2*) If something is worthy of being desired, then it is good.
∴(3) If something is desired, then it is good.

This argument is clearly not valid. To make the charge of equivocation stick, however, it has to be shown that the argument is not valid when the meaning of the word "desirable" is used in the same sense in the two premises. This produces two cases to be examined:

(1*) If something is desired, then it is capable of being desired.
(2**) If something is capable of being desired, then it is good.
∴(3) If something is desired, then it is good.

We now have a valid argument, but the second premise is not true, for sometimes people are capable of desiring things that are not good. The second way of restoring validity takes the following form:

(1**) If something is desired, then it is worthy of being desired.
(2*) If something is worthy of being desired, then it is good.
∴(3) If something is desired, then it is good.

Again, we have a valid argument, but this time the first premise is false, since sometimes people do desire things that they should not desire. Thus, in both cases, altering the premises to produce a valid argument produces a false premise, so the argument cannot be sound.

This is a pattern that emerges when dealing with arguments that involve the fallacy of equivocation. When the premises are interpreted in a way that produces a valid argument, then at least one of the premises is false. When the premises are interpreted in a way that makes them true, then the argument is not valid. Here, then, is the strategy for dealing with arguments that may involve a fallacy of equivocation:

1. Distinguish the possible meanings of the potentially ambiguous expressions in the argument.
2. For each possible meaning, restate the argument so that each expression clearly has the same meaning in all of the premises and the conclusion.
3. Evaluate the resulting arguments separately.

If the argument fails whenever each term has a consistent meaning throughout the argument, then the argument is guilty of equivocation.

EXERCISE IV

Each of the following arguments trades on an ambiguity. For each, locate the ambiguity by showing that one or more of the statements can be interpreted in different ways.

1. We shouldn't hire Peter, because our company has a policy against hiring drug users, and I saw Peter take aspirin, which is a drug.
2. Man is the only rational animal, and no woman is a man, so women are not rational.
3. My doctor has been practicing medicine for thirty years, and practice makes perfect, so my doctor must be nearly perfect.
4. Our cereal is all natural, for there is obviously nothing supernatural about it.
5. Ice cream is never all natural, since it never appears in nature without human intervention.
6. I have a right to spend all my money on lottery tickets. Therefore, when I spend all my money on lottery tickets, I am doing the right thing.
7. You passed no one on the road; therefore, you walked faster than no one.
8. Everything must have some cause; therefore, something must be the cause of everything.
9. The apostles were twelve. Matthew was an apostle. Hence, Matthew was twelve. (attributed to Bertrand Russell)
10. If I have only one friend, then I cannot say that I have any number of friends. So one is not any number. (from Timothy Duggan)

(continued)

11. "Our bread does have fiber, because it contains wood pulp." (The Federal Trade Commission actually ordered the Continental Baking Company to indicate in their advertising that this is the kind of fiber in their Fresh Horizons bread.)

12. Anyone who tries to violate a law, even if the attempt fails, should be punished. People who try to fly are trying to violate the law of gravity. So they should be punished. (This argument is reported to have been used in an actual legal case during the nineteenth century, but compare Stephen Colbert, "Physics is the ultimate Big Government interference—universal laws meant to constrain us at every turn. . . . Hey, is it wrong that I sometimes want to act without having to deal with an equal and opposite reaction?"[1])

DISCUSSION QUESTIONS

1. When a newspaper was criticized as a scandalous rumormonger, its editor responded with the following argument (as paraphrased by Deni Elliot). Does the editor's argument commit the fallacy of equivocation?

   It's not wrong for newspapers to pass on rumors about sex scandals. Newspapers have a duty to print stories that are in the public interest, and the public clearly has a great interest in rumors about sex scandals, since, when newspapers print such stories, their circulation increases, and they receive a large number of letters.

2. In the following passage, Tom Hill Jr. claims that a common argument against affirmative action commits a fallacy of equivocation. Do you agree that this argument equivocates? Why or why not?

   Some think that the injustice of all affirmative action programs is obvious or easily demonstrated. [One argument] goes this way: "Affirmative action, by definition, gives preferential treatment to minorities and women. This is discrimination in their favor and against non-minority males. All discrimination by public institutions is unjust, no matter whether it is the old kind or the newer 'reverse discrimination.' So all affirmative action programs in public institutions are unjust."

   This deceptively simple argument, of course, trades on an ambiguity. In one sense, to "discriminate" means to "make a distinction," to pay attention to a difference. In this evaluatively neutral sense, of course, affirmative action programs do discriminate. But public institutions must, and justifiably do, "discriminate" in this sense, for example, between citizens and noncitizens, freshmen and seniors, the talented and the retarded, and those who pay their bills and those who do not. Whether it is unjust to note and make use of a certain distinction in a given context depends upon many factors: the nature of the institution, the relevant rights of the parties involved, the purposes and effects of making that distinction, and so on.

   All this would be obvious except for the fact that the word "discrimination" is also used in a pejorative sense, meaning (roughly) "making use of a distinction in an unjust or illegitimate way." To discriminate in this sense is obviously wrong, but now it remains an open question whether the use of gender and race distinctions in affirmative action programs is really "discrimination" in this sense. The simplistic argument uses the evaluatively neutral sense of "discrimination" to show that affirmative action discriminates; it then shifts to the pejorative sense when it asserts that discrimination is always wrong. Although one may, in the end, *conclude* that all public use of racial and gender distinctions is unjust, to do so requires more of an *argument* than the simple one (just given) that merely exploits an ambiguity of the word "discrimination."[2]

3. Many people argue that homosexuality is immoral because it is unnatural. In the following reading,[3] Burton Leiser criticizes this argument for equivocating on five meanings of the term "natural." Does the argument really equivocate? Why or why not?

HOMOSEXUALITY AND NATURAL LAW

by Burton Leiser

When theologians and moralists speak of homosexuality, contraception, abortion, and other forms of human behavior as being unnatural and say that for that reason such behavior must be considered to be wrong, in what sense are they using the word *unnatural*? Are they saying that homosexual behavior and the use of contraceptives are [1] *contrary to the scientific laws of nature*, are they saying that they are [2] *artificial* forms of behavior, or are they using the terms *natural* and *unnatural* in some third sense?

They cannot mean that homosexual behavior (to stick to the subject presently under discussion) violates the laws of nature in the first sense [including, for example, Boyle's law that the volume of a gas varies inversely with the pressure that is applied to it], for . . . in *that* sense it is impossible to violate the laws of nature. Those laws, being merely descriptive of what actually does happen, would have to *include* homosexual behavior if such behavior does actually take place. . . .

If those who say that homosexual behavior is unnatural are using the term *unnatural* in the second sense as artificial, it is difficult to understand their objection. That which is artificial is often far better than what is natural. . . . [Moreover,] homosexual behavior can hardly be considered unnatural in this sense. There is nothing artificial about such behavior. On the contrary, it is quite natural, in this sense, to those who engage in it. And, even if it were not, this is not in itself a ground for condemning it.

It would seem, then, that those who condemn homosexuality as an unnatural form of behavior must mean something else by the word *unnatural*, something not covered by either of the preceding definitions. A third possibility is this:

3. *Anything uncommon or abnormal is unnatural.* If this is what is meant by those who condemn homosexuality on the ground that it is unnatural, it is quite obvious that their condemnation cannot be accepted without further argument. The fact that a given form of behavior is uncommon provides no justification for condemning it. . . . Great artists, poets, musicians, and scientists are uncommon in this sense; but clearly the world is better off for having them, and it would be absurd to condemn them or their activities for their failure to be common and normal. If homosexual behavior is wrong, then, it must be for some reason other than its unnaturalness in this sense of the word.

(continued)

4. *Any use of an organ or an instrument that is contrary to its principal purpose or function is unnatural.* Every organ and every instrument—perhaps even every creature—has a function to perform, one for which it is particularly designed. Any use of those instruments and organs that is consonant with their purposes is natural and proper, but any use that is inconsistent with their principal functions is unnatural and improper, and to that extent evil or harmful. Human teeth, for example, are admirably designed for their principal functions—biting and chewing the kinds of food suitable for human consumption. But they are not particularly well suited for prying the caps from beer bottles. If they are used for that purpose, they are likely to crack or break under the strain. . . .

What are the sex organs peculiarly suited to do? . . . Our sexual organs are uniquely adapted for procreation, but that is obviously not the only function for which they are adapted. Human beings may—and do—use those organs for a great many other purposes, and it is difficult to see why any *one* use should be considered to be the only proper one. The sex organs seem to be particularly well adapted to give their owners and others intense sensations of pleasure. Unless one believes that pleasure itself is bad, there seems to be little reason to believe that the use of the sex organs for the production of pleasure in oneself or in others is evil. In view of the peculiar design of these organs, with their great concentration of nerve endings, it would seem that they were designed (if they *were* designed) with that very goal in mind, and that their use for such purposes would be no more unnatural than their use for the purpose of procreation.

Nor should we overlook the fact that human sex organs may be and are used to express, in the deepest and most intimate way open to man, the love of one person for another. Even the most ardent opponents of "unfruitful" intercourse admit that sex does serve this function. They have accordingly conceded that a man and his wife may have intercourse even though she is pregnant, or past the age of child bearing, or in the infertile period of her menstrual cycle. . . .

To sum up, then, the proposition that any use of an organ that is contrary to its principal purpose or function is unnatural assumes that organs *have* a principal purpose or function, but this may be denied on the ground that the purpose or function of a given organ may vary according to the needs or desires of its owner. It may be denied on the ground that a given organ may have more than one principal purpose or function, and any attempt to call one use or another the only natural one seems to be arbitrary, if not question-begging. Also, the proposition suggests that what is unnatural is evil or depraved. This goes beyond the pure description of things, and enters into the problem of the evaluation of human behavior, which leads us to the fifth meaning of *natural*.

5. *That which is natural is good, and whatever is unnatural is bad.* . . . Clearly, [people who say this] cannot have intended merely to reduce the word *natural* to a synonym of *good, right,* and *proper,* and *unnatural* to a synonym of *evil, wrong, improper, corrupt,* and *depraved.* If that were all they had intended to do, . . . it would follow inevitably that whatever is good must be natural, and vice versa, by definition. This is certainly not what the opponents of homosexuality have been saying when they claim that homosexuality, being unnatural, is evil. For if it were, their claim would be quite empty. They would be saying merely that homosexuality, being evil, is evil—a redundancy that could as easily be reduced to the simpler assertion that homosexuality is evil. This

assertion, however, is not an argument. . . . "Unnaturalness" and "wrongful-ness" are not synonyms, then, but different concepts.

The problem with which we are wrestling is that we are unable to find a meaning for *unnatural* that enables us to arrive at the conclusion that homosexuality is unnatural or that if homosexuality is unnatural, it is therefore wrongful behavior. We have examined [five] common meanings of *natural* and *unnatural,* and have seen that none of them performs the task that it must perform if the advocates of this argument are to prevail. Without some more satisfactory explanation of the connection between the wrongfulness of homosexuality and its alleged unnaturalness, the argument [that homosexuality is wrong because it is unnatural] must be rejected.

DEFINITIONS

It is sometimes suggested that a great many disputes could be avoided if people simply took the precaution of defining their terms. To some extent this is true. People do sometimes seem to disagree just because they are using terms in different ways, even though they agree on the nonverbal issues.

Nonetheless, definitions will not solve all problems, and a mindless insistence on definitions can turn a serious discussion into a semantic quibble. If you insist on defining every term, you will never be satisfied, because every definition will introduce new terms to be defined. Furthermore, definitions themselves can be confusing or obfuscating as, for example, when an economist tells us:

I define "inflation" as too much money chasing too few goods.

Not only is this definition metaphorical and obscure, it also has a theory of the causes of inflation built into it.

To use definitions correctly, we must realize that they come in various forms and serve various purposes. There are at least five kinds of definitions that need to be distinguished:

1. *Lexical* or *dictionary definitions* are the most common kind of definition. We consult a dictionary when we are ignorant about the meaning of a word in a particular language. If you do not happen to know what the words "jejune," "ketone," or "Kreis" mean, then you can look these words up in an English, a scientific, and a German dictionary, respectively.

Except for an occasional diagram, dictionaries explain the meaning of a word by using other words that the reader presumably already understands. These explanations often run in a circle, such as when the *Oxford American Dictionary* defines "car" as "automobile" and "automobile" as "car." Circular definitions can still be useful, because if you know what one of the terms in the circle means, you can use that background knowledge plus the definition to figure out what the other terms mean.

The goal of dictionary definitions is to supply us with factual information about the standard meanings of words in a particular language. As dictionary definitions are, in effect, factual claims about how people in general actually use certain words, dictionary definitions can be either accurate or inaccurate. The *Oxford American Dictionary* defines one meaning of "fan" as "a device waved in the hand or operated mechanically to create a current of air." This is, strictly speaking, incorrect because a bellows also meets these conditions but is not a fan. Dictionary definitions can be criticized or defended on the basis of a speaker's sense of the language or, more formally, by empirical surveys of what speakers accept as appropriate or reject as inappropriate uses of the term.

2. *Disambiguating definitions* specify a sense in which a word or phrase is or might be being used by a particular speaker on a particular occasion. ("When I said that the banks were collapsing, I meant river banks, not financial institutions.") Disambiguating definitions can tell us which dictionary definition actually is intended in a particular context, or they can distinguish several meanings that might be intended. They can also be used to remove syntactic ambiguity or amphiboly. ("When I said that all of my friends are not students, I meant that not all of them are students, not that none of them are students.")

Whether the ambiguity is semantic or syntactic, the goal of a disambiguating definition is to capture what the speaker intended, so such definitions can be justified by asking the speaker what he or she meant. This is a different question than asking what a word means. Whereas dictionary definitions say what words mean or how they are used by most speakers of the language, a disambiguating definition focuses on a particular speaker and specifies which meaning that speaker intended on a particular occasion.

Such disambiguating definitions can be used in response to arguments that seem to commit the fallacy of equivocation. A critic can use disambiguating definitions to distinguish possible meanings and then ask, "Did you mean this or that?" The person who gave the argument can answer by picking one of these alternatives or by providing another disambiguating definition to specify what was meant. Speakers are sometimes not sure which meaning they intended, and then the critic needs to show that the argument cannot work if a single disambiguating definition is followed throughout. Whether one sides with the arguer or the critic, arguments that use terms ambiguously cannot be evaluated thoroughly without the help of disambiguating definitions.

3. *Stipulative definitions* are used to assign a meaning to a new (usually technical) term or to assign a new or special meaning to a familiar term. They have the following general form: "By such and such expression I (or we) will mean so and so." Thus, mathematicians introduced the new term "googol" to stand for the number expressed by 1 followed by 100 zeroes. Physicists use words like "charm," "color," and "strangeness" to stand for certain features of subatomic particles. Stipulative definitions do not report

what a word means; they give a new word a meaning or an old word a new meaning.

Notice that if I say, "I stipulate that . . . " I thereby stipulate that . . . ; so such utterances are explicit performatives, and stipulation is a speech act. (See Chapter 2.) This explains why stipulative definitions cannot be false, since no performatives can be false. Stipulative definitions can, however, be criticized in other ways. They can be vague or ambiguous. They can be useless or confusing. Someone who stipulates a meaning for a term might go on to use the term with a different meaning (just as people sometimes fail to keep their promises). Still, stipulative definitions cannot be false by virtue of failing to correspond to the real meaning of a word, because they give that meaning to that word.

4. *Precising definitions* are used to resolve vagueness. They are used to draw a sharp (or sharper) boundary around the things to which a term refers, when this collection has a fuzzy or indeterminate boundary in ordinary usage. For example, it is not important for most purposes to decide how big a population center must be in order to count as a city rather than as a town. We can deal with the borderline cases by using such phrases as "very small city" or "quite a large town." It will not make much difference which phrase we use on most occasions. Yet it is not hard to imagine a situation in which it might make a difference whether a center of population is a city or not. As a city, it might be eligible for development funds that are not available to towns. Here a precising definition—a definition that draws a sharp boundary where none formerly existed—would be useful.

Precising definitions are, in effect, combinations of stipulative definitions and dictionary definitions. Like stipulative definitions, they involve a choice. One could define a city as any population center with more than 50,000 people, or one could decide to decrease the minimum to 30,000 people. Precising definitions are not completely arbitrary, however, because they usually should conform to the generally accepted meaning of a term. It would be unreasonable to define a city as any population center with more than seventeen people. Dictionary definitions, thus, set limits to precising definitions.

Precising definitions are also not arbitrary in another way: There can be good reasons to prefer one precising definition over another, when adopting the preferred definition will have better effects than the alternative. If development funds are to be distributed only to cities, then to define cities as having more than 50,000 people will deny those funds to smaller population centers with, say, 10,000 people. Consequently, we need some reason to resolve the vagueness of the term "city" in one way rather than another. In this case, the choice might be based on the amount of funds available for development. In a more dramatic example, a precising definition of "death" might be used to resolve controversial issues about euthanasia—about what doctors may or must do to patients who are near death—and then our choices between possible precising definitions might be based on our deepest value commitments. In any case, we need some argument to show that one precising definition is better than other alternatives.

Such arguments often leave some leeway. Even if one can justify defining cities as having a minimum of 50,000 people instead of 10,000, one's reason is not likely to justify a cutoff at 50,000 as opposed to 49,000. A different kind of defense would be needed if someone used a slippery-slope argument to show that it is unfair to provide development funds to one city with 50,000 people but to deny such funds to its neighbor with only 49,000 people. Against this kind of charge, the only way to defend a precising definition might be to show that some precising definition is needed, the cutoff should lie inside a certain general area, one's preferred definition does lie within that area, and no alternative is any better. Such responses might also apply to nearby alternatives, but they are still sometimes enough to support a precising definition. If responses like these are not available, then a precising definition can be criticized as unjustified.

5. *Systematic or theoretical definitions* are introduced to give a systematic order or structure to a subject matter. For example, in geometry, every term must be either a primitive (undefined) term or a term defined by means of these primitive terms. Thus, if we take points and distances as primitives, we can define a straight line as the shortest distance between two points. Then, assuming some more concepts, we can define a triangle as a closed figure with exactly three straight lines as sides. By a series of such definitions, the terms in geometry are placed in systematic relationships with one another.

In a similar way, we might try to represent family relationships using only the primitive notions of parent, male, and female. We could then construct definitions of the following kind:

"*A* is the brother of *B*." = "*A* and *B* have the same parents and *A* is male."

"*A* is *B*'s grandmother." = "*A* is a parent of a parent of *B* and *A* is female."[4]

Things become more complicated when we try to define such notions as "second cousin once removed" or "stepfather." Yet, by extending some basic definitions from simple to more complicated cases, all family relationships can be given a systematic presentation.

Formulating systematic definitions for family relationships is relatively easy, but similar activities in science, mathematics, and other fields can demand genius. It often takes deep insight into a subject to see which concepts are genuinely fundamental and which are secondary and derivative. When Sir Isaac Newton defined force in terms of mass and acceleration, he was not simply stating how he proposed to use certain words; he was introducing a fundamental conceptual relationship that improved our understanding of the physical world.

Such theoretical definitions can be evaluated on the basis of whether they really do help us formulate better theories and understand the world. Evaluating theoretical definitions often requires a great deal of empirical investigation. When water was defined as H_2O,[5] this made it possible to formulate more precise laws about how water interacted with other chemicals. Other alternatives were available. Whereas molecules count as H_2O, and hence as water, even if they contain unusual isotopes of hydrogen and oxygen, chemists could define water so that it would have to contain only the most common isotopes of hydrogen and oxygen. Why don't they? Because they discovered that differences among isotopes generally do not affect how molecules of H_2O react with other chemicals. As a result, the simplest and most useful generalizations about the properties of water can be formulated in terms of H_2O without regard to certain isotopes of hydrogen and oxygen. This illustrates one way in which choosing one theoretical definition over another can lead to a better theory.

Definitions can play important roles in the presentation of arguments, but demands for definitions can also hinder the progress of an argument. In the middle of discussions people often ask for definitions or even state, usually with an air of triumph, that everything depends on the way you define your terms. We saw in Chapter 2 that definitions are not always needed, and most issues do not turn on the way in which words are defined. When asked for a definition, it is appropriate to reply: "What sort of definition do you want, and why do you want it?" Of course, if you are using a word in a way that departs from customary usage, or using it in some special way of your own, or using a word that is too vague for the given context, or using a word in an ambiguous way, then the request for a definition is perfectly in order. In such cases, the demand for a definition represents an important move within the argument rather than a distraction from it.

EXERCISE V

Look up lexical or dictionary definitions for the following words. (For fun, you might try to guess the meanings of these words before you look them up, as in the game "Balderdash.")

1. jejune
2. ketone
3. fluvial
4. xebec
5. plangent

EXERCISE VI

1. Give a stipulative definition for the word "klurg."
2. Stipulate a word to stand for the chunks of ice that form under car fenders in winter.
3. Describe something that does not have a common name, for which it would be useful to stipulate a name. Explain how the name would be useful.

Give precising definitions for the following words. In each case, supply a context that gives your precising definition a point.

1. book
2. alcoholic beverage
3. crime
4. warm
5. fast

Give disambiguating definitions for the following words. In each case, supply a context in which your definition might be needed to avoid confusion.

1. run
2. pen
3. game
4. painting
5. fast

Using the notions of parents, male, and female as basic, give systematic definitions of the following family relationships:

1. *A* and *B* are sisters.
2. *A* and *B* are siblings.
3. *A* is *B*'s half-brother.
4. *A* is *B*'s niece.
5. *A* is *B*'s cousin.

1. The United States federal criminal prohibition against torture (18 U.S.C. §§ 2340-2340A) prohibits conduct "specifically intended to inflict severe physical or mental pain or suffering." On August 1, 2002, the United States attorney general's office issued a statement that "severe" pain under the statute was limited to pain "equivalent in intensity to the pain

accompanying serious physical injury, such as organ failure, impairment of bodily function, or even death." (This interpretation was withdrawn in 2004.) What kind of a definition is this? Is it justified or not? What does this controversy show about the nature and importance of definitions?

2. The definition of "sexual relations" was crucial to the issue of whether President Bill Clinton committed perjury. Find and distinguish the various definitions of "sexual relations" at play in the following selection from President Clinton's testimony before the independent counsel, Kenneth Starr, on August 17, 1998.[6] In your opinion, does either President Clinton or the lawyers who are questioning him use definitions improperly? Why or why not?

Q: (BY MR. BITTMAN): Mr. President, were you physically intimate with Monica Lewinsky? . . .

A: (BY PRESIDENT CLINTON): When I was alone with Ms. Lewinsky on certain occasions in early 1996 and once in early 1997, I engaged in conduct that was wrong. These encounters did not consist of sexual intercourse. They did not constitute sexual relations as I understood that term to be defined at my January 17th, 1998 deposition. . . .

Q: Let us then move to the definition that was provided you during your deposition. We will have that marked as Grand Jury Exhibit WJC-2. . . .

> [Definition of Sexual Relations] For the purposes of this deposition, a person engages in "sexual relations" when the person knowingly engages in or causes—(1) contact with the genitalia, anus, groin, breast, inner thigh, or buttocks of any person with an intent to arouse or gratify the sexual desire of any person; (2) contact between any part of the person's body or an object and the genitals or anus of another person; or (3) contact between the genitals or anus of the person and any part of another person's body. "Contact" means intentional touching, either directly or through clothing.

. . . I'm sure you remember from the deposition that paragraph (1) of the definition remained in effect. Judge Wright ruled that that was to be the guiding definition, and that paragraphs (2) and (3) were stricken. . . . I suppose, since you have now read portions of the transcript again, that you were reminded that you did not ask for any clarification of the terms. Is that correct? Of the definition?

A: No, sir. I thought it was . . . a rather strange definition. But it was the one the Judge decided on and I was bound by it. So, I took it. . . .

Q: And you remember that Ms. Lewinsky's affidavit said that she had had no sexual relationship with you. Do you remember that?

A: I do.

Q: And do you remember in the deposition that Mr. Bennett asked you . . . whether the statement that Ms. Lewinsky made in her affidavit was . . . true. And you indicated that it was absolutely correct.

(continued)

A: I did. . . . I believe at the time that she filled out this affidavit, if she believed that the definition of sexual relationship was two people having intercourse, then this is accurate. And I believe that is the definition that most ordinary Americans would give it. If you said Jane and Harry have a sexual relationship, and you're not talking about people being drawn into a lawsuit and being given definitions, and then a great effort to trick them in some way, but you are just talking about people in ordinary conversations, I'll bet the grand jurors, if they were talking about two people they know, and said they have a sexual relationship, they meant they were sleeping together; they meant they were having intercourse together. So, I'm not at all sure that this affidavit is not true and was not true in Ms. Lewinsky's mind at the time she swore it out. . . .

Q: (BY MR. WISENBERG): Mr. President, I want to, before I go into a new subject area, briefly go over something you were talking about with Mr. Bittman. The statement of your attorney, Mr. Bennett, at the Paula Jones deposition, "Counsel is fully aware . . . that Ms. Lewinsky has filed, has an affidavit which they are in possession of saying that there is absolutely no sex of any kind in any manner, shape or form, with President Clinton." That statement is made by your attorney in front of Judge Susan Webber Wright, correct?

A: That's correct.

Q: That statement is a completely false statement. Whether or not Mr. Bennett knew of your relationship with Ms. Lewinsky, the statement that there was "no sex of any kind in any manner, shape or form, with President Clinton," was an utterly false statement. Is that correct?

A: It depends on what the meaning of the word "is" is. If . . . "is" means is and never has been, . . . that is one thing. If it means there is none, that was a completely true statement. . . .

Q: I just want to make sure I understand, Mr. President. Do you mean today that because you were not engaging in sexual activity with Ms. Lewinsky during the deposition that the statement of Mr. Bennett might be literally true?

A: No, sir. I mean that at the time of the deposition, it had been—that was well beyond any point of improper contact between me and Ms. Lewinsky. So that anyone generally speaking in the present tense, saying there is not an improper relationship, would be telling the truth if that person said there was not, in the present tense; the present tense encompassing many months. That's what I meant by that. . . .

Q: If Monica Lewinsky has stated that her affidavit that she didn't have a sexual relationship with you is, in fact, a lie, I take it you disagree with that?

A: No. I told you before what I thought the issue was there. I think the issue is how do you define sexual relationship. And there was no definition imposed on her at the time she executed the affidavit. Therefore, she was free to give it any reasonable meaning. . . .

Q: Well, the grand jury would like to know, Mr. President, why it is that you think that oral sex performed on you does not fall within the definition of sexual relations as used in your deposition.

A: Because that is—if the deponent is the person who has oral sex performed on him, then the contact is with—not with anything on that list, but with the lips of another person. It seems to be self-evident that that's what it is. And I thought it was curious. . . .

NOTES

[1] Stephen Colbert, *I Am America (And So Can You!)* (New York: Grand Central Publishing, 2007), 201.

[2] Thomas E. Hill Jr., "The Message of Affirmative Action," in *Autonomy and Self-Respect*, ed. Thomas E. Hill Jr., 193–94 (New York: Cambridge University Press, 1991).

[3] Burton Leiser, "Homosexuality and Natural Law," in *Liberty, Justice and Morals*, 3rd ed., 52–57 (New York: Macmillan, 1986).

[4] Notice that in these definitions an individual word is not defined in isolation. Instead, a whole sentence containing the word is replaced by another whole sentence in which the defined word does not appear. Definitions of this kind are called "contextual definitions" because a context containing the word is the unit of definition. Dictionary, disambiguating, stipulative, and precising definitions can also be presented in this contextual form.

[5] If you doubt that the identity "Water is H_2O" is used as a definition, just consider how you would react to someone who claims to have discovered some water that is *not* H_2O. We would dismiss this person as linguistically confused, as the discovered stuff cannot properly be called "water" if it is not H_2O.

[6] Reprinted in Kenneth Starr, *Appendices to the Referral . . . by the Office of the Independent Counsel . . .* (House Document 105-311) (Washington, DC: U.S. Government Printing Office, 1998), 393, 460–61, 464, 466, 469–70, 472–74, 509–10, 571–72, 601–2.

15

Fallacies of Relevance

This chapter will consider a different kind of defect in arguments. Fallacies of relevance arise when a premise, true or not, is not adequately related to the conclusion. Such irrelevance comes in endless varieties, but we will focus on two of the most common forms: arguments ad hominem *and* appeals to authority. *Arguments of these kinds are not always fallacious, so we will discuss various factors that determine when such arguments are defective and when they are not.*

RELEVANCE

In a good argument, we present statements that are true in order to offer support for some conclusion. One way to depart from this ideal is to state things that are true themselves, but have no bearing on the truth of the conclusion.

We might wonder why irrelevant remarks can have any influence at all. The answer is that we generally assume that a person's remarks are relevant, for this is one of the conditions for smooth and successful conversation (as Grice pointed out in his rule of Relevance, discussed in Chapter 2). That it is possible to exploit people by violating this natural assumption is shown in the following passage from *The Catcher in the Rye*.

> The new elevator boy was sort of on the stupid side. I told him, in this very casual voice, to take me up the Dicksteins'. . . .
>
> He had the elevator doors all shut and all, and was all set to take me up, and then he turned around and said, "They ain't in. They're at a party on the fourteenth floor."
>
> "That's all right," I said. "I'm supposed to wait for them. I'm their nephew."
>
> He gave me this sort of stupid, suspicious look. "You better wait in the lobby, fella," he said.
>
> "I'd like to—I really would," I said. "But I have a bad leg. I have to hold it in a certain position. I think I'd better sit down in the chair outside their door."
>
> He didn't know what the hell I was talking about, so all he said was "oh" and took me up. Not bad, boy. It's funny. All you have to do is say something nobody understands and they'll do practically anything you want them to.[1]

It is clear what is going on here. When you offer something as a reason, it is conversationally implied that there is some connection between it and the thing you are arguing for. In most cases, the connection is obvious, and there is no need to spell it out. In other cases, the connection is not obvious, but in the spirit of cooperation others are willing to assume that the connection exists. In the present case, there seems to be no connection between having a bad leg and sitting in one particular chair. Why, then, does the elevator operator not challenge this statement? Part of the reason is that it is not easy to challenge what people say; among other things, it is not polite. But politeness does not seem to hold the elevator operator back; instead, he does not want to appear stupid. The person who offers a reason conversationally implies a connection, and we do not like to admit that we fail to see this connection. This combination of generosity and fear of looking stupid leads us to accept all sorts of irrelevant statements as reasons.

Fallacies of relevance are surprisingly common in everyday life. People often introduce irrelevant details or tangents in order to mislead by diverting attention from the real issue. The irrelevant distraction is sometimes described as a *red herring* (after a man who dragged a red herring across his trail in order to throw pursuing hounds off his scent). The best strategy for dealing with such tricks is simply to cross out all irrelevant claims and then see what is left. Sometimes nothing is left.

On the other hand, we should not be heavy-handed in making charges of irrelevance. Sometimes the occurrence of irrelevance is innocent; good arguments often contain irrelevant asides. More important, relevance is often secured by way of a conversational implication, so we really have to know what is going on in a given context to decide whether a remark is relevant or not. We can illustrate this last point by examining two kinds of arguments that often involve fallacies of irrelevance: *arguments ad hominem* and *appeals to authority.*

AD HOMINEM ARGUMENTS

Literally, an argument ad hominem is an argument directed against a person who is making a claim rather than against that person's claim or argument for it. On the face of it, this move seems to involve irrelevance, for the character or social position or status of a person should have nothing to do with the truth of what that person says or with the soundness or strength of that person's arguments. Even when protesters dress shabbily or fail to bathe, their clothing and hygiene show nothing about the legitimacy of their protest. A speaker's ethnicity, race, sex, or sexual orientation almost never give us any good reason to challenge the truth of what that person says or the soundness of his or her argument. And the fact that a judge was appointed by a Democrat (or Republican) does not show that the judge's legal decisions are incorrect or unfounded. Ad hominem fallacies very often deal in such irrelevant personal characteristics. They are often introduced just to distract us from the real point at issue.

In rare and unusual cases, however, a speaker's character or position *is* a reason to doubt the truth of what he says. Suppose that Lucy is suspected of committing murder, but Louie testifies that he was with her at the time of the murder. Then the prosecution shows that Louie provided a similar alibi for an accused murderer at ten trials in the past year, and every time he was found to have lied in exchange for money. Louie never testifies without being paid, he says whatever he is paid to say, and people do not hire him if they have any better defense. This background about Louie provides some reason to believe that what Louie said was false—that he was not with Lucy at the time of the murder. Lucy still might not have committed the murder, but we can't take Louie's word for it. Ad hominem arguments like this can be called *deniers*, since they deny the truth of what is said or the strength or soundness of an argument. Although most ad hominem deniers are fallacious, the case of Louie shows that a few are not.

A different kind of ad hominem argument questions a person's right to make a claim or present an argument. Imagine that the Senate is debating tax rates. During one session, Tad stands up and argues for a reduction in taxes. Tad can be criticized if he is not a senator, because then he lacks the status that confers the right to speak in this setting. Even outside of any formal institution, if a neighbor tells someone that she ought to take her children to a certain church, the mother might respond, "Mind your own business, you busybody." Responses like this can be called *silencers*, because they revoke the right to speak without necessarily denying the truth of what is said.

A third variety of ad hominem argument is more subtle. Consider the following exchange:

NORM: The cold war is over, and bad relations between Cuba and the United States hurt both countries, so it is time for the United States to develop normal relations with Cuba.

CLIFF: Yeah, so you can make a bundle importing cigars from those commies.

Cliff's reply is an attack on the motives of Norm and not on the truth of what Norm said. Nor is Cliff denying that Norm has a right to speak. Yet the remark is not without some relevance—it is not off the wall. In a conversational exchange, we rely on the integrity of the person who is speaking, and when we have reasons to believe that the person's integrity is questionable, we sometimes say so. This is the significance of Cliff's remark. Cliff points to a fact that gives some reason for us not to trust Norm's integrity in a discussion of the United States' relations with Cuba.

Cliff's attack might or might not be justified. If the only reason why Norm favors normal relations between the United States and Cuba is that this would enable Norm to make more money, then Cliff's ad hominem attack is well founded. But if Norm's real reason for saying what he does is that he honestly believes that normal relations would be beneficial both to the

United States and to Cuba, then Norm's position does not depend on any lack of integrity. In that case, Cliff's attack is not well founded, even if it so happens that Norm would profit from normal relations.

Whether justified or not, ad hominem arguments of this third variety can be called *dismissers*, because they dismiss the speaker as untrustworthy and unreliable. Their point is not to deny the truth of the claim or the speaker's right to say it. Instead, a dismisser is supposed to show why the fact that this speaker supports a claim is not a good reason to believe that claim (or to deny it, for that matter).

These three variations are all ad hominem arguments because they start from premises about the person's character or status. Where they differ is in their conclusions: Deniers conclude that a claim is untrue or that an argument is unsound or weak. Silencers conclude that someone lacks the right to speak in a certain context. Dismissers conclude that someone is untrustworthy or unreliable. Each can be either justified or unjustified, so there are six kinds that can be diagrammed like this:

Ad Hominem Arguments	Justified	Not Justified
Deniers	Louie, the hired perjurer	Shabby protesters
Silencers	Tad if he is not a senator	Tad if he is a senator
Dismissers	Cliff's reply if Norm lacks integrity	Cliff's reply if Norm does not lack integrity

What logicians usually call ad hominem fallacies are unjustified deniers. Even when the premises of such an argument are true, they are irrelevant to the conclusion. That makes them fallacies of relevance. Once you get used to spotting ad hominem fallacies, they seem common and obvious.

When assessing an ad hominem argument, the first step is to determine whether its conclusion is about someone's right to speak, about someone's reliability, or about the truth, soundness, or strength of what is claimed. The second step is to determine whether its premises provide adequate justification for its conclusion. These steps will enable you to place the argument in the above table, but they will often not be easy or obvious. Although perjurers for hire almost always lie, most people exhibit some middling degree of reliability. When people are known for passing on rumors without checking their truth, this might be a reason to doubt what they say when they pass on yet another rumor (even if it is not a reason to believe that what they say is false). In assessing what they say, it would be best to look for additional evidence. If none is available, then we need to ask how often their testimony is true on matters of this kind. Only by careful inspection of individual cases can we determine the strength of such ad hominem arguments.

A related case occurs when someone is accused of inconsistency over time. If your neighbor says that the best time to prune roses is in the autumn, but then the next spring she tells you that the spring is the best time to prune roses, this inconsistency would give you some reason to doubt her expertise as a gardener. Maybe over the winter she got new information that changed her mind, but her reliability is in question until you have some explanation of why she would say different things at different times. If she wavers between contrary positions, no more than half of her views can be correct, so you have reason to ask your neighbor, "Why should I trust you?"

What she is saying now still might be correct. Maybe spring is the right time to prune roses. Moreover, if she gave an argument for her claim (such as that pruned roses grow back more quickly in the spring, and it is better to prune roses when they grow back more quickly), then that argument still might be sound. Her current claim and argument do not depend on what she said last fall. For this reason, it is normally a fallacy to reject people's views on the basis of an inconsistency with their views at other times. Their current positions need to be assessed as they stand now. (Whether we want political leaders whose views blow with the wind is, of course, another issue.)

A different kind of inconsistency occurs in the traditional fallacy called *tu quoque*, a Latin term that means "you are another." When a parent tells a child to quit smoking, the child might respond, "Look who's talking. You've been smoking for years. If it's so bad, why don't you stop?" The force of this charge might be just that the parent is hypocritical or that one has no right to criticize others for doing something that one does oneself. If that is the point, this response is a silencer, and it might or might not be justified. In any case, the parent's smoking does not give any reason at all to conclude that smoking is not bad. To use a *tu quoque* argument to reach *that* conclusion would be an unjustified denier (and an ad hominem fallacy). Even hypocrites can make true claims and give good arguments. Thus, to show that someone's claims and arguments are defective, one normally needs to look at those claims and arguments themselves, not at the behavior of the speaker.

Instead of citing past beliefs or acts of a speaker, some ad hominem arguments aim at the source or origin of the speaker's belief. Stephen Colbert, for example, dismisses scientists by explaining how they got caught up in science: "They're physically awkward and lonely, so they spent their adolescence down by the creek studying the creatures that live there. 'I may be ridiculed at school,' they think, 'but a crawfish would never judge me.'"[2] This parody, of course, is supposed to show how silly it is to reject science because of its origin (even if this origin were plausible). When its origin is irrelevant to the truth of a claim, such arguments commit what is called the *genetic fallacy*. Whole movements are sometimes accused of genetic fallacies. Marxists often reject opposing views because those views arose under capitalism. Freudians sometimes dismiss critics on the basis of how those critics were raised as children. Usually, the same kind of argument is available to their opponents as well. Critics of Freud sometimes cite his childhood and training to explain away his views. The fact that genetic arguments can be used just as well for contrary conclusions suggests that they do not really support either side.

The problem with genetic arguments is that lots of good ideas have questionable origins. Much mathematics originated within Pythagorean cults. Gravity and much of chemical theory were first discussed by alchemists who were trying to turn lead into gold. The structure of the benzene ring is reported to have come to Kekule von Stradonitz in a dream about a snake biting its tail. Early religions were close to magic and were used by rich and powerful leaders to control their subordinates. In all of these cases, the origin of the ideas cannot be used to refute those views or the arguments for them. Learning the genesis of an idea can help improve one's understanding of its content and of the process of discovery. Origins sometimes indicate where to look for evidence or for objections. Still, to evaluate an idea or an argument, one should focus on that idea or argument, not on its origin.

EXERCISE I

For each of the following arguments, indicate whether it involves (1) an ad hominem denier against a speaker's claim or argument, (2) an ad hominem silencer against a person's right to speak, (3) an ad hominem dismisser against someone's trustworthiness, or (4) none of these. Explain your answer. Be sure to focus on what is explicitly said and not on what might be conversationally implied in each example.

> Example: Sure, Sara says she saw me cheat in the game, but Sara's stupid, so you shouldn't pay any attention to her.
>
> Answer: This is an ad hominem dismisser, since the point is that Sara is unreliable. The speaker does not deny what Sara says or that she has a right to say it.

1. Sure, Sadie says she saw me cheat, but it was very dark, and her vision is horrible, so she must have seen something else and thought it was me cheating.
2. Sure, Sam says he saw me cheat, but the only reason he says it is that he wants to win the game. He's a real jerk.
3. Sure, Steve says she saw me cheat, but he wasn't even playing the game. It's not his place to accuse those of us who were playing.
4. Sure, Sybill says she saw me cheat, but I didn't even take the exam, so I couldn't have cheated on it.
5. Sure, Sally says she saw me cheat, but she accuses everyone, and she's almost always wrong, so you should know that she is wrong this time, too.

EXERCISE II

Explain the point of each of the following remarks. Indicate whether each remark involves an ad hominem silencer, dismisser, denier, or none of these. Then say whether the argument provides an adequate justification for its conclusion, and why or why not.

1. The American Tobacco Company has argued for years that smoking is not really unhealthy, but what would you expect the company to say? It would take the same position regardless of any evidence, so I can't trust them.

2. The Joint Chiefs of Staff argue that the U.S. government needs to increase its military budget, but an opponent responds, "Well, of course, *they* will want as much money as they can get for their departments. They always ask for more money even though most of the time they don't really need it. So this time, again, they probably don't need it."

3. After Congress passes a military draft during a war, an opponent says, "If members of Congress were eligible for the draft, they would not vote for it. So we must not really need a draft."

4. Of course, the party in power is opposed to term limits. That's just because they want to stay in power.

5. The main opposition to tax reductions comes from people who depend on government programs funded by taxes, so they can hardly be impartial, but only those who are impartial should be allowed to speak on such a crucial issue for our whole country.

6. The main support for tax reductions comes from people who pay taxes, so their views can't be a reliable indicator of what the best policy is.

7. Very few citizens have studied the entire tax code, and nobody understands the effect of taxes on the economy, so we have little reason to believe them when they say that present tax policies will destroy the economy.

8. An economist cites recent trends in sales of raw materials as evidence of an upturn in the economy, and then a critic, who doubts the economist's prediction, responds, "If you're so smart, why ain't you rich?"

9. As a criticism of pro-choice activists, Ronald Reagan said, "I've noticed that everybody who is for abortion has already been born."

10. Attacking male opponents of abortion, a feminist claims, "Most opponents of abortion are men."

11. When a member of a fraternity argued for co-ed houses in place of fraternities, a critic responded, "When he quits his fraternity in protest and joins a co-ed house, then he will earn the right to criticize us."

12. When Fred argues at a fraternity meeting that his house should admit women, another member announces, "Let me remind you all that Fred held exactly the opposite position last year."

13. Let he who is without sin among you cast the first stone. (John 8:7)

DISCUSSION QUESTIONS

1. In a heated discussion, people will sometimes ask an opponent, "Why are you being so defensive?" This is obviously a rhetorical question. What is the point of this question? Does it implicitly involve an ad hominem fallacy?

2. In the biblical story of Job, Job is described as a person who "was blameless and upright, one who feared God and turned away from evil" (Job 1:1). Satan challenges God to allow him to subject Job to the worst

(continued)

calamities to see if Job's faith will remain unchanged. After the most extreme misfortunes, Job finally cries out and asks why he should be made to suffer so (Job 38:1–4):

> Then the Lord answered Job out of the whirlwind:
> Who is this that darkens counsel by words without knowledge?
> Gird up your loins like a man.
> I will question you, and you shall declare to me.
> Where were you when I laid the foundation of the earth?
> Tell me, if you have understanding.

Does God's response to Job involve an ad hominem silencer, dismisser, or denier? Is it justified? Why or why not?

3. Nietzsche is often accused of committing the genetic fallacy when he uses speculation about the origin of Christian moral beliefs as part of his critique of what he called slave morality. In your opinion, does Nietzsche commit a genetic fallacy in the following passage? Why or why not? Can the origin of a moral belief ever show that that moral belief is false or unjustified or indefensible? Why or why not?

> Let us articulate this new demand: we need a critique of moral values, the value of these values themselves must first be called into question—and for that there is needed a knowledge of the conditions and circumstances in which they grew, under which they evolved and changed, . . . a knowledge of a kind that has never yet existed or even been desired. One has taken the value of these "values" as given, as factual, as beyond all question; one has hitherto never doubted or hesitated in the slightest degree in supposing "the good man" to be of greater value than "the evil man," of greater value in the sense of furthering the advancement and prosperity of man in general (the future of man included). But what if the reverse were true? What if a symptom of regression were inherent in the "good," likewise a danger, a seduction, a poison, a narcotic, through which the present was possibly living at the expense of the future? Perhaps more comfortably, less dangerously, but at the same time in a meaner style, more basely?—So that precisely morality would be to blame if the highest power and splendor actually possible to the type man was never in fact attained? So that precisely morality was the danger of dangers?[3]

APPEALS TO AUTHORITY

Often in the midst of an argument, we cite an authority to back up what we say. As we saw in Chapter 3, this is a standard way of offering assurances. In citing an authority, instead of giving reasons for what we say, we indicate that someone (the authority cited) could give them.

Although logicians sometimes speak of the *fallacy* of appealing to authorities, there is often nothing wrong with citing authorities or experts to support what we say. An authority is a person or institution with a privileged position concerning certain information. Through training, a doctor is an expert on certain diseases. A person who works in the Department of Agriculture can be an expert on America's soybean production. Someone who grew up in the swamps might be an expert on trapping muskrats. Because some people stand in a better position to know things than others, there is nothing improper about citing them as authorities. In fact, an appeal to experts and authorities is essential if we are to make up our minds on subjects outside our own range of competence.

At the same time, appeals to authority can be abused, and there are some obvious questions we should ask whenever such an appeal is made. Most obviously, we should always ask whether the person cited is, in fact, an authority at all. Moreover, it is not enough to be an authority in some area or other. We need to ask whether the person cited is an authority in the particular area under discussion. If the answer to this question is "No," then we are dealing with a *fallacy of relevance*. For example, being a movie star does not qualify a person to speak on the merits of a particular brand of toothpaste. Endorsements by athletes of hair creams, deodorants, beer, and automobiles are in the same boat. Of course, we have to be careful in making this charge. It is possible that certain athletes make systematic studies of deodorants before giving one deodorant their endorsement. But it is not likely.

Most people realize that athletes, movie stars, and the like are featured in advertisements primarily to attract attention and not because they are experts concerning the products they are endorsing. It is more surprising how often the wrong authorities are brought in to judge serious matters. To cite one example, Uri Geller had little difficulty convincing a group of distinguished British scientists that he possessed psychic powers. In particular, he was able to convince them that he could bend spoons by mental powers alone. In contrast, James Randi, a professional magician, had little difficulty detecting and duplicating the tricks that bamboozled the scientific observers. The remarkable feature of this case was not that a group of scientists could be fooled by a magician, but rather that these scientists assumed that they had the expertise necessary to decide whether a paranormal phenomenon had taken place or not. After all, the most obvious explanation of Geller's feats was that he had somehow cheated. To test this possibility, what was needed was not a scientist with impeccable scholarly credentials, but a magician who could do the same tricks himself and therefore knew what to look for.[4]

It is, of course, difficult to decide whether someone is an expert in a field when you yourself are not, but certain clues will help you make this decision. If the supposed authority claims to have knowledge of things that he or she could not possibly possess (for example, about private conversations the person could not have heard), then you have little reason to trust other things that person has to say. You know that he or she has no qualms about making things up. Furthermore, it is often possible to spot-check certain claims in order to make sure that they are correct. It may take one expert to determine another, but it often takes little more than good common sense and an unwillingness to be fooled to detect a fraud.

Even when it is clear that the person cited is an expert in the appropriate field, we can still ask whether the question is of the kind that can now be settled by an appeal to experts. One sign that a question cannot yet be settled by experts is that experts in that area do not agree with each other. It does not do much good to cite one authority in support of a claim if another authority with just as much expertise would endorse the opposite claim. Moreover, even the best experts sometimes simply get things wrong. For example, in 1932 Albert Einstein, who was surely an expert in the field, declared, "There is not the slightest indication that [nuclear] energy will ever be obtainable. It would mean that the atom would have to be shattered at will." Just a year later, the atom was, in fact, split. Even so, a leading British physicist, Ernest Lord Rutherford, insisted that the splitting of the atom would not lead to the development of nuclear power, saying, "The energy produced by the atom is a very poor kind of thing. Anyone who expects a source of power from the transformation of these atoms is talking moonshine."[5] Given the knowledge available at the time, both Einstein and Rutherford may have been justified in their claims, but their assertions were, after all, more speculations than scientifically supported statements of fact. The lesson to be learned from this is that the best experts are sometimes fallible, and become more fallible when they go beyond established facts in their discipline to speculate about the future.

Although the next question may seem obvious, we often forget to ask whether the authority has been cited correctly. When a person cites an authority, he or she is making a factual claim that so-and-so holds some particular view. Sometimes the claim is false. If someone told you, "According to medical authorities, the rash from poison ivy is contagious when it is oozing," you would probably believe it. In fact, the citation is incorrect. According to medical authorities, the rash from poison ivy is never contagious. Yet many people hold that it is contagious, and they think that they have medical opinion on their side. It is hard to deal with people who cite authorities incorrectly, for we do not carry an almanac or encyclopedia around with us. Yet, again, it is a good idea to spot-check appeals to authority, for people often twist authorities to support their own opinions.

It is also worth asking whether the authority cited can be trusted to tell the truth. To put this more bluntly, we should ask whether a particular authority has any good reason to lie or misrepresent facts. Presumably, the officials who know most about food production in China will be the heads of the various agricultural bureaus. But it would be utterly naive to take their reports at face value. Inadequate agricultural production has been a standing embarrassment of the Chinese economy. As a consequence, there is pressure at every level to make things look as good as possible. Even if the state officials were inclined to tell the truth, which is a charitable assumption, the information they receive is probably not very accurate.

Experts also lie because it can bring fame and professional advancement. Science, sometimes at the highest level, has been embarrassed by problems of the falsification and misrepresentation of data. Consider the case of Sir Cyril Burt's research on the inheritance of intelligence. Burt wanted to show that there is a significant correlation between the IQs of parents and their children.

The difficulty was to find a way to screen out other influences—for example, that of home environment. To overcome this, Burt undertook a systematic study of identical twins who had been separated at birth and raised in various social settings. His study revealed a very high correlation between the IQs of these twins, and that gave strong reason to believe that IQ, to some significant extent, depends on heredity rather than environment.

Unfortunately, Burt's data, or at least a significantly large portion of them, were cooked—that is, made up. It is interesting that Burt's bogus research could go unchallenged for so long. It is also interesting how he was finally unmasked. First, to many his results seemed too good to be true. He claimed to have found more than fifty identical twins who had been separated at birth and raised in contrasting environments. Given the rarity of such creatures, that is a very large number to have found. Second, the correlations he claimed to find were extremely high—indeed, much higher than those usually found in research in this area. Both of these facts raised suspicions. Stephen Jay Gould describes Burt's final undoing as follows:

> Princeton psychologist Leon Kamin first noted that, while Burt had increased his sample of twins from fewer than twenty to more than fifty in a series of publications, the average correlation between pairs for IQ remained unchanged to the third decimal place—a statistical situation so unlikely that it matches the vernacular definition of impossible. Then, in 1976, Oliver Gillie, medical correspondent of the London *Sunday Times*, elevated the charge from inexcusable carelessness to conscious fakery. Gillie discovered, among many other things, that Burt's two "collaborators" . . . the women who supposedly collected and processed his data, either never existed at all, or at least could not have been in contact with Burt while he wrote the papers bearing their names.[6]

Of course, Burt's claims still might be correct: genes and IQ might be correlated. Nonetheless the point here is just that Burt and his studies should not be trusted as authorities. Outright fraud of this kind by someone so prominent is rare, but even a few cases provides a reason for being suspicious of authorities, at least when their results have not been given independent confirmation.

One last question we can ask is why the appeal to authority is being made at all. To cite an authority is to give assurances. As we noticed in Chapter 3, people usually give assurances to strengthen weak points in their arguments. It is surprising how often we can see what is wrong with an argument just by noticing where it is backed by appeals to authority. Beyond this, we should be suspicious of arguments that rely on too many authorities. (We might call this the fallacy of *excessive footnotes*.) Good arguments tend to stand on their own.

To summarize, reliance on experts and authorities is unavoidable in our complicated and specialized world. Yet we still need to be critical of appeals to authority by asking these questions:

1. Is the cited authority in fact an authority in the appropriate area?
2. Is this the kind of question that can now be settled by expert consensus?

3. Has the authority been cited correctly?

4. Can the cited authority be trusted to tell the truth?

5. Why is an appeal to authority being made at all?

If the answers to questions 1–4 are "Yes," then the appeal to authority is probably justified. Still, even the best authorities make mistakes, so the conclusion of any appeal to authority might turn out to be false. We can reduce errors by appealing to better authorities, but no authority can guarantee the truth.

EXERCISE III

Answer the five questions in the text about each of the following appeals to authority, and then decide whether each appeal to authority is legitimate or fallacious.

1. The surgeon general says that smoking is hazardous to your health, so it is.

2. The surgeon general says that abortion is immoral, so it is.

3. Michael Jordan says that Air Jordan sneakers are springier, so they must be springier.

4. This must be a great movie, because the billboard says that *Time* magazine called it "terrific."

5. My friend Joe says that this new movie is hilarious, so it must be worth watching.

6. Ben and Jerry's ice cream must be the best, because Fat Fred eats more ice cream than anyone else I know, and he says that Ben and Jerry's is the best.

7. There must be life on other planets, because many great scientists are looking for it, so they must think it is there.

8. Lefty Lopez must be the best pitcher of the year, because he won the Cy Young Award (awarded by the Baseball Writers Association to the best pitcher of the year).

9. Vanna must be the most beautiful woman in America, because she won the Miss America contest.

10. There were 250,000 protesters at the rally, because organizers gave that figure.

11. There were 25,000 protesters at the rally, because its opponents said so.

12. True Christians ought to give away all their money, because the Bible says, "Blessed are the poor."

MORE FALLACIES OF RELEVANCE

Questions like those used to evaluate appeals to authority can also be used to assess some other common styles of reasoning that are often accused of being fallacious. Here is one example:

The American people are convinced that, if we get involved in North Korea, we will be stuck there for a long time. So we shouldn't invade in the first place.

This argument, of course, depends on suppressed premises. On one reconstruction, the argument is that, because Americans fear getting stuck in North Korea, they oppose American involvement, and a democratic government should not do what the people oppose, so we should not get involved in North Korea. The argument also seems to suggest another reason why America should not get involved—namely, that if we do, our troops will be stuck in North Korea. The only reason given for believing this is that lots of American people believe it. So the argument seems to be that, because so many Americans believe it, it must be true.

Such an argument is not an appeal to authority, since no person is claimed to be an authority or an expert. Instead, the argument is an *appeal to popular opinion*. When the popular opinion is supposed to have been shared for a long time, the argument can be called an *appeal to tradition*. Such arguments assume that, when many people agree on some issue or agree for a long time, they are likely to be right. This assumption is often incorrect. An opinion might be shared by many people just because they all learned it from a common source, such as television or some prominent politicians. Then the shared opinion is not reliable unless its source is reliable. Of course, the shared opinion *might* be true; America might get stuck in North Korea if it got involved. But the argument for this conclusion is still fallacious, because the mere fact that an opinion is widely held is not enough to show that the opinion is true.

Although such appeals to popular opinion are often fallacious, there are also some areas where popular opinion is evidence of truth. If most people think that a book is entertaining and easy to understand, then it is entertaining and easy to understand. If most people think that the sky looks blue, this is evidence that the sky does look blue. Thus, not all appeals to popular opinion are defective or fallacious.

To determine whether or not a particular appeal to popular opinion is fallacious, we need to ask questions that are much like the questions we asked about appeals to authority. These include:

1. Is this opinion actually widely held?
2. Is this the kind of area where popular opinion is likely to be right?
3. Why is an appeal to popular opinion being made at all?

Even when superficial examination reveals that an appeal to popular opinion is fallacious, such arguments still seem to convince many people. This might be because many people want to agree with others so that they will be popular and will not have to think for themselves.

Other appeals are not to beliefs, but instead to emotions. One common form of appeal to emotion is an *appeal to pity*. Defense lawyers often dwell on the sad circumstances in which a defendant grew up or on how badly the defendant's family will be hurt if the defendant goes to prison. Such an appeal to pity might show that the defendant should not receive the maximum sentence. But when such an appeal to pity is used to argue that the defendant is not guilty or should not be found guilty, then the argument is almost always fallacious.

Appeals to fear are also common, especially since al Qaeda's destruction of the World Trade Center towers in New York on September 11, 2001. After another terrorist attack occurred in London in 2005, television news anchors and talk-show hosts flashed headlines like "Who's at risk?", "Are we next in America?", "How safe are we in America?", "How prepared are we?", "Can we prevent a subway or a bus attack in the US?", and "You have to wonder, will we ever truly feel safe again?" To be fair, televisions stations asked these questions because they knew that their audiences wanted answers to those very questions. A problem arises only when the media stirs up fears and fails to provide a balanced estimation of the real dangers. Such fearmongering is parodied in Stephen Colbert's segment, "The Threat Down," which lists more and more outrageous fears. An even more serious problem arises when politicians use exaggerated fears to gain support for costly policies that could not be justified by the actual threats that people face. Of course, it is controversial how much fear and which policies are justified. Democrats accuse Republicans of distortion when Republicans use fear of terrorism to justify their counterterrorist policies; Republicans accuse Democrats of exaggeration when Democrats paint a scary picture of the effects of global warming. Defenders of any particular policy can reply that it really is needed to ward off peril. Some fears are justified, including some fears of terrorism and of global warming, of course. Appeals to fear are fallacious only when they are overdone or exaggerated in order to lead people away from an accurate assessment of the risks that really exist. But this happens all-too often; so, whenever anyone appeals to fear, we need to ask whether those fears are being amplified and abused.

Outrage is another emotion that many arguments appeal to. On Day 3 of the 2004 Republican National Convention, for example, Democratic Senator Zell Miller proclaimed, "Today's Democratic leaders see America as an occupier, not a liberator; and nothing makes this marine madder than someone calling American troops occupiers rather than liberators!" This line drew thunderous applause, even though Miller did not give any reason either against calling American troops occupiers or for describing them as liberators. Nonetheless, a receptive audience will tend to assume that, if such an impressive speaker is *that* outraged (and if others in the audience share that outrage), then there must be something terribly objectionable about whatever the outrage is directed against. To assess such appeals to outrage, as for other emotions, we need to become aware of these common assumptions so that they can be critically evaluated.

Appeals to emotion can also be positive. Many advertisements work by linking a product to positive feelings. Everyone knows that a car does not become better just because it is displayed in beautiful scenery, but it is amazing how much the scenery in advertisements can affect people's inclinations to buy a certain car. Similarly, advocates of a treaty or government program often paint pictures of how wonderful life will be if the treaty or program works out well. Such appeals to emotion might provide some reason to adopt their plan, but these arguments can be very misleading if it is unlikely that everything will work out so well and if serious dangers will arise when something goes wrong.

Thus, even when emotional reactions are relevant to some extent, one must be careful not to let them cloud the other side of the issue.

EXERCISE IV

For each of the following arguments, indicate whether it is an appeal to popular opinion, an appeal to tradition, or an appeal to emotion. (The argument might fit into more than one of these categories. If so, explain why.) Then determine whether it is fallacious, and why.

1. For centuries throughout Europe, women were burned for being witches, so there must have been lots of witches.

2. There must be life on other planets, because most people think there is. Just read a few tabloids.

3. Most people who live in the United States think that it is the greatest country ever, so it must be.

4. There are more Buddhists than followers of any other religion, so there must be more truth in Buddhism.

5. Incest must be immoral, because people all over the world for many centuries have seen it as immoral.

6. The Golden Rule is accepted in almost every system of ethics both in the past and in the present, so there is probably something to it.

7. Chris must not be guilty, because twelve jurors, who saw all the evidence, agreed on a verdict of not guilty.

8. "Polls show an overwhelming majority of the American people want a lot less immigration or even an immigration moratorium. . . . These are persistent results over time. Most of the people cannot be wrong all of the time!" (from an advertisement placed by Federation for American Immigration Reform, *Atlantic Monthly* [June 1995], 67)

NOTES

[1] J. D. Salinger, *The Catcher in the Rye* (New York: Bantam Books, 1951), 157–58.

[2] Stephen Colbert, *I Am America (and So Can You!)* (New York: Grand Central Publishing, 2007), 193.

[3] Friedrich Nietzsche, *On the Genealogy of Morals*, trans. Walter Kaufmann, in *Basic Writings of Nietzsche* (New York: Random House, 1968), 456. Nietzsche goes on to argue that (slave) morality is the danger of dangers, so the reader is supposed to answer the rhetorical questions at the end of the passage in the affirmative.

[4] For an entertaining and instructive account of this case, see James Randi, *The Magic of Uri Geller* (New York: Ballantine Books, 1975).

[5] Both quotations are from Christopher Cerf and Victor Navasky, *The Experts Speak* (New York: Pantheon Books, 1984), 215. This work contains a marvelous collection of false and sometimes just plain stupid things that have been claimed by experts. One notable example is the remark made by the Union general John B. Sedgwick just before being fatally shot in the head by a Confederate marksman: "They couldn't hit an elephant at this dist—"(135).

[6] Stephen Jay Gould, *The Mismeasure of Man* (New York: Norton, 1981), 235.

16

FALLACIES OF VACUITY

Arguments are vacuous when they don't go anywhere. This happens in two main ways. Sometimes an argument begins by assuming its conclusion or some independent reason for its conclusion, so the argument makes no real progress beyond its own assumptions. In other cases, the argument's conclusion is empty, so the argument has nowhere in particular to go. Both kinds of argument are fallacious and vacuous, so we call them fallacies of vacuity. Circular arguments and arguments that beg the question fall into this category. So do positions that make themselves immune to criticism by being self-sealing.

CIRCULARITY

One purpose of arguments is to establish the truth of a claim to someone who doubts it. In a typical situation, one person, A, makes a claim; another person, B, raises objections to it; then A tries to find arguments that respond to the objections and justify the original statement. Schematically:

A asserts that *p* is true.

B raises objections *x, y,* and *z* against it.

A then offers reasons to overcome these objections.

What must A's responses be like to meet B's objections? To start with the simplest case, A cannot meet B's challenge simply by repeating the original assertion. If someone is maintaining that terrorists can't be stopped without torture, it will not help to offer as a justification for this the very claim that is in dispute—that terrorists can't be stopped without torture. The argument would look like this:

> Terrorists can't be stopped without torture.
> ∴ Terrorists can't be stopped without torture.

This argument is, of course, *valid,* since the premise cannot be true without the conclusion being true as well. Furthermore, if the premise is true, then the argument is also *sound.* All the same, the argument has no force in this conversational setting because any objection that B has to the conclusion is straight off an objection to the premise, since they are identical.

Unfortunately, people usually do not make it so easy to tell when they reason in a circle. Often, circular reasoning is disguised by restating the conclusion in different words. Someone might argue that terrorists can't be stopped without torture, because, if you do not use torture, there is no other way to stop terrorists. This premise means the same as the conclusion, so this reasoning is still circular.

Another way to hide circularity is by suppressing the premise that repeats the conclusion. (See Chapter 5 on suppressed premises.) Suppose someone argues that terrorists cannot be stopped without torture, because they are so callous that their goal is to kill and maim innocent civilians. This argument depends on the suppressed premise that anyone whose goal is to kill and maim innocent civilians cannot be stopped without torture. If terrorists are then defined as people whose goal is to kill and maim innocent civilians, then this suppressed premise reduces to the conclusion that terrorists cannot be stopped without torture. So this argument is also circular.

Yet another trick is to put forward a statement first as a conclusion to be proved, and then only much later—after several subarguments or tangents—use the same statement as a premise on its own behalf. Consider this simple argument:

> The only way to prevent terrorists from committing their horrible crimes is to inflict enough pain on them either to scare them off or to force them to reveal information that enables the police to head off terrorist attacks. Because these are the only methods that work, we cannot reason with them or talk them into giving up. We cannot make friends or sign a treaty with them. We cannot buy them off or satisfy their demands. Therefore, terrorists cannot be stopped without torture.

If the first sentence is supposed to provide a reason for the next three sentences, then those three sentences cannot later be used as a reason for the last sentence without the whole argument becoming circular, because the last sentence, "Terrorists can't be stopped without torture," means pretty much the same as the first sentence, "The only way to prevent terrorists . . . is to inflict enough pain on them. . . ." Although this trick is often harder to detect in a long and complex argument, such reasoning is still indirectly circular if any premise in a chain of arguments repeats or restates the eventual conclusion. Thus, we have *circular reasoning* if and only if one of the premises that is used directly or indirectly to support a conclusion is equivalent to the conclusion itself.

BEGGING THE QUESTION

Reasoning in a circle is normally bad reasoning, but it is not easy to say exactly what is bad about it. The problem with circular reasoning becomes clearer when we notice that the same basic defect is shared by arguments that are not circular. Instead of arguing, "Terrorists can't be stopped without torture, so they can't," we could avoid circularity by adding a few words to get this new argument:

> If terrorists can be stopped without torture, then I'm a monkey's uncle.
> I'm not a monkey's uncle.
> ∴ Terrorists can't be stopped without torture.

This argument is not circular, because neither premise repeats the conclusion. It is also valid, and it might even be sound. Still, it is no good as an argument for the same reason as "Terrorists can't be stopped without torture, so it can't." The problem lies in its first premise. The consequent of the first premise ("I'm a monkey's uncle") is obviously false, so that first premise is false unless its antecedent ("Terrorists can be stopped without torture.") is false. But that means that the conclusion must be true in order for the first premise to be true. Thus, one could not have any reason to believe the first premise if one did not already have the very same reason to believe the conclusion. One's reason to believe the premise depends on one's prior belief in the conclusion or on one's reason to believe the conclusion. In short, one has no independent reason for the premise.

This is a problem if the conclusion is disputed and the argument is being used to get someone who rejects the conclusion to change his or her mind and accept it. Anyone who rejects the conclusion will simply reject the premise. For the argument to show someone that he or she ought to accept the conclusion, the arguer would need an independent reason to believe the premise. But then that independent reason does all of the real work, and the argument as stated does nothing to establish the conclusion. It is, in a word, vacuous.

The point is not just that an opponent would deny the premise. If that were enough to make an argument fail, then arguments would almost never succeed. The point is instead that, when an opponent objects to a premise, the arguer cannot show that the opponent has reason to accept that premise simply by asserting what the opponent denies. Bare assertion and reassertion do nothing to overcome objections. To show that the opponent has reason to accept the premise and, hence, the conclusion, the arguer needs some independent evidence for the premise. Because there needs to be—but cannot be—an independent reason for the premise, "If terrorists can be stopped without torture, then I'm a monkey's uncle," the argument with this premise must beg the question in any normal context.

More generally, we can say that an argument *begs the question* in a context if and only if (1) it depends on a premise that is not supported by any reason that is independent of the conclusion, and (2) there is a need for such an independent reason.

To say that an argument begs the question in this sense is not, of course, to say that it raises the question. That is what a sports announcer means, for example, when she says, "His injury begs the question of whether he will return in time for the playoffs." This common use of the phrase "begs the question" is separate from the fallacy, but they are not completely unrelated. An argument can also be seen as begging the question when its context raises the question of why anyone who denies its conclusion should accept its premises and when that question has no adequate answer.

More precisely, the need for an independent justification arises from the context and the purpose for which the argument is being used. A premise *needs* support from an independent reason, for example, when it is in dispute or subject to objection and the arguer's goal is to give an audience some reason to accept the premise and, on that basis, to accept the conclusion. That such a need for an independent reason exists but is not satisfied explains why the argument can be criticized by saying that it commits the fallacy of *begging the question*.

This fallacy is often very hard to detect, both because it is affected by the context and because there are many ways to hide the fact that a premise depends on the conclusion. Consequently, people often use arguments that beg the question when they have nothing better to say, especially on a controversial issue. It is common, for example, to hear an argument something like the following:

> It's always wrong to murder human beings.
> Capital punishment involves murdering human beings.
> ∴ Capital punishment is wrong.

Here the first premise is true by definition, since calling something murder implies that it is a wrongful killing. The second premise is, however, question begging, for calling capital punishment murder assumes the point at issue— that capital punishment is wrong. As a result, anyone who objects to the conclusion would or should raise exactly the same objections to the second premise, and one could not give any adequate reason for the second premise without first arguing for the conclusion.

More subtly than this, opponents of abortion typically refer to the human fetus as an unborn baby or simply as a baby. It may seem a matter of indifference how the fetus is referred to, but this is not true. One of the central points in the debate over abortion is whether the fetus has the status of a person and thus has the rights that any person has. It is generally acknowledged in our society that babies are persons and therefore have the rights of persons. By referring to the fetus as an unborn baby (or simply as a baby), a point that demands argument is taken for granted without argument. That counts as begging the question. Of course, many opponents of abortion argue for the claim that a human fetus has the moral status of a person and thus do not beg this central question in the debate. Still, if they give no such independent argument, then they do beg the question.

Similarly, if someone argues for the pro-choice position simply on the grounds that a woman has a right to control the destiny of her own body, this also begs an important question, because it takes for granted the claim that the fetus is part of a woman's body, not an independent being with rights of its own. Of course, defenders of the pro-choice position need not beg the question in this way, but they often do. Whether a particular argument or premise is question begging will depend on whether there is a need for an independent reason, which in turn depends on the context in which the argument is given. One way for an argument to beg the question is for it to rely, either explicitly or implicitly, on an unsupported premise that is a matter of dispute in the particular argumentative context. Thus, referring to a human fetus as a baby will be question begging in contexts in which the moral status of the fetus is at issue, but it may not be question begging when this is not an issue.

Because begging the question depends in this way on context, we should be careful before charging opponents with begging the question. Some people charge every opponent with begging the question, almost like a knee-jerk reaction. However, even if an opponent uses a premise that you reject, this does not yet show that the argument begs the question, since your opponent might have plenty of independent evidence for the premise. Before you accuse people of begging the question, you should ask them to give you their reasons for the disputed premise. If they can come up with an independent reason, then they did not beg the question, and you might learn something from them. However, if they do not have any independent reason for the premise, then they did indeed beg the question.

EXERCISE I

For each of the following arguments, does it involve circular reasoning? Does it beg the question in any context? If so, in which contexts? Explain your answers.

1. A student of mine told me that I am her favorite professor, and I know that she is telling the truth, because no student would lie to her favorite professor.

2. Intoxicating beverages should be banned, because they can make people drunk.

3. Capitalism is the only correct economic system, because without it free enterprise would be impossible.

4. Free trade is good for the country, because it brings the country all of the advantages of an unimpeded flow of goods.

5. Gun-control laws are wrong, because they violate the citizen's right to bear arms.

6. When *B* applies for a job from *A:*

   A: How can we know that you are trustworthy?

   B: Mr. Davidson will write me a recommendation.

   A: But why should we trust him?

   B: I assure you that he is honest and accurate.

   (continued)

7. The Bible is the inerrant word of God, because God speaks only the truth, and repeatedly in the Bible God tells us that the Bible consists of His words.

8. We have to accept change, because without change there is no progress.

9. Premarital sex is wrong, because premarital sex is fornication, and fornication is a sin.

10. The drinking age should be lowered to eighteen, because eighteen-year-olds are mature enough to drink.

11. We should never give security clearances to homosexuals, because they can be blackmailed into revealing classified information. They are subject to blackmail, because we will revoke their security clearances if we find out they are gay.

12. People with suicidal tendencies are insane, because they want to kill themselves.

13. Jeffrey can't really be insane, because he says he is.

DISCUSSION QUESTIONS (ADVANCED)

1. Explanations are often presented in the form of arguments that sometimes seem circular. Are the following arguments circular? Do they beg the question? Are they defective in some other way? Why or why not? More generally, when, if ever, can circular arguments provide good explanations?

   A. **TOM:** Why are so many people moving out of Claremont this year?

      SUE: Because its economy is going down so fast.

      TOM: But why is its economy going down so fast?

      SUE: Because so many people are moving out of town.

   B. **AMY:** Why is Jarred going down on the seesaw right now?

      JOHN: Because Jeremiah is going up on the other side of the seesaw.

      AMY: But why is Jeremiah going up right now?

      JOHN: Because Jarred is going down.

2. Explain John Stuart Mill's argument in the following passage (from *A System of Logic* [London, 1843], book 2, chapter 3, section 2). Do you agree? Why or why not?

   It must be granted that in every syllogism, considered as an argument to prove the conclusion, there is a *petitio principii* [a begging of the question]. When we say,

   All men are mortal.
   Socrates is a man.
   ∴ Socrates is mortal;

   it is unanswerably urged by the adversaries of the syllogistic theory that the proposition, "Socrates is mortal," is presupposed in the more general assumption, "All men are mortal"; that we cannot be assured of the mortality of all men unless we are already certain of the mortality of every individual man. . . . That, in short, no reasoning from generals to particulars can, as such, prove anything, since from a general principle we cannot infer any particulars but those which the principle itself assumes as known.

3. Suppose Andrea asks, "How many days are there in November?" In response, Cummings says, "Let's see. How does that mnemonic go? Oh yeah: Thirty days has September, April, June, and November. So November has thirty days." Is this argument circular? Does it beg the question? Why or why not?

4. Does the following argument (from Roy Sorensen) beg the question in any contexts? If so, in which contexts? Why?

> Some arguments beg the question.
> ∴ Some arguments beg the question.

5. St. Thomas Aquinas gave the following argument for the existence of God:

> In the world of sense we find there is an order of efficient causes. There is no case known (neither is it, indeed, possible) in which a thing is found to be the efficient cause of itself; for so it would be prior to itself, which is impossible. Now in efficient causes it is not possible to go on to infinity, because in all efficient causes following in order, the first is the cause of the intermediate cause, and the intermediate is the cause of the ultimate cause, whether the intermediate cause be several, or only one. Now to remove the cause is to remove the effect. Therefore, if there be no first cause among efficient causes, there will be no ultimate, nor any intermediate cause. But if in efficient causes it is possible to go on to infinity, there will be no first efficient cause, neither will there be an ultimate effect, nor any intermediate efficient causes; all of which is plainly false. Therefore it is necessary to admit a first efficient cause, to which everyone gives the name of God.[1]

In response, John Mackie accused Aquinas of begging the question:

> Unfortunately this argument is unsound. Although in a *finite* ordered series of causes the intermediate (or the earliest intermediate) is caused by the first item, this would not be so if there were an infinite series. In an infinite series, every item is caused by an earlier item. The way in which the first item is "removed" if we go from a finite to an infinite series does not entail the removal of the later items. In fact, Aquinas . . . has simply begged the question against an infinite regress of causes. . . .[2]

Explain and evaluate Mackie's objection. Does Aquinas beg the question? Why or why not?

SELF-SEALERS

It is characteristic of certain positions that no evidence can *possibly* refute them. This may seem to be a wonderful feature for a position to have. In fact, however, it *usually* makes the position useless. We can start with a silly example. A Perfect Sage claims to be able to predict the future in detail. The Perfect Sage's predictions take the following form:

> Two weeks from today at 4:37 you are going to be doing *exactly* what you will be doing.

Of course, whatever you are doing at that time will be exactly what you are doing, so this prediction cannot possibly be wrong. But this is only because it does not tell us anything in particular about the future. *Whatever* happens, the prediction is going to be true, and this is just what is wrong with it. The prediction is *empty* or *vacuous*.

People do not, of course, go around making predictions of this kind, but they do sometimes hold positions that are empty or vacuous in much the same way. A clairvoyant claims to be able to predict the future, but every time a prediction fails, she says that this just proves that someone set up bad vibrations that interfered with her visions. So, if the prediction turns out to be true, she claims that this shows her clairvoyance; if it turns out to be false, she cites this as evidence of interference. No matter what happens, then, the clairvoyant's claim to be clairvoyant cannot be refuted. Her claim to clairvoyance is as empty and vacuous as the Perfect Sage's prediction.

Positions that are set up in this way so that nothing can possibly refute them are called *self-sealers*. A self-sealing position is one that is so constructed that no evidence can possibly be brought against it no matter what happens. This shows its vacuity, and it is precisely for this reason that we reject it.

People do not usually hold self-sealing positions in a blatant way; they tend to back into them. A person who holds that the American economy is controlled by an international Jewish conspiracy will point out people of Jewish extraction (or with Jewish names) who occupy important positions in financial institutions. This at least counts as evidence, though very weak evidence. And there seems to be much stronger evidence on the other side: There are a great many people in these institutions who are not Jews. To counter this claim, the person now argues that many of these other people are secretly Jews or are tools of the Jewish conspiracy. The Jews have allowed some non-Jews to hold important positions in order to conceal their conspiracy. What evidence is there for this? Well, none really, but that only helps prove how sneaky the Jewish conspiracy is. At this point, the position has become self-sealing, for all evidence cited against the existence of the conspiracy will be converted into evidence for its cleverness.

Self-sealing arguments are hard to deal with, because people who use them will often shift their ground. A person will begin by holding a significant position that implies that facts are one way rather than another, but under the pressure of criticism will self-seal the position so that no evidence can possibly count against it. That is, the person will slide back and forth between two positions—one that is not self-sealed (and so is significant but subject to refutation) and another that is self-sealed (and so is not subject to criticism but is also not significant). The charge that is leveled against a theory that vacillates in this way is that it is either *vacuous* or *false*. It is vacuous if self-sealing, false if not.

One way of challenging a self-sealing position is to ask what possible fact could prove it wrong. This is a good question to ask, but it can be misunderstood and met with the triumphant reply: "Nothing can prove my position wrong, because it is right." A better way to show the insignificance of a self-sealing theory is to put the challenge in a different form: "If your position has any significance, it should tell us that certain things will occur whereas certain other things will not occur. If it cannot do this, it really tells us nothing at all; so please make some specific predictions, and we will see how they come out."

Ideologies and worldviews tend to be self-sealing. The Marxist ideology sometimes has this quality. If you fail to see the truth of the Marxist ideology, that just shows that your social consciousness has not been raised. The very fact that you reject the Marxist ideology shows that you are not yet capable of understanding it and that you are in need of re-education. This is perfect self-sealing. Sometimes psychoanalytic theory gets involved in this same kind of self-sealing. People who vigorously disagree with certain psychoanalytic claims can be accused of repressing these facts. If a boy denies that he wants to murder his father and sleep with his mother, this itself can be taken as evidence of the strength of these desires and of his unwillingness to acknowledge them. If this kind of reasoning gets out of hand, then psychoanalytic theory also becomes self-sealing and empty. Freud was aware of this danger and warned against it.

So far, we have seen two ways in which an argument can be self-sealing: (1) It can invent an ad hoc or arbitrary way of dismissing every possible criticism. The clairvoyant can always point to interfering conditions without going to the trouble of saying what they are. The anti-Semite can always cite Jewish cleverness to explain away counterevidence. We might call this self-sealing *by universal discounting.* (2) A theory can also counter criticism by attacking its critics. Critics of Marxism are charged with having a decadent bourgeois consciousness that blinds them to the facts of class conflict. The critic's response to psychoanalytic theory is analyzed (and then dismissed) as repression, a reaction formation, or something similar. Here self-sealing is achieved through an ad hominem fallacy. We might call this self-sealing *by going upstairs,* because the theorist is looking down on the critic.

Yet another form of self-sealing is this: (3) Words are used in such a way that a position becomes true *by definition.* For example, a person makes the strong claim that all human actions are selfish. This is an interesting remark, but it seems to be false, for it is easy to think of cases in which people have acted in self-sacrificing ways. To counter these obvious objections, the argument takes the following turn: When a person acts in a self-sacrificing way, what that person *wants* to do is help another even at her own expense. This is her desire or her motive, and that is what she acts to fulfill. So the action is selfish after all, because the person is acting to achieve what she wants. This is a self-sealing move, for it will not help to cite any behavior—even heroic self-destructive behavior—as counterevidence. If a person desires to do something even if it involves the sacrifice of her life, then she acts to fulfill her desire, and the act is again called selfish.

It is not hard to see what has happened in this case. The arguer has chosen to use the word "selfish" in a new and peculiar way: A person is said to act selfishly if she acts to do what she desires to do. This is not what we usually mean by this word. We ordinarily say that a person acts selfishly if she is too much concerned with her own interests at the expense of the interests of others. On this standard use of the word "selfish," there are any number of counterexamples to the claim that all human actions are selfish. But these counterexamples do not apply when the word "selfish" is used in a new way, where "acting selfishly" comes close to meaning just "acting." The point is that under this new meaning of "selfish," it becomes empty (or almost empty) to say that all human actions are selfish. We are thus back to a familiar situation. Under one interpretation (the ordinary interpretation), the claim that all human actions are selfish is interesting but false. Under another interpretation (an extraordinary interpretation), the claim is true but vacuous. The position gets all its *apparent* interest and plausibility from a rapid two-step back-and-forth between these positions.

Self-sealing arguments are not easy to handle, for they change their form under pressure. One good strategy is to begin by charging a person who uses such an argument with saying something trivial, vacuous, or boring. If, to meet this charge, he or she says something quite specific and important, then argument can proceed along normal lines. But it is not always easy to get down to brass tacks in this way. This becomes clear if you examine an argument between a Marxist and an anti-Marxist, between a psychoanalyst and a critic of psychoanalysis, or between individuals with different religious views. Their positions are often sealed against objections from each other, and then their arguments are almost always at cross-purposes.

Although we have emphasized how large-scale ideologies can become self-sealing, small-scale claims in everyday life are also often sealed against any possible refutation. In fact, a number of common words are used to this end. If someone says, "All true conservatives support school prayer," and a critic points out a conservative who opposes school prayer, then the original claim might be defended by saying, "He is not *truly* (or *really*) a conservative." If this response is trotted out in every case, it turns out that the original claim does not exclude anything. Similarly, the claim that "some students need to work harder than others, but if any student works hard enough, he or she will get good grades" can be protected simply by declaring that any student who works hard but does not get good grades does not work hard *enough*. Finally, someone who says, "If you think it over thoroughly, you will agree with me" can dismiss anyone who disagrees simply by denying that he thought it over *thoroughly*. Of course, these terms—"true," "real," "thorough(ly)," and "enough"—do not always make positions self-sealing. Nonetheless, these and other common terms are often used to seal positions against any possible criticism. When these terms are used in these ways, the resulting positions are empty and can be criticized in the same ways as self-sealing ideologies.

1. Antony Flew famously wrote:

   Now it often seems to people who are not religious as if there was no conceivable event or series of events the occurrence of which would be admitted by sophisticated religious people to be a sufficient reason for conceding "There wasn't a God after all" or "God does not really love us then." Someone tells us that God loves us as a father loves his children. We are reassured. But then we see a child dying of inoperable cancer of the throat. His earthly father is driven frantic in his efforts to help, but his Heavenly Father shows no obvious sign of concern. Some qualification is made— God's love is "not merely human love" or it is "an inscrutable love," perhaps—and we realize that such offerings are quite compatible with the truth of the assertion that "God loves us as a father (but, of course . . .)." We are reassured again. But then perhaps we ask: what is this assurance of God's (appropriately qualified) love worth, what is this apparent guarantee really a guarantee against? Just what would have to happen not merely (morally and wrongly) to tempt us but also (logically and rightly) to entitle us to say "God does not love us" or even "God does not exist"?[3]

   How would you answer Flew's question? If the answer to Flew's question were that nothing could entitle us to say this, as Flew suggests, then would this show that religious positions like this are self-sealing? That they are empty? Why or why not?

2. During the nineteenth century, evidence mounted that apparently showed that the Earth had existed for millions, perhaps hundreds of millions, of years. This seemed to contradict the account given in Genesis that holds that the Earth was created less than 10,000 years ago. In response to this challenge, Philip Henry Gosse, an English theist, replied roughly as follows: In creating Adam and Eve, God would endow them with navels, and thus it would seem that they had been born in the normal way, and thus also seem that they had existed for a number of years before they were created by God. Beyond this, their hair, fingernails, bones, and so on would all show evidence of growth, again giving evidence of previous existence. The same would be true of the trees that surrounded them in the Garden of Eden, which would have rings. Furthermore, the sediment in the rivers should suggest that they had flowed for very many years in the past. In sum, although the Earth was created fairly recently, God would have created it in a way that would make it appear that it had existed for many more years, perhaps millions of years in the past. Thus, the actual creation of the Earth less than 10,000 years ago is compatible with scientific evidence that suggests that it is much older than this. Evaluate this line of reasoning.

3. Some creationist critics of Darwin's theory of natural selection argue as follows:

   Natural selection is a tautologous concept (circular reasoning) because it simply requires the fittest organisms to leave the most offspring and at the same time it identifies the fittest organisms as those that leave the most offspring. Thus natural selection seemingly does not provide a testable explanation of how mutation would produce more fit organisms.[4]

(continued)

> Does this argument show that Darwin's theory is self-sealing? How could defenders of natural selection best respond?
>
> 4. Christina Hoff Sommers wrote:
>
> > The women currently manning—womanning—the feminist ramparts do not take well to criticism. How could they? As they see it, they are dealing with a massive epidemic of male atrocity and a constituency of benighted women who have yet to comprehend the seriousness of their predicament. Hence, male critics must be "sexist" and "reactionary," and female critics "traitors," "collaborators," or "backlashers." This kind of reaction has had a powerful inhibiting effect. It has alienated and silenced women and men alike.[5]
>
> Do you agree? Why or why not? If feminists are guilty of what Sommers claims, does this make their positions self-sealing? Does it make their positions empty?

NOTES

[1] *The Summa Theologica of St. Thomas Aquinas,* Part I, Question 2, Article 3, 2nd and rev. ed., 1920, trans. Fathers of the English Dominican Province. Online edition © 2002 by Kevin Knight, http://www.newadvent.org/summa/100203.htm. We replaced the phrase "take away" with the word "remove" to fit Mackie's objection.

[2] J. L. Mackie, "The Regress of Causes" in *The Miracle of Theism* (Oxford: Oxford University Press, 1982), 90.

[3] Antony Flew, "Theology and Falsification," in *New Essays in Philosophical Theology,* ed. A. Flew and A. MacIntyre (New York: Macmillan, 1955), 98–99.

[4] Duane T. Gish, Richard B. Bliss, and Wendell R. Bird, "Summary of Scientific Evidence for Creation," *Impact* 95–96 (May/June 1981).

[5] Christina Hoff Sommers, *Who Stole Feminism? How Women Have Betrayed Women* (New York: Simon & Schuster, 1994), 18.

17

REFUTATION

Chapter 1 showed how arguments can be used for justification and for explanation, but arguments can also be used for another purpose: refutation. *This chapter will explain the nature of refutation and explore some of the main ways in which arguments can refute another argument or claim. These methods of refutation include counterexamples, reductio ad absurdum, and parallel reasoning. This last kind of refutation can reveal a large variety of fallacies in addition to those studied in previous chapters.*

WHAT IS REFUTATION?

In addition to justifying and explaining their conclusions, arguments are also sometimes used to refute other arguments. To *refute* an argument is to show that it is no good. Some writers, however, incorrectly use the term "refute" to mean something much weaker. They say such things as that Bill Clinton refuted the charges brought against him by those attempting to impeach him, meaning nothing more than that he rejected or replied to the charges. This, however, is not what the word "refute" means. To refute the charges brought against him, Clinton would have to *give reason to believe* that these charges were erroneous. Refuting a charge requires giving an adequate argument against it. This takes a lot more work than simply denying it.

On the other hand, it is also important to remember that we can refute an argument without proving that its conclusion is false. A refutation of an argument is sufficient if it raises objections that cannot be answered. Consequently, the patterns of successful refutations mirror the criteria for a good argument, because the point of a refutation is to show that one of these criteria has not been met. Refutations, then, take four main forms: (1) We can argue that some of the premises are dubious or even false. (2) We can argue that the conclusion of the argument leads to absurd results. (3) We can show that the conclusion does not follow from the premises (or, in the case of an inductive argument, that the premises do not provide strong enough support for the conclusion). (4) We can show that the argument begs the question. This last charge was discussed in Chapter 16, so here we will focus on the first three methods of refutation.

Is refuting an argument the same as justifying a belief that its conclusion is false? Is it the same as justifying a belief that the argument is invalid or weak? Why or why not?

COUNTEREXAMPLES

The first main way to attack an argument is to challenge one of its premises. We can argue that there is no good reason to accept a particular premise as true, asking, for example, "How do you know that?" If the premise is not justified, then the argument fails to justify its conclusion. More strongly, we can argue that the premise is actually false. In this second case, we refute an argument by refuting one of its premises.

One common way to refute a premise by showing that it is false is by producing a counterexample. Counterexamples are typically aimed at universal claims. This is true because a *single* contrary instance will show that a universal claim is false. If someone claims that *all* snakes lay eggs, then pointing out that rattlesnakes bear their young alive is sufficient to refute this universal claim. If the person retreats to the weaker claim that *most* snakes lay eggs, the guarding term makes it much harder to refute the claim. A single example of a snake that bears its young alive is not enough to refute this claim; we would have to show that a majority of snakes do not lay eggs. Here, instead of trying to refute the statement, we may ask the person to produce his *argument* on behalf of it. We can then attack this argument. Finally, if the person retreats to the very weak claim that at least *some* snakes lay eggs, then this statement becomes very difficult to refute. Even if it were false (which it is not), to show this we would have to check every single snake and establish that it does not lay eggs. So, as a rough-and-ready rule, we can say that the stronger a statement is, the more subject it is to refutation; the weaker it is, the less subject it is to refutation.

When a universal claim is refuted by a single case, that case is a *counterexample* to the universal claim. The pattern of reasoning is perfectly simple: To refute a claim that *everything* of a certain kind has a certain feature, we need find only *one* thing of that kind lacking that feature. In response to a counterexample, many people just repeat the misleading saying, "That's the exception that proves the rule." What most people do not realize is that "proves" originally meant "tests," so all this saying means is that an apparent exception can be used to test a rule or a universal claim. When the exception is a true counterexample, the universal claim fails the test.

There are only two ways to defend a universal claim against a purported counterexample. Because the universal claim says that all things of a certain kind have a certain feature, (1) one can deny that the apparent counterexample really is a thing of that kind, or (2) one can deny that the supposed counterexample really lacks that feature. For example, a defender of the claim that all snakes lay eggs might deny (1) that rattlesnakes are snakes, or (2) that rattlesnakes bear their young alive. Neither of these responses is plausible in this case. That is what makes this counterexample *decisive*.

Other counterexamples are not decisive. Indeed, some purported counterexamples miss their targets entirely. If a person claims that all snakes except rattlesnakes lay eggs, someone might respond with another counterexample: male snakes. This counterexample does not really refute the intended claim, since that claim was meant to be about the methods by which female snakes of various species give birth when they do give birth.

When a counterexample can be answered with a simple clarification or modification that does not affect the basic force of the original claim, it is a *shallow* counterexample. A *deep* counterexample is one that requires the original claim to be modified in more important or interesting ways. Shallow counterexamples can sometimes be fun as jokes, but they are usually not much help in refuting arguments, since basically the same argument can be resurrected in a slightly different form. Indeed, people who give too many shallow counterexamples can be annoying. If you really want to understand a subject matter, you should look for counterexamples that are deep.

Deep and decisive counterexamples are not always easy to think up, but Socrates was a genius in this respect. In one dialogue by Plato, Theaetetus and Socrates are trying to define "knowledge." They notice an important difference between knowledge and mere belief: It is possible for someone to *believe* something that is false, but it is not possible for someone to *know* something that is false. This leads Theaetetus to suggest a simple definition of knowledge: Knowledge equals true belief. This proposed definition is refuted in the following exchange:

SOCRATES: [There is] a whole profession to prove that true belief is not knowledge.

THEAETETUS: How so? What profession?

SOCRATES: The profession of those paragons of intellect known as orators and lawyers. There you have men who use their skill to produce conviction, not by instruction, but by making people believe whatever they want them to believe. You can hardly imagine teachers so clever as to be able, in the short time allowed by the clock, to instruct their hearers thoroughly in the true facts of a case of robbery or other violence which those hearers had not witnessed.

THEAETETUS: No, I cannot imagine that; but they can convince them.

SOCRATES: And by convincing you mean making them believe something.

THEAETETUS: Of course.

SOCRATES: And when a jury is rightly convinced of facts which can be known only by an eye-witness, then, judging by hearsay and accepting a true belief, they are judging without knowledge, although, if they find the right verdict, their conviction is correct?

THEAETETUS: Certainly.

SOCRATES: But if true belief and knowledge were the same thing, the best of jurymen could never have a correct belief without knowledge. It now appears that they must be different things.[1]

One thing to notice about this discussion is that Theaetetus does not dig in his heels and insist that the ignorant members of the jury do know that the person is innocent provided only that they believe it and it is true. Faced with the counterexample, he retreats at once. Why is this? Why not stay with the definition and reject the counterexample as false? The answer is that for many concepts, there is general agreement about their application to particular cases, even if there is no general agreement about a correct definition. To take an extreme example, everyone agrees that Hitler was a dictator (even Hitler), and no one supposes that Thomas Jefferson was a dictator (even his enemies). So any definition of "dictator" must be wrong if it implies that Hitler was not a dictator or that Thomas Jefferson was a dictator. Of course, people do disagree about borderline cases, so there might be no perfectly exact definition of "dictator." Nonetheless, any definition that does not square with the clear cases can be refuted by citing one of these clear cases as a counterexample.

Ethics is an area where arguments often turn on counterexamples. Consider the traditional moral precept "Do unto others as you would have them do unto you." This principle captures an important moral insight, but, if taken quite literally, it is also subject to counterexamples. Jones, a sadomasochist, enjoys beating other people. When asked whether he would like to be treated in that way, he replies, "Yes." It is obvious that the Golden Rule was not intended to approve of Jones's behavior. The task, then, is to reformulate this rule to avoid this counterexample. That is not as easy as it might seem.

No discussion of counterexamples is complete without a mention of the Morgenbesser retort. Though the exact story is now shrouded in the mists of time, it has come down to us from the 1950s in the following form: In a lecture, a British philosopher remarked that he knew of many languages in which a double negative means an affirmative, but not one language in which a double affirmative means a negative. From the back of the room came Morgenbesser's retort: "Yeah, yeah."

EXERCISE I

Find a counterexample to each of the following claims, if possible.

Example: *Claim:* "Sugar" is the only word in which an *s* is pronounced *sh.*
        Counterexample: Oh, sure.

1. No prime number is even.
2. Three points always determine a plane.

3. Balloons that are filled with helium always rise in the air.

4. All mammals bear their young live.

5. You can never get too much of a good thing.

6. What you don't know can't hurt you.

7. You can't be too careful.

8. You should never look a gift horse in the mouth.

9. It is always wrong to tell a lie.

10. You should never ask someone else to do something that you are not willing to do yourself.

11. If lots of people do something, then it must not be wrong for me to do it.

12. If it would be horrible for everyone to do something, then it would be morally wrong for anyone to do it.

13. If it would not be horrible for everyone to do something, then it would not be morally wrong for anyone to do it.

14. Wherever you use the word "nearly," you could use the word "almost" instead, without affecting the truth or the good sense of what you have said.

EXERCISE II

There cannot possibly be any counterexamples to the following claims. Explain why.

1. There is life on the moon.

2. Killing is usually wrong.

3. Any short person is a person.

4. Every horse is an animal.

5. $2 + 2 = 4$.

6. Everything with a size has a shape.

7. Everything that is green has a shape.

8. There's no way to turn a right-hand glove around to get a left-hand glove.

DISCUSSION QUESTIONS

1. How can the Golden Rule best be reformulated to avoid the above counterexample of the sadomasochist? Can you think of any counterexamples to this reformulation of the Golden Rule?

2. Is the Morgenbesser retort a shallow counterexample or a deep counterexample? Why?

(continued)

3. When theologians claim that God can do anything, atheists sometimes respond that God cannot make a stone that is so large that God cannot lift it, or that God cannot make a circle with four sides. Are these really counterexamples to the theologians' claim? Why or why not?

4. Suppose there are only two balls in a bag, and someone claims, "Most of the balls in the bag are red." Does a single black ball in the bag refute this claim? Is it a counterexample to this claim? Is it also a counterexample to the claim that no counterexamples can refute any claim that is not universal?

5. When people today respond to counterexamples by saying, "That's the exception that proves the rule," they usually do not mean, "That's the exception that tests the rule," which was its original meaning. What do they mean?

REDUCTIO AD ABSURDUM

Particular counterexamples can normally be used to refute claims only if those claims are universal, so how can we refute claims that are not universal? One method is to show that the claim to be refuted implies something that is ridiculous or absurd in ways that are independent of any particular counterexample. This mode of refutation is called a *reductio ad absurdum*, which means a reduction to absurdity. Reductios, as they are called for short, can refute many different kinds of propositions. They are sometimes directed at a premise in an argument, but they can also be used to refute a conclusion. This method of refutation will not show exactly *what* is wrong with the argument for that conclusion, but it will show that *something* is wrong with the argument, because it cannot be sound if its conclusion is false. That might be enough in some situations.

For example, suppose someone argues that because there is a tallest mountain and a heaviest human, there must also be a largest integer. We might respond by arguing as follows: Suppose there is a largest integer. Call it N. Since N is an integer, $N + 1$ is also an integer. Moreover, $N + 1$ is larger than N. But it is absurd to think that any integer is larger than the largest integer. Therefore, our supposition—that there is a largest integer—must be false.

In this mathematical example a contradiction is derived, but absurdity also comes in other forms. Suppose a neighbor tells a parent, "The local public schools are so bad that you ought to send your kids to private school," and the parent responds, "Do you think I'm rich?" The point of this rhetorical question is that it is absurd to think that the parent is rich, presumably because of her lifestyle or house, which the neighbor can easily see. Without being rich, the parent cannot afford a private school, so the neighbor's advice is useless.

Often the absurdity is derived indirectly. A wonderful example occurred in the English parliamentary debate on capital punishment. One member of

Parliament was defending the death penalty on the grounds that the alternative—life in prison—was much more cruel than death. This claim was met with the following reply: On this view, those found guilty of first-degree murder ought to be given life in prison, and the death penalty should be given to those who commit some lesser offense. The first speaker could respond in several ways, because this reductio depends on background assumptions that the first speaker could question. First, he might deny that the most severe crime should receive the most severe penalty possible. If the first speaker sees life in prison as too cruel to be inflicted on anyone, then he might call for the abolition of life imprisonment and keep the death penalty as the most severe punishment. Alternatively, the first speaker could claim that, even though the death penalty is less severe than life in prison, it is still fitting in some other way for the most severe crime, first-degree murder. Finally, of course, the first speaker could simply *accept* the supposedly absurd result and apply life imprisonment to first-degree murder, while using the death penalty for lesser crimes. In fact, however, the first speaker was unwilling to accept any of these alternatives. He simply tried a rhetorical trick and got caught.

These reductios are fairly good, but other reductios fail for a variety of reasons. To succeed in refuting a claim, a reductio ad absurdum argument must meet two main requirements. First, the result must really be *absurd*. Often opponents try to reduce a view to absurdity but really only draw out implications of the view that are not absurd at all. For example, in a famous debate in which Thomas Huxley defended a theory of evolution, Bishop Wilberforce asked Huxley whether he had descended from apes on his mother's side or on his father's side of the family. This question was intended to draw laughter from the crowd, and it did, partly because they and Wilberforce thought that any answer to the question would be absurd. Nonetheless, Huxley could respond that he had descended from apes on both sides of his family. Because that response was not really absurd—regardless of how absurd it seemed to Wilberforce—the bishop's attempt did not really refute Huxley's claim.

In other cases, one cannot deny that a certain result really would be absurd, but the reductio still fails because the claim to be refuted does not really *imply* that absurdity. For example, opponents sometimes say that the theory of evolution implies that animals are constantly evolving, so they cannot be divided into separate species. This would be absurd, because it is easy to observe distinct species. The theory of evolution, however, does not really imply this absurdity, so this reductio fails to refute that theory. It fails to meet the second requirement for successful reductios, which is that the claim to be refuted must actually imply the absurdity.

Finally, it is important to notice that reductios can be deep or shallow in much the same way as counterexamples. Sometimes a claim really does imply a result that is absurd, but it can be modified in some minor way so as to avoid the absurd result. For example, if a fan says, "Tiger Woods is better than any golfer ever," someone might respond that Woods is himself a golfer, so this claim implies that Woods is better than himself, which is absurd.

Of course, the fan meant to say, "Woods is better than any *other* golfer ever," so this reductio is shallow. The reductio does refute the original form of the claim, but the main force of the claim is restored by the minor modification. A reductio ad absurdum is deep only if it reveals that a claim implies an absurd result that cannot be avoided without modifying the claim in essential respects or giving it up entirely.

In sum, then, a reductio ad absurdum argument tries to show that one claim, X, is false because it implies another claim, Y, that is absurd. To evaluate such an argument, the following questions should be asked:

1. Is Y really absurd?
2. Does X really imply Y?
3. Can X be modified in some minor way so that it no longer implies Y?

If either of the first two questions is answered in the negative, then the reductio fails; if the third question receives an affirmative answer, then the reductio is shallow. Otherwise, the reductio ad absurdum argument is both successful and deep.

EXERCISE III

Evaluate the following reductio ad absurdum arguments by asking the above three questions.

1. CLAIM TO BE REFUTED: Even the worst of enemies can become friends.

   REDUCTIO: If people are enemies, then they are not friends. If they do become friends, then they are not enemies. So it's absurd to think that enemies can be friends.

2. CLAIM TO BE REFUTED: This ball is both red all over and green all over.

   REDUCTIO: If it is red, it reflects light within a certain range of wavelengths. If it is green, it reflects light within a different range of wavelengths. These ranges do not overlap, so it is absurd to think that anything can reflect both kinds of light. Thus, a ball cannot be both red and green all over.

3. CLAIM TO BE REFUTED: Most children in Lake Wobegon are above average (in intelligence).

   REDUCTIO: If so, the average (intelligence) would really be higher than it is; and then it would not be true that most children in Lake Wobegon are above the real average (intelligence).

4. ARGUMENT TO BE REFUTED: Your brain is mostly empty space, because the subatomic particles in it are very far apart.

   REDUCTIO: That's absurd, because my brain is solid, and it works pretty well.

5. CLAIM TO BE REFUTED: Some things are inconceivable.

   REDUCTIO: Consider something that is inconceivable. Since you are considering it, you are conceiving it. But then it is conceivable as well as inconceivable. That is absurd. So nothing is inconceivable.

Spell out a reductio ad absurdum argument to refute each of the following claims. If no such reductio is possible, explain why.

1. Some sisters are nephews.
2. Some fathers were never children.
3. Most students scored better than the median grade on the last test.
4. Almost everyone in this class is exceptional.
5. There is an exception to every universal claim.
6. I know that I do not know anything.
7. Some morally wrong actions are morally permitted.
8. God exists outside of time, and we will meet Him someday.
9. There is a male barber in this town who shaves all and only the men in this town who do not shave themselves. (Hint: Does he shave himself?)
10. Most of the sentences in this exercise are true.

1. Marc Antony's funeral oration, quoted in a Discussion Question in Chapter 2, uses several reductio ad absurdum arguments to refute Brutus's claim that Caesar was ambitious. Are these reductios deep or shallow? How could Brutus respond?

2. The legal case of *Plessy v. Ferguson*, 163 U.S. 537 (1896), questioned the constitutionality of a law requiring racial segregation in railroad cars. Opponents of the law gave the following reductio argument. How could defenders of segregation respond to this argument? Is their response adequate? Is any response adequate? Why or why not?

   The same argument that will justify the state legislature in requiring railways to provide separate accommodations for the two races will also authorize them to require separate cars to be provided for people whose hair is of a certain color, or who are aliens, or who belong to certain nationalities, or to enact laws requiring colored people to walk upon one side of the street, and white people upon the other, or requiring white men's houses to be painted white, and colored men's black, or their vehicles or business signs to be of different colors, upon the theory that one side of the street is as good as the other, or that a house or vehicle of one color is as good as one of another color.

3. Many atheists try to refute belief in God with the following reductio ad absurdum argument: God is defined to be all-good and all-powerful (as well as all-knowing). If God is all-good, then God prevents as much evil as He can. If God is all-powerful (and all-knowing), then God can prevent all evil. Thus, if a traditional God did exist, there would be no evil in the world. But that's absurd. There is obviously lots of evil in the world. Therefore, God does not exist. (Compare Chapter 21 in Part V on Religious Reasoning.) Evaluate this reductio argument. How could religious believers best respond?

STRAW MEN AND FALSE DICHOTOMIES

Very often when trying to refute either by counterexample or by reductio, people move too quickly. The general rule is this: Before trying to refute someone's claim, it is important to make sure that you understand his or her position. If you misunderstand what your opponent is claiming, but you go ahead and attack a specific claim anyway, then the claim you attack will not be the claim that your opponent made. You might even fail to refute any position that anyone ever really held. This is called the fallacy of *attacking a straw man*.

Sometimes people attack a straw man intentionally. They mischaracterize their opponents' position on purpose in order to make their opponents look silly by associating their opponents with a position that really is silly. One example comes from the 2004 presidential election, when John Kerry suggested that the United States should have conferred more with its allies, including the French, before attacking Iraq. In response, at the Republican National Convention Senator Zell Miller said that Kerry would "let Paris decide when America needs defending." Surely Miller knew that this mischaracterization of Kerry's position was unfair, but it achieved the desired reaction from the crowd.

The fallacy of attacking a straw man can also arise from an honest mistake. Some people get so wrapped up in their own arguments that they forget the view against which they are arguing. The opponent can also be partly to blame. If someone states her position obscurely, it might not be clear whether the speaker would go so far as to make a certain claim. Then someone might attack that further claim, honestly believing that the speaker had adopted it. Alternatively, a critic might refute that further claim simply to make the speaker clarify her position by explicitly saying that that is not what she meant to say. In such ways, it might be useful to refute a position that the speaker does not really hold, even though, of course, doing so does not refute any position that the speaker actually does hold.

In more insidious cases, straw men are often set up by means of a related fallacy—*false dichotomy*. With regard to the Iraq war, President Bush often said something like this: "I had a choice to make: Either take the word of a madman [Saddam Hussein] or defend America. Given that choice, I will defend America every time." The crucial phrase, of course, is "given that choice." If those were the only options, then Bush's critics would also defend America every time. The problem lies in Bush's suggestion that his opponents do not want to defend America and would instead "take the word of a madman." That insinuation sets up a straw man.

Political rhetoric is filled with such false dichotomies that set up straw men. A cable news host is reported to have said, "Sure, it's not great having the government collect our telephone records, but it is better than having them collect our body parts." Let's hope there is a third option! Opponents of the government collecting phone records, of course, think that there is another way to avoid having to collect body parts. But then they sometimes add, "Either you are opposed to the government collecting phone records or you don't care about civil rights." This is just a false dichotomy on the other side.

Those who favor the government collecting phone records do care about civil rights, even though they favor some intrusions (which they see as minor intrusions) on those rights in order to fight terrorism.

False dichotomies like these are parodied by Stephen Colbert when he says, "Either you are with us or you are with the terrorists," "Either you're for the war [in Iraq] or you hate America," and his best, "George W. Bush: great president or the greatest president?" The trick here is obviously to give you some choice, so that you end up committed to the option that you choose, but your choices are limited to ones that Colbert gives you.

After listing his dichotomy, Colbert usually adds, "It's that simple!" The best response is to recognize that these issues are usually not simple at all. These tricks work partly because many people long for simple choices or they fail to notice any third option. Whenever someone tells you that you have only two alternatives, you should look carefully for other possibilities. And whenever your choice among the options seems obvious, you should ask whether the rejected options have been set up as straw men rather than characterized fairly.

EXERCISE V

Do the following arguments attack straw men? Why or why not?

1. Anyone who thinks that the United States should not have sent troops to Iraq must think that the suffering Saddam Hussein inflicted on his own citizens doesn't matter much.

2. Anyone who thinks that the United States should have sent troops to Iraq must think that they will only be there for a short time.

3. Humans could not have been created in the image of God, because God is not a physical being, and only physical beings can have images.

4. Atheists think that God does not exist, so everything is permitted. But even atheists must admit that I would not be permitted to kill them! So atheism is nonsense.

5. The theory of evolution says that humans are no different from apes, but humans are clearly smarter than apes, so the theory of evolution must be wrong.

6. Stephen Colbert again: "Evolutionists' main claim is that one day we decided to stop being monkeys and turned ourselves into humans. Well, if that's true, why aren't more monkeys escaping from zoos? Think about it. They could turn into humans, then disguise themselves as janitors and walk out of their cages. But I guess evolution doesn't have an answer for that one."[2]

DISCUSSION QUESTION

Find five more examples of attacking straw men in your local newspaper, in a talk show on television, or in a college course.

REFUTATION BY PARALLEL REASONING

Even if its premises and conclusion cannot be refuted by any counterexample or reductio, a deductive argument can also be refuted by showing that it is invalid. We know that an argument is not valid if it starts from true premises and leads to a false conclusion. Often, however, we cannot point this out to refute an argument, because the truth or falsity of the conclusion is the very thing at issue. When this problem arises, a typical device is to point out that by arguing in the same way, or a similar way, we can reach a conclusion that is unsatisfactory.

Here is a simple example:

> **CARY:** Most of the people in this class are college students. Most college students study hard. Therefore, most of the people in this class study hard.

> **DAVID:** That's just like arguing that most whales live in the sea, and most animals that live in the sea are fish, so most whales are fish.

At first sight, it might not be clear how the second argument could show anything about the first argument. What do whales have to do with students? The point, however, is simply that the two arguments share a basic form. Thus, if the second argument is not valid by virtue of that form, then the first is also not valid by virtue of that same form. The second argument is obviously not valid, since its premises are true but its conclusion is false. This shows that the first argument is not valid, at least by virtue of this shared form. Even though the first argument still might be valid on some other basis, its defenders at least owe an alternative account of its validity. Often there will be none.

Refuting an argument by showing that it is *just like* another argument that is obviously no good is a common device in everyday discussions. Here's another example:

> **MATTHEW:** If I had a higher salary, I could buy more things; so, if everyone had higher salaries, everyone could buy more things.

> **KIRSTY:** That's just like arguing that, if one person stands up at a ball game, he will get a better view; so, if everyone stands up, everyone will get a better view.

At first sight, it may not be obvious whether Matthew's style of reasoning is valid or not. Kirsty's response shows that Matthew's argument is invalid by providing an instance in which the same style of reasoning takes us from something true to something that is obviously false, because, if everyone stands up at a ball game, only the tallest people will be able to see better. Kirsty's response also shows *why* Matthew's argument is invalid: Just as one person's ability to see can be affected by other people standing up, because this raises the height that is necessary to see, so one person's ability to buy can be affected by other people having more money, if this raises prices and thereby raises the amount of money that is necessary to buy things.

This fallacy is often called a *fallacy of composition*, because it rests on the mistaken assumption that what is true of the parts is also true of the whole that is composed out of those parts. Each person in a class has a mother, but the whole class does not have a mother. The earth might be heating up on average in the long run even if some locations on earth have a cool summer one year. These obvious mistakes can be cited to show that and why potentially misleading arguments with the same form are no better. Lots of new fallacies can be revealed in this way by deploying this method of refutation by parallel reasoning.

Of course, not every refutation of this kind is so simple or so successful. To understand the criteria that must be met for such a refutation to work, it will be useful to consider a more complex example that reveals some of the ways to respond to a charge of "That's just like arguing. . . ." The example concerns proposed legal restrictions on gun ownership. The National Rifle Association (NRA) feared that these restrictions would lead to a total ban on guns, which they opposed, so they widely distributed a bumper sticker that read:

(1) If guns are outlawed, only outlaws will have guns.

The point, presumably, was that most people would add the suppressed premise:

(2) It would be bad if only outlaws had guns,

and then reach the conclusion:

(3) Therefore, guns should not be outlawed.

This argument is not completely clear, partly because it is not clear who counts as an "outlaw." Some critics poke fun at this bumper sticker because (1) seems true by definition if outlaws include anyone who breaks any law, because anyone with a gun breaks a law if guns are outlawed. But what the NRA probably means by "outlaws" are people who commit violent crimes, such as robbery and murder. It is not strictly true that these will be the only people with guns if guns are outlawed, since police and some present gun owners would keep their guns. Nonetheless, these exceptions do not touch the NRA's main claim, which is that law-abiding people who would give up their guns if guns were outlawed would then not have guns to defend themselves against violent criminals.

How can an opponent try to refute this argument? There are several possibilities, but what defenders of gun control in fact did was distribute other bumper stickers. One of them read:

(1*) If gum is outlawed, only outlaws will have gum.

The main point might be just to parody the NRA bumper sticker, but, if we take it more seriously, (1*) also suggests an application of the method of refutation by parallel reasoning. The parallel argument would continue like this:

> (2*) It would be bad if only outlaws had gum.
>
> ∴(3*) Therefore, gum should not be outlawed.

This conclusion, however, is not obviously false. Indeed, it seems true: People should be allowed to chew gum. Moreover, (2*) seems false, because nothing particularly bad would happen if only outlaws chewed gum. For these reasons, this bumper sticker cannot really refute the original argument. This failure illustrates two general tests: A refutation by parallel reasoning works only if the conclusion of the parallel argument really is unacceptable and only if the premises of the parallel argument really are true.

But opponents of the NRA did not stop there. They distributed a third bumper sticker:

> (1**) If guns are outlawed, only outlaws will shoot their children by mistake.

The argument behind this new bumper sticker is again not clear. If it is a straightforward instance of refutation by parallel reasoning, then the parallel argument would add, "It would be bad if only outlaws shot their children by mistake" and conclude, "Guns should not be outlawed." But that is the very conclusion the NRA wants to reach; so this newest argument could not refute the original one. Nonetheless, a different argument might lie behind this third bumper sticker. The point seems to be that gun owners sometimes shoot their children by mistake, and we can minimize such tragedies by reducing the number of gun owners through laws against guns. The argument then runs something like this:

> (1**) If guns are outlawed, only outlaws will shoot their children by mistake.
>
> (2**) It would be good if outlaws were the only ones who shot their children by mistake.
>
> ∴(3**) Therefore, guns should be outlawed.

This conclusion would seem false to the NRA, and this argument might also seem to suggest that the same form of reasoning could lead to opposite conclusions: (3) and (3**). Moreover, (2**) seems true. This premise does not say that it is good for outlaws to shoot their children by mistake. Instead, it says that it would be good if nobody else shot their children by mistake. So far, so good. Notice, however, that this latest argument, (1**)–(3**), does not have the same form as the original argument, (1)–(3), because (2**) and (3**) are about what is good and what ought to be law, whereas (2) and (3) are about what is bad and what ought not to be law.

The next question is whether this disanalogy is *important*. If not, the latest bumper sticker still might refute the original one. The NRA, however, might argue that this difference *is* important. The fact that a law has bad effects overall *does* show that the law should not be passed, whereas the fact that a law would have good effects overall is *not* enough to show that the law should be passed, since the law still might violate individual rights that cannot be overridden by good effects on others. This claim is controversial, but, if it can be defended, then this parallel argument, (1**)–(3**), fails to show that the original argument, (1)–(3), is invalid. More generally, then, a refutation by parallel reasoning works only if the two arguments really do have relevantly similar structures—that is, only if one argument really is *just like* the other in relevant respects.

In sum, the method of refutation by parallel reasoning can be used to show that an argument is invalid by presenting another argument with essentially the same form in which the inference takes us from obvious truths to an obvious falsehood. In response to such an attack, a defender of the original argument has three main options. The defender might

1. deny that the conclusion of the parallel argument is false,

2. deny that the premises of the parallel argument are true, or

3. deny that the supposedly parallel argument really has essentially the same form.

If any of these responses is justified, then the attempt to refute the original argument by parallel reasoning fails.

This procedure is admittedly imprecise. There will sometimes be disputes about whether the premises of the parallel argument really are true, or clearly true, and whether the conclusion of the parallel argument really is false, or clearly false. Moreover, we have given no general explanation of the notion that two arguments have the *same basic form*. Some forms of argument were discussed in previous chapters, but they are only part of the story. We have not discussed and cannot discuss all possible forms of argument. Yet it remains a fact that people can often see that two arguments have the same essential form and, through seeing this, decide that an argument presented to them is invalid. This ability is the basis of sound logical judgment. It is also the basis of wit. It is at best mildly funny to say that if God had wanted us to fly, He would have given us wings. You have to be fairly clever to reply at once, "If God had wanted us to stay on the ground, He would have given us roots."

EXERCISE VI

In each of the following examples, does the parallel argument succeed in refuting the original argument? Why or why not? Consider the three possible responses listed above. If the original argument is refuted, is there some simple way to fix it so that it cannot be refuted by this parallel reasoning? If so, how? (You might try to add a premise whose analogue would be false in the parallel argument.)

(continued)

1. **CHRIS:** The United States is wealthy, so its citizens are wealthy as well.

   PAT: That's just like arguing that a building is expensive, so the nails in its walls are expensive as well.

2. **CHAUVINIST:** Since women are the only people who can bear children, they should bear children.

   FEMINIST: That's like arguing that, if I am the only person who can wiggle my own ears, then I should wiggle my ears.

3. **NEWT:** Orphanages are fine places, as the movie *Boys Town* shows.

   CRITIC: That's just like saying that Oz is a fine place, as *The Wizard of Oz* shows.

4. **A YOUNG CHILD AT 6:00 AM:** It's morning. Morning is the time to wake up. So it's time to wake up.

   THE CHILD'S SLEEPY PARENT: That's just like arguing that it's daytime, and daytime is the time to eat lunch, so it's time to eat lunch.

5. **MARK:** You shouldn't walk on that grass, because if everybody did that, the grass would die.

   BOB: That's just like arguing that I shouldn't go to this movie right now, because if everybody did that, the theater would be packed like a can of sardines.

6. **THOMAS:** Everything in the world has a cause, so the world itself must have a cause.

   TONY: That's just like arguing that every leg in the relay race was run by a single runner, so the entire race itself must have been run by a single runner.

7. **HAWK:** Nuclear deterrence must work, because we have never had a nuclear exchange as long as we have maintained nuclear deterrence.

   DOVE: That's just like arguing that hanging garlic by the front door must keep thieves away, because I put garlic there and my house has never been robbed.

8. **LIBERAL:** We ought to provide condoms for high school students, because they are going to have sex anyway.

   CONSERVATIVE: That's just like arguing that we should provide high school students with guns, because they are going to use guns anyway.

9. **SCIENTIST:** My initial steps toward human cloning, no matter how controversial, are important because they bring the debate out into the public.

   OPPONENT: That's just like arguing that we should start a fire in a house in order to bring the debate about getting a new fire engine out into the public. (paraphrased from an actual interview on National Public Radio)

10. **KING:** "In your statement you asserted that our actions, even though peaceful, must be condemned because they precipitate violence. But can this assertion be logically made? Isn't this like condemning the robbed man because his possession of money precipitated the evil act of robbery?" (from Martin Luther King's "Letter from Birmingham Jail")

11. **A:** He owns a red car, so he owns a car.

   B: That's just like arguing that he owns a toy duck, so he owns a duck.

12. **A:** He is holding a baby girl, so he is holding a baby.

   B: That's just like arguing that he is driving a fire truck, so he is driving a fire.

Exercise VII

For each of the following arguments, find another argument with the same basic form in which the premise or premises are clearly true and the conclusion is clearly false.

1. If tea is dangerous, so is coffee. Tea isn't dangerous. So coffee isn't either.

2. If it were about to rain, it would be cloudy. It is cloudy. So it's about to rain.

3. Fred had either ice cream or cake for dessert. He had cake. So he must not have had ice cream.

4. You cannot pass laws against dangerous drugs, because there is no way to draw a sharp line between dangerous and nondangerous drugs.

5. If you have never written a novel, then you are in no position to make judgments about novels. So don't presume to criticize mine.

6. Since I have written several novels, I am in a position to know which novels are good. So you ought to trust me when I say that this one is great.

7. There's nothing wrong with smoking, since the longer you smoke, the longer you live.

8. If one has nothing to hide, one should not be afraid of being investigated. So no one should object to being investigated.

9. Radicals should not be granted freedom of speech, because they deny this freedom to others.

10. In nature, a species is more likely to survive when its weak members die out, so we should let the weak in our society die out.

11. Buses use more gas than cars, so the city cannot reduce gas consumption by providing more buses.

12. Boxing can't be very bad, since so many people like it.

13. This war is just, for to say otherwise in public would be to aid our enemies.

14. If you don't buy the most expensive shoes, you buy cheap ones. You don't want cheap shoes. So you should buy the most expensive shoes.

15. I'd rather be smart than strong, so I am going to quit exercising and spend all day in the library.

16. You don't want to be this murderer's next victim, so you had better convict her and send her to prison where she can't hurt you.

17. If it weren't for America, these refugees would have nowhere to go; so they should adopt the American way of life and give up their old culture.

18. You can't be right, because, if the answer were that obvious, someone would have thought of it before.

1. In Chapter 22 below, Searle tries to refute Turing by means of parallel reasoning about a Chinese room. Using the standards discussed above, assess Searle's attempted refutation.

2. In *St. Anselm's Proslogion with a Reply on Behalf of the Fool by Gaunilo and the Author's Reply to Gaunilo*, trans. M. J. Charlesworth (Oxford: Clarendon Press, 1965), St. Anselm gives an ontological argument (in the form of a reductio ad absurdum) for the existence of God and then Gaunilo replies with a refutation by parallel reasoning. Reconstruct and assess both of their arguments, using the standards discussed above.

GOD TRULY EXISTS

by St. Anselm

Well then, Lord, You who give understanding to faith, grant me that I may understand, as much as You see fit, that You exist as we believe You to exist, and that You are what we believe You to be. Now we believe that You are something than which nothing greater can be thought. Or can it be that a thing of such a nature does not exist, since "the Fool has said in his heart, there is no God" [Ps. xiii. I, lii. I]? But surely, when this same Fool hears what I am speaking about, namely, "something-than-which-nothing-greater-can-be-thought," he understands what he hears, and what he understands is in his mind, even if he does not understand that it actually exists. For it is one thing for an object to exist in the mind, and another thing to understand that an object actually exists. Thus, when a painter plans beforehand what he is going to execute, he has [the picture] in his mind, but he does not yet think that it actually exists because he has not yet executed it. However, when he has actually painted it, then he both has it in his mind and understands that it exists because he has now made it. Even the Fool, then, is forced to agree that something-than-which-nothing-greater-can-be-thought exists in the mind, since he understands this when he hears it, and whatever is understood is in the mind. And surely that-than-which-a-greater-cannot-be-thought cannot exist in the mind alone. For if it exists solely in the mind even, it can be thought to exist in reality also, which is greater. If then that-than-which-a-greater-cannot-be-thought exists in the mind alone, this same that-than-which-a-greater-*cannot*-be-thought is that-than-which-a-greater-*can*-be-thought. But this is obviously impossible. Therefore, there is absolutely no doubt that something-than-which-a-greater-cannot-be-thought exists both in the mind and in reality.

A REPLY TO THE FOREGOING BY A CERTAIN WRITER ON BEHALF OF THE FOOL

—————————■—————————

by Gaunilo

. . . they say that there is in the ocean somewhere an island which, because of the difficulty (or rather the impossibility) of finding that which does not exist, some have called the "Lost Island." And the story goes that it is blessed with all manner of priceless riches and delights in abundance, much more even than the Happy Isles, and, having no owner or inhabitant, it is superior everywhere in abundance of riches to all those other lands that men inhabit. Now, if anyone tell me that it is like this, I shall easily understand what is said, since nothing is difficult about it. But if he should then go on to say, as though it were a logical consequence of this: You cannot any more doubt that this island that is more excellent than all other lands truly exists somewhere in reality than you can doubt that it is in your mind; and since it is more excellent to exist not only in the mind alone but also in reality, therefore it must needs be that it exists. For if it did not exist, any other land existing in reality would be more excellent than it, and so this island, already conceived by you to be more excellent than others, will not be more excellent. If, I say, someone wishes thus to persuade me that this island really exists beyond all doubt, I should either think that he was joking, or I should find it hard to decide which of us I ought to judge the bigger fool—I, if I agreed with him, or he, if he thought that he had proved the existence of this island with any certainty, unless he had first convinced me that its very excellence exists in my mind precisely as a thing existing truly and indubitably and not just as something unreal or doubtfully real. . . .

NOTES

[1] Plato, *Theaetetus,* trans. Francis M. Cornford, in Cornford's *Plato's Theory of Knowledge* (New York: Liberal Arts Press, 1957), 141.

[2] Stephen Colbert, *I Am America (And So Can You!)* (New York: Grand Central Publishing, 2007), 198.

AREAS OF ARGUMENTATION

Particular subject matters often give rise to new kinds of arguments and special standards for assessing arguments. One reason is that arguments in different areas have different purposes. Much scientific reasoning is aimed at explaining observations, including findings in experiments, whereas the point of moral reasoning is not to explain what happens but, rather, to evaluate and to determine which acts are justified. The audience also varies from one area of argumentation to another. Some religious reasoning is addressed only to people who already accept certain basic claims of a religious tradition, such as that the Bible is inspired, whereas philosophical reasoning typically prides itself in questioning common assumptions and authorities. Similarly, arguments about different topics often take place within different institutional contexts with distinctive rules. Legal arguments, for example, often assume specified burdens of proof, certain basic laws (such as in a constitution), and other fundamental features of the legal system in the jurisdiction; whereas moral reasoning is sometimes used to overturn those very same features of legal systems. Because these areas of argumentation differ in so many ways, we need to look at each of them separately and carefully to see which standards are at play in each area. That is one main goal of Part V. Another goal is to provide extensive examples of arguments both as targets for criticism and as models of how to construct a good argument. We can get better at arguing for our own views if we learn to appreciate the strengths in arguments given by other people, including our opponents. Toward these ends, Part V will discuss and give illustrations of legal, moral, scientific, religious, and philosophical reasoning in Chapters 18–22, respectively.

18

LEGAL REASONING

Law is a prime example of how institutional setting affects standards of argumentation, for legal systems have their own procedures and authorities. Legal decisions are often based on statutes, constitutions, and precedents that are peculiar to a particular legal system. These sources of law are often vague, and they can conflict, so they need to be interpreted. This chapter will discuss legal interpretation and legal reasoning in general. The general forms of legal arguments will then be illustrated by looking in more detail at the law of discrimination and affirmative action.

Legal decisions have concrete effects on people's lives. In criminal cases, judges can deprive people of their freedom or even their lives. In civil cases, judges often take away large sums of money, the custody of children, and so on. Constitutional decisions can affect the basic rights of all citizens, even those who have never been in a courtroom. These decisions are made because certain legal arguments are accepted and others are rejected.

Unfortunately, it is sometimes difficult to find any good reason for a legal decision. Crucial facts might not be known, and the law is sometimes unclear or inconsistent. Some cases "fall between the cracks," so no law seems to apply. Human beings have a remarkable ability to produce weird cases that would tax the wisdom of Solomon.

Even in the toughest cases, judges and juries must reach *some* decision. Outside the law, we can often just let matters ride—we can postpone a decision until further facts are established, or even declare that the issues are too vague to admit of any decision. This is rarely an option in a legal case. If *A* sues *B*, either *A* or *B* must win. The judge cannot say, "This case is too tough for me. I'm not going to rule on it." Throwing the case out of court amounts to ruling in favor of the defendant. A decision must be made, usually in a relatively short period of time.

These pressures have led lawyers and judges to develop many ingenious ways to argue. Lawyers cite statutes, precedents, and historical contexts. They claim the authority of common sense and science, and they cite scholarly articles, even some by philosophers. They deploy metaphors and rhetorical devices—almost anything to convince the judge or jury to decide in favor of their clients. The variety of these arguments makes legal reasoning complex and also fascinating.

Despite this variety, some rough generalizations can be made: A decision in a legal case usually depends on (1) questions of fact and (2) questions of law.

COMPONENTS OF LEGAL REASONING

QUESTIONS OF FACT

A *criminal law* prohibits a certain kind of behavior and assigns a punishment to those who violate it. When a person is accused of violating this law, a trial is held to determine whether *in fact* he or she has done so. The judge instructs the jury on the law bearing on the case. If the members of the jury then decide that the accused has violated the law, they find him or her guilty, and the judge usually hands down the punishment stated in the statute.

In a *civil* suit, one party sues another, say, for breach of contract. Because states have laws governing contracts, once more a trial is held to decide whether *in fact* there was a contract (instead of some other speech act) and whether *in fact* it was breached. If a breach of contract is found, the judge or jury awards damages as the law specifies.

Although questions of fact arise in all cases, criminal and civil cases do differ in the *burden of proof*—in who is required to establish the facts and to what degree of certainty. In a criminal procedure, the prosecution must establish its case *beyond a reasonable doubt*. In a civil case, the burden of proof is less. Generally, the case is won by the party who shows that the *preponderance* of evidence favors his or her side of the case. Although this is a bit too simple, it is sometimes said that if the scales tip ever so slightly in favor of *A* rather than *B*, then *A* wins the case.

The only way to carry the burden of proof is to present *evidence*. This evidence can contain conflicts and unclarities, which make it hard to prove the facts. Sometimes the facts are so complex that they simply cannot be proved one way or the other, and sometimes the distinction between facts and law is not so clear.

These problems arise often in cases that raise larger social issues. For example, in the famous case of *Brown v. Board of Education* (347 U.S. 483 [1954]), which found segregated schools unconstitutional, the Supreme Court answered the question of law at issue by saying "the opportunity of an education . . . is a right which must be available to all on equal terms." The Court next asked: "Does segregation of children in public schools solely on the basis of race . . . deprive the children of the minority group of equal educational opportunities?" This question was presented as a question of fact. The Court answered in the affirmative and tried to justify its answer by citing various psychological studies of the performance of minority children from segregated schools. This answer would be accepted by most people today, but the studies used as proof were controversial and inconclusive, so the Court had to decide whether studies of this kind were reliable enough to serve as evidence in this case. Moreover, the answer to the above question also depends on what counts as "equal educational opportunities" for the purposes of the law. For example, the studies cited by the Court found that segregated schools "affect the motivation of a child to learn," but these factual studies could not determine whether lowered *motivation* to learn counts as lowered *opportunity* to learn. The Court had to decide this issue because it in effect determines what the law is— what it prohibits and what it allows. Thus, what was presented as a question of fact turned out to be at least partly a question of law. In such cases, it is not clear where law ends and facts begin.

QUESTIONS OF LAW

Even after the facts are determined, no decision can be reached without determining what the law is. The law varies from place to place and from time to time, so we have to know what the law is at the right time and place. This is determined mainly by looking at the legal institutions that actually exist. In our legal system, there are three main sources of the law: statutes, the Constitution, and precedents.

STATUTES. Roughly, statutes are general rules of law passed by legislatures. Statutes are made at various levels (federal, state, and local), and they cover various subjects, including crimes as well as property, contracts, and other areas of civil law. There are also statutes governing the procedures and kinds of evidence that can be presented in court.

When a general statute is applied to a particular case, the legal argument is often primarily deductive. For example, Sally drove ninety-five miles per hour in front of Hanover High School at 4 PM on a school day. It is illegal to drive over fifteen mph in front of any school at 4 PM on a school day. Therefore, Sally's driving was illegal. Of course, there are lots of suppressed premises, such as that ninety-five mph is over fifteen mph. Other assumptions are trickier: Sally might not be found guilty if she had an excuse or justification, such as that a terrorist held a gun to her head. Still, it is often obvious that Sally had no excuse or justification. If we add this claim as a premise, then, with a little fiddling, the legal argument against Sally can be made deductively sound.

Such simple cases are common, but they are also boring. Things get much more difficult and interesting when a statute is *vague*, so that it is not clear whether the statute applies to the case at issue. Then the statute must be *interpreted*. We need some way to tell more precisely what the law prohibits and what it allows.

The first step in interpreting a statute is to look carefully at the *words* in the statute and their literal *meanings*. But the courts must often look beyond the mere words of the statute. This need arises when the words are unclear and when they lead to absurd results. For example, suppose a city council passes an ordinance requiring zoos to provide clean, dry cages for all mammals. This works fine until one zoo puts a whale in its aquarium. The whale would be in trouble if the courts stuck to the words of the ordinance. Fortunately, the courts can also consider the *intentions* of the legislators, which can be gleaned from their debates about the law. Of course, the city council might not have thought at all about whales, or they might have thought that whales are fish instead of mammals. Thus, if their intentions are what the legislators consciously had in mind, then we also need to consider the deeper, more general *purpose* of the legislators—the goal they were trying to reach or the moral outlook they were trying to express. This purpose is revealed by the wider historical context and by other laws made by the same legislature. In our example, the purpose of the statute was obviously to provide a healthy environment for mammals in zoos. This purpose is best served by interpreting the ordinance so that it does not require dry cages for whales.

In addition to words, intentions, and purposes, *moral beliefs* are often used to interpret statutes. Judges often argue that a statute should be interpreted one way by claiming that any other interpretation would lead to some kind of practical difficulty or moral unfairness. Such arguments are effective when everyone agrees about what is immoral or unfair, but judges often depend on more controversial moral beliefs. Critics claim that judges should not use their own moral views in this way, but there is no doubt that many or even all judges do in fact reason from such moral premises.

It should be clear that none of these methods of interpretation is mechanical, and none guarantees a single best interpretation of every statute. Part of the legal controversy is often over which factors can or should be used to argue for an interpretation. When all is said and done, legal reasoning from statutes is often far from the straightforward deduction that it appears to be in simple cases.

THE CONSTITUTION.   Even when a statute has been interpreted, it is sometimes not clear whether the statute is *valid*—whether it has any legal force. This is determined by the Constitution. The Constitution occupies a special place in the legal system of the United States. If any statute conflicts with the Constitution, including its amendments, that statute has no legal force. Generally it is not the role of courts to enact laws, but the courts do have the power to strike down laws if they conflict with provisions in our Constitution.

It is easy to imagine clear cases of laws that violate constitutional provisions. If the state of Kansas began printing its own money, that would plainly violate the constitutional provision that reserves this right to the federal government. But, typically, those constitutional questions that reach the courts are not clear-cut. Even more so than statutes, provisions in the Constitution are very general and sometimes vague. This vagueness serves a purpose: The framers of the Constitution recognized that they could not foresee every eventuality, so they wanted to allow future courts to interpret the Constitution as cases arose. But the vagueness of the Constitution also creates problems. Interpretations can often conflict and fuel controversy. As with statutes, arguments for and against interpretations of the Constitution usually refer to the words of the Constitution, the intentions and purposes of the framers of the Constitution, the effects of adopting an interpretation, moral beliefs, and so on. Such arguments are often inconclusive. The Supreme Court is then the final arbiter on questions of constitutionality.

PRECEDENTS.   The United States legal system is not only a constitutional system; it is also partly a system of common law. This means that lawyers and judges often cite precedents in arguments for present decisions. A *precedent* is simply a past case or decision that is supposed to be similar to the present case.

The practice of citing precedents might seem strange at first sight. Why should one case provide any reason for a decision in a different case? The answer is that the cases resemble each other in important respects. Of course, when there is an important enough difference between the cases, they should be *distinguished,* and then the precedent provides no argument in the present case. But, when there is no important enough difference, like cases should be treated alike. If similar precedents were not followed, the legal system would lack continuity, and this would make it unfair and ineffective. Of course, past decisions that were mistaken or immoral should not be continued. That is why precedents can be *overturned.* Nonetheless, our legal system assumes that, if there is no adequate reason to overturn a precedent or to distinguish the precedent from the present case, then the precedent provides some reason to decide the present case in the same way as the precedent. This general doctrine of precedent is often called *stare decisis*—to adhere to previous decisions.

Precedents are used for many different purposes. When a statute is vague, precedents are often used to argue for one interpretation over another. When no statute applies directly, precedents are often used to argue about what the law is. Precedents can also be used in arguments for general questions of fact, or simply as sources of persuasive rhetoric.

The form of arguments from precedents also varies. Often a judge or lawyer merely quotes part of the opinion in the precedent and treats that quotation as an authoritative pronouncement of the law. Arguments from precedents are then similar to arguments from legislative statutes, and there often arises a similar need to interpret the judicial pronouncement in the precedent. In other precedents, the judge chooses to make the decision without explicitly formulating any general rule of law. The precedent can still be used to argue for future decisions by emphasizing analogies and discounting differences between the precedent and the present case.

One example occurs in the case of *Plessy v. Ferguson,* 163 U.S. 537 (1896). Louisiana passed a statute that required blacks and whites to use "separate but equal" cars in trains. Plessy refused to comply, and he claimed that the Louisiana law violated the Fourteenth Amendment to the Constitution, which forbids states to deprive anyone of "the equal protection of the laws."

In his argument for this claim, Plessy cited the precedent of *Yick Wo v. Hopkins,* 118 U.S. 356 (1886). That case was about an ordinance in San Francisco that required a permit from the Board of Supervisors for any public laundry not operated in a brick or stone building. On its face, this ordinance was supposed simply to prevent fires. In practice, however, the Board of

Supervisors granted permits to all but one of the non-Chinese applicants and denied permits to all the Chinese applicants. Because of this practice, Yick Wo claimed that the ordinance violated the equal protection clause. The Supreme Court agreed and declared the ordinance unconstitutional, at least insofar as it gave the city power to grant and refuse permits "without regard to the competency of the persons applying, or the propriety of the places selected for the carrying on of business."

The argument from a precedent to a decision in a present case is often presented as an argument from *analogy*. In this form, the argument emphasizes similarities between the cases, and then concludes that the decision in the present case should be the same as in the precedent. Plessy's argument then appears to run something like this:

> (1) The ordinance in *Yick Wo* was declared unconstitutional.
> (2) The ordinance in *Yick Wo* is similar to the statute in *Plessy* in several respects.
> ∴ (3) The statute in *Plessy* also ought to be declared unconstitutional.

This argument is not very good as it stands, so we need to add some suppressed premises.

The first step is to construct a list of the respects in which the cases are similar. That is not always easy. When we are evaluating someone else's argument, we can focus on the similarities that he or she mentions. But when we are constructing our own legal arguments, we have to be more creative; we have to formulate the respects in which the cases are supposed to be similar. Some similarities do not matter: It is clearly irrelevant that the laws in *Yick Wo* and *Plessy* both contain more than ten words or that both apply to large cities. This much is assumed by both sides in the case, and legal reasoning would be impossible without assuming that many such similarities are irrelevant. Likewise, not all differences matter: It is not important, even if true, that Yick Wo was married and over fifty years old, but Plessy was not. To discount or distinguish the precedent, one must show that some difference between *Yick Wo* and *Plessy* is important enough to justify reaching different decisions in these cases. The central question, then, asks which factors—similarities and differences—*do* matter. In general, the answer is that a factor is relevant when it is needed to justify the decision in the precedent. These factors are often called the *ratio decidendi*—the reason for the decision.

Incorporating the doctrine of precedents as a suppressed premise, the argument from *Yick Wo* to *Plessy* can now be reconstructed as follows:

> (1) The ordinance in *Yick Wo* was declared unconstitutional.
> (2) The ordinance in *Yick Wo* is similar to the statute in *Plessy* in several respects (*A, B, C, D,* and so on).
> (3) These are the features that justified declaring the ordinance in *Yick Wo* unconstitutional.
> (4) There are no important enough differences between *Yick Wo* and *Plessy* to justify distinguishing the precedent.

(5) *Yick Wo* ought not to be overturned.

(6) If a precedent is similar to a present case in the respects that justified the decision in the precedent, and if the precedent ought not to be either overturned or distinguished, then the present case ought to be decided in the same way as the precedent.

∴ (7) The statute in *Plessy* ought to be declared unconstitutional.

This argument is now valid, but validity does not get us very far. We still need to know whether its premises are true.

Clearly, the crucial question is this: How do we determine which features of the precedent are needed to justify that decision? What we need to do is to extract a general rule of law that provides the best justification for the precedent decision.

The most obvious way to argue that a certain feature is important is to look at the written opinion in the precedent and see what the Court said—more specifically, what reasons it gave for its decision. In *Yick Wo*, the Court wrote:

> whatever may have been the intent of the ordinances as adopted, . . . though the law itself be fair on its face and impartial in appearance, yet, if it is applied and administered by public authority with an evil eye and an unequal hand, so as practically to make unjust and illegal discriminations between persons in similar circumstances, material to their rights, the denial of equal justice is still within the prohibition of the Constitution.

Here the Court explicitly announces that the intent of the ordinance and its appearance (for example, whether the ordinance explicitly mentions race or ethnic background) did *not* matter to their decision. The Court also declares that it *did* matter that the ordinance in practice creates inequalities in rights. Such official pronouncements by a court have considerable force for future courts in legal arguments.

Another way to determine which factors matter is to apply the necessary condition test or the sufficient condition test from Chapter 9 to a group of precedents. These tests had to be passed by each side in the *Plessy* case. Plessy claimed that a sufficient condition of unconstitutionality is that a law has a discriminatory *effect* on the rights of a particular racial or ethnic group. This claim would fail the sufficient condition test if there were any precedent still in force in which a law was found to have a discriminatory effect but the law was not held unconstitutional. Because there was no such precedent, the sufficient condition test does not exclude Plessy's claim that discriminatory effect is sufficient by itself to make a law unconstitutional.

On the other side, the Court claimed that discriminatory effect is not sufficient, because discriminatory *motive* is a necessary condition for a law to be unconstitutional under the equal protection clause. For this claim to pass the necessary condition test, there must have been no precedent still in force in which a law was held unconstitutional under the equal protection clause but the Court did not find any discriminatory motive. Plessy claimed that *Yick Wo* was such a case, but the Court responded that, even if those who passed the ordinance had no discriminatory motive, the administration of the ordinance in *Yick Wo* "was held to be a covert attempt on the part of the municipality to make an arbitrary and unjust discrimination against the Chinese race." If so, the necessary condition test does not rule out the Court's claim that discriminatory motive is necessary for unconstitutionality in this case.

This disagreement reveals the limits on the tests of necessary conditions and sufficient conditions. These tests are useful when there is a rich body of coherent precedents. But when there are not enough precedents of the right kinds, and when the precedents are not coherent, the necessary condition test and the sufficient condition test cannot be used to rule out conflicting interpretations of the precedents.

When the actual precedents are not enough, judges sometimes refer to *hypothetical cases*. In *Plessy*, a judge might imagine a law with discriminatory effect but no discriminatory motive. If the judge can show why this law should be found unconstitutional, this would suggest that a discriminatory motive is not really necessary for a violation of the equal protection clause. This takes some imagination, and it also requires judges to apply their moral beliefs about which laws should be allowed. Some critics deny that moral arguments should have any legal force, because they are so controversial. Nonetheless, there is no doubt that judges often do in fact assume such moral beliefs in arguments from precedents.

A final point to remember is that arguments from precedents are usually defeasible, like other inductive arguments (see Chapter 8). One reason is that more precedents might be found, and these new precedents might conflict with the precedents in the original argument. Another reason is that any precedent can be overturned. Precedents are not supposed to be overturned unless they are very badly mistaken or immoral, but this is always a possibility. Nonetheless, even though arguments from precedents always might be refuted in such ways, precedents can still provide reasons for legal decisions.

So far we have looked at arguments from precedents as ways to determine what is necessary or sufficient to violate the law. Even after this is determined, the law still must be applied to the facts in the present case. In *Plessy*, the Court held that there was no intent to discriminate, because the statute in *Plessy* was "reasonable" and "enacted in good faith for the promotion of the public good and not for the annoyance or oppression of a particular class." This claim is highly questionable. In his famous dissent, Justice Harlan denies it when he writes:

> Everyone knows that the statute in question had its origin in the purpose,
> not so much to exclude white persons from railroad cars occupied by blacks,
> as to exclude colored people from coaches occupied by or assigned to white
> persons. . . . No one would be so wanting in candor as to assert the contrary.

If Harlan is right, the Court's argument has a false premise, so the statute in *Plessy* should have been found unconstitutional even if the Court was right about what was necessary to find a law unconstitutional.

We can summarize this discussion by listing various ways in which arguments from precedents can fail:

1. The precedent and the present case might not *truly* resemble each other in the ways that the argument claims.

2. The respects in which the cases resemble each other might not be *important* enough to justify the same decision in the present case.

3. The precedent and the present case might also differ from each other in important respects that justify *distinguishing* the precedent.

4. The precedent might be mistaken or immoral enough to be *overturned*.

5. There might be other, stronger precedents that *conflict* with the precedent in the argument.

Whenever you evaluate or present any argument from a precedent, you need to ask whether the argument fails in any of these ways.

THE LAW OF DISCRIMINATION

These general methods of legal reasoning can be seen at work in a particular area of constitutional law—the law of discrimination. To understand the cases in this area, some background will be helpful.

THE EQUAL PROTECTION CLAUSE

The provision of the Constitution that governs discrimination is the equal protection clause of the Fourteenth Amendment. It provides as follows:

> No state shall make or enforce any law which shall . . . deny to any person within its jurisdiction the equal protection of the laws.

The clearest thing about this clause is that it is not clear. Whatever it means, it cannot mean that laws cannot ever treat people unequally. Criminal laws treat those who commit crimes quite differently from those who do not. The general idea behind the clause seems to be that like cases should be treated in like ways. Put negatively, the clause prohibits unequal treatment when there is no significant difference. This, however, is still both general and vague, for we need principles that determine what sorts of likenesses matter and what kinds of differences are significant.

Going back to the historical context in which the Fourteenth Amendment was adopted, we know that it was *intended* to prohibit unequal treatment on the basis of "race, color, or previous condition of servitude" (a phrase that occurs in the companion Fifteenth Amendment on voting rights).

More specifically, it was one of those constitutional provisions intended to protect the newly emancipated slaves. This was the primary *purpose* of these provisions, but the *language* is more general, giving like protection to all citizens of the United States.

APPLYING THE EQUAL PROTECTION CLAUSE

After the Fourteenth Amendment was adopted, many questions arose concerning its interpretation and application. The amendment explicitly refers only to state laws, but the state does many things besides pass laws, so the courts had to determine what counts as a *state action*. In a series of cases, the amendment was interpreted to mean that only positive actions of the state fell under the amendment. Thus, when thugs broke up a black political rally, with the police standing by doing nothing to protect the demonstrators, the Supreme Court ruled that this was not a violation of the equal protection clause because the state itself had not participated in the action (*U.S. v. Cruikshank*, 1875). On this view, the state was forbidden to aid discrimination, but it was not required to protect anyone against it.

Another issue that arose concerned what the state has to do to justify treating people differently. Here the courts decided that it was not their business to examine the details of legislation to make sure that the laws were as equitable as possible. The task of making laws, they held, falls to legislatures, and the courts gave legislatures wide latitude in formulating these laws. Flagrant violations of the equal protection clause could lead to the decision that the law was unconstitutional, but only if the law failed what became known as the *rational-relation test*. This test required only that the unequal treatment of individuals be reasonably likely to achieve some legitimate end.

A final issue was whether the Fourteenth Amendment protected only the civil rights of citizens or also rights of other kinds. In *Strauder v. West Virginia* (1880), a law that made blacks ineligible for jury duty was struck down on the grounds that the equal protection clause prohibits discrimination in areas of civil rights. In *Yick Wo v. Hopkins* (1886), the Court applied the equal protection clause to discrimination in areas of economic rights. *Yick Wo* also established that the equal protection clause protects not only blacks but also other groups (such as Chinese) and that laws that do not explicitly mention racial or ethnic groups can violate the equal protection clause if they are applied unequally in practice.

In 1896, the Supreme Court decided the case of *Plessy v. Ferguson*, which was about a Louisiana statute enforcing racial segregation in public transportation. This was clearly a state action, and the Court continued to apply the rational-relation test. The main issues were whether the equal protection clause extends to social rights, whether the segregation law served any reasonable purpose, and whether the separate facilities were truly equal. The Court held that the segregation statute did not violate the equal protection clause so long as the facilities were equal. This became known as the *separate-but-equal doctrine*.

THE STRICT SCRUTINY TEST

As soon as *Plessy* was decided, Southern and some border states rapidly passed a whole series of segregation laws. These were subsequently upheld by the courts on the precedent of *Plessy* and its separate-but-equal doctrine. The result was the introduction of a system of racial segregation throughout much of the country.

The doctrine of the rational-relation test remained basically unchanged until the 1940s. During World War II, the Supreme Court had to decide whether it was constitutional to relocate Japanese Americans away from Pacific ports. In *Korematsu v. United States,* 323 U.S. 214 at 216 (1944), the Court announced that

> all legal restrictions which curtail the rights of a single racial group are immediately suspect. That is not to say that all such restrictions are unconstitutional. It is to say that the courts must subject them to the most rigid scrutiny.

It is ironic that the Court did not strike down the Japanese relocation orders, but these cases established a new interpretation of equal protection that eventually greatly increased the power of the courts to strike down discriminatory laws.

On this new interpretation of the equal protection clause, most laws still need to pass only the rational-relation test, but there are two features of a law that serve as *triggers* of strict scrutiny. A law must pass *strict scrutiny* if the law either restricts a *fundamental right* or employs a *suspect classification.* Fundamental rights concern such things as the right to vote or the right to procreate. A classification is suspect if it concerns race, religion, national origin, and so on. Under the new interpretation of the equal protection clause, states could still pass laws restricting fundamental rights, and these laws could still employ suspect classifications, but, when they did so, a heavy burden of proof fell on them. To justify such a law, the state had to show that (1) the legislation serves a *legitimate* and *compelling* state interest, and that (2) it does so in the *least intrusive* way possible (or, as later courts put it, the legislation must be "narrowly tailored" to fit the interest). This is the *strict-scrutiny test.*

It should be clear that the rational-relation test is easy to meet, whereas the test of strict scrutiny is nearly impossible to satisfy. It is not hard to show that a piece of legislation has some chance of serving some legitimate goal and, thus, passes the rational relation test. It is difficult to show that the purpose of a law is compelling—that is, of overwhelming importance; and it is even more difficult to show that the stated purpose cannot be achieved by any less intrusive means. Thus, in adopting this new test, the Court no longer showed great deference to state legislatures, as it did in *Plessy,* when it applied the rational-relation test. Instead, the heaviest burden was shifted to the states in areas that involved what the Court declared to be suspect classifications or fundamental rights.

This new test was crucial for the decision of *Brown v. Board of Education* (1954), which declared segregation in public schools unconstitutional. The *Brown* opinion does not directly mention strict scrutiny, but this test looms in the background. Segregation clearly involves a suspect classification, but the Court emphasizes, "the opportunity of an education . . . is a *right* which must be available to all on equal terms" (emphasis added). The next step is to argue that segregated schools violate this right by their very nature, even if all "tangible" factors are equal. This violation of a fundamental right triggers strict scrutiny, and the *Brown* opinion then simply assumes that segregation in education will fail this test. Separate but equal is thus found unconstitutional, at least in education, and *Plessy* is in effect overturned.

THE *BAKKE* CASE

After *Brown,* the Supreme Court struck down segregation in many other areas—transportation, parks, libraries, and so on—as well as laws against racial intermarriage (though not until 1967, after Barack Obama's parents were married). Another string of decisions required states to use busing as a means to end segregation in school systems. The Court also required some employers to hire or promote minimum percentages of minorities to overcome the effects of illegal discrimination in employment.

In response to these court decisions, some schools and companies voluntarily took steps to overcome what they saw as the effects of past discrimination. These steps required them to use racial classifications, and that raised the issue of reverse discrimination. Part of the issue was about what to call such programs. Their opponents label them "reverse discrimination," but their defenders refer to them as "affirmative action." Both names clearly involve evaluation. A more neutral description might be "preferential treatment."

The classic case in this area is *Regents of the University of California v. Bakke* (1978) (hereafter, *Bakke*). The basic situation was that the medical school of the University of California at Davis had very few minority students, so they created a special admissions program that set aside 16 seats for minorities who were disadvantaged. Bakke, who was not a member of any of the specified minorities, applied to the school but was rejected even though he had higher scores on admissions tests than some minority members who were admitted under the special admissions program.

Bakke claimed that Davis's special admissions program violated the equal protection clause of the U.S. Constitution, the California Constitution, and Title VI of the Civil Rights Act of 1964, which provides:

> No person in the United States shall, on the ground of race, color, or national origin, be excluded from participation in, be denied the benefits of, or be subjected to discrimination under any program or activity receiving Federal financial assistance.

The Supreme Court was thus asked to rule on four main issues:

1. Did the Davis special admissions program violate the equal protection clause of the Constitution?

2. Does reference to race without judicial findings of particular past discrimination violate this constitutional guarantee?

3. Did the Davis special admissions program violate Title VI of the Civil Rights Act?

4. Should Davis be required to admit Bakke into its medical school?

The decision of the Supreme Court on these issues is so complicated that it takes a scorecard to follow it:

Question Ruled On	Brennan, Marshall, Blackmun, and White	Powell	Burger, Stewart, Stevens, and Rehnquist	The majority
1	No	Yes	No decision	No decision
2	No	No	No decision	No
3	No	Yes	Yes	Yes
4	No	Yes	Yes	Yes

Because the justices split into two groups of four, the remaining justice, Powell, determined the majority on most issues. Powell, however, was the only justice who argued that the Davis program was unconstitutional. Four others (Brennan, Marshall, Blackmun, and White) dissented. The remaining four (Burger, Stevens, Stewart, and Rehnquist) chose not to address this constitutional issue because they had already ruled out the Davis program under Title VI. Since a majority did not join Powell in his opinion, the Court did *not* explicitly declare the Davis program unconstitutional. But the Davis program was held to violate Title VI, and Davis was ordered to admit Bakke, because Burger, Stevens, Stewart, and Rehnquist did join Powell on these issues. Despite Davis's loss, the Court took the opposite position on the second issue. Powell argued that it was not always unconstitutional for the state to refer to race, and he created a majority when he was joined by Brennan, Marshall, Blackmun, and White. Thus, each group of justices got part of what it wanted.

The constitutional issues are raised most directly in the opinions of Powell and Brennan (excerpted below). These opinions differ not only in their conclusions but also in their interpretations of the equal protection clause. Powell argued that the Davis program and any consideration of race must be subjected to the test of strict scrutiny. He held that the Davis program did not meet the high standards of strict scrutiny, but some other consideration of race might, such as in the Harvard College admissions program, which used race as a "goal" rather than as a "quota" (much like the University of Michigan Law School admissions program in the *Grutter* case below).

In contrast, Brennan argued for a new interpretation of the equal protection clause. On this new interpretation, strict scrutiny would still be applied to most racial classifications, but strict scrutiny need not be passed when the state uses a racial classification to serve a *benign, remedial purpose.* The purpose of a racial classification is benign when it does not stigmatize anyone and was not adopted out of any discriminatory motive, and it is remedial if the state used the racial classification because the state found that, without the racial classification, an underprivileged group would suffer harm or differential impact because of past discrimination in society at large.

Powell criticized Brennan's conditions on the grounds that the notion of stigma is too vague and that it is not groups but individuals who are protected by the equal protection clause. Brennan responded by distinguishing stigma from other harms and by emphasizing the importance of groups. The heart of the controversy was, thus, about the conditions under which to apply strict scrutiny.

REGENTS OF THE UNIVERSITY OF CALIFORNIA V. BAKKE

■

(438 U.S. 268, 1978)

Excerpts from Justice Powell's opinion:

Racial and ethnic classifications . . . are subject to stringent examination without regard to . . . additional characteristics. We declared as much in the first cases explicitly to recognize racial distinctions as suspect: ". . . [A]ll legal restrictions which curtail the rights of a single racial group are immediately suspect. That is not to say that all such restrictions are unconstitutional. It is to say that courts must subject them to the most rigid scrutiny" (*Korematsu*, 323 U.S. 214 at 216 [1944]). The Court has never questioned the validity of those pronouncements. . . .

Petitioner urges us to adopt for the first time a more restrictive view of the Equal Protection Clause and hold that discrimination against members of the white "majority" cannot be suspect if its purpose can be characterized as "benign." The clock of our liberties, however, cannot be turned back to 1868. It is far too late to argue that the guarantee of equal protection to *all* persons permits the recognition of special wards entitled to a degree of protection greater than that accorded others.

Moreover, there are serious problems of justice connected with the idea of preference itself. First, it may not always be clear that a so-called preference is in fact benign. Courts may be asked to validate burdens imposed upon individual members of particular groups in order to advance the group's general interest. . . . Nothing in the Constitution supports the notion that individuals may be asked to suffer otherwise impermissible burdens in order to enhance the societal standing of their ethnic groups. Second, preferential programs may only reinforce common stereotypes holding that certain groups are unable to achieve success without special protection based on a factor having no relationship to individual worth. . . . Third, there is a measure of inequity in forcing innocent persons in respondent's position to bear the burdens of redressing grievances not of their making.

Petitioner contends that on several occasions this Court has approved preferential classifications without applying the most exacting scrutiny. Most of the cases upon which petitioner relies are drawn from three areas: school desegregation, employment discrimination, and sex discrimination. Each of the cases cited presented a situation materially different from the facts of this case. . . . [W]e have never approved preferential classifications in the absence of proven constitutional or statutory violations. . . . When a classification denies an individual opportunities or benefits enjoyed by others solely because of his race or ethnic background, it must be regarded as suspect. . . .

Excerpts from Justice Brennan's opinion:

. . . Unquestionably we have held that a government practice or statute which restricts "fundamental rights" or which contains "suspect classifications" is to be subjected to "strict scrutiny" and can be justified only if it furthers a compelling government purpose and, even then, only if no less restrictive alternative is available. . . . But no fundamental right is involved here. . . . Nor do whites as a class have any of the "traditional indicia of suspectness: the class is not saddled with such disabilities, or subjected to such a history of purposeful unequal treatment, or relegated to such a position of political powerlessness as to command extraordinary protection from the majoritarian political process." . . .

[The] fact that this case does not fit neatly into our prior analytic framework for race cases does not mean that it should be analyzed by applying the very loose rational-basis standard of review that is the very least that is always applied in equal protection cases. . . .

[B]ecause of the significant risk that racial classifications established for ostensibly benign purposes can be misused, causing effects not unlike those created by invidious classifications, it is inappropriate to inquire only whether there is any conceivable basis that might sustain such a classification. Instead, to justify such a classification an important and articulated purpose for its use must be shown. In addition, any statute must be stricken that stigmatizes any group or that singles out those least well represented in the political process to bear the brunt of a benign program. Thus our review under the Fourteenth Amendment should be strict—not "'strict' in theory and fatal in fact," because it is stigma that causes fatality—but strict and searching nonetheless. . . .

DISCUSSION QUESTION

Do you agree with Powell or with Brennan in their debate about whether strict scrutiny should be applied to affirmative actions programs in admissions? Why?

LEGAL DEVELOPMENTS SINCE *BAKKE*

The legal story of affirmative action gets very complicated after the *Bakke* decision. Because of the split within the Court, it was not clear which parts, if any, of Powell's opinion had force as precedent. It was also not clear which kinds of programs were close enough to the Harvard program that Powell endorsed; and it was not clear how to extend Powell's emphasis on diversity in education to other areas, such as employment and government contracts. As a result, some affirmative action programs were struck down and others were upheld while commentators scrambled to explain the underlying pattern and rationale for the Court's decisions.

The year after *Bakke*, in *United Steelworkers of America v. Weber*, 445 U.S. 193 (1979), the Supreme Court upheld a preferential treatment quota in employment. Later, in *Richmond v. J. A. Croson Co.*, 488 U.S. 469 (1989), the Court struck down a local program that set aside a specified percentage of municipal contracts for minority-controlled firms. Then, in *Metro Broadcasting v. FCC*, 497 U.S. 547 (1990), the Court allowed a Federal Communications Commission "distress sale" policy that permitted a broadcaster whose license or renewal application has been designated for a revocation hearing to sell the license to a buyer if, but only if, that buyer is at least 50 percent minority-owned. Of course, the majority opinions gave reasons for each decision, but dissents were common and fierce, and it was hard to see how the pieces of the puzzle fit together.

The law was somewhat clearer in college admissions. As Justice O'Connor put it, "Since this Court's splintered decision in *Bakke*, Justice Powell's opinion announcing the judgment of the Court has served as the touchstone for constitutional analysis of race-conscious admissions policies. Public and private universities across the nation have modelled their own admissions programs on Justice Powell's views on permissible race-conscious policies." Still, there was great uncertainty about exactly which kinds of admissions programs were allowed by Powell's reasoning in *Bakke*. Some critics also held that the precedent of *Bakke* should be overturned or disregarded, and the Court should hold, instead, that all race-conscious programs are unconstitutional.

This issue came to a head in 2003, when the Court considered two very different kinds of admissions programs practiced at the University of Michigan under its president, Lee Bollinger (hence the names of the cases below). Michigan's Law School admissions program was very much like the Harvard program that Powell endorsed, so that program was upheld. The admissions program at Michigan's undergraduate College of Literature, Science, and the Arts, in contrast, gave a specific number of points to all applicants in underrepresented minority groups. Critics claimed that this program amounted to a "quota" more like the Davis Medical School admissions program that Powell had struck down in *Bakke*, and the Court struck it down. The differences between these programs thus define the line between what is and is not permitted in college admissions today.

GRUTTER V. BOLLINGER

■

(539 U.S. 306, 2003)

Syllabus:

The University of Michigan Law School (Law School), one of the Nation's top law schools, follows an official admissions policy that seeks to achieve student body diversity through compliance with *Regents of Univ. of Cal. v. Bakke*. Focusing on students' academic ability coupled with a flexible assessment of their talents, experiences, and potential, the policy requires admissions officials to evaluate each applicant based on all the information available in the file, including a personal statement, letters of recommendation, an essay describing how the applicant will contribute to Law School life and diversity, and the applicant's undergraduate grade point average (GPA) and Law School Admissions Test (LSAT) score. Additionally, officials must look beyond grades and scores to so-called "soft variables," such as recommenders' enthusiasm, the quality of the undergraduate institution and the applicant's essay, and the areas and difficulty of undergraduate course selection. The policy does not define diversity solely in terms of racial and ethnic status and does not restrict the types of diversity contributions eligible for "substantial weight," but it does reaffirm the Law School's commitment to diversity with special reference to the inclusion of African-American, Hispanic, and Native-American students, who otherwise might not be represented in the student body in meaningful numbers. By enrolling a "critical mass" of underrepresented minority students, the policy seeks to ensure their ability to contribute to the Law School's character and to the legal profession.

When the Law School denied admission to petitioner Grutter, a white Michigan resident with a 3.8 GPA and 161 LSAT score, she filed this suit, alleging that respondents had discriminated against her on the basis of race in violation of the Fourteenth Amendment, Title VI of the Civil Rights Act of 1964, and 42 U.S.C. § 1981; that she was rejected because the Law School uses race as a "predominant" factor, giving applicants belonging to certain minority groups a significantly greater chance of admission than students with similar credentials from disfavored racial groups; and that respondents had no compelling interest to justify that use of race. . . .

Justice O'Connor delivered the opinion of the Court, in which
Justices Stevens, Souter, Ginsburg, and Breyer joined:

. . . We have held that all racial classifications imposed by government "must be analyzed by a reviewing court under strict scrutiny." This means that such classifications are constitutional only if they are narrowly tailored to further compelling governmental interests. . . .

With these principles in mind, we turn to the question whether the Law School's use of race is justified by a compelling state interest. Before this Court, as they have throughout this litigation, respondents assert only one justification for their use of race in the admissions process: obtaining "the educational benefits that flow from a diverse student body." . . .

The Law School's educational judgment that such diversity is essential to its educational mission is one to which we defer. The Law School's assessment that diversity will, in fact, yield educational benefits is substantiated by respondents and their amici. Our scrutiny of the interest asserted by the Law School is no less strict for taking into account complex educational judgments in an area that lies primarily within the expertise of the university. Our holding today is in keeping with our tradition of giving a degree of deference to a university's academic decisions, within constitutionally prescribed limits. . . .

As part of its goal of "assembling a class that is both exceptionally academically qualified and broadly diverse," the Law School seeks to "enroll a 'critical mass' of minority students." The Law School's interest is not simply "to assure within its student body some specified percentage of a particular group merely because of its race or ethnic origin." That would amount to outright racial balancing, which is patently unconstitutional. Rather, the Law School's concept of critical mass is defined by reference to the educational benefits that diversity is designed to produce.

These benefits are substantial. As the District Court emphasized, the Law School's admissions policy promotes "cross-racial understanding," helps to break down racial stereotypes, and "enables [students] to better understand persons of different races." These benefits are "important and laudable," because "classroom discussion is livelier, more spirited, and simply more enlightening and interesting" when the students have "the greatest possible variety of backgrounds." . . .

Moreover, universities, and in particular, law schools, represent the training ground for a large number of our Nation's leaders. . . . In order to cultivate a set of leaders with legitimacy in the eyes of the citizenry, it is necessary that the path to leadership be visibly open to talented and qualified individuals of every race and ethnicity. All members of our heterogeneous society must have confidence in the openness and integrity of the educational institutions that provide this training. . . .

Even in the limited circumstance when drawing racial distinctions is permissible to further a compelling state interest, government is still "constrained in how it may pursue that end: [T]he means chosen to accomplish the [government's] asserted purpose must be specifically and narrowly framed to accomplish that purpose." The purpose of the narrow tailoring requirement is to ensure that "the means chosen 'fit' . . . the compelling goal so closely that there is little or no possibility that the motive for the classification was illegitimate racial prejudice or stereotype.". . .

To be narrowly tailored, a race-conscious admissions program cannot use a quota system. . . . We are satisfied that the Law School's admissions program, like the Harvard plan described by Justice Powell, does not operate as a quota. Properly understood, a "quota" is a program in which a certain fixed number or proportion of opportunities are "reserved exclusively for certain minority groups.". . . The Law School's goal of attaining a critical mass of underrepresented minority students does not transform its program into a quota. As the Harvard plan described by Justice Powell recognized, there is of course "some relationship between numbers and achieving the benefits to be derived from a diverse student body, and between numbers and providing a reasonable environment for those students admitted." . . . Nor, as Justice Kennedy posits, does the Law School's consultation of the "daily reports," which keep track of the racial and ethnic composition of the class (as well as of residency and gender), "suggest[ ] there was no further attempt at individual review save for race itself" during the final stages of the admissions process. To the contrary, the Law School's admissions officers testified without contradiction that they never gave race any more or less weight based on the information contained in these reports. Moreover, . . . the number of African-American, Latino, and Native-American students in each class at the Law School varied from 13.5 to 20.1 percent, a range inconsistent with a quota.

That a race-conscious admissions program does not operate as a quota does not, by itself, satisfy the requirement of individualized consideration. When using race as a "plus" factor in university admissions, a university's admissions program must remain flexible enough to ensure that each applicant is evaluated as an individual and not in a way that makes an applicant's race or ethnicity the defining feature of his or her application. The importance of this individualized consideration in the context of a race-conscious admissions program is paramount. Here, the Law School engages in a highly individualized, holistic review of each applicant's file, giving serious consideration to all the ways an applicant might contribute to a diverse educational environment. The Law School affords this individualized consideration to applicants of all races. There is no policy, either *de jure* or *de facto,* of automatic acceptance or rejection based on any single "soft" variable. Unlike the program at issue in *Gratz v. Bollinger* [see below], the Law School awards no mechanical, predetermined diversity "bonuses" based on race or ethnicity. . . .

What is more, the Law School actually gives substantial weight to diversity factors besides race. The Law School frequently accepts nonminority applicants with grades and test scores lower than underrepresented minority applicants (and other nonminority applicants) who are rejected. This shows that the Law School seriously weighs many other diversity factors besides race that can make a real and dispositive difference for nonminority applicants as well. By this flexible approach, the Law School sufficiently takes into account, in practice as well as in theory, a wide variety of characteristics besides race and ethnicity that contribute to a diverse student body. . . .

Petitioner and the United States argue that the Law School's plan is not narrowly tailored because race-neutral means exist to obtain the educational benefits of student body diversity that the Law School seeks. We disagree. Narrow tailoring does not require exhaustion of every conceivable race-neutral alternative. Nor does it require a university to choose between maintaining a reputation for excellence or fulfilling a commitment to provide educational opportunities to members of all racial groups. Narrow tailoring does, however, require serious, good faith consideration of workable race-neutral alternatives that will achieve the diversity the university seeks.

We agree with the Court of Appeals that the Law School sufficiently considered workable race-neutral alternatives. The District Court took the Law School to task for failing to consider race-neutral alternatives such as "using a lottery system" or "decreasing the emphasis for all applicants on undergraduate GPA and LSAT scores." But these alternatives would require a dramatic sacrifice of diversity, the academic quality of all admitted students, or both. . . . The United States advocates "percentage plans," recently adopted by public undergraduate institutions in Texas, Florida, and California to guarantee admission to all students above a certain class-rank threshold in every high school in the State. The United States does not, however, explain how such plans could work for graduate and professional schools. Moreover, even assuming such plans are race-neutral, they may preclude the university from conducting the individualized assessments necessary to assemble a student body that is not just racially diverse, but diverse along all the qualities valued by the university. We are satisfied that the Law School adequately considered race-neutral alternatives currently capable of producing a critical mass without forcing the Law School to abandon the academic selectivity that is the cornerstone of its educational mission. . . .

We take the Law School at its word that it would "like nothing better than to find a race-neutral admissions formula" and will terminate its race-conscious admissions program as soon as practicable. It has been 25 years since Justice Powell first approved the use of race to further an interest in student body diversity in the context of public higher education. Since that time, the number of minority applicants with high grades and test scores has indeed increased. We expect that 25 years from now, the use of racial preferences will no longer be necessary to further the interest approved today.

In summary, the Equal Protection Clause does not prohibit the Law School's narrowly tailored use of race in admissions decisions to further a compelling interest in obtaining the educational benefits that flow from a diverse student body. Consequently, petitioner's statutory claims based on Title VI and 42 U.S.C. § 1981 also fail.

Chief Justice Rehnquist, with whom
Justices Scalia, Kennedy, and Thomas join, dissenting:

I do not believe . . . that the University of Michigan Law School's means are narrowly tailored to the interest it asserts. The Law School claims it must take the steps it does to achieve a "'critical mass'" of underrepresented minority students. But its actual program bears no relation to this asserted goal. . . .

From 1995 through 2000, the Law School admitted between 1,130 and 1,310 students. Of those, between 13 and 19 were Native American, between 91 and 108 were African-Americans, and between 47 and 56 were Hispanic. If the Law School is admitting between 91 and 108 African-Americans in order to achieve "critical mass," thereby preventing African-American students from feeling "isolated or like spokespersons for their race," one would think that a number of the same order of magnitude would be necessary to accomplish the same purpose for Hispanics and Native Americans. . . .

Only when the "critical mass" label is discarded does a likely explanation for these numbers emerge. . . . [F]rom 1995 through 2000 the percentage of admitted applicants who were members of these minority groups closely tracked the percentage of individuals in the school's applicant pool who were from the same groups. . . . The tight correlation between the percentage of applicants and admittees of a given race, therefore, must result from careful race based planning by the Law School. . . . The Law School has offered no explanation for its actual admissions practices and, unexplained, we are bound to conclude that the Law School has managed its admissions program, not to achieve a "critical mass," but to extend offers of admission to members of selected minority groups in proportion to their statistical representation in the applicant pool. But this is precisely the type of racial balancing that the Court itself calls "patently unconstitutional."

Justice Thomas, with whom
Justice Scalia joins . . . , concurring in part and dissenting in part:

The Law School adamantly disclaims any race-neutral alternative that would reduce "academic selectivity," which would in turn "require the Law School to become a very different institution, and to sacrifice a core part of its educational mission." In other words, the Law School seeks to improve marginally the education it offers without sacrificing too much of its exclusivity and elite status.

The proffered interest that the majority vindicates today, then, is not simply "diversity." Instead the Court upholds the use of racial discrimination as a tool to advance the Law School's interest in offering a marginally superior education while maintaining an elite institution. Unless each constituent part of this state interest is of pressing public necessity, the Law School's use of race is unconstitutional. I find each of them to fall far short of this standard. . . .

Under the proper standard, there is no pressing public necessity in maintaining a public law school at all and, it follows, certainly not an elite law school. Likewise, marginal improvements in legal education do not qualify as a compelling state interest. . . .

The absence of any articulated legal principle supporting the majority's principal holding suggests another rationale. I believe what lies beneath the Court's decision today are the benighted notions that one can tell when racial discrimination benefits (rather than hurts) minority groups, and that racial discrimination is necessary to remedy general societal ills. . . .

I must contest the notion that the Law School's discrimination benefits those admitted as a result of it. . . . [N]owhere in any of the filings in this Court is any evidence that the purported "beneficiaries" of this racial discrimination prove themselves by performing at (or even near) the same level as those students who receive no preferences. . . . The Law School tantalizes unprepared students with the promise of a University of Michigan degree and all of the opportunities that it offers. These overmatched students take the bait, only to find that they cannot succeed in the cauldron of competition. . . . While these students may graduate with law degrees, there is no evidence that they have received a qualitatively better legal education (or become better lawyers) than if they had gone to a less "elite" law school for which they were better prepared. . . .

Beyond the harm the Law School's racial discrimination visits upon its test subjects, no social science has disproved the notion that this discrimination "engenders attitudes of superiority or, alternatively, provoke[s] resentment among those who believe that they have been wronged by the government's use of race." "These programs stamp minorities with a badge of inferiority and may cause them to develop dependencies or to adopt an attitude that they are 'entitled' to preferences."

It is uncontested that each year, the Law School admits a handful of blacks who would be admitted in the absence of racial discrimination. Who can differentiate between those who belong and those who do not? The majority of blacks are admitted to the Law School because of discrimination, and because of this policy all are tarred as undeserving. This problem of stigma does not depend on determinacy as to whether those stigmatized are actually the "beneficiaries" of racial discrimination. When blacks take positions in the highest places of government, industry, or academia, it is an open question today whether their skin color played a part in their advancement. . . .

DISCUSSION QUESTIONS

1. Reconstruct Justice O'Connor's main argument in the selection from her majority opinion in *Grutter*.

2. Reconstruct Chief Justice Rehnquist's main arguments in the selection from his dissenting opinion in *Grutter*. How could Justice O'Connor best respond? Is this response adequate? Why or why not?

3. What are Justice Thomas's main points in the selection from his dissenting opinion in *Grutter*? How could Justice O'Connor best respond? Is this response adequate? Why or why not?

4. How would you have decided the *Grutter* case? Why?

GRATZ V. BOLLINGER

■

(539 U.S. 244, 2003)

Syllabus:

Petitioners Gratz and Hamacher, both of whom are Michigan residents and Caucasian, applied for admission to the University of Michigan's (University) College of Literature, Science, and the Arts (LSA) in 1995 and 1997, respectively. Although the LSA considered Gratz to be well qualified and Hamacher to be within the qualified range, both were denied early admission and were ultimately denied admission. [The] University's Office of Undergraduate Admissions (OUA) . . . considers a number of factors in making admissions decisions, including high school grades, standardized test scores, high school quality, curriculum strength, geography, alumni relationships, leadership, and race. During all relevant periods, the University has considered African-Americans, Hispanics, and Native Americans to be "underrepresented minorities," and it is undisputed that the University admits virtually every qualified applicant from these groups. The current guidelines use a selection method under which every applicant from an underrepresented racial or ethnic minority group is automatically awarded 20 points of the 100 needed to guarantee admission. . . .

Chief Justice Rehnquist delivered the opinion of the Court, in which Justices O'Connor, Scalia, Kennedy, and Thomas joined:

We granted *certiorari* in this case to decide whether "the University of Michigan's use of racial preferences in undergraduate admissions violates the Equal Protection Clause of the Fourteenth Amendment, Title VI of the Civil Rights Act of 1964 . . ., or 42 U.S.C. § 1981. . . ." Because we find that the manner in which the University considers the race of applicants in its undergraduate admissions guidelines violates these constitutional and statutory provisions, we reverse that portion of the District Court's decision upholding the guidelines. . . .

It is by now well established that "all racial classifications reviewable under the Equal Protection Clause must be strictly scrutinized." . . . To withstand our strict scrutiny analysis, respondents must demonstrate that the University's use of race in its current admission program employs "narrowly tailored measures that further compelling governmental interests." . . . We find that the University's policy, which automatically distributes 20 points, or one-fifth of the points needed to guarantee admission, to every single "underrepresented minority" applicant solely because of race, is not narrowly tailored to achieve the interest in educational diversity that respondents claim justifies their program.

In *Bakke*, Justice Powell . . . explained . . . that in his view it would be permissible for a university to employ an admissions program in which "race or ethnic background may be deemed a 'plus' in a particular applicant's file." . . . Justice Powell's opinion in *Bakke* emphasized the importance of considering each particular applicant as an individual, assessing all of the qualities that individual possesses, and in turn, evaluating that individual's ability to contribute to the unique setting of higher education. The admissions program Justice Powell described, however, did not contemplate that any single characteristic automatically ensured a specific and identifiable contribution to a university's diversity. . . . Instead, under the approach Justice Powell described, each characteristic of a particular applicant was to be considered in assessing the applicant's entire application.

The current LSA policy does not provide such individualized consideration. The LSA's policy automatically distributes 20 points to every single applicant from an "underrepresented minority" group, as defined by the University. The only consideration that accompanies this distribution of points is a factual review of an application to determine whether an individual is a member of one of these minority groups. Moreover, unlike Justice Powell's example, where the race of a "particular black applicant" could be considered without being decisive, the LSA's automatic distribution of 20 points has the effect of making "the factor of race . . . decisive" for virtually every minimally qualified underrepresented minority applicant.

Also instructive in our consideration of the LSA's system is the example provided in the description of the Harvard College Admissions Program, which Justice Powell both discussed in, and attached to, his opinion in *Bakke*. The example was included to "illustrate the kind of significance attached to race" under the Harvard College program. It provided as follows:

> The Admissions Committee, with only a few places left to fill, might find itself forced to choose between A, the child of a successful black physician in an academic community with promise of superior academic performance, and B, a black who grew up in an inner-city ghetto of semi-literate parents whose academic achievement was lower but who had demonstrated energy and leadership as well as an apparently abiding interest in black power. If a good number of black students much like A but few like B had already been admitted, the Committee might prefer B; and vice versa. If C, a white student with extraordinary artistic talent, were also seeking one of the remaining places, his unique quality might give him an edge over both A and B. Thus, the critical criteria are often individual qualities or experience *not dependent upon race but sometimes associated with it.* (emphasis added)

This example further demonstrates the problematic nature of the LSA's admissions system. Even if student C's "extraordinary artistic talent" rivaled that of Monet or Picasso, the applicant would receive, at most, five points under the LSA's system. At the same time, every single underrepresented minority applicant, including students A and B, would automatically receive 20 points for submitting an application. Clearly, the LSA's system does not offer applicants the individualized selection process described in Harvard's example. Instead of considering how the differing backgrounds, experiences, and characteristics of students A, B, and C might benefit the University, admissions counselors reviewing LSA applications would simply award both A and B 20 points because their applications indicate that they are African-American, and student C would receive up to 5 points for his "extraordinary talent."

Respondents emphasize the fact that the LSA has created the possibility of an applicant's file being flagged for individualized consideration by the ARC. We think that the flagging program only emphasizes the flaws of the University's system as a whole when compared to that described by Justice Powell. Again, students A, B, and C illustrate the point. First, student A would never be flagged. This is because, as the University has conceded, the effect of automatically awarding 20 points is that virtually every qualified underrepresented minority applicant is admitted. Student A, an applicant "with promise of superior academic performance," would certainly fit this description. Thus, the result of the automatic distribution of 20 points is that the University would never consider student A's individual background, experiences, and characteristics to assess his individual "potential contribution to diversity." Instead, every applicant like student A would simply be admitted.

It is possible that students B and C would be flagged and considered as individuals. This assumes that student B was not already admitted because of the automatic 20-point distribution, and that student C could muster at least 70 additional points. But the fact that the "review committee can look at the applications individually and ignore the points," once an application is flagged is of little comfort under our strict scrutiny analysis. The record does not reveal precisely how many applications are flagged for this individualized consideration, but it is undisputed that such consideration is the exception and not the rule in the operation of the LSA's admissions program. Additionally, this individualized review is only provided after admissions counselors automatically distribute the University's version of a "plus" that makes race a decisive factor for virtually every minimally qualified underrepresented minority applicant.

Respondents contend that "the volume of applications and the presentation of applicant information make it impractical for [LSA] to use the . . . admissions system" upheld by the Court today in *Grutter*. But the fact that the implementation of a program capable of providing individualized consideration might present administrative challenges does not render constitutional an otherwise problematic system. Nothing in Justice Powell's opinion in *Bakke* signalled that a university may employ whatever means it desires to achieve the stated goal of diversity without regard to the limits imposed by our strict scrutiny analysis.

We conclude, therefore, that because the University's use of race in its current freshman admissions policy is not narrowly tailored to achieve respondents' asserted compelling interest in diversity, the admissions policy violates the Equal Protection Clause of the Fourteenth Amendment. . . .

Justice Souter, with whom Justice Ginsburg joins as to Part II, dissenting:

The record does not describe a system with a quota like the one struck down in *Bakke*, which "insulated" all nonminority candidates from competition from certain seats. . . . The plan here, in contrast, lets all applicants compete for all places and values an applicant's offering for any place not only on grounds of race, but on grades, test scores, strength of high school, quality of course of study, residence, alumni relationships, leadership, personal character, socioeconomic disadvantage, athletic ability, and quality of a personal essay. A nonminority applicant who scores highly in these other categories can readily garner a selection index exceeding that of a minority applicant who gets the 20-point bonus.

Subject to one qualification to be taken up below, this scheme of considering, through the selection index system, all of the characteristics that the college thinks relevant to student diversity for every one of the student places to be filled fits Justice Powell's description of a constitutionally acceptable program: one that considers "all pertinent elements of diversity in light of the particular qualifications of each applicant" and places each element "on the same footing for consideration, although not necessarily according them the same weight." In the Court's own words, "each characteristic of a particular applicant [is] considered in assessing the applicant's entire application." An unsuccessful nonminority applicant cannot complain that he was rejected "simply because he was not the right color"; an applicant who is rejected because "his combined qualifications . . . did not outweigh those of the other applicant" has been given an opportunity to compete with all other applicants.

The one qualification to this description of the admissions process is that membership in an underrepresented minority is given a weight of 20 points on the 150-point scale. On the face of things, however, this assignment of specific points does not set race apart from all other weighted considerations. Nonminority students may receive 20 points for athletic ability, socioeconomic disadvantage, attendance at a socioeconomically disadvantaged or predominantly minority high school, or at the Provost's discretion; they may also receive 10 points for being residents of Michigan, 6 for residence in an underrepresented Michigan county, 5 for leadership and service, and so on.

The Court nonetheless finds fault with a scheme that "automatically" distributes 20 points to minority applicants because "the only consideration that accompanies this distribution of points is a factual review of an application to determine whether an individual is a member of one of these minority groups." The objection goes to the use of points to quantify and compare characteristics, or to the number of points awarded due to race, but on either reading the objection is mistaken.

The very nature of a college's permissible practice of awarding value to racial diversity means that race must be considered in a way that increases some applicants' chances for admission. Since college admission is not left entirely to inarticulate intuition, it is hard to see what is inappropriate in assigning some stated value to a relevant characteristic, whether it be reasoning ability, writing style, running speed, or minority race. Justice

Powell's plus factors necessarily are assigned some values. The college simply does by a numbered scale what the [Michigan] law school accomplishes in its "holistic review"; the distinction does not imply that applicants to the undergraduate college are denied individualized consideration or a fair chance to compete on the basis of all the various merits their applications may disclose.

Nor is it possible to say that the 20 points convert race into a decisive factor comparable to reserving minority places as in *Bakke*. Of course we can conceive of a point system in which the "plus" factor given to minority applicants would be so extreme as to guarantee every minority applicant a higher rank than every nonminority applicant in the university's admissions system. But petitioners do not have a convincing argument that the freshman admissions system operates this way. The present record obviously shows that nonminority applicants may achieve higher selection point totals than minority applicants owing to characteristics other than race, and the fact that the university admits "virtually every qualified underrepresented minority applicant," may reflect nothing more than the likelihood that very few qualified minority applicants apply, as well as the possibility that self-selection results in a strong minority applicant pool. It suffices for me, as it did for the District Court, that there are no Bakke-like set-asides and that consideration of an applicant's whole spectrum of ability is no more ruled out by giving 20 points for race than by giving the same points for athletic ability or socioeconomic disadvantage. . . .

In contrast to the college's forthrightness in saying just what plus factor it gives for membership in an underrepresented minority, it is worth considering the character of one alternative thrown up as preferable, because supposedly not based on race. Drawing on admissions systems used at public universities in California, Florida, and Texas, the United States contends that Michigan could get student diversity in satisfaction of its compelling interest by guaranteeing admission to a fixed percentage of the top students from each high school in Michigan.

While there is nothing unconstitutional about such a practice, it nonetheless suffers from a serious disadvantage.[*] It is the disadvantage of deliberate obfuscation. The "percentage plans" are just as race conscious as the point scheme (and fairly so), but they get their racially diverse results without saying directly what they are doing or why they are doing it. In contrast, Michigan states its purpose directly and, if this were a doubtful case for me, I would be tempted to give Michigan an extra point of its own for its frankness. Equal protection cannot become an exercise in which the winners are the ones who hide the ball.

———————————————■———————————————

[*]Of course it might be pointless in the State of Michigan, where minorities are a much smaller fraction of the population than in California, Florida, or Texas.

```
                    ┌──────────────────────────┐
                    │   DISCUSSION QUESTIONS    │
                    └──────────────────────────┘
```

1. Describe the main differences among the following admissions programs. Which of these differences are relevant to the constitutionality of these programs, in your opinion?

   a. The admissions program at Michigan Law School

   b. The admissions program at Michigan's College of Literature, Science, and the Arts

   c. The percentage plan used in California, Florida, and Texas

   d. A lottery among all qualified candidates

2. In your opinion, would the admissions program at Michigan's College of Literature, Science, and the Arts be unconstitutional if, instead of twenty points, it awarded only five points to members of underrepresented minority groups? What if it awarded fifty points? Does the number of points matter at all? Why or why not?

3. Much of the debate between Justices Rehnquist and Souter in *Gratz* concerns whether applicants receive "individualized consideration." What exactly does this mean? Why is it important in this context?

4. What are the implications of *Grutter* and *Gratz* for admissions policies in private colleges and universities? For preferential treatment in hiring? In government contracts?

5. Find out what kinds of preferential treatment programs exist in your own school or town, and then argue either that these programs are constitutional or that they are not.

BURDEN OF PROOF

A remarkable feature of the line of cases from *Plessy* through *Brown* to *Bakke*, *Grutter*, and *Gratz* is the extent to which interpretations of the equal protection clause turn on the matter of *burden of proof.* Under the rational-relation test that governed *Plessy*, the state bears a light burden when it is asked to show that its actions do not conflict with the equal protection clause. In contrast, the strict-scrutiny test that governed *Brown*, that Powell applied in *Bakke*, and that the Court applies in *Grutter* and *Gratz* places a very heavy burden on the state to justify any use of a suspect classification or any interference with fundamental rights.

It may seem peculiar that an important legal decision can turn on such a technical and procedural matter as burden of proof. But the question of burden of proof often plays a decisive role in a legal decision, so it is worth knowing something about it.

The two basic questions concerning burden of proof are (1) *who* bears this burden and (2) how *heavy* is the burden. In our system of criminal justice, the rules governing burden of proof are fairly straightforward. The state has the burden of establishing the guilt of the accused. The defendant has no obligation to establish his or her innocence. That is what is meant by saying that the defendant is *innocent until proven guilty*. The burden of proof is also very heavy on the state in criminal procedures, for it must show *beyond a reasonable doubt* that the accused is guilty. If the prosecution shows only that it is more likely than not that the accused has committed a crime, then the jury should vote for acquittal.

Turning to civil law, there is no simple way to explain burden of proof. Very roughly, the plaintiff (the one who brings the suit) has an initial burden to establish a *prima facie* case—that is, a case that is strong enough that it needs to be rebutted—on behalf of his or her complaint. The burden then shifts to the respondent (the one against whom the suit is being brought) to answer these claims. The burden may then shift back and forth depending on the nature of the procedure. Provided that both sides have met their legally required burdens of proof, the case is then decided on the basis of the *preponderance of evidence;* that is, the judge or jury decides which side has made the stronger case.

Burden of proof is primarily a legal notion, but it is sometimes used, often loosely, outside the law. The notion of burden of proof is needed within the law because law cases are adversarial and the court has to come to a decision. Outside the law, people have a general burden to *have* good reasons for what they say. That is the second part of Grice's rule of Quality (described in Chapter 2). More specifically, people have a burden to be able to *present* some reasons when they make accusations or statements that run counter to common opinion.

The important thing to see is that you cannot establish the truth of something through an appeal to the burden of proof. The following argument is perfectly weird:

> There is life in other parts of the universe, because you can't prove otherwise.

Of course, no one can prove that there is *not* life elsewhere in the universe, but this has no tendency to show that there *is*. Attempts to prove the truth of something through appeals to burden of proof—often called arguments from ignorance—are another example of a fallacy of *relevance*. (See Chapter 15.)

Nonetheless, the importance of burden of proof in the law does give force to another kind of argument. In a criminal case, the following argument would be perfectly fine:

> The defendant ought to be found not guilty, because the prosecution has not proven beyond a reasonable doubt that she is guilty.

This argument would also be a fallacy of relevance if the burden of proof were not so important. But the relevant burden of proof makes this argument strong in a court of law. Who bears the burden of proof and how heavy the burden is determine which legal arguments work. Consider the following argument:

This law uses a suspect classification, and the state has not shown that it serves any compelling purpose, so the law is unconstitutional.

This argument is strong if the strict-scrutiny interpretation is accepted (assuming the premises are true). But this argument fails if a weaker burden of proof is required, as in the rational-relation test. When one chooses between interpretations of the equal protection clause and between different burdens of proof, one also chooses which arguments will have force in courts of law. This is another example of a general phenomenon that has been stressed throughout this book—that background assumptions can determine whether an argument is any good.

DISCUSSION QUESTION

Try to formulate general rules governing who has the burden of proof when people disagree. Be sure to consider a variety of areas, such as science, religion, philosophy, morality, and personal life.

19

MORAL REASONING

Many acts—such as lying to a friend—are not illegal, but they still seem immoral. Thus, even if such an act is legally *permitted, this does not show that it is* morally *permitted. That is a separate issue, and it is one that many people care deeply about, because they want to do what is moral and avoid doing what is immoral. But how can we show that an act is moral or immoral? One kind of argument will not do. We can often show that an act is illegal by citing official pronouncements by judges and legislators, such as precedents and statutes. In contrast, morality is not decided by any official. There are no authoritative books in which we can look up whether a certain act is immoral without asking whether that book is correct. This affects the nature of moral arguments and the criteria for evaluating them. We cannot appeal to any documents or officials to justify our moral beliefs, so moral beliefs must be based on something else. The kinds of arguments that can be used to justify moral beliefs will be the topic of this chapter.*

MORAL DISAGREEMENTS

People often disagree on moral questions. When these disagreements arise, it is often difficult—and sometimes impossible—to resolve them. At times these disagreements turn on questions of fact. If one person thinks that an action will have a particular consequence, and another thinks that it will not, they might well disagree on the moral worth of that action. For example, those who have defended the United States' decision to drop atomic bombs on Japan have often claimed that it was the only way to end the war quickly without creating a great number of casualties on both sides. Many critics of this decision have denied this factual claim.

Moral disagreements can also arise from disagreements about moral principles. To many people, it is immoral to have sex outside marriage. To others, it is immoral to interfere with such acts.

Despite such disagreements, it is surprising how much agreement there is on general moral principles. In our society, most people accept a great many moral principles as a matter of course. If a policy has no other consequence but to produce widespread misery, it is rejected out of hand. We share a conception of justice that includes, among other things, equality of opportunity and equality before the law. Most people also have a conception of human dignity: A human being is not a thing to be used and disposed of for personal advantage.

With all this agreement, how does moral disagreement arise at all? One answer is that in certain circumstances, our moral principles *conflict* with one another, and people are inclined to resolve these conflicts in different ways. People often agree on principles about welfare, justice, and human dignity, and yet, by weighing these principles differently or seeing the situation in a different light, they arrive at opposing moral conclusions.

Another kind of moral disagreement concerns the *range* or *scope* of moral principles. Even if everyone agrees that death and suffering are bad, they often disagree about *whose* death and suffering count. With few exceptions, it is thought to be wrong to inflict death and suffering on human beings. Most people have a similar attitude toward their pet dogs or cats. Some, however, go further and claim that it is also immoral to kill any animals—including cows, chickens, and fish—just to produce tasty food for humans.

The hardest problems combine issues of *range* with *conflicts of principles*. It is a disagreement of this complex kind that we will focus on in this chapter. The problem is abortion. The main issues are (1) whether fetuses lie within the range of a standard moral principle against killing, and (2) how to resolve conflicts between the principles that protect fetuses and other principles concerning, for example, human welfare and a woman's control over her body.

THE PROBLEM OF ABORTION

When faced with a moral problem, it often seems clear what the problem is, but this assumption can be mistaken. Sometimes a problem is formulated so vaguely that there is no way even to begin to solve it. People can argue for hours or even years without realizing that they are really talking about different things.

To clarify a moral problem, the first step is to specify precisely what is being judged—which action or kind of action is at issue. In the problem of abortion, the first step is to specify exactly what counts as an abortion. It is common to define abortion as the termination of a pregnancy. This includes spontaneous abortions or miscarriages, but these raise no moral problems because they are not the result of human action. Furthermore, the moral problem of abortion arises only when the death of the fetus is an expected consequence of terminating the pregnancy. To focus on these problematic cases, from now on we will take "abortion" to mean the intentional termination of a pregnancy with the expected consequence that the fetus dies as a result.

After the class of actions is picked out, we need to determine what is being asked about this class of actions—what kind of moral judgment is at stake. It is one thing to ask whether abortion is *morally wrong*, and another thing to ask whether abortion *should be illegal*. These are both moral questions (because the second asks what the law should be and not what it is), but they can be answered differently. It is not uncommon for people to claim that abortion is morally wrong but should not be made illegal, because it is a matter of personal, not public, morality. It is also important to distinguish the question of whether abortion is or is not morally *wrong* from the separate question of whether abortion is or is not *good*. People who deny that abortion is morally wrong do not hold that abortion is a positive good. They do not, for example, recommend that people get pregnant so that they can have abortions. So, from now on, we will focus on the issue of the moral wrongness of abortion.

THE "PRO-LIFE" ARGUMENT

We can begin to understand this problem if we reconstruct the main argument against abortion, using the method sketched in Chapter 5. Most opponents of abortion call themselves "pro-life" and base their position on an appeal to a moral principle involving the "right to life." Of course, most opponents of abortion are not opposed to killing weeds, germs, or even fish. What they have in mind, then, is probably a principle such as this:

It is always morally wrong to kill a human being.

This principle by itself does not rule out abortion. To reach this conclusion, we need further premises of the following kind:

Abortion involves killing a human fetus.

A human fetus is a human being.

With these premises, the anti-abortion argument will have the following form:

(1) It is always morally wrong to kill a human being.
(2) Abortion involves killing a human fetus.
(3) A human fetus is a human being.
∴ (4) Abortion is always morally wrong.

This argument is valid and reasonably charitable, so we have completed the first stage of reconstruction.

We next ask if the premises of this argument are true. The second premise is not controversial, given our definition of abortion; but the third premise raises many problems. Much of the debate concerning abortion turns on the question of whether a fetus is a human being. We will examine this question later on. For now, we will assume for the sake of argument that a fetus is a human being. That leaves only the first premise.

Some people—for example, strong pacifists—accept premise (1), but most people who adopt strong anti-abortion positions do not. This comes out in the following way. Many of those who oppose abortion are in favor of the death penalty for certain crimes. Therefore, they do not accept the general principle that it is always wrong to take a human life. What they need, then, is a principle that allows taking a human life in some instances but not in others. In an effort to achieve this, those who oppose abortion could reformulate the first premise in these words:

(1*) It is always morally wrong to kill an *innocent* human being.

Here the word "innocent" allows an exception for the death penalty being imposed on those who are found guilty of certain crimes. Of course, if we simply stick this premise into the previous argument, the result is invalid:

(1*) It is always morally wrong to kill an innocent human being.
(2) Abortion involves killing a human fetus.
(3) A human fetus is a human being.
∴(4) Abortion is always morally wrong.

To make it valid, we need to add a new premise, so that the whole argument looks like this:

(1*) It is always morally wrong to kill an innocent human being.
(2) Abortion involves killing a human fetus.
(3) A human fetus is a human being.
(4*) A human fetus is innocent.
∴(5) Abortion is always morally wrong.

Even stated this way, however, the first premise seems to admit of counterexamples. If someone's life is threatened by a madman, it is generally thought that the person has the right to use whatever means are necessary against the madman to prevent being killed. This may include killing the madman, even though the insane are usually thought to be morally innocent of their deeds. If so, the moral principle must be modified again, and then we get something like this:

(1**) It is always morally wrong to kill an innocent human being *except in self-defense.*

It is still possible to find difficulties with this principle that will lead some to add further modifications or clarifications. Children, for example, are often the innocent victims of bombing raids, yet the raids are often thought to be justified, because these deaths are not intended, even though they are foreseeable. At this point it is common to modify the principle again by including a reference to intentions. We shall not, however, pursue this complex line of reasoning here.[1]

We have arrived, then, at a principle that seems to make sense out of a position that is against abortion but in favor of the death penalty and self-defense. With these modifications included, the argument now looks like this:

(1**) It is always morally wrong to kill an innocent human being except in self-defense.
(2) Abortion involves killing a human fetus.
(3) A human fetus is a human being.
(4*) A human fetus is innocent.
∴(5) Abortion is always morally wrong.

Again, however, by making the premises more plausible, we created a new problem: The argument is invalid as it stands, since the qualification "except in self-defense" is missing from the conclusion. The proper conclusion of the argument should be:

(5*) Abortion is always morally wrong except in self-defense.

Rewriting the conclusion in this way has an important consequence: The argument no longer leads to a conclusion that abortion is *always* wrong. This qualified conclusion could permit abortion in those cases in which it is needed to defend the life of the pregnant woman who bears the fetus. In fact, this is the position that many people who are generally opposed to abortion adopt: Abortion is wrong except in those cases in which it is necessary to save the life of the mother. Although this does not lay down an absolute prohibition, it is still a strong anti-abortion position, since it would condone abortion in only a few exceptional cases.

"PRO-CHOICE" RESPONSES

We can now examine the way in which those who adopt the liberal or "pro-choice" position will respond to the conservative or "pro-life" argument as it has just been spelled out. The second premise should not be a subject for controversy, given our definition of abortion. Nor does it seem likely that the fourth premise will be attacked on the ground that the fetus is not innocent. How could a fetus be guilty of anything?

This leaves three strategies for the liberal: (1) Further modify the moral principle in the first premise to allow more exceptions. (2) Deny the third premise—that the fetus is a human being. (3) Oppose this conservative argument with a different argument based on a different moral principle.

FURTHER MODIFICATIONS. Even if it is agreed that abortion is justified when it saves the mother's life, we still need to ask whether this is the only exception or whether abortion is justified in other cases as well. Many pro-life conservatives admit that abortion is also justified when the pregnancy results from rape or incest. It is not easy to see how to modify the moral principle against killing to allow an exception in cases of rape and incest, so this exception is controversial. We will return to this issue later. But even if exceptions are made both for life-threatening pregnancies and for pregnancies due to rape and incest, the range of morally permissible abortions will still be very small.

Pro-choice liberals can, however, argue for a wider range of morally permissible abortions by extending the self-defense exception. It can be argued that a woman has a right to defend not only her life but also her physical and psychological well-being. Liberals can also argue that the exception of rape shows that abortion is allowed when the woman is not responsible for her pregnancy, and this might include cases in which the woman tried to prevent pregnancy by using contraceptives. Granting exceptions of this kind does not provide the basis for an absolute right to an abortion, but it does move things away from a "pro-life" position in the direction of a "pro-choice" position.

THE STATUS OF THE FETUS. So far we have assumed for the sake of argument that a human fetus is a human being. But pro-choice liberals often deny this premise. It may seem hard to deny that a human fetus is human. After all, it is not an aardvark. Liberals, however, claim that the real issue is not about biological species. The real issue is whether a human fetus is covered by the moral principle against killing, and whether it is protected to the same extent as an adult human. Anything that is protected to this extent is said to have a "right to life" and will be called a "person." The issue, then, is whether a human fetus is a person. If a fetus is a person, the burden of proof is on those who defend abortion to show why the moral principle against killing should be set aside or modified. If a fetus is *not* a person, this moral principle cannot show that there is anything wrong with abortion for any reason—with what is called "abortion on demand."

Any argument that a fetus either is a person or is not a person must proceed from some idea of which properties make something a person—which properties warrant the protection of moral principles. To argue that a fetus is not a person, pro-choice liberals need to find some feature that fetuses lack and that is necessary for personhood. In response, pro-life conservatives need to find some feature that fetuses have and that is sufficient for personhood.

Many conditions of personhood have been suggested. This list is not complete:

Genetic code (which determines biological species)

Ensoulment (when a soul enters the body)

Brain activity (first detected around eight weeks)

Sentience (capacity to feel pain and pleasure)

Viability (when the fetus can survive outside the womb)

Rationality (and other related capacities)

Pro-life conservatives usually emphasize tests such as genetic code (which is formed at conception) or ensoulment (which is supposed to occur at or shortly after conception). In contrast, pro-choice liberals usually employ tests such as viability (which is reached during the second trimester) or rationality (which comes sometime after birth, depending on what counts as rationality—ability to choose and plan, self-consciousness, and so on). Thus, the personhood of fetuses during the first trimester is usually asserted by conservatives and denied by liberals on this issue.

How can we determine whether a feature is necessary or sufficient for personhood? We can start by rejecting any test of personhood that leads to *implausible* results. Pro-life conservatives argue that rationality is not necessary for personhood, because, whatever rationality is, newborn babies and severely retarded adults are not rational, but it is still morally wrong to kill them. Other tests of personhood are ruled out because they do not seem *important* enough. Pro-choice liberals argue that a certain genetic code is not sufficient to make something a person, because there is no reason to favor one genetic code over another except that it later produces other important features, such as rationality. It is also common to rule out a test of personhood if we cannot *know* when the test is passed. For example, many people reject ensoulment as a criterion of personhood, because they see no way to tell when, if ever, a fetus has a soul. And tests of personhood are also often rejected if they depend on factors that are *extraneous*. Conservatives often argue that viability cannot be a test of personhood, because the point when a fetus can survive outside the womb depends on what technology happens to be available to doctors at the time.

In addition to features that fetuses have when they are fetuses, they also seem to have the *potential* to develop many more, including rationality. Opponents of abortion often use this premise to argue that fetuses are persons and have a right to life. The first problem with this argument is that it seems to assume that something has a right if it has the potential to come to have that right. But this is clearly too strong. A three-year-old child does not have the right to vote even though it has the potential to develop into someone who will have the right to vote. Furthermore, the notion of potential is not clear. If the fetus has the potential, why do the egg and sperm not have it? This does not refute potentiality as a test of personhood, but much more must be done to show what potentiality is and why it is sufficient to make something a person even before the potential is realized.

All these positions on personhood are controversial, and many people feel uncertain about which is the correct one. A major issue in many moral problems is how to deal with uncertainties such as this. One reaction is a position called "gradualism."[2] We have assumed so far that the fetus either has a full right to life or has no right to life at all, but rights sometimes come in varying strengths. Gradualists claim that a fetus slowly develops a right to life that is at first very weak. As pregnancy progresses, this right gets stronger, so it takes more to justify abortion. Late abortions still might be permitted, but only in extreme circumstances. This position is still vague, but it is attractive to some people who want to avoid placing too much emphasis on any single point in fetal development.

Uncertainty is also exploited in other ways. We already discussed slippery-slope arguments in Chapter 13. Another way to exploit uncertainty is to put the burden on the other side to produce a reason for drawing a line at some point. For example, Ronald Reagan said, "Anyone who doesn't feel sure whether we are talking about a second human life should clearly give life the benefit of the doubt." However, the same kind of argument is also available to defenders of abortion: Since we are not sure whether the fetus is a person, but we are sure that the pregnant woman has rights over her body, we should give the benefit of the doubt to the pregnant woman. We should always suspect that there is something wrong with an argument that can be used equally well in opposing directions.

CONFLICTING PRINCIPLES. A third kind of pro-choice response is to invoke another principle, which conflicts with the pro-life principle against killing. Pro-choice liberals often emphasize two such principles: one about the rights of the pregnant woman to control her own body and another about overall human welfare. We will focus for now on human welfare.

Defenders of abortion often argue that abortion can sometimes be justified in terms of the welfare of the woman who bears the fetus, or in terms of the welfare of the family into which it will be born, or even in terms of the welfare of the child itself (if it were to be born with a severe disability or into an impoverished situation). This argument, when spelled out, looks like this:

> (1) An action that best increases overall human welfare is not morally wrong.
> (2) Abortion is sometimes the best way of increasing overall human welfare.
> ∴ (3) Abortion is sometimes not morally wrong.

What are we to say about this argument? It seems valid in form, so we can turn to the premises themselves and ask whether they are acceptable. The first (and leading) premise of the argument is subject to two immediate criticisms. First, it is vague. Probably what a person who uses this kind of argument has in mind by speaking of human welfare is a certain level of material and psychological well-being. Of course, this is still vague, but it is clear enough to make the premise a target of the second, more important, criticism: Although maximizing human welfare may, in general, be a good thing, it is not the only relevant consideration in deciding how to act. For example, it might be true that our society would be much more prosperous on the whole if 10 percent of the population were designated slaves who would do all the menial work. Yet even if a society could be made generally happy in this way, most people would reject such a system on the grounds that it is unfair to the slave class. (See the discussion of counterexamples in Chapter 17.) For reasons of this kind, most people would modify premise (1) in the following way:

> (1*) An action that best increases human welfare is not morally wrong, provided that it is not unfair.

But if the first premise is modified in this way, then the entire argument must be restated to reflect this revision. It will now look like this:

(1*) An action that best increases human welfare is not morally wrong, provided that it is not unfair.

(2*) Abortion is sometimes an action that best increases human welfare.

∴(3*) Abortion is sometimes not morally wrong, provided that it is not unfair.

It should be obvious how opponents of abortion will reply to this argument. They will maintain that abortion almost always involves unfairness—namely, to the fetus—so abortion is still wrong in almost all cases, as the pro-life argument claimed. Once more we have encountered a standard situation: Given a strong premise (premise 1), it is possible to derive a particular conclusion, but this strong premise is subject to criticism and therefore must be modified. When the premise is modified as in 1*, it no longer supports the original conclusion that the person presenting the argument wishes to establish.

The argument does not stop here. A defender of abortion might reply in a number of ways. Some theory of fairness might be developed to argue that many abortions are not unfair to the fetus, because the fetus has no right to use the pregnant woman's body. (See the reading from Thomson, page 446.) The burden of the argument may shift to the question of whether or not a human fetus is a person and therefore possessed of a right to fair treatment. It might also be argued that questions of human welfare are sometimes more important than issues of fairness. During war and some emergencies, for example, members of a certain segment of the population are called on to risk their lives for the good of the whole in ways that might seem unfair to them.

When the argument is put on this new basis, the question becomes this: Are there circumstances in which matters of welfare become so urgent that the rights of the fetus (assuming the fetus has rights) are overridden? The obvious case in which this might happen is when the life of the bearer of the fetus is plainly threatened. For many conservatives on abortion, abortion is permitted in such cases. Some who hold a pro-choice position will maintain that severe psychological, financial, or personal losses to the pregnant woman may also take precedence over the life of the fetus. Furthermore, if not aborted, many fetuses would live in very deprived circumstances, and some would not develop very far or live very long, because they have deadly diseases, such as Tay-Sachs. How severe must these losses, deprivations, and diseases be? From our previous discussion of slippery-slope arguments in Chapter 13, we know that we should not expect any sharp lines here. Indeed, people will tend to be spread out in their opinions along a continuum ranging from a belief in complete prohibition to no prohibition.

ANALOGICAL REASONING IN ETHICS

Using the method for reconstructing arguments, we now have a fairly clear idea of the main options on the abortion issue. But understanding the structure of the debate—though essential for dealing with it intelligently—does not settle it. If the reasons on all sides are fully spelled out and disagreement remains, what is to be done?

At this stage, those who do not simply turn to abuse often appeal to *analogical arguments*. The point of an analogical argument is to reach a conclusion in a controversial case by comparing it to a similar situation in which it is clearer what is right or wrong. In fact, a great deal of ethical reasoning uses such analogies. We have already seen one simple analogy between an abortion to save the life of the mother and self-defense against an insane person. To get a better idea of how analogical reasoning works in ethics, we will concentrate on a more complex analogy, which raises the issue of whether abortion is morally permissible in cases of pregnancy due to rape.

A classic analogical argument is given by Judith Jarvis Thomson in "A Defense of Abortion" (reprinted page 446). Thomson grants for the sake of argument that a fetus is a person. Then she tells the following story:

> You wake up in the morning and find yourself back to back in bed with an unconscious violinist. A famous unconscious violinist. He has been found to have a fatal kidney ailment, and the Society of Music Lovers has canvassed all the available medical records and found that you alone have the right blood type to help. They have therefore kidnapped you, and last night the violinist's circulatory system was plugged into yours, so that your kidneys can be used to extract poisons from his blood as well as your own. The director of the hospital now tells you, "Look, we're sorry the Society of Music Lovers did this to you—we would never have permitted it if we had known. But still, they did it, and the violinist now is plugged into you. To unplug you would be to kill him. But never mind, it's only for nine months. By then he will have recovered from his ailment, and can safely be unplugged from you."

Thomson claims that it is not wrong for you to unplug yourself from the violinist in this situation, and most people seem to agree with this judgment. By analogy, abortion after rape is not wrong either, or so she says.

The basic assumption of this analogical argument is that we should not make different moral judgments in cases that do not differ. More positively:

> (1) If two actions are similar in all morally relevant respects, and if one of the acts is not morally wrong, then the other act is also not morally wrong.

Now we can apply this principle to Thomson's story:

> (2) It is not morally wrong for you to unplug the violinist in Thomson's example.
> (3) To unplug the violinist and to abort a pregnancy due to rape are similar in all morally relevant respects.

∴(4) It is not morally wrong for a woman to abort a pregnancy due to rape.

This argument is valid, so, following the normal procedure, we can ask whether the premises are true. The first premise seems plausible, and it is accepted in most moral theories. Most people also accept the second premise. Consequently, the discussion usually focuses on the third premise—on the similarities and differences between Thomson's story and abortion in a pregnancy due to rape.

First, consider these similarities between Thomson's story and abortion after rape:

1. Both the fetus and the violinist are on or near the Earth.
2. Kidnapping is immoral and illegal, like rape.
3. The hospital stay lasts nine months, like pregnancy.
4. The violinist is innocent and a human being, like the fetus (given our present assumption).
5. Unplugging the violinist is supposed to be killing, like an abortion.

Now here are some differences between the situations:

6. The fetus cannot play the violin, but the violinist can.
7. The person who is plugged into the violinist might not be female.
8. The person who is plugged into the violinist cannot leave the hospital room, but pregnant women can still move around, even if they have some difficulty.
9. Abortion involves killing, but unplugging the violinist is merely refusing to save.

It is obvious that some of the similarities and differences are *not* relevant. It does not matter whether killing occurs near the Earth. Killing is usually wrong, even on the starship *Enterprise*. It is also accepted that differences in musical talent and in sex cannot justify killing. The other similarities and differences on our list *do* seem important. They each concern harm and responsibility, matters that must be considered in reaching a moral judgment about these actions. The force of Thomson's analogical argument is that the very features that lead us to conclude that it would not be wrong to unplug the violinist are also found in the case of pregnancy due to rape. Furthermore, there are no relevant differences that are important enough to override the significance of these similarities. These considerations, if correct, provide a reason for treating the two cases in the same way. If we agree, as Thomson thinks we will, that it is not wrong to unplug the violinist, then we have a reason to conclude that abortion after rape is not wrong either.

Responses to Thomson's argument have largely turned on emphasizing the differences between the two situations. Many critics claim that Thomson's argument fails because abortion involves *killing*, whereas unplugging does not. If you stay plugged to the violinist, this will save the violinist, so to unplug yourself is to *fail to save* the violinist. But critics deny that to unplug yourself from the violinist is the same as to *kill* the violinist, or to take the violinist's life. They argue that there is a crucial difference between killing and failing to save, because a negative duty not to kill is much stronger than any positive duty to save another person's life.

To determine whether unplugging the violinist is more like acts of killing or more like other acts of refusing to save, we might consider more analogies. Thomson also introduces additional analogies that seem more like abortions in which the pregnancy is not due to rape. In the end, our sense of which features seem most important will determine how we evaluate all such analogical arguments. The analogies bring certain features to our attention, but we have to decide which features are important, and how important they are.

WEIGHING FACTORS

Our discussion has brought us to the following point: Disagreements concerning abortion in general cannot be reduced to a yes-no dispute. Most opponents of abortion acknowledge that abortion is permissible in some (though very few) cases. Most defenders of abortion admit that there are some (though not restrictively many) limitations on when abortion is permissible. Where people place themselves on this continuum does not depend on any simple acceptance of one argument over another, but instead on the weight they give certain factors. To what extent does a fetus have rights? The pro-life position we examined earlier grants the fetus a full (or close to full) right to life. The pro-choice position usually grants few or no rights to the fetus. In what areas do questions of welfare override certain individual rights? The conservative in this matter usually restricts this to those cases in which the very life of the mother is plainly threatened. As the position on abortion becomes more liberal, the more extensive becomes the range of cases in which the rights, if any, of the fetus are set aside in favor of the rights of the bearer of the fetus. Where a particular person strikes this balance is not only a function of basic moral beliefs but also a function of different weights assigned to them.

How can one deal with such bedrock disagreements? The first thing to see is that logic alone will not settle them. Starting from a certain conception of persons, it is possible to argue coherently for a pro-choice view on abortion; starting from another point of view, it is possible to argue coherently for a pro-life view on abortion. The next important thing to see is that it is possible to *understand* an opposing view—that is, get a genuine feeling for its inner workings—even if you disagree with it completely. Logical analysis might show that particular arguments are unsound or have unnoticed and unwanted implications. This might force clarification and modification. But the most important service that logical analysis can perform is to lay bare the fundamental principles that lie beneath surface disagreements. Analysis will sometimes show that these disagreements are fundamental and perhaps irreconcilable. Dealing with such irreconcilable differences in a humane way is one of the fundamental tasks of a society dedicated to freedom and a wide range of civil liberties.

1. Reconstruct and evaluate the arguments against abortion that are stated or suggested in the following short passages from Ronald Reagan, *Abortion and the Conscience of the Nation* (New York: Thomas Nelson, 1984). Be sure to specify the exact conclusion and spell out important suppressed premises. How would an opponent best respond to each argument?

   a. "We cannot diminish the value of one category of human life—the unborn—without diminishing the value of all human life" (18).

   b. "I have often said that when we talk about abortion, we are talking about two lives—the life of the mother and the life of the unborn child. Why else do we call a pregnant woman a mother?" (21).

   c. "I have also said that anyone who doesn't feel sure whether we are talking about a second human life should surely give life the benefit of the doubt. If you don't know whether a body is alive or dead, you would never bury it. I think this consideration itself should be enough for all of us to insist on protecting the unborn" (21).

   d. "Medical practice confirms at every step the correctness of these moral sensibilities. Modern medicine treats the unborn child as a patient. Medical pioneers have made great breakthroughs in treating the unborn—for genetic problems, vitamin deficiencies, irregular heart rhythms, and other medical conditions" (21–22).

   e. "I am convinced that Americans do not want to play God with the value of human life. It is not for us to decide who is worthy to live and who is not" (30).

   f. "Malcolm Muggeridge, the English writer, goes right to the heart of the matter: 'Either life is always and in all circumstances sacred, or intrinsically of no account; it is inconceivable that it should be in some cases the one and in some the other'" (34).

2. Reconstruct and evaluate the arguments in defense of abortion that are stated or suggested in the following short passages from Mary Gordon, "A Moral Choice," *Atlantic Monthly*, April 1990, 78–84. Be sure to specify the exact conclusion and spell out important suppressed premises. How would an opponent best respond to each argument?

   a. "Common sense, experience, and linguistic usage point clearly to the fact that we habitually consider, for example, a seven-week-old fetus to be different from a seven-month-old one. . . . We have different language for the experience of the involuntary expulsion of the fetus from the womb depending upon the point of gestation at which the expulsion occurs. If it occurs early in the pregnancy, we call it a miscarriage; if late, we call it a stillbirth" (80).

   b. "Our ritual and religious practices underscore the fact that we make distinctions among fetuses. If a woman took the bloody matter—indistinguishable from a heavy period—of an early miscarriage and insisted upon putting it in a tiny coffin and marking its grave, we would have serious concerns

   (continued)

about her mental health. By the same token, we would feel squeamish about flushing a seven-month-old fetus down the toilet—something we would normally do with an early miscarriage. There are no prayers for the matter of a miscarriage, nor do we feel there should be. Even a Catholic priest would not baptize the issue of an early miscarriage" (80).

c. "We must make decisions on abortion based on an understanding of how people really do live. We must be able to say that poverty is worse than not being poor, that having dignified and meaningful work is better than working in conditions of degradation, that raising a child one loves and has desired is better than raising a child in resentment and rage, that it is better for a twelve-year-old not to endure the trauma of having a child when she is herself a child" (81–82).

d. "It is possible for a woman to have a sexual life unriddled by fear only if she can be confident that she need not pay for a failure of technology or judgment (and who among us has never once been swept away in the heat of a sexual moment?) by taking upon herself the crushing burden of unchosen motherhood" (82).

e. "There are some undeniable bad consequences of a woman's being forced to bear a child against her will. First is the trauma of going through a pregnancy and giving birth to a child who is not desired, a trauma more long-lasting than that experienced by some (only some) women who experience an early abortion. The grief of giving up a child at its birth—and at nine months it is a child one has felt move inside one's body—is underestimated both by anti-choice partisans and by those for whom access to adoptable children is important. This grief should not be forced on any woman—or, indeed, encouraged by public policy" (84).

f. "We must be realistic about the impact on society of millions of unwanted children in an overpopulated world" (84).

g. "Making abortion illegal will result in the deaths of women, as it has always done. Is our historical memory so short that none of us remember aunts, sisters, friends, or mothers who were killed or rendered sterile by septic abortions? . . . Can anyone genuinely say that it would be a moral good for us as a society to return to those conditions?" (84).

A DEFENSE OF ABORTION[3, *]
***

by Judith Jarvis Thomson

. . . Opponents of abortion commonly spend most of their time establishing that the fetus is a person, and hardly any time explaining the step from there to the impermissibility of abortion. Perhaps they think the step too simple and obvious to require much comment. Or perhaps instead they are simply being

---

* I am very much indebted to James Thomson for discussion, criticism, and many helpful suggestions.

economical in argument. Many of those who defend abortion rely on the premise that the fetus is not a person, but only a bit of tissue that will become a person at birth; and why pay out more arguments than you have to? Whatever the explanation, I suggest that the step they take is neither easy nor obvious, that it calls for closer examination than it is commonly given, and that when we do give it this closer examination we shall feel inclined to reject it.

I propose, then, that we grant that the fetus is a person from the moment of conception. How does the argument go from here? Something like this, I take it. Every person has a right to life. So the fetus has a right to life. No doubt the mother has a right to decide what shall happen in and to her body; everyone would grant that. But surely a person's right to life is stronger and more stringent than the mother's right to decide what happens in and to her body, and so outweighs it. So the fetus may not be killed; an abortion may not be performed.

It sounds plausible. But now let me ask you to imagine this. You wake up in the morning and find yourself back to back in bed with an unconscious violinist. A famous unconscious violinist. He has been found to have a fatal kidney ailment, and the Society of Music Lovers has canvassed all the available medical records and found that you alone have the right blood type to help. They have therefore kidnapped you, and last night the violinist's circulatory system was plugged into yours, so that your kidneys can be used to extract poisons from his blood as well as your own. The director of the hospital now tells you, "Look, we're sorry the Society of Music Lovers did this to you—we would never have permitted it if we had known. But still, they did it, and the violinist now is plugged into you. To unplug you would be to kill him. But never mind, it's only for nine months. By then he will have recovered from his ailment, and can safely be unplugged from you." Is it morally incumbent on you to accede to this situation? No doubt it would be very nice of you if you did, a great kindness. But do you have to accede to it? What if it were not nine months, but nine years? Or longer still? What if the director of the hospital says, "Tough luck, I agree, but you've now got to stay in bed, with the violinist plugged into you, for the rest of your life. Because remember this. All persons have a right to life, and violinists are persons. Granted you have a right to decide what happens in and to your body, but a person's right to life outweighs your right to decide what happens in and to your body. So you cannot ever be unplugged from him." I imagine you would regard this as outrageous, which suggests that something really is wrong with that plausible-sounding argument I mentioned a moment ago.

In this case, of course, you were kidnapped; you didn't volunteer for the operation that plugged the violinist into your kidneys. Can those who oppose abortion on the ground I mentioned make an exception for a pregnancy due to rape? Certainly. They can say that persons have a right to life only if they didn't come into existence because of rape; or they can say that all persons have a right to life, but that some have less of a right to life than others, in particular, that those who came into existence because of rape have less. But these statements have a rather unpleasant sound. Surely the question of whether you have a right to life at all, or how much of it you have, shouldn't turn on the question of whether or not you are the product of a rape. And in fact the people who oppose abortion on the ground I mentioned do not make this distinction, and hence do not make an exception in the case of rape.

Nor do they make an exception for a case in which the mother had to spend the nine months of her pregnancy in bed. They would agree that would be a great pity, and hard on the mother; but all the same all persons have a right to life, the fetus is a person, and so on. I suspect, in fact, that they would not make an exception for a case in which, miraculously enough, the pregnancy went on for nine years or even the rest of the mother's life.

Some won't even make an exception for a case in which continuation of the pregnancy is likely to shorten the mother's life; they regard abortion as impermissible even to save the mother's life. Such cases are nowadays very rare, and many opponents of abortion do not accept this extreme view. All the same, it is a good place to begin: a number of points of interest come out in respect to it.

1. Let us call the view that abortion is impermissible even to save the mother's life "the extreme view." I want to suggest first that it does not issue from the argument I mentioned earlier without the addition of some fairly powerful premises. Suppose a woman has become pregnant, and now learns that she has a cardiac condition such that she will die if she carries the baby to term. What may be done for her? The fetus, being a person, has a right to life, but as the mother is a person too, so has she a right to life. Presumably they have an equal right to life. How is it supposed to come out that an abortion may not be performed? If mother and child have an equal right to life, shouldn't we perhaps flip a coin? Or should we add to the mother's right to life her right to decide what happens in and to her body which everybody seems to be ready to grant—the sum of her rights now outweighing the fetus's right to life?

The most familiar argument here is the following. We are told that performing the abortion would be directly killing* the child, whereas doing nothing would not be killing the mother, but only letting her die. Moreover, in killing the child, one would be killing an innocent person, for the child has committed no crime, and is not aiming at his mother's death. And then there are a variety of ways in which this might be continued. (1) But as directly killing an innocent person is always and absolutely impermissible, an abortion may not be performed. Or, (2) as directly killing an innocent person is murder, and murder is always and absolutely impermissible, an abortion may not be performed.** Or, (3) as one's duty to refrain from directly killing

---

* The term "direct" in the arguments I refer to is a technical one. Roughly what is meant by "direct killing" is either killing as an end by itself, or killing as a means to some end, for example, the end of saving someone else's life. See [the following] note for an example of its use.

** Cf. *Encyclical Letter of Pope Pius XI on Christian Marriage*, St. Paul Editions (Boston, n.d.), 32: "[H]owever much we may pity the mother whose health and even life is gravely imperiled in the performance of the duty allotted to her by nature, nevertheless what could ever be a sufficient reason for excusing in any way the direct murder of the innocent? This is precisely what we are dealing with here." Noonan (*The Morality of Abortion*, p. 43) reads this as follows: "What cause can ever avail to excuse in any way the direct killing of the innocent? For it is a question of that."

an innocent person is more stringent than one's duty to keep a person from dying, an abortion may not be performed. Or, (4) if one's only options are directly killing an innocent person or letting a person die, one must prefer letting the person die, and thus an abortion may not be performed.[*]

Some people seem to have thought that these are not further premises which must be added if the conclusion is to be reached; but that they follow from the very fact that an innocent person has a right to life.[**] But this seems to me to be a mistake, and perhaps the simplest way to show this is to bring out that while we must certainly grant that innocent persons have a right to life, the theses in (1) through (4) are all false. Take (2), for example. If directly killing an innocent person is murder, and thus is impermissible, then the mother's directly killing the innocent person inside her is murder, and thus is impermissible. But it cannot seriously be thought to be murder if the mother performs an abortion on herself to save her life. It cannot seriously be said that she *must* refrain, that she *must* sit passively by and wait for her death. Let us look again at the case of you and the violinist. There you are, in bed with the violinist, and the director of the hospital says to you, "It's all most distressing, and I deeply sympathize, but you see this is putting an additional strain on your kidneys, and you'll be dead within the month. But you *have* to stay where you are all the same. Because unplugging you would be directly killing an innocent violinist, and that's murder, and that's impermissible." If anything in the world is true, it is that you do not commit murder, you do not do what is impermissible, if you reach around to your back and unplug yourself from that violinist to save your life.

The main focus of attention in writings on abortion has been on what a third party may or may not do in answer to a request from a woman for an abortion. This is in a way understandable. Things being as they are, there isn't much a woman can safely do to abort herself. So the question asked is what a third party may do, and what the mother may do, if it is mentioned at all, is deduced, almost as an afterthought, from what it is concluded that third parties may do. But it seems to me that to treat the matter in this way is to refuse to grant to the mother that very status of person which is so firmly insisted on for the fetus. For we cannot simply read off what a person may do from what a third party may do. Suppose you find yourself trapped in a tiny house with a growing child. I mean a very tiny house, and a rapidly growing child—you are already up against the wall of the house and in a few

---

[*] The thesis in (4) is in an interesting way weaker than those in (1), (2), and (3): They rule out abortion even in cases in which both mother *and* child will die if the abortion is not performed. By contrast, one who held the view expressed in (4) could consistently say that one needn't prefer letting two persons die to killing one.

[**] Cf. the following passage from Pius XII, *Address to the Italian Catholic Society of Midwives:* "The baby in the maternal breast has the right to life immediately from God—Hence there is no man, no human authority, no science, no medical, eugenic, social, economic or moral 'indication' which can establish or grant a valid juridical ground for a direct deliberate disposition of an innocent human life, that is a disposition which looks to its destruction either as an end or as a means to another end perhaps in itself not illicit. The baby, still not born, is a man in the same degree and for the same reason as the mother" (quoted in Noonan, *The Morality of Abortion,* p. 45).

minutes you'll be crushed to death. The child on the other hand won't be crushed to death; if nothing is done to stop him from growing he'll be hurt, but in the end he'll simply burst open the house and walk out a free man. Now I could well understand it if a bystander were to say, "There's nothing we can do for you. We cannot choose between your life and his, we cannot be the ones to decide who is to live, we cannot intervene." But it cannot be concluded that you too can do nothing, that you cannot attack it to save your life. However innocent the child may be, you do not have to wait passively while it crushes you to death. Perhaps a pregnant woman is vaguely felt to have the status of house, to which we don't allow the right of self-defense. But if the woman houses the child, it should be remembered that she is a person who houses it.

I should perhaps stop to say explicitly that I am not claiming that people have a right to do anything whatever to save their lives. I think, rather, that there are drastic limits to the right of self-defense. If someone threatens you with death unless you torture someone else to death, I think you have not the right, even to save your life, to do so. But the case under consideration here is very different. In our case there are only two people involved, one whose life is threatened, and one who threatens it. Both are innocent: the one who is threatened is not threatened because of any fault, the one who threatens does not threaten because of any fault. For this reason we may feel that we bystanders cannot intervene. But the person threatened can.

In sum, a woman surely can defend her life against the threat to it posed by the unborn child, even if doing so involves its death. And this shows not merely that the theses in (1) through (4) are false; it shows also that the extreme view of abortion is false, and so we need not canvass any other possible ways of arriving at it from the argument I mentioned at the outset.

2. The extreme view could of course be weakened to say that while abortion is permissible to save the mother's life, it may not be performed by a third party, but only by the mother herself. But this cannot be right either. For what we have to keep in mind is that the mother and the unborn child are not like two tenants in a small house which has, by an unfortunate mistake, been rented to both: the mother *owns* the house. The fact that she does adds to the offensiveness of deducing that the mother can do nothing from the supposition that third parties can do nothing. But it does more than this: it casts a bright light on the supposition that third parties can do nothing. Certainly it lets us see that a third party who says "I cannot choose between you" is fooling himself if he thinks this is impartiality. If Jones has found and fastened on a certain coat, which he needs to keep him from freezing, but which Smith also needs to keep him from freezing, then it is not impartiality that says "I cannot choose between you" when Smith owns the coat. Women have said again and again "This is *my* body!" and they have reason to feel angry, reason to feel that it has been like shouting into the wind. Smith, after all, is hardly likely to bless us if we say to him, "Of course it's your coat; anybody would grant that it is. But no one may choose between you and Jones who is to have it."

We should really ask what it is that says "no one may choose" in the face of the fact that the body that houses the child is the mother's body. It may be simply a failure to appreciate this fact. But it may be something more interesting, namely the sense that one has a right to refuse to lay hands on people, even where it would be just and fair to do so, even where justice seems to require that somebody do so. Thus justice might call for somebody to get Smith's coat back from Jones, and yet you have a right to refuse to be the one to lay hands on Jones, a right to refuse to do physical violence to him. This, I think, must be granted. But then what should be said is not "no one may choose," but only "I cannot choose," and indeed not even this, but "I will not act," leaving it open that somebody else can or should, and in particular that anyone in a position of authority, with the job of securing people's rights, both can and should. So this is no difficulty. I have not been arguing that any given third party must accede to the mother's request that he perform an abortion to save her life, but only that he may.

I suppose that in some views of human life the mother's body is only on loan to her, the loan not being one which gives her any prior claim to it. One who held this view might well think it impartiality to say "I cannot choose." But I shall simply ignore this possibility. My own view is that if a human being has any just, prior claim to anything at all, he has a just, prior claim to his own body. And perhaps this needn't be argued for here anyway, since, as I mentioned, the arguments against abortion we are looking at do grant that the woman has a right to decide what happens in and to her body.

But although they do grant it, I have tried to show that they do not take seriously what is done in granting it. I suggest the same thing will reappear even more clearly when we turn away from cases in which the mother's life is at stake, and attend, as I propose we now do, to the vastly more common cases in which a woman wants an abortion for some less weighty reason than preserving her own life.

3. Where the mother's life is not at stake, the argument I mentioned at the outset seems to have a much stronger pull. "Everyone has a right to life, so the unborn person has a right to life." And isn't the child's right to life weightier than anything other than the mother's own right to life, which she might put forward as grounds for an abortion?

This argument treats the right to life as if it were unproblematic. It is not, and this seems to me to be precisely the source of the mistake.

For we should now, at long last, ask what it comes to, to have a right to life. In some views having a right to life includes having a right to be given at least the bare minimum one needs for continued life. But suppose that what in fact is the bare minimum a man needs for continued life is something he has no right at all to be given? If I am sick unto death, and the only thing that will save my life is the touch of Henry Fonda's cool hand on my fevered brow, then all the same, I have no right to be given the touch of Henry Fonda's cool hand on my fevered brow. It would be frightfully nice of him to fly in from the West Coast to provide it. It would be less nice, though no doubt well meant, if my friends flew out to the West Coast and carried Henry Fonda back with them. But I have no right at all against anybody that he should do this for me. Or again, to return to the story I told earlier, the fact that for continued life that violinist needs the continued use of your kidneys does not establish that he has a right to be given the continued use of your kidneys. He certainly has no right against *you* that you should give him continued use of your kidneys. For nobody has any right to use your kidneys unless you give him such a right; and nobody has the right against you that you shall give him this right—if you do allow him to go on using your kidneys, this is a kindness on your part, and not something he can claim from you as his due. Nor has he any right against anybody else that *they* should give him continued use of your kidneys. Certainly he had no right against the Society of Music Lovers that they should plug him into you in the first place. And if you now start to unplug yourself, having learned that you will otherwise have to spend nine years in bed with him, there is nobody in the world who must try to prevent you, in order to see to it that he is given something he has a right to be given.

Some people are rather stricter about the right to life. In their view, it does not include the right to be given anything, but amounts to, and only to, the right not to be killed by anybody. But here a related difficulty arises. If everybody is to refrain from killing that violinist, then everybody must refrain from doing a great many different sorts of things. Everybody must refrain from slitting his throat, everybody must refrain from shooting him—and everybody must refrain from unplugging you from him. But does he have a right against everybody that they shall refrain from unplugging you from him? To refrain from doing this is to allow him to continue to use your kidneys. It could be argued that he has a right against us that we should allow him to continue to use your kidneys. That is, while he had no right against us that we should give him the use of your kidneys, it might be argued that he anyway has a right against us that we shall not now intervene and deprive him of the use of your kidneys. I shall come back to third-party interventions later. But certainly the violinist has no right against you that *you* shall allow him to continue to use your kidneys. As I said, if you do allow him to use them, it is a kindness on your part, and not something you owe him.

The difficulty I point to here is not peculiar to the right to life. It reappears in connection with all the other natural rights; and it is something which an adequate account of rights must deal with. For present purposes it is enough just to draw attention to it. But I would stress that I am not arguing that people do not have a right to life—quite to the contrary, it seems to me that the primary control we must place on the acceptability of an account of rights is that it should turn out in that account to be a truth that all persons have a right to life. I am arguing only that having a right to life does not guarantee having either a right to be given the use of or a right to be allowed continued use of another person's body—even if one needs it for life itself. So the right to life will not serve the opponents of abortion in the very simple and clear way in which they seem to have thought it would.

4. There is another way to bring out the difficulty. In the most ordinary sort of case, to deprive someone of what he has a right to is to treat him unjustly. Suppose a boy and his small brother are jointly given a box of chocolates for Christmas. If the older boy takes the box and refuses to give his brother any of the chocolates, he is unjust to him, for the brother has been given a right to half of them. But suppose that, having learned that otherwise it means nine years in bed with that violinist, you unplug yourself from him. You surely are not being unjust to him, for you gave him no right to use your kidneys, and no one else can have given him any such right. But we have to notice that in unplugging yourself, you are killing him; and violinists, like everybody else, have a right to life, and thus in the view we were considering just now, the right not to be killed. So here you do what he supposedly has a right you shall not do, but you do not act unjustly to him in doing it.

The emendation which may be made at this point is this: the right to life consists not in the right not to be killed, but rather in the right not to be killed unjustly. This runs a risk of circularity, but never mind: it would enable us to square the fact that the violinist has a right to life with the fact that you do not act unjustly toward him in unplugging yourself, thereby killing him. For if you do not kill him unjustly, you do not violate his right to life, and so it is no wonder you do him no injustice.

But if this emendation is accepted, the gap in the argument against abortion stares us plainly in the face: it is by no means enough to show that the fetus is a person, and to remind us that all persons have a right to life—we need to be shown also that killing the fetus violates its right to life, i.e., that abortion is unjust killing. And is it?

I suppose we may take it as a datum that in a case of pregnancy due to rape the mother has not given the unborn person a right to the use of her body for food and shelter. Indeed, in what pregnancy could it be supposed that the mother has given the unborn person such a right? It is not as if there were unborn persons drifting about the world, to whom a woman who wants a child says, "I invite you in."

But it might be argued that there are other ways one can have acquired a right to the use of another person's body than by having been invited to use it by that person. Suppose a woman voluntarily indulges in intercourse, knowing of the chance it will issue in pregnancy, and then she does become pregnant; is she not in part responsible for the presence, in fact the very existence of the unborn person inside her? No doubt she did not invite it in. But doesn't her partial responsibility for its being there itself give it a right to the use of her body?* If so, then her aborting it would be more like the boy's taking away the chocolates, and less like your unplugging yourself

---

* The need for a discussion of this argument was brought home to me by members of the Society for Ethical and Legal Philosophy, to whom this paper was originally presented.

from the violinist—doing so would be depriving it of what it does have a right to, and thus would be doing it an injustice.

And then, too, it might be asked whether or not she can kill it even to save her own life: If she voluntarily called it into existence, how can she now kill it, even in self-defense?

The first thing to be said about this is that it is something new. Opponents of abortion have been so concerned to make out the independence of the fetus, in order to establish that it has a right to life, just as the mother does, that they have tended to overlook the possible support they might gain from making out that the fetus is *dependent* on the mother, in order to establish that she has a special kind of responsibility for it, a responsibility that gives it rights against her which are not possessed by an independent person— such as an ailing violinist who is a stranger to her.

On the other hand, this argument would give the unborn person a right to its mother's body only if her pregnancy resulted from a voluntary act, undertaken in full knowledge of the chance a pregnancy might result from it. It would leave out entirely the unborn person whose existence is due to rape. Pending the availability of some further argument, then, we would be left with the conclusion that unborn persons whose existence is due to rape have no right to the use of their mothers' bodies, and thus that aborting them is not depriving them of anything they have a right to and hence is not unjust killing.

And we should also notice that it is not at all plain that this argument really does go even as far as it purports to. For there are cases and cases, and the details make a difference. If the room is stuffy, and I therefore open a window to air it, and a burglar climbs in, it would be absurd to say, "Ah, now he can stay, she's given him a right to the use of her house—for she is partially responsible for his presence there, having voluntarily done what enabled him to get in, in full knowledge that there are such things as burglars, and that burglars burgle." It would be still more absurd to say this if I had had bars installed outside my windows, precisely to prevent burglars from getting in, and a burglar got in only because of a defect in the bars. It remains equally absurd if we imagine it is not a burglar who climbs in, but an innocent person who blunders or falls in. Again, suppose it were like this: people-seeds drift about in the air like pollen, and if you open your windows, one may drift in and take root in your carpets or upholstery. You don't want children, so you fix up your windows with fine mesh screens, the very best you can buy. As can happen, however, and on very, very rare occasions does happen, one of the screens is defective; and a seed drifts in and takes root. Does the person-plant who now develops have a right to the use of your house? Surely not—despite the fact that you voluntarily opened your windows, you knowingly kept carpets and upholstered furniture, and you knew that screens were sometimes defective. Someone may argue that you are responsible for its rooting, that it does have a right to your house, because after all you *could* have lived out your life with bare floors and furniture, or with sealed windows and doors. But this won't do—for by the same token anyone can avoid a pregnancy due to rape by having a hysterectomy, or anyway by never leaving home without a (reliable!) army.

It seems to me that the argument we are looking at can establish at most that there are *some* cases in which the unborn person has a right to the use of its mother's body, and therefore *some* cases in which abortion is unjust killing. There is room for much discussion and argument as to precisely which, if any. But I think we should side-step this issue and leave it open, for at any rate the argument certainly does not establish that all abortion is unjust killing.

5. There is room for yet another argument here, however. We surely must all grant that there may be cases in which it would be morally indecent to detach a person from your body at the cost of his life. Suppose you learn that what the violinist needs is not nine years of your life, but only one hour: all you need do to save his life is to spend one hour in that bed with him. Suppose also that letting him use your kidneys for that one hour would not affect your health in the slightest. Admittedly you were kidnapped. Admittedly you did not give anyone permission to plug him into you. Nevertheless it seems to me plain you *ought* to allow him to use your kidneys for that hour—it would be indecent to refuse.

Again, suppose pregnancy lasted only an hour, and constituted no threat to life or health. And suppose that a woman becomes pregnant as a result of rape. Admittedly she did not voluntarily do anything to bring about the existence of a child. Admittedly she did nothing at all which would give the unborn person a right to the use of her body. All the same it might well be said, as in the newly emended violinist story, that she *ought* to allow it to remain for that hour—that it would be indecent of her to refuse. . . .

So my own view is that even though you ought to let the violinist use your kidneys for the one hour he needs, we should not conclude that he has a right to do so—we should say that if you refuse, you are, like [a] boy who owns all the chocolates and will give none away, self-centered and callous, indecent in fact, but not unjust. And similarly, that even supposing a case in which a woman pregnant due to rape ought to allow the unborn person to use her body for the hour he needs, we should not conclude that he has a right to do so; we should conclude that she is self-centered, callous, indecent, but not unjust, if she refuses. The complaints are no less grave; they are just different. However, there is no need to insist on this point. If anyone does wish to deduce "he has a right" from "you ought," then all the same he must surely grant that there are cases in which it is not morally required of you that you allow that violinist to use your kidneys, and in which he does not have a right to use them, and in which you do not do him an injustice if you refuse. And so also for mother and unborn child. Except in such cases as the unborn person has a right to demand it— and we were leaving open the possibility that there may be such cases— nobody is morally *required* to make large sacrifices, of health, of all other interests and concerns, of all other duties and commitments, for nine years, or even for nine months, in order to keep another person alive.

6. We have in fact to distinguish between two kinds of Samaritan: the Good Samaritan and what we might call the Minimally Decent Samaritan. The story of the Good Samaritan, you will remember, goes like this:

> A certain man went down from Jerusalem to Jericho, and fell among thieves, which stripped him of his raiment, and wounded him, and departed, leaving him half dead.
>
> And by chance there came down a certain priest that way; and when he saw him, he passed by on the other side.
>
> And likewise a Levite, when he was at the place, came and looked on him, and passed by on the other side.
>
> But a certain Samaritan, as he journeyed, came where he was and when he saw him he had compassion on him.
>
> And went to him, and bound up his wounds, pouring in oil and wine, and set him on his own beast, and brought him to an inn, and took care of him.
>
> And on the morrow, when he departed, he took out two pence, and gave them to the host, and said unto him, "Take care of him: and whatsoever thou spendest more, when I come again, I will repay thee." (Luke 10:30–35)

The Good Samaritan went out of his way, at some cost to himself, to help one in need of it. We are not told what the options were, that is, whether or not the priest and the Levite could have helped by doing less than the Good Samaritan did, but assuming they could have, then the fact they did nothing at all shows they were not even Minimally Decent Samaritans, not because they were not Samaritans, but because they were not even minimally decent.

These things are a matter of degree, of course, but there is a difference, and it comes out perhaps most clearly in the story of Kitty Genovese, who, as you will remember, was murdered while thirty-eight people watched or listened, and did nothing at all to help her. A Good Samaritan would have rushed out to give direct assistance against the murderer. Or perhaps we had better allow that it would have been a Splendid Samaritan who did this, on the ground that it would have involved a risk of death for himself. But the thirty-eight not only did not do this, they did not even trouble to pick up a phone to call the police. Minimally Decent Samaritanism would call for doing at least that, and their not having done it was monstrous.

After telling the story of the Good Samaritan, Jesus said "Go, and do thou likewise." Perhaps he meant that we are morally required to act as the Good Samaritan did. Perhaps he was urging people to do more than is morally required of them. At all events it seems plain that it was not morally required of any of the thirty-eight that he rush out to give direct assistance at the risk of his own life, and that it is not morally required of anyone that he give long stretches of his life—nine years or nine months—to sustaining the life of a person who has no special right (we were leaving open the possibility of this) to demand it.

Indeed, with one rather striking class of exceptions, no one in any country in the world is *legally* required to do anywhere near as much as this for anyone else. The class of exceptions is obvious. My main concern here is not the state of the law in respect to abortion, but it is worth drawing attention to the fact that in no state in this country is any man compelled by law to be even a Minimally Decent Samaritan to any person; there is no law under which charges could be brought against the thirty-eight who stood by while Kitty Genovese died. By contrast, in most states in this country women are compelled by law to be not merely Minimally Decent Samaritans, but Good Samaritans to unborn persons inside them. This doesn't by itself settle anything one way or the other, because it may well be argued that there should be laws in this country—as there are in many European countries—compelling at least Minimally Decent Samaritanism.[*] But it does show that there is a gross injustice in the existing state of the law. And it shows also that the groups currently working against liberalization of abortion laws, in fact working toward having it declared unconstitutional for a state to permit abortion, had better start working for the adoption of Good Samaritan laws generally, or earn the charge that they are acting in bad faith.

I should think, myself, that Minimally Decent Samaritan laws would be one thing, Good Samaritan laws quite another, and in fact highly improper. But we are not here concerned with the law. What we should ask is not whether anybody should be compelled by law to be a Good Samaritan, but whether we must accede to a situation in which somebody is being compelled—by nature, perhaps—to be a Good Samaritan. We have, in other words, to look now at third-party interventions. I have been arguing that no person is morally required to make large sacrifices to sustain the life of another who has no right to demand them, and this even where the sacrifices do not include life itself; we are not morally required to be Good Samaritans or anyway Very Good Samaritans to one another. But what if a man cannot extricate himself from such a situation? What if he appeals to us to extricate him? It seems to me plain that there are cases in which we can, cases in which a Good Samaritan would extricate him. There you are, you were kidnapped, and nine years in bed with that violinist lie ahead of you. You have your own life to lead. You are sorry, but you simply cannot see giving up so much of your life to the sustaining of his. You cannot extricate yourself, and ask us to do so. I should have thought that—in light of his having no right to the use of your body—it was obvious that we do not have to accede to your being forced to give up so much. We can do what you ask. There is no injustice to the violinist in our doing so.

7. Following the lead of the opponents of abortion, I have throughout been speaking of the fetus merely as a person, and what I have been asking is whether or not the argument we began with, which proceeds only from the fetus being a person, really does establish its conclusion. I have argued that it does not.

But of course there are arguments and arguments, and it may be said that I have simply fastened on the wrong one. It may be said that what is important

---

[*] For a discussion of the difficulties involved, and a survey of the European experience with such laws, see *The Good Samaritan and the Law*, ed. James M. Ratcliffe (Garden City, NY: Doubleday Anchor, 1966).

is not merely the fact that the fetus is a person, but that it is a person for whom the woman has a special kind of responsibility issuing from the fact that she is its mother. And it might be argued that all my analogies are therefore irrelevant—for you do not have that special kind of responsibility for that violinist, Henry Fonda does not have that special kind of responsibility for me. And our attention might be drawn to the fact that men and women both *are* compelled by law to provide support for their children.

I have in effect dealt (briefly) with this argument in section 4 above; but a (still briefer) recapitulation now may be in order. Surely we do not have any such "special responsibility" for a person unless we have assumed it, explicitly or implicitly. If a set of parents do not try to prevent pregnancy, do not obtain an abortion, and then at the time of birth of the child do not put it out for adoption, but rather take it home with them, then they have assumed responsibility for it, they have given it rights, and they cannot *now* withdraw support from it at the cost of its life because they now find it difficult to go on providing for it. But if they have taken all reasonable precautions against having a child, they do not simply by virtue of their biological relationship to the child who comes into existence have a special responsibility for it. They may wish to assume responsibility for it, or they may not wish to. And I am suggesting that if assuming responsibility for it would require large sacrifices, then they may refuse. A Good Samaritan would not refuse—or anyway, a Splendid Samaritan, if the sacrifices that had to be made were enormous. But then so would a Good Samaritan assume responsibility for that violinist; so would Henry Fonda, if he is a Good Samaritan, fly in from the West Coast and assume responsibility for me.

8. My argument will be found unsatisfactory on two counts by many of those who want to regard abortion as morally permissible. First, while I do argue that abortion is not impermissible, I do not argue that it is always permissible. There may well be cases in which carrying the child to term requires only Minimally Decent Samaritanism of the mother, and this is a standard we must not fall below. I am inclined to think it a merit of my account precisely that it does *not* give a general yes or a general no. It allows for and supports our sense that, for example, a sick and desperately frightened fourteen-year-old schoolgirl, pregnant due to rape, may *of course* choose abortion, and that any law which rules this out is an insane law. And it also allows for and supports our sense that in other cases resort to abortion is even positively indecent. It would be indecent in the woman to request an abortion, and indecent in a doctor to perform it, if she is in her seventh month, and wants the abortion just to avoid the nuisance of postponing a trip abroad. The very fact that the arguments I have been drawing attention to treat all cases of abortion, or even all cases of abortion in which the mother's life is not at stake, as morally on a par ought to have made them suspect at the outset.

Secondly, while I am arguing for the permissibility of abortion in some cases, I am not arguing for the right to secure the death of the unborn child. It is easy to confuse these two things in that up to a certain point in the life of the fetus it is not able to survive outside the mother's body; hence removing it from her body guarantees its death. But they are importantly different. I have argued that you are not morally required to spend nine months in bed, sustaining the life of that violinist; but to say this is by no means to say that if, when you unplug yourself, there is a miracle and he survives, you then have a right to turn around and slit his throat. You may detach yourself even if this costs him his life; you have no right to be guaranteed his death by some other means, if unplugging yourself does not kill him. There are some people who will feel dissatisfied by this feature of my argument. A woman may be utterly devastated by the thought of a child, a bit of herself, put out for adoption and never seen or heard of again. She may therefore want not merely that the child be detached from her, but more, that it die. Some opponents of abortion are inclined to regard this as beneath contempt—thereby showing insensitivity to what is surely a powerful source of despair. All the same, I agree that the desire for the child's death is not one which anybody may gratify, should it turn out to be possible to detach the child alive.

At this place, however, it should be remembered that we have only been pretending throughout that the fetus is a human being from the moment of conception. A very early abortion is surely not the killing of a person, and so is not dealt with by anything I have said here.

DISCUSSION QUESTIONS

1. Exactly what is Thomson trying to show with her examples of the burglar and the people-seeds? Reconstruct and evaluate these arguments from analogy. Remember to say which similarities and differences are important, and why.

2. Thomson distinguishes what is morally indecent from what is morally wrong. Explain her distinction. Are any acts morally indecent but not morally wrong? If so, give examples. If not, why not? Does Thomson deny that abortion is morally indecent? If so, does she argue for this denial?

AN ARGUMENT THAT ABORTION IS WRONG[4]

by Don Marquis

The purpose of this essay is to set out an argument for the claim that abortion, except perhaps in rare instances, is seriously wrong. One reason for these exceptions is to eliminate from consideration cases whose ethical analysis should be controversial and detailed for clear-headed opponents of abortion. Such cases include abortion after rape and abortion during the first fourteen days after conception when there is an argument that the fetus is not definitely an individual. Another reason for making these exceptions is to allow for those cases in which the permissibility of abortion is compatible with the argument of this essay. Such cases include abortion when continuation of a pregnancy endangers a woman's life and abortion when the fetus is anencephalic. When I speak of the wrongness of abortion in this essay, a reader should presume the above qualifications. I mean by an abortion an action intended to bring about the death of a fetus for the sake of the woman who carries it. (Thus, as is standard on the literature on this subject, I eliminate spontaneous abortions from consideration.) I mean by a fetus a developing human being from the time of conception to the time of birth. (Thus, as is standard, I call embryos and zygotes, fetuses.)

The argument of this essay will establish that abortion is wrong for the same reason as killing a reader of this essay is wrong. I shall just assume, rather than establish, that killing you is seriously wrong. I shall make no attempt to offer a complete ethics of killing. Finally, I shall make no attempt to resolve some very fundamental and difficult general philosophical issues into which this analysis of the ethics of abortion might lead.

WHY THE DEBATE OVER ABORTION SEEMS INTRACTABLE

Symmetries that emerge from the analysis of the major arguments on either side of the abortion debate may explain why the abortion debate seems intractable. Consider the following standard anti-abortion argument: Fetuses are both human and alive. Humans have the right to life. Therefore, fetuses have the right to life. Of course, women have the right to control their own bodies, but the right to life overrides the right of a woman to control her own body. Therefore, abortion is wrong.

Thomson's View

Judith Thomson (1971) has argued that even if one grants (for the sake of argument only) that fetuses have the right to life, this argument fails. Thomson invites you to imagine that you have been connected while sleeping, bloodstream to bloodstream, to a famous violinist. The violinist, who suffers from a rare blood disease, will die if disconnected. Thomson argues that you surely have the right to disconnect yourself. She appeals to our intuition that having to lie in bed with a violinist for an indefinite period is too much for morality to demand. She supports this claim by noting that the body being used is your body, not the violinist's body. She distinguishes the right to life, which the violinist clearly has, from the right to use someone else's body when necessary to preserve one's life, which it is not at all obvious the violinist has. Because the case of pregnancy is like the case of the violinist, one is no more morally obligated to remain attached to a fetus than to remain attached to the violinist.

It is widely conceded that one can generate from Thomson's vivid case the conclusion that abortion is morally permissible when a pregnancy is due to rape (Warren, 1973, p. 49; Steinbock, 1992, p. 79). But this is hardly a general right to abortion. Do Thomson's more general theses generate a more general right to an abortion? Thomson draws our attention to the fact that in a pregnancy, although a fetus uses a woman's body as a life-support system, a pregnant woman does not use a fetus's body as a life-support system. However, an opponent of abortion might draw our attention to the fact that in an abortion the life that is lost is the fetus's, not the woman's. This symmetry seems to leave us with a stand-off.

Thomson points out that a fetus's right to life does not entail its right to use someone else's body to preserve its life. However, an opponent of abortion might point out that a woman's right to use her own body does not entail her right to end someone else's life in order to do what she wants with her body. In reply, one might argue that a pregnant woman's right to control her own body doesn't come to much if it is wrong for her to take any action that ends the life of the fetus within her. However, an opponent of abortion can argue that the fetus's right to life doesn't come to much if a pregnant woman can end it when she chooses. The consequence of all of these symmetries seems to be a stand-off. But if we have the stand-off, then one might argue that we are left with a conflict of rights: a fetal right to life *versus* the right of a woman to control her own body. One might then argue that the right to life seems to be a stronger right than the right to control one's own body in the case of abortion because the loss of one's life is a greater loss than the loss of the right to control one's own body in one respect for nine months. Therefore, the right to life overrides the right to control one's own body and abortion is wrong. Considerations like these have suggested to both opponents of abortion and supporters of choice that a Thomsonian strategy for defending a general right to abortion will not succeed (Tooley, 1972; Warren, 1973; Steinbock, 1992). In fairness, one must note that Thomson did not intend her strategy to generate a general moral permissibility of abortion.

Do Fetuses have the Right to Life?

The above considerations suggest that whether abortion is morally permissible boils down to the question of whether fetuses have the right to life. An argument that fetuses either have or lack the right to life must be based upon some general criterion for having or lacking the right to life. Opponents of abortion, on the one hand, look around for the broadest possible plausible criterion, so that fetuses will fall under it. This explains why classic arguments against abortion appeal to the criterion of being human (Noonan, 1970; Beckwith, 1993). This criterion appears plausible: The claim that all humans, whatever their race, gender, religion or age, have the right to life seems evident enough. In addition, because the fetuses we are concerned with do not, after all, belong to another species, they are clearly human. Thus, the syllogism that generates the conclusion that fetuses have the right to life is apparently sound.

On the other hand, those who believe abortion is morally permissible wish to find a narrow, but plausible, criterion for possession of the right to life so that fetuses will fall outside of it. This explains, in part, why the standard pro-choice arguments in the philosophical literature appeal to the criterion of being a person (Feinberg, 1986; Tooley, 1972; Warren, 1973; Benn, 1973; Engelhardt, 1986). This criterion appears plausible: The claim that only persons have the right to life seems evident enough. Furthermore, because fetuses neither are rational nor possess the capacity to communicate in complex ways nor possess a concept of self that continues through time, no fetus is a person. Thus, the syllogism needed to generate the conclusion that no fetus possesses the right to life is apparently sound. Given that no fetus possesses the right to life, a woman's right to control her own body easily generates the general right to abortion. The existence of two apparently defensible syllogisms which support contrary conclusions helps to explain why partisans on both sides of the abortion dispute often regard their opponents as either morally depraved or mentally deficient.

Which syllogism should we reject? The anti-abortion syllogism is usually attacked by attacking its major premise: the claim that whatever is biologically human has the right to life. This premise is subject to scope problems because the class of the biologically human includes too much: human cancer-cell cultures are biologically human, but they do not have the right to life. Moreover, this premise also is subject to moral-relevance problems: the connection between the biological and the moral is merely assumed. It is hard to think of a good *argument* for such a connection. If one wishes to consider the category of "human" a moral category, as some people find it plausible to do in other contexts, then one is left with no way of showing that the fetus is fully human without begging the question. Thus, the classic anti-abortion argument appears subject to fatal difficulties.

These difficulties with the classic anti-abortion argument are well known and thought by many to be conclusive. The symmetrical difficulties with the classic pro-choice syllogism are not as well recognized. The pro-choice syllogism can be attacked by attacking its major premise: Only persons have the right to life. This premise is subject to scope problems because the class of persons includes too little: infants, the severely retarded, and some of the mentally ill seem to fall outside the class of persons as the supporter of choice understands the concept. The premise is also subject to moral-relevance problems: Being a person is understood by the pro-choicer as having certain psychological attributes. If the pro-choicer questions the connection between the biological and the moral, the opponent of abortion can question the connection between the psychological and the moral. If one wishes to consider "person" a moral category, as is often done, then one is left with no way of showing that the fetus is not a person without begging the question.

Pro-choicers appear to have resources for dealing with their difficulties that opponents of abortion lack. Consider their moral-relevance problem. A pro-choicer might argue that morality rests on contractual foundations and that only those who have the psychological attributes of persons are capable of entering into the moral contract and, as a consequence, being a member of the moral community. (This is essentially Engelhardt's [1986] view.) The great advantage of this contractarian approach to morality is that it seems far more plausible than any approach the anti-abortionist can provide. The great disadvantage of this contractarian approach to morality is that it adds to our earlier scope problems by leaving it unclear how we can have the duty not to inflict pain and suffering on animals.

Contractarians have tried to deal with their scope problems by arguing that duties to some individuals who are not persons can be justified even though those individuals are not contracting members of the moral community. For example, Kant argued that, although we do not have direct duties to animals, we "must practice kindness towards animals, for he who is cruel to animals becomes hard also in his dealings with men" (Kant, 1963, p. 240). Feinberg argues that infanticide is wrong, not because infants have the right to life, but because our society's protection of infants has social utility. If we do not treat infants with tenderness and consideration, then when they are persons they will be worse off and we will be worse off also (Feinberg, 1986, p. 271).

These moves only stave off the difficulties with the pro-choice view; they do not resolve them. Consider Kant's account of our obligations to animals. Kantians certainly know the difference between persons and animals. Therefore, no true Kantian would treat persons as she would treat animals. Thus, Kant's defense of our duties to animals fails to show that Kantians have a duty not to be cruel to animals. Consider Feinberg's attempt to show that infanticide is wrong even though no infant is a person. All Feinberg really shows is that it is a good idea to treat with care and consideration the infants we intend to keep. That is quite compatible with killing the infants we intend to discard. This point can he supported by an analogy with which any pro-choicer will agree. There are plainly good reasons to treat with care and consideration the fetuses we intend to keep. This is quite compatible with aborting those fetuses we intend to discard. Thus, Feinberg's account of the wrongness of infanticide is inadequate.

Accordingly, we can see that a contractarian defense of the pro-choice personhood syllogism fails. The problem arises because the contractarian cannot account for our duties to individuals who are not persons, whether these individuals are animals or infants. Because the pro-choicer wishes to adopt a narrow criterion for the right to life so that fetuses will not be included, the scope of her major premise is too narrow. Her problem is the opposite of the problem the classic opponent of abortion faces.

The argument of this section has attempted to establish, albeit briefly, that the classic antiabortion argument and the pro-choice argument favored by most philosophers both face problems that are mirror images of one another. A stand-off results. The abortion debate requires a different strategy.

THE "FUTURE LIKE OURS" ACCOUNT OF THE WRONGNESS OF KILLING

Why do the standard arguments in the abortion debate fail to resolve the issue? The general principles to which partisans in the debate appeal are either truisms most persons would affirm in the absence of much reflection, or very general moral theories. All are subject to major problems. A different approach is needed.

Opponents of abortion claim that abortion is wrong because abortion involves killing someone like us, a human being who just happens to be very young. Supporters of choice claim that ending the life of a fetus is not in the same moral category as ending the life of an adult human being. Surely this controversy cannot be resolved in the absence of an account of what it is about killing us that makes killing us wrong. On the one hand, if we know what property we possess that makes killing us wrong, then we can ask whether fetuses have the same property. On the other hand, suppose that we do not know what it is about us that makes killing us wrong. If this is so, we do not understand even easy cases in which killing is wrong. Surely, we will not understand the ethics of killing fetuses, for if we do not understand easy cases, then we will not understand hard cases. Both pro-choicer and anti-abortionist agree that it is obvious that it is wrong to kill us. Thus, a discussion of what it is about us that makes killing us not only wrong, but seriously wrong, seems to be the right place to begin a discussion of the abortion issue.

Who is primarily wronged by a killing? The wrong of killing is not primarily explained in terms of the loss to the family and friends of the victim. Perhaps the victim is a hermit. Perhaps one's friends find it easy to make new friends. The wrong of killing is not primarily explained in terms of the brutalization of the killer. The great wrong to the victim explains the brutalization, not the other way around. The wrongness of killing us is understood in terms of what killing does to us. Killing us imposes on us the misfortune of premature death. That misfortune underlies the wrongness.

Premature death is a misfortune because when one is dead, one has been deprived of life. This misfortune can be more precisely specified. Premature death cannot deprive me of my past life. That part of my life is already gone. If I die tomorrow or if I live thirty more years my past life will be no different. It has occurred on either alternative. Rather than my past, my death deprives me of my future, of the life that I would have lived if I had lived out my natural life span.

The loss of a future biological life does not explain the misfortune of death. Compare two scenarios: in the former I now fall into a coma from which I do not recover until my death in thirty years. In the latter I die now. The latter scenario does not seem to describe a greater misfortune than the former.

The loss of our future conscious life is what underlies the misfortune of premature death. Not any future conscious life qualifies, however. Suppose that I am terminally ill with cancer. Suppose also that pain and suffering would dominate my future conscious life. If so, then death would not be a misfortune for me.

Thus, the misfortune of premature death consists of the loss to us of the future goods of consciousness. What are these goods? Much can be said about this issue, but a simple answer will do for the purposes of this essay. The goods of life are whatever we get out of life. The goods of life are those items toward which we take a "pro" attitude. They are completed projects of which we are proud, the pursuit of our goals, aesthetic enjoyments, friendships, intellectual pursuits, and physical pleasures of various sorts. The goods of life are what makes life worth living. In general, what makes life worth living for one person will not be the same as what makes life worth living for another. Nevertheless, the list of goods in each of our lives will overlap. The lists are usually different in different stages of our lives.

What makes the goods of my future good for me? One possible, but wrong, answer is my desire for those goods now. This answer does not account for those aspects of my future life that I now believe I will later value, but about which I am wrong. Neither does it account for those aspects of my future that I will come to value, but which I don't value now. What is valuable to the young may not be valuable to the middle-aged. What is valuable to the middle-aged may not be valuable to the old. Some of life's values for the elderly are best appreciated by the elderly. Thus it is wrong to say that the value of my future to me is just what I value now. What makes my future valuable to me are those aspects of my future that I will (or would) value when I will (or would) experience them, whether I value them now or not.

It follows that a person can believe that she will have a valuable future and be wrong. Furthermore, a person can believe that he will not have a valuable future and also be wrong. This is confirmed by our attitude toward many of the suicidal. We attempt to save the lives of the suicidal and to convince them that they have made an error in judgment. This does not mean that the future of an individual obtains value from the value that others confer on it. It means that, in some cases, others can make a clearer judgment of the value of a person's future *to that person* than the person herself. This often happens when one's judgment concerning the value of one's own future is clouded by personal tragedy. (Compare the views of McInerney, 1990, and Shirley, 1995.)

Thus, what is sufficient to make killing us wrong, in general, is that it causes premature death. Premature death is a misfortune. Premature death is a misfortune, in general, because it deprives an individual of a future of value. An individual's future will be valuable to that individual if that individual will come, or would come, to value it. We know that killing us is wrong. What makes killing us wrong, in general, is that it deprives us of a future of value. Thus, killing someone is wrong, in general, when it deprives her of a future like ours. I shall call this "an FLO."

ARGUMENTS IN FAVOR OF THE FLO THEORY

At least four arguments support this FLO account of the wrongness of killing.

The Considered Judgment Argument

The FLO account of the wrongness of killing is correct because it fits with our considered judgment concerning the nature of the misfortune of death. The analysis of the previous section is an exposition of the nature of this considered judgment. This judgment can be confirmed. If one were to ask individuals with AIDS or with incurable cancer about the nature of their misfortune, I believe that they would say or imply that their impending loss of an FLO makes their premature death a misfortune. If they would not, then the FLO account would plainly be wrong.

The Worst of Crimes Argument

The FLO account of the wrongness of killing is correct because it explains why we believe that killing is one of the worst of crimes. My being killed deprives me of more than does my being robbed or beaten or harmed in some other way because my being killed deprives me of all of the value of my future, not merely part of it. This explains why we make the penalty for murder greater than the penalty for other crimes.

As a corollary the FLO account of the wrongness of killing also explains why killing an adult human being is justified only in the most extreme circumstances, only in circumstances in which the loss of life to an individual is outweighed by a worse outcome if that life is not taken. Thus, we are willing to justify killing in self-defense, killing in order to save one's own life, because one's loss if one does not kill in that situation is so very great. We justify killing in a just war for similar reasons. We believe that capital punishment would be justified if, by having such an institution, fewer premature deaths would occur. The FLO account of the wrongness of killing does not entail that killing is always wrong. Nevertheless, the FLO account explains both why killing is one of the worst of crimes and, as a corollary, why the exceptions to the wrongness of killing are so very rare. A correct theory of the wrongness of killing should have these features.

The Appeal to Cases Argument

The FLO account of the wrongness of killing is correct because it yields the correct answers in many life-and-death cases that arise in medicine and have interested philosophers.

Consider medicine first. Most people believe that it is not wrong deliberately to end the life of a person who is permanently unconscious. Thus we believe that it is not wrong to remove a feeding tube or a ventilator from a permanently comatose patient, knowing that such a removal will cause death. The FLO account of the wrongness of killing explains why this is so. A patient who is permanently unconscious cannot have a future that she would come to value, whatever her values. Therefore, according to the FLO theory of the wrongness of killing, death could not, *ceteris paribus*, be a misfortune to her. Therefore, removing the feeding tube or ventilator does not wrong her.

By contrast, almost all people believe that it is wrong, *ceteris paribus*, to withdraw medical treatment from patients who are temporarily unconscious. The FLO account of the wrongness of killing also explains why this is so. Furthermore, these two unconsciousness cases explain why the FLO account of the wrongness of killing does not include present consciousness as a necessary condition for the wrongness of killing.

Consider now the issue of the morality of legalizing active euthanasia. Proponents of active euthanasia argue that if a patient faces a future of intractable pain and wants to die, then, *ceteris paribus*, it would not be wrong for a physician to give him medicine that she knows would result in his death. This view is so universally accepted that even the strongest *opponents* of active euthanasia hold it. The official Vatican view (Sacred Congregation, 1980) is that it is permissible for a physician to administer to a patient morphine sufficient (although no more than sufficient) to control his pain even if she foresees that the morphine will result in his death. Notice how nicely the FLO account of the wrongness of killing explains this unanimity of opinion. A patient known to be in severe intractable pain is presumed to have a future without positive value. Accordingly, death would not be a misfortune for him and an action that would (foreseeably) end his life would not be wrong.

Contrast this with the standard emergency medical treatment of the suicidal. Even though the suicidal have indicated that they want to die, medical personnel will act to save their lives. This supports the view that it is not the mere *desire* to enjoy an FLO which is crucial to our understanding of the wrongness of killing. *Having* an FLO is what is crucial to the account, although one would, of course, want to make an exception in the case of fully autonomous people who refuse life-saving medical treatment. Opponents of abortion can, of course, be willing to make an exception for fully autonomous fetuses who refuse life support.

The FLO theory of the wrongness of killing also deals correctly with issues that have concerned philosophers. It implies that it would be wrong to kill (peaceful) persons from outer space who come to visit our planet even though they are biologically utterly unlike us. Presumably, if they are persons, then they will have futures that are sufficiently like ours so that it would be wrong to kill them. The FLO account of the wrongness of killing shares this feature with the personhood views of the supporters of choice. Classical opponents of abortion who locate the wrongness of abortion somehow in the biological humanity of a fetus cannot explain this.

The FLO account does not entail that there is another species of animals whose members ought not to be killed. Neither does it entail that it is permissible to kill any non-human animal. On the one hand, a supporter of animals' rights might argue that since some non-human animals have a future of value, it is wrong to kill them also, or at least it is wrong to kill them without a far better reason than we usually have for killing non-human animals. On the other hand, one might argue that the futures of non-human animals are not sufficiently like ours for the FLO account to entail that it is wrong to kill them. Since the FLO account does not specify which properties a future of another individual must possess so that killing that individual is wrong, the FLO account is indeterminate with respect to this issue. The fact that the

FLO account of the wrongness of killing does not give a determinate answer to this question is not a flaw in the theory. A sound ethical account should yield the right answers in the obvious cases; it should not be required to resolve every disputed question.

A major respect in which the FLO account is superior to accounts that appeal to the concept of person is the explanation the FLO account provides of the wrongness of killing infants. There was a class of infants who had futures that included a class of events that were identical to the futures of the readers of this essay. Thus, reader, the FLO account explains why it was as wrong to kill you when you were an infant as it is to kill you now. This account can be generalized to almost all infants. Notice that the wrongness of killing infants can be explained in the absence of an account of what makes the future of an individual sufficiently valuable so that it is wrong to kill that individual. The absence of such an account explains why the FLO account is indeterminate with respect to the wrongness of killing non-human animals.

If the FLO account is the correct theory of the wrongness of killing, then because abortion involves killing fetuses and fetuses have FLOs for exactly the same reasons that infants have FLOs, abortion is presumptively seriously immoral. This inference lays the necessary groundwork for a fourth argument in favor of the FLO account that shows that abortion is wrong.

The Analogy with Animals Argument

Why do we believe it is wrong to cause animals suffering? We believe that, in our own case and in the case of other adults and children, suffering is a misfortune. It would be as morally arbitrary to refuse to acknowledge that animal suffering is wrong as it would be to refuse to acknowledge that the suffering of persons of another race is wrong. It is, on reflection, suffering that is a misfortune, not the suffering of white males or the suffering of humans. Therefore, infliction of suffering is presumptively wrong no matter on whom it is inflicted and whether it is inflicted on persons or nonpersons. Arbitrary restrictions on the wrongness of suffering count as racism or speciesism. Not only is this argument convincing on its own, but it is the only way of justifying the wrongness of animal cruelty. Cruelty toward animals is clearly wrong. (This famous argument is due to Singer, 1979.)

The FLO account of the wrongness of abortion is analogous. We believe that, in our own case and the cases of other adults and children, the loss of a future of value is a misfortune. It would be as morally arbitrary to refuse to acknowledge that the loss of a future of value to a fetus is wrong as to refuse to acknowledge that the loss of a future of value to Jews (to take a relevant twentieth-century example) is wrong. It is, on reflection, the loss of a future of value that is a misfortune; not the loss of a future of value to adults or loss of a future of value to non-Jews. To deprive someone of a future of value is wrong no matter on whom the deprivation is inflicted and no matter whether the deprivation is inflicted on persons or nonpersons. Arbitrary restrictions on the wrongness of this deprivation count as racism, genocide or ageism. Therefore, abortion is wrong. This argument that abortion is wrong should be convincing because it has the same form as the argument for the claim that causing pain and suffering to non-human animals is wrong. Since the latter argument is convincing, the former argument should be also. Thus, an analogy with animals supports the thesis that abortion is wrong.

REPLIES TO OBJECTIONS

The four arguments in the previous section establish that abortion is, except in rare cases, seriously immoral. Not surprisingly, there are objections to this view. There are replies to the four most important objections to the FLO argument for the immorality of abortion.

The Potentiality Objection

The FLO account of the wrongness of abortion is a potentiality argument. To claim that a fetus *has* an FLO is to claim that a fetus now has the potential to be in a state of a certain kind in the future. It is not to claim that all ordinary fetuses *will* have FLOs. Fetuses who are aborted, of course, will not. To say that a standard fetus has an FLO is to say that a standard fetus either will have or would have a life it will or would value. To say that a standard fetus would have a life it would value is to say that it will have a life it will value if it does not die prematurely. The truth of this conditional is based upon the nature of fetuses (including the fact that they naturally age) and this nature concerns their potential.

Some appeals to potentiality in the abortion debate rest on unsound inferences. For example, one may try to generate an argument against abortion by arguing that because persons have the right to life, potential persons also have the right to life. Such an argument is plainly invalid as it stands. The premise one needs to add to make it valid would have to be something like: "If Xs have the right to Y, then potential Xs have the right to Y." This premise is plainly false. Potential presidents don't have the rights of the presidency; potential voters don't have the right to vote.

In the FLO argument potentiality is not used in order to bridge the gap between adults and fetuses as is done in the argument in the above paragraph. The FLO theory of the wrongness of killing adults is based upon the adult's potentiality to have a future of value. Potentiality is in the argument from the very beginning. Thus, the plainly false premise is not required. Accordingly, the use of potentiality in the FLO theory is not a sign of an illegitimate inference.

The Argument from Interests

A second objection to the FLO account of the immorality of abortion involves arguing that even though fetuses have FLOs, nonsentient fetuses do not meet the minimum conditions for having any moral standing at all because they lack interests. Steinbock (1992, p. 5) has presented this argument clearly:

> Beings that have moral status must be capable of caring about what is done to them. They must be capable of being made, if only in a rudimentary sense, happy or miserable, comfortable or distressed. Whatever reasons we may have for preserving or protecting non-sentient beings, these reasons do not refer to their own interests. For without conscious awareness, beings cannot have interests. Without interests, they cannot have a welfare of their own. Without a welfare of their own, nothing can be done for their sake. Hence, they lack moral standing or status.

Medical researchers have argued that fetuses do not become sentient until after 22 weeks of gestation (Steinbock, 1992, p. 50). If they are correct, and if Steinbock's argument is sound, then we have both an objection to the FLO account of the wrongness of abortion and a basis for a view on abortion minimally acceptable to most supporters of choice.

Steinbock's conclusion conflicts with our settled moral beliefs. Temporarily unconscious human beings are nonsentient, yet no one believes that they lack either interests or moral standing. Accordingly, neither conscious awareness nor the capacity for conscious awareness is a necessary condition for having interests.

The counter-example of the temporarily unconscious human being shows that there is something internally wrong with Steinbock's argument. The difficulty stems from an ambiguity. One cannot *take* an interest in something without being capable of caring about what is done to it. However, something can be *in* someone's interest without that individual being capable of caring about it, or about anything. Thus, life support can be *in* the interests of a temporarily unconscious patient even though the temporarily unconscious patient is incapable of *taking* an interest in that life support. If this can be so for the temporarily unconscious patient, then it is hard to see why it cannot be so for the temporarily unconscious (that is, non-sentient) fetus who requires placental life support. Thus the objection based on interests fails.

The Problem of Equality

The FLO account of the wrongness of killing seems to imply that the degree of wrongness associated with each killing varies inversely with the victim's age. Thus, the FLO account of the wrongness of killing seems to suggest that it is far worse to kill a five-year-old than an 89-year-old because the former is deprived of far more than the latter. However, we believe that all persons have an equal right to life. Thus, it appears that the FLO account of the wrongness of killing entails an obviously false view (Paske, 1994).

However, the FLO account of the wrongness of killing does not, strictly speaking, imply that it is worse to kill younger people than older people. The FLO account provides an explanation of the wrongness of killing that is sufficient to account for the serious presumptive wrongness of killing. It does not follow that killings cannot be wrong in other ways. For example, one might hold, as does Feldman (1992, p. 184), that in addition to the wrongness of killing that has its basis in the future life of which the victim is deprived, killing an individual is also made wrong by the admirability of an individual's past behavior. Now the amount of admirability will presumably vary directly with age, whereas the amount of deprivation will vary inversely with age. This tends to equalize the wrongness of murder.

However, even if, *ceteris paribus*, it is worse to kill younger persons than older persons, there are good reasons for adopting a doctrine of the legal equality of murder. Suppose that we tried to estimate the seriousness of a crime of murder by appraising the value of the FLO of which the victim had been deprived. How would one go about doing this? In the first place, one would be confronted by the old problem of interpersonal comparisons of utility. In the second place, estimation of the value of a future would involve putting oneself, not into the shoes of the victim at the time she was killed, but rather into the shoes the victim would have worn had the victim survived, and then estimating from that perspective the worth of that person's future. This task seems difficult, if not impossible. Accordingly, there are reasons to adopt a convention that murders are equally wrong.

Furthermore, the FLO theory, in a way, explains why we do adopt the doctrine of the legal equality of murder. The FLO theory explains why we regard murder as one of the worst of crimes, since depriving someone of a future like ours deprives her of more than depriving her of anything else. This gives us a reason for making the punishment for murder very harsh, as harsh as is compatible with civilized society. One should not make the punishment for younger victims harsher than that. Thus, the doctrine of the equal legal right to life does not seem to be incompatible with the FLO theory.

The Contraception Objection

The strongest objection to the FLO argument for the immorality of abortion is based on the claim that, because contraception results in one less FLO, the FLO argument entails that contraception, indeed, abstention from sex when conception is possible, is immoral. Because neither contraception nor abstention from sex when conception is possible is immoral, the FLO account is flawed.

There is a cogent reply to this objection. If the argument of the early part of this essay is correct, then the central issue concerning the morality of abortion is the problem of whether fetuses are individuals who are members of the class of individuals whom it is seriously presumptively wrong to kill. The properties of being human and alive, of being a person, and of having an FLO are criteria that participants in the abortion debate have offered to mark off the relevant class of individuals. The central claim of this essay is that having an FLO marks off the relevant class of individuals. A defender of the FLO view could, therefore, reply that since, at the time of contraception, there is no individual to have an FLO, the FLO account does not entail that contraception is wrong. The wrong of killing is primarily a wrong to the individual who is killed; at the time of contraception there is no individual to be wronged.

However, someone who presses the contraception objection might have an answer to this reply. She might say that the sperm and egg are the individuals deprived of an FLO at the time of contraception. Thus, there are individuals whom contraception deprives of an FLO and if depriving an individual of an FLO is what makes killing wrong, then the FLO theory entails that contraception is wrong.

There is also a reply to this move. In the case of abortion, an objectively determinate individual is the subject of harm caused by the loss of an FLO. This individual is a fetus. In the case of contraception, there are far more candidates (see Norcross, 1990). Let us consider some possible candidates in order of the increasing number of individuals harmed: (1) The single harmed individual might be the combination of the particular sperm and the particular egg that would have united to form a zygote if contraception had not been used. (2) The two harmed individuals might be the particular sperm itself, and, in addition, the ovum itself that would have physically combined to form the zygote. (This is modeled on the double homicide of two persons who would otherwise in a short time fuse. (1) is modeled on harm to a single entity some of whose parts are not physically contiguous, such as a university.) (3) The many harmed individuals might be the millions of *combinations* of sperm and the released ovum whose (small) chances of having an FLO were reduced by the successful contraception. (4) The even larger class of harmed individuals (larger by one) might be the class consisting of all of the individual sperm in an ejaculate and, in addition, the individual ovum released at the time of the successful contraception. (1) through (4) are all candidates for being the subject(s) of harm in the case of successful contraception or abstinence from sex. Which should be chosen? Should we hold a lottery? There seems to be no non-arbitrarily determinate subject of harm in the case of successful contraception. But if there is no such subject of harm, then no determinate thing was harmed. If no determinate thing was harmed, then (in the case of contraception) no wrong has been done. Thus, the FLO account of the wrongness of abortion does not entail that contraception is wrong.

CONCLUSION

This essay contains an argument for the view that, except in unusual circumstances, abortion is seriously wrong. Deprivation of an FLO explains why killing adults and children is wrong. Abortion deprives fetuses of FLOs. Therefore, abortion is wrong. This argument is based on an account of the wrongness of killing that is a result of our considered judgment of the nature of the misfortune of premature death. It accounts for why we

regard killing as one of the worst of crimes. It is superior to alternative accounts of the wrongness of killing that are intended to provide insight
into the ethics of abortion. This account of the wrongness of killing is supported by the way it handles cases in which our moral judgments are settled. This account has an analogue in the most plausible account of the
wrongness of causing animals to suffer. This account makes no appeal to
religion. Therefore, the FLO account shows that abortion, except in rare
instances, is seriously wrong.

REFERENCES

Beckwith, F. J., *Politically Correct Death: Answering Arguments for Abortion Rights* (Grand Rapids, Michigan: Baker Books, 1993).

Benn, S. I., "Abortion, Infanticide, and Respect for Persons," *The Problem of Abortion*, ed. J. Feinberg (Belmont, California: Wadsworth, 1973), pp. 92–104.

Engelhardt, Jr [sic], H. T., *The Foundations of Bioethics* (New York: Oxford University Press, 1986).

Feinberg, J., "Abortion," *Matters of Life and Death: New Introductory Essays in Moral Philosophy*, ed. T. Regan (New York: Random House, 1986).

Feldman, F., *Confrontations with the Reaper. A Philosophical Study of the Nature and Value of Death* (New York: Oxford University Press, 1992).

Kant, I., *Lectures on Ethics*, trans. L. Infeld (New York: Harper, 1963).

Marquis, D. B., "A Future like Ours and the Concept of Person: a Reply to McInerney and Paske," *The Abortion Controversy: A Reader*, ed. L. P. Pojman and F. J. Beckwith (Boston: Jones and Bartlett, 1994), pp. 354–68.

——,"Fetuses, Futures and Values: a Reply to Shirley," *Southwest Philosophy Review* 11 (1995): 263–5.

——,"Why Abortion Is Immoral," *Journal of Philosophy* 86 (1989): 183–202.

McInerney, P., "Does a Fetus Already Have a Future like Ours?," *Journal of Philosophy* 87 (1990): 264–8.

Noonan, J., "An Almost Absolute Value in History," in *The Morality of Abortion*, ed. J. Noonan (Cambridge, MA: Harvard University Press, 1970).

Norcross, A., "Killing, Abortion, and Contraception: a Reply to Marquis," *Journal of Philosophy* 87 (1990): 268–77.

Paske, G., "Abortion and the Neo-natal Right to Life: a Critique of Marquis's Futurist Argument," *The Abortion Controversy: A Reader*, ed. L. P. Pojman and F. J. Beckwith (Boston: Jones and Bartlett, 1994), pp. 343–53.

Sacred Congregation for the Propagation of the Faith, *Declaration on Euthanasia* (Vatican City, 1980).

Shirley, E. S., "Marquis' Argument Against Abortion: a Critique," *Southwest Philosophy Review* 11 (1995): 79–89.

Singer, P., "Not for Humans Only: the Place of Nonhumans in Environmental Issues," *Ethics and Problems of the 21st Century*, ed. K. E. Goodpaster and K. M. Sayre (South Bend: Notre Dame University Press, 1979).

Steinbock, B., *Life Before Birth: The Moral and Legal Status of Embryos and Fetuses* (New York: Oxford University Press, 1992).

Thomson, J. J., "A Defense of Abortion," *Philosophy and Public Affairs* 1 (1971): 47–66.

Tooley, M., "Abortion and Infanticide," *Philosophy and Public Affairs* 2 (1972): 37–65.

Warren, M. A., "On the Moral and Legal Status of Abortion," *Monist* 57 (1973): 43–61.

DISCUSSION QUESTIONS

1. Explain and evaluate Marquis's criticisms of Thomson's argument.

2. Explain why Marquis thinks that the problem of abortion cannot be solved by asking whether fetuses have a right to life.

3. Marquis's argument against abortion can be seen as an inference to the best explanation of why it is morally wrong to kill normal adult human beings. What does Marquis take to be the best explanation of this? Why does he think that it is better than the alternatives? Can you give an even better explanation that accounts for the cases that Marquis discusses?

4. Is Marquis's argument different in important ways from traditional arguments based on the premise that a fetus is a person or a potential person? If so, how? If not, why not?

5. Explain the contraception objection to Marquis's argument and his response. Is his response adequate? Why or why not?

6. How could Thomson respond to Marquis's argument. Is her best response good enough? Why or why not?

7. Determine whether you think abortion is morally wrong in the following cases:

    a. Where the mother is in danger of dying if she does not have an abortion.

    b. Where the pregnancy is due to rape.

    c. Where contraception was used, but it failed.

    d. Where the fetus has a disease that usually causes death within a year or two.

    e. Where the fetus has a disease that usually causes severe mental retardation.

    f. Where the pregnant woman is mentally or physically unable to be a good mother.

    g. Where the mother will suffer severe personal losses if the pregnancy continues.

Now try to formulate principles and analogies to justify your positions in these controversial cases.

8. Which underlying principles, if any, could protect human lives with only a few exceptions, yet allow us to take lives of:

    a. Contract killers sentenced to capital punishment

    b. Humans who are in irreversible comas

    c. Ourselves in suicide

    d. Children who live next to munitions factories that are bombed in a war

    e. Animals for food, clothing, and entertainment

9. Describe a moral problem that you have faced in your personal life, and apply the methods of moral reasoning that you have learned in this chapter.

NOTES

[1] For a discussion of this approach, and for a model of how to argue about a moral principle, see Philippa Foot, "The Problem of Abortion and the Doctrine of Double Effect," in Foot, *Virtues and Vices and Other Essays in Moral Philosophy* (Berkeley: University of California Press, 1978), 19–32.

[2] Gradualism is discussed in more detail in Joel Feinberg, "Abortion," in *Matters of Life and Death*, 2nd ed., ed. Tom Regan (New York: Random House, 1986), 256–93.

[3] *Philosophy and Public Affairs* 1, no. 1 (Fall 1971), 47–66.

[4] From *Ethics in Practice: An Anthology*, Second Edition, ed. Hugh LaFollette (Malden, Mass.; Blackwell, 2002), pp. 83–93. This essay was originally published in the first edition of this anthology. This is an updated version of a view that first appeared in the *Journal of Philosophy* (1989). This essay incorporates attempts to deal with the objections of McInerney (1990), Norcross (1990), Shirley (1995), Steinbock (1992), and Paske (1994) to the original version of the view.

20

SCIENTIFIC REASONING

The products of science are all around us. We depend on science when we drive cars, listen to compact discs, and cook food in microwaves. Still, few people understand how science operates. To some, the scientific enterprise seems to consist of nothing more than amassing huge quantities of data to prove or disprove some hypothesis. There is more to science than that. Scientists also seek theories that are profound and far-reaching, or even elegant and beautiful, as is shown by how scientists themselves speak about their theories. The goal of scientific theory is not just to list and describe natural phenomena but to make sense of nature—that is, to explain it, make it more intelligible. To choose among conflicting scientific theories, we have to decide which theory makes the most sense and provides the best explanations. This chapter will bring out this complex nature of science by discussing the scientific enterprise in general and then focusing on a particular debate about biological evolution.

STANDARD SCIENCE

The beginning of science lies in observation. When we look at the world around us, we see that many things happen. Apples fall off trees, the leaves of some trees change color in the autumn, the tides come in and go out, chickens lay eggs, and so on. One job of scientists is to describe and classify what happens and what exists. But scientists also wonder *why* some things happen rather than others. Maple trees change color in the fall, and spruce trees do not, but why? Chickens lay eggs, and monkeys do not, but why? A sphere of wood floats in water, and a gold sphere does not, but why? And why does gold float when pressed into the shape of a boat? These questions ask for *explanations*.

To provide an explanation, scientists often give arguments of the kind discussed in Chapter 1. The event to be explained is derived from a general principle plus a statement of initial conditions or particular facts. For example, given the general principle that a solid sphere floats in water if and only if it is less dense than water, and also given the particular facts that wood is less dense than water, whereas gold is denser than water, we can explain why a wooden sphere floats in water and a gold sphere does not.

Scientists often seek *deeper* explanations by asking why certain general principles themselves are true. The principle that a sphere floats in water only when it is less dense than water can be explained as an instance of the more general principle that *anything* floats only when it displaces more than its own weight in water. This broader principle not only explains why a wooden sphere floats in water but also why a piece of gold will float when molded into the form of a boat. This broader principle is in turn explained by deriving it from even more basic principles about gravity and the mutual repulsion of molecules. A larger scientific theory is thus used to explain not only why particular things happen but also why certain general principles hold.

Of course, scientists often put forward conflicting theories, so we need some way to test which theory is correct. One simple method is to use the theory to make *predictions*. Since an explanation depends on principles that are general, these principles have implications beyond the particular phenomenon that they were originally intended to explain. The theory thus predicts what will happen in circumstances that the scientist has not yet observed. We can then test the theory by seeing whether these predictions hold true. For example, we can make spheres out of a wide variety of materials, calculate their densities, and then see which ones float. If any sphere floats that is denser than water, then we have to give up our principle that a sphere floats in water *only if* it is less dense than water. (This is an application of the necessary condition test, discussed in Chapter 9.) If we find a sphere that is less dense than water but does not float, then we have to give up the principle that a sphere floats if it is less dense than water. (This is an application of the sufficient condition test, discussed in Chapter 9.)

These methods help us rule out certain scientific principles, but the fact that a principle implies true predictions does not, by itself, prove that the principle is true. That argument would commit something like the fallacy of affirming the consequent (see Exercise XXI in Chapter 6). Nonetheless, we can still say that a theory is *confirmed* if it yields true predictions, and it is confirmed more strongly if it yields more, more varied, and more unexpected true predictions.

Scientific method is actually much more complex than this simple example suggests. This becomes apparent when we encounter *anomalies*. Suppose we have confirmed and explained the principle that a sphere floats in water if and only if it is less dense than water. Suppose also that another principle is well confirmed: A substance gets smaller and denser as it gets colder. Taken together, these principles predict that a sphere of ice should sink in water. Ice is colder than water, so, according to the second principle, ice should be denser than water, and that, given the first principle, means that it should not float in water. Of course, our prediction is wrong, since spheres of ice do float in water. What do we do now? The obvious solution is to modify the principle that a substance gets smaller and denser as it gets colder. This holds for most substances, but not for water. Water expands and thus gets less dense as it freezes.

We could have tried another solution. We could have denied the other principle: that a sphere floats in water if and only if it is less dense than water. Why do scientists not do this? One reason is that we have independent evidence that water expands when it freezes. That is why jars of water burst when they are left in a freezer. Another reason is that we could not give up this principle alone, because it follows from more basic principles about gravity and the mutual repulsion of molecules. Thus, many other areas of science would be affected if we gave up the principle that a sphere floats in water if and only if it is less dense than water. Scientific theories work together, so we cannot throw out one without undermining the others. That all these other scientific theories are not only well confirmed but useful is what makes scientists give up one principle rather than another when an anomaly arises.

At this point we might seek an even deeper explanation and ask why water expands when it freezes. In fact, to this day, nobody seems to have a fully adequate explanation of this common phenomenon. There are various theories but no agreement about how to explain the expansion of water. It has something to do with the way in which liquid water crystallizes to form ice, but nobody is quite sure why water crystallizes in that way. Does this show that certain phenomena are beyond scientific understanding? Probably not. But it does suggest that science may never be complete. More questions arise as science progresses, and there will always be questions that remain unanswered. As scientists discover and explain more and more phenomena and see connections among principles in different areas, every new step gives rise to more questions that need to be answered. That is one way in which science makes progress.

SCIENTIFIC REVOLUTIONS

Another type of scientific development is more radical—knowledge is not simply extended, but, instead, one scientific framework is replaced (or largely replaced) by another. What changes is not just particular claims, but large-scale ways of doing science. In biology, the germ theory of disease and the theory of evolution through natural selection are examples of such revolutionary developments. Einstein's theory of relativity and the rise of quantum mechanics were also revolutionary developments in physics. Indeed, every branch of science has undergone at least one such revolutionary change during the past few centuries.

There are some important differences between scientific progress within a framework and the replacement of one framework by another.[1] In the first place, such changes in framework usually meet with strong resistance. A new conceptual framework will be unfamiliar and hard to understand and may even seem absurd or unintelligible. Even today, for example, the thought that the Earth is spinning on its axis and revolving around the sun seems completely counter to our commonsense view of the world. Also, arguments on behalf of a new framework will be very different from arguments that occur *within* a framework. Disputes over conceptual frameworks cannot be settled by a straightforward appeal to facts. The long debate between Albert Einstein and Niels Bohr concerning quantum theory did not turn on matters of fact but on their interpretation. Einstein could not accept the indeterminacy involved in the quantum theory's interpretation of the world, and he worked until the end of his life to find some alternative to it. At present, few scientists share Einstein's reservations.

One of the most important and fascinating revolutions in science was Darwin's theory of evolution through natural selection in biology. The Darwinian revolution challenged—and continues to challenge—many common assumptions about the nature of science and also the nature of humankind. As a result, Darwin's views on evolution and natural selection encountered vehement opposition right from the start.

These conflicts have attracted public attention when school boards have tried either to prevent the teaching of evolution in public schools or to require or allow alternative views, such as so-called "intelligent design," to be taught alongside standard evolutionary biology. In one recent case, the school board of Dover, Pennsylvania, passed a resolution requiring teachers to read a statement about "intelligent design" aloud in ninth-grade science classes whenever evolution was taught. Eleven parents of high-school students challenged this requirement in the case of *Kitzmiller v. Dover Area School District*, 400 F. Supp. 2d 707 (M.D. Pa. 2005). In his opinion, U.S. District Judge John E. Jones III ruled that intelligent design is not science, partly because it depends on "its creationist, and thus religious, antecedents," so the school district's requirement therefore violated the Establishment Clause of the First Amendment to the U.S. Constitution.

This debate between natural selection and intelligent design, thus, has not only scientific but also legal and religious dimensions. The following selections represent this debate at its best. Michael Behe (professor of biochemistry at Lehigh University in Pennsylvania) is one of the most prominent proponents of intelligent design, and Philip Kitcher (professor of philosophy at Columbia University) is one of his most profound critics. They focus on simple examples that are supposed to cause problems for the Darwinian approach to evolution. These case studies raise more general issues about the nature of religion, the nature of science, and the relation between religion and science—issues that remain alive today in pulpits, classrooms, and courts.

DISCUSSION QUESTION

To get simplistic objections out of the way first, explain what is wrong with Stephen Colbert's satirical refutation of Darwin's theory of evolution in the following passage:

Hey kids! Now you can disprove evolution in your own backyard. Here's what you'll need: one fishbowl, one pitcher of water, one hamster, alive, and one hardbound copy, Charles Darwin's *Origin of Species* . . . and now here's the experiment. . . .

STEP 1: Fill your fishbowl with the water. I don't want to give anything away, but soon it's going to be a bowl for another kind of animal.

STEP 2: Drop the hamster (you can call it "Skip") into the fishbowl.

STEP 3: Cover the fishbowl with Charles Darwin's *Origin of Species*.

STEP 4: Seems like a pretty desperate situation Skip has gotten himself into. This would be an ideal time for evolution to kick in.

STEP 5: Follow the scientific method—observe! Is the hamster "evolving" gills? Has he "evolved" a jackhammer to drill through the fishbowl, or "adapted to his environment" with a tiny hamster flamethrower to burn through *Origin of Species?* Don't think so.

STEP 6: Let the hamster go. Just because Darwin was a sick twist with a God complex doesn't mean we have to buy into his power trip. (You could also call the hamster "Teddy.")[2]

MOLECULAR MACHINES: EXPERIMENTAL SUPPORT FOR THE DESIGN INFERENCE

by Michael J. Behe

from *Cosmic Pursuit 1*, no. 2 (1998), 27–35

DARWINISM'S PROSPERITY

Within a short time after Charles Darwin published *The Origin of Species* the explanatory power of the theory of evolution was recognized by the great majority of biologists. The hypothesis readily resolved the problems of homologous resemblance, rudimentary organs, species abundance, extinction, and biogeography. The rival theory of the time, which posited creation of species by a supernatural being, appeared to most reasonable minds to be much less plausible, since it would have a putative Creator attending to details that seemed to be beneath His dignity.

As time went on the theory of evolution obliterated the rival theory of creation, and virtually all working scientists studied the biological world from a Darwinian perspective. Most educated people now lived in a world where the wonder and diversity of the biological kingdom were produced by the simple, elegant principle of natural selection.

However, in science a successful theory is not necessarily a correct theory. In the course of history there have also been other theories which achieved the triumph that Darwinism achieved, which brought many experimental and observational facts into a coherent framework, and which appealed to people's intuitions about how the world should work. Those theories also promised to explain much of the universe with a few simple principles. But, by and large, those other theories are now dead.

A good example of this is the replacement of Newton's mechanical view of the universe by Einstein's relativistic universe. Although Newton's model accounted for the results of many experiments in his time, it failed to explain aspects of gravitation. Einstein solved that problem and others by completely rethinking the structure of the universe.

Similarly, Darwin's theory of evolution prospered by explaining much of the data of his time and the first half of the 20th century, but my article will show that Darwinism has been unable to account for phenomena uncovered by the efforts of modern biochemistry during the second half of this century. I will do this by emphasizing the fact that life at its most fundamental level is irreducibly complex and that such complexity is incompatible with undirected evolution.

A SERIES OF EYES

How do we see?

In the 19th century the anatomy of the eye was known in great detail and the sophisticated mechanisms it employs to deliver an accurate picture of the outside world astounded everyone who was familiar with them. Scientists of the 19th century correctly observed that if a person were so unfortunate as to be missing one of the eye's many integrated features, such as the lens, or iris, or ocular muscles, the inevitable result would be a severe loss of vision or outright blindness. Thus it was concluded that the eye could only function if it were nearly intact.

As Charles Darwin was considering possible objections to his theory of evolution by natural selection in *The Origin of Species* he discussed the problem of the eye in a section of the book appropriately entitled "Organs of extreme perfection and complication." He realized that if in one generation an organ of the complexity of the eye suddenly appeared, the event would be tantamount to a miracle. Somehow, for Darwinian evolution to be believable, the difficulty that the public had in envisioning the gradual formation of complex organs had to be removed.

Darwin succeeded brilliantly, not by actually describing a real pathway that evolution might have used in constructing the eye, but rather by pointing to a variety of animals that were known to have eyes of various constructions, ranging from a simple light sensitive spot to the complex vertebrate camera eye, and suggesting that the evolution of the human eye might have involved similar organs as intermediates.

But the question remains, how do we see? Although Darwin was able to persuade much of the world that a modern eye could be produced gradually from a much simpler structure, he did not even attempt to explain how the simple light sensitive spot that was his starting point actually worked. When discussing the eye Darwin dismissed the question of its ultimate mechanism by stating: "How a nerve comes to be sensitive to light hardly concerns us more than how life itself originated."

He had an excellent reason for declining to answer the question: 19th century science had not progressed to the point where the matter could even be approached. The question of how the eye works—that is, what happens when a photon of light first impinges on the retina—simply could not be answered at that time. As a matter of fact, no question about the underlying mechanism of life could be answered at that time. How do animal muscles cause movement? How does photosynthesis work? How is energy extracted from food? How does the body fight infection? All such questions were unanswerable.

The Calvin and Hobbes Approach

Now, it appears to be a characteristic of the human mind that when it lacks understanding of a process, then it seems easy to imagine simple steps leading from nonfunction to function. A happy example of this is seen in the popular comic strip *Calvin and Hobbes*. Little boy Calvin is always having adventures in the company of his tiger Hobbes by jumping in a box and traveling back in time, or grabbing a toy ray gun and "transmogrifying" himself into various animal shapes, or again using a box as a duplicator and making copies of himself to deal with worldly powers such as his mom and his teachers. A small child such as Calvin finds it easy to imagine that a box just might be able to fly like an airplane (or something), because Calvin doesn't know how airplanes work.

A good example from the biological world of complex changes appearing to be simple is the belief in spontaneous generation. One of the chief proponents of the theory of spontaneous generation during the middle of the 19th century was Ernst Haeckel, a great admirer of Darwin and an eager popularizer of Darwin's theory. From the limited view of cells that 19th century microscopes provided, Haeckel believed that a cell was a "simple little lump of albuminous combination of carbon," not much different from a piece of microscopic Jell-O®. Thus it seemed to Haeckel that such simple life could easily be produced from inanimate material.

In 1859, the year of the publication of *The Origin of Species*, an exploratory vessel, the H.M.S. Cyclops, dredged up some curious-looking mud from the sea bottom. Eventually Haeckel came to observe the mud and thought that it closely resembled some cells he had seen under a microscope. Excitedly he brought this to the attention of no less a personage than Thomas Henry Huxley, Darwin's great friend and defender, who observed the mud for himself. Huxley, too, became convinced that it was Urschleim (that is, protoplasm), the progenitor of life itself, and Huxley named the mud *Bathybius haeckelii* after the eminent proponent of abiogenesis.

The mud failed to grow. In later years, with the development of new biochemical techniques and improved microscopes, the complexity of the cell was revealed. The "simple lumps" were shown to contain thousands of different types of organic molecules, proteins, and nucleic acids, many discrete subcellular structures, specialized compartments for specialized processes, and an extremely complicated architecture. Looking back from the perspective of our time, the episode of *Bathybius haeckelii* seems silly or downright embarrassing, but it shouldn't. Haeckel and Huxley were behaving naturally, like Calvin: since they were unaware of the complexity of cells, they found it easy to believe that cells could originate from simple mud.

Throughout history there have been many other examples, similar to that of Haeckel, Huxley, and the cell, where a key piece of a particular scientific puzzle was beyond the understanding of the age. In science there is even a whimsical term for a machine or structure or process that does something, but the actual mechanism by which it accomplishes its task is unknown: it is called a "black box." In Darwin's time all of biology was a black box: not only the cell, or the eye, or digestion, or immunity, but every biological structure and function because, ultimately, no one could explain how biological processes occurred.

Biology has progressed tremendously due to the model that Darwin put forth. But the black boxes Darwin accepted are now being opened, and our view of the world is again being shaken.

Take our modern understanding of proteins, for example.

PROTEINS

In order to understand the molecular basis of life it is necessary to understand how things called "proteins" work. Proteins are the machinery of living tissue that build the structures and carry out the chemical reactions necessary for life. For example, the first of many steps necessary for the conversion of sugar to biologically-usable forms of energy is carried out by a protein called hexokinase. Skin is made in large measure of a protein called collagen. When light impinges on your retina it interacts first with a protein called rhodopsin. A typical cell contains thousands and thousands of different types of proteins to perform the many tasks necessary for life, much like a carpenter's workshop might contain many different kinds of tools for various carpentry tasks.

What do these versatile tools look like? The basic structure of proteins is quite simple: they are formed by hooking together in a chain discrete subunits called amino acids. Although the protein chain can consist of anywhere from about 50 to about 1,000 amino acid links, each position can only contain one of 20 different amino acids. In this they are much like words: words can come in various lengths but they are made up from a discrete set of 26 letters.

Now, a protein in a cell does not float around like a floppy chain; rather, it folds up into a very precise structure which can be quite different for different types of proteins. Two different amino acid sequences—two different proteins—can be folded to structures as specific and different from each other as a three-eighths inch wrench and a jigsaw. And like the household tools, if the shape of the proteins is significantly warped then they fail to do their jobs.

THE EYESIGHT OF MAN

In general, biological processes on the molecular level are performed by networks of proteins, each member of which carries out a particular task in a chain.

Let us return to the question, how do we see? Although to Darwin the primary event of vision was a black box, through the efforts of many biochemists an answer to the question of sight is at hand. The answer involves a long chain of steps that begin when light strikes the retina and a photon is absorbed by an organic molecule called 11-cis-retinal, causing it to rearrange itself within picoseconds. This causes a corresponding change to the protein, rhodopsin, which is tightly bound to it, so that it can react with another protein called transducin, which in turn causes a molecule called GDP to be exchanged with a molecule called GTP.

To make a long story short, this exchange begins a long series of further bindings between still more specialized molecular machinery, and scientists now understand a great deal about the system of gateways, pumps, ion channels, critical concentrations, and attenuated signals that result in a current to finally be transmitted down the optic nerve to the brain, interpreted as vision. Biochemists also understand the many chemical reactions involved in restoring all these changed or depleted parts to make a new cycle possible.

To Explain Life

Although space doesn't permit me to give the details of the biochemistry of vision here, I have given the steps in my talks. Biochemists know what it means to "explain" vision. They know the level of explanation that biological science eventually must aim for. In order to say that some function is understood, every relevant step in the process must be elucidated. The relevant steps in biological processes occur ultimately at the molecular level, so a satisfactory explanation of a biological phenomenon such as sight, or digestion, or immunity, must include a molecular explanation.

It is no longer sufficient, now that the black box of vision has been opened, for an "evolutionary explanation" of that power to invoke only the anatomical structures of whole eyes, as Darwin did in the 19th century and as most popularizers of evolution continue to do today. Anatomy is, quite simply, irrelevant. So is the fossil record. It does not matter whether or not the fossil record is consistent with evolutionary theory, any more than it mattered in physics that Newton's theory was consistent with everyday experience. The fossil record has nothing to tell us about, say, whether or how the interactions of 11-cis-retinal with rhodopsin, transducin, and phosphodiesterase could have developed, step by step.

"How a nerve comes to be sensitive to light hardly concerns us more than how life itself originated," said Darwin in the 19th century. But both phenomena have attracted the interest of modern biochemistry in the past few decades. The story of the slow paralysis of research on life's origin is quite interesting, but space precludes its retelling here. Suffice it to say that at present the field of origin-of-life studies has dissolved into a cacophony of conflicting models, each unconvincing, seriously incomplete, and incompatible with competing models. In private even most evolutionary biologists will admit that science has no explanation for the beginning of life.

The same problems which beset origin-of-life research also bedevil efforts to show how virtually any complex biochemical system came about. Biochemistry has revealed a molecular world which stoutly resists explanation by the same theory that has long been applied at the level of the whole organism. Neither of Darwin's black boxes—the origin of life or the origin of vision (or other complex biochemical systems)—has been accounted for by his theory.

IRREDUCIBLE COMPLEXITY

In *The Origin of Species* Darwin stated:

> If it could be demonstrated that any complex organ existed which could not possibly have been formed by numerous, successive, slight modifications, my theory would absolutely break down.

A system which meets Darwin's criterion is one which exhibits irreducible complexity. By irreducible complexity I mean a single system which is composed of several interacting parts that contribute to the basic function, and where the removal of any one of the parts causes the system to effectively cease functioning. An irreducibly complex system cannot be produced directly by slight, successive modification of a precursor system, since any precursor to an irreducibly complex system is by definition nonfunctional.

Since natural selection requires a function to select, an irreducibly complex biological system, if there is such a thing, would have to arise as an integrated unit for natural selection to have anything to act on. It is almost universally conceded that such a sudden event would be irreconcilable with the gradualism Darwin envisioned. At this point, however, "irreducibly complex" is just a term, whose power resides mostly in its definition. We must now ask if any real thing is in fact irreducibly complex, and, if so, then are any irreducibly complex things also biological systems?

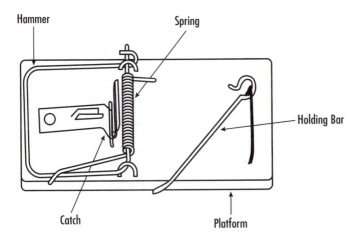

Figure 20.1 A household mousetrap. The working parts of the trap are labeled. If any of the parts is missing, the trap does not function.

Consider the humble mousetrap (Figure 20.1). The mousetraps that my family uses in our home to deal with unwelcome rodents consist of a number of parts. There are: (1) a flat wooden platform to act as a base; (2) a metal hammer, which does the actual job of crushing the little mouse; (3) a wire spring with extended ends to press against the platform and the hammer when the trap is charged; (4) a sensitive catch which releases when slight pressure is applied; and (5) a metal bar which holds the hammer back when the trap is charged and connects to the catch. There are also assorted staples and screws to hold the system together.

If any one of the components of the mousetrap (the base, hammer, spring, catch, or holding bar) is removed, then the trap does not function. In other words, the simple little mousetrap has no ability to trap a mouse until several separate parts are all assembled.

Because the mousetrap is necessarily composed of several parts, it is irreducibly complex. Thus, irreducibly complex systems exist.

MOLECULAR MACHINES

Now, are any biochemical systems irreducibly complex? Yes, it turns out that many are.

Earlier we discussed proteins. In many biological structures proteins are simply components of larger molecular machines. Like the picture tube, wires, metal bolts, and screws that comprise a television set, many proteins are part of structures that only function when virtually all of the components have been assembled.

A good example of this is a cilium. Cilia are hairlike organelles on the surfaces of many animal and lower plant cells that serve to move fluid over the cell's surface or to "row" single cells through a fluid. In humans, for example, epithelial cells lining the respiratory tract each have about 200 cilia that beat in synchrony to sweep mucus towards the throat for elimination.

A cilium consists of a membrane-coated bundle of fibers called an axoneme. An axoneme contains a ring of 9 double microtubules surrounding two central single microtubules. Each outer doublet consists of a ring of 13 filaments (subfiber A) fused to an assembly of 10 filaments (subfiber B). The filaments of the microtubules are composed of two proteins called alpha and beta tubulin. The 11 microtubules forming an axoneme are held together by three types of connectors: subfibers A are joined to the central microtubules by radial spokes; adjacent outer doublets are joined by linkers that consist of a highly elastic protein called nexin; and the central microtubules are joined by a connecting bridge. Finally, every subfiber A bears two arms, an inner arm and an outer arm, both containing the protein dynein.

But how does a cilium work? Experiments have indicated that ciliary motion results from the chemically-powered "walking" of the dynein arms on one microtubule up the neighboring subfiber B of a second microtubule so that the two microtubules slide past each other (Figure 20.2). However, the protein cross-links between microtubules in an intact cilium prevent neighboring microtubules from sliding past each other by more than a short distance. These cross-links, therefore, convert the dynein-induced sliding motion to a bending motion of the entire axoneme.

Now, let us sit back, review the workings of the cilium, and consider what it implies. Cilia are composed of at least a half dozen proteins: alpha-tubulin, beta-tubulin, dynein, nexin, spoke protein, and a central bridge protein. These combine to perform one task, ciliary motion, and all of these proteins must be present for the cilium to function. If the tubulins are absent, then there are no filaments to slide; if the dynein is missing, then the cilium remains rigid and motionless; if nexin or the other connecting proteins are missing, then the axoneme falls apart when the filaments slide.

What we see in the cilium, then, is not just profound complexity, but it is also irreducible complexity on the molecular scale. Recall that by "irreducible complexity" we mean an apparatus that requires several distinct components for the whole to work. My mousetrap must have a base, hammer, spring, catch, and holding bar, all working together, in order to function. Similarly, the cilium, as it is constituted, must have the sliding filaments, connecting proteins, and motor proteins for function to occur. In the absence of any one of those components, the apparatus is useless.

The components of cilia are single molecules. This means that there are no more black boxes to invoke; the complexity of the cilium is final, fundamental. And just as scientists, when they began to learn the complexities of the cell, realized how silly it was to think that life arose spontaneously in a

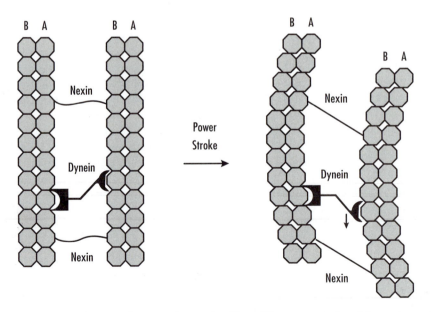

Figure 20.2 Schematic drawing of part of a cilium. The power stroke of the motor protein dynein, attached to one microtubule, against subfiber B of a neighboring microtubule causes the fibers to slide past each other. The flexible linker protein, nexin, converts the sliding motion to a bending motion.

single step or a few steps from ocean mud, so too we now realize that the complex cilium cannot be reached in a single step or a few steps.

But since the complexity of the cilium is irreducible, then it cannot have functional precursors. Since the irreducibly complex cilium cannot have functional precursors, it cannot be produced by natural selection, which requires a continuum of function to work. Natural selection is powerless when there is no function to select. We can go further and say that, if the cilium cannot be produced by natural selection, then the cilium was designed.

A NON-MECHANICAL EXAMPLE

A non-mechanical example of irreducible complexity can be seen in the system that targets proteins for delivery to subcellular compartments. In order to find their way to the compartments where they are needed to perform specialized tasks, certain proteins contain a special amino acid sequence near the beginning called a "signal sequence."

As the proteins are being synthesized by ribosomes, a complex molecular assemblage called the signal recognition particle or SRP, binds to the signal sequence. This causes synthesis of the protein to halt temporarily. During the pause in protein synthesis the SRP is bound by the transmembrane SRP receptor, which causes protein synthesis to resume and which allows passage of the protein into the interior of the endoplasmic reticulum (ER). As the protein passes into the ER the signal sequence is cut off.

For many proteins the ER is just a way station on their travels to their final destinations (Figure 20.3). Proteins which will end up in a lysosome are enzymatically "tagged" with a carbohydrate residue called mannose-6-phosphate while still in the ER. An area of the ER membrane then begins to concentrate several proteins; one protein, clathrin, forms a sort of geodesic dome called a coated vesicle which buds off from the ER. In the dome there is also a receptor protein which binds to both the clathrin and to the mannose-6-phosphate group of the protein which is being transported. The coated vesicle then leaves the ER, travels through the cytoplasm, and binds to the lysosome through another specific receptor protein. Finally, in a maneuver involving several more proteins, the vesicle fuses with the lysosome and the protein arrives at its destination.

During its travels our protein interacted with dozens of macromolecules to achieve one purpose: its arrival in the lysosome. Virtually all components of the transport system are necessary for the system to operate, and therefore the system is irreducible. And since all of the components of the system are comprised of single or several molecules, there are no black boxes to invoke. The consequences of even a single gap in the transport chain can be seen in the hereditary defect known as I-cell disease. It results from a deficiency of the enzyme that places the mannose-6-phosphate on proteins to be targeted to the lysosomes. I-cell disease is characterized by progressive retardation, skeletal deformities, and early death.

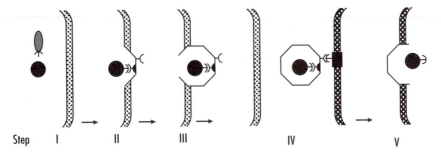

Figure 20.3 Transport of a protein from the ER to the lysosome. Step I: A specific enzyme (gray oval) places a marker on the protein (black sphere). This takes place within the ER, which is de-limited by a barrier membrane (cross-hatched bar with ends curving to the left). Step II: The marker is specifically recognized by a receptor protein and the clathrin vesicle (hexagonal shape) begins to form. Step III: The clathrin vesicle is completed and buds off from the ER mem-brane. Step IV: The clathrin vesicle crosses the cytoplasm and attaches through another specific marker to a receptor protein (dark gray box) on the lysosomal membrane and releases its cargo.

The Study of "Molecular Evolution"

Other examples of irreducible complexity abound, including aspects of pro-tein transport, blood clotting, closed circular DNA, electron transport, the bacterial flagellum, telomeres, photosynthesis, transcription regulation, and much more. Examples of irreducible complexity can be found on virtually every page of a biochemistry textbook. But if these things cannot be ex-plained by Darwinian evolution, how has the scientific community regarded these phenomena of the past forty years?

A good place to look for an answer to that question is in the *Journal of Molecular Evolution*. *JME* is a journal that was begun specifically to deal with the topic of how evolution occurs on the molecular level. It has high scientific standards, and is edited by prominent figures in the field. In a re-cent issue of *JME* there were published eleven articles; of these, all eleven were concerned simply with the analysis of protein or DNA sequences. None of the papers discussed detailed models for intermediates in the de-velopment of complex biomolecular structures. In the past ten years *JME* has published 886 papers. Of these, 95 discussed the chemical synthesis of molecules thought to be necessary for the origin of life, 44 proposed mathe-matical models to improve sequence analysis, 20 concerned the evolution-ary implications of current structures and 719 were analyses of protein or polynucleotide sequences. However, there weren't any papers discussing detailed models for intermediates in the development of complex biomole-cular structures. This is not a peculiarity of *JME*. No papers are to be found that discuss detailed models for intermediates in the development of com-plex biomolecular structures in the *Proceedings of the National Academy of Sci-ence, Nature, Science,* the *Journal of Molecular Biology* or, to my knowledge, any journal whatsoever.

Sequence comparisons overwhelmingly dominate the literature of molec-ular evolution. But sequence comparisons simply can't account for the development of complex biochemical systems any more than Darwin's comparison of simple and complex eyes told him how vision worked. Thus in this area science is mute.

DETECTION OF DESIGN

What's going on? Imagine a room in which a body lies crushed, flat as a pancake. A dozen detectives crawl around, examining the floor with magnifying glasses for any clue to the identity of the perpetrator. In the middle of the room next to the body stands a large, gray elephant. The detectives carefully avoid bumping into the pachyderm's legs as they crawl, and never even glance at it. Over time the detectives get frustrated with their lack of progress but resolutely press on, looking even more closely at the floor. You see, textbooks say detectives must "get their man," so they never consider elephants.

There is an elephant in the roomful of scientists who are trying to explain the development of life. The elephant is labeled "intelligent design." To a person who does not feel obliged to restrict his search to unintelligent causes, the straightforward conclusion is that many biochemical systems were designed. They were designed not by the laws of nature, not by chance and necessity. Rather, they were planned. The designer knew what the systems would look like when they were completed; the designer took steps to bring the systems about. Life on earth at its most fundamental level, in its most critical components, is the product of intelligent activity.

The conclusion of intelligent design flows naturally from the data itself—not from sacred books or sectarian beliefs. Inferring that biochemical systems were designed by an intelligent agent is a humdrum process that requires no new principles of logic or science. It comes simply from the hard work that biochemistry has done over the past forty years, combined with consideration of the way in which we reach conclusions of design every day.

What is "design"? Design is simply the purposeful arrangement of parts. The scientific question is how we detect design. This can be done in various ways, but design can most easily be inferred for mechanical objects.

Systems made entirely from natural components can also evince design. For example, suppose you are walking with a friend in the woods. All of a sudden your friend is pulled high in the air and left dangling by his foot from a vine attached to a tree branch.

After cutting him down you reconstruct the trap. You see that the vine was wrapped around the tree branch, and the end pulled tightly down to the ground. It was securely anchored to the ground by a forked branch. The branch was attached to another vine—hidden by leaves—so that, when the trigger-vine was disturbed, it would pull down the forked stick, releasing the spring-vine. The end of the vine formed a loop with a slipknot to grab an appendage and snap it up into the air. Even though the trap was made completely of natural materials you would quickly conclude that it was the product of intelligent design.

Intelligent design is a good explanation for a number of biochemical systems, but I should insert a word of caution. Intelligent design theory has to be seen in context: it does not try to explain everything. We live in a complex world where lots of different things can happen. When deciding how various rocks came to be shaped the way they are a geologist might consider a whole range of factors: rain, wind, the movement of glaciers, the activity of moss and lichens, volcanic action, nuclear explosions, asteroid impact, or the hand of a sculptor. The shape of one rock might have been determined primarily by one mechanism, the shape of another rock by another mechanism.

Similarly, evolutionary biologists have recognized that a number of factors might have affected the development of life: common descent, natural selection, migration, population size, founder effects (effects that may be due to the limited number of organisms that begin a new species), genetic drift (spread of "neutral," nonselective mutations), gene flow (the incorporation of genes into a population from a separate population), linkage (occurrence of two genes on the same chromosome), and much more. The fact that some biochemical systems were designed by an intelligent agent does not mean that any of the other factors are not operative, common, or important.

Conclusion

It is often said that science must avoid any conclusions which smack of the supernatural. But this seems to me to be both bad logic and bad science. Science is not a game in which arbitrary rules are used to decide what explanations are to be permitted. Rather, it is an effort to make true statements about physical reality. It was only about sixty years ago that the expansion of the universe was first observed. This fact immediately suggested a singular event—that at some time in the distant past the universe began expanding from an extremely small size.

To many people this inference was loaded with overtones of a supernatural event—the creation, the beginning of the universe. The prominent physicist A. S. Eddington probably spoke for many physicists in voicing his disgust with such a notion:

> Philosophically, the notion of an abrupt beginning to the present order of Nature is repugnant to me, as I think it must be to most; and even those who would welcome a proof of the intervention of a Creator will probably consider that a single winding-up at some remote epoch is not really the kind of relation between God and his world that brings satisfaction to the mind.

Nonetheless, the big bang hypothesis was embraced by physics and over the years has proven to be a very fruitful paradigm. The point here is that physics followed the data where it seemed to lead, even though some thought the model gave aid and comfort to religion. In the present day, as biochemistry multiplies examples of fantastically complex molecular systems, systems which discourage even an attempt to explain how they may have arisen, we should take a lesson from physics. The conclusion of design flows naturally from the data; we should not shrink from it; we should embrace it and build on it.

In concluding, it is important to realize that we are not inferring design from what we do not know, but from what we do know. We are not inferring design to account for a black box, but to account for an open box. A man from a primitive culture who sees an automobile might guess that it was powered by the wind or by an antelope hidden under the car, but when he opens up the hood and sees the engine he immediately realizes that it was designed. In the same way biochemistry has opened up the cell to examine what makes it run and we see that it, too, was designed.

It was a shock to the people of the 19th century when they discovered, from observations science had made, that many features of the biological world could be ascribed to the elegant principle of natural selection. It is a shock to us in the twentieth century to discover, from observations science has made, that the fundamental mechanisms of life cannot be ascribed to natural selection, and therefore were designed. But we must deal with our shock as best we can and go on. The theory of undirected evolution is already dead, but the work of science continues.

DISCUSSION QUESTIONS

1. Explain what Behe means by "irreducible complexity." Give examples of what is and of what is not irreducibly complex, according to Behe, then explain why he takes the former to be and the latter not to be irreducibly complex. Why is irreducible complexity supposed to be a problem for Darwin's theory of evolution?

2. Behe cites the human eye as evidence against Darwin's theory of evolution. Explain Behe's claims and arguments using this example. How could Darwin best respond? Do you think Darwin's theory of evolution can explain the eye? Why or why not?

3. Behe next cites cilia to argue against Darwin's theory of evolution. Answer the same questions as in Discussion Question 2 about this example.

4. In addition to arguing against Darwin, Behe argues positively that "the conclusion of intelligent design flows naturally from the data itself—not from sacred books or sectarian beliefs." Explain Behe's conclusion here and his argument for that conclusion. Do you agree with Behe? Why or why not?

LIVING WITH DARWIN

———————■———————

by Philip Kitcher

(New York: Oxford University Press, 2007)

. . . Darwin's own consideration of the concrete case argument focused on some complex organs and structures that he rightly believed to be hard to understand in terms of natural selection. Two examples are prominent in the *Origin*, the eye and the electric organs found in some fish. The latter example disconcerted Darwin because the fish with electric organs are of very different types, and have their organs in different parts of their bodies. Much to his relief, research on electric fish carried out by a contemporary who was not sympathetic to evolutionary ideas—"McDonnell of Dublin (a first-rate man)"*—revealed that, for each type of fish with an electric organ, there is a related fish with a similar organ (not functionally electric) in the same position. What had initially appeared to be the challenge of understanding how different electric organs had been built from scratch, became the much simpler question of how a similar change had occurred in each instance.

Darwin himself offered a tentative proposal about the evolution of the eye. He supposed that sensitivity to light might come in degrees, and that it might be possible to find, among existing organisms, some with a crude ability to respond to light, others with a more refined capacity and so on in something like a series. Perhaps, he speculated, research on these creatures might expose reasons why the different levels of sensitivity provided an advantage over rival organisms who had less, thus providing a way of answering (or sidestepping) the creationist quip, "What use is half an eye?"

It has taken more than a century of research on a wide variety of organisms to demonstrate that Darwin's hunch was basically right. Appearances to the contrary, organs and structures sensitive to light can be assembled piecemeal, with the intermediates enjoying some advantage over the competition. Biologists have studied organisms that respond to the light that impinges on their surfaces, organisms with indentations of the superficial layer that are able to acquire information about the direction of the light, organisms with deeper indentations whose light detection is more fine grained, organisms that have a structure resembling a pinhole camera, organisms that interpose a translucent medium between the surface and the aperture through which the light comes—and so on. By studying this sequence of organisms, they have been able to explore the transitions through which relatively crude abilities to detect light were successively refined.** One feature of the story deserves emphasis. Darwin didn't start with a comparison between the fully formed eye—in a human being or an octopus, say—and then think of the component parts as being

---

* Francis Darwin, ed., *Life and Letters of Charles Darwin*, vol. 2 (London: John Murray, 1888), 352.

** For a superbly accessible presentation of this research, see Richard Dawkins, *Climbing Mount Improbable* (New York: Norton, 1996). Another lucid, and concise, account by one of the scientists involved is Dan-Eric Nilsson, "Vision Optics and Evolution" in *Bioscience*, 39, 1989, 298–307.

introduced, one at a time. He resisted the challenge to explain first the advantage of an eighth of an eye, then the advantage of a quarter of an eye, and so on, and focused instead on a function, light sensitivity, that might have been refined from an initial state of absence. To put it more bluntly, he didn't allow his envisaged challengers to define the sequence of "intermediates" for him.

Savvy champions of the concrete case argument know this story. They appreciate Darwin's ingenuity in responding to the challenge, and, although they think the response ultimately fails, their reasons for this judgment depend on a more general problem for evolution under natural selection. That more general problem derives from the fine structure of the components of complex organs (like eyes), the molecular mechanisms that have to be in place for eyes to work. For all Darwin's cleverness, he failed to appreciate the full depth, and the full generality of the difficulty confronting him.

The principal exponent of the complex case argument is Michael Behe, a professor of biochemistry, who argues at length in *Darwin's Black Box* that the real troubles of natural selection become visible when you appreciate the molecular components of complex biological systems. Almost everywhere you look in nature, there are complicated structures and processes, with many molecular constituents, and all the constituents need to be present and to fit together precisely for things to work as they should. Biochemical pathways require numerous enzymes to interact with one another, in appropriate relative concentrations, so that some important process can occur. If you imagine a mutation in one of the genes that directs the formation of some essential protein, or if you suppose that the genetic material becomes shuffled in a way that allows for differences in the rates at which proteins are formed, it looks as though disaster will ensue. Crucial pieces will be missing, or won't be present in the right proportions, so that everything will break down. How then could organisms with the pertinent structures or processes have evolved from organisms that lacked them?

Behe offers numerous instances of molecular machines that, he claims, could not have been built up in stages by natural selection. Among his most influential examples is a discussion of devices that some bacteria use for motion, flagella. He contrasts the bacterial flagellum with a different motor, used by other cells, the cilium. "In 1973 it was discovered that some bacteria swim by rotating their flagella. So the bacterial flagellum acts as a rotary propeller—in contrast to the cilium, which acts more like an oar."[*] Both flagella and cilia are intricate structures, and Behe describes the many molecular parts and systems that have to be present if they are to do their jobs. He concludes that the complexity of the organization dooms any attempt to explain its emergence as the result of natural selection. "As biochemists have begun to examine apparently simple structures like cilia and flagella, they have discovered staggering complexity, with dozens or even hundreds of

[*] Behe, *Darwin's Black Box*, 70. Behe uses the example of the bacterial flagellum as a parade case in many of his writings and presentations. See, for example, "Design at the Foundation of Life" in *Science and Evidence for Design in the Universe* (San Francisco: Ignatius Press, 2000), 120 ff.

precisely tailored parts. It is very likely that many of the parts we have not considered here are required for any cilium to function in a cell. As the number of required parts increases, the difficulty of gradually putting the system together skyrockets, and the likelihood of indirect scenarios plummets. Darwin looks more and more forlorn."[*] Indeed, the most famous portraits of Darwin hardly make him look exactly cheerful, but it's worth asking why examples like these should render him more forlorn.

Perhaps it seems obvious. Natural selection depends upon mutations that are not produced in response to the organism's needs. The bacteria are at the mercy of chance, which will fling in this variant protein or that, with negligible probability that the latest novelty will fit with what went before or will contribute to the design project of building a flagellum. In essentials, however, this is precisely parallel to an old creationist strategy, just the one that Darwin sidestepped in the case of the eye. Behe has specified how the intermediates are to be formed, and it isn't surprising that his preferred scenario has the air of impossibility.

What exactly is known about the bacterial flagellum? During the past few decades, careful molecular studies have identified the genes that direct the assembly of the motor, and have explored the ways in which it is put together in the development of an individual bacterium. Some mutations in these genes allow for bacteria to move, albeit less efficiently. What is currently missing, however, is that systematic study of the differences among bacteria with flagella and bacteria without that would parallel the knowledge attained in the case of vision. A sufficiently intensive study of the genomes of bacteria that lack flagella would enable biologists to explore the potential role of some of the crucial genes, and of the proteins they give rise to, when others are absent, and thus enable them to make more progress with Behe's apparently formidable challenge.

Most sciences face unsolved problems—indeed the exciting unsolved problems are the motivators for talented people to enter a field. Chemists still struggle to understand how newly made proteins fold into their three-dimensional shapes as they are synthesized. To take an instance closer to hand, Behe's own discussion acknowledges that there's still a lot to learn about the molecular structure and functions of cilia. Unsolved questions are not typically written off as unsolvable—nobody proposes that there's some special force, unknown to current chemistry (an "intelligent force" perhaps?) that guides the proteins to their proper forms, or some hand that assembles the cilium in the development of an individual bacterium. Why, then, should we believe that the problem of the bacterial flagellum is unsolvable? Just because, in the absence of systematic molecular studies of bacteria with and without flagella, we can't currently give a satisfactory scenario for the evolution of the bacterial flagellum under natural selection, why should we conclude that further research couldn't disclose how that evolution occurred?

---

[*] Behe, *Darwin's Black Box*, 73.

We are beguiled by the simple story line Behe rehearses. He invites us to consider the situation by supposing that the flagellum requires the introduction of some number—20, say—of proteins that the ancestral bacterium doesn't originally have. So Darwinians have to produce a sequence of 21 organisms, the first having none of the proteins, and each subsequent organism having one more than its predecessor. Darwin is forlorn because however he tries to imagine the possible pathway along which genetic changes successively appeared, he appreciates the plight of numbers 2–20, each of which is clogged with proteins that can't serve any function, proteins that interfere with important cellular processes. These organisms will be targets of selection, and will wither in the struggle for existence. Only number 1, and number 21, in which all the protein constituents come together to form the flagellum, have what it takes. Because of the dreadful plight of the intermediates, natural selection couldn't have brought the bacterium from there to here.

The story is fantasy, and Darwinians should disavow any commitment to it. First, there is no good reason for supposing that the ancestral bacterium lacked all, or even any, of the proteins needed to build the flagellum. It's a common theme of evolutionary biology that constituents of a cell, a tissue, or an organism are put to new uses because of a modification of the genome. Perhaps the immediate precursor of the bacterium with the flagellum is an organism in which all the protein constituents are already present, but are employed in different ways. Then, at the very last step there's a change in the genome that removes whatever chemical barrier previously prevented the building of the flagellum. In this organism (the precursor), the function of one of the proteins is to increase the efficiency of a particular energy-transfer process. The precursor of the precursor lacked that protein, so that the genetic change that led to the precursor improved a process that was previously adequate. So it goes, back down a sequence of ancestors, all quite capable of functioning in their environments but all at a selective disadvantage to the bacteria that succeeded them.

Isn't this all fantasy too? Of course*—but it is no more the product of speculative imagination than Behe's seemingly plausible assumption that the components of the flagellum would have had to be added one by one, and would have sat around idly (at best) until the culminating moment when all were present. Moreover, we were supposed to be offered a proof of impossibility, and that won't be complete until Behe and his allies have shown that all the conceivable scenarios through which bacteria might acquire flagella are flawed. Really demonstrating impossibility—or even improbability—here and in kindred instances, is extremely difficult, precisely because it would require a much more systematic survey of the molecular differences among bacteria.

* Perhaps not complete fantasy. The account I offer here is concordant with a recent review of the molecular details of the bacterial flagellum. See Howard C. Berg, "The Rotary Motor of Bacterial Flagella," *Annual Review of Biochemistry*, 72, 2003, 19–54. (For this reference, I'm indebted to Mel Simon.)

The serious way forward is to amend our ignorance, by sequencing the genomes of different bacteria, with and without flagella. Using our current knowledge of the genetic basis of the flagellum, researchers would be able to specify more clearly what the intermediate forms—those with some, but not all, of the crucial genes—might have been like, and what functions the relevant proteins might have served. Until we know these things, efforts to describe intermediates will be so much whistling in the dark. Behe's examples rely on guesses that simply anticipate what this hard work would reveal.

So we have the illusion of an impossibility proof. Allegedly there could be no sequence of intermediates concluding with the fortunate, flagellum-bearing bacterium, in which each member of the sequence enjoyed a selective advantage over its predecessor. Behe's story (quite charmingly told in *Darwin's Black Box*) offers his own preferred version of what the sequence would have to be like. Since Darwinians have no commitment to simpleminded stories of sequential addition of components, there is no reason to accept Behe's description. Because the same rhetorical strategy pervades his entire book, showing up in all the instances of the concrete case argument he provides, all the parade of examples really shows is that there are some interesting problems for molecularly minded evolutionists to work on, problems they might hope to solve in the light of increased understanding from comparative studies of the genetics and development of a wide variety of organisms.

The computational argument occurs in a variety of forms in current intelligent design literature, sometimes with relatively simple calculations of infinitesimal probabilities, on other occasions with much more technical specification of conditions under which we should make the "design inference" and conclude that some aspect of life has been intelligently designed.[*] Whether or not intelligent designers attempt to be fully explicit about the requirements for invoking design, all their versions require the preliminary step of arguing that it is highly improbable that various aspects of life on earth could have emerged through natural selection. To use an analogy much beloved by earlier creationists, Darwinian claims about selection and the organization of life are equivalent to the idea that a hurricane in a junkyard could assemble a functioning airplane.

Besides providing the concrete case argument, Behe offers several versions of its computational cousin. Here's his attack on a scenario for the evolution of a blood-clotting mechanism, tentatively proposed by the eminent biochemist Russell Doolittle:

> Let's do our own quick calculation. Consider that animals with blood-clotting cascades have roughly 10,000 genes, each of which is divided into an average of three pieces. This gives a total of about 30,000 gene pieces. TPA [tissue plasminogen activator] has four different types of domains. By "variously shuffling," the odds

[*] For the full-dress treatment of the design inference, see William Dembski, *The Design Inference* (Cambridge: Cambridge University Press, 1998). For an incisive rebuttal, see Brandon Fitelson, Christopher Stephens and Elliot Sober, "How Not to Detect Design" in Robert Pennock, ed., *Intelligent Design Creationism and its Critics* (Cambridge, MA: MIT Press, 2001).

of getting those four domains together is 30,000 to the fourth power [presumably Behe means that the chance is one-thirty-thousandth to the fourth power], which is approximately one-tenth to the eighteenth power. Now, if the Irish Sweepstakes had odds of winning of one-tenth to the eighteenth power, and if a million people played the lottery each year, it would take about a thousand billion years before *anyone* (not just a particular person) won the lottery. . . . Doolittle apparently needs to shuffle and deal himself a number of perfect bridge hands to win the game.[*]

At first sight, this looks very powerful, since, given the time available for the evolution of life on earth (four billion or so years), it seems extremely improbable that the clotting mechanism could have evolved through natural selection.

Yet we should think carefully about the ways in which the pertinent probabilities are calculated. Behe is relying on two general ideas about probability. One is the thought that, when events are independent of one another, the probability that both will occur is the product of the individual probabilities—if you toss a fair die twice, then the chance of getting two sixes is 1 in 36; for, on each toss, the probability is 1 in 6, and, since the tosses are independent of one another, you multiply. The other idea is that, when you have a range of alternatives and don't have any reasons for thinking that one is more likely to occur than another, each of the possibilities has an equal chance. This idea, the notorious "principle of indifference," is known to be problematic, but, judiciously employed, it serves us well in some everyday contexts—as, for example, when we conclude that each side of the die has the same probability of falling uppermost.

Even in ordinary life, however, there are occasions on which applications of these principles would lead us to obviously unacceptable conclusions, so that we would rethink our computations. Consider a humdrum phenomenon suggested by Behe's analogy with bridge. You take a standard deck of cards and deal 13 to yourself. What is the probability that you get exactly those cards in exactly that order? The answer is 1 in 4×10^{21}. Suppose you repeat the process 10 times. You'll now have received 10 standard bridge hands, 10 sets of 13 cards, each one delivered in a particular order. Scrupulously, you record just the order in which all these cards were received, and calculate the chance that this event occurs. The probability; you claim, is 1 in $4^{10} \times 10^{210}$, which is approximately 1 in 10^{216}—notice that this denominator is enormously larger than Behe's 10^{18}. It must be really improbable that you (or anyone else) would ever receive just those cards in just that order in the entire history of the universe. But you did, and you have witnesses to testify that your records are correct. Excitedly, you contact Michael Behe to announce this quite miraculous event, surely evidence of some kind of Intelligence at work in the universe.

Your report would not be well received. Like everyone else, Behe knows how to understand this commonplace occurrence. Given the way in which the cards were initially arranged, the first deal was bound to go as it did. Given the shuffling that produced the ordering prior to the second deal, that

[*] Behe, *Darwin's Black Box*, 94.

deal, too, was sure to give rise to just those cards in that order; and so on. So there was a perspective, unknown to you, from which the probability of that sequence of cards wasn't some infinitesimally small number, but one (as high as chances go). If you describe events that actually occur from a perspective that lacks crucial items of knowledge, you can make them look improbable. We know enough about card dealing and coin tossing to understand this, and to see the calculation I attributed to you as perverse—for, although you don't know what the initial setup was, you should have recognized that there was some initial setup that would determine the sequence. Hence you should have known that application of the two general principles of probability in this context would provide a misleading view of the chance that this particular sequence would result.

In the case of the evolution of blood clotting, our ignorance is deeper. Not only do we not know what the initial molecular conditions—the prior state of the organisms in the population in which blood clotting emerged—were, we also don't know whether that initial state favored certain sorts of molecular changes rather than others. We have reason to think that Behe's assumption that there's a precise chance of 1 in 30,000 that each gene piece will participate in the "shuffling" process is incorrect. For, given what we know about mechanisms within the genome, the idea of exactly equal chances is suspect. But we don't know whether, given the initial molecular state, the chance of the cascade Doolittle hypothesizes remains infinitesimally small or whether it is actually one. Any estimate of the probability here is an irresponsible guess.

My imagined experiment with the deck of cards suggests a different way to think about the problem. Imagine that all the hands you were dealt were mundane—fairly evenly distributed among the four suits, with a scattering of high cards in each. If you calculated the probability of receiving ten mundane hands in succession, it would naturally be a lot higher than the chance of being dealt those very particular mundane hands, with the cards arriving in precisely that sequence (although it wouldn't be as high as you might expect). Blood clotting might also work in the same way, depending on how many candidates there are among the 30,000 "gene pieces" to which Behe alludes, that would yield a protein product able to play the necessary role. Suppose that there are a thousand acceptable candidates for each of the four positions in the molecule we need (TPA). The chance of success on any particular draw is now about 1 in 2.5 million. If there were 10,000 tries a year, it would take, on average, two or three centuries to find an appropriate combination, a flicker of an instant in evolutionary time.

My assumptions are no better—and no worse—than Behe's, for neither of us knows how tolerant the blood-clotting system is of the molecular combinations that the animals in question (whatever they were) might have supplied. We simply don't know what the right way to look at this problem is. But, given our ignorance, we shouldn't make wild guesses and then declare that the probabilities are so low that evolution under natural selection is impossible. A better research strategy would be to try to assemble information that will replace the guesses with serious estimates.

Moreover, even when the chance of a particular event turns out to be extremely small, it is important to resist the idea that that event could not have occurred. Imagine that you own a ticket in a lottery with an extremely large number of tickets—a million, say—and that the lottery is decided by a fundamentally random process, one that has no underlying causal basis by which the outcome will be determined. (You might suppose that each ticket is associated with a specific atomic nucleus of some radioactive element, and that the prize will go to the person whose nucleus decays first.) On any perspective we might justifiably adopt, there is a probability of one in a million that you will win, and similarly for all the other ticket holders (nobody has more than one ticket). Clearly, somebody will be lucky, and, after the fact, we'll have to admit that something very improbable has occurred. Moreover, this conclusion remains valid even if the number of tickets is vastly expanded. However small a probability we compute, it would be wrong to suppose that an outcome with that probability would be impossible. Finally, even if some people had massive numbers of tickets, it would still be possible for someone holding only one to win. That shows that an extremely improbable outcome, one much less probable than alternatives, is still possible.*

So there is another way to think about the allegedly minute probabilities of life as we know it. Our galaxy has roughly 200 billion stars, and the total number of galaxies, each with similar numbers of stars is—literally—astronomical. Some fraction of these stars has planets that are potentially suitable for sustaining life. Each such planet could be conceived as "buying a ticket" in an enormous lottery, with the prize, or one of the prizes, consisting in the emergence of life. For any of those planets, the probability of gaining that prize is extremely small, but if there are enough of them, one will win. That lucky planet may have been ours. . . .

So far I have focused on the negative doctrine of intelligent design, the identification of unsolved evolutionary problems. We now have to consider the positive thesis, the claim that the phenomena to which Darwin's detractors point are produced by a process that deserves the label "intelligent." Two issues need to be considered. First, on what grounds should we apply the label? Second, what help can intelligent design provide in understanding the phenomena in question? . . .

Making any judgment about whether a mechanism is intelligent or not appears rather difficult until we have been told considerably more about the way in which that mechanism operates. Officially, of course, we aren't supposed to personify this mechanism, and it's hard to understand just what the attribution of Intelligence even means if we resist the personification. If something counts as intelligent, wouldn't it have psychological states and engage in psychological processes—and wouldn't anything like that be very like a person? Intelligent design-ers do not address such questions. . . .

---

* For advice about these probabilistic considerations, I am grateful to Isaac Levi and Erick Weinberg.

It's simply a fallacy to suppose that because a particular structure or mechanism appears complex, then the causal agent that brought it about must be appropriately characterized as having "foreseen" or "planned" or "designed" the outcome. Even if intelligent design-ers were right in supposing that the phenomena they indicate couldn't have evolved by natural selection, only a more explicit identification of the causal mechanism that was at work could justify the conclusion that that mechanism is intelligent.

So, turning to the second question posed above, what help can intelligent design provide when we try to understand the difficulties it takes to beset Darwinism? How does it deal with the bacterial flagellum, for example?

If we take Behe at his word when he declares that he finds "the idea of common descent" to be "fairly convincing," and that he has "no particular reason to doubt it,"[*] then we should suppose that bacteria with flagella emerged from ancestors who lacked flagella. In line with the simple additive story he uses to make a history of natural selection appear implausible, he must suppose that the ancestors were missing a number of crucial proteins that the lucky descendants acquired, proteins that, once present, fit themselves together in the flagellum. If the intelligent design perspective is to help settle the unsolved problems of evolution, it would be good to have an alternative account that tells us how Intelligence facilitated the transition.

Unfortunately, the rest is silence. Neither in Behe's writings, nor in those of any other intelligent design-er, is there the slightest indication of how Intelligence performs the magic that poor, limited, natural selection cannot. On the face of it, there are just two basic possibilities. The first option is that Intelligence arranges the environment so that the intermediates—the apparently hapless organisms, cluttered with useless proteins—are protected against elimination under natural selection. (If we were unofficially inclined, we might say that the good Lord tempers the wind to the shorn bacterium.) The second option is that Intelligence provides for coordinated mutations to arise. If 20 genetic changes are needed, it brings about all of them at once. Or we can mix elements of both options and suppose that Intelligence introduces mutations in clumps—first ten, say, and then another ten, or first seven, then another seven, then six—and arranges protective environments for the intermediates. Of course, any story along these lines raises serious doubts. Just how does the coordination of the genetic changes or the modification of the environment work?

In presenting the possibilities in this way, I may seem to be forcing words into the mouths of the intelligent design-ers. Their core position, after all, is that at crucial moments in the history of life, descendants of some ancestors who lacked some trait (or organ or structure) came to possess the pertinent trait (organ, structure) by some causal process that is, unlike natural selection, intelligent. Why, then, do they have to talk about genes, mutations, and the need for protection against natural selection? The answer is that the traits in question are heritable—they are not introduced in each generation

[*] Behe, *Darwin's Black Box*, 7.

by some continued activity on the part of Intelligence, but emerge through the interactions of genes and environments. As in the case of the bacterial flagellum, there are underlying genes, and hence there have to be genetic changes in the passages from the ancestors to the descendants. If these changes occur over several generations, then, on the intelligent design-ers' own principles, there has to be protection against the tendency of natural selection to weed out the hapless intermediates. If they happen in one step, then, again by the favored principles, there must be coordinated mutations. Hence, even if the position would prefer to talk more vaguely of "novelties," it is committed to one of the options I have presented.

What intelligent design urgently needs if it's going to make any progress in understanding these transitions, in tackling the problems it claims to raise, is a set of coherent principles that identify the ways in which Intelligence is directed and what its powers and limitations are. If we lapse from the official story for a moment, we have to have some idea about what Intelligence "wants to achieve" and what kinds of things "it can do to work toward what it wants." What basis do we have to think that Intelligence aims to remedy the plight of the flagellumless bacteria, who can't evolve into bacteria-with-a-flagellum under natural selection? What basis is there to believe that Intelligence—or anything else, for that matter—can coordinate genetic changes or modify environments?

In fact, we need two distinct kinds of principles. First, there have to be principles that specify when Intelligence swings into action. Perhaps they will tell us that Intelligence operates when there are potentially advantageous complex traits that can't evolve by natural selection. Second, there must be principles that explain what Intelligence does when it acts. Perhaps these will identify the sorts of genetic changes Intelligence can arrange, or the ways in which it can inhibit the normal operation of selection.

It is already clear that these principles will be hard to state precisely. For, if Intelligence has been waiting in the wings throughout the history of life, seizing opportunities as they arise, we know that there are all sorts of things it hasn't done. Apparently Intelligence isn't directed toward eliminating the junk from genomes or removing vestigial structures like the whale's pelvis or generating radically new arrangements for mammalian forelimbs. It's possible, of course, that although directed toward these ends, Intelligence is simply unable to bring them about. So any satisfactory principles must differentiate between the bacterial flagellum, blood-clotting cascade, and similar places where Intelligence shows its prowess, and the accumulated junk, vestigial structures, and genetic blunders, where it remains in abeyance. . . .

Why do intelligent design-ers ignore the basic problem of explaining the power and direction of the mechanism they invoke, a problem that strikes at the heart of their theory? Apparently, their preferred perspective faces a multitude of currently unsolved puzzles about the scope and direction of Intelligence. Yet, unlike their counterparts in other scientific ventures, they are reluctant to suggest their strategies for seeking solutions. Their reticence provokes the charge that what they are doing is not science, but perhaps breaking their silence would be theologically unwise. Saying too much might disrupt the harmony between the sanitized version of intelligent design elaborated in the classroom during the week and the richer account delivered from the pulpit on Sunday. Moreover, saying anything that would genuinely respond to the puzzles might be saying too much.

Yet, I suspect many people would simply reject the terms in which I have posed the problem. Friends of intelligent design would prefer not to talk about evolutionary transitions at all. So, they might say, the complex structures are built from scratch. Intelligence is a creative force that replaces older types of organisms with new, individually designed species. Conceived in this way, intelligent design disavows Behe's acceptance of descent with modification, drawing bars across the tree of life to mark the places of radical discontinuity, of events of special creation. . . .

The real situation is that intelligent design-ers oscillate. . . . Yet however they wriggle, they find no satisfactory positive doctrine, no set of principles about Intelligence that can adequately account for the phenomena. This is why readers hunt through their literature seeking fragments of positive theory in vain. They won't find it. Because to advance any such theory would expose the corpse of dead science.

DISCUSSION QUESTIONS

1. How does Kitcher explain the evolution of the human eye? Is this explanation adequate? Why or why not?
2. How does Kitcher explain the evolution of the bacterial flagellum? Is this explanation adequate? Why or why not?
3. How does Kitcher explain the evolution of the blood-clotting mechanism? Is this explanation adequate? Why or why not?
4. Are there other examples that Darwinian theory cannot explain?
5. Can intelligent design theory itself explain the examples that are supposed to cause trouble for Darwinian theories of evolution?
6. Is "intelligent design" a scientific theory? Why or why not?
7. In your opinion, should "intelligent design" be required (or allowed) to be taught in public high schools alongside evolution and natural selection as part of the science curriculum? Why or why not? (It might help to read Judge Jones's opinion in *Kitzmiller v. Dover Area School District*.)

NOTES

[1] Thomas Kuhn gives prominence to this difference in his important work, *The Structure of Scientific Revolutions*, 2nd ed. (Chicago: University of Chicago Press, 1970).

[2] Stephen Colbert, *I Am America (And So Can You!)* (New York: Grand Central Publishing, 2007), 207.

21

RELIGIOUS REASONING

Religion is central to the lives of many people across the world. They attend religious ceremonies and pray or meditate, sometimes several times a day. Even when they are not engaged in explicitly religious practices, religion also affects believers' views in morality, politics, and even science. (See Chapter 20.) Critics of religion disdain these influences and claim that religions depend on false or unjustified beliefs, especially the belief that God exists. Both sides of this debate present ingenious arguments, which will be explored in this chapter.

What is religion? That's not an easy question to answer. Religions are varied and complex. They include rituals, communities, institutions, texts, and beliefs. You cannot understand religion as a whole by looking merely at religious *beliefs*. Moreover, religious beliefs cover many topics, from the afterlife and the meaning of life to creation and miracles. You also cannot understand religion by considering only beliefs *about God*. Nonetheless, since belief in God is so central to so many religions, it is crucial to ask whether God exists.

People who believe that God exists are called *theists*. People who deny the existence of God (or any other god) are called *atheists*. Many people accept neither belief and claim that we cannot know whether God exists. They are called *agnostics*.

It is also important to realize, however, that people who believe in a traditional God within Christianity, say, usually deny the existence of other kinds of gods. Their position is, thus, theism with respect to their own religion and God but atheism regarding other religions and gods. Hence, when asking whether someone is a theist or an atheist, it is crucial to specify the kind of God at issue.

Who or what is God? Different religions include different beliefs about God or gods. Nonetheless, the dominant traditions in the Western world—Judaism, Christianity, and Islam—all derive from Abraham and share certain central beliefs about God. In traditional views, God is a person with the three "omnis": omnipotent (or all-powerful), omniscient (or all-knowing), and omnibenevolent (or all-good). Some theologians add that God is omnipresent (or equally present at all spaces and times), but many see God as eternal or existing outside of all time and space.

Nonetheless, God is supposed to be active in time, such as when He causes miracles or answers prayers. Not all Jews, Christians, and Moslems share all of these claims about God, but they are accepted by traditional theologians.

The readings in this chapter are about the traditional Christian God. William Lane Craig argues for the existence of a traditional Christian God. Edwin Curley then argues against the existence of such a God. These readings are slightly revised transcripts of a live debate that occurred at the University of Michigan in 1999, so they bear some marks of that setting.

FIVE REASONS TO BELIEVE IN GOD
■

by William Lane Craig

Good Evening! I want to begin by thanking [Michigan Christian Grads] for inviting me to participate in tonight's debate. And I want to say what a privilege it is to be debating so eminent a scholar as Professor Curley. When I was a doctoral student writing my dissertation on the cosmological argument for God's existence, Dr. Curley's work on the famous philosopher Benedict de Spinoza was a valuable resource to me in trying to analyze Spinoza's own argument for God. So it's a genuine honor to be sharing the podium with Dr. Curley tonight.

Now in tonight's debate it seems that there are two basic questions that we need to ask ourselves:

I. Are there any good reasons to think that God does not exist?

And

II. Are there good reasons to think that God does exist?

Now with respect to the first question, I'll leave it up to Dr. Curley to present the reasons why he thinks that God does not exist. Atheist philosophers have tried for centuries to disprove the existence of God. But no one has ever been able to come up with a convincing argument. So rather than attack straw men at this point, I'll just wait to hear Professor Curley's answer to the following question: What good reasons are there to think that God does not exist?

So let's move on, then, to that second question: Are there good reasons to think that God does exist? Tonight I'm going to present five reasons why I think that God exists. Whole books have been written on each one of these, so all I can present here is a brief sketch of each argument and then go into more detail as Dr. Curley responds to them.[*] These reasons are independent

---

[*] For a popular presentation of these arguments and responses to typical objections, see my booklet "God, Are You There?" (Atlanta: RZIM, 1999).

of one another, so that if even one of them is sound, it furnishes good grounds for believing that God exists. Taken together, they constitute a powerful cumulative case that God exists.

1: God makes sense of the origin of the universe. Have you ever asked yourself where the universe came from? Why everything exists instead of just nothing? Typically atheists have said that the universe is eternal, and that's all. But surely this doesn't make sense. Just think about it for a minute. If the universe never began to exist, then that means that the number of events in the past history of the universe is infinite. But mathematicians recognize that the idea of an actually infinite number of things leads to self-contradictions. For example, what is infinity minus infinity? Well, mathematically, you get self-contradictory answers. This shows that infinity is just an idea in your mind, not something that exists in reality. David Hilbert, perhaps the greatest mathematician of this century states, "The infinite is nowhere to be found in reality. It neither exists in nature nor provides a legitimate basis for rational thought. The role that remains for the infinite to play is solely that of an idea."[*]

But that entails that since past events are not just ideas, but are real, the number of past events must be finite. Therefore, the series of past events can't just go back forever. Rather the universe must have begun to exist.

This conclusion has been confirmed by remarkable discoveries in astronomy and astrophysics. The astrophysical evidence indicates that the universe began to exist in a great explosion called the "Big Bang" about 15 billion years ago. Physical space and time were created in that event, as well as all the matter and energy in the universe. Therefore, as Cambridge astronomer Fred Hoyle points out, the Big Bang theory requires the creation of the universe from nothing. This is because, as you go back in time, you reach a point in time at which, in Hoyle's words, the universe was "shrunk down to nothing at all."[**] Thus, what the Big Bang model requires is that the universe began to exist and was created out of nothing.

Now this tends to be very awkward for the atheist. For as Anthony Kenny of Oxford University urges, "A proponent of the Big Bang theory, at least if he is an atheist, must believe that the universe came from nothing and by nothing."[†]

But surely that doesn't make sense! Out of nothing, nothing comes. So why does the universe exist instead of just nothing? Where did it come from? There must have been a cause which brought the universe into being. And from the very nature of the case, this cause must be an uncaused, changeless, timeless, and immaterial being which created the universe. It must be uncaused because there cannot be an infinite regress of causes. It

[*] David Hilbert, "On the Infinite," in *Philosophy of Mathematics,* ed. with an Introduction by Paul Benacerraf and Hillary Putnam (Englewood Cliffs, NJ: Prentice-Hall, 1964), 139, 141.

[**] Fred Hoyle, *Astronomy and Cosmology* (San Francisco: Freeman, 1975), 658.

[†] Anthony Kenny, *The Five Ways: St. Thomas Aquinas' Proofs of God's Existence* (New York: Schocken Books, 1969), 66.

must be timeless and therefore changeless—at least without the universe—because it created time. Because it also created space, it must transcend space as well and therefore be immaterial, not physical.

Moreover, I would argue, it must also be personal. For how else could a timeless cause give rise to a temporal effect like the universe? If the cause were an impersonal set of sufficient conditions, then the cause could never exist without the effect. If the sufficient conditions were timelessly present, then the effect would be timelessly present as well. The only way for the cause to be timeless but for the effect to begin in time is if the cause is a personal agent who freely chooses to create an effect in time without any prior determining conditions. And, thus, we are brought, not merely to the transcendent cause of the universe, but to its personal Creator.

Isn't it incredible that the Big Bang theory thus fits in with what the Christian theist has always believed: that in the beginning God created the universe? Now I put it to you, which do you think makes more sense: that the Christian theist is right or that the universe just popped into being, uncaused, out of nothing? I, at least, have no trouble assessing these alternatives.

2: God makes sense of the complex order in the universe. During the last 30 years, scientists have discovered that the existence of intelligent life depends upon a delicate and complex balance of initial conditions simply given in the Big Bang itself. We now know that life-prohibiting universes are vastly more probable than any life-permitting universe like ours. How much more probable?

Well, the answer is that the chances that the universe should be life-permitting are so infinitesimal as to be incomprehensible and incalculable. For example, Stephen Hawking has estimated that if the rate of the universe's expansion one second after the Big Bang had been smaller by even one part in a hundred thousand million million, the universe would have recollapsed into a hot fireball.[*] P. C. W. Davies has calculated that the odds against the initial conditions being suitable for star formation (without which planets could not exist) is one followed by a thousand billion billion zeroes, at least.[**] [He also] estimates that a change in the strength of gravity or of the weak force by only one part in 10 raised to the 100th power would have prevented a life-permitting universe.[†] There are around 50 such constants and quantities present in the Big Bang which must be fine-tuned in this way if the universe is to permit life. And it's not just each quantity which must be finely tuned; their ratios to each other must also be exquisitely finely tuned. So improbability is multiplied by improbability by improbability until our minds are reeling in incomprehensible numbers.

There is no physical reason why these constants and quantities should posses the values they do. The onetime agnostic physicist P. C. W. Davies comments, "Through my scientific work I have come to believe more and

---

[*] Stephen W. Hawking, *A Brief History of Time* (New York: Bantam Books, 1988), 123.

[**] P. C. W. Davies, *Other Worlds* (London: Dent, 1980), 160–61, 168–69.

[†] P. C. W. Davies, "The Anthropic Principle," *Particle and Nuclear Physics* 10 (1983): 28.

more strongly that the physical universe is put together with an ingenuity so astonishing that I cannot accept it merely as a brute fact."* Similarly, Fred Hoyle remarks, "A common sense interpretation of the facts suggests that a super-intellect has monkeyed with physics."** Robert Jastrow, the head of NASA's Goddard Institute for Space Studies, calls this the most powerful evidence for the existence of God ever to come out of science.†

So, once again, the view that Christian theists have always held, that there is an intelligent Designer of the universe, seems to make much more sense than the atheistic interpretation that the universe, when it popped into being, uncaused, out of nothing, just happened to be, by chance, fine-tuned for intelligent life with an incomprehensible precision and delicacy.

3: God makes sense of objective moral values in the world. If God does not exist, then objective moral values do not exist. Many theists and atheists alike concur on this point. For example, the late J. L. Mackie of Oxford University, one of the most influential atheists of our time, admitted: "If . . . there are . . . objective values, they make the existence of a god more probable than it would have been without them. Thus, we have a defensible argument from morality to the existence of God."‡ But in order to avoid God's existence, Mackie therefore denied that objective moral values exist. He wrote, "It is easy to explain this moral sense as a natural product of biological and social evolution."§

Professor Michael Ruse, a philosopher of science at the University of Guelph, agrees. He explains:

> Morality is a biological adaptation no less than are hands and feet and teeth. Considered as a rationally justifiable set of claims about an objective something, ethics is illusory. I appreciate that when somebody says, "Love thy neighbor as thyself," they think they are referring above and beyond themselves. Nevertheless, such reference is truly without foundation. Morality is just an aid to survival and reproduction . . . and any deeper meaning is illusory.§§

Friedrich Nietzsche, the great atheist of the last century who proclaimed the death of God, understood that the death of God meant the destruction of all meaning and value in life. I think that Friedrich Nietzsche was right.

But we've got to be very careful here. The question here is not: Must we believe in God in order to live moral lives? I'm not claiming that we must. Nor is the question: can we recognize objective moral values without believing in God? I think we can.

---

* Paul Davies, *The Mind of God* (New York: Simon & Schuster, 1992), 169.

** Fred Hoyle, "The Universe: Past and Present Reflections," *Engineering and Science* (November 1981): 12.

† Robert Jastrow, "The Astronomer and God," in *The Intellectuals Speak Out About God*, ed. Roy Abraham Varghese (Chicago: Regenery Gateway, 1984), 22.

‡ J. L. Mackie, *The Miracle of Theism* (Oxford: Clarendon Press, 1982), 115–16.

§ Ibid., 117–18.

§§ Michael Ruse, "Evolutionary Theory and Christian Ethics," in Ruse, *The Darwinian Paradigm* (London: Routledge, 1989), 262–69.

Rather the question is: If God does not exist, do objective moral values exist? Like Mackie and Ruse, I just don't see any reason to think that in the absence of God, the morality evolved by homo sapiens is objective. After all, if there is no God, then what's so special about human beings? They're just accidental by-products of nature which have evolved relatively recently on an infinitesimal speck of dust lost somewhere in a hostile and mindless universe and which are doomed to perish individually and collectively in a relatively short time. On the atheistic view, some action, say, rape, may not be socially advantageous, and so in the course of human development has become taboo. But that does absolutely nothing to prove that rape is really wrong. On the atheistic view, there's nothing really wrong with your raping someone. Thus, without God there is no absolute right and wrong which imposes itself on our conscience.

But the problem is that objective moral values do exist, and deep down we all know it. There's no more reason to deny the objective reality of moral values than the objective reality of the physical world. Actions like rape, torture, and child abuse aren't just socially unacceptable behavior; they're moral abominations. Some things, at least, are really wrong. Similarly, love, equality, and self-sacrifice are really good. But if objective values cannot exist without God, and objective values do exist, then it follows logically and inescapably that God exists.

4: God makes sense of the historical facts concerning the life, death and resurrection of Jesus. The historical person, Jesus of Nazareth, was a remarkable individual. New Testament critics have reached something of a consensus that the historical Jesus came on the scene with an unprecedented sense of divine authority, the authority to stand and speak in God's place. That's why the Jewish leadership instigated his crucifixion for the charge of blasphemy. He claimed that in himself the Kingdom of God had come, and as visible demonstrations of this fact, he carried out a ministry of miracle-working and exorcisms. But the supreme confirmation of his claim was his resurrection from the dead. If Jesus did rise from the dead, then it would seem that we have a divine miracle on our hands and, thus, evidence for the existence of God.

Now most people would think that the resurrection of Jesus is just something you believe in by faith or not. But, in fact, there are three established facts, recognized by the majority of New Testament historians today, which I believe support the resurrection of Jesus: the empty tomb; Jesus' postmortem appearances; and the origin of the disciples' belief in his resurrection. Let me say a word about each one of these.

Fact # 1: On the Sunday following his crucifixion, Jesus' tomb was found empty by a group of his women followers. According to Jacob Kremer, an Austrian scholar who has specialized in the study of the resurrection, "By far most scholars hold firmly to the reliability of the Biblical statements about the empty tomb."[*]

---

[*] Jacob Kremer, *Die Osterevangelien Geschichten um Geschichte* (Stuttgart: Katholisches Bibelwerk, 1977), 49–50.

According to the New Testament critic, D. H. van Daalen, it is extremely difficult to object to the empty tomb on historical grounds; those who deny it do so on the basis of theological or philosophical assumptions.

Fact # 2: On separate occasions different individuals and groups saw appearances of Jesus alive after his death. According to the prominent, skeptical German New Testament critic Gerd Ludemann, "It may be taken as historically certain that . . . the disciples had experiences after Jesus' death in which Jesus appeared to them as the risen Christ."[*] These appearances were witnessed not only by believers, but also by unbelievers, skeptics, and even enemies.

Fact # 3: The original disciples suddenly came to believe in the resurrection of Jesus despite having every predisposition to the contrary. Jews had no belief in a dying, much less a rising, Messiah, and Jewish beliefs about the afterlife precluded anyone's rising from the dead prior to the end of the world. Luke Johnson, a New Testament scholar at Emory University, muses, "Some sort of powerful, transformative experience is required to generate the sort of movement earliest Christianity was . . ."[**] N. T. Wright, an eminent British scholar, concludes, "That is why, as an historian, I cannot explain the rise of early Christianity unless Jesus rose again, leaving an empty tomb behind him."[†]

Therefore, it seems to me, the Christian is amply justified in believing that Jesus rose from the dead and was who he claimed to be. But that entails that God exists.

5: God can be immediately known and experienced. This isn't really an argument for God's existence; rather it's the claim that you can know God exists wholly apart from arguments simply by immediately experiencing Him. This was the way people in the Bible knew God, as Professor John Hick explains:

God was known to them as a dynamic will interacting with their own wills, a sheer given reality, as inescapably to be reckoned with as a destructive storm and life-giving sunshine . . . To them God was not . . . an idea adopted by the mind, but an experiential reality which gave significance to their lives.[‡]

Now if this is so, then there's a danger that proofs for God could actually distract our attention from God Himself. If you're sincerely seeking God, then God will make His existence evident to you. The Bible promises, "Draw near to God and He will draw near to you" (James 4. 8). We mustn't so concentrate on the proofs that we fail to hear the inner voice of God speaking to our own heart. For those who listen, God becomes an immediate reality in their lives.

So, in conclusion, we've yet to see any arguments to show that God does not exist, and we have seen five reasons to think that God does exist. And, therefore, I think that theism is the more plausible worldview.

[*] Gerd Lüdemann, *What Really Happened to Jesus?*, trans. John Bowden (Louisville, KY: Westminster John Knox Press, 1995), 8.

[**] Luke Timothy Johnson, *The Real Jesus* (San Francisco: Harper San Francisco, 1996), 136.

[†] N. T. Wright, "The New Unimproved Jesus," *Christianity Today*, September 13, 1993, 26.

[‡] John Hick, Introduction, in *The Existence of God*, ed. with an Introduction by John Hick, Problems of Philosophy Series (New York: Macmillan, 1964), 13–14.

1. Reconstruct each of Craig's five arguments in standard form.

2. For each of Craig's arguments, what is the main objection that an opponent could raise? What is the best way for Craig to respond to that objection? Is his best response good enough? Why or why not?

3. Craig cites authorities at many points in his speech. Assess his appeals to authorities using the standards in Chapter 15.

4. Is there any strong reason to believe in God that Craig left out? If so, present that reason in argument form as forcefully as you can.

SEVEN DEADLY OBJECTIONS TO BELIEF IN THE CHRISTIAN GOD

■

by Edwin Curley

Contrary to the impression Dr. Craig's talk may have given you, I am not here tonight to argue for an unqualified atheism. People use the term 'God' with many different meanings. Some of them use it to refer to a being whose existence I might be able to accept. If by 'God' you mean what I think Spinoza meant by that term—an impersonal system of eternal and immutable laws of nature, which explains everything that happens in the universe, but does not itself require explanation—then I think it quite likely that there is a God. What I'm here to argue against is just the God of Christianity.

I assume that by 'God' Christians generally mean an eternal, personal, first cause of the universe, who has infinite perfections—omnipotence, omniscience, perfect goodness, and so on—*and* who has revealed himself to man in the Christian scriptures. The idea of God as an eternal, personal, first cause of the universe, possessing all perfections, is common not only in Christianity, but also in Judaism and Islam. I take it that the most important thing which distinguishes *Christian* theism from these other forms of theism is the acceptance of the Christian scriptures as the revealed word of God.* And that's what I shall be arguing against tonight. If the Christian scriptures are supposed to be God's revelation of himself to man, then he is not the perfect being Christians claim he is.

When I was a child, I accepted the Christian religion in which my parents raised me. But when I became a man, I put away the faith of my childhood. For a while I called myself an agnostic, because I felt that I could neither

---

* I thought, when I accepted the challenge to debate Dr. Craig, that we had agreed to debate only the existence of the Christian God. This limitation was central to my argumentative strategy here, which relies on the tension between the perfections Christian philosophers and theologians typically ascribe to God and the beliefs they might form about him as a consequence of accepting the Christian scriptures as revealed truth.

affirm nor deny the existence of God as I then understood that term. I felt that I had to suspend judgment about matters of religion. I thought perhaps the truth about religion might be unknowable. But if it should turn out to be knowable, I knew that I, at least, did not know it. This doubting spirit led me, while I was in college, to study philosophy and its history. Many of the philosophers I studied were Christians, for whom the rational defense of their religion was very important. My reading of their works did not lessen my doubts; it increased them. Eventually I came to think there is hardly any chance the Christian religion might be true. "Agnostic" no longer seemed the right label, not when we're talking about the Christian God.

Finding a good label for my position is not easy. Sometimes people who have embraced Christianity and then rejected it are called heretics or apostates. I have no objection to either of those labels, now that we've agreed to abolish the death penalty for these offenses.

What started me on this path to apostasy was reading the prayer book my mother gave me when I was 16. At the back were printed the Thirty-nine Articles of Religion which members of my church, the Episcopal Church, were expected to accept. I had not read them carefully when I was preparing for confirmation. Then I was only 13, and there was much I did not understand. Our minister seemed to me a good man: highly intelligent, cultured, and humane. At 13, I was content to accept what he told me, simply on his authority.

Then, at 16, I read those Articles of Religion, carefully and critically for the first time. I was disturbed that my church accepted predestination. Before the foundation of the world, the Articles said, God had chosen some vessels for honor and others for dishonor.[*] One of the first principles of my church was that no one should be required to believe, as necessary for salvation, any doctrine which could not be proved from scripture.[**] So far as I could see, there was as good scriptural foundation for the doctrine of predestination as there was for any doctrine the church affirmed.[†]

---

[*] Article XVII: "Predestination to life is the everlasting purpose of God, whereby, before the foundations of the world were laid, He hath constantly decreed by His counsel secret to us, to deliver from curse and damnation those whom He hath chosen in Christ out of mankind, and to bring them by Christ to everlasting salvation as vessels made to honour." The complete text of the Thirty-nine Articles is available at http://anglicansonline.org/basics/thirty-nine_articles.htm.

[**] See Article VI on the sufficiency of the Holy Scriptures for salvation: "Holy Scripture containeth all things necessary to salvation: so that whatsoever is not read therein, nor may be proved thereby, is not to be required of any man, that it should be believed as an article of the Faith, or be thought requisite or necessary to salvation."

[†] The authors of the Articles clearly had in mind Romans 9:10–33. In the debate Dr. Craig replied by arguing that what I was rejecting was, not Christianity, but Calvin's erroneous version of Christianity. I'm told that this displeased the numerous Calvinist members of our Michigan audience. However that may be, it should be realized that predestination is not only a Calvinist doctrine. It will be found in any theologian who takes the letters of St. Paul seriously. See, for example, St. Augustine, *The Gift of Perseverance* § 15 (citing Ephesians 1:4–11), § 34 (citing Philippians 2:12–13), § 47 (citing Romans 11:1–7), and St. Thomas Aquinas, *Summa theologiae*, Part I, Qu. 23, (citing Romans 8:28–30).

There also seemed to be strong philosophical reasons for accepting pre-destination. If God is omniscient, if he knows everything, he must have fore-knowledge of his creatures' fates. That suggests that there is a fact of the matter about what my fate will be, which is knowable with certainty well in advance of my birth. It doesn't follow from this that God determined what my fate will be. But it does seem to follow that my fate is not indeterminate. Moreover, if God is omnipotent, and can do anything, or anything it is logi-cally possible to do, then nothing happens except by his will. So if I wind up in Hell, he will not only have known that from eternity, he will also have willed it from eternity.

Predestination is not so widely accepted now as it was when my church was founded in the 16th century. I find many Christians who reject it. And I sympathize with them. Their hearts are in the right place, certainly. I cannot believe that a just and loving God would create beings he knew, and had pre-determined, would spend eternity in hell. But Christians can reject predesti-nation only at the cost of ignoring the authority of their scriptures and the implications of their theology. I would not insist that a good Christian must be a fundamentalist, who thinks that everything Scripture says is literally true. But it does seem to me that if someone calls himself a Christian, he ought at least to believe that the Christian scriptures are not seriously misleading about central matters, such as salvation and damnation.

Let us set predestination to one side. Even if the Christian scriptures did not contain that commitment, there would still be a problem about Hell, to which they are committed by an even wider range of texts.[*] The philosoph-ical support for Hell, though, seems much weaker than the support for pre-destination. I see no philosophical reason for believing in an eternal punishment for sinners. Indeed, philosophy is against it. Philosophy teaches that the punishment should be proportionate to the crime. Let's concede, for the sake of argument, that we are all, in some sense, sinners. Which of us, looking into his heart, can honestly say that he has never done anything seriously wrong, at least once in his life? But the doctrine of Hell requires that most of us sinners will suffer eternal torment.[**]

Perhaps in some cases that is just. Hitler was responsible for the horrify-ing deaths of millions of Jews, not to mention gypsies, Slavs, and homo-sexuals. Perhaps for crimes of that magnitude eternal punishment can

---

[*] So far as I can see, the strongest scriptural support for predestination comes from the letters of St. Paul. There seems to be relatively little support for it in the gospels. This might suggest that it was not part of the original teaching of Jesus. But texts supporting the idea of Hell are easy to find in the gospels.

[**] The most explicit passage I know on the question of the proportion of the saved to the damned is Matthew 22:14, "Many are called, but few are chosen." But if salvation depends on acceptance of Jesus as one's savior, as Christian exclusivists hold, and if the great majority of people have not accepted Jesus as their savior, the texts supporting exclusivism do imply that comparatively few are chosen. I say more about exclusivism below.

be justified.* But can it really be justified for those of us who are only sinners in the sense I have just specified, people who have done something seriously wrong, at least once in our lives?

I am, in that sense, a sinner. But, in all candor, I must say that to me my sins seem pretty minor compared to those of Hitler. I haven't killed anyone, or tortured anyone, or been responsible for anyone's torture or death, let alone the torture and death of millions. Yet, if the doctrine of hell is correct, I shall be keeping Hitler company in Hell. No doubt I'm not an impartial judge in this case, but that doesn't seem fair.

In spite of these difficulties, Hell was part of the teaching of my church, and is part of the teaching of many Christian churches. This is no accident. The doctrine has strong support in the Christian scriptures.**

Hell, too, is less widely believed in now than it was when my church was founded. I find many Christians who reject Hell. Their hearts are in the right place, certainly. I cannot believe that a just and loving God would send the majority of his creatures to spend eternity in Hell. But Christians who reject Hell can do so only at the cost of rejecting also the authority of their scriptures.

I conceded, for the sake of argument, that we are all sinners. Now let me qualify that. Very likely all of us, in this room, are sinners *provided* it's enough, to be a sinner, that once in your life you did something seriously wrong. But I don't concede that absolutely all humans are sinners, even in that rather loose sense.

I have a granddaughter, whom I love. She's a sweet girl, but she's seven. By now she must have committed quite a number of sins. I know that sometimes she doesn't mind her mother very well. Sometimes she's mean to her baby brother. I don't find any of this serious enough to deserve eternal punishment, or even significant finite punishment. Perhaps she has committed more serious sins which I don't know about. Perhaps she has even done something so wicked as to steal pears from a neighbor's orchard, not to eat, but to throw at pigs.†

---

* I concede this for the sake of argument. But in fact I am not sure that even Hitler deserved eternal punishment. Mightn't the demands of justice have been satisfied if God had tortured him for, say, 1000 years for each of his victims? Eternal punishment looks like overkill, even for someone like Hitler. What I principally object to, though, in the doctrine of hell, is the idea that all sinners deserve eternal punishment, even those whose sins pale by comparison with those of a monster like Hitler (or Stalin, or Pol Pot, or Idi Amin, etc.). The essential problem here is that to make the doctrine of the universality of sin plausible we must define sin in a way which makes sinners even of those whose offenses, though serious, are comparatively minor, whereas the seriousness of the punishment they are to receive seems appropriate (if it is ever appropriate) only for those who are extremely wicked. I say more about the doctrine that sin is universal below.

** See, for example, Matthew 5:22, 29–30, 8:11–12, 13:36–50, 18:8–9, 23:29–33, 25:31–46, Mark 3:28–29, 9:42–48, Luke 16:19–31, 2 Thessalonians 1:5–10.

† Readers of Augustine's *Confessions* will recall that he cites this incident from his childhood to illustrate his wickedness. (*Confessions* II.iv.9)

In any case, I wouldn't claim that she's completely innocent of serious wrong-doing at this stage of her life. Probably no child that age is completely innocent. And Jesus did say that we should be perfect, as our Father in heaven is perfect.[*] That's a tough standard.

But when I think about my granddaughter at an earlier age, lying, say, in the neonatal intensive care unit, where she spent the first three months of her life, with an oxygen tube, and a feeding tube, and a heart monitor, all taped to her tiny body—for she was born in the 29th week of my daughter's pregnancy, and weighed less than 3lbs. at birth—I cannot think of her, at that stage of her life, as a sinner, deserving of Hell. She did not even cry greedily for her mother's milk.[**]

In the Christian tradition it is normal to baptize infants at an early age because it is believed that they come into the world tainted by the sin of Adam and Eve.[†] This is the doctrine of original sin. I cannot believe in original sin. My granddaughter may be a sinner now, but not when she was in the intensive care unit.

Original sin is also less widely accepted now than when my church was founded. I find many Christians who reject original sin. I sympathize with them. Their hearts are in the right place, certainly. But, Christians can reject original sin only at the cost of a substantial reinterpretation of their scriptures and traditions.[‡]

---

[*] I was surprised to discover, from email I received after the debate, that not all of my Christian critics recognized this allusion to Matthew 5:48.

[**] Another example from St. Augustine, who uses it to illustrate his sinfulness even as an infant. See *Confessions* I.vii.11. An unhealthy sense of sin seems to be characteristic of a certain kind of Christian. It is unfortunate that that kind of Christian has been so influential in the history of this religion.

[†] This seems to have been the original justification for this practice, though like much else in early Christianity it subsequently became controversial. Some abandoned the practice. Others found other justifications for it. For a good brief account see Alister McGrath, *Christian Theology*, 2nd edition, Blackwell, 1997, pp. 514–518.

[‡] As Article IX puts it: "Original sin standeth not in the following of Adam (as the Pelagians do vainly talk), but it is the fault and corruption of the Nature of every man that naturally is engendered of the offspring of Adam; whereby man is very far gone from original righteous-ness, and is of his own nature inclined to evil, so that the flesh lusteth always contrary to the Spirit; and therefore in every person born into this world, it deserveth God's wrath and damnation. And this infection of nature doth remain, yea in them that are regenerated; whereby the lust of the flesh . . . is not subject to the Law of God. And although there is no condemnation for them that believe and are baptized; yet the Apostle doth confess, that con-cupiscence and lust hath of itself the nature of sin." The principal scriptural authority for this doctrine is found in the letters of St. Paul (the source of so much that is appalling in tra-ditional Christian teaching), notably in Romans 3:9–20, 5:12–21, and 1 Corinthians 15:20–22. I had thought from something Dr. Craig said later in our debate that this doctrine might be rejected in the Wesleyan tradition to which he adheres. But the Articles of Religion of the Methodist Church (available at http://archives.umc.org/interior.asp?ptid=1&mid=1649) seem very similar.

Consistently with the doctrine of original sin, it is common among Christians to believe that if we are justified, it is by faith in Jesus.* Since we are all sinners, we cannot earn salvation by our works. But we can be forgiven and treated as if we were righteous. The mark of our having been forgiven is that God, by an act of grace, gives us faith.

This doctrine has implications I find appalling. It implies that those among us who lack faith in Jesus have not received grace, have not been forgiven, and will, if we continue in that state, go to Hell. So the doctrine of justification by faith, which has strong support in the Christian scriptures, leads inevitably to exclusivism, to the idea that all who reject Christian doctrine must be damned, no matter how good they may be in other respects.

If God chose the beneficiaries of his grace on the ground of some distinctive merit they possessed, this might not be unfair to those he didn't choose, whom we would presume to lack that merit. But that would be contrary to the idea of grace, which implies a free gift, not something given to someone who deserves it on account of merit.

So usually it is held that God has no reason for choosing some and not others. He acts quite arbitrarily. It's a hard and ugly doctrine, this doctrine of grace. Of course if you have already accepted Hell and original sin, you may find this doctrine "full of comfort," as my church put it. You may be grateful for having this chance at salvation, even if it does seem to be a lottery in which the odds are not on your side. And if you think you have faith, then you may also think you have won the lottery. Still even the faithful may not be able to entirely set aside thoughts about the unlucky losers. Sometimes they love nonbelievers and then the doctrine of salvation by faith can cause them great grief.

---

* This was certainly the doctrine of my church. See Article XIII: "We are accounted righteous before God, only for the merit of our Lord and Saviour Jesus Christ by Faith, and not for our own works or deservings. Wherefore, that we are justified by Faith only, is a most wholesome Doctrine, and very full of comfort . . . " Scriptural support for this doctrine may be found in Mark 16:16; John 3:16–18, 5:24, 14:6–7; Acts 4.12; Romans 3:9–26, 5:12–21; Ephesians 2.12; I John 2.22–23; 4.3; II John 9. It should, however, be acknowledged that this doctrine seems to be much more common in the works of Paul, and in the fourth gospel, than it is in the synoptic gospels, which tend to suggest that obedience to the commandments, supplemented only by selling all you have and giving it to the poor, is sufficient for salvation. See the story told (with some variations) in Matthew 19:16–22, Mark 10:17–22, Luke 18:18–23. The gospel of John is generally dated late enough that its account of Jesus's teaching might have been influenced by the letters of Paul. (On the dating of Paul's letters and John's gospel, see Raymond Brown's *Introduction to the New Testament*, Yale University Press, 1997.) We should concede also that the exceptional passage from Mark comes from the 'longer ending of Mark,' which is not found in the earliest manuscripts. (See *The New Oxford Annotated Bible*, ed. by Bruce Metzger and Roland Murphy, Oxford University Press, 1991.) I would not, of course, be thought to suggest that any member of the early Christian Church might have tampered with the text of Mark, to bring it into line with Pauline theology. To do that would be to embrace the kind of radical skepticism for which Bart Ehrman's *Misquoting Jesus* (HarperOne, 2007) has been so widely and justly censured. Still, these textual data are puzzling. A Christian who took his scriptures seriously might think they require some explanation.

So far my objections have been mainly theological; they are objections to teachings whose basis is primarily scriptural rather than philosophical. The main exception to that generalization is the doctrine of predestination, which has philosophical grounds as well as scriptural grounds. I know many Christians here tonight will not feel that their understanding of Christianity requires them to accept all these doctrines, either because they do not think their scriptures clearly require these views, or because they do not regard the Christian scriptures as absolutely authoritative in determining their beliefs and conduct. I've said I think those Christians who adopt a freer attitude toward scripture and do not feel that their acceptance of Christianity commits them to predestination, or Hell, or original sin, or justification by faith, or exclusivism—those Christians have their hearts in the right place. But I also think their feet may be planted on the slippery slope to heresy, and that more conservative Christians, who would accord greater authority to scripture, have a clearer right to consider themselves Christians. How much of traditional Christianity can you reject and still be entitled to call yourself a Christian? This was a question I found extremely difficult as I moved gradually from Christianity to apostasy.

Let's turn now to objections not so scripturally based. It is common among Christians to believe that God is a personal being, who created the universe, and who is omnipotent, omniscient, and perfectly good. Indeed, it is commonly said that God must possess all perfections.

Yet we observe that the world this perfect being created has many imperfections: there is much joy in the world; but there is also much suffering, much of it apparently undeserved; and there is sin. We call these things evil. How can they exist in a world which owes its origin to a God with the attributes Christians believe their God to possess?

The usual response now is to say that, though God could have created a world without evil, it was better for him to have created the world he did, in spite of the evils it contains. The occurrence of those evils was necessary for goods which are even greater. If God had so created the world that it contained no evil at all, that world would have been less good, all things considered, than it is even with all the evil it contains. This is called the greater goods defense.

The Christian may say: we humans rightly do many things we expect to cause avoidable harm. We build a bridge from San Francisco to Marin County, knowing that in the construction some workmen will fall into the water and die. We could avoid their deaths by not building the bridge. But the bridge is a great good. Given our human limitations, we cannot build it without some people dying a result. So we build it and accept their deaths as part of the cost of bridging those waters. And God's permission of evil may also be justified by the greater goods it leads to.

An omnipotent being, of course, does not face all the hard choices we do. If he wants a bridge across those waters, he need only say, "Let there be a bridge." And there will be. This fact that God is supposed to be omnipotent puts constraints on the kinds of good he might be able to use to justify his acceptance of the evils he allows. What kind of good could be so intimately connected with evil that even an omnipotent being would have to accept the evil, as the price of realizing that good? And what good could be so great that it would justify such a being's accepting the amount of evil there is in the world as the price of attaining that good?

The usual answer is: freedom. There must be freedom, if there is to be moral goodness. And the price of giving humans freedom is that sometimes they will misuse it. Even an omnipotent being can't cause a person to freely do good. If he caused one of his creatures to behave well, that person would no longer be acting freely. His 'acts' would no longer be *his* acts, and he would not deserve moral credit for them. Freedom, with the moral goodness which sometimes results from it, is a good sufficiently great that it makes the evils which also result worth accepting. This is what is called the free will defense.

There is a problem, of course, about appealing to human freedom to solve the problem of evil when you also believe in divine foreknowledge and pre-destination. This is a problem of long standing, which many philosophers have wrestled with. No solution has gained general acceptance. If Dr. Craig accepts the doctrines of predestination and divine foreknowledge and also appeals to human freedom to solve the problem of evil, he will have worked out a way of explaining how these things are consistent, and I will listen with interest to that explanation.

In the meantime, though, there are other problems about the appeal to freedom. There are evils whose occurrence has no discernible connection with freedom. Theologians call them natural evils, meaning by that such things as earthquakes, floods, tornadoes, diseases, and so on. If a deer dies in a forest fire, suffering horribly as it does so, that is an evil. It is not only human suffering we must take into account, when we are weighing good against evil in this world.

Now, if you accept anything like the theory of evolution,[*] you will be-lieve there were other animals on this planet long before humans appeared on the scene. Many of them must have suffered horribly as their species became extinct. None of that suffering can be justified as a necessary con-sequence of permitting humans freedom. We weren't around then. So none of it seems beyond the power of omnipotence to prevent without the loss of that good.

Another objection: The greater goods defense can easily lead to a kind of cost-benefit analysis which is deeply repugnant to our moral sense. Con-sider the kind of case which troubled Ivan in Dostoevsky's great novel, *The Brothers Karamazov*.[**] A little girl is treated quite brutally by her parents, who

[*] You don't, of course, have to accept the full Darwinian explanation of evolution for this to be a problem, so long as you accept what the evidence of geology and paleontology seems to make as certain as anything in science can be: that the earth has been around for a very long time, and that many, many different species of animals flourished and then became extinct before man appeared on the scene.

[**] See Part II, Book V: Pro and Contra, Chapter 4: Rebellion. The text is available online at: http://www.online-literature.com/booksearch.php.

beat her because she has done something which made them angry. Perhaps she wets the bed repeatedly, and they think she ought to be old enough to control her bladder. Or perhaps the father is an alcoholic who abuses his daughter sexually. *The Brothers Karamazov* is fiction, but to hear about real cases like this, you need only listen regularly to the 11 o'clock news.

The free will defense seems to say, in cases of this kind: well, it's all very unfortunate, of course, but this is the price we must pay for having freedom. For the father to have the opportunity to display moral goodness, God must give him the opportunity to choose evil. You can't have the one opportunity without the other. And the father's having the opportunity to display moral goodness is such a great good that it outweighs the fact that he chooses evil.

But notice who gets the good here. It's the father. And notice who suffers the evil. It's the little girl. Let us grant, for the sake of argument, that the benefit outweighs the cost. Freedom is a very great good. Still it makes some difference who pays the cost. Freedom may be a great good, even a good so great that it would outweigh really horrendous suffering. But justice requires some attention, not only to the net amount of good, after you have subtracted the evil, but also to the way the goods and evils are distributed. Some distributions just aren't fair.*

The mention of Ivan Karamazov brings me to my final objection. Ivan claims that if God does not exist, everything is permissible. Dr. Craig believes the same thing. Dostoevsky, speaking through Ivan, may have stated the problem of evil as powerfully as any atheist; but he was himself a Christian, who believed that God must exist if we are to make sense of morality.

I think the opposite is true. I think Christian belief makes morality, as we normally think of it, unintelligible. Consider the story of Abraham and Isaac. One day God put Abraham to the test. He said to Abraham: "Take your only son, Isaac, whom you love, and go to the land of Moriah, and offer him there as a burnt offering."** God gives no reason for this horrifying command. And Abraham asks none. He simply sets out to obey the command. And he nearly does obey. He has the knife raised to kill his son, when God sends down an angel to stay his hand. God then says he is satisfied with Abraham: "Now I know that you fear God, since you have not withheld your son, your only son, from me." (Gen. 22:12) In the end God does not actually require the sacrifice. But he does require that Abraham demonstrate his willingness to carry out the sacrifice.

What's the moral of this story? I suggest it's this: as God's creatures, our highest loyalty must be to God, even if this requires the sacrifice of our

---

* I first became aware of the importance of this by reading Michael Tooley's "The Argument from Evil" (in *Philosophical Perspectives, 5 – Philosophy of Religion, 1991*, ed. by James E. Tomberlin, Ridgeview Publishing, 1991, 89–134). But I think acknowledgment of this point underlies Marilyn Adams' rejection of the free will defense in her *Horrendous Evils and the Goodness of God* (Cornell University Press, 2000).

** Genesis 22:2, quoted in the New Revised Standard Version, as given in *The New Oxford Annotated Bible*.

deepest human loyalties; God is our Creator, our Lord, and we owe him absolute obedience, no matter what he commands. And he might command anything. There are no constraints on his will; so we might be required to do anything. There is no predicting what he might require; and there is nothing to say that his commands will not change from one moment to the next. At the beginning of the story, God commands Abraham to kill Isaac; in the middle he commands Abraham not to kill Isaac.

If there is a God who is liable to command anything; and if our highest loyalty must be to this God, there is no act save disobedience to God which we can safely say is out of bounds, no act of a kind which simply must not be done, even rape, to use Dr. Craig's example. If this God exists, and we must obey him unconditionally, then anything whatever might turn out to be permissible. This view is destructive of morality as we normally think of it.

So there you have my opening argument. I have offered seven objections, seven deadly objections, I would say, to Christian theism: it is committed to predestination, to Hell, to original sin, to justification by faith, and to exclusivism; it has no good solution to the problem of evil; and it is destructive of morality as we understand it. These are only some of the objections which make it impossible for me to believe in the Christian God. But they are enough to make me wonder how anyone who has thought seriously about the Christian faith can accept it.

DISCUSSION QUESTIONS

1. The opening parts of Curley's speech tell some of his life story. What is the point of this opening? Does this narrative contribute to his argument?

2. Explain and evaluate each of Curley's "seven deadly objections" to belief in a Christian God. How could a traditional Christian best respond to each objection? Is that response adequate? Why or why not?

3. Some of Curley's arguments depend on specific doctrines of traditional Christianity. Does this make his arguments weaker? Why or why not?

4. Is there any better reason to deny the existence of God that Curley overlooked? If so, present it as forcefully as you can.

22

PHILOSOPHICAL REASONING

It is not easy to explain the character of philosophical reasoning. Indeed, the nature of philosophical reasoning is itself a philosophical problem. We can, however, acquire some sense of it by comparing philosophical reasoning with reasoning as it occurs in daily life. In the opening chapters of this book, we noticed that, in everyday discussions, much is taken for granted and left unsaid. In general, there is no need to state points that are already a matter of agreement. In contrast, philosophers usually try to make underlying assumptions explicit and then subject them to critical examination. Still, even for the philosopher, something must trigger an interest in underlying assumptions. This usually arises when the advance of knowledge creates fundamental conflicts within the system of hitherto accepted assumptions. Thus, much that counts as modern philosophy is an attempt to come to terms with the relationship between modern science and the traditional conception of humankind's place in the universe. This chapter explores one such conflict arising from advances in computer theory.

In recent years, the rise of computer technology has generated a conflict with traditional concepts about human beings. Traditionally, humans have cited the capacity to think as the feature that sets them apart from and, of course, above all other creatures. Humans have been defined as rational animals. But we now live in an age in which computers seem able to perform tasks that, had a human being performed them, would certainly count as thinking. Not only can computers perform complex calculations very rapidly, they can also play an excellent game of chess. Do machines think? The question seems forced on us, and it is more than a semantic quibble. In deciding it, we are also reevaluating the status of an aspect of humanity that has long been considered its unique or distinctive feature. Once we decide whether machines can think, the next question is whether human beings are not themselves merely thinking machines.

The two essays presented in this chapter address such questions. The writer of the first essay, Alan Turing, is one of the geniuses of the twentieth century. He not only developed much of the mathematics that underlies modern computer theory but also helped give computers their first remarkable application: the cracking of the German secret codes during World War II. In this essay, Turing considers whether machines can or cannot think. The brilliance of the essay does not depend on the answer he gives to the question, but rather on his attempt to formulate it in a way that would allow reasonable debate to take place concerning it. For this reason, Turing's essay has been considered a classic work on the subject for more than fifty years. In the second essay, John Searle presents and defends an analogy intended to refute not only Turing's argument but also any other claim that machines could ever think solely by virtue of having the right formal program.

COMPUTING MACHINERY AND INTELLIGENCE[1]

■

by A. M. Turing

1. THE IMITATION GAME

I propose to consider the question "Can machines think?" This should begin with definitions of the meaning of the terms "machine" and "think." The definitions might be framed so as to reflect so far as possible the normal use of the words, but this attitude is dangerous. If the meaning of the words "machine" and "think" are to be found by examining how they are commonly used, it is difficult to escape the conclusion that the meaning and the answer to the question, "Can machines think?" is to be sought in a statistical survey such as a Gallup poll. But this is absurd. Instead of attempting such a definition I shall replace the question by another, which is closely related to it and is expressed in relatively unambiguous words.

The new form of the problem can be described in terms of a game which we call the "imitation game." It is played with three people, a man (A), a woman (B), and an interrogator (C) who may be of either sex. The interrogator stays in a room apart from the other two. The object of the game for the interrogator is to determine which of the other two is the man and which is the woman. He knows them by labels X and Y, and at the end of the game he says either "X is A and Y is B" or "X is B and Y is A." The interrogator is allowed to put questions to A and B thus:

C: Will X please tell me the length of his or her hair?

Now suppose X is actually A, then A must answer. It is A's object in the game to try to cause C to make the wrong identification. His answer might therefore be

"My hair is shingled, and the longest strands are about nine inches long."

In order that tones of voice may not help the interrogator the answers should be written, or better still, typewritten. The ideal arrangement is to have a teleprinter communicating between the two rooms. Alternatively the question and answers can be repeated by an intermediary. The object of the game for the third player (B) is to help the interrogator. The best strategy for her is probably to give truthful answers. She can add such things as "I am the woman, don't listen to him!" to her answers, but it will avail nothing as the man can make similar remarks.

We now ask the question, "What will happen when a machine takes the part of A in this game?" Will the interrogator decide wrongly as often when the game is played like this as he does when the game is played between a man and a woman? These questions replace our original, "Can machines think?"

2. CRITIQUE OF THE NEW PROBLEM

As well as asking, "What is the answer to this new form of the question," one may ask, "Is this new question a worthy one to investigate?" This latter question we investigate without further ado, thereby cutting short an infinite regress.

The new problem has the advantage of drawing a fairly sharp line between the physical and the intellectual capacities of a man. No engineer or chemist claims to be able to produce a material which is indistinguishable from the human skin. It is possible that at some time this might be done, but even supposing this invention available we should feel there was little point in trying to make a "thinking machine" more human by dressing it up in such artificial flesh. The form in which we have set the problem reflects this fact in the condition which prevents the interrogator from seeing or touching the other competitors, or hearing their voices. Some other advantages of the proposed criterion may be shown up by specimen questions and answers. Thus:

Q: Please write me a sonnet on the subject of the Forth Bridge.

A: Count me out on this one. I never could write poetry.

Q: Add 34957 to 70764.

A: (Pause about 30 seconds and then give as answer) 105621.

Q: Do you play chess?

A: Yes.

Q: I have K at my K1, and no other pieces. You have only K at K6 and R at R1. It is your move. What do you play?

A: (After a pause of 15 seconds) R–R8 mate.

The question and answer method seems to be suitable for introducing almost any one of the fields of human endeavor that we wish to include. We do not wish to penalize the machine for its inability to shine in beauty competitions, nor to penalize a man for losing in a race against an airplane. The conditions of our game make these disabilities irrelevant. The "witnesses" can brag, if they consider it advisable, as much as they please about their charms, strength or heroism, but the interrogator cannot demand practical demonstrations.

The game may perhaps be criticized on the ground that the odds are weighted too heavily against the machine. If the man were to try and pretend to be the machine, he would clearly make a very poor showing. He would be given away at once by slowness and inaccuracy in arithmetic. May not machines carry out something which ought to be described as thinking but which is very different from what a man does? This objection is a very strong one, but at least we can say that if, nevertheless, a machine can be constructed to play the imitation game satisfactorily, we need not be troubled by this objection.

It might be urged that when playing the "imitation game" the best strategy for the machine may possibly be something other than imitation of the behavior of a man. This may be, but I think it is unlikely that there is any great effect of this kind. In any case there is no intention to investigate here the theory of the game, and it will be assumed that the best strategy is to try to provide answers that would naturally be given by a man.

3. THE MACHINES CONCERNED IN THE GAME

The question which we put in § 1 will not be quite definite until we have specified what we mean by the word "machine." It is natural that we should wish to permit every kind of engineering technique to be used in our machines. We also wish to allow the possibility that an engineer or team of engineers may construct a machine which works, but whose manner of operation cannot be satisfactorily described by its constructors because they have applied a method which is largely experimental. Finally, we wish to exclude from the machines men born in the usual manner. It is difficult to frame the definitions so as to satisfy these three conditions. One might for instance insist that the team of engineers should be all of one sex, but this would not really be satisfactory, for it is probably possible to rear a complete individual from a single cell of the skin (say) of a man. To do so would be a feat of biological technique deserving of the very highest praise, but we would not be inclined to regard it as a case of "constructing a thinking machine." This prompts us to abandon the requirement that every kind of technique should be permitted. We are the more ready to do so in view of the fact that the present interest in "thinking machines" has been aroused by a particular kind of machine, usually called an "electronic computer" or "digital computer." Following this suggestion we only permit digital computers to take part in our game.

This restriction appears at first sight to be a very drastic one. I shall attempt to show that it is not so in reality. . . . The digital computers considered [here] are classified among the "discrete state machines." These are the machines which move by sudden jumps or clicks from one quite definite state to another. . . . [A] special property of digital computers [is] that they can mimic any discrete state machine. [This property] is described by saying that they are *universal* machines. The existence of machines with this property has the important consequence that, considerations of speed apart, it is unnecessary to design various new machines to do various computing processes. They can all be done with one digital computer, suitably programmed for each case. It will be seen that as a consequence of this all digital computers are in a sense equivalent. . . .

It was suggested tentatively that the question, "Can machines think?" should be replaced by "Are there imaginable digital computers which would do well in the imitation game?" If we wish we can make this superficially more general and ask "Are there discrete state machines which would do well?" But in view of the universality property we see that either of these questions is equivalent to this, "Let us fix our attention on one particular digital computer C. Is it true that by modifying this computer to have an adequate storage, suitably increasing its speed of action, and providing it with an appropriate program, C can be made to play satisfactorily the part of A in the imitation game, the part of B being taken by a man?" . . .

6. CONTRARY VIEWS ON THE MAIN QUESTION

We may now consider the ground to have been cleared and we are ready to proceed to the debate on our question, "Can machines think?" and the variant of it quoted at the end of the last section. We cannot altogether abandon the original form of the problem, for opinions will differ as to the appropriateness of the substitution and we must at least listen to what has to be said in this connection.

It will simplify matters for the reader if I explain first my own beliefs in the matter. Consider first the more accurate form of the question. I believe that in about fifty years' time it will be possible to program computers, with a storage capacity of about 10^9, to make them play the imitation game so well that an average interrogator will not have more than 70 per cent chance of making the right identification after five minutes of questioning. The original question, "Can machines think?" I believe to be too meaningless to deserve discussion. Nevertheless I believe that at the end of the century the use of words and general educated opinion will have altered so much that one will be able to speak of machines thinking without expecting to be contradicted. I believe further that no useful purpose is served by concealing these beliefs. The popular view that scientists proceed inexorably from well-established fact to well-established fact, never being influenced by any unproved conjecture, is quite mistaken. Provided it is made clear which are proved facts and which are conjectures, no harm can result. Conjectures are of great importance since they suggest useful lines of research.

I now proceed to consider opinions opposed to my own.

1. *The Theological Objection.* Thinking is a function of man's immortal soul. God has given an immortal soul to every man and woman, but not to any other animal or to machines. Hence no animal or machine can think.

I am unable to accept any part of this, but will attempt to reply in theological terms. I should find the argument more convincing if animals were classed with men, for there is a greater difference, to my mind, between the typical animate and the inanimate than there is between man and the other animals. The arbitrary character of the orthodox view becomes clearer if we consider how it might appear to a member of some other religious community. How do Christians regard the Moslem view that women have no souls? But let us leave this point aside and return to the main argument. It appears to me that the argument quoted above implies a serious restriction of the omnipotence of the Almighty. It is admitted that there are certain things that He cannot do such as making one equal to two, but should we not believe that He has freedom to confer a soul on an elephant if He sees fit? We might expect that He would only exercise this power in conjunction with a mutation which provided the elephant with an appropriately improved brain to minister to the needs of this soul. An argument of exactly similar form may be made for the case of machines. It may seem different because it is more difficult to "swallow." But this really only means that we think it would be less likely that He would consider the circumstances suitable for conferring a soul. The circumstances in question are discussed in the rest of this paper. In attempting to construct such machines we should not be irreverently usurping His power of creating souls, any more than we are in the procreation of children: rather we are, in either case, instruments of His will providing mansions for the souls that He creates.

However, this is mere speculation. I am not very impressed with theological arguments whatever they may be used to support. Such arguments have often been found unsatisfactory in the past. In the time of Galileo it was argued that the texts, "And the sun stood still . . . and hasted not to go down about a whole day" (Joshua x. 13) and "He laid the foundations of the earth, that it should not move at any time" (Psalm cv. 5) were an adequate refutation of the Copernican theory. With our present knowledge such an argument appears futile. When that knowledge was not available it made a quite different impression.

2. *The "Heads in the Sand" Objection.* "The consequences of machines thinking would be too dreadful. Let us hope and believe that they cannot do so."

This argument is seldom expressed quite so openly as in the form above. But it affects most of us who think about it at all. We like to believe that Man is in some subtle way superior to the rest of creation. It is best if he can be shown to be *necessarily* superior, for then there is no danger of him losing his commanding position. The popularity of the theological argument is clearly connected with this feeling. It is likely to be quite strong in intellectual people, since they value the power of thinking more highly than others, and are more inclined to base their belief in the superiority of Man on this power.

I do not think that this argument is sufficiently substantial to require refutation. Consolation would be more appropriate: perhaps this should be sought in the transmigration of souls.

3. *The Mathematical Objection.* There are a number of results of mathematical logic which can be used to show that there are limitations to the powers of discrete state machines. The best known of these results is known as

Gödel's theorem, and shows that in any sufficiently powerful logical system statements can be formulated which can neither be proved nor disproved within the system, unless possibly the system itself is inconsistent. . . . This is the mathematical result: it is argued that it proves a disability of machines to which the human intellect is not subject.

The short answer to this argument is that although it is established that there are limitations to the powers of any particular machine, it has only been stated, without any sort of proof, that no such limitations apply to the human intellect. But I do not think this view can be dismissed quite so lightly. Whenever one of these machines is asked the appropriate critical question, and gives a definite answer, we know that this answer must be wrong, and this gives us a certain feeling of superiority. Is this feeling illusory? It is no doubt quite genuine, but I do not think too much importance should be attached to it. We too often give wrong answers to questions ourselves to be justified in being very pleased at such evidence of fallibility on the part of the machines. Further, our superiority can only be felt on such an occasion in relation to the one machine over which we have scored our petty triumph. There would be no question of triumphing simultaneously over *all* machines. In short, then, there might be men cleverer than any given machine, but then again there might be other machines cleverer again, and so on.

Those who hold to the mathematical argument would, I think, mostly be willing to accept the imitation game as a basis for discussion. Those who believe in the two previous objections would probably not be interested in any criteria.

4. *The Argument from Consciousness.* This argument is very well expressed in Professor Jefferson's Lister Oration for 1949, from which I quote, "Not until a machine can write a sonnet or compose a concerto because of thoughts and emotions felt, and not by the chance fall of symbols, could we agree that machine equals brain—that is, not only write it but know that it had written it. No mechanism could feel (and not merely artificially signal, an easy contrivance) pleasure at its successes, grief when its values fuse, be warmed by flattery, be made miserable by its mistakes, be charmed by sex, be angry or depressed when it cannot get what it wants."

This argument appears to be a denial of the validity of our test. According to the most extreme form of this view the only way by which one could be sure that a machine thinks is to *be* the machine and to feel oneself thinking. One could then describe these feelings to the world, but of course no one would be justified in taking any notice. Likewise according to this view the only way to know that a *man* thinks is to be that particular man. It is in fact the solipsist point of view [which claims that only oneself exists]. It may be the most logical view to hold but it makes communication of ideas difficult. A is liable to believe "A thinks but B does not" while B believes "B thinks but A does not." Instead of arguing continually over this point it is usual to have the polite convention that everyone thinks.

I am sure that Professor Jefferson does not wish to adopt the extreme and solipsist point of view. Probably he would be quite willing to accept the imitation game as a test. The game (with the player B omitted) is frequently used in practice under the name of *viva voce* to discover whether someone really understands something or has "learned it parrot fashion." Let us listen in to a part of such a *viva voce*:

> **INTERROGATOR:** In the first line of your sonnet which reads "Shall I compare thee to a summer's day," would not "a spring day" do as well or better?
>
> **WITNESS:** It wouldn't scan.
>
> **INTERROGATOR:** How about "a winter's day." That would scan all right.
>
> **WITNESS:** Yes, but nobody wants to be compared to a winter's day.
>
> **INTERROGATOR:** Would you say Mr. Pickwick reminded you of Christmas?
>
> **WITNESS:** In a way.
>
> **INTERROGATOR:** Yet Christmas is a winter's day, and I do not think Mr. Pickwick would mind the comparison.
>
> **WITNESS:** I don't think you're serious. By a winter's day one means a typical winter's day, rather than a special one like Christmas.

And so on. What would Professor Jefferson say if the sonnet-writing machine was able to answer like this in the *viva voce*? I do not know whether he would regard the machine as "merely artificially signaling" these answers, but if the answers were as satisfactory and sustained as in the above passage I do not think he would describe it as "an easy contrivance." This phrase is, I think, intended to cover such devices as the inclusion in the machine of a record of someone reading a sonnet, with appropriate switching to turn it on from time to time. In short then, I think that most of those who support the argument from consciousness could be persuaded to abandon it rather than be forced into the solipsist position. They will then probably be willing to accept our test.

I do not wish to give the impression that I think there is no mystery about consciousness. There is, for instance, something of a paradox connected with any attempt to localize it. But I do not think these mysteries necessarily need to be solved before we can answer the question with which we are concerned in this paper.

5. *Arguments from Various Disabilities.* These arguments take the form, "I grant you that you can make machines do all the things you have mentioned but you will never be able to make one to do X." Numerous features X are suggested in this connection. I offer a selection:

> Be kind, resourceful, beautiful, friendly, have initiative, have a sense of humor, tell right from wrong, make mistakes, fall in love, enjoy strawberries and cream, make someone fall in love with it, learn from experience, use words properly, be the subject of its own thought, have as much diversity of behavior as a man, do something really new.

No support is usually offered for these statements. I believe they are mostly founded on the principle of scientific induction. A man has seen thousands of machines in his lifetime. From what he sees of them he draws a number of general conclusions. They are ugly, each is designed for a very limited purpose, when required for a minutely different purpose they are useless, the variety of behavior of any one of them is very small, etc., etc. Naturally he concludes that these are necessary properties of machines in general. Many of these limitations are associated with the very small storage capacity of most machines. (I am assuming that the idea of storage capacity is extended in some way to cover machines other than discrete state machines. The exact definition does not matter as no mathematical accuracy is claimed in the present discussion.) A few years ago, when very little had been heard of digital computers, it was possible to elicit much incredulity concerning them, if one mentioned their properties without describing their construction. That was presumably due to a similar application of the principle of scientific induction. These applications of the principle are of course largely unconscious. When a burned child fears the fire and shows that he fears it by avoiding it, I should say that he was applying scientific induction. (I could of course also describe his behavior in many other ways.) The works and customs of mankind do not seem to be very suitable material to which to apply scientific induction. A very large part of space-time must be investigated if reliable results are to be obtained. Otherwise we may (as most English children do) decide that everybody speaks English, and that it is silly to learn French.

There are, however, special remarks to be made about many of the disabilities that have been mentioned. The inability to enjoy strawberries and cream may have struck the reader as frivolous. Possibly a machine might be made to enjoy this delicious dish, but any attempt to make one do so would be idiotic. What is important about this disability is that it contributes to some of the other disabilities, e.g., to the difficulty of the same kind of friendliness occurring between man and machine as between white man and white man, or between black man and black man.

The claim that "machines cannot make mistakes" seems a curious one. One is tempted to retort, "Are they any the worse for that?" But let us adopt a more sympathetic attitude, and try to see what is really meant. I think this criticism can be explained in terms of the imitation game. It is claimed that the interrogator could distinguish the machine from the man simply by setting them a number of problems in arithmetic. The machine would be unmasked because of its deadly accuracy. The reply to this is simple. The machine (programmed for playing the game) would not attempt to give the *right* answers to the arithmetic problems. It would deliberately introduce mistakes in a manner calculated to confuse the interrogator. . . .

The claim that a machine cannot be the subject of its own thought can of course only be answered if it can be shown that the machine has *some* thought with *some* subject matter. Nevertheless, "the subject matter of a machine's operations" does seem to mean something, at least to the people who deal with it. If, for instance, the machine was trying to find a solution of the equation $x^2 - 40x - 11 = 0$ one would be tempted to describe this equation as part of the machine's subject matter at that moment. In this sort of sense a machine undoubtedly can be its own subject matter. It may be used to help in making up its own programs, or to predict the effect of alterations in its own structure. By observing the results of its own behavior it can modify its own programs so as to achieve some purpose more effectively. These are possibilities of the near future, rather than Utopian dreams.

The criticism that a machine cannot have much diversity of behavior is just a way of saying that it cannot have much storage capacity. Until fairly recently a storage capacity of even a thousand digits was very rare.

The criticisms that we are considering here are often disguised forms of the argument from consciousness. Usually if one maintains that a machine *can* do one of these things, and describes the kind of method that the machine could use, one will not make much of an impression. It is thought that the method (whatever it may be, for it must be mechanical) is really rather base. Compare the parenthesis in Jefferson's statement quoted above.

6. *Lady Lovelace's Objection.* Our most detailed information of Babbage's Analytical Engine [a digital computer planned in the 1830s] comes from a memoir by Lady Lovelace. In it she states, "The Analytical Engine has no pretensions to *originate* anything. It can do *whatever we know how to order it* to perform" (her italics). This statement is quoted by Hartree who adds: "This does not imply that it may not be possible to construct electronic equipment which will 'think for itself,' or in which, in biological terms, one could set up a conditioned reflex, which would serve as a basis for 'learning.' Whether this is possible in principle or not is a stimulating and exciting question, suggested by some of these recent developments. But it did not seem that the machines constructed or projected at the time had this property."

I am in thorough agreement with Hartree over this. It will be noticed that he does not assert that the machines in question had not got the property, but rather that the evidence available to Lady Lovelace did not encourage her to believe that they had it. It is quite possible that the machines in question had in a sense got this property. For suppose that some discrete state machine has the property. The Analytical Engine was a universal digital computer, so that, if its storage capacity and speed were adequate, it could by suitable programming be made to mimic the machine in question. Probably this argument did not occur to the Countess or to Babbage. In any case there was no obligation on them to claim all that could be claimed. . . .

A variant of Lady Lovelace's objection states that a machine can "never do anything really new." This may be parried for a moment with the saw, "There is nothing new under the sun." Who can be certain that "original work" that he has done was not simply the growth of the seed planted in him by teaching, or the effect of following well-known general principles. A better variant of the objection says that a machine can never "take us by surprise." This statement is a more direct challenge and can be met directly. Machines take me by surprise with great frequency. This is largely because I do not do sufficient calculation to decide what to expect them to do, or rather because, although I do a calculation, I do it in a hurried, slipshod fashion, taking risks. Perhaps I say to myself, "I suppose the voltage here ought to be the same as there: anyway let's assume it is." Naturally I am often wrong, and the result is a surprise for me, for by the time the experiment is done these assumptions have been forgotten. These admissions lay me open to lectures on the subject of my vicious ways, but do not throw any doubt on my credibility when I testify to the surprises I experience.

I do not expect this reply to silence my critic. He will probably say that such surprises are due to some creative mental act on my part, and reflect no credit on the machine. This leads us back to the argument from consciousness, and far from the idea of surprise. It is a line of argument we must consider closed, but it is perhaps worth remarking that the appreciation of something as surprising requires as much of a "creative mental act" whether the surprising event originates from a man, a book, a machine or anything else.

The view that machines cannot give rise to surprises is due, I believe, to a fallacy to which philosophers and mathematicians are particularly subject. This is the assumption that as soon as a fact is presented to a mind all consequences of that fact spring into the mind simultaneously with it. It is a very useful assumption under many circumstances, but one too easily forgets that it is false. A natural consequence of doing so is that one then assumes that there is no virtue in the mere working out of consequences from data and general principles.

7. *Argument from Continuity in the Nervous System.* The nervous system is certainly not a discrete state machine. A small error in the information about the size of a nervous impulse impinging on a neuron, may make a large difference to the size of the outgoing impulse. It may be argued that, this being so, one cannot expect to be able to mimic the behavior of the nervous system with a discrete state system.

It is true that a discrete state machine must be different from a continuous machine. But if we adhere to the conditions of the imitation game, the interrogator will not be able to take any advantage of this difference. The situation can be made clearer if we consider some other simpler continuous machine. A differential analyzer will do very well. (A differential analyzer is a certain kind of machine not of the discrete state type used for some kinds of calculation.) Some of these provide their answers in a typed form, and so are suitable for taking part in the game. It would not be possible for a digital computer to predict exactly what answers the differential analyzer would give to a problem, but it would be quite capable of giving the right sort of answer. For instance, if asked to give the value of *pi* (actually about 3.1416) it would be reasonable to choose at random between the values 3.12, 3.13, 3.14, 3.15, 3.16 with the probabilities of 0.05, 0.15, 0.55, 0.19, 0.06 (say). Under these circumstances it would be very difficult for the interrogator to distinguish the differential analyzer from the digital computer.

8. *The Argument from Informality of Behavior.* It is not possible to produce a set of rules purporting to describe what a man should do in every conceivable set of circumstances. One might for instance have a rule that one is to stop when one sees a red traffic light, and to go if one sees a green one, but what if by some fault both appear together? One may perhaps decide that it

is safest to stop. But some further difficulty may well arise from this decision later. To attempt to provide rules of conduct to cover every eventuality, even those arising from traffic lights, appears to be impossible. With all this I agree.

From this it is argued that we cannot be machines. I shall try to reproduce the argument, but I fear I shall hardly do it justice. It seems to run something like this. "If each man had a definite set of rules of conduct by which he regulated his life he would be no better than a machine. But there are no such rules, so men cannot be machines." The undistributed middle is glaring. I do not think the argument is ever put quite like this, but I believe this is the argument used nevertheless. There may however be a certain confusion between "rules of conduct" and "laws of behavior" to cloud the issue. By "rules of conduct" I mean precepts such as "Stop if you see red lights," on which one can act, and of which one can be conscious. By "laws of behavior" I mean laws of nature as applied to a man's body such as "if you pinch him he will squeak." If we substitute "laws of behavior which regulate his life" for "laws of conduct by which he regulates his life" in the argument quoted the undistributed middle is no longer insuperable. For we believe that it is not only true that being regulated by laws of behavior implies being some sort of machine (though not necessarily a discrete state machine), but that conversely being such a machine implies being regulated by such laws. However, we cannot so easily convince ourselves of the absence of complete laws of behavior as of complete rules of conduct. The only way we know of for finding such laws is scientific observation, and we certainly know of no circumstances under which we could say, "We have searched enough. There are no such laws." . . .

7. LEARNING MACHINES

The reader will have anticipated that I have no very convincing arguments of a positive nature to support my views. If I had, I should not have taken such pains to point out the fallacies in contrary views. Such evidence as I have I shall now give. . . .

The only really satisfactory support that can be given for the view expressed at the beginning of § 6, will be that provided by waiting for the end of the century and then doing the experiment described. But what can we say in the meantime? What steps should be taken now if the experiment is to be successful? . . .

Instead of trying to produce a programme to simulate the adult mind, why not rather try to produce one which simulates the child's? If this were then subjected to an appropriate course of education, one would obtain the adult brain. Presumably the child brain is something like a notebook as one buys it from the stationer's. Rather little mechanism and lots of blank sheets. (Mechanism and writing are from our point of view almost synonymous.) Our hope is that there is so little mechanism in the child brain that something like it can be easily programmed. The amount of work in the education we can assume, as a first approximation, to be much the same as for the human child. . . .

We normally associate punishments and rewards with the teaching process. Some simple child machines can be constructed or programmed on this sort of principle. The machine has to be so constructed that the events which shortly preceded the occurrence of a punishment signal are unlikely to be repeated, whereas a reward signal increased the probability of repetition of the events which led up to it. These definitions do not presuppose any feelings on the part of the machine. . . .

We may hope that machines will eventually compete with men in all purely intellectual fields. But which are the best ones to start with? Even this is a difficult decision. Many people think that a very abstract activity, like the playing of chess, would be best. It can also be maintained that it is best to provide the machine with the best sense organs that money can buy, and then teach it to understand and speak English. This process could follow the normal teaching of a child. Things would be pointed out and named, etc. Again I do not know what the right answer is, but I think both approaches should be tried.

We can only see a short distance ahead, but we can see plenty there that needs to be done.

DISCUSSION QUESTIONS

1. Why does Turing replace the question "Can machines think?" with the question "Can any machine ever win the imitation game?" Must anyone who answers "Yes" to the first question also answer "Yes" to the second question? Must anyone who answers "No" to the first question also answer "No" to the second question? Is Turing's replacement fair to his opponents? Why or why not?

2. Turing predicted that by 2000, average interrogators would be fooled 70 percent of the time by machines after playing the imitation game for five minutes. We are now beyond 2000, but no machine is even close to this degree of success. Thus, Turing's prediction seems false (and not even close to true). Does this show that Turing's main argument is fallacious? Why or why not?

3. Turing claims that Jefferson's argument from consciousness lands him in solipsism. Reconstruct and evaluate this *reductio ad absurdum* refutation. How could Jefferson best reply? Is this reply adequate? Why or why not?

4. One variant of Lady Lovelace's objection claims that machines are programmed, so they "never do anything really new." Turing responds by arguing that machines can "take us by surprise." Is this response adequate? Why or why not? What does it mean to do something "really new"? Is there any sense in which humans do things that are really new but machines cannot? How can you tell?

(continued)

5. Some MP3 players are of such high quality that it is sometimes impossible to distinguish the sound of the MP3 player from the sound of a live human voice. Would the Turing test show that such MP3 players can sing? Why or why not?

THE MYTH OF THE COMPUTER[2]

by John R. Searle

[A] theory, which is fairly widely held in cognitive science, can be summarized in three propositions.

1. *Mind as Program.* What we call minds are simply very complex digital computer programs. Mental states are simply computer states and mental processes are computational processes. Any system whatever that had the right program, with the right input and output, would have to have mental states and processes in the same literal sense that you and I do, because that is all there is to mental states and processes, that is all that you and I have. The programs in question are "self-updating" or "self-designing" "systems of representations."

2. *The Irrelevance of the Neurophysiology of the Brain.* In the study of the mind actual biological facts about actual human and animal brains are irrelevant because the mind is an "abstract sort of thing" and human brains just happen to be among the indefinitely large number of kinds of computers that can have minds. Our minds happen to be embodied in our brains, but there is no essential connection between the mind and the brain. Any other computer with the right program would also have a mind. . . .

3. *The Turing Test as the Criterion of the Mental.* The conclusive proof of the presence of mental states and capacities is the ability of a system to pass the Turing test, the test devised by Alan Turing and described in his article in this book. If a system can convince a computer expert that it has mental states then it really has those mental states. If, for example, a machine could "converse" with a native Chinese speaker in such a way as to convince the speaker that it understood Chinese then it would literally understand Chinese. . . .

We might call this collection of theses "strong artificial intelligence" (strong AI).* These theses are certainly not obviously true and they are seldom explicitly stated and defended.

---

*"Strong" to distinguish the position from "weak" or "cautious" AI, which holds that the computer is simply a very useful tool in the study of the mind, not that the appropriately programmed computer literally has a mind.

Let us inquire first into how plausible it is to suppose that specific bio-chemical powers of the brain are really irrelevant to the mind. . . . [I]f you consider specific mental states and processes—being thirsty, wanting to go to the bathroom, worrying about your income tax, trying to solve math puzzles, feeling depressed, recalling the French word for "butterfly"—then it seems at least a little odd to think that the brain is so irrelevant.

Take thirst, where we actually know a little about how it works. Kidney secretions of renin synthesize a substance called angiotensin. This substance goes into the hypothalamus and triggers a series of neuron firings. As far as we know these neuron firings are a very large part of the cause of thirst. Now obviously there is more to be said, for example, about the relations of the hypothalamic responses to the rest of the brain, about other things going on in the hypothalamus, and about the possible distinctions between the *feeling* of thirst and the *urge* to drink. Let us suppose we have filled out the story with the rest of the biochemical causal account of thirst.

Now the theses of the mind as program and the irrelevance of the brain would tell us that what matters about this story is not the specific biochemi-cal properties of the angiotensin or the hypothalamus but only the formal computer programs that the whole sequence instantiates. Well, let's try that out as a hypothesis and see how it works. A computer can simulate the for-mal properties of the sequence of chemical and electrical phenomena in the production of thirst just as much as it can simulate the formal properties of anything else—we can simulate thirst just as we can simulate hurricanes, rainstorms, five-alarm fires, internal combustion engines, photosynthesis, lactation, or the flow of currency in a depressed economy. But no one in his right mind thinks that a computer simulation of a five-alarm fire will burn down the neighborhood, or that a computer simulation of an internal com-bustion engine will power a car or that computer simulations of lactation and photosynthesis will produce milk and sugar. To my amazement, however, I have found that a large number of people suppose that computer simulations of mental phenomena, whether at the level of brain processes or not, literally produce mental phenomena.

Again, let's try it out. Let's program our favorite PDP-10 computer with the formal program that simulates thirst. We can even program it to point out at the end "Boy, am I thirsty!" or "Won't someone please give me a drink?" etc. Now would anyone suppose that we thereby have even the slightest reason to suppose that the computer is literally thirsty? Or that any simulation of any other mental phenomena, such as understanding stories, feeling depressed, or worrying about itemized deductions, must therefore produce the real thing? The answer, alas, is that a large number of people are committed to an ideology that requires them to believe just that. So let us carry the story a step further.

The PDP-10 is powered by electricity and perhaps its electrical properties can reproduce some of the actual causal powers of the electrochemical fea-tures of the brain in producing mental states. We certainly couldn't rule out that eventuality *a priori*. But remember: the thesis of strong AI is that the mind is "independent of *any* particular embodiment" because the mind is just a program and the program can be run on a computer made of anything whatever provided it is stable enough and complex enough to carry the program. The actual physical computer could be an ant colony . . . , a collection of beer cans, streams of toilet paper with small stones placed on the squares, men sitting on high stools with green eye shades—anything you like.

So let us imagine our thirst-simulating program running on a computer made entirely of old beer cans, millions (or billions) of old beer cans that are rigged up to levers and powered by windmills. We can imagine that the program simulates the neuron firings at the synapses by having beer cans bang into each other, thus achieving a strict correspondence between neuron firings and beer-can bangings. And at the end of the sequence a beer can pops up on which is written "I am thirsty." Now, to repeat the question, does anyone suppose that this Rube Goldberg apparatus is literally thirsty in the sense in which you and I are?

Notice that the thesis of [strong AI] is not that *for all we know* the collection of beer cans might be thirsty but rather that if it has the right program with the right input and output it *must* be thirsty (or understand Proust or worry about its income tax or have any other mental state) because that is all the mind is, a certain kind of computer program, and any computer made of anything at all running the right program would have to have the appropriate mental states.

I believe that everything we have learned about human and animal biology suggests that what we call "mental" phenomena are as much a part of our biological natural history as any other biological phenomena, as much a part of biology as digestion, lactation, or the secretion of bile. Much of the implausibility of the strong AI thesis derives from its resolute opposition to biology; the mind is not a concrete biological phenomenon but "an abstract sort of thing."

Still, in calling attention to the implausibility of supposing that the specific causal powers of brains are irrelevant to minds I have not yet fully exposed the preposterousness of the strong AI position, so let us press on and examine a bit more closely the thesis of mind as program.

Digital computer programs by definition consist of sets of purely formal operations on formally specified symbols. The ideal computer does such things as print a 0 on the tape, move one square to the left, erase a 1, move back to the right, etc. It is common to describe this as "symbol manipulation" or . . . the whole system as a "self-updating representational system"; but these terms are at least a bit misleading since as far as the computer is concerned the symbols don't *symbolize* anything or *represent* anything. They are just formal counters.

The computer attaches no meaning, interpretation, or content to the formal symbols; and *qua* computer it couldn't, because if we tried to give the computer an interpretation of its symbols we could only give it more uninterpreted symbols. The interpretation of the symbols is entirely up to the programmers and users of the computer. For example, on my pocket calculator if I print "3 × 3 =," the calculator will print "9" but it has no idea that "3" means 3 or that "9" means 9 or that anything means anything. We might put this point by saying that the computer has a syntax but no semantics. The computer manipulates formal symbols but attaches no meaning to them, and this simple observation will enable us to refute the thesis of mind as program.

Suppose that we write a computer program to simulate the understanding of Chinese so that, for example, if the computer is asked questions in Chinese the program enables it to give answers in Chinese; if asked to summarize stories in Chinese it can give such summaries; if asked questions about the stories it has been given it will answer such questions.

Now suppose that I, who understand no Chinese at all and can't even distinguish Chinese symbols from some other kinds of symbols, am locked in a room with a number of cardboard boxes full of Chinese symbols. Suppose that I am given a book of rules in English that instruct me how to match these Chinese symbols with each other. The rules say such things as that the "squiggle-squiggle" sign is to be followed by the "squoggle-squoggle" sign. Suppose that people outside the room pass in more Chinese symbols and that following the instructions in the book I pass Chinese symbols back to them. Suppose that unknown to me the people who pass me the symbols call them "questions" and the book of instructions that I work from they call "the program"; the symbols I give back to them they call "answers to the questions" and me they call "the computer." Suppose that after a while the programmers get so good at writing the programs and I get so good at manipulating the symbols that my answers are indistinguishable from those of native Chinese speakers. I can pass the Turing test for understanding Chinese. But all the same I still don't understand a word of Chinese and neither does any other digital computer because all the computer has is what I have: a formal program that attaches no meaning, interpretation, or content to any of the symbols.

What this simple program shows is that no formal program by itself is sufficient for understanding, because it would always be possible in principle for an agent to go through the steps in the program and still not have the relevant understanding. And what works for Chinese would also work for other mental phenomena. I could, for example, go through the steps of the thirst-simulating program without feeling thirsty. The argument also, *en passant*, refutes the Turing test because it shows that a system, namely me, could pass the Turing test without having the appropriate mental states.* . . .

The details of how the brain works are immensely complicated and largely unknown, but some of the general principles of the relations

---

*The "Chinese room argument" is stated in detail in my article "Minds, Brains, and Programs," . . . [which] originally appeared in *The Behavioral and Brain Sciences*, Vol. 3 (Cambridge: Cambridge University Press, 1980), along with twenty-seven responses and a reply to the responses.

between brain functioning and computer programs can be stated quite simply. First, we know that brain processes cause mental phenomena. Mental states are caused by and realized in the structure of the brain. From this it follows that any system that produced mental states would have to have powers equivalent to those of the brain. Such a system might use a different chemistry, but whatever its chemistry it would have to be able to cause what the brain causes. We know from the Chinese room argument that digital computer programs by themselves are never sufficient to produce mental states. Now since brains do produce minds, and since programs by themselves can't produce minds, it follows that the way the brain does it can't be by simply instantiating a computer program. (Everything, by the way, instantiates some program or other, and brains are no exception. So in that trivial sense brains, like everything else, are digital computers.) And it also follows that if you wanted to build a machine to produce mental states, a thinking machine, you couldn't do it solely in virtue of the fact that your machine ran a certain kind of computer program. The thinking machine couldn't work solely in virtue of being a digital computer but would have to duplicate the specific causal powers of the brain.

A lot of the nonsense talked about computers nowadays stems from their relative rarity and hence mystery. As computers and robots become more common, as common as telephones, washing machines, and forklift trucks, it seems likely that this aura will disappear and people will take computers for what they are, namely useful machines. In the meantime one has to try to avoid certain recurring mistakes that keep cropping up in . . . current discussions.

The first is the idea that somehow computer achievements pose some sort of threat or challenge to human beings. But the fact, for example, that a calculator can outperform even the best mathematician is no more significant or threatening than the fact that a steam shovel can outperform the best human digger. (An oddity of artificial intelligence, by the way, is the slowness of the programmers in devising a program that can beat the very best chess players. From the point of view of games theory, chess is a trivial game since each side has perfect information about the other's position and possible moves, and one had to assume that computer programs will soon be able to outperform any human chess player.)

A second fallacy is the idea that there might be some special human experience beyond computer simulation because of its special humanity. We are sometimes told that computers couldn't simulate feeling depressed or falling in love or having a sense of humor. But as far as simulation is concerned you can program your computer to print out "I am depressed," "I love Sally," or "Ha, ha," as easily as you can program it to print out "3 × 3 = 9." The real mistake is to suppose that simulation is duplication, and that mistake is the same regardless of what mental states we are talking about.

A third mistake, basic to all the others, is the idea that if a computer can simulate having a certain mental state then we have the same grounds for supposing it really has that mental state as we have for supposing that human beings have that state. But we know from the Chinese room argument as well as from biology that this simple-minded behaviorism of the Turing test is mistaken.

Until computers and robots become as common as cars and until people are able to program and use them as easily as they now drive cars we are likely to continue to suffer from a certain mythological conception of digital computers. . . .

DISCUSSION QUESTIONS

1. Reconstruct and evaluate Searle's Chinese room argument in the form of an argument from analogy. Be sure to state his conclusion as precisely as you can.

2. Is Searle's analogy undermined by the fact that computers are much faster than any person in a Chinese room? Why or why not?

3. Could any future developments of more sophisticated computers (such as computers that can reprogram themselves) undermine Searle's argument? Why or why not?

4. Could any future discoveries about how the brain works (such as that brains work just like computers) undermine Searle's argument? Why or why not?

5. Searle admits that, in a "trivial sense brains, like everything else, are digital computers." Does this admission weaken his argument? Why or why not?

6. Some defenders of strong AI respond that, even if the person in the Chinese room does not understand Chinese, the system consisting of the person, room, and manual together does understand Chinese. Is this "systems reply" plausible? Why or why not?

7. Some opponents reply that Searle's Chinese room would have understanding if it had arms and legs so that it could move around as well as a television camera so that it could perceive its environment. Is this "robot reply" plausible? Why or why not?

8. Some critics charge that, given Searle's requirements, we cannot know whether other people have minds, because we cannot see whether they mean anything by the symbols they put out. Is Searle really committed to such a skeptical view? Why or why not?

9. Suppose that a friend of yours for many years is seriously injured in an accident and the doctors discover that she is made from wires, transistors, and so on. Would this be sufficient to show that your "friend" never really thought or felt anything? Why or why not?

(continued)

10. Suppose that you are seriously injured in an accident and the doctors discover that *you* are made from wires, transistors, and so on. Would this convince you that you had never really thought or felt anything? If your answer to this question is different from your answer to the previous question, explain why.

11. Searle predicts that, "As computers and robots become more common, . . . people will take computers for what they are, namely useful machines." Do you agree? Why or why not?

NOTES

[1]*Mind* LIX, no. 236 (1950): 433–60.

[2]*The New York Review of Books,* April 29, 1982, 3. Searle is here reviewing Hofstadter and Dennett, *The Mind's I.* We removed references to that particular book, since Searle's argument is much more general.

INDEX

Note: Page numbers followed by letter n indicate footnotes.

n = footnote

n = footnote

n = footnote

n = footnote

n = footnote

n = footnote

n = footnote

n = footnote

n = footnote

n = footnote

n = footnote

n = footnote

n = footnote

n = footnote

n = footnote